MAGILL'S LITERARY ANNUAL 2012

*Essay-Reviews of 200 Outstanding Books
Published in the United States During 2011*

With an Annotated List of Titles

Volume Two
K-Z

Edited by
JOHN D. WILSON
STEVEN G. KELLMAN

SALEM PRESS
A Division of EBSCO Publishing
Ipswich, Massachusetts   Hackensack, New Jersey

LIBRARY OF CONGRESS CATALOG CARD NO
ISBN (set): 978-1-58765-964-5
ISBN (vol. 1): 978-1-58765-965-2
ISBN (vol. 2): 978-1-58765-966-9

FIRST PRINTING

PRINTED IN THE UNITED STATES OF AMERICA

CONTENTS

Complete Annotated List of Titles vii

The Keats Brothers: The Life of John and George—*Denise Gigante* 413
The King James Bible: A Short History from Tyndale to Today—
    David Norton 417

The Land at the End of the World—*António Lobo Antunes*. 421
Last Man in Tower—*Aravind Adiga* 425
Lee Krasner: A Biography—*Gail Levin*. 429
The Leftovers—*Tom Perrotta*. 434
The Lessons—*Joanne Diaz* 438
The Letters of Ernest Hemingway: Volume 1, 1907–1922—
    Sandra Spanier and Robert W. Trogdon. 442
Liberty's Exiles: American Loyalists in the Revolutionary World—
    Maya Jasanoff. 447
Life Itself: A Memoir—*Roger Ebert* 452
Life on Mars—*Tracy K. Smith* 456

Malcolm X: A Life of Reinvention—*Manning Marable* 460
The Marriage Plot—*Jeffrey Eugenides* 465
Metropole—*Geoffrey G. O'Brien*. 469
Micro—*Michael Crichton and Richard Preston* 473
Miss New India—*Bharati Mukherjee*. 477
Modigliani: A Life—*Meryle Secrest* 481
Moonwalking with Einstein: The Art and Science of Remembering
    Everything—*Joshua Foer* 485
Mr. Fox—*Helen Oyeyemi*. 489
Music for Silenced Voices: Shostakovich and His Fifteen Quartets—
    Wendy Lesser 493
My Father's Fortune: A Life—*Michael Frayn* 497
My New American Life—*Francine Prose* 501

Nanjing Requiem—*Ha Jin* 505
Never Say Die: The Myth and Marketing of the New Old Age—*Susan Jacoby* . . . 509
The Night Circus—*Erin Morgenstern*. 513
Night Soul and Other Stories—*Joseph McElroy* 517
Nod House—*Nathaniel Mackey*. 521
No Regrets: The Life of Edith Piaf—*Carolyn Burke* 526

Once Upon a River—*Bonnie Jo Campbell* 530
On China—*Henry Kissinger* 534

One Day I Will Write about This Place—*Binyavanga Wainaina* 539
One Hundred Names For Love: A Stroke, a Marriage, and the Language of
    Healing—*Diane Ackerman* 543
1Q84—*Haruki Murakami* 548
One Was a Soldier—*Julia Spencer-Fleming* 552
Open City—*Teju Cole* 556
Orientation: And Other Stories—*Daniel Orozco* 561
Otherwise Known as the Human Condition: Selected Essays and Reviews—
    Geoff Dyer 565

The Pale King—*David Foster Wallace* 569
The Paper Garden: An Artist Begins Her Life's Work at Seventy-Two—
    Molly Peacock 574
A People of One Book: The Bible and the Victorians—*Timothy Larsen* 578
The Philosophical Breakfast Club: Four Remarkable Friends Who
    Transformed Science and Changed the World—*Laura J. Snyder* 583
Please Look After Mom—*Kyung-sook Shin* 588
The Pleasures of Reading in an Age of Distraction—*Alan Jacobs* 592
The Prague Cemetery—*Umberto Eco* 596
The Preacher—*Camilla Läckberg* 601
The Psychopath Test: A Journey Through the Madness Industry—
    Jon Ronson 605
Pulphead: Essays—*John Jeremiah Sullivan* 609
Pym—*Mat Johnson* 613

Reading My Father: A Memoir—*Alexandra Styron* 617
Redeemers: Ideas and Power in Latin America—*Enrique Krauze* 621
Rodin's Debutante—*Ward Just* 625

Sacred Trash: The Lost and Found World of the Cairo Geniza—
    Adina Hoffman and Peter Cole 629
The Saturday Big Tent Wedding Party—*Alexander McCall Smith* 633
Say Her Name—*Francisco Goldman* 637
The Seamstress and the Wind—*César Aira* 641
The Selected Stories of Mercè Rodoreda—*Mercè Rodoreda* 645
Seven Years—*Peter Stamm* 649
The Shadow of What We Were—*Luis Sepúlveda* 653
She-Wolves: The Women Who Ruled England before Elizabeth—
    Helen Castor 657
Silver Sparrow—*Tayari Jones* 662
A Singular Woman: The Untold Story of Barack Obama's Mother—
    Janny Scott 666
The Sly Company of People Who Care—*Rahul Bhattacharya* 670

CONTENTS

Smoking Typewriters: The Sixties Underground Press and the Rise of
    Alternative Media in America—*John McMillian* 674
Sobbing Superpower: Selected Poems of Tadeusz Różewicz—*Tadeusz Różewicz* . . . 679
The Social Animal: The Hidden Sources of Love, Character, and
    Achievement—*David Brooks* 683
Songs of Kabir—*Kabir* 687
Space, in Chains—*Laura Kasischke* 691
The Splendor of Portugal—*António Lobo Antunes* 695
Steve Jobs—*Walter Isaacson* 699
Stone Arabia—*Dana Spiotta* 704
The Stranger's Child—*Alan Hollinghurst* 708
The Summer Without Men—*Siri Hustvedt* 712
Swamplandia!—*Karen Russell* 716
The Swerve: How the World Became Modern—*Stephen Greenblatt* 720
Swim Back to Me—*Ann Packer* 724

Tabloid City—*Pete Hamill* 728
Taller When Prone—*Les Murray* 732
The Tiger's Wife—*Téa Obreht* 736
To End All Wars: A Story of Loyalty and Rebellion: 1914–1918—
    Adam Hochschild 740
Tolstoy: A Russian Life—*Rosamund Bartlett* 745
Tough Without a Gun: The Life and Extraordinary Afterlife of Humphrey
    Bogart—*Stefan Kanfer* 749
Townie: A Memoir—*Andre Dubus III* 754
The Tragedy of Arthur—*Arthur Phillips* 758
Traveler—*Devin Johnston* 762
The Trouble Ball—*Martín Espada* 767
The Troubled Man—*Henning Mankell* 771
Twice a Spy—*Keith Thomson* 775

The Uncoupling—*Meg Wolitzer* 779
Unseen Hand—*Adam Zagajewski* 783

Vaclav and Lena—*Haley Tanner* 787

We, the Drowned—*Carsten Jensen* 791
We Others: New and Selected Stories—*Steven Millhauser* 795
When the Killing's Done—*T. C. Boyle* 799
Widow—*Michelle Latiolais* 803
A Widow's Story: A Memoir—*Joyce Carol Oates* 808
Words Made Fresh: Essays on Literature and Culture—*Larry Woiwode* 813
The Words of Others: From Quotations to Culture—*Gary Saul Morson* 817
The Wrong War: Grit, Strategy, and the Way Out of Afghanistan—*Bing West* . . 821

You and Three Others Are Approaching a Lake—*Anna Moschovakis* 825
You Think That's Bad—*Jim Shepard* 829

Category Index 833
Title Index 837
Author Index 841

COMPLETE ANNOTATED LIST OF TITLES

VOLUME 1

After Midnight—*Irmgard Keun*. 1
*A satire set in the closing years of the Weimar Republic that exposes the brutali-
ties and intolerance of the rising Nazi Party from the perspective of a teenage girl
with little interest in politics.*

Alan Lomax: The Man Who Recorded the World— *John Szwed* 5
*A thorough examination of the life and career of the man who brought Lead Belly,
Muddy Waters, and Woody Guthrie to the world's attention, this biography is at its
finest when interweaving musical history with cultural history.*

Alfred Kazin's Journals—*Richard M. Cook* 9
*The collected journal entries of esteemed American critic and intellectual Alfred
Kazin reveal his preoccupations and personal musings.*

All Our Worldly Goods—*Irène Némirovsky* 13
*Chronicling the lives of four generations of the Hardelot family, this novel por-
trays bourgeois French society during the first half of the twentieth century and the
struggle for individual happiness within this highly regulated social milieu.*

Almost a Family: A Memoir—*John Darnton*. 17
*John Darnton presents a compelling memoir about growing up in the shadow of a
father killed in World War II. He reflects on his father's mythic presence in his life as
he searches for the truth about his parents' marriage and his father's death.*

Alone Together: Why We Expect More from Technology and Less from
Each Other—*Sherry Turkle* 21
*Alone Together presents a cautionary tale of how technology is changing human
society by reducing the instances in which individuals interact with one another in
person and with their full attention. Turkle proposes a need to scale back reliance on
technology in order to prevent a crisis in human society.*

American Eden—*Wade Graham* 25
*A history of American landscape design from the colonial era to the early twenty-
first century, this book introduces key themes, personages, and problems in landscape design and demonstrates the consistent presence of gardening throughout the
history and culture of the United States.*

The Anatomy of Influence: Literature as a Way of Life—*Harold Bloom* 29
   The eminent critic's self-described "swan song" recapitulates the interpretive and critical principles that have informed his fifty-five years of teaching and writing about literature.

And So It Goes: Kurt Vonnegut, A Life—*Charles J. Shields*. 33
   This biography of the popular late-twentieth-century American novelist paints Kurt Vonnegut's life and career in great detail but leaves large questions unanswered.

Apricot Jam: And Other Stories—*Aleksandr Solzhenitsyn* 37
   In this posthumous collection, nine short stories expose Communist misrule in the Soviet Union and the failures of post-Soviet Russia.

Art and Madness: A Memoir of Lust without Reason—*Anne Roiphe* 41
   Roiphe's memoir discusses her search for love and identity in the sexist world of writers and artists in New York City during the late 1950s and early 1960s.

The Art of Asking Your Boss for a Raise—*Georges Perec*. 45
   Appearing for the first time in English translation, this short novella adapts the methodology of a computer program in an experimental text. With only occasional punctuation and capitalization, Perec describes the mind of an office employee summoning the courage to ask his boss for a raise.

The Art of Fielding—*Chad Harbach* 49
   A wise and winning debut novel about how baseball players at a small Wisconsin college learn to make life choices.

An Atlas of Impossible Longing—*Anuradha Roy* 53
   In this debut novel, three generations of a Bengali family struggle with personal, romantic, and economic challenges as India gains independence from Great Britain.

Attack of the Difficult Poems: Essays and Inventions—*Charles Bernstein* 57
   Writing with a verve and edge uncommon in literary discourse, Bernstein presents a practical program for an active engagement with literature through a variety of essays.

Bad Intentions—*Karin Fossum* 61
   A veteran detective's investigation of two suspicious drownings evolves into a larger exploration of conscience, culpability, and the relationship between crime and peer pressure.

Baseball in the Garden of Eden: The Secret History of the Early Game—
John Thorn. 65
   The author addresses the myth that American baseball originated with Abner Doubleday, while examining the sport's likely origin and evolution during the 1800s.

Battle Hymn of the Tiger Mother—*Amy Chua* 70
A controversial account of how one parent deals with the successes and failures of attempting to raise her American-born daughters the Chinese way.

Beautiful and Pointless: A Guide to Modern Poetry—*David Orr*. 74
Offers a fascinating, instructive, and provocative discussion of the place that modern poetry holds in the contemporary world.

Believing Is Seeing: Observations on the Mysteries of Photography—
Errol Morris. 78
Filmmaker Errol Morris interrogates the relationship between image and reality, examining the stories behind several popular and controversial photographs.

Binocular Vision: New and Selected Stories—*Edith Pearlman* 82
This collection of short fiction includes eighteen stories from Edith Pearlman's first three collections, plus sixteen new stories.

Bismarck: A Life—*Jonathan Steinberg*. 87
Jonathan Steinberg presents a critical biography of Otto von Bismarck, the statesman who became a master of power politics and unified Germany by force.

The Bitter Waters of Medicine Creek: A Tragic Clash Between White
and Native America—*Richard Kluger*. 91
A historical account of the conflict between white settlers and the Nisqually nation of Washington State during and after the Puget Sound Indian War.

Blake and the Bible—*Christopher Rowland* 95
Christopher Rowland combines interpretations of William Blake's written and visual work to present an analysis of the artist as biblical theologian, self-styled prophet, and radical religious thinker.

Blood, Bones, and Butter: The Inadvertent Education of a Reluctant Chef—
Gabrielle Hamilton 99
A candid, funny, and unsparing memoir of a life lived mainly in kitchens, Hamilton's story celebrates the pleasures of the table without concealing the dirty work of cooking.

Blue Nights—*Joan Didion* 103
Didion provides an intimate, unflinching look at her relationship with her adopted daughter, a promising photographer who died of natural causes at the age of thirty-nine.

A Book of Secrets: Illegitimate Daughters, Absent Fathers—
Michael Holroyd. 107
*An innovative British biographer explores the lives of Eve Fairfax, Alice Keppel,
Violet Trefusis, and other women who played important roles in the life of Ernest
Beckett, 2nd Baron Grimthorpe.*

Bowstring: On the Dissimilarity of the Similar—*Viktor Shklovsky*. 111
*The author's significant revision of his earlier theory of estrangement is trans-
lated into English for the first time.*

The Brilliant Disaster: JFK, Castro, and America's Doomed Invasion of
Cuba's Bay of Pigs—*Jim Rasenberger* 115
*An account and analysis of the events leading up to the Bay of Pigs invasion, its
preparation and execution, its outcome, its lingering aftermath, and the roles played
by its major and minor protagonists.*

The Buddha in the Attic—*Julie Otsuka* 119
*An experimental novel that recreates the experiences of the generation of Japa-
nese women who immigrated to the United States shortly after World War I, the so-
called picture brides sent to marry Japanese men already in California.*

Bye-and-Bye: Selected Late Poems—*Charles Wright* 123
*Wright presents a collection of meditative and penetrating poems selected from
five of his previous volumes.*

Caleb's Crossing—*Geraldine Brooks* 127
*Brooks's historical novel about a Puritan girl in seventeenth-century Massachu-
setts who befriends a Wampanoag boy is based on the true story of Caleb Cheeshah-
teaumauk, the first Native American to graduate from Harvard University.*

The Call—*Yannick Murphy* 131
*This innovative novel draws on magical realism, mystery, and children's literature
to present a moving and entertaining story of family love and community spirit.*

The Captain Asks for a Show of Hands—*Nick Flynn*. 136
*This fragmented and lyric collection of poems is Flynn's first book of poetry in
nearly a decade. In language that draws freely from other poets, musicians, and government files, Flynn explores how language fails to adequately express the horrors of
warfare and torture.*

The Chameleon Couch—*Yusef Komunyakaa* 140
*This poetry collection deepens Komunyakaa's enduring involvement with three
elements of inquiry central to his writing: music, myth, and mystery.*

Changó's Beads and Two-Tone Shoes—*William Kennedy* 144
This riveting novel, the eighth in Kennedy's Albany cycle, links such tumultuous events as the Cuban Revolution and the civil rights movement.

Charles Dickens: A Life—*Claire Tomalin* 148
Claire Tomalin presents a lively biography of Charles Dickens that balances an acute appreciation of the great novelist's literary output with an engrossing account of his complicated private life.

China in Ten Words—*Yu Hua* 152
Yu Hua presents a series of personal essays centered on ten key words: "people," "leader," "reading," "writing," "revolution," "disparity," "grassroots," "copycat," "bamboozle," and "Lu Xun." As he meditates on each word, Yu Hua reflects on the China of his boyhood and the China of his middle age, describing the two eras' similarities and differences.

Civilization: The West and the Rest—*Niall Ferguson* 156
Ferguson argues that the countries of the West became dominant world powers because of six "killer apps" that other nations, particularly China, have now begun to "download": competition, science, the rule of law, modern medicine, consumerism, and the work ethic.

Cloud of Ink—*L. S. Klatt* 160
This varied collection of tight, clear, and determined poems generally aims to understand the world through the examination and presentation of small details, subtle surrealism, and casual absurdity.

Coda—*René Belletto* 164
In this French Voices Award winner, a widower father follows a strange sequence of events in the wake of his wife's mysterious murder. Along the way, he encounters old and new friends and has brushes with death and fate itself in an accidental quest for immortality.

The Cold War—*Kathleen Ossip* 168
Ossip's poetry collection captures the latter half of the twentieth century in the United States: a time of progress and paranoia, change and conformity.

The Color of Night—*Madison Smartt Bell* 172
The novel is a disturbing investigation into the erotic thrill of violence in American culture through the story of a fugitive killer who attempts to reunite with a former lover in New York City following the terrorist attacks of September 11, 2001.

Come and See—*Fanny Howe* 176
Showcasing her meditative and lyrical strengths, Howe's collection of poems explores perception, misperception, and social justice in the rapidly changing world of the twenty-first century.

Confessions of a Young Novelist—*Umberto Eco* 180
This collection of lectures can be read as a memoir, a guide to novel writing, and a treatise on literary theory that provides insight into Eco's mind and career as well as the art of writing.

Conversations with Scorsese—*Richard Schickel* 184
Schickel interviews noted filmmaker Martin Scorsese, eliciting detailed comments about his early life and film career and his thoughts on art, morality, religion, and life.

The Convert: A Tale of Exile and Extremism—*Deborah Baker* 188
Baker narrates a primarily factual story about an ethnically Jewish woman from suburban New York City who converted to Islam, moved to Pakistan, and wrote in support of her new religion in its struggle against the West. Her unusual life story raises numerous questions about the relations between East and West and about the nature of truth.

A Covert Affair: Julia Child and Paul Child in the OSS—*Jennet Conant* 193
A historical account of Jane Foster, an artist and employee in the United States Office of Strategic Services (OSS) who was accused of working as a Soviet spy during World War II. The book discusses her life in the 1940s and 1950s, during which time she was friends with iconic chef Julia Child and her husband Paul.

Crazy U: One Dad's Crash Course in Getting His Kid into College—
Andrew Ferguson 197
With self-deprecating humor and critical scrutiny, Ferguson and his oldest child struggle through the college application process, uncovering research on the SAT, college rankings, and admissions.

Culture of One—*Alice Notley* 201
This innovative collection of poetry tells the story of Marie, a woman living in a desert town in the American Southwest.

The Curfew—*Jesse Ball* 205
Jesse Ball's third novel takes place in a totalitarian state and follows a father's dangerous night journey through the city after curfew while his daughter waits his return at home and imagines, reinvents, and possibly retells their past, present, and future.

Dante in Love—*A. N. Wilson* 209
Wilson offers a detailed overview of Dante's life and the political and religious conflicts, cultural concepts, and historical events that informed The Divine Comedy.

Devotions—*Bruce Smith* 213
In the tradition of Walt Whitman, Bruce Smith's sixth collection is an expansive, celebratory portrait of the United States.

Don't Shoot: One Man, a Street Fellowship, and the End of Violence in
Inner-City America—*David M. Kennedy* 217
A self-trained criminologist offers a possible solution to the problem of gang-related homicides in America's inner cities.

The Drop—*Michael Connelly*. 221
The seventeenth entry of the Harry Bosch police procedural series follows the detective on a baffling cold case and an apparent suicide, two cases that present a multitude of political implications.

A Drop of the Hard Stuff—*Lawrence Block* 225
In the seventeenth entry in the Scudder crime series, private investigator Matthew Scudder tells the story of his childhood friend and reflects on how their lives were entwined despite their being on opposite sides of the law.

The Eichmann Trial—*Deborah E. Lipstadt*. 229
Lipstadt provides an account and analysis of the 1961 trial in Jerusalem that brought SS Lieutenant Colonel Adolf Eichmann to justice.

1861: The Civil War Awakening—*Adam Goodheart* 233
Goodheart describes events that took place during the first months of the American Civil War, primarily from the perspectives of lesser-known historical figures.

Electric Eden:Unearthing Britain's Visionary Music—*Rob Young* 237
Young provides a historical overview of the mid-twentieth-century folk music revival in Great Britain that examines the genre's roots as well as its culture, contributors, and legacy.

11/22/63—*Stephen King* 241
King conjures up an intriguing time-travel tale about an English teacher from Lisbon Falls, Maine, who journeys from 2011 back to 1963 in order to stop the assassination of President John F. Kennedy.

Elizabeth Bishop and the *New Yorker*: The Complete Correspondence—
Joelle Biele 245
*Spanning from 1933 to 1979, the correspondence between poet Elizabeth Bishop
and her editors at the New Yorker illustrates details of Bishop's life and writing
process and gives new insights into the background and inspiration behind many of
her poems.*

Embassytown—*China Miéville* 250
*When a human's voice has unexpected effects on an alien race, a group of hu-
mans and Ariekei must find a new way to use language to save their society.*

Emily, Alone—*Stewart O'Nan* 254
*Stewart O'Nan chronicles a year in the life of eighty-year-old Emily Maxwell as
she tries to cope with declining health, loneliness, a constantly changing world, and
memories of the past. The novel provides an objective and perceptive look at a period
of life not often treated in fiction.*

An Empty Room—*Mu Xin* 258
*The thirteen short stories of this collection span life experiences from childhood
to death, reflecting on lives shaped by family and history.*

Endgame: Bobby Fischer's Remarkable Rise and Fall—From America's
Brightest Prodigy to the Edge of Madness—*Frank Brady* 262
*This comprehensive biography of controversial world chess champion Bobby
Fischer uses new information from friends, family, and FBI and KGB documents to
build a more complete picture of Fischer as a person. Endgame focuses on Fischer's
personality and personal relationships more than the details of his chess games.*

The Evolution of Bruno Littlemore—*Benjamin Hale* 266
*Author Benjamin Hale presents the fictional memoir of an erudite and loquacious
talking chimpanzee, who reflects on his life and on the nature of being human.*

The Fates Will Find Their Way—*Hannah Pittard* 270
*In this debut novel, sixteen-year-old Nora Lindell is missing and missed. The
story that follows, narrated by the boys she left behind, imagines where she may have
gone and what her disappearance might mean.*

The Fear: Robert Mugabe and the Martyrdom of Zimbabwe—
Peter Godwin 274
*Godwin describes an extended trip back to his native country of Zimbabwe to
observe the change of government after the violently disputed 2008 presidential and
parliamentary elections.*

COMPLETE ANNOTATED LIST OF TITLES

Feeding on Dreams: Confessions of an Unrepentant Exile—*Ariel Dorfman* . . . 279
This memoir relates the experiences of loss, exile, and self-discovery of Ariel Dorfman after his flight from Chile. Dorfman's book makes an important contribution to the area of human rights by insisting on the necessity of valuing human community over membership in political parties.

Field Gray—*Philip Kerr* 283
The seventh novel in the popular Bernie Gunther detective series finds the hero hiding in Cuba, but he is soon forced back to Europe to confront his checkered past.

The Fifth Witness—*Michael Connelly* 287
Mickey Haller, the hero of Michael Connelly's popular Lincoln Lawyer series, returns to criminal law to defend a client who has been accused of murder.

The Forgotten Founding Father: Noah Webster's Obsession and the Creation
of an American Culture—*Joshua Kendall*. 291
This biography of Noah Webster offers a colorful portrait of the man who compiled the first American English dictionary and helped the country discover its national identity.

Founding Gardeners: The Revolutionary Generation, Nature, and the Shaping
of the American Nation—*Andrea Wulf* 295
Author Andrea Wulf examines the botanical interests of America's founding fathers and how those interests shaped their political endeavors.

1493: Uncovering the New World Columbus Created—*Charles C. Mann*. . . . 299
Using the background of Christopher Columbus's voyage to the Americas, Mann describes the impact of European exploration not only in the West but also on global changes and events.

The Girl in the Blue Beret—*Bobbie Ann Mason* 304
An American pilot reevaluates his life while searching for the resistance workers who helped him escape from Nazi-occupied Europe.

The Girl in the Polka Dot Dress—*Beryl Bainbridge* 308
Bainbridge assembles an eccentric cast of characters whose lives intersect with the novel's two protagonists on their westward journey across the United States seeking an enigmatic man whose location, the travelers' final destination, is the site of the assassination of Senator Robert F. Kennedy.

G. K. Chesterton—*Ian Ker* 312
A comprehensive look at the life of G. K. Chesterton, a leading journalist, essayist, novelist, and apologist for Roman Catholicism during the early twentieth century.

Grand Pursuit:The Story of Economic Genius—*Sylvia Nasar* 316
Nasar's latest work is a history of economics that discusses how humankind has attempted to understand and control the often-mercurial boom and bust cycles of free-market capitalism.

The Greater Journey: Americans in Paris—*David McCullough* 321
McCullough describes the stories of American students, artists, and politicians who worked, studied, and lived in Paris during the nineteenth century.

The Great Night—*Chris Adrian*. 326
William Shakespeare's fantastical romantic comedy of errors A Midsummer Night's Dream *is retold for modern times, as three troubled mortals find themselves in the thick of the faerie queen Titania's annual bacchanalian festival. Adrian's take on this classic story provides some dark and profound twists on the original.*

Great Soul:Mahatma Gandhi and His Struggle with India—*Joseph Lelyveld* . . 330
A probing, well-researched biography of one of the most influential social and political figures of the twentieth century.

The Great Stagnation—*Tyler Cowen* 335
Cowen argues that before the 1970s, the United States benefited from unusually favorable economic conditions, including free land, cheap immigrant labor, and major technological innovations. He contends that all these examples of "low-hanging fruit" have now disappeared, making further rapid economic progress unlikely unless truly major innovations are conceived.

The H.D. Book: The Collected Writings of Robert Duncan—*Robert Duncan* . . 339
Appearing for the first time in book form, this diverse collection of writings by a well-known poet of the San Francisco Renaissance celebrates his literary hero and friend, the poet and feminist revisionist H.D.

Heat Wave: The Life and Career of Ethel Waters—*Donald Bogle* 343
Donald Bogle has written a comprehensive biography of Ethel Waters, the first black woman to sing on radio and perform in a dramatic role on Broadway. Bogle traces her career from early vaudeville and Harlem nightclubs through sixty years as an entertainer on stage, in films, and on television.

Hemingway's Boat: Everything He Loved in Life, and Lost, 1934–1961—
Paul Hendrickson 347
This meticulously researched biography of writer Ernest Hemingway uses his beloved boat, Pilar, as a conceit to trace his prodigious life and literary career.

The Hemlock Cup: Socrates, Athens and the Search for the Good Life—
Bettany Hughes 351
This vivid reconstruction of the life of Socrates places the self-styled gadfly within the rich, turbulent context of Athens during the fifth century BCE.

The Hidden Reality: Parallel Universes and the Deep Laws of the Cosmos—
Brian Greene 355
Greene's The Hidden Reality *is an introduction to the theory of the existence of the multiverse, outlining nine variations of the theory and providing the lay reader with the necessary physics history and background to fully understand these concepts.*

Horoscopes for the Dead—*Billy Collins* 359
In this engaging and touching collection of poetry, Collins once again mines everyday life for inspiration.

The Illumination—*Kevin Brockmeier*. 363
One Friday night, for no apparent reason, human wounds become visible in the form of radiating light.

The Immortalization Commission: Science and the Strange Quest to Cheat
Death—*John Gray*. 367
Gray traces the efforts of Victorian and Edwardian scientists to prove that life existed after death, arguing that since Darwinism had undermined traditional religious belief, proof of immortality was sometimes sought by experimental means; he then suggests that Soviet efforts to prove the existence of immortality led to the brutalities and mass murders committed by the Communist regime.

In Other Worlds: SF and the Human Imagination—*Margaret Atwood* 371
This eclectic collection of essays, reviews, and short fiction explores Margaret Atwood's personal connections with the genre of science fiction, as well as science fiction's roots in mythology, utopian fiction, and Victorian literature.

In the Garden of Beasts: Love, Terror, and an American Family in Hitler's
Berlin—*Erik Larson*. 376
Larson's book is a historical reconstruction of what life was like for the family of William E. Dodd, the American ambassador to Germany from 1933 to 1937, the period in which the newly elected Nazi leader Adolf Hitler was consolidating his grip on Germany.

Into the Silence: The Great War, Mallory, and the Conquest of Everest—
Wade Davis 380
This meticulously researched account of the British attempts to climb Mount Everest in the early 1920s examines the national significance of the expeditions, the legacies of mountaineer George Mallory and his fellow climbers, and the effects of World War I on the men involved.

Iphigenia in Forest Hills: Anatomy of a Murder Trial—*Janet Malcolm* 384
  Malcolm's account of a murder trial reveals layer upon layer of complexities
  and absurdities and seeming contradictions, leading the reader to question the very
  nature of truth and ambiguity.

A Jane Austen Education: How Six Novels Taught Me about Love, Friendship,
  and the Things That Really Matter—*William Deresiewicz* 389
  Literary critic William Deresiewicz reflects on how he overcame his bias against
  author Jane Austen and became a more thoughtful and understanding person in the
  process.

J. D. Salinger: A Life—*Kenneth Slawenski* 393
  Slawenski offers a new biography of J. D. Salinger, the enigmatic and secretive
  author of such works as The Catcher in the Rye, *who ceased publishing long before*
  he died and went out of his way to protect his personal privacy.

Jerusalem: The Biography—*Simon Sebag Montefiore* 397
  Montefiore presents a detailed narrative history of Jerusalem, studying the conti-
  nuity of the city in the face of changing empires, dynasties, and religions.

Joan Mitchell: Lady Painter, A Life—*Patricia Albers* 401
  As the first full-scale biography of Joan Mitchell, this well-researched tome
  builds upon primary sources such as Mitchell's letters and interviews with her fam-
  ily, friends, and peers to provide an intimate and detailed portrayal of the abstract
  expressionist painter who came of age in the 1950s and 1960s.

Joe Dimaggio: The Long Vigil—*Jerome Charyn* 405
  Jerome Charyn examines Joe DiMaggio, separating "the greatest living ballplay-
  er" from the man haunted by the demons of loneliness and passion.

Just One Catch: A Biography of Joseph Heller—*Tracy Daugherty* 409
  Just One Catch is the first comprehensive biography of writer Joseph Heller,
  the author of Catch-22, *one of the most important American novels of the twentieth*
  century

VOLUME 2

The Keats Brothers: The Life of John and George—*Denise Gigante* 413
  This biography of the Keats brothers traces their parallel lives from John's first
  poetic success to their deaths, examining in particular the nature of their relation-
  ship and the effect of George's migration to the American Midwest.

The King James Bible: A Short History from Tyndale to Today—
David Norton 417
Norton presents a scholarly examination of the nearly ninety-year process by which English translations of the Bible culminated in the so-called King James Version, as well as a summary account of this version's continuing influence on the present and potential impact for the future.

The Land at the End of the World—*António Lobo Antunes*. 421
A man recounts his traumatic experience as a military doctor during Portugal's colonial wars in Angola.

Last Man in Tower—*Aravind Adiga* 425
When an ambitious, somewhat shady developer seeks to raze two old Mumbai condominium towers in favor of a luxury complex, he offers owners an above-market price, with the catch that they all have to agree to sell; soon, vicious peer pressure begins breaking apart the existing social harmony. The novel reflects on the effect of greed but also raises questions about one person going against the will of the community.

Lee Krasner: A Biography—*Gail Levin*. 429
Levin presents Lee Krasner as an independent, talented avant-garde artist whose stature should be assessed outside of the shadow of her more famous husband, Jackson Pollock.

The Leftovers—*Tom Perrotta*. 434
After one-third of the world's population mysteriously disappears, a suburban American family completely unravels.

The Lessons—*Joanne Diaz* 438
With striking imagery and lush language, Joanne Diaz's first collection of poetry addresses topics such as travel, family, illness, and mortality.

The Letters of Ernest Hemingway: Volume 1, 1907–1922—
Sandra Spanier and Robert W. Trogdon. 442
The letters in this first volume reveal two forces that shaped the young Hemingway and made their mark on him for life: his middle-class upbringing in Oak Park and his experience in the war.

Liberty's Exiles: American Loyalists in the Revolutionary World—
Maya Jasanoff. 447
Jasanoff discusses the diversity of loyalists living in North American colonies, examining how they extended the British Empire after the American Revolution by migrating to numerous locations where their activities affected imperial policies.

Life Itself: A Memoir—*Roger Ebert* 452
Film critic Roger Ebert recalls his encounters with famous stars and filmmakers, his successful career, and his struggles with cancer and debilitating surgeries.

Life on Mars—*Tracy K. Smith* 456
Tracy K. Smith's third collection of poetry uses outer space, science fiction, and interplanetary travel to examine the human condition on Earth while exemplifying the author's vivid and affecting use of language and imagery

Malcolm X: A Life of Reinvention—*Manning Marable* 460
This detailed and scholarly biography of Malcolm X focuses on the evolution in his thinking about race and revolution, including much controversial information about his private life.

The Marriage Plot—*Jeffrey Eugenides* 465
Set on an Ivy League campus during the heyday of deconstruction, Eugenides's third novel takes on the archetypal story line of middle-class fiction.

Metropole—*Geoffrey G. O'Brien* 469
O'Brien's startling and intriguing poetry collection examines what a globalized world has done to humanity's ability to value loved ones, the self, possessions, and language.

Micro—*Michael Crichton and Richard Preston* 473
A posthumous techno-thriller begun by Michael Crichton and completed by Richard Preston, Micro *pits a group of young graduate students in various fields of sciences against a sinister villain, killer micro-robots, and the implacable forces of nature.*

Miss New India—*Bharati Mukherjee* 477
A young Indian woman rejects her impecunious family and its traditions and seeks a new life in the modern city of Bangalore. Her ambiguous mix of success and failure becomes a symbol of an emerging India.

Modigliani: A Life—*Meryle Secrest* 481
An in-depth portrait of Amedeo Modigliani, the twentieth-century master painter and sculptor, this biography aims to discern the truth about the man behind the myth.

Moonwalking with Einstein: The Art and Science of Remembering
Everything—*Joshua Foer* 485
An often-humorous exploration into the human memory, this book chronicles the journey that transformed author Joshua Foer, a journalist investigating the 2005 US Memory Championship, into a participant and record-setting champion at the same event in 2006.

Mr. Fox—*Helen Oyeyemi* 489
A novel composed of short stories, Oyeyemi's fourth book is a modern retelling of several classic fairy tales.

Music for Silenced Voices: Shostakovich and His Fifteen Quartets—
Wendy Lesser 493
This book, designed for the layperson rather than for the professional musician, describes the intertwining of Shostakovich's life with his string quartets.

My Father's Fortune: A Life—*Michael Frayn* 497
Author Michael Frayn recalls his father, his family life, and his own pursuits while growing up in early to mid-twentieth century London.

My New American Life—*Francine Prose* 501
This light-hearted look at an immigrant's pursuit of the American Dream sheds light on why so many people from other countries want to live in the United States— and why they are willing to leave their homeland for a new country.

Nanjing Requiem—*Ha Jin* 505
A fictionalized account of the Japanese capture of the Chinese city of Nanjing in 1937 and its effect on the Chinese population and the community of foreigners.

Never Say Die: The Myth and Marketing of the New Old Age—
Susan Jacoby 509
A history of old age in the United States that challenges optimistic assumptions about aging, suggesting that only a new social contract can help prevent generational conflict as more baby boomers retire.

The Night Circus—*Erin Morgenstern* 513
In this immersive debut novel about an intoxicatingly stylish circus and its performers, a talented pair of magicians-turned-lovers duel to the death in a competition of illusion and skill.

Night Soul and Other Stories—*Joseph McElroy* 517
This is the first short story collection by a highly praised postmodernist author best known for his long, complex novels.

Nod House—*Nathaniel Mackey* 521
Lyric and rhythmic, the world described in Nod House *is a mythic version of our own, constantly in the process of change and reinvention. Continuing two serial poems from his previous collections, Mackey describes travelers, exiled from their home and wandering instead through a world of the dead, of dream states, and of music.*

No Regrets: The Life of Edith Piaf—*Carolyn Burke* 526
In this descriptive biography of the life of Édith Piaf, Burke chronicles the vocal artist's origins, meteoric career, and long struggles with cancer.

Once Upon a River—*Bonnie Jo Campbell* 530
After her father's death, Margo Crane goes in search of her mother, setting off by herself on the Stark River.

On China—*Henry Kissinger* 534
A key figure in US-Chinese diplomacy recounts his experience and attempts to elucidate the underlying principles of China's foreign policy in the twenty-first century.

One Day I Will Write about This Place—*Binyavanga Wainaina* 539
In this memoir, the author uses strong, descriptive language to depict a diverse Kenya, recounting his experiences inside and outside of his country as the political landscape in postcolonial Africa rapidly shifts.

One Hundred Names For Love: A Stroke, a Marriage, and the Language
of Healing—*Diane Ackerman* 543
Ackerman presents an account of her husband's stroke, its devastating aftermath, and her efforts to help him heal.

1Q84—*Haruki Murakami* 548
Aomame finds herself pulled into an alternate reality, which may be the fictional creation of a seventeen-year-old girl and her ghostwriting partner, a young man with whom Aomame had an encounter during her childhood.

One Was a Soldier—*Julia Spencer-Fleming* 552
This seventh novel in the Clare Fergusson and Russ Van Alstyne murder mystery series follows a group of veterans as they return home to Millers Kill from tours of duty in Iraq.

Open City—*Teju Cole* 556
This impressive debut novel provides a case history of New York City from the perspective of a Nigerian German psychiatrist finishing his residency.

Orientation: And Other Stories—*Daniel Orozco* 561
A debut collection of nine stories about the loneliness and deadening daily life of work.

Otherwise Known as the Human Condition: Selected Essays and Reviews—
Geoff Dyer 565
This collection of Dyer's essays and critical reviews encompasses a wide range of topics, including war photography, Americana, aviation, music, and much more.

COMPLETE ANNOTATED LIST OF TITLES

The Pale King—*David Foster Wallace* 569
The last and unfinished novel of David Foster Wallace considers the monotony of working life and the significance of boredom through a group of IRS examiners working at the Midwest Regional Examination Center in Peoria, Illinois.

The Paper Garden: An Artist Begins Her Life's Work at Seventy-Two—
Molly Peacock 574
This biography of artist Mary Delany is at once the portrait of a fascinating woman and a meditation on creativity, womanhood, and age. Poet Molly Peacock crafts the narrative with beautiful language, highlighted by reproductions of Delany's flower mosaics.

A People of One Book: The Bible and the Victorians—*Timothy Larsen* 578
Religious studies scholar Timothy Larsen investigates how Victorians of many different Christian denominations, as well as agnostics and atheists, were influenced by the Bible.

The Philosophical Breakfast Club: Four Remarkable Friends Who
Transformed Science and Changed the World—*Laura J. Snyder* 583
The story of four accomplished scientists who became friends while students at Cambridge in the mid-nineteenth century and formed an informal society for the discussion of science.

Please Look After Mom—*Kyung-sook Shin* 588
When their elderly mother goes missing after becoming separated from her husband at a subway platform at Seoul Station, her two oldest adult children try to find her. In the course of their quest, the mother's boundless love for her children and her acceptance of a difficult husband is revealed.

The Pleasures of Reading in an Age of Distraction—*Alan Jacobs* 592
Literary and cultural critic Alan Jacobs presents an extended argument in defense of reading and offers suggestions for making the experience more enjoyable.

The Prague Cemetery—*Umberto Eco.* 596
Set in a nineteenth-century Europe obsessed with theories of conspiracy, Umberto Eco's The Prague Cemetery *is the story of Simone Simonini, a master forger of documents who is driven by hatred.*

The Preacher—*Camilla Läckberg.* 601
The gruesome murder of a young woman in the small village of Fjällbacka, Sweden—and the discovery of decades-old remains located beneath her body—challenge the skills of police detective Patrik Hedström and his wife, writer Erica Falck.

The Psychopath Test: A Journey Through the Madness Industry—
Jon Ronson 605
The author offers a comic yet insightful exploration of psychiatric diagnostic methods past and present, as well as a critique of their effects on individuals and society.

Pulphead: Essays—*John Jeremiah Sullivan* 609
John Jeremiah Sullivan presents an engaging collection of essays that provides many unexpected perspectives on American popular culture.

Pym—*Mat Johnson* 613
An African American professor of literature travels to Antarctica in order to prove that the outlandish events related in Edgar Allen Poe's novel The Narrative of Arthur Gordon Pym of Nantucket *actually took place.*

Reading My Father: A Memoir—*Alexandra Styron* 617
Alexandra Styron's memoir of life with her late father, American novelist William Styron, chronicles the celebrated author's achievements and struggles, as well as his lifelong battle with clinical depression.

Redeemers: Ideas and Power in Latin America—*Enrique Krauze* 621
The author analyzes the ideas of the thinkers, writers, and revolutionaries who have influenced politics in Latin America, making a significant contribution to the history of the region.

Rodin's Debutante—*Ward Just* 625
A young man comes of age in Chicago and reflects on the direct and indirect events and relationships that have profoundly shaped his life.

Sacred Trash: The Lost and Found World of the Cairo Geniza—
Adina Hoffman and Peter Cole 629
This nonfiction book delves into the work of scholars who spent over a century rediscovering lost Jewish history in the nearly 280,000 assorted documents of the Cairo Geniza, a diverse collection of documents from one Jewish community between 870 and 1880.

The Saturday Big Tent Wedding Party—*Alexander McCall Smith* 633
The twelfth volume of Alexander McCall Smith's series about Botswana's "No.1 Lady Detective," Precious Ramotswe, tells the story of an intriguing mystery dealing with cattle while exploring the complex daily lives of Precious's family and friends.

Say Her Name—*Francisco Goldman* 637
This fictionalized memoir from the award-winning journalist and novelist is a testament of the narrator's love for his deceased wife, Aura Estrada, as well as a testimony to how grief can morph into guilt.

The Seamstress and the Wind—*César Aira*. 641
A highly experimental, elaborate rendering of the dynamics of the imagination and the process of literary creation, The Seamstress and the Wind presents a dream tale of a distraught mother, tracking down her missing child in the forbidding wastes of Argentina's Patagonia region.

The Selected Stories of Mercè Rodoreda—*Mercè Rodoreda*. 645
Representing over two decades of work by one of the most important Catalan authors, the stories in this collection focus on themes of obsessive love, personal loss, violence, and warfare.

Seven Years—*Peter Stamm* 649
Set in Germany during reunification, this novel breathes new life into the cliché of the seven-year itch.

The Shadow of What We Were—*Luis Sepúlveda*. 653
A rainy day in Santiago, Chile, is the backdrop for the reunion of three aging leftists who survived the violent and oppressive Pinochet regime.

She-Wolves: The Women Who Ruled England before Elizabeth—
Helen Castor. 657
Castor examines how perceptions of gender affected the inheritance of royal titles and access to power by medieval women who were descended from kings or related to monarchs through marriage or motherhood, analyzing how their experiences influenced the acceptance of queens in later centuries.

Silver Sparrow—*Tayari Jones* 662
The eventual meeting of two half sisters, daughters of a bigamist father, shapes their personal identities and feelings of self-worth.

A Singular Woman: The Untold Story of Barack Obama's Mother—
Janny Scott. 666
Scott presents a meticulously researched account of the life of cultural anthropologist Ann Dunham, whose groundbreaking contributions had a profound impact on the lives of the poor in Indonesia and whose values shaped the life of her son, US president Barack Obama.

The Sly Company of People Who Care—*Rahul Bhattacharya*. 670
Bhattacharya's engaging debut novel chronicles the impressions, adventures, and realizations of a young man from India who spends a year in Guyana.

Smoking Typewriters: The Sixties Underground Press and the Rise of
Alternative Media in America—*John McMillian* 674
*McMillian offers a historical overview of the 1960s underground press and its
legacy in the modern alternative press and Internet publishing industries.*

Sobbing Superpower: Selected Poems of Tadeusz Różewicz—
Tadeusz Różewicz 679
*This extensive overview of Różewicz's poetry is drawn from over twenty individ-
ual collections. Long considered the most influential contemporary poet in Poland,
Różewicz's work has been largely unread in the United States. This collection seeks
to introduce new audiences to the philosophical poet's dark, stripped-down verse.*

The Social Animal: The Hidden Sources of Love, Character, and
Achievement—*David Brooks* 683
*Brooks's study traces the lives of two invented characters, Harold and Erica, as a
way of presenting a great deal of scientific and sociological information about how
humans develop and how the mind, and especially the brain, influence this development.*

Songs of Kabir—*Kabir* 687
*Mehrotra's translation of sixty of Kabir's poems is the latest of a long line of
translations of the Indian mystic and poet. It is a sampler done in idiomatic English,
but it provides a set of notes and a preface to give Western readers some context.*

Space, in Chains—*Laura Kasischke* 691
*A lyric and emotional exploration of grief, Space, in Chains focuses on the death
of the poet's parents and her own realizations of mortality and aging.*

The Splendor of Portugal—*António Lobo Antunes* 695
*Another psychologically driven novel from successful storyteller António Lobo
Antunes, this story examines the high price paid by a dysfunctional Portuguese settler family as they lose their African farm in the devastating postindependence civil
war in Angola.*

Steve Jobs—*Walter Isaacson* 699
*Isaacson offers an extremely detailed and appreciative biography of Steve
Jobs, the computer and marketing genius who helped transform the lives of people
throughout the world through one innovative product after another. Isaacson presents Jobs as a driven, inspired, and inventive man who could be both abrasive and
abusive in dealing with others.*

Stone Arabia—*Dana Spiotta* 704
*Spiotta presents a fragmented and fascinating portrait of a brother and sister who
wrestle with the past in order to come to terms with where they are in the present.*

The Stranger's Child—*Alan Hollinghurst*. 708
Hollinghurst's fifth novel, The Stranger's Child, is a complex study of English society, sexual mores, literary creation, and the reliability of memory and biography told through the history of the Valance and Sawle families from 1913 to 2008.

The Summer Without Men—*Siri Hustvedt* 712
Faced with a midlife crisis and turbulence in her marriage, a poet returns to her hometown and finds strength in forging connections with teenage girls, older women, and a young mother.

Swamplandia!—*Karen Russell* 716
After the failure of their family's business, their mother's death, and their father's abandonment, Ava Bigtree and her siblings embark on very different journeys in strange and unfamiliar surroundings as they try to cope with their losses.

The Swerve: How the World Became Modern—*Stephen Greenblatt*. 720
The author presents a comprehensive overview of the origins, rediscovery, and influence of a famous poem by Lucretius that foreshadowed the rise of modern thinking.

Swim Back to Me—*Ann Packer* 724
Packer's collection of stories about Northern California bring the reader into the heart of true-to-life experiences in which ordinary suburban characters navigate their way through loss and longing.

Tabloid City—*Pete Hamill* 728
Hamill's tale about the end of a tabloid tells the story of how a man who has lived in the tabloid world far too long discovers life outside of his work. Hamill also explores the stories of a cross section of New Yorkers dealing with their own endings.

Taller When Prone—*Les Murray* 732
A thoughtful, mischievous, and masterful collection of poems by one of Australia's most accomplished living poets.

The Tiger's Wife—*Téa Obreht* 736
A young doctor's humanitarian mission to the Balkans also sends her on a quest to solve the mystery of her grandfather's death.

To End All Wars: A Story of Loyalty and Rebellion: 1914–1918—
Adam Hochschild 740
Adam Hochschild presents a brilliantly written account of Great Britain in World War I, focusing on individuals who opposed as well as supported the war

Tolstoy: A Russian Life—*Rosamund Bartlett* 745
 Focusing on the last thirty years of Tolstoy's life, this biography vividly captures the writer's epic life and conducts readers on a fascinating journey through Russian history and culture.

Tough Without a Gun: The Life and Extraordinary Afterlife of Humphrey
 Bogart—*Stefan Kanfer* 749
 Kanfer chronicles the life of Humphrey Bogart, from childhood through a struggling early career to his breakthrough as a film star in his early forties, and offers a thorough examination of the lore and legend of Bogart as a larger-than-life icon after his death.

Townie: A Memoir—*Andre Dubus III* 754
 Andre Dubus III's memoir is a story of a boy who, terrified by his inability to stand up for himself and those he loves, turns to physical strength and violence as a young man and then eventually to the art of writing.

The Tragedy of Arthur—*Arthur Phillips* 758
 This book explores the psychological character of its narrator, his relationships with his twin sister and criminal father, and the authenticity of the manuscript of The Tragedy of Arthur, *a play purportedly penned by William Shakespeare.*

Traveler—*Devin Johnston* 762
 In poems that favor careful observation, studious details, and deliberate structure, Johnston explores travel, the natural world, and the experience of being a father.

The Trouble Ball—*Martín Espada* 767
 A riveting and instructive poetry collection, The Trouble Ball *focuses on the personal struggles and insults that countless members of the minority community have had to endure.*

The Troubled Man—*Henning Mankell* 771
 In the tenth and final book of the author's popular series, taciturn police detective Kurt Wallander is drawn into a mystery from the Cold War when a former naval commander—the father of his daughter's fiancé—disappears.

Twice a Spy—*Keith Thomson* 775
 Thomson's father-son spy duo returns to grapple with a terrorist intent on detonating a nuclear device during an international economic summit in Mobile, Alabama.

The Uncoupling—*Meg Wolitzer* 779
 A modern fairy tale set against American involvement in Afghanistan and Iraq, Wolitzer's story uses the premise of Aristophanes' play Lysistrata *to explore the relationship between passion and love when women in suburban New Jersey suddenly become bewitched and inexplicably lose interest in sex.*

COMPLETE ANNOTATED LIST OF TITLES

Unseen Hand—*Adam Zagajewski*. 783
Zagajewski's sixth book of poetry to be translated into English, Unseen Hand
*explores memory, history, and family, all while maintaining a firm grounding in the
physicality of place and everyday life.*

Vaclav and Lena—*Haley Tanner* 787
*In this debut novel, Tanner brings to life two young Russian immigrants and tells
the story of how they learn to navigate the difficulties of love and life in a new land.*

We, the Drowned—*Carsten Jensen* 791
*The history of a town and a way of life, this epic novel tells the story of genera-
tions of sailors from the Danish port of Marstal who went to sea to earn their living
and the women and children they left behind.*

We Others: New and Selected Stories—*Steven Millhauser*. 795
*Millhauser's latest collection of short stories features selected works from his four
previous collections, plus seven new and previously uncollected stories.*

When the Killing's Done—*T. C. Boyle* 799
*This environmental-ecological novel centers on two opposing factions, bringing to
the surface the questions of who and what is right when, despite the best of intentions
of both sides, fanatical adherence to principles leads to unintended consequences.*

Widow—*Michelle Latiolais*. 803
*This collection of short stories has propelled its author into the national spotlight
in part for its exposé of the anger, depression, and vulnerability of widowhood that is
so often misunderstood by society.*

A Widow's Story: A Memoir—*Joyce Carol Oates* 808
*The author describes in harrowing detail her grief after the death of her husband
of nearly forty-eight years.*

Words Made Fresh: Essays on Literature and Culture—*Larry Woiwode* 813
*This book presents an intriguing and stimulating set of essays discussing issues
that are close to Woiwode's heart.*

The Words of Others: From Quotations to Culture—*Gary Saul Morson*. 817
*This book presents a discussion of the relevance and power of the use of quota-
tions throughout literature and culture.*

The Wrong War: Grit, Strategy, and the Way Out of Afghanistan—
Bing West 821
*This book offers a critique of American military strategy in Afghanistan, includ-
ing recommendations on how to bring the war to a successful conclusion.*

You and Three Others Are Approaching a Lake—*Anna Moschovakis* 825
Largely spoken in the language of modern technology, Moschovakis's second poetry collection is an investigation into the morals and lifestyles of contemporary society.

You Think That's Bad—*Jim Shepard* 829
Jim Shepard's new collection of short fiction examines the domestic and large-scale cataclysms that befall a wide cast of characters, from an explorer in 1930s Lebanon to a hydraulic engineer in the near future.

The Keats Brothers
The Life of John and George

Author: Denise Gigante (b. 1965)
Publisher: Harvard University Press (Cambridge, MA). 552 pp. $35.00
Type of work: Biography
Time: 1816–1841
Locale: London and southern England; Louisville, Kentucky

This biography of the Keats brothers traces their parallel lives from John's first poetic success to their deaths, examining in particular the nature of their relationship and the effect of George's migration to the American Midwest.

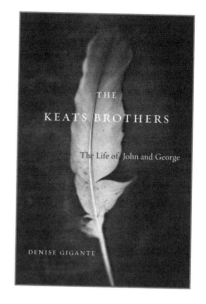

Principal personages:
JOHN KEATS (1795–1821), a leading English romantic poet, eldest of the Keats children
GEORGE KEATS (1797–1841), the second of the Keats boys, seeking fortune abroad
TOM KEATS (1799–1818), the youngest of the three boys, who died early of consumption
FANNY KEATS (1803–1889), the youngest child of the family, separated from her brothers
FANNY BRAWNE (1800–1865), John's unofficial fiancée and the love of his life
GEORGIANA WYLIE (1802–1879), George's wife, married to him shortly before emigration

Writing a literary biography on more than one person at a time presents many challenges. Successful examples include the books on the Brontë sisters by Inga-Stina Ewbank, Phyllis Bentley, and Juliet Barker. The Brontë and Keats families are remarkably similar in many ways, both being intimately connected to the English romantic movement and both having family members who suffered tragic deaths from that scourge of the nineteenth century, consumption (tuberculosis). Despite their respective tragedies, each family contributed gems of brilliance that continue to be some of the finest works of English literature. The poetry of John Keats is a clear example, and while Denise Gigante's *The Keats Brothers: The Life of John and George* does not prove to be quite as successful a study as others, it does offer generous rewards.

The life of John Keats has been well mapped over the years, ever since early Victorian poets such as Alfred, Lord Tennyson confirmed his status as a major English poet. Tennyson's friend Richard Monckton Milnes produced the first biography, *Life and Letters of Keats* (1848), and many other fine biographies have been written in recent years, including Robert Gittings's *The Mask of Keats* (1956), W. J. Bate's *John Keats* (1963), and poet Andrew Motion's *Keats: A Biography* (1997). The brilliance of Keats's letters to friends and family also has long been recognized and studied.

(Raúl Díaz)

Denise Gigante is a professor of English at Stanford University. She completed her Ph.D. in romanticism at Princeton University and has since written extensively on the topic. She is working on a book about Charles Lamb.

Collections of Keats-related documents are kept in the Houghton Library at Harvard University, and, to lesser extents, in the British Library in London, the Keats House in Hampstead, the Keats-Shelley House in Rome, and the Morgan Library and Museum in New York City.

There would seem, then, to be very little more to discover about Keats. However, with *The Keats Brothers*, Gigante provides new information on the family in general, including a thorough study of John's brother George. She makes this a true family affair by also including details about Tom, the youngest son—whose death in 1818 prefigured John's own death three years later—and Fanny, their sister, who was kept closely confined by their guardian, Richard Abbey. Generally, *The Keats Brothers* attempts to examine the family dynamics that helped produce John's great poetic works, much in the same way that other biographers have examined how the dynamics between the Brontës influenced each one's literary output. In the Keats family, of course, only one family member generated literary work. Part of Gigante's argument is that George produced a body of work of his own, as a pioneer on the American frontier in the 1820s, and she tries to plot their works' similarities in the context of romanticism.

No less central to Gigante's agenda is an exploration of the effect George's absence had on John. She argues that by going abroad at the beginning of his brother's literary career, George removed a major stabilizing factor from John's life, leaving him to deal with his dying brother and an uncertain income by himself. Gigante portrays a John Keats who was unable to deal well with money or the affairs of life in general. However, it was out of this very sense of loss that he produced some of his best poetry, and Gigante wonders if his work would have been so compelling had George remained in England.

The strength of the book is not so much its pursuit of this thesis as it is Gigante's description of the American frontier and the effect it had on romantic perceptions. She traces the large number of people emigrating from Great Britain to the United States despite the War of 1812, many as a result of Britain's depressed economy, but also due in part to political publications such as those of Morris Birkbeck. Many of Gigante's sources, including information gathered from surviving members of the Keats family, were previously collected and preserved at the Filson Historical Society in Louisville, Kentucky, where they remained boxed and neglected until she discovered them. To students of the American frontier, accounts such as those she produces about settlements in Kentucky and Illinois throughout the nineteenth century will be familiar. To students of English literature, however, these accounts will be a fascinating discovery. The contrasts between the romantic project of founding a new Eden and the reality of the immigrant situation in America are striking, the latter fulfilling Thomas Hobbes's popular description of life as "nasty, brutish, and short."

The young, newly married George Keats invested what money he had in his venture abroad, inspired by Birkbeck's glowing account in *Notes on a Journey in America from the Coast of Virginia to the Territory of Illinois* (1817). He and his wife headed to the English Prairie settlement in Illinois, thinking they could easily acquire the necessary skills for farming, George's only skills at that time being those he had developed as the clerk of Abbey's tea-importing business. Upon discovering that his wife, Georgiana, was pregnant and that Birkbeck's accounts were less than reliable, George moved to Louisville, where he encountered John Audubon. Some biographers of Keats have painted Audubon as a frontier swindler who successfully disposed of the rest of the Keats's money. Gigante is kinder to him, suggesting that most frontier economy ran on credit, and that in any financial disaster, everybody lost.

George's plan to remit money to his brother failed, and he was forced to return to London to raise money for a joint venture lumber mill. There has been some controversy surrounding the moral dynamics of financial transactions between John and George, and whether John owed George money. Most biographers have their own accounts of the Keatses' finances and the part their guardian played in them. Gigante's take is that Abbey dealt as fairly as he could, especially given the grandmother's inheritance and that he did not get on well with John. Nobody, it seems, is to be blamed exclusively for the situation—not the "man of genius," as John is called, and not the "man of power," George.

Eventually, George's business enterprises flourished in response to the growing influx of immigrants until the financial crash of 1837, when he lost everything again. During this period, he acquired a sizable house in Louisville, enjoyed a large family, and owned slaves, but remained modest on the subject of his famous dead brother. He died of tuberculosis, "the family disease," in 1841. The narrative finishes with Irish writer and poet Oscar Wilde visiting Louisville to lecture on John Keats, only to discover one of George's descendants in possession of many of Keats's letters, manuscripts, and poems.

Gigante's narrative begins in 1816, as essayist and poet Leigh Hunt is on the verge of publishing John's first poem. At the same time, George is working for Abbey, and Tom is already too sick to work at all. The text is divided into four parts, with the first part dealing with the years 1816–17, the next two focusing on 1818 and 1819 respectively, and the fourth covering 1820 onward. Every chapter represents the fruits of Gigante's research, offering extensive historical detail and background. She attempts to draw attention to the parallels between John and George, but this parallelism does not always work successfully. A detailed discussion of "The Fall of Hyperion," for example, abruptly morphs into an equally detailed account of the American frontier, and the fact that these two events transpired simultaneously does not necessarily yield the significance Gigante's methodology seems to suggest. Most literary readers, at least, would prefer to learn more about "Hyperion" and less about which family member married which. Other times, however, Gigante's style brings events to life. This is especially the case in passages that describe life on the frontier, which prove that there is something of the novelist in Gigante. Additionally, accounts of Tom's and John's deaths remain unbearably sad and painful, particularly in light of John's having cared for and nursed his brother Tom during his own case of tuberculosis.

Still, Gigante's style features certain qualities that readers may find irritating. One of these is the patronizing way the term "cockney" is thrown around. "The Cockney Poet" and "the Cockney Pioneer" present themselves whenever they can. Critic John Lockhart used the term as a sneer at "uneducated" poets who dared to use classical material in their poetry; when used to refer to Keats, it still retains an element of opprobrium, and to that end Gigante might be suspected of being of the Lockhart party. Readers may also find themselves being weighed down with too many details from time to time, specifically details that are not directly relevant to George's life on the frontier. And there are trivial mistakes: Procne is confused with Philomela (p. 218), while the Irish Sea is variously placed on the wrong side of the St. George's Channel (p. 161) and confused with the North Sea (p. 336).

More importantly, Gigante's fundamental claim that George's absence influenced John's poetry is not tackled in any systematic way, thus becoming somewhat speculative. Many of Keats's biographers have drawn attention to particular friends as having a significant influence on his work, and with *The Keats Brothers*, Gigante seems to be adding her own candidate to the list. John clearly stated that George was his best friend, but the argument that his mere absence so heavily inspired and motivated Keats's poetry is unpersuasive. The effects of absence are most evident in the brothers' correspondence, and while John did write many significant letters to George, he also wrote such letters to Brown, Bailey, Haydon, and a host of others who were often no more than a mile or two down the road. Thus, Gigante's literary argument does little to privilege her work over other biographical accounts. It is in the Americana portion of the book that she has uncovered new, exciting territory. Her rendering of the American frontier evokes the romantic paradox of plenty and beauty that can only be realized in a sordid, deceptive world, a paradox that John and George, in their different ways, lived out.

David Barratt

Review Sources

Publishers Weekly 258, no. 35 (August 29, 2011): 55–56.
The New York Times Book Review, October 14, 2011, p. 22.

The King James Bible
A Short History from Tyndale to Today

Author: David Norton (b. 1962)
Publisher: Cambridge University Press (Cambridge). 232 pp. $24.99
Type of work: History
Time: 1523–1611
Locale: England, mainly Westminster, Oxford, and Cambridge

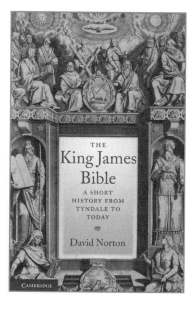

Norton presents a scholarly examination of the nearly ninety-year process by which English translations of the Bible culminated in the so-called King James Version, as well as a summary account of this version's continuing influence on the present and potential impact for the future.

Principal personages:

WILLIAM TYNDALE (1494? –1536), English cleric and translator of the first English Bible

MYLES COVERDALE (1488? –1569), bishop of Exeter and biblical translator

JOHN BOIS (1560–1643), translator of the Bible and compiler of an account of the Second Cambridge Company's work on the King James Bible

MATTHEW PARKER (1504–1575), archbishop of Canterbury (1559–1575) and inspirational leader behind the translation known as the Bishops' Bible

LANCELOT ANDREWES (1555–1626), bishop of Winchester, former bishop of Chichester and Ely, and chair of the First Westminster Company of biblical translators

EDWARD LIVELY (1545–1605), professor of Hebrew at Trinity College, Cambridge, and chair of the First Cambridge Company of translators

JOHN HARDING (?–1610), president of Magdalen College, Oxford University, and chair of the First Oxford Company of translators

WILLIAM BARLOW (?–1613), bishop of Lincoln and chair of the Second Westminster Company of translators

JOHN DUPORT (?–1617-18), master of Jesus College, Cambridge University, and chair of the Second Cambridge Company of translators

THOMAS RAVIS (1560?–1609), bishop of London and chair of the Second Oxford Company of translators

In *The King James Bible*, David Norton views the Authorized Version (AV) of the Bible, also called the King James Bible or the King James Version, as being the end product of a long period of development and the fruit of many individual minds, having precious little to do with King James I of England. Norton begins with a summary sketch of the historical development of biblical texts and the various kinds of texts that were available for study and translation in the early sixteenth century before focusing on William Tyndale, well known for undertaking the first major translation of the Bible into English. Tyndale suffered martyrdom for several reasons, including but not limited to his activities as a biblical translator. Norton rightly credits Tyndale, the first to translate scripture directly from the original Hebrew and Greek, as the true author of what would become known as the King James Bible. Indeed, the subsequent translator companies of the early 1600s fully acknowledged that they were only building on Tyndale's foundations. In spite of Norton's acknowledgments, though, Tyndale is passed over rather quickly, as the narrative continues with his disciple, Myles Coverdale, and the draft revisions he undertook.

Norton spends a good deal of time grudgingly praising Coverdale for his energy and desire to continue Tyndale's work. Mainly, however, he criticizes Coverdale's shortcomings as a scholar, accusing him of proceeding in the "false direction" and relying more on the work of secondary sources than on the original material. He even casts doubt on Coverdale's spectacular achievement in completing his revisions within the space of a year. Norton is similarly ambivalent in his assessment of the Matthew Bible, a revised translation by John Rogers (alias Thomas Matthew), first dismissing it as unoriginal and then extolling it as the primary inspiration for the Great Bible of 1541.

The Great Bible itself, the first version to be royally authorized—in this case, by King Henry VIII of England—was shepherded by Thomas Cranmer, archbishop of Canterbury (some sources accordingly labeling it "Cranmer's Bible"), as well as Thomas Cromwell, the Lord Privy Seal. Coverdale was heavily involved in the work of compiling the Great Bible, complementing Tyndale's translation with his own. However, the Great Bible was soon superseded in popularity and dissemination by the Geneva Bible of 1560. This new version was assembled by a group of English exiles in Calvinist Geneva under the direction of scholar William Whittingham, which meant that Continental scholars such as John Calvin and Theodore Beza exerted at least a certain measure of influence on the text, while the work of translators and editors like Coverdale foreshadowed the work of the companies of scholars who would hammer out the King James Bible from 1604 to 1611. However, in the conservative climate that prevailed in the late 1560s, the Geneva Bible was too suggestive of Calvinism, particularly in its annotations. Therefore, with the authorization of Queen Elizabeth I of England and Matthew Parker, archbishop of Canterbury, the Bishops' Bible was published in 1568 as a partial reconfiguration of the Great Bible. Parker, a moderately conservative churchman, sought to replace the radical reformist connotations of the Geneva Bible with a translation that would align more closely to the queen's Elizabethan Religious Settlement of 1559, which sought a middle path between the extremes of Calvinism and Roman Catholicism. The Bishops' Bible was significantly reedited in 1572 and in 1602. Although not as widely read among the general English population as the Geneva Bible, it had a significant influence on the translator companies.

Norton largely abandons the historical chronology when it comes to describing the actual translation process of the AV, focusing instead on selected extant translators'

David Norton worked as a taxicab driver in Cambridge, England, before graduating from Cambridge University with a master's degree in English. He is a professor of English at Victoria University in Wellington, New Zealand, and has published an edition of the King James Bible *(2006) as well as several previous books on the English* Bible, *including* A History of the English Bible as Literature *(2000) and* A Textual History of the King James Bible *(2005).*

notes and John Bois's diary. He characterizes King James I as having a strictly passive role, merely giving a "rubber stamp" endorsement to ideas that were already widely recognized. Norton also downplays and glosses over the Hampton Court Conference of 1604, where James I met with leaders of the Church of England. One might be pardoned for thinking that perhaps this revisionism has gone too far, and that King James's true role was somewhere between those of a nonparticipant and an engaged scholar. The facts still suggest that in seeking an accurate, authorized, and more Anglican version of the Bible, James I urged the undertaking of this massive project, which entailed translating the Old Testament from the original Hebrew, the New Testament from the Greek, and the Books of the Apocrypha from the Latin. To this end, he appointed scholar-translators whose assemblies in Westminster, Oxford, and Cambridge would later become known as companies. Each company assumed the responsibility of translating a portion of the scriptures, with the First Westminster Company taking on Genesis to 2 Kings; the First Cambridge Company, 1 Chronicles to the Song of Solomon; the First Oxford Company, Isaiah to Malachi; the Second Westminster Company, the Epistles; the Second Cambridge Company, the Apocrypha; and the Second Oxford Company, the Gospels, the Acts of the Apostles, and Revelation. Norton performs a singular service and demonstrates his scholarship by compiling as complete a list as possible of potential company members and adding a thumbnail biography for each. Estimates vary as to the total number of translators; Norton asserts that James I appointed 54 translators, while other speculative figures range from as few as 45 to as many as 450.

What makes *The King James Bible* such a valuable contribution to biblical scholarship is the way in which Norton weaves his primary source research into an interesting narrative account that successfully illuminates the context of these translator companies. Notably, Norton's sources include the entire personal library of William Branthwaite, vice-chancellor of Caius College, Cambridge University, as well as the notes and personal diary of John Bois, fellow at St. John's College, Cambridge. His treatment of Bois's diary is historical writing at its finest, as Norton manages to extract truths and insights from even the homeliest of details—truly, a scholar and researcher's fondest dream. Branthwaite's library provides a unique glimpse into what resources each translator might have had at his disposal, while the pithy details of Bois's diary reveal the inconvenience of a leaky chamber pot, a spat with his wife, and the deaths of two children in rapid succession. Many of Norton's primary sources provide irreplaceable gems to add to the reader's knowledge of history and the human experience.

While the actual mechanics of drafting a biblical translation might ordinarily prove rather dry, Norton makes the topic quite interesting through the addition of a chapter devoted to the process, in which he provides two examples: one from Genesis 3:1–13 (the temptation of Adam and Eve in the Garden of Eden and their fall from grace) and one from Matthew 1:18–21 (when Joseph discovers that his future bride, Mary, is pregnant and ponders what course of action he should take, only to be visited by an angel and informed that all is as it should be). Norton offers the reader these textual examples so that one might compare the different renditions, from Tyndale's translation to the AV.

The final chapters deal with the numerous editions that have appeared since the AV's completion in 1611 and how these subsequent editions have varied. Though they make for somewhat heavy reading for the nonspecialist, these chapters nevertheless serve to explode some of the myths surrounding the AV. For example, this version of the Bible remained controversial and was never universally accepted in England. Only with significant difficulty did the AV supplant the Geneva Bible in popular use. To that end, Puritan radicalism and the politics of the English Restoration—a movement presided over in 1660 by Charles II, grandson of James I—may have contributed most significantly.

Reading *The King James Bible*, one might wish for more coverage of the actual influence of the AV on the politics of Great Britain or the United States, but such subjects do not seem to be within the author's purview. What has been proved beyond doubt, throughout the changes and upheavals of the last four centuries, is the enduring quality of the King James Bible, whether one reads it as literature, history, or religious text. The narrow focus of Norton's work in *The King James Bible* is, to use a biblical allusion, a double-edged sword, insofar as it examines the history at hand on an intentionally limited scale while still hinting at the tantalizing fringes—the social, political, psychological, and historical issues surrounding the making of what has become, by whatever means, the best-known version of the Christian scriptures in the English-speaking world.

Raymond Pierre Hylton

Review Sources

The Financial Times, April 29, 2011 (Web).
Library Journal 136, no. 2 (February 1, 2011): 70.
London Review of Books 33, no. 3 (February 3, 2011): 20–22.
New Statesman 140, no. 5036 (January 20, 2011): 47.
Times Literary Supplement, February 11, 2011 (Web).

The Land at the End of the World

Author: António Lobo Antunes (b. 1942)
First published: *Os Cus de Judas*, 1979, in
  Portugal
Translated from the Portuguese by Margaret
  Jull Costa
Publisher: W. W. Norton (New York). 224 pp.
  $26.95
Type of work: Fiction
Time: 1960s and 1970s
Locale: Angola and Portugal

*A man recounts his traumatic experience as a
military doctor during Portugal's colonial wars
in Angola.*

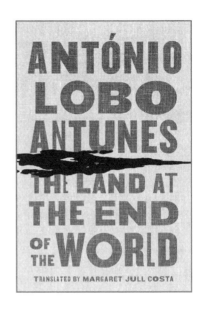

Many critics have commented on the hints
of autobiography in António Lobo Antunes's
novel *The Land at the End of the World*, first
published in Portuguese as *Os Cus de Judas*;
literally, "Judas's asshole." Like the novel's haunted narrator, Lobo Antunes survived
Portugal's brutal colonial war in Angola, in which Prime Minister António de Oliveira
Salazar sent conscripts to fight guerrillas and defend Portugal's colonial stake in the
country. The novel takes place during and immediately after Salazar's regime, depicting both the events of the war and life in postrevolutionary Lisbon, two time periods
that converge as the narrator recounts his story to a woman he meets in a bar. The relationship between fact and fiction continues to be debated, but critics agree that much
in Lobo Antunes's disturbing novel reads with the horrible clarity of fact. Lobo Antunes describes his narrator's attitude toward his post as military doctor with the same
visceral absurdity that characterizes much of the novel: "I helped them to die with my
useless drugs and their eyes were protesting, protesting, they didn't understand, is this
what dying is." The sheer absurdity of Portugal's war, in which a soldier's death war-
rants a scant few lines on paper and all those who survive return home as disturbed
men, has seemingly driven the narrative voice into hysteria.

The speaker, his sense of humanity destroyed by his experience, both transcends and
expresses his painful memories through references to art and film. As the narrator rambles to the woman, interspersing bizarre images, he imagines that "if you and I were
anteaters, rather than two people sitting in a bar, I might feel more comfortable with the
silence." Moving from fantasy to Mae West films, he remembers how military service
was supposed to make him a man, how "the tribe" gathered as he embarked for Angola
to make his dramatic metamorphosis possible. He recalls masturbating at the base, "feeling like your body was a tiny seed lost in the vast, rumpled, tremulous mattress," and
the desire to "disappear through the city walls just as Chagall's violinists merge with the

dense blue of the canvas." As he leaves the
base, the narrator fantasizes about escaping
into another Chagall painting, "flapping the
clumsy cotton wings" of his military sleeves,
after which he will come to rest in Paris to
live a life of revolutionary exile. Similarly absurd is his account of a visit from the ladies
of the National Women's Movement, whose
pubic hair he "always imagined . . . to be like a
fox-fur stole and thought that, when aroused,
drops of Ma Griffe and poodle drool would
dribble from their vaginas, leaving shiny snail
trails on their wrinkled thighs." These fantasies—paranoid, bizarre, and deliberately
nonsensical—testify to the way in which the
narrator's wartime experiences have wounded
his entire worldview.

(Luis Miguel Palomares)

*António Lobo Antunes is the author
of over twenty novels, including* What
Can I Do When Everything Is on Fire?
*(2001). His work has been translated
into more than twenty languages. He has
won many awards, including the Jerusalem Prize for the Freedom of the Individual in Society in 2005.*

The narrator shares his first impressions
of Africa, where white birds dissolve into
palm trees and he gazes at women working
as prostitutes. He recalls minute details, such
as what they ate and drank, and it is in these
details that Lobo Antunes's writing is stron-
gest. The writing itself is directly involved in the story, as the narrator uses his story's
twists and turns to seduce the woman. He narrates his origins, his "apprenticeship in
dying," as he calls his medical training, and how he ran from police during protest
demonstrations in 1962. Likening himself to Che Guevara, he describes the helplessness of treating malaria. He imagines hearing the news of a cease-fire in the form of a
scene from Charlie Chaplin's *Modern Times* (1936).

He asks, "Why the hell doesn't anyone talk about this? I'm beginning to think that
one million five hundred thousand men who went to Africa never existed and that I'm
giving you some spiel, the ludicrous plot of a novel, a story I invented to touch your
heart." This sweeping bitterness depicts his alienation from the society he serves but
from which his experiences have separated him. The feeling is intensified when his
daughter is born in Lisbon while he is confined to his post in a foreign land, unable to
see her. In the jungle, the narrator watches a man writhe in agony after losing his leg
to a mine, and a lieutenant places a hand on his shoulder, "one of the rare moments"
when he does not feel alone. Even the narrator's sense of connection to others has been
wounded, derived at random from a scene of carnage. In the story's present, struggling to find any sense of connection, he offers to pay his conversation partner's bill
in a gesture of cynical chivalry: "seriously, let me pretend to be the young Portuguese
technocrat, circa 1970."

The dissociation he feels pursues him as he returns to civilization. In the airport,
he observes that "the female voice, coming from nowhere and announcing in three

languages the departure of planes, floated, immaterial, above my head, like a cloud painted by Delvaux, before dissolving gradually into a foam of syllables in which echoed the names of strange cities." He experiences the shock of reentry when an airline official checking his bags says, "You guys come back from Angola thinking you're really big men, but this isn't a jungle here, soldier." A sense of otherness pursues him everywhere; he feels eyes watching him "the way they look at cripples hauling themselves along on crutches near the Military Hospital." When he finally arrives home, he finds his family asleep and observes them in a "defenseless pose, fragile and abandoned."

The above passage hints at the narrator's eventual separation from his wife. Subsequently, his love life plays out in a desperate scramble:

> I stumbled from house to house and woman to woman like a blind child frenziedly groping for an elusive arm, and I often woke up alone in hotels as impersonal as the faces of psychoanalysts, to find myself connected by a numberless phone to the friendly but vaguely suspicious receptionist, who was clearly intrigued by my meager luggage.

He dwells on the persistent lack of connectedness in his life, feigning indifference but implying the crisis of his situation. He is aware that, unlike him, the woman he is talking to lives in the present, but he cannot leave his life of eight years ago. He creates a portrait of universal loneliness: "I'm sure that if I were to lock myself in and stay here for a whole month . . . I would gradually metamorphose into the perfect insect of a colonel in the army reserves or a retiree from a savings and loan." His cynical view of love betrays his anxiety, loathing, and isolation; later, he describes the act of love as being "like sticking a knife in someone's belly in a brawl in a bar." This view, Lobo Antunes suggests, has resulted in part from sexual practices during the war. The narrator at one point couples with a washwoman only to learn that the entire brigade had done the same with her. Later, he witnesses the rape of a prisoner. There is a grim reason to his offering the woman in the bar "A double, no ice?" and espousing the value of drunkenness.

The narrator seems aware that alcohol only exacerbates his feelings of alienation and loneliness, and as he tells the story of what he suffered, he implies his desire to hide in the alcohol as well as in a woman's body to escape despair. He feels abandoned to "endless night" and to waiting for the morning that never comes, feeling no refuge or way out of anguish, and wants the woman he has picked up to agree to making love in solidarity with the melancholy of a shared disaster. Lobo Antunes suggests a kind of solidarity of guilt. Rather than accusing merely the Portuguese government of responsibility for what he has experienced, Lobo Antunes assumes the guilt of each and every character indiscriminately. "[W]e distrust humanity as much as we distrust ourselves," he writes, and later: "We lack someone to blame for our deep dissatisfaction for ourselves."

As the novel progresses, one hopes for a redemptive turn of events in the present, a confession from the narrator about how he is afraid to love. Embracing the woman, he pleads, "let me return from Africa to here and feel happy." However, such hopes are thrown into serious question when the narrator imagines sex with his new partner: "We will come together like two great Tertiary-age monsters, bristling with cartilage and bones, bleating out the onomatopoetic groans of vast lizards." He so quickly reverts from the present moment back to Angola that the reader understands why his wife must have left him in the first place.

The next chapter opens with postcoital conversation, as the narrator apologizes for his performance; soon he is appealing to her to carry him, to save him from his despair, just as years ago he had carried a black man whose leg had been bitten off by a crocodile. Suddenly, he is back in Africa again, describing the red ants marching determinedly along their arms. Aware that he has wandered, the narrator tries to make a connection: "In a way we are still in Angola, you and I, and I am making love to you as I did in the village." He disappears into flashbacks of another woman in a marijuana grove, "the one place in Angola where the war had not touched." Finally, he confesses to liking the woman he has just seduced and admits to being tired of solitude.

Ending the novel here, Lobo Antunes foregrounds the narrator's relationship with the woman as a powerful counterpoint to his recollections of war. In interviews, the author has commented that it was with their relationship, not his personal involvement in the war, that his work on the novel initially began. In the end, the reader is left to consider the emotional and personal ramifications of trauma and alienation and the difficulty of relationships themselves, which are, according to Lobo Antunes, "something like a war."

Batya Weinbaum

Review Sources

Book Forum, May 16, 2011 (Web).
The Guardian, July 21, 2011 (Web).
The New York Times, June 29, 2011 (Web).
Paris Review, July 26, 2011 (Web).

Last Man in Tower

Author: Aravind Adiga (b. 1974)
Publisher: Alfred A. Knopf (New York). 400 pp.
$26.95
Type of work: Novel
Time: May 11, 2007–December 23, 2007
Locale: Mumbai, India

When an ambitious, somewhat shady developer seeks to raze two old Mumbai condominium towers in favor of a luxury complex, he offers owners an above-market price, with the catch that they all have to agree to sell; soon, vicious peer pressure begins breaking apart the existing social harmony. The novel reflects on the effect of greed but also raises questions about one person going against the will of the community.

Principal characters:

YOGESH A. MURTHY, also known as MASTERJI, a retired, widowed schoolteacher and is the last man in Tower A of Vishram Cooperative Society to hold out against the developer's offer

DHARMEN SHAH, a ruthless, self-made real estate developer who sets his sights on Towers A and B of Vishram Cooperative Society to best a rival developer

SHANMUGHAM, a young man picked from Mumbai's slums to become Shah's lackey, also performing some criminal duties

ASHVIN KOTHARI, the secretary of Vishram Cooperative Society, who seeks to persuade Masterji to sell like all the other owners

IBRAHIM KUDWA, an Internet store owner and a Muslim, who reluctantly agrees to sell and to pressure Masterji

GEORGINA REGO, an embittered social worker of leftist leanings and single mother of two teenagers, whose initial opposition to Shah's offer evaporates in light of its genuine financial benefits

RAMESH AJWANI, a real estate broker and early ally of Shah among the apartment owners

RAM KHARE, Hindu security guard of Tower A

MARY, the cleaning lady of Tower A

ROSIE, the battered young mistress of Shah, who accepts his abuse in hopes of big material gains from their relationship

ALBERT AND SHELLEY PINTO, a retired accountant and his almost blind wife, Masterji's closest friends

SANJIV and SANGEETA PURI, a couple in their early fifties whose son, Ramesh, suffers from Down syndrome; Sangeeta becomes Masterji's strongest opponent

Last Man in Tower, by Aravind Adiga, is a multifaceted novel that entices its readers on several levels. Out of personal pride and desire to beat a competitor, a developer offers the owners of two old, run-down condominium towers an above-market price for their dwellings. His plan is to raze the towers to build a luxury compound. However, one resident opposes him.

Last Man in Tower is a story of the fight of one man, Masterji, against the system of brash capitalism. However, the novel also relays an understanding of the common goal of the other characters: They want to better their lives as the result of an unexpected windfall. Once it becomes clear that the developer will not cheat the apartment owners out of their homes and will pay the sum promised, it becomes somewhat hard to understand the utter resistance of one man to the detriment of the dreams of all the others. In a sense, Masterji is a Don Quixote type who fights to the end the windmills of change and modernity.

The book opens with a panoramic view of the respectable, middle-class twin condominium complex of the Vishram Society Cooperative, located near Mumbai's international airport. The area represents an urban zone in transition: What was once an island amid slums has become an area desired by developers catering to the urban sprawl of affluent Mumbai inhabitants.

Adiga describes, with a keen eye for human frailty, how the ambitious developer Dharmen Shah begins to worm his way into his target. Assessing the cooperative through his ambitious, lowborn, and occasionally criminal lackey Shanmugham, Shah comes up with an attractive offer. If, as required by their cooperative bylaws, all owners of Towers A and B agree to sell their apartments, Shah will pay them a generous, above-market price. Adiga illustrates all the tricks of a Mumbai developer's trade, with Shah offering candy gift boxes and other enticements to the owners.

While some of the owners immediately begin to dream of the possibilities this opportunity offers, others are more critical. The social worker Georgina Rego suspects the offer is a trick. Albert and Shelley Pinto, the retired couple, fear that the new place into which they would have to move would disorient the almost blind wife. However, nobody is as opposed as the retired teacher and widower, Yogesh A. Murthy, called Masterji. Masterji refuses, for understandable reasons, to hand over his wife's jewelry to his greedy son Gaurav and his wife, and he is adamant in his refusal to sell his apartment. He insists on his right to make his own decisions about where to live, regardless of the will of the others in the Vishram Cooperative Society.

Adiga makes sure readers realize that developer Shah is not a kind man. He is abusive to his girlfriend Rosie, who only clings to him because she hopes for material benefits. Shah's own son, Satish, is an unrepentant juvenile delinquent who tells his father that he has to learn to be a criminal to be a worthy successor in the development business. The shady underling, Shanmugham, is just a tool to be discarded once he tries to blackmail his employer.

Nonetheless, for all these negative traits, Adiga never hints that Shah will cheat those who sign his deal. Instead, Shah is willing to pay a generous price to ensure his ambitious development vision. This fact makes it somewhat hard for readers to sympathize with Masterji's intransigence. After all, those who sign will reap benefits

Aravind Adiga began his writing career as a journalist covering financial topics. Switching to freelance work, he wrote his first novel, The White Tiger *(2008), which won the prestigious British Man Booker Prize for the year. He went on to publish a series of twelve connected short stories in* Between the Assassinations, *published in India in 2008 and the United States in 2009.* Last Man in Tower *is his third published book.*

and will be able to leave a run-down condominium tower for a more upscale dwelling. Thus, a key problem of the novel is presented. It makes Masterji's decision to hold out seem contrarian instead of wise. While Masterji's principled move may have merit, his decision affects many others, and this is the central dilemma in the novel.

The long tradition of communitarian society makes coming to decision hard for the owners in Tower A. The young people owning property in Tower B immediately take up developer Shah's high-priced offer. In Tower A, resistance emanates from Masterji and his shrinking group of friends. Suddenly, for the sake of material advantage, the solid secretary of the society, Ashvin Kothari, caves in to the prospects of a good offer. He is even willing to bend the law to further the tower's sale.

Masterji has some support from the Hindu security guard, Ram Khare, whose daughter Masterji taught even though she did not belong to the middle class. Masterji also expresses sympathy toward the cleaning woman, Mary. Ultimately, though, neither Ram nor Mary pulls much weight in the struggle between Masterji and the other apartment owners.

Exasperated with Masterji's refusal to accept the offer, the opposition coalesces around Sangeeta Puri. Mother to a developmentally disabled son, Ramesh, and domineering toward her accountant husband, Sanjiv, she takes it upon herself to force Masterji to agree to the developer's price. At first, she and the others resort to bullying, but as time goes by, they turn to increasingly disturbing forms of intimidation.

Shah plays his own hand. Paying off the owners of Tower B ahead of schedule, an unprecedented event, he fuels the jealously of Tower A dwellers. Eventually, Sangeeta Puri and her allies decide to physically assault Masterji. Tellingly, on the birthday of India's revered Mahatma Gandhi, the spiritual father of nonviolent opposition, Kothari has the key to Masterji's apartment copied illegally by a fly-by-night locksmith. With this key, some teenage would-be toughs enter Masterji's apartment, only to be soundly defeated by the old man, and the misadventure results in a comic rout of the louts. Thereafter, however, the plot turns decidedly dark. In the final pages of the novel, the moral corruption of the residents of Vishram Cooperative Society is made complete, and violence prevails.

Adiga's novel is a bitter indictment of what people are willing to do for money. In observant detail, Adiga describes how the previous social harmony among the owners of the apartments of Tower A unravels in face of the developer's tempting offer. Money triumphs over allegiance and friendship. At the same time, readers may wonder what good Masterji's intransigence does for his community. Tower A is described as decrepit. As developer Shah, for all his personal faults, will not cheat the owners of their money, they will all be able to afford better living conditions. That they cannot come to an agreement that allows all of them to profit from the situation is a sad commentary on the notion of community.

Magill's Literary Annual 2012

Adiga's style conveys a concise sense of the details of life in contemporary Mumbai. He is careful to show that all his characters but Masterji, regardless of their Hindu, Muslim, or Christian religion, ultimately succumb to the temptations of Shah's offer. Ironically, Shah, a dark presence who seduces members of the cooperative to commit acts of evil, lives in a building adorned by Ganesh, the jovial Hindu elephant god of wine and festivals.

Although *Last Man in Tower* did not receive quite the universal praise American critics gave Adiga's first novel, *The White Tiger* (2008), with its focus on a picaresque hero, this latest novel conjures up an enticing dilemma. In working out the dramatic conflict of one man's principled opposition to his pragmatic community, Adiga touches on the limits of personal freedom and self-determination versus obligation to community. The novel is told in a lively, moving style and is sure to fascinate readers with its views on a complex moral problem.

R. C. Lutz

Review Sources

Booklist 108, no. 1 (September 1, 2011): 42.
The Christian Science Monitor, September 27, 2011 (Web).
The Economist 399, no. 8743 (July 23, 2011): 82.
Kirkus Reviews 79, no. 16 (August 15, 2011): 1401.
Library Journal 136, no. 14 (September 1, 2011): 95.
New Statesman 140, no. 5062 (July 18, 2011): 57.
Newsweek 158, no. 10 (September 5, 2011): 62–63.
Publishers Weekly 258, no. 30 (July 25, 2011): 30.
Times Literary Supplement, no. 5651 (July 22, 2011): 21.
The Wall Street Journal, September 17, 2011, C8.

Lee Krasner
A Biography

Author: Gail Levin (b. 1948)
Publisher: HarperCollins (New York). Illustrated. 560 pp. $30.00
Type of work: Biography
Time: 1908–1984
Locale: New York City

Levin presents Lee Krasner as an independent, talented avant-garde artist whose stature should be assessed outside of the shadow of her more famous husband, Jackson Pollock.

Principal personages:

LEE KRASNER (1908–1984), an abstract expressionist painter

JACKSON POLLOCK (1912–1956), Krasner's husband, an abstract expressionist artist best known for his drip paintings

IGOR PANTUHOFF (1911–1972), a portraitist and Krasner's first partner

WILLEM DE KOONING (1905–1997), an abstract expressionist painter

CLEMENT GREENBERG (1909–1994), an art critic who was responsible in part for the early exposure of Jackson Pollock

JEANNE MERCEDES CORDOBA (MATTER) CARLES (1913–2001), an abstract artist

PEGGY GUGGENHEIM (1898–1979), a patron of the arts and founder of the Guggenheim Museum

HANS HOFFMAN (1880–1966), an abstract artist and theorist

ALFONSO OSSORIO (1916–1990), an abstract expressionist painter

Lee Krasner has been a familiar name since her husband, Jackson Pollock, became known for his drip paintings in the 1940s. Because of the significance of Pollock's art and Krasner's role in supporting and promoting him, both before and after his death in 1956, Krasner has long been known primarily as Pollock's widow rather than as an artist in her own right. Historical interest in Krasner's work began in the 1970s; with this biography, Gail Levin introduces her to a broader readership as a key figure in twentieth-century art. Levin presents Krasner as an intelligent, independent, and talented woman whose significance within the New York City art scene was by no means limited to her relationship with Pollock. Krasner is presented as a colorful Jewish American woman with a deep-seated interest in avant-garde abstraction. Art was a constant throughout her life, in which her years with Pollock were simply one exceptionally vibrant period.

(Randy Parsons)

Gail Levin is an art historian and a Distinguished Professor of art history, American studies, and women's studies at the Graduate Center and Baruch College of the City University of New York. She has previously published biographies of Edward Hopper and Judy Chicago.

Lee Krasner: A Biography begins with an introduction in which Levin presents Krasner as a complex historical figure, introduces key themes of Krasner's art, and positions this biography within the extant literature (a more thorough discussion of sources is included at the end of the book). Most important in this introduction is Levin's discussion of her own friendship with Krasner, which began in February 1971 and continued until Krasner's death in 1984. The friendship between Levin and Krasner is a crucial element of this biography because it positions the text as both an ambitious scholarly product and a personal project. As Levin states in the introduction, "Knowing Krasner enriched my life. She . . . deeply affected me." Levin's personal investment in Krasner, as well as her admiration of, and affection for, the artist, is evident throughout the text and lends it a personal tone. Although Levin did not begin to work seriously on Krasner's biography until after her death, the artist supplied Levin with a variety of primary-source materials. Their conversations also provided a starting point from which Levin could launch her research. The relationship between subject and biographer is of most obvious significance in Levin's discussion of Krasner's final years, which is particularly influenced by Levin's own observations.

The first four chapters of the book narrate the artist's life from her birth in Brooklyn in 1908 through her art education—first at the Cooper Union for the Advancement of Science and Art and then at the National Academy of Design, both in New York City. The reader is introduced to Krasner as an independent young woman, motivated from an early age by her passion for art and strongly influenced by her upbringing in a Jewish family that had relocated to New York City from Russia shortly before her birth. Born Lena Krassner, the fifth child of struggling immigrant parents, she gradually transformed herself into Lee Krasner, an ambitious young female artist who experimented with abstraction even while following a traditional artistic curriculum. This narrative of Krasner's youth is remarkable because, although it reveals endemic sexism and anti-Semitism, it also illustrates the routes through which a young woman with no financial resources could gain an art education and develop an independent personal and professional path in New York City, moving in the city's highest circles of professional art practice.

Subsequent chapters of the biography follow Krasner's life from 1932 through 1941. Here, Levin describes Krasner as a professional artist prior to her acquaintance with Jackson Pollock. Equally important to Levin is the discussion of Krasner's relationship with artist Igor Pantuhoff. Krasner and Pantuhoff lived together for most of the 1930s, and Krasner became known by family, friends, and professional acquaintances as "Mrs. Igor Pantuhoff." Much of Levin's narrative demonstrates the significance of their relationship within the New York City art world at that time. Because of their conjoined personal and professional association, the Pantuhoff-Krasner relationship had complexities akin to those that Krasner would again encounter with Pollock, though without the heightened drama of the latter's exceptional professional success. Krasner and Pantuhoff's separation in 1940, precipitated in part by the extreme financial pressures of the 1930s, represents a significant turning point in Levin's narrative of Krasner's life. As the author states, "This definitive break left Krasner bereft after living so long together and sharing so much. After all, they had given the impression that they were married, perhaps not only to others. Socially this was tantamount to a divorce."

More important is the information that Levin provides about Krasner's professional practice across this decade. These chapters capture the difficulties of professionalism during the difficult years of the 1930s. They contain extensive information about Krasner's work for the federal government, beginning with a position providing illustrations and large-scale murals for the Public Works of Art Project. Krasner's deep investment in the development of modernist trends in art in New York City is also key to Levin's narrative of these years. Levin closely documents Krasner's artistic activities, as well as her friendships with a range of prominent artists and theorists. Finally, these chapters also consider Krasner's proactive role as an activist for artists in New York City at this time, though they refute suggestions of Krasner's long-term affiliation with communism.

The following chapters encompass Krasner's relationship with Jackson Pollock, which began in 1942 and ended with Pollock's death in 1956. For obvious reasons, the material in these chapters will be the most familiar for readers. Although Levin resolutely focuses the narrative on Krasner, these chapters are also inevitably about Jackson Pollock. For this reason, it is somewhat harder to follow the development of Krasner's persona and artistic production across these years than in the preceding and subsequent chapters. This is certainly the result, in part, of the breadth of existing literature that considers the relationship of Krasner and Pollock as driven by the genius of Pollock's art. However, Levin succeeds in reminding the reader that Krasner's independent personality and achievements should not be subsumed within the myth of Pollock.

The narrative in these chapters is particularly significant for two reasons beyond the important events that it reviews. First, it highlights the trauma that Krasner endured during the final years of her marriage to Pollock, when he was suffering from alcoholism. Although she continued championing her husband and his art, and loyally managed his artistic legacy following his death, it is crucial to understand the effect that these painful years had on Krasner despite her resilient personality. Second, Levin takes pains to accentuate Krasner's own testimony that Pollock supported her work as an artist and encouraged her to continue painting. If Krasner did not always make progress in her art during her relationship with Pollock, it was not necessarily because Pollock intentionally prevented her from painting. Levin further notes that Pollock's insistence that Krasner not work outside of their home allowed her more time for painting than was available for some other female artists of her generation who needed to find other work to support the artistic careers of their partners.

The narrative in these chapters complicates the prevailing understanding of the relationship between Krasner and Pollock, though it also reflects the irresolvable complexities of both individuals and their conjoined legacies. Throughout, the writing is strongly influenced by Levin's own agendas both as a scholar and as a friend of Krasner's; these chapters will certainly bear the greatest critical scrutiny as they attempt, in part, to credit Krasner with helping to shape Pollock's artistic genius, beyond merely acting as his agent and domestic support system. In her reflections on Pollock's death, for example, Levin cites the critic Clement Greenberg's statement that "Lee was the one who really got to [Pollock] . . . . He could talk about art only with her—well, he could with me *mostly when Lee was there to join in,*" an assertion that comes close to suggesting that the ideas behind Pollock's most successful art would not have existed without Krasner's guidance.

The final chapters of the book examine Krasner's life and career following Pollock's death. These chapters explore the pressures that Krasner endured in the later decades of her life, which involved maneuvering among competing, self-interested parties who hoped to gain access to the Pollock estate, working to advance her own artistic career independent of her identity as Pollock's widow, and struggling with a series of debilitating illnesses. A final interesting piece of this narrative is Krasner's negotiation of her own legacy, in particular her conflicted relationship with the budding feminist scholarship of the 1970s. In searching to find her course within these challenges, Krasner did not always remain the unscathed heroine of her own drama. Although Levin is clearly inclined to deal gently with Krasner's faults, she does highlight instances in which Krasner took missteps during these years. One such example was her relationship with David Gibbs, a British art dealer. Levin traces the opportunistic manner in which Gibbs insinuated himself into Krasner's life when she was extremely vulnerable following Pollock's death. However, Levin also suggests that Krasner may have successfully used Gibbs in order to achieve her own goals (which included increasing Pollock's profile in the international art world) even as Gibbs was likewise exploiting her.

Levin's discussion of the recognition that Krasner received late in life is the most important aspect of these chapters. Krasner exerted a consistent effort to place her own work in galleries and to develop a national and an international audience. At the same time, she resisted joining the ranks of consciously feminist artists and was often hesitant to exhibit her work in shows specifically for women. Nevertheless, Krasner's reputation as an artist was significantly advanced by the interest and advocacy of feminist art historians. The final chapter of the book deals with Krasner's retrospective exhibition, which opened at the Museum of Fine Arts in Houston, Texas, in October 1983. Krasner died in July 1984, before the exhibition could open in its second venue at the Museum of Modern Art in New York City.

Levin's biography of Krasner is a major achievement that may well shift some of the directions from which scholars approach Krasner's art. Levin offers a narrative that is always mediated by her own voice as a scholar and a friend of Krasner's, and the book has received some criticism for this tendency. It is also somewhat surprising that Levin does not conclude the text with a chapter offering a scholarly assessment of Krasner's legacy, given that the biography is so openly a project of conjoined scholarship and personal investment. The book nevertheless balances several agendas; those of the scholar, the biographer, and the friend are all intertwined with competing concerns over the legacies of Pollock, Krasner, Greenberg, and others. Likewise, it can be difficult to reconcile the scholarly assessment of Krasner's art with Levin's sometimes voyeuristic emphasis on Krasner's personal and sensual life, such as the detailed exploration of the sexual attraction between her and Pantuhoff. Given the high stakes of its subject matter for the art world and its unabashedly personal agenda, this biography will certainly continue to receive a range of critical responses. In its close attention to Krasner and respect for her both as an individual and as an artist, this book makes a substantive contribution to literature and art history.

Julia A. Sienkewicz

Review Sources

Booklist 107, no. 13 (March 1, 2011): 11.
Chicago Sun-Times, March 24, 2011 (Web).
Kirkus Reviews 79, no. 4 (February 15, 2011): 290.
Library Journal 136, no. 6 (April 1, 2011): 90.
Los Angeles Times, March 20, 2011 (Web).
The New York Times Book Review, July 10, 2011, p. 14.
The Wall Street Journal, March 19, 2011, p. C7.

The Leftovers

Author: Tom Perrotta (b. 1961)
Publisher: St. Martin's (New York). 368 pp.
$25.99
Type of work: Novel
Time: 2006
Locale: A suburb in the northeastern United States

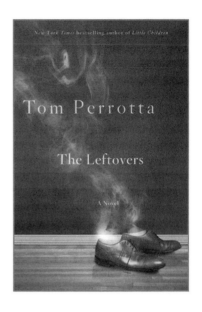

After one-third of the world's population mysteriously disappears, a suburban American family completely unravels.

Principal characters:
KEVIN GARVEY, the mayor of Mapleton
LAURIE GARVEY, his wife
TOM GARVEY, his college-age son
JILL GARVEY, his teenage daughter
CHRISTINE, Tom's friend
AIMEE, Jill's friend
NORA, Kevin's girlfriend
MEG, Laurie's friend

The premise of Tom Perrotta's *The Leftovers* references the evangelical Christian expectation of a supernatural event known as the Rapture, which will drastically disrupt ordinary life and lead the chosen few to a heavenly destination. But what happens in this novel is far more ambiguous. What is called the "Sudden Departure" of one-third of the population of the world cannot be said to pose a clear religious message, because while the group of the departed includes some evangelical Christians, it also includes Hindus, Muslims, Jews, atheists, and a mix of prominent figures such as Jennifer Lopez, Shaquille O'Neill, Vladimir Putin, the pope, and numerous celebrity chefs. In addition, a number of alcoholics, faithless husbands, and ne'er-do-wells are also among those who have disappeared. The event, therefore, remains inexplicable to those left behind.

It also demoralizes mainstream religion. The Reverend Matt Jamison, disconsolate that he was not among the departed, deems as disreputable those who were, handing out flyers denouncing them on the streets. New cults proliferate. There is the Healing Hug Movement, initiated by a man who calls himself Holy Wayne and offers sympathetic hugs that he claims can absorb the fear and sense of abandonment of those who have been left behind. Tom Garvey, the son of the mayor of Mapleton, joins this cult, which sees Holy Wayne rapidly transition from the purveying of harmless hugs to the predatory sexual exploitation of teenage girls. Tom is given the task of escorting Christine, an impregnated teenager, to Boston, where she will give birth to Wayne's son, who is believed to be the new messiah. When authorities finally get around to arresting Wayne, and when Christine gives birth not to a son but to a daughter, Tom and Christine come crashing to earth. Unable to nurture her infant, Christine sinks into a depression that does not let up until she abandons Tom and the baby and joins the Barefoot People. This new cult is composed of young people whose response to the Sudden Departure is to embrace good times; they live raggle-taggle lives, holding big celebratory gatherings in various venues across the country. After leaving the baby in front of his father's house, Tom also joins the cult.

Similarly unable to return to normal life, Tom's mother, Laurie, joins a different and far more sinister group, the Guilty Remnant, which discourages anyone from moving on with their lives. According to this ascetic cult, the Sudden Departure has brought history to an end; not only is there no return to normalcy, there is no hope for the future. Members must leave their families behind, wear white at all times, and take a vow of silence. To demonstrate their detachment from the world, their confidence that everything is about to end, and their mastery of their desire to live, they must chain-smoke cigarettes. Laurie Garvey is a true believer, finding in the hard regimen an expression of her own anguish and a way to defend herself against further pain. When Jill, her daughter, gives her a lighter as a Christmas present, she throws it down a grate precisely because it is an object that would strengthen her attachment to her daughter, thus making her that much more vulnerable to loss.

Laurie is assigned to team up with Meg, a new recruit, to form a unit the cult refers to as the Watchers, whose task it is to silently stalk outsiders as if they are emissaries from a condemning and vigilant God. Lonely and deprived, Laurie and Meg find in each other a nourishing friendship. Although the cult officially forbids the formation of any worldly attachments, Laurie and Meg's relationship is encouraged. Eventually, Laurie understands that the cult is creating this friendship only to break it; to cleanse its members of the capacity for love and friendship, the cult requires one member of a Watcher team to murder the other. Laurie herself is assigned to murder Meg as a nec-essary step in her utter withdrawal from the world and from human attachment. But Laurie cannot bring herself to shoot Meg, so Meg must take the gun and shoot herself. Satisfied that Laurie has done the deed, the cult spirits Laurie away to some undetect-able place, as if she too has become one of the disappeared.

The other two members of the Garvey family, Kevin and Jill, do not join cults and remain in their suburban home as before. Abandoned by her brother and her mother, Jill feels as though she has been raised to live in a world that no longer exists. She fails to study in school, joins a group of kids whose pastime is mainly sex parties, and befriends Aimee, a dissolute fellow student who moves in and exerts an unsettling in-fluence on Jill and her father. Surprisingly, Aimee comes to understand that her way of life is unsustainable and bound to end badly, eventually finding work and moving out of the Garvey house to start a new life. But Jill, feeling abandoned once again, accepts her old grade-school teacher's highly suspicious invitation to join the Guilty Remnant. As she is about to be recruited by this mother-surrogate, however, Jill hears Meg shoot herself. Intuiting that this is a warning, Jill walks away, refusing the dubious consola-tions of the cult and letting go of the futile hope that she will be reconciled with her mother. Like Aimee, Jill makes a fresh start; instead of joining the cult that night, she plays a game of ping-pong with two ordinary high-school boys who have always wanted her as a friend.

Tom Perrotta is the author of six works of fiction, including Joe College *(2000) and* The Abstinence Teacher *(2008). His novels* Election *(1998) and* Little Children *(2004) have been made into acclaimed and award-winning movies. He lives outside of Boston.*

At the center of this thoughtful novel is Kevin's story. While the novel's many cults enable their members to avoid the work of mourning, Kevin is genuinely stricken with grief. The loss of his wife and son leaves him bewildered and sad, and he similarly finds it difficult to come to terms with a changed Mapleton. He cannot bring himself to let go of his memories of the world that he fears is never coming back. He also finds it impossible to build a new love life after Laurie's abandonment, which leaves him in a condition of self-doubt and deep melancholy. He is, however, attracted to Nora Durst, a fellow Mapletonian, but the relationship does not go well. Nora has lost her husband and two children, all of whom mysteriously disappeared in the middle of a fractious family dinner. Nora's bereavement is complicated by the news that her husband was having a love affair, so she feels herself to be not so much a tragic widow as the ex-wife of a selfish, uncaring man. Although she loved her family, the moment of their disappearance coincided with her wish that they would all die and disappear forever. Overcome with remorse and sorrow, Nora spends her days disconsolately watching reruns of *SpongeBob SquarePants*, her little boy's favorite television show, in an attempt to somehow sustain a connection with her lost family.

Even though Kevin wants to hold on to the way things were, he and Nora attempt to start a new relationship. During a dinner date, the mention of Tom brings Kevin to tears, ruining the possibility of a romantic evening. Nora cannot comfort Kevin, as her enduring grief has made her unable to risk any new relationships, perhaps indefinitely. Despite their shared status as survivors of the Sudden Departure, they feel abandoned and bereft. Neither is sure if there can ever be love after such losses, and they both feel too damaged to pick up the pieces and start over. Despite the discouraging setback of the bad dinner date, there are indications that Kevin and Nora are still capable of loving and being loved. One positive sign is Kevin's coaxing Nora to recall her best friends from when she was a girl, a therapeutic effort that reminds Nora of a time when she could be a good friend. This small, telling moment, as Nora recalls their names, marks her coming to understand that her heart is not truly deadened.

In fact, it is Nora who rescues Christine's baby after Tom leaves her on Kevin's doorstep. This baby was meant to be the redemptive miracle child of the Healing Hug movement, but she is also a leftover of Tom and Christine, as they attempt to begin again among the Barefoot People. Christine, in particular, has failed to form an attachment to the baby girl, abandoning her in a sudden departure that mirrors the larger one. Christine's failure to care for the baby also reflects the way in which the many post-crisis relationships that follow the disappearances are somehow contaminated by the event itself. As a result, Aimee and Jill must go their separate ways, there is no future for Laurie and Meg, and Tom and Christine must start again in a completely new context, free of the poisonous cult. Nora and Kevin also are convinced that their relationship is too much a product of the crisis, but when Nora finds the baby and brings her to Kevin, it is as if they have found a purpose that will enable them to form new lives. They intend to make sure that the new baby will not be a leftover but will instead begin her life with the basic trust that she will need in order to negotiate the rest of her life. It is that sense of primal trust that has risen from the ashes of the mysterious and tragic upheaval.

In addition to being speculative fiction, the novel also works as a historical metaphor. The sense of epic collapse is evident at a variety of junctures in American history, from the September 11 terrorist attacks to the economic crisis of 2008. The true achievement of the novel, however, lies in the way Perrotta concentrates not on the disaster itself but on the lives of those who have survived, which allows him to probe into the psychology of loss and abandonment. While its premise may suggest a work of science fiction or theological conjecture, this fine novel's real center is its exploration of garden-variety tribulations that will be familiar to denizens of the average American suburb, including issues such as death, divorce, suicide, family breakup, child abandonment, emotional desertion, and infidelity. Although he is often praised for his witty, satirical humor, here Perrotta's powerful imagination and emotional intelligence venture naturally into the precincts of the human heart.

Margaret Boe Birns

Review Sources

Booklist 107, no. 21 (July 1, 2011): 25.
The Boston Globe, August 28, 2011 (Web).
The New York Times, August 25, 2011, p. C1.
Star Tribune, August 28, 2011, p. 13.
The Wall Street Journal, August 27, 2011, p. C7.
The Washington Post, August 31, p. C1.

The Lessons

Author: Joanne Diaz
Publisher: Silverfish Review (Eugene, OR). 72 pp. $14.95
Type of work: Poetry

With striking imagery and lush language, Joanne Diaz's first collection of poetry addresses topics such as travel, family, illness, and mortality.

The world of Joanne Diaz's *The Lessons* is above all a physical one. While the poems in this brief collection adopt several different modes—some strictly narrative, others lyrically descriptive or philosophical—they consistently maintain a focus on concrete images and sensations of life. Clearly a writer interested in her own history and experiences, Diaz uses an autobiographical style to root her reader in the world of the poem, recreating the physical experiences of a Boston childhood or a trip to Spain to such vivid effect that the emotional content is itself physical and inescapable. The winner of the Gerald Cable First Book Award in 2009, *The Lessons* will serve as an introduction to a new poet for many readers. While many first books (including others in the Gerald Cable series) distinguish themselves with stylistic leaps, formal experimentation, or postmodern playfulness, Joanne Diaz relies instead on traditional poetic devices. This collection is hardly predictable or familiar, however; rather, it is surprising in both its engrossing imagery and its ability to tie the physical world to the abstractions of emotions, loss, and memory.

In poems concerned with the concrete and the tactile, Diaz utilizes her selected images to full effect. The poem "Violin," for instance, addresses the construction of the musical instrument itself, an object that "lives as both horse and tree," a reference to the maple of the violin's body and the horse intestine out of which strings are sometimes made. Although rooted in the physical construction of the instrument, Diaz conveys a sort of magical rapture at the reality of the object's history. She wonders that

> Its treble cry holds memories of pulp
> and root. Its sloped hips remember the race
>
> through a leaf's narrow veins. Here a crow cleaned
> his beak; there an owl turned its neck. Even
>
> before music, the rosin did its work—

The horse and the tree, although long dead, are still present in the body itself, indistinguishable from the "treble cry" of the instrument's music. In this yoking together of physicality and memory, Diaz manages to transcend both; she cannot hear the music without recalling the birds that landed on the tree, nor can she think of the tree's rosin without hearing the music that will eventually come from it. The poem lingers over this transcendence, imagining the "horse's desire for rhythm" and delighting in the sensory details of the violin's construction. While the lyrical description is rewarding enough, Diaz goes one step further, solidifying the link between memory and object with the poem's surprising conclusion. She notes that the violin falls apart from use, as though it is "longing for what it was, not unlike // my father as he stood by the open mailbox, / reading my brother's first letter home." This jump to the father, made more abrupt by the stanza break that precedes it, is connected to the remainder of the poem only by the metaphor of the violin. We are not given the details of where the brother has gone or why, as this is not a poem about the family itself. Instead, it is about the memories that come rushing forth from an object, whether that object is an unexpected letter in the mailbox or a violin alive with the forest.

(Jason Reblando)

A scholar of Renaissance literature, Joanne Diaz has published her poetry widely in literary magazines. The Lessons (2011) is her first book of poetry and was the recipient of the Gerald Cable First Book Award.

Not surprisingly for a collection so concerned with imagery, Diaz maintains a consistent sense of music and innovation in her descriptions. The individual poems are often loosely metered, indulgent in alliteration and sound play, and filled with internal rhyme. As a result, many of the best poems are like songs, lending themselves to being read out loud. Whether describing the "pepperbush / standing as straight as physics / will permit" or the "slice of speed / and threat of flight" that comes with sledding down a hill, there are few lines that do not ring with musicality. As an academic with a focus in English Renaissance poetry, Diaz has a finely tuned ear for meter and sound, the Renaissance being a time of strict forms and regular meters. While there are many contemporary poets who make use of these devices, Diaz employs them both with unusual regularity and to surprisingly evocative results. The heightened music of descriptions makes them almost magical, so that the physical world she describes, although often mundane and familiar to us, becomes new and unusual: the pepperbush is an object that tests the limits of the natural world; a sled risks actual flight. All of this succeeds not only in creating a pleasurable reading experience but also in bridging the gap that separates the concrete world from the memory and imagination that is never far away.

The physical world is a place of unending beauty in these poems, but it is also a place of danger and disease, where death is constantly present. This is one of the most exciting qualities of Diaz's work; she takes the natural world as fully as she can, not romanticizing it but instead extracting from it both loss and joy, beauty as well as decay. In "Linnaeus and the Patient," she imagines the famous botanist during his brief career as a doctor, during which he primarily treated patients with venereal disease. Linnaeus begins,

> To cure I had to touch
> without knowing what touch
> would do. I had to ease
> his trousers down and see
> the mucus, shiny and constant
> on his swollen sex, the red
> pustules burning to break

The description is grotesque and diseased, yet it appears in imagery as rich and detailed as the imagery of flowers and wine elsewhere in the collection. Diaz does not elevate the sentimental objects of beauty above others, but instead takes the world as a whole, in the totality of its details. This is, ultimately, what attracts her to Linnaeus as well. A master botanist, she imagines him comparing the human body to plants, drawing parallels between human beings and the nature in which they live. These parallels do not just help Linnaeus confront the diseased body; they are the means by which he reaches greater insight into life itself, even though he does not know what his touch will accomplish. He declares that "everyone must die a little / in order for me to cure them," accepting death as a fundamental aspect of existence. Although death and health (like beauty and the grotesque) seem disparate, they are brought together in the physical world, made one for a brief moment.

The confrontation with physical decay also plays a fundamental role in helping Diaz understand her aging family. Seeing her mother at work in the kitchen, she wonders,

> how long until she vanishes, until
> the pinkish-white of each bone's glow becomes
> Venetian glass, the chipped mosaic,
> the dust

The experience of losing her mother, while heart wrenching, is portrayed less through recollections of a mother-daughter connection and more through the physical decay of the older woman's body. This is not an avoidance of that loss, but a way to see it fully—the absence of the mother physically made manifest long before she is actually gone. In "On My Father's Loss of Hearing," this acceptance is taken a step further. Diaz begins to accept the decline in her father's health by noting, "What else / is there but loss?" She goes so far as to wonder if the loss of hearing is a relief, the father no longer held to the physical world by sound, "no noisy cruelty, no baffled rage, / no aging children sullen in their lack." Although she runs the risk of pessimism, these poems avoid despair in their treatment of loss. Instead, they recognize loss as part of the natural order, rendering it in beautiful language. Diaz does her best to recognize what is gained while something is lost, just as her father's "desires / release like saffron pistils in the wind."

Despite her insistence on tactile truth, Diaz does occasionally depart into fancy and metaphor. "Love Poem" transforms the narrator into an omnipresent force, describing itself as "the warmth that lifted / from your piled sheets" and "the rush / in the vein of every oak leaf / that crowded your window." Beautiful, evocative, and flush with concrete images, the poem is nonetheless a step away from the preference for verifiable truth that characterizes much of the book. Likewise, the poem "Christmas in Southern California" declares, "I am certain that this vision is a lie," the speaker unable to reconcile the sunny weather with the "singular loveliness of the cold" of Christmases from her childhood. It is surprising to hear the speaker of this collection casting doubt on what she sees, just as it is surprising when she moves so fully into the imagination in "Love Poem." However, these departures balance out the poems that offer no obvious link to the speaker's life and rely entirely on image. Bridged by their reliance on lyrical imagery, these poems still earn their place in the text, even if the philosophy behind the imagery is not as rewarding as it is in other places.

A satisfying, musical book, *The Lessons'* greatest success lies in the beauty of its language, regardless of the ends to which that beauty is applied. Again and again, Diaz summons the knowledge of life with the "sound that secrets make / as they return from that other world / of teeth and blood and fire." Her poems indulge themselves, so that the description of eating a pomegranate can last line after line, "the translucent membrane gently parting / seed from luscious crimson seed." Ultimately, these descriptions not only provide lessons and metaphors but also urge the reader further into the physical world, like the subject of the title poem, a young girl learning to swim who "won't put [her] face in the water, won't / lie like a discarded doll on the surface, / won't hold [her] breath." After this long narrative, however, the girl sees her mother, a woman who rarely smiles, yet "her light laugh / makes her tall, young, warm." Taken by this physical power, the girl dives in, experiencing the magic of life underwater for the first time. This is the urging of *The Lessons*: to resist fear of the natural world—of death, disease, and the grotesque. Instead, Diaz persuades her readers to accept life for what it is and dive into the water, suggesting that they will find there a lyric beauty that is somehow redemptive.

T. Fleischmann

The Letters of Ernest Hemingway
Volume 1, 1907–1922

Author: Ernest Hemingway (1899–1961)
Editors: Sandra Spanier and Robert W. Trogdon
Publisher: Cambridge University Press (New York). 516 pp. $40.00
Type of work: Letters, biography
Time: 1907–1922
Locale: United States

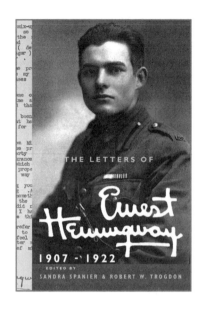

The letters in this first volume reveal two forces that shaped the young Hemingway and made their mark on him for life: his middle-class upbringing in Oak Park and his experience in the war.

When writing his novels and short stories, Ernest Hemingway used a journalistic style and simple, unadorned prose to capture the everyday lives of men and women caught up in some of history's most momentous events. Indeed, the title of his first published book, *In Our Time* (1925), a collection of short stories and experimental modernist prose, reflects his desires to chronicle the triumphs and failures of his own modern culture in an intimate and knowing fashion. His unforgettable portraits of a generation of writers and artists grab readers and transport them to that time, giving them the experience of rubbing shoulders with such luminaries as Gertrude Stein, Sherwood Anderson, F. Scott Fitzgerald, and Ezra Pound. In *The Sun Also Rises* (1926), Hemingway shrewdly depicts the boredom and disillusionment with politics that marked the famous Lost Generation. His *A Farewell to Arms* (1929) portrays the ugliness of World War I and the cynicism of Hemingway's circle of literary friends. In *To Have and Have Not* (1937), he probes the despair, hopelessness, and injustices brought on by the Great Depression and in *For Whom the Bell Tolls* (1940), he explores the complex web of cynicism, patriotism, loyalty, individualism, and nationalism that arose out of the awful conflicts of the Spanish Civil War. In one of his most widely read novels, *The Old Man and the Sea* (1952), Hemingway eloquently captures the brokenness of human hopes and desires, as a fisherman struggles mightily against forces of nature that are destined to overcome him and his dreams. More than any of the writers who were his contemporaries—Fitzgerald, Stein, William Faulkner—Hemingway vividly captured the lives of individuals as they struggled against society, nature, and each other in an attempt to preserve their hopes and dreams against the backdrop of a culture in turmoil.

As much as Hemingway's novels and stories offer a record of a tumultuous time in twentieth-century history, his own life fascinates biographers and readers of his fiction. More than a dozen biographies have explored the many facets of Hemingway's adventurous and often raucous life. Many films have also attempted to portray Hemingway as a legendary hardfisted, hard-drinking writer who often tried to hide his insecurities behind a false bravado, embarking on big-game hunting or running with the bulls in Pamplona, Spain. Despite the depth of these biographies, however, certain aspects of Hemingway's life have remained unavailable until the publication of his letters, which come closer than any other of his writings to providing his autobiography.

During his life, Hemingway never intended his letters for publication. The great English novelist and critic Ford Maddox Ford once told Hemingway that he should always write his letters thinking about how posterity would read them. In a letter to Fitzgerald, Hemingway writes that he had such an adverse reaction to Ford's advice that he burned all of his own letters, including Ford's letters to him. Hemingway goes on to remark that he writes letters because it is fun to get letters back. It is through his letters that readers come to best know Hemingway, and he presents himself vividly in the ones that editors Sandra Spanier and Robert W. Trogdon have collected for what will be a multivolume edition, the first volume of which covers his childhood, youth, and earliest forays into journalism and fiction.

As Spanier and Trogdon point out, Hemingway's parents cultivated the habit of letter writing in their children when their children were young. At age three, the young Ernest wrote a letter to his mother describing his Christmas gifts from Santa Claus. When he was a teenager heading off to camp, his father provided him with postcards that he used to write to his family while away. The habit of letter writing was so firmly a part of his life that Hemingway always encouraged his friends and family to write with all the news of their own lives. Yet as much as he loved to receive letters, he often put off writing them. As a writer, Hemingway was sometimes afraid that if he spent too much time consumed in writing letters, his best content would end up there rather than in his stories or articles. He often apologized for the dullness of his letters, such as in one sent to his mother in 1915, in which he tells her that he is so exhausted from writing articles as a reporter for the *Toronto Star* that he feels his letters are quite commonplace. Hemingway writes his letters in a range of voices, and as this collection of his earliest letters makes clear, he always has a clear sense of his audience (public or private) when writing. Hemingway's distinct voice booms loudly through his letters, even as he performs for whatever audience to which he is writing. He corresponded with many of the twentieth century's greatest artists and writers, including Fitzgerald, Pound, Stein, Anderson, John Dos Passos, Pablo Picasso, Ingrid Bergman, Marlene Dietrich, and Gary Cooper.

As prolific a letter writer as he was, Hemingway was often afraid that his words might be regarded as libelous and offensive. Although some of his letters, such as those to the editors of newspapers or magazines, were intended for publication, his letters to family and friends were private ones, and he was constantly wary of biographers getting too close to these materials and publishing them. In May 1958, Hemingway directed his literary executors not to publish, or consent to allow others to publish, any of the letters he wrote during his lifetime. In one of the most fascinating stories of this volume, the editors trace the long and winding chronicle surrounding the fate of Hemingway's letters following his death. In 1981, his fourth wife and literary executor, Mary Hemingway, did decide to publish *Ernest Hemingway: Selected Letters, 1917–1961*. Hailed as a major literary event, this publication set numerous Hemingway scholars on a quest to uncover and recover as much of his surviving correspondence as could be located. When it is completed, *The Letters of Ernest Hemingway* will include more than six thousand of Hemingway's surviving letters in more than a dozen volumes; approximately 85 percent of these letters have never before been published.

This first volume of *The Letters of Ernest Hemingway* captures a young writer's attempt to carve out his career. It contains letters he wrote during his youth in his native Oak Park, Illinois; his teenage years of camping and fishing in northern Michigan;

(The Pennsylvania State University Press)

Sandra Spanier is a professor of English at Pennsylvania State University.

his early years as a journalist at the *Kansas City Star*; his wounding in Italy in World War I; his return to the northern Michigan haunts of his youth for about a year and a half following the war; and his earliest days and experiences in Paris. Hemingway's early letters reflect his ambivalent relationship with his parents (strong and tender in his early years, but often tortured after his return from the war), his loves, and his struggles as a writer. The youthful letters often swagger and boast and reveal a young man who is absorbed in his own interests. As one of the volume's editors observes, the letters in this first volume reveal two forces that shaped the young Hemingway and made their mark on him for life: his middle-class upbringing in Oak Park and his experience in the war. During the war, his letters to his parents and brothers and sisters are affectionate, often concentrating on descriptions of the beauty of the Italian countryside so as not to disturb his family with glimpses of the real horrors of the conflict. In some of his earliest letters from this period, he exclaims how glad he is to be amid the fighting and to be a participant in the glories of war. Later, though, after being wounded, he admits in his letters that he is not the go-getter that he originally made himself out to be.

The book is nicely divided into four sections that correspond to the four major periods of Hemingway's life between 1907 and 1922: his childhood and youth in Oak Park and northern Michigan; his years in Kansas City and as an ambulance driver in Italy; his almost two years in Michigan and Chicago following the war; and his first year in Paris in 1922, when he began his literary apprenticeship. Of the 264 letters collected in this volume, more than half of them are addressed to family members, thus underscoring the importance of family to Hemingway, an aspect of his life and work that has not yet been adequately explored. These early letters reflect how places and

Robert W. Trogdon is professor of English and director of the Institute for Bibliography and Editing at Kent State University. He is the editor of Ernest Hemingway: A Literary Reference *(1999).*

people in his youth deeply shaped Hemingway and his sense of self, firing his creativity and imagination throughout his work.

The letters from Hemingway's childhood and youth display his love of fishing, hunting, and sports. His letters home from northern Michigan contain observations about wildlife, reflections on sports teams, and requests for advice from his father about making various purchases. After his high school graduation, Hemingway moved to Kansas City to become a cub reporter for the *Kansas City Star*; in the letters from this time, he mostly writes about the long hours he spends on the job, but he also writes reflectively about his interviews with sports figures and politicians.

In 1917, wanting to contribute in some way to the war effort, he joined the Red Cross and arrived in Italy. Not long after his arrival, he was wounded, and during his recovery he met Agnes von Kurowsky, an American nurse with whom he fell in love and about whom he wrote home frequently to his parents. The letters he wrote about her and their relationship resemble the love story he would later tell about Frederic Henry and the nurse Catherine Barkley in *A Farewell to Arms*. In a letter to his parents, Hemingway expresses his disillusionment with the war by observing that there are no heroes in this war.

The third section of letters chronicles Hemingway's life at home following his return from Italy. The letters during this period reveal the young author's resolve to focus more and more on his writing, especially on his fiction. His relationships with Kate Smith and Marjorie Bump during these years (1919–21) provide the raw material for stories such as "Big Two-Hearted River" and "Summer People." His letters also reveal an increasing alienation from his parents. Perhaps the most important event during this period of his life was meeting Elizabeth Hadley Richardson, a cultured young woman with whom Hemingway fell deeply in love. The two married in September 1921 and soon left to begin a new life in Paris.

The final section of letters in this volume covers Hemingway's first year in Paris, where he discovered nineteenth-century French and Russian literature and formed lifelong relationships with Pound and Stein. The letters from this time in his life emphasize the great significance of these writers to his own career as a novelist. They also highlight just how instrumental these other writers were in their support of Hemingway's career, often referring his writing to their editors.

The Letters of Ernest Hemingway: Volume 1, 1907–1922 contributes significantly to readers' knowledge of Hemingway. For the first time, they are afforded an important glimpse of Hemingway as a young man and of the forces that shaped him. Moreover, readers see him engaged in the art of writing from his earliest boyhood and the ways in which writing became a part of the very fabric of his life. These letters reveal Hemingway at his most vulnerable, most tender, and most self-critical, as well as at his funniest. Spanier and Trogdon provide deeply engaging introductions as well as chronologies and other useful material to put the letters in context. Hemingway's letters provide a compelling portrait of the artist as a young man, learning to take in all the elements of his life and transform them into the beautiful and memorable novels and stories that have so shaped American literature and culture.

Henry L. Carrigan Jr.

Review Sources

Hemingway Review 31, no. 1 (Fall 2011): 124–7.
Library Journal 136, no. 17 (October 15, 2011): 82–83.
The New York Times Book Review, November 13, 2011, p. 8.

Liberty's Exiles
American Loyalists in the Revolutionary World

Author: Maya Jasanoff (b. 1974)
Publisher: Random House (New York). 480 pp. $30.00
Type of work: Biography, history
Time: Eighteenth and nineteenth centuries
Locale: North America, Caribbean, Great Britain, Africa, India, Australia

Jasanoff discusses the diversity of loyalists living in North American colonies, examining how they extended the British Empire after the American Revolution by migrating to numerous locations where their activities affected imperial policies.

Principal personages:

BEVERLEY ROBINSON (1723–1792), a New York loyalist

ELIZABETH LICHTENSTEIN JOHNSTON (1764–1848), the wife of a Georgia loyalist officer

DAVID GEORGE (1742–1810), a freed Virginia slave and Baptist minister

JOSEPH BRANT / THAYENDANEGEA (1743–1807), a Mohawk leader

WILLIAM AUGUSTUS BOWLES (1763–1805), a Maryland loyalist and Creek leader

GUY CARLETON (1724–1808), first Baron Dorchester, governor of Quebec and British North America, and commander in chief of North American British forces

JOHN MURRAY (1732–1809), fourth Earl of Dunmore and loyalist governor of New York, Virginia, and the Bahamas

JOSEPH GALLOWAY (1731–1803), a Pennsylvania loyalist lawyer and legislator

WILLIAM FRANKLIN (1731–1813), a loyalist governor of New Jersey

Liberty's Exiles: American Loyalists in the Revolutionary World explores the post–American Revolution global distribution of North American colonists and indigenous peoples who had supported Great Britain during the war. Dividing her text into three parts to examine the loyalists as refugees, as settlers in loyalist communities, and as British subjects into the early nineteenth century, Maya Jasanoff presents biographical examples of the differing experiences of loyalists. She counters the stereotypes perpetuated in many historical depictions of the British subjects living in American colonies who remained faithful to King George III. In contrast to the generalization that loyalists were primarily wealthy white men, Jasanoff emphasizes their diversity, noting that they represented the colonies' complex demographics. Loyalists included both men and women, ranging from children to the elderly, and were associated with

Maya Jasanoff is a professor at the Harvard University Center for European Studies. She has written articles for The Age of Revolutions in Global Context, c. 1760–1840 *(2010) and the* William and Mary Quarterly. *Her book* Edge of Empire: Lives, Culture, and Conquest in the East, 1750–1850 *(2005) won the Duff Cooper Prize.*

various socioeconomic classes, occupations, ethnicities, and regional concerns. Her study develops various themes that characterize the loyalists and their experiences, including commitment, loss, movement, perseverance, and reinvention.

Jasanoff conducted her research in archives all over the world. The vast primary resources she consulted—encompassing such documents as Loyalist Claims Commission records, passenger lists, correspondence, journals, and pamphlets (such as those composed by New York rector Charles Inglis)—preserve details essential to comprehending who the loyalists were, their allegiances to the British monarchy, and the circumstances they encountered in the North American colonies and areas where they sought sanctuary. Her scrutiny of these archival materials enabled Jasanoff to understand aspects of the loyalists that previous historians have misunderstood or dismissed. As a result, her book presents new information and corrects errors, particularly regarding the number of loyalists who departed the colonies after the American Revolution. By assessing ship manifests, claim applications, and other documentation, Jasanoff calculates that the number of emigrating loyalists totaled approximately seventy-five thousand.

She contemplates how loyalists dealt with their dual identity as Americans and British subjects and how they differentiated between those roles. Her study reveals that they often shared characteristics with patriots, such as business skills, devotion to their families, and religious faith, that enabled them to function economically and socially in their communities. Loyalists had various reasons for retaining their affiliation with Great Britain and its monarchy. Some believed Britain would prevail militarily. Jasanoff notes that both the Declaration of Independence and a Continental Congress resolution passed on June 24, 1776, intensified division between patriotic and loyalist colonists. That resolution stated that loyalists' properties could be seized and their rights, including free speech, could be denied if they refused to pledge devotion to the government formed by the patriots.

After the British defeat, loyalists evacuated aboard Royal Navy vessels departing from New York City (the site of the largest loyalist population during the revolution, totaling almost thirty thousand) as George Washington's army marched through Manhattan's streets in November 1783. Rewarding their commitment during the revolution, Great Britain transported loyalists to new locations. Waiting was a constant theme, as the resettlement process from all the former colonies sometimes proceeded slowly, with affected loyalists living in floating communities offshore before passage to East Florida, the Caribbean, Great Britain, Africa, India, or Australia could be arranged. According to Jasanoff, the majority of loyalists fled to Canada, primarily the provinces of Nova Scotia, Quebec, and New Brunswick. She explains that Great Britain's leaders encouraged Canadian settlement so they could maintain that country's influence on North American policies. Jasanoff estimates that eight thousand white loyalists and approximately five thousand black loyalists immigrated to Great Britain.

Jasanoff outlines three major postrevolution developments associated with the loyalists and what she refers to as the "spirit of 1783." First, she emphasizes that the 1780s was a significant decade in the reshaping and transformation of the British Empire, with the loyalists aiding global expansion of Great Britain's colonies. King George III and Britain's political leaders envisioned how the loyalists could strengthen and extend the empire's territories. Next, Jasanoff states that the plight of the loyalists reinforced Britain's efforts to assure legal and humanitarian rights for its subjects wherever they lived. Third, many loyalists voiced frustration and disappointment at decisions of British officials that did not consider those subjects' sacrifices and perspectives, which influenced government policies in their new communities.

Jasanoff emphasizes the losses of property, family, and income that many loyalists suffered and notes that the British government provided for their compensation. Some loyalists required immediate assistance to replace basic clothing and essential items for their evacuation. They also needed assistance to survive in unfamiliar locations while they attempted to adapt. Jasanoff evaluates how the Loyalist Claims Commission aided exiles. The commission required applicants to submit claims with proof, preparing documentation or speaking with commission representatives. Some claims agents verified property values by going to Canada and the United States. The application process hindered many claimants, and only one-third of all claims were approved, for a total of more than three million pounds distributed. Upset that many loyalists were denied compensation, William Franklin and Joseph Galloway urged Parliament to help loyalists instead of neglect them. Often loyalists were confused by British officials' dismissing their needs or forcing them to abandon their new homes, such as when England ceded East Florida, where many loyalists and Native American allies had settled, to Spain.

Jasanoff explains that many loyalists saw opportunities despite their losses. In their new communities, they attempted to rebuild their lives, seeking financial stability. Some provided leadership in government positions. Arrival of loyalist exiles impacted existing residents; for example, Cajuns in Canada were expelled in order to free land and housing for loyalists. Assimilation occurred as loyalists appropriated aspects of their new cultures into their lifestyles while adding British influences to communities, such as placing a monument at Spanish Town, Jamaica, to recognize Great Britain's success in the Battle of the Saintes in 1782. Occasionally, loyalists married indigenous people, resulting in biracial descendants; these included Benedict Arnold's Eurasian granddaughter, who was born in India. Many loyalists voiced similar criticisms of British rule over colonial subjects as the revolutionary patriots had. Several aspired to regain lost territory in the former colonies or adjacent areas. While serving as the governor of the Bahamas, John Murray supported attempts focused on restoring East Florida to loyalists.

Beverley Robinson's experiences symbolize the personal losses many loyalists suffered. Robinson had delayed committing to becoming a loyalist, contemplating pleas from patriot associates to fight the British. His eventual decision tore his family apart.

A loyalist regiment commander, Robinson abandoned his valuable New York properties after Great Britain's defeat and left his family to seek sanctuary in England. The dispersal of his kin in Canada and England resulted in many of them never being reunited, while others located relatives in their new homes years later. Some children returned to the former colonies as adults to see sites they had been forced to leave when young.

Similarly, Elizabeth Lichtenstein Johnston stands as a symbol of how female loyalists endured disruptions and physical and emotional sacrifices associated with postrevolution relocation. The wife of a captain in the loyalist military forces, Johnston wrote a narrative in 1837 that describes leaving her Savannah, Georgia, home for refuge in Charleston, South Carolina. She moved to St. Augustine in East Florida, a popular settlement where many loyalists from southern colonies relocated. Soon, however, those loyalists were forced to leave again when Spain acquired that territory. Jasanoff stresses Johnston's resilience, traveling by ship with her children between North America, Scotland, and Jamaica, and enduring yellow-fever epidemics, the deaths of two of her children, depression, and her physician husband's absences. She eventually settled in Nova Scotia with other loyalists, and her descendants became provincial leaders.

Many blacks chose to become loyalists to secure their freedom, which Great Britain offered to slaves who fought for the British, prompting around twenty thousand to run away from their colonial owners. This wartime emancipation resulted in ample documentation of those loyalists' legal status, providing Jasanoff valuable primary materials. The free black loyalists represented another aspect of postrevolution distribution of British subjects. After Great Britain's defeat, many feared being enslaved. North American British forces commander Guy Carleton oversaw their evacuation to Nova Scotia, in the process transgressing the Treaty of Paris provision that forbade loyalists from transporting "Negroes, or other Property of the American Inhabitants" out of the former colonies.

Some black loyalists who sought refuge in Great Britain struggled to survive. Shadrack Furman, for example, was maimed by Americans because he concealed military intelligence he was delivering to British troops. Evacuated to London, Furman survived by begging. The Committee for the Black Poor arranged for approximately three hundred black loyalists to depart Great Britain for Africa to settle in Sierra Leone. In Nova Scotia, two thousand blacks insisted on being sent to Sierra Leone as well. Emigrants included David George, a former Virginia slave who initially moved to Nova Scotia, where he preached to a Baptist congregation he organized. By 1792, George, confronted by racism, decided to move to the Freetown settlement in Sierra Leone. Ironically, many black loyalists immigrating to Sierra Leone lived near slave depots and survived assaults by French troops during the Napoleonic Wars. Most slaves belonging to southern white loyalists were transferred to their owners' properties in the Caribbean or East Florida, where they were often tormented by racial violence, heat, humidity, and disease.

Jasanoff discusses alliances established between Native Americans and Great Britain before the American Revolution to control the colonists encroaching on the frontier. Mohawk sachem Thayendanegea, known as Joseph Brant, had fought in the

Seven Years' War with British troops; later, with his wife Molly Brant, he rallied and supplied Mohawk and Iroquois fighters for the British in the American Revolution. After the revolution, these loyalists and members of their tribes settled on Canadian lands provided by the British. In the south, loyalist William Augustus Bowles became a Creek leader and aspired to regain lost loyalist lands by establishing Muskogee, a Creek state, in Florida. He petitioned King George III regarding his idea, but his plans failed when he was imprisoned in Cuba and then the Philippines by the Spanish.

Most critics have described Jasanoff's work as revisionist and groundbreaking, recognizing the uniqueness of her book and its resources, which include an appendix enumerating loyalist emigration. Reviewers have remarked that Jasanoff's biographical approach and inclusion of excerpts from loyalists' writings provides readers access to contemporary mindsets and realities. Many have praised her global view of the loyalists' emigration, as most previous books have only discussed their Canadian settlement, and noted that Jasanoff's text is useful in perceiving how military loss influenced the British government's later decisions regarding war as well as its colonial policies and treatment of its subjects. Some critics have stated that Jasanoff's writing style is more appropriate for popular rather than scholarly audiences, suggesting she has not sufficiently analyzed political ideology, while others criticize her omission of loyalists living in Spanish West Florida. Overall, however, critics recognize the complexities of the text as well as the new information and insights Jasanoff presents, all of which inspire reconsideration and further examination of an often-overlooked historical group that contributed to shaping world history.

Elizabeth D. Schafer

Review Sources

The American Spectator 44, no. 4 (May 2011): 74–75.
Booklist 107, no. 11 (February 1, 2011): 26.
Choice: Current Reviews for Academic Libraries 48, no. 11 (July 2011): 2170.
Kirkus Reviews 78, no. 22 (November 15, 2010): 146.
Library Journal 135, no. 20 (December 1, 2010): 125.
The New York Times Book Review, May 1, 2011, p. 16.
Publishers Weekly 257, no. 46 (November 22, 2010): 53.
Spectator 315, no. 9521 (February 19, 2011): 34.
Wilson Quarterly 35, no. 2 (Spring 2011): 94–96.

Life Itself
A Memoir

Author: Roger Ebert (b. 1942)
Publisher: Grand Central (New York).
 448 pp. $27.99
Type of work: Memoir
Time: 1942–the present

Film critic Roger Ebert recalls his encoun-
ters with famous stars and filmmakers, his
successful career, and his struggles with can-
cer and debilitating surgeries.

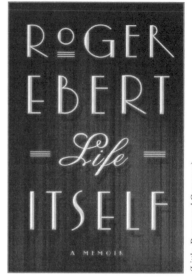

(Little, Brown and Company)

Principal personages:
ROGER EBERT (b. 1942), film critic for the
 Chicago Sun-Times and television per-
 sonality
CHARLIE "CHAZ" HAMMELSMITH EBERT
 (b. 1952), his wife
GENE SISKEL (1946–1999), film critic for the
 Chicago Tribune and Ebert's longtime
 television partner
ROBERT F. "BOB" ZONKA (1928–1985), features editor of the *Chicago Sun-Times*,
 Ebert's mentor and close friend
RUSS MEYER (1922–2004), film director, Ebert's mentor and friend
MARTIN SCORSESE (b. 1942), film director, Ebert's friend
STUDS TERKEL (1912–2008), Chicago-based, Pulitzer Prize–winning author, historian,
 radio personality, and Ebert's friend

Some celebrities seem to write memoirs in order to bring their self-analysis into an autobiographical forum. Fortunately for the reader, Roger Ebert's *Life Itself* is more about his observations of others than his personal introspection. There is some intro-spection, but nothing too deep, and nothing like self-pity. A writer by profession, he does not need to resort to the amanuensis format that lends itself to most celebrity memoirs. One of the best aspects of the book, and one of the things that has made Roger Ebert one of the most successful film critics of all time, is his well-informed and eminently readable writing style. Whether discussing childhood memories, or his years at the University of Illinois, Champaign-Urbana, and the *Chicago Sun-Times*, Ebert manages to make his prose as smooth and entertaining as it is erudite. Perhaps that is one of the keys to his success: his ability to elevate the conversation without ever speaking down to the reader.

 Of the memoir's fifty-five chapters, many are as much about Ebert's love of travel as they are about him or his favorite films. He references his travel-related books *Two*

Weeks in the Midday Sun: A Cannes Notebook (1987), about his annual trips to the Cannes Film Festival, and *The Perfect London Walk* (1986; co-authored with Daniel Curley), about his favorite home-away-from-home. His descriptions of London, in particular, are some of the most entertaining of the book. While Ebert does not seem to care for the more modern, energetic London of the twenty-first century, he nonetheless embraces it and lovingly recounts the day-to-day experiences of his many trips in vivid detail. He also provides long passages about restaurants and romantic times with his wife in Venice, and about the best bars, neighborhoods, and hangouts of his beloved hometown, Chicago.

The author spends a considerable number of pages recounting anecdotes about his many colorful friends, which are so numerous that one begins to wonder if some have been embellished by memory; however, they certainly make for entertaining reading. These short chapters are not so much about Ebert as the people he has met throughout his life, including close friends and mentors like Bob Zonka and Studs Terkel, film stars such as John Wayne, and many other people who were all larger than life and influenced Ebert. Many local Chicago media personalities, from *Sun-Times* entertainment columnist Irv Kupcinet to talk show hosts Oprah Winfrey and Phil Donohue, are also mentioned throughout the book, although they do not receive individual chapters.

The portions of the book that deal with Ebert's childhood in Urbana, Illinois, are reminiscent of experiences related by humorist and fellow Illinois resident Jean Shepherd. Although Ebert was born twenty years after Shepherd, many of his life experiences, from grammar school and neighborhood pranks to family recollections, have the spirit and humor of Shepherd's short story collection *In God We Trust, All Others Pay Cash* (1966; portions of which were adapted into the popular 1984 film *A Christmas Story*). A pre–baby boomer, Ebert fondly recalls listening to radio programs and going to Saturday matinees, in which popular Western B-movie heroes such as Lash LaRue prevailed.

Though reared as a Roman Catholic, Ebert drifted away from the church. Unlike many writers, however, he does not seem to bear the church ill will, speaking very fondly of the Dominican nuns who taught him and the excellent education he received. He is a reverential and almost fanatical alumnus of the University of Illinois, where he attended both undergraduate and graduate school, and where his father was an electrician while young Roger, an only child, grew up. Whether out of school loyalty or nostalgia, Ebert quite emphatically states that being an editor of the university newspaper, *The Daily Illini*, was the best job he ever had.

Many of the chapters are named after Ebert's friends or famous people he has known. He does not spend time trashing people he does not like, even though he implies that he could. Instead, he offers three chapters about three down-to-earth tough guys, three actors for whom he has a particular fondness and affinity: Lee Marvin, Robert Mitchum, and John Wayne. Marvin was the subject of Ebert's earliest published celebrity interview, and Mitchum and Wayne represent, for Ebert, an earlier, less guarded time. On reflection, though, Ebert indicates that it is not just these three men that resonate with him, but also the early years in the 1960s and 1970s, when being an international star did not mean having an army of people to guard the celebrity from everyone else. Though

Mitchum and Marvin were often considered hostile to the press, Ebert's style proved successful, as he did not ask too many questions and simply allowed his subjects to be who they really were. His first interview with Marvin set the precedent for Ebert's style of letting celebrities say whatever they wanted, then formulating the story later on his typewriter. There are several hilarious anecdotes about Mitchum, one while filming the 1970 epic *Ryan's Daughter* in Dingle, Ireland, and

Roger Ebert was the first film critic to win a Pulitzer Prize in criticism, and he has been awarded numerous film and journalism awards before and since. Despite the loss of his ability to speak, Ebert participates in the annual Ebertfest at the University of Illinois, continues to write for the Chicago Sun-Times, *and produces a popular daily blog at http://rogerebert.suntimes.com.*

another, while Mitchum was filming the obscure film *Going Home* in McKeesport, Pennsylvania, in 1971, and vainly attempting to drive to a location.

Another significant aspect that these three actors shared, particularly Mitchum and Marvin, was that they were hard drinkers, something Ebert embraced as a young adult but gave up in the late 1970s, when he realized he was an alcoholic. On the subject of alcoholism, Ebert permits himself some self-reflection, as he ponders the possibly hereditary nature of his alcoholism. His father, as far as Ebert was able to deduce from his mother and other relatives, had been an alcoholic, but had stopped drinking before Ebert was born. Ebert's mother became an alcoholic later in life, drinking with her son at first and then holding some resentment when he joined Alcoholics Anonymous. Even in reflecting on his mother's problems, though, Ebert never fails to write about her in loving terms.

One important figure to whom Ebert devotes two chapters is the late Gene Siskel. Siskel and Ebert began their groundbreaking television series in 1975 as a monthly PBS show called *Sneak Previews*, which eventually became the nationally syndicated weekly show *Siskel & Ebert at the Movies*. Their intellectually argumentative banter, including the "thumbs up," "thumbs down" film ratings, became a cultural icon of the 1980s and 1990s; however, for unfathomable reasons, Ebert only mentions "thumbs up" and "thumbs down" once in the book, and even then not within the context of the show. Ebert mentions the rating in passing as he is describing how life since his surgeries has deprived him of speech, saying that charades-like hand signals have led him to "more uses of 'thumbs-up' and 'thumbs-down' than I ever dreamed of."

Ebert describes the enigmatic Siskel as intelligent and argumentative, extremely closed-mouthed and private, and, despite their many differences, something of an intellectual soul mate. Their on-air squabbles often led to charges that the two men really disliked each other off the air, but Ebert denies that this was ever the case. He does take exception to being known as "the fat one" of the pair, but otherwise he speaks very nostalgically of his on-air partner. Siskel died of brain cancer in 1999 but, according to Ebert, he has been in his television partner's thoughts ever since.

Among the directors whom Ebert has allotted a chapter are some of the greats of the latter half of the twentieth century; the group includes Ingmar Bergman, Martin Scorsese, Robert Altman, and Woody Allen, all of whom he has met and, with the exception of Bergman, interviewed many times. Though Russ Meyers can hardly be considered on the same artistic plane as the other directors, his personal relationship with Ebert, who wrote the screenplay for the director's cult classic *Beyond the Valley of the Dolls* (1970), makes him a worthy selection for a chapter. In fact, of all of the film industry figures allotted profiles in the book, Meyers comes off the best in terms of kindness. If there are conclusions to be gleaned from Ebert's chapters, it is that they are almost all about characters and, aside from his mother and his wife, they are all men. Ebert seems most at ease in the company of so-called "man's men," hard-drinking raconteurs who often were hard-smoking womanizers as well.

Ebert's wife Chaz receives the most loving treatment in the book, as much for her down-to-earth good nature as her unabashed willingness to stand by him during his horrific surgeries and treatment for thyroid cancer. Married in his late forties, Ebert embraced her affectionate, extended African American family as his own, crediting Chaz for helping him finally achieve adulthood. Although not previously interested in film, Chaz has nonetheless been by his side for the last twenty years at screenings and film festivals, and for the past few years she has successfully managed his career. Although her full appearance in the book does not come until the final third, she is mentioned throughout the memoir and frequently brought in as a point of reference for Ebert's travels and thoughts.

Ebert's catastrophic illness is mentioned periodically throughout the book, but Ebert does not focus on his condition in earnest until chapters forty-seven and forty-eight, "Good News and Bad News" and the poignantly named "Nil by Mouth." While the reader will have a hard time getting through chapters about the diagnosis, surgery, and painful post-operative experience that left him unable to speak, drink, or eat, Ebert does not turn these experiences into extended periods of self-pity. Instead, he speaks lovingly of his wife and friends alongside descriptions of his struggles, balancing the two so that his memoir is never depressing. Despite what has certainly been an excruciating experience on physical and emotional levels, Ebert has reaffirmed his will to speak not through his voice but via a daily blog, which is read by millions around the world. In Janet Maslin's review for *The New York Times*, she, like many other critics, commented that this book's many short chapters are reminiscent of "the vitality of blog entries without the sloppiness that often goes with them." Although Ebert occasionally reintroduces characters that were previously mentioned and has a habit of going back and forth in time, there is absolutely nothing sloppy in his writing style, which is both thoughtful and entertaining at the same time.

Patricia King Hanson

Review Sources

Chicago Tribune, September 7, 2011 (Web).
Entertainment Weekly, no. 1171/1172 (September 9, 2011): 139.
The New York Times, September 22, 2011 (Web).
Publishers Weekly 258, no. 30 (July 25, 2011): 1.
Time 178, no. 12 (September 11, 2011): 58.

Life on Mars

Author: Tracy K. Smith (b. 1972)
Publisher: Graywolf (Minneapolis). 88 pp.
$15.00
Type of work: Poetry
Locale: Various settings, including outer space, Brooklyn, and a public library

Tracy K. Smith's third collection of poetry uses outer space, science fiction, and interplanetary travel to examine the human condition on Earth while exemplifying the author's vivid and affecting use of language and imagery.

Principal personages:

FLOYD WILLIAM SMITH (1935–2008), the poet's father, an engineer who worked on the lenses of the Hubble Space Telescope

DAVID BOWIE (b. 1947), an English musician whose song "Life on Mars" inspired the title of the collection

CHARLTON HESTON (1923– 2008), an American actor known for his roles in science-fiction films such as *Planet of the Apes* (1968) and *Soylent Green* (1973)

STANLEY KUBRICK (1928–1999), an American film director whose work includes the science-fiction film *2001: A Space Odyssey* (1968)

With *Life on Mars*, award-winning poet Tracy K. Smith continues her examination of the human condition through her lyrical and often revelatory verse. In her third collection of poems, she directs her gaze outward toward the cosmos before turning it inward to her own childhood and private life. At each stopping point in her poetry, she examines perceptions of time, love, God, and death, reminding readers that the concept of closeness is best understood when juxtaposed against great distance—that space can reveal intimacy and that darkness can cast light. Indeed, the use of outer space creates a sense of perspective for readers, inviting them to examine their lives while also considering the vastness of the unknown far, far beyond. Like her earlier works, *The Body's Question* (2003) and *Duende* (2007), which explore the world of personal and existential connections, this collection sends readers to the stars in order to illuminate the here and now.

The cover of the book is an astounding and ethereal photograph of the Cone Nebula, a red dust and gas cloud over 2,500 light-years from Earth. Smith's father, Floyd William Smith, worked as an optical engineer on the Hubble telescope project, and Smith would have seen this and other similar images as a child, perhaps even before they were made available to the public. It should therefore be no surprise that cosmic images have found their way into her poetry. The first section of the collection is imbued with vibrant images, much like the magnificent, otherworldly photographs of space first seen by the Hubble telescope.

In this first section, Smith's references to David Bowie, a music icon of the 1970s, evoke memories of lunar landings, campy science fiction, Martians, and saucer-flying aliens. The collection takes its name from the Bowie song "Life on Mars," which contains a stirring, yearning melody and vivid poetic images. In the poem "Don't You Wonder, Sometimes," Smith conjures images of Bowie, both in space and on Earth:

> After dark, stars glisten like ice, and the distance they span
> Hides something elemental. Not God, exactly. More like
> Some thin-hipped glittering Bowie being—a Starman
> Or cosmic ace hovering, swaying, aching to make us see.

In this first section of *Life on Mars*, Smith's poems look beyond the confines of the earth with titles like "The Weather in Space," "The Museum of Obsolescence," and "The Universe: Original Motion Picture Soundtrack," while playfully addressing the cultural obsession with science fiction and the unknown.

Rather than question the mystery of the universe, Smith seems to accept it for what it is: an immense body of magic and morality. Her consistent use of the pronoun "it" in situations with no antecedent, as in the phrase "it sprawls" and exemplified in the poem "It & Co.," highlights the insatiable need for explanation and, in doing so, redirects readers' attention to the questions themselves. In "The Weather in Space," she ponders the nature of control in the universe:

> Is God being or pure force? The wind
> Or what commands it? When our lives slow
> And we can hold all that we love, it sprawls
> In our laps like a gangly doll.

The author's cultural references are similarly evocative. In addition to David Bowie, she incorporates Charlton Heston, an actor known for his roles in kitschy science-fiction films, into her work. She also alludes to science-fiction director Stanley Kubrick and his 1968 film *2001: A Space Odyssey*. These references act as a cultural bridge to internal reflection:

> In those last scenes of Kubrick's *2001*
> When Dave is whisked into the center of space
> . . .
> Who knows what blazes through his mind?
> Is it still his life he moves through, or does
> That end at the end of what he can name?

The jarring last stanza brings the reader decidedly back to Earth. Having delved into the nature of Dave, the film's protagonist, and his existence as a man alone in the center of space, Smith meditates on the human condition, linking it to the actors on the set: "On set, it's shot after shot till Kubrick is happy, / Then the costumes go back on their racks / And the great gleaming set goes black." Other images also create a link between the visual and emotional effect, tying the familiar and the alien together for readers. In "Sci-Fi," the sun becomes a Standard Uranium-Neutralizing device; in "The Universe is a House Party," the cosmos is portrayed as a party to which the reader has not been invited.

Much of the first section and the brilliant poem "The Speed of Belief," which takes up a majority of the second section, are elegies to Smith's father. In "The Speed of Belief," space shifts from a metaphor about the fundamental question of human existence to an allegory for the individual journey of grief and solace. The cosmos is part of the continuum into which Smith's father has vanished, and what follows is the hope that his existence has merely changed, not ceased altogether: "My father won't lie still, though his legs are buried in trousers and socks. / But where does all he knew—all he must now know—walk?" The poems about Floyd are affecting and hauntingly convey Smith's grief as she attempts to cope with his death. In referring to the unknowable expanses of the universe, she is able to express her feelings of both loss and hope.

(Tina Chang)

Tracy K. Smith is the author of the poetry collections The Body's Question *(2003) and* Duende *(2007). Her poetry awards include the James Laughlin Award of the Academy of American Poets and the Cave Canem Poetry Prize. She is an assistant professor of creative writing at Princeton University.*

The breathy pace and lightness of her work, especially the poem "Don't You Wonder, Sometimes?," are reminiscent of the New York school of poetry in the 1960s, characterized by abstract expressionism, surrealism, and urban and ironic sensibilities. One reviewer notes that Smith owes a debt to poets such as John Ashbery, Barbara Guest, and Frank O'Hara, all of whom relied on vivid imagery to reflect both light and violent subject matter. For Smith, violence and dark humor are subjects of significant interest, as is evident in the title poem. In "Life on Mars" Smith utilizes images of confinement to create a feeling of imprisonment that, while invoking darkness, nevertheless contrasts the vastness of space.

In the book's third section, Smith addresses issues in popular culture and current events, drawing attention to the helplessness she feels toward violence in the world. These poems present scenes in which prisoners are strung up like beef and ridden like mules, children live indoors like sullen sages, and pirates celebrate for days after white men leave on their white ships. In "Solstice," Smith laments the state of the world, writing, "They're gassing geese outside of JFK / Tehran will likely fill up soon with blood. / The *Times* is getting smaller by the day." She uses the poetic form of a villanelle to make this point; here, the form's unusual structure and rigid rhyme and meter create a melancholy mood that conveys the author's feelings of loss and vulnerability. This structure, juxtaposed against the title of the poem, seems to imply that change can occur only as the result of internal and the external reflection, a repeated message throughout the collection.

The lines in "Solstice" and in other poems in this section of the book reveal humankind's limitations and the "dark matter" that resides within the self. This simultaneously defined and undefined darkness also suggests that the realities of life are as equally unfathomable as the mysteries of the cosmos. Although this section of the collection was criticized by at least one reviewer as "haphazard," it could be said that these poems offer Smith's unique vision of a paternalistic and racially motivated reality. The perpetrators of violence in these poems, while perhaps evil, are still human and thus part of the earth as a whole.

In the fourth and final section of the collection, the setting and tone are more focused and the questions posed are more domestic and concrete. The imagery is rooted in the realistic and the mundane: writer's block, walking the dog, noisy children. The science-fiction foil that worked so well in the earlier sections is gone, and in comparison, these later poems run the risk of feeling incidental or even extraneous to the work as a whole. While some critics have argued that these poems are weaker than the previous ones, Smith has defended her work, noting that, to her, poetry is primarily a private endeavor and the public aspects of it are secondary to her. During the writing of this collection, she experienced both her father's death and the birth of her child. In this context, these latter poems reflect a natural progression or cycle: death to life, cosmos to reality, and where we came from to where we go.

Life on Mars takes the reader on an extraordinary journey to the edge of the universe and back. At times, the ride is evocative and astonishing. Smith's skill as a poet is very much in evidence through her use of imagery and structure. More importantly, this ambitious collection resonates in a way that makes it challenging but still accessible to the reader. While the subject matter stretches through space and even to alternate realities, it never fails to be grounded in real emotion. It is no wonder that Tracy K. Smith is considered unique in her generation of poets.

Cheryl Lawton Malone

Review Sources

The New Yorker 87, no. 23 (August 8, 2011): 71-73.
The New York Times Book Review, August 26, 2011 (Web).
NPR, September 6, 2011 (Web).
Publishers Weekly 258, no. 12 (March 21, 2011): 54.

Malcolm X
A Life of Reinvention

Author: Manning Marable (1950–2011)
Publisher: Viking (New York). 608 pp. $30.00; paperback $18.00
Type of work: Biography
Time: 1925–1965
Locale: Major US cities, including Detroit, Boston, New York City, and Chicago

This detailed and scholarly biography of Malcolm X focuses on the evolution in his thinking about race and revolution, including much controversial information about his private life.

Principal personages:

MALCOLM X, born MALCOLM LITTLE (1925–1965), a dynamic and militant African American leader

ELIJAH MUHAMMAD (1897–1975), founder and head of the Nation of Islam (NOI)

BETTY SHABAZZ (1934–1997), Malcolm's wife

LOUIS FARRAKHAN (b. 1933), NOI leader after the death of Elijah Muhammad

WARITH DEEN MUHAMMAD (1933–2008), born WALLACE DELANEY MUHAMMAD, Elijah Muhammad's son who converted to orthodox Islam

MARTIN LUTHER KING JR. (1929–1968), Protestant minister and civil rights leader who emphasized nonviolent strategies

ALEX HALEY (1921–1992), coauthor of *The Autobiography of Malcolm X*

TALMADGE HAYER (b. 1942), Malcolm's murderer who was paroled in 2010

ELLA LITTLE COLLINS (1914–1996), Malcolm's half sister

As many critics have noted, the subtitle of Manning Marable's biography, "A Life of Reinvention," accurately expresses its major theme: the continuing transformations in the political and personal identities of the Black Power icon. At the age of twenty-three, while in prison for burglary, Malcolm X converted to the Nation of Islam (NOI), an African American religious organization that preached racial separatism from white society. Following his parole, he quickly emerged as the group's most effective spokesperson and recruiter, known for his support of violence. After breaking with the organization in late 1963, however, he converted to orthodox Islam. In contrast to his earlier positions, Malcolm X began to speak favorably about the goals of the civil rights movement, even giving qualified endorsement for nonviolent strategies.

Although no historical work can ever be definitive, it is unlikely that Marable's biography will ever be surpassed in its scholarship. Utilizing the rich collection of oral histories and other materials at Columbia University, Marable researched Malcolm's life and career for at least twenty years. In addition to archival materials, he interviewed Malcolm's associates and accessed FBI records as well as other government documents through the Freedom of Information Act. The book's extensive notes section also reveals that he gained much material from previous biographical studies, most notably those by Bruce Perry, Kofi Natambu, Rodnell Collins, and Louis Anthony DeCaro Jr.

As in any historical account, the emphasis and interpretations of the book tends to reflect the author's point of view. Praising "the revolutionary visionary's faith," Manning is in complete agreement with Malcolm's goals of expanding the economic conditions, racial pride, and cultural development of African Americans. In an earlier book, *How Capitalism Underdeveloped Black America* (2000), Marable endorsed Malcolm's radical criticisms of American capitalism, which both men believed to be based on exploitation and controlled by a relatively small number of white elites, a commonality that appears in this text as well.

Marable, however, is highly critical of Malcolm's longstanding support for the NOI version of black nationalism and appears to have little, if any, appreciation for the group's religious teachings. While emphasizing Malcolm's secular messages, Marable acknowledges that as late as December 1963 he claimed to believe all of Elijah Muhammad's doctrines, including the divinity of Wallace Fard and the special creation of whites by the evil Dr. Yacub. However, Marable suggests that this statement may have been motivated by Malcolm's desire for his family to continue to occupy a NOI-owned house.

One of many interesting aspects of the book is its deconstruction of Malcolm's famous *The Autobiography of Malcolm X*, which was based on his numerous discussions with author Alex Haley and was released shortly after Malcolm's death. Marable argues that the structure and major themes of the book tend to reflect Haley's perspective. With the goal of increased sales, the book tended to exaggerate and emphasize drama and conflict. For instance, the book suggests that the murder of Malcolm's father by white supremacists was an established fact, even though the cause of his death remains highly questionable. Likewise, there is no way of knowing whether Malcolm's light complexion resulted from a white man raping his maternal grandmother. Because of the great appeal of a story about a personal conversion from evil ways, Haley described "Detroit Red," as Malcolm was known in his youth, as more of a hardened criminal than had actually been the case. Indeed, had Malcolm lived to review the final edition, it is entirely possible that he might have made a number of changes.

While admiring Malcolm as a larger-than-life figure, Marable does not attempt to minimize his personal flaws, including sexism, anti-Semitism, extreme hatred, and authoritarianism. Marable is particularly offended by his willingness to cooperate with the Ku Klux Klan and the American Nazi Party because of their common support for racial segregation. Some readers will be more distressed to learn about Malcolm's frequent advocacy and defense of violence. In 1962, for instance, following the killing of NOI officer Ronald Stokes by Los Angeles police, he was surprised and angered

Manning Marable, who died mere days before the book's publication, was a professor at Columbia University and founding director of its Institute for Research in African American Studies and Center for Contemporary Black History. Recipient of numerous awards for his scholarship, he authored fifteen acclaimed books and published over four hundred articles.

when the NOI leadership refused to authorize an assassination to kill those responsible. Shortly thereafter, he publically attributed a plane crash killing over one hundred white Atlanta residents to answered prayer: "We call on our God—He gets rid of 120 of them." Marable observes that the speech was "a public relations disaster," even to the point of encouraging the FBI to increase its anti-NOI activities.

Marable's discussion of Malcolm's sexual behavior has aroused a considerable amount of controversy, particularly the suggestion that during his youth, Malcolm probably received money from a wealthy, older white man, William Paul Lennon, in exchange for homosexual acts. Observing that Bruce Perry arrived at the same conclusion in his 1991 biography, Marable offers additional evidence from Malcolm's half sister Ella and letters to Lennon. He also provides much information about Malcolm's marital problems with Betty Shabazz. When she complained in 1959 about his inability to satisfy her sexually, he reacted by spending more and more time away from home. Marable asserts, moreover, that much circumstantial evidence suggests that both partners were involved in extramarital liaisons during the 1960s. All of these allegations about Malcolm's personal life are somewhat speculative, based almost entirely on inference and hearsay evidence. Family members and admirers make a valid point when they argue that the biography lends legitimacy to such unproven rumors, thereby distracting from Malcolm's public career and legacy.

By 1962, Malcolm had become increasingly frustrated by Elijah Muhammad's separatism because he believed it was important to fight for the civil rights and political power of African Americans. This ideological disagreement, according to Marable, was the fundamental reason for Malcolm's break with the NOI. Elijah Muhammad "silenced" him because he had publically celebrated President John Kennedy's death, declaring "the chickens coming home to roost . . . always made me glad," and this further alienated him from the organization. Earlier, he had made the mistake of telling Louis Farrakhan and other NOI leaders about Elijah Muhammad impregnating several teenage secretaries, but it was only after the silencing that he began to emphasize this scandal, eventually claiming in public forums that the "real reason" for the silencing was to stop him from talking about the matter. It was impossible for a NOI member to make such accusations against Elijah Muhammad and to remain a member in good standing, and Malcolm well knew that many NOI members believed that death was the appropriate penalty for anyone harming the organization.

When reconciliation with the NOI became impossible, Malcolm began to take a new interest in the orthodox Sunni sect of Islam. Influenced by Warith Deen Muhammad and traditional Muslim scholars, he began to reject nonorthodox doctrines such as Fard's divinity and Yacub's creation of the white race. Following his pilgrimage to

Mecca, Malcolm told associates that he had been surprised to observe that, contrary to NOI teachings, many pious Muslims had blue eyes and blond hair, and he further claimed that this was the first time he had ever observed people of all races interacting on the basis of equality. In addition to making conciliatory statements about the courage of civil-rights workers, he ceased to use the term "black nationalism," and he no longer demanded a separate country for African Americans. These modifications in his speeches during the last year of his life have caused many middle-class liberals to believe that he was moving toward Martin Luther King Jr.'s positions on integration and the repudiation of violence.

According to Marable, however, there continued to be fundamental differences between the ideas of Malcolm and those of the liberal civil rights movement. Malcolm was always a revolutionary who did not think that incremental changes could produce great social transformations. He still perceived himself as primarily a black man who happened to be a citizen of an oppressive country founded upon white supremacy. Having very little confidence in the US judicial system, he insisted on the necessity for a fundamental restricting of power and wealth. While coming to believe that racial hierarchies might be dismantled, he assumed that such a restricting would require cooperation among persons of color throughout the world. Subtly praising communist leaders Mao Zedong and Che Guevara, whom he greatly admired, Malcolm's 1964 speech, "The Ballot or the Bullet" espoused violence if peaceful means were unsuccessful. His views, however, were still in flux, and it is impossible to know how they might have evolved had he not died at the young age of thirty-nine.

Marable's biography contains a detailed narrative and analysis of Malcolm's assassination in Manhattan's Audubon Ballroom on February 21, 1965. The guilt of NOI member Talmadge Hayer, who was seized and beaten at the crime scene, was unquestionably proven. Although Marable does not doubt that additional NOI members were accomplices, he concludes that the two men convicted with Hayer were probably innocent. In addition to finding some evidence of involvement by police informants, he persuasively argues that the police were incompetent in their attempts to provide security at the Audubon, and he criticizes their failure to investigate whether members of the Newark mosque were involved. Although no clear evidence proves that Elijah Muhammad ordered Malcolm's death, Marable writes that evidence might eventually appear in FBI records. He argues that while Louis Farrakhan was most likely not directly involved, his extremist rhetoric helped to create a climate that justified the murder.

Marable's biography constitutes a valuable contribution to the growing literature devoted to African American history, the civil rights movement, and American society from the 1930s until the 1960s. Anyone intrigued by the life, ideas, and career of the militant black leader should not neglect this fascinating book.

Thomas Tandy Lewis

Review Sources

The American Spectator 44, no. 6 (July/August 2011): 79–81.
Atlantic Monthly 307, no. 4 (May 2011): 100–107.
Chronicle of Higher Education 57, no. 35 (May 6, 2011): B6–9.
The Economist 398, no. 8728 (April 9, 2011): 94.
Nation, October 10, 2011 (Web).
New African 509 (August/September 2011): 88–91.
New Statesman 140, no. 5052 (May 9, 2011): 51–55.
The New Yorker 87, no. 10 (April 25, 2011): 74–78.
The New York Review of Books 58, no. 14 (September 29, 2011): 72–75.
Wilson Quarterly 35 (Spring 2011): 90–93.

The Marriage Plot

Author: Jeffrey Eugenides (b. 1960)
Publisher: Farrar, Straus and Giroux (New York). 406 pp. $28.00
Type of work: Novel
Time: Early 1980s
Locale: Providence, Rhode Island; Prettybrook, New Jersey; New York City; Cape Cod, Massachusetts; Paris; Athens; Calcutta; Monaco

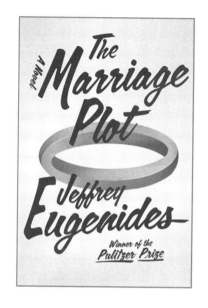

Set on an Ivy League campus during the heyday of deconstruction, Eugenides's third novel takes on the archetypal story line of middle-class fiction.

Principal characters:
MADELEINE HANNA (MADDY; MAD), a rich, beautiful English major at Brown
LEONARD BANKHEAD, a tobacco-chewing double major in biology and philosophy who has bipolar disorder
MITCHELL GRAMMATICUS, a brilliant religious studies major whose failure to secure Madeleine's love sends him on a physical and existential journey across Europe and India
ALTON AND PHYLLIDA HANNA, Madeleine's parents

In Jeffrey Eugenides's first novel, *The Virgin Suicides* (1993), he used an intimate point of view to tell the story of five teenage sisters who commit suicide. His second novel, *Middlesex* (2002), a major hit and a Pulitzer Prize winner, took a step back in viewpoint and time, using both first- and third-person narration to tell the historically sweeping, multigenerational story of a misunderstood hermaphrodite. In his latest novel, *The Marriage Plot*, Eugenides returns to the close-up perspective of his first work and employs a setting he knows well from his own college days during the early 1980s. Like his characters, Eugenides was an undergraduate student at Brown University when the study of semiotics, which he explains as a literary theory that "examines how the text gives meaning" instead of trying to find out what the text means, was coming into fashion on campus. In fact, Eugenides admits that his own study of semiotics helped him develop his protagonist, Madeleine Hanna, a privileged, preppy, tennis-playing English major.

Madeleine is not a virgin, but her orderly love life is governed by a set of self-imposed rules: no nervous men, no men who hate their parents, and no men who will not ask her out first. She is a capable student, but the hip new literary theories evade her, as seen in her first encounter with Jacques Derrida's seminal work of deconstructionist criticism in her own kitchen:

Then, one Sunday morning, before winter break, Abby's boyfriend, Whitney, materialized at their kitchen table, reading something called *Of Grammatology*. When Madeleine asked what the book was about, she was given to understand by Whitney that the idea of a book being "about" something was exactly what this book was against, and that, if it was "about" anything, then it was about the need to stop thinking of books as being about things.

Secretly, Madeleine prefers her comfortable library of Jane Austen, Henry James, T. S. Eliot, Charles Dickens, and the Brontë sisters. She does not connect with the semiotic studies crowd until she reads *A Lover's Discourse* by French philosopher Roland Barthes, which postulates that love is in fact about solitude. Just as she is grappling with a literary theory that "deconstructs the very notion of love," she falls in love herself.

According to Eugenides, *The Marriage Plot* is not just a romance; it is also a twenty-first-century look at the literary device known as the marriage plot. Not coincidentally, Madeleine is writing her English honors thesis is on the device, and she is also at the vertex of her own marriage plot: the love triangle that she is stuck in with two of her fellow students, Leonard Bankhead and Mitchell Grammaticus, both of whom she meets in her semiotics class. The adoring Mitchell loves her, while she loves the fatally flawed Leonard, who is so damaged that he cannot sustain a relationship. Though Leonard breaks all of her self-imposed rules and despite his poverty and manic depression, she falls for him deeply. When Madeleine finally moves in with Leonard, Mitchell sets off on a journey of self-realization, traveling first to Europe and then to India, where he does a stint as a volunteer for Mother Theresa. Despite his brilliance, Mitchell spends all but the last few pages of the novel expressing his unrequited love. The thread of Madeleine and Leonard's romance eventually intersects with Mitchell's meandering trip when the three characters meet in New York City. While the setup may seem familiar, the characters, their motivations, and the setting are distinctly and intentionally modern.

Eugenides once said that he likes "to have at my disposal complicated hybrid emotions," and *The Marriage Plot* is a good example of this. Madeleine's life is filled with angst and tension. In the opening scene, her cheerfully uptight suburban parents arrive at her apartment on the morning of her college graduation, waking Madeleine from an alcoholic and sexual stupor. She handles the situation by inviting Mitchell, whom she runs into by chance, to join them at breakfast. Mitchell accepts eagerly. He already knows and likes her parents, previously having spent Thanksgiving at their home on Madeleine's invitation. Madeleine, on the other hand, cannot wait to get away from all three.

Some critics have argued that *The Marriage Plot* is not about matrimony or love at all, except perhaps secondarily, and at least one commentator points out that Eugenides does not succeed in his attempt to impose this meaning. Eugenides acknowledges that his characters do not carry out the conventions of the traditional marriage plot. Under a traditional scenario, Madeleine would fall in love with Leonard (the wrong man) initially, spurning Mitchell (the right man) because of some deceit or error. Once the mystery was unraveled or the error rectified, Madeleine would fall in love with the right man and marry. In Shakespeare's hands, the wrong man often found the right woman and married, too. Eugenides, however, toys with these classic plotlines. Madeleine is drawn to Leonard, not because of some mistake or misunderstanding, but precisely because of his flaws. Although she is not aware of his illness at the start of their relationship, her love only grows when she finds him commit-

Jeffrey Eugenides is a professor of creative writing at Princeton University. He has won many awards for his work, including the Pulitzer Prize in 2003 for his second novel, Middlesex *(2002). His first novel,* The Virgin Suicides *(1993), was adapted by director Sofia Coppola into a successful feature film and has been translated into thirty-four languages.*

ted to the psych ward in a Providence hospital. She willingly misses her college graduation to be with him and moves into his apartment even before he is released. Not even a horrific summer in Provincetown dealing with his symptoms and medications deter her from marrying him.

Leonard and Mitchell play more classic roles. Leonard's world spins between his manic and depressive poles, his brilliant academic and sexual achievements and his emotional and physical breakdown. His illness leads to numerous hospitalizations that only encourage his reluctance to take his medication, making the reader wonder why the practical Madeleine would ever agree to marry him. As the villain, he selfishly holds on to Madeleine's love at every decision point in the relationship, except the very end. Meanwhile, smart, sane, and parent-pleasing Mitchell struggles to reconcile his religious scholarship with Madeleine's love for Leonard and the real world of postgraduate adulthood. Notwithstanding his intelligence and mysticism, Mitchell manages to bore Madeleine with his eligibility. He plays a traditional Victorian lover by pursuing Madeleine doggedly, thereby creating the expectation that he will ultimately secure her love. Both of these story lines set up the reader for the double twist at the end.

In casting the plot, themes, and characters as he has, Eugenides claims to question whether marriage, and its nineteenth-century equivalent, happiness, is still an appropriate goal for all characters. His novel represents a present-day fictional experiment. In defense of the query, Eugenides references the gay marriage debate. The institution of marriage, he argues, is still relevant in our culture and is therefore an appropriate topic for modern fiction.

With few mythic overtones and metaphors, *The Marriage Plot* is firmly anchored in realism, achieved in part through authentic 1980s references: dresses with shoulder pads, Trinitron portable televisions, Saab convertibles, Annie Lennox albums, letters written on typewriters and sent by mail to American Express offices overseas. These references are woven throughout the novel, but occasional passages, such as the following, are rife with them: "A Course listing like 'English 274: Lyly's Euphues' excited Madeleine the way a pair of Fiorucci cowboy boots did Abby. 'English 450A: Hawthorne and James' filled Madeleine with an expectation of sinful hours in bed not unlike what Olivia got from wearing a Lycra skirt and leather blazer to Danceteria."

Eugenides's tone is funny but serious. Readers may chuckle at his spot-on observations of the students' pretensions and self-important naïveté:

> Mitchell . . . wrote, "Maddy, give me a call. Mitchell." Then he erased this and wrote, "Permit a colloquy. M."

> Back in his own room, Mitchell examined himself in the mirror. He turned sideways, trying to see his profile. He pretended to be talking to someone at a party to see what he was really like.

Eugenides's student characters are not the only ones who are pretentious and twee. Alton and Phyllida Hanna, Madeleine's clueless, privileged parents, provide humor that might make some readers wince in recognition:

> "Speaking of religious dignitaries," Alton cut in, "did I ever tell you about the time we met the Dalai Lama? It was at this fund-raiser at the Waldorf. We were in the receiving line. Must have been three hundred people at least. Anyway, when we finally got up to the Dalai Lama, I asked him, 'Are you any relation to Dolly Parton?'"

> "I was mortified!" Phyllida cried. "Absolutely mortified."

More than a few critics have noted Eugenides's belabored treatment of his subordinate themes of deconstructionism, campus politics, and spirituality. One such critic asserts that the narrative in these sections is claustrophobic. Another finds that the characters are flat and diffuse, unlike the teenage sisters in the author's earlier work *The Virgin Suicides*. Most commentators agree, however, that the story shines when the narrative focuses on the Madeleine-Leonard-Mitchell romantic triangle.

Regardless of whether the reader feels that Eugenides has succeeded in his contemporary examination of the marriage plot, the novel also succeeds as a coming-of-age story, with its engaging narrative about the characters' struggles as they journey into young adulthood.

Cheryl Lawton Malone

Review Sources

The Guardian, October 12, 2011 (Web).
Los Angeles Times, October 9, 2011 (Web).
The New York Times, October 7, 2011 (Web).
The *New York Times Book Review*, October 16, 2011 (Web).
NPR, October 11, 2010 (Web).
Star Tribune, October 29, 2011 (Web).

Metropole

Author: Geoffrey G. O'Brien (b. 1969)
Publisher: University of California Press
(Berkeley). 112 pp. $21.95
Type of work: Poetry

*O'Brien's startling and intriguing poetry
collection examines what a globalized world has
done to humanity's ability to value loved ones,
the self, possessions, and language.*

Geoffrey G. O'Brien is the author of two previous poetry collections, *The Guns and Flags
Project* (2002), and *Green and Gray* (2007),
both of which were included in the New California Poetry series. Many of the poets that
have been included in the series—such as
Fanny Howe, Harryette Mullen, Mark Levine,
Ron Silliman, Cole Swensen, Keith Waldrop,
and Laura Mullen—have produced the most inventive poetry in twenty-first century
America. With his first collection, O'Brien was compared to such influential poets
as John Ashbery, T. S. Eliot, W. S. Auden, and Wallace Stevens. Certainly, one can
trace his approach back to modernism, the literary movement ushered in during the
early decades of the twentieth century. While O'Brien understands the comparison,
he does not appreciate being identified with one particular school of poetry. Skeptical
of the clutter and noise that seems to attend struggling poets who push themselves
into the public arena, he has remained reluctant to increase his presence in the public
eye. O'Brien is suspicious of anything that might taint the full impact of the poetry
itself, whether it be his own personality, politics, or anything else. For there to be an
intelligent discussion between a poet and his public, there must be a certain alignment
of factors. Yet O'Brien is all too aware of his sometimes irrational fear of any public
forum for the promotion of his poetry. With time, however, this fear may recede, and
the public may get the chance to interact with this important poetic voice.

The Guns and Flags Project* was praised by critics who appreciated the influence
of the language poets on the work. For his second collection, *Green and Gray*, the
poet examined the layering that exists within memory and experience. In his poetry,
O'Brien seems to be constantly probing, taking apart language, the self, and everyday
items in order to look more closely at what makes these things function. For *Metropole*,
O'Brien has gathered together twenty-one poems. All but the title poem and "Three
Years" are of a short to modest length. While "Three Years" consists of fifteen pages,
the title poem is forty pages and concludes the collection. The poet values the poetic
rules and, therefore, breaks them with ease as needed. The seemingly relaxed nature of
his approach helps to balance each poem. For O'Brien, meaning must be served first

and foremost, not merely the poetic form he has employed. The title poem reads like an iambic prose piece that swirls in and out of an urban setting, a life controlled by technology, and a wider, contemporary consciousness. O'Brien has mentioned that the poem "records the falling of verse into prose." O'Brien understands how massive the poem is, and that even the most diligent reader may not consume the poem in a single sitting. The poet believes that readers should visit this poem, and poetry in general, on several occasions. He even realizes that, just as a poet may decide that he or she cannot continue in the composition of a poem, a reader also may abandon a poem.

The shorter poems of *Metropole* almost serve as preambles to the longer, more meditative title poem, which inhabits all points on the map at one time. It is a curious dichotomy, how O'Brien combines elements of avant-garde with a more structured poetic hardware. He is willing to thrive within the framework that many of his contemporaries have long discarded as unnecessary and constricting. Within the book's shorter poems, there is a strong sense of the pastoral. It is the speakers and figures inhabiting these poems that seem to be no longer at ease with their possessions, their success, and their version of America. O'Brien has been averse to formal closure and sceptical of the need for poems to have a manufactured ending. Most readers are accustomed to a poem's arrival at a conclusion wherein all questions or ideas introduced in the poem are either answered or resolved. O'Brien has suggested an alternative: a "poem's close as a last instance of what it does everywhere else rather than emphasizing [the] finish as a special region of the poem." He admits that the poems of his first collection tended to close in a "very loud" manner, but in each subsequent collection, O'Brien has attempted to construct poems that are quieter at their "formal demise." Since he has taken to renouncing the end of a poem "as a place in which to dramatize" a poem's conclusion, his work now provides the reader with a more purposeful encounter. The reader cannot merely go straight to the ending in order to find out how everything turns out. For O'Brien, reading poetry is supposed to be different from reading a romance novel. His poetry is full of ideas, observations, mischief, mayhem, but not necessarily closure; traditional patterns are to be broken, or, at the very least, challenged. Since he does not want to be strictly associated with any one school of poetry, he relishes the opportunity to take elements from a variety of traditions.

Writing for the *Boston Review*, a reviewer observes that O'Brien's sentences "rush off toward somewhere they forget about along the way." The fullness of what O'Brien is saying may be a fantastic mirage, something seen that cannot be reached. In "Poem Beginning to End," O'Brien begins by announcing that "the trees are men, men strange, / Strangers come into a house to speak / Across a table made of trees." This makes for an intriguing beginning, but where is the poet going with this image? There is a house and the objects that can fill a house. For the poet, the daily life of a house looks to be vague at best. The "reasons escape," and yet activity still takes place. There is a cup that may be used as a tool for talking or gesturing. Everything seemingly has been made into a tool for something else. The reader may ask what form of labor created such things as the table and the cup. Even the night, which is "deaf as a mural," has been "assembled from memories of those / Who couldn't get out of the

Geoffrey G. O'Brien is the author of the poetry collections The Guns and Flags Project *(2002) and* Green and Gray *(2007). His poetry has also appeared in many well-regarded poetry journals. He teaches at the University of California, Berkeley, and at San Quentin State Prison in California.*

way." In the end, "Morning is the answer" to all that has happened. Other poems in the collection with similar titles are "Poem with No Good Lines" and "To Be Read in Either Direction." O'Brien is not above mocking his own approach to poetry. It is the opening poem, "Vague Cadence," that sets the tone for what is to come. In this startling poem, O'Brien describes "a hapless river filled with sand / For years it flows like unmarked rope / Years of saying as it moves away." The key words of the poem seem to be "hapless," "flow," "child," and "useless." There is a certain tug-of-war between opposite ideas, meaning that when "the lights are on so the dark is out / Like the useless children others are." This leads the poet to confirm "a certain building dream within / A part of speech without a name."

In response to the title, *Metropole*, the reader will most likely conjure up images of a primary city, or the proverbial mother city. Here, O'Brien has focused on America as an imperial power; however, O'Brien's vision of America is not confident or secure, and there is no utopia on a sunny hillside. O'Brien's version of a globalized empire is wrought with alienation and fearfulness. Individuals become prisoners within their own empire. As the poet splinters thoughts, so too are the citizens of this empire detached from one another and all they have built. In "Forms of Battle," the poet speaks of an "open fate / All ills flower from." He goes on to divulge various forms of conflict, various ways to be defeated. It is necessary to comprehend how "you can shoot the future through," and that it "reminds me of a fallen sound." Once again, O'Brien introduces the image of falling. There seemingly is nothing that will not fall: people, possessions, empire, and even poetry will fall into despair, fall from grace, and fall from view. As the poem tumbles toward an end, even lights are "ashamed to be on." What is left are the "bitter verbs / Of manner of motion away from a source." It is as though, in defeat or disgust, the speaker of the poem puts his head "under her arm / As though to leave America." The massive title poem opens: "Inaudibly, technologies lament their falling into parts have scattered / anywhere a world extends. I'm thinking of the loneliness of wheels, word / processors conserving single lines in short-term memory." There is an urban swirl of activity to the poem that is at once riveting and rambling. The reader is expected to do much of the heavy lifting. As the poem moves forward, it becomes obvious that O'Brien is employing an irregular syntax with iambic meter, so that the poem may fall forward in a similar way.

O'Brien has produced a work of art to be relished over the course of repeated encounters. The reader may emerge exhausted from the experience, but one can only hope that *Metropole* will not be permanently abandoned. O'Brien has gone the distance and initiated a challenging vision for those willing to engage the arguments his poems present. He reveals a version of the sometimes-inspired but primarily mundane lives of modern humankind. As O'Brien himself writes, "fatigue and anger, vitamins, of being born at some remove from Sunday, / leaving any world untouched, I guess I sing." The question becomes, what is the appropriate response to the current configuration of life? This is O'Brien's blistering and babbling answer to all that is around him. As soon as one subject or issue takes center stage, another emerges, moving the speakers of these poems one step forward and two steps somewhere else. O'Brien has jumbled the jigsaw of the eternal moment and discovered this scant revelation: "the sun revolves around the earth revolves around the sun."

Jeffry Jensen

Review Sources

Boston Review, September/October 2011 (Web).
Publishers Weekly 258, no. 12 (March 21, 2011): 56.

Micro

Authors: Michael Crichton (1942–2008) and Richard Preston (b. 1956)
Publisher: HarperCollins (New York). 429 pp. $28.99
Type of work: Novel
Time: The present
Locale: Cambridge, Massachusetts; Oahu, Hawaii

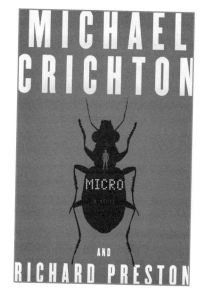

A posthumous techno-thriller begun by Michael Crichton and completed by Richard Preston, Micro pits a group of young graduate students in various fields of sciences against a sinister villain, killer micro-robots, and the implacable forces of nature.

Principal characters:

PETER JANSEN, a Harvard University graduate student interested in venoms produced by snakes, frogs, and spiders

VINCENT "VIN" DRAKE, a venture capitalist and head of Nanigen MicroTechnologies, a Hawaii-based company that develops pharmaceuticals and manufactures miniaturized robots

ERIC JANSEN, Peter's brother, vice president of technology at Nanigen

RICK HUTTER, a Harvard graduate student specializing in rainforest analgesics, particularly those used in native medicines

KAREN KING, a Harvard graduate student specializing in spider venom and spiderwebs

ERIKA MOLL, a German graduate student in entomology at Harvard who specializes in beetles

AMAR SINGH, an East Indian graduate student in botany at Harvard specializing in plant hormones

JENNY LINN, an Asian graduate student in biochemistry at Harvard examining plant and animal pheromones

DANNY MINOT, a graduate student at Harvard specializing in science studies, a blend of psychology, sociology, and comparative literature

BEN ROURKE, inventor of the Nanigen shrinking device, who has survived in a miniaturized state in the wild

ALYSON BENDER, the chief financial officer of Nanigen and the sometimes-girlfriend of both Eric Jansen and Vincent Drake

DON MAKELE, an ex-Marine and head of security at Nanigen

TELIUS AND JOHNSTONE, a pair of ex-military mercenaries who are miniaturized in order to hunt the micro-sized students

(WireImage and Robert Lewis)

Michael Crichton was a best-selling author, with over 200 million copies of his books sold worldwide, as well as a screenwriter, film director, and television producer. He won the 1969 Mystery Writers of America Edgar Award for Best Novel for A Case of Need *(1968),* and won a second Edgar in 1980 for The Great Train Robbery *(1975).* His best-known novels include The Andromeda Strain *(1969) and* Jurassic Park *(1990)*

During a productive career that flourished between the late 1960s and the first decade of the twenty-first century, Michael Crichton became one of the world's best-known writers of speculative fiction centered on concepts from hard science. He was particularly skilled at writing techno-thrillers—action-adventure stories that often demonstrate the potential consequences and downsides of advanced technology. Few other authors could compare with Crichton in his heyday at playing the game of "what if?" with science and nature. What if, as in *The Andromeda Strain* (1969), a malevolent and constantly mutating extraterrestrial microorganism was accidentally brought to Earth from outer space? What if, as in *Terminal Man* (1972), sophisticated electronics and a miniaturized computer were implanted in a human being's body to control aberrant brain impulses? What if, as in the screenplay for the movie *Westworld* (1972), humans interacted with lifelike androids at a futuristic amusement park and the androids began to go haywire? What if, as in *Jurassic Park* (1990), extinct dinosaurs could be recreated from DNA extracted from blood contained in prehistoric mosquitoes preserved in amber? What if, as in *Prey* (2002), instruments from nanotechnology combined to create a form of artificial intelligence detrimental to humans? What if, as in *Next* (2006), humans could be successfully crossbred with other primates?

Even after his death from cancer in 2008, Crichton's fiction continues to explore the boundaries and question the ethics of science. *Micro* is the second Crichton novel to be released since 2008, after the historic action novel *Pirate Latitudes* (2009). This suspenseful and entertaining novel revisits themes from several of his previous works and borrows liberally from other fictional traditions. Crichton had written one-third of *Micro* at the time of his death, and coauthor Richard Preston completed the novel based on his notes, outlines, and extensive research.

The plot of *Micro* is relatively straightforward. In part 1, the novel begins with an intriguing scenario that foreshadows the denouement: three men die under mysterious circumstances from multiple hairline cuts to the body and throat. The pace afterward slows precipitously, however, due to numerous perfunctory character introductions and lengthy information dumps. At the center of the story is Nanigen, a billion-dollar high-tech company in Hawaii, representatives of which are touring

American colleges and universities to recruit rainforest researchers who will help the company develop profitable new drugs from nature-based sources. At Harvard University in Cambridge, Massachusetts, Nanigen representatives Vin Drake, Alyson Bender, and Eric Jansen meet a group of seven outstanding graduate students, including Eric's younger brother Peter, with specialties relevant to Nanigen's interests. The students are quickly convinced to travel to Hawaii to visit the company's facilities there. The day before they are scheduled to fly west, Peter receives a cryptic message from Eric warning him not to come. Shortly afterward, Peter is informed that his brother has gone missing in a boating accident.

Richard Preston was selected by Crichton's publisher and estate to complete Micro *after the manuscript was discovered in 2008. Preston is a writer for the* New Yorker *and is the best-selling author of several books, including* The Hot Zone *(1994),* The Cobra Event *(1998), and* The Demon in the Freezer *(2002).*

Upon the group's arrival in Hawaii, Peter learns from the police that Eric's disappearance may not have been an accident, and he jumps to the conclusion (rightly, as it happens) that Nanigen might have been involved in Eric's sudden removal. During the students' tour of the company facilities, Peter rashly confronts Vin Drake with his knowledge and suspicions. In an unguarded moment, Drake admits his complicity, and the other students inadvertently overhear his confession. Drake is thus forced to take drastic action: he holds the group hostage and uses Nanigen technology to shrink the students to a height of one half-inch.

Of course, miniaturization in fiction is nothing new. Literary works like *Gulliver's Travels* (1726), movies like *Dr. Cyclops* (1940), *The Incredible Shrinking Man* (1957), and *Fantastic Voyage* (1966), and television series like *Land of the Giants* (1968–70) have all dealt with the concept in its various forms. *Micro*'s particular use of this trope requires a suspension of disbelief from readers, but once that barrier is crossed, the novel charges ahead full bore. Crichton's main contribution to the tradition lies in his imaginative and well-realized presentation of how it would look, smell, sound, and feel to be a miniature human. These vivid descriptions create a rich world for the characters, one in which the familiar becomes alien and the benign becomes deadly.

Part 2 of *Micro* ratchets up the action to a fever pitch as the novel evolves into an old-fashioned action-adventure story. Vin Drake, like any mad scientist worth his salt, plans to kill the shrunken students, enlisting the aid of security head Don Makele by promising him millions of dollars in company stock. However, with the help of a conscience-stricken Alyson Bender, the students escape into Hawaii's Manoa Valley rainforest, where nature does its best to eliminate them. This section of the novel focuses on the miniaturized students' efforts to survive in a hostile natural world where ants, spiders, wasps, birds, bats, and even rainfall constitute lethal threats; they employ their skills from their education and scientific specialties, including making curare-tipped darts and extracting irritant chemicals from a beetle, to avoid injury and death.

There are many close calls, and some characters are wounded or killed. These chapters of *Micro* also rely heavily on another long-standing tradition: the last-person-standing device, wherein a group of imperiled characters is slowly whittled away as the story progresses. As in many novels, films, and television programs, the audience is kept in suspense, wondering who will be next to die and who be alive at the end. Crichton provides an additional incentive that increases the tension: miniaturization causes side effects in the human body that are similar to symptoms of the bends, and if the survivors are not restored to normal size within a few days, they will die horribly. As if that were not enough, Drake also miniaturizes two mercenaries, Telius and Johnstone, and sends them out with specialized equipment and tracking devices to hunt down any students still alive and ensure their permanent silence.

Part 3 of *Micro* continues the exciting battle of the surviving students against nature and their human pursuers. Characters are killed off, unexpected allies emerge, and Honolulu police investigators make an important discovery about the mysterious deaths that opened the novel. A new character also comes to aid the surviving students in their rainforest environment: Ben Rourke, inventor of the miniaturization machinery and enemy of Drake, who has learned how to survive the deleterious effects of his shrinkage. In the tense and action-packed final confrontation, the authors pit the students against the villains, testing their loyalty and cunning in the face of death. The book's conclusion also reveals Nanigen's true and sinister purpose, thus increasing the stakes even further for both the characters and the readers.

Like most techno-thrillers, *Micro* often sacrifices literary aspirations for the sake of a hard-driving and high-concept plot. Characters, barely described physically or psychologically, are reduced to cardboard cutouts, and the emotional relationships between them are fairly pat and predictable. The novel's dialogue is serviceable, pedestrian, and generally unmemorable. Similes, metaphors, and other such literary devices are also virtually nonexistent throughout the story. Critics have noted that the writing is generally flat and formulaic, but have been reluctant to blame the joint authorship for these flaws.

The main strength of *Micro* lies in its action, which is almost nonstop in the novel's second half. Descriptions are also well done, particularly those of everyday objects made gigantic from the perspective of the wondering, wandering mini-characters. This particular facet of the story continues Crichton's—who stood six feet nine inches tall—fascination with relative size, along the continuum from microscopic (as in alien bacterium) to enormous (as in a cloned brontosaurus), and with humankind's place as the norm against which other life is measured. Relative size is also reflected on the cover of *Micro*, where Michael Crichton's name is printed twice as large as Richard Preston's. Though neither as original as Crichton's other science-based works nor as plausible, *Micro* will probably nonetheless eventually be adapted for film, due to its high potential for visual impact.

Jack Ewing

Review Sources

Entertainment Weekly, no. 1182 (November 25, 2011): 75–76.
Nature 479, no. 7374 (November 24, 2011): 476.
The Wall Street Journal, September 9, 2011, p. D5.
The Wall Street Journal, November 18, 2011, p. D4.

Miss New India

Author: Bharati Mukherjee (b. 1940)
Publisher: Houghton Mifflin Harcourt (Boston). 336 pp. $25.00
Type of work: Novel
Time: The present
Locale: Gauripur in the northeastern province of Bihar and Bangalore in southern India

A young Indian woman rejects her impecunious family and its traditions and seeks a new life in the modern city of Bangalore. Her ambiguous mix of success and failure becomes a symbol of an emerging India.

Principal characters:
ANJALI "ANGIE" BOSE, an ambitious young woman from a small city
PETER CHAMPION, an American expatriate and former hippie who teaches English and business in Gauripur
ALI, Peter's young Indian lover
MR. GG, also known as GIRISH GUJRAL or DYNAMO, a columnist for an English-language Bangalore newspaper
MINNIE BAGEHOT, an Anglicized Indian, now a relic of the past
TOOKIE D'MELLO, a "Bagehot girl" boarder at Minnie Bagehot's mansion
HUSSEINA SHIRAZ, a secretive Muslim girl, another "Bagehot girl"
MONISH "MONI" LAHIRI, a Bangalore photographer
RABI CHATTERJEE, Angie's friend and a member of the wealthy Chatterjee family
PARVATI BANERJI, a wealthy Indian woman

Like Bharati Mukherjee's previous novels, *Miss New India* explores contemporary Indians in the midst of change and migration. However, while her earlier novels depict characters largely coping with assimilating into American society, this novel takes place exclusively in India; American influence in India is represented in the form of the city of Bangalore. Bangalore is "New India," a site for new apartment complexes, call centers, and enterprises outsourced from the United States and a place where small-town Indians enter a world at odds with the values of their parents. The ethos of the city is expressive individualism, which privileges freedom, autonomy, and personal fulfillment over family or community responsibilities and which, in the context of the novel, has been yoked to the neoliberal economy that gives its young aspiring provincial migrants opportunities for wealth and status hitherto out of reach.

Mukherjee's story concerns the way Bangalore not only serves American economic interests but also embraces American culture. As a result, it is as if heroine Anjali "Angie" Bose has not so much journeyed from one Indian city to another but has emigrated from India to the United States. In Bangalore, she joins an Americanized youth culture populated by fugitives from the provinces, who see themselves as part of a cultural revolution in which they are not defined by their families or communities but can instead largely reinvent themselves.

Like her contemporaries, Anjali has an adventurous spirit and finds in Bangalore the opportunity to change her life. However, while the novel is told from her perspective, that point of view is inherently complicated. From the outset, the protagonist possesses two identities: the Angie who wears American blue jeans and T-shirts and dreams of a life of greater liberty and the Anjali who dutifully wears generic Indian garb for a photograph preparatory to an arranged marriage. The alternation between blue jeans and traditional Indian clothing is one way that Mukherjee reminds readers that Angie is a divided self; one side of her identity is fixed in the traditional Indian culture, and the other side of herself is part of a new wave of innovation and Americanization. Similarly, Angie's Indian name, Anjali, points to her identity as a dutiful daughter, while her American-style name, "Angie," indicates her rebellious, free-spirited wish to join an evolving India. Throughout the novel, she seems to move in an unstable way between these two names and identities, never quite resolving into one or the other.

As Anjali, she is the obedient daughter of an impoverished Bengali family that time has left behind. Anjali's parents attempt to preserve the traditional ways, but the text indicates such is impossible. Anjali's older sister is divorced, and her work as a secretary appears to shade into prostitution. Additionally, the man her parents have arranged for Anjali to marry proves to be a sociopathic grifter only pretending to be a traditional eligible bachelor. When this would-be suitor assaults her on their first date, it is as if Angie's bridges to the past have been burned—she uses this crisis as an opportunity to run off to Bangalore immediately. While this decision leads to a measure of freedom for Angie, the ensuing mess leads to a tragedy within the family and leaves her with a legacy of guilt.

While Angie's traumatic experience with her would-be bridegroom is the catalyst for her departure, the possibility of escape is first planted by her former teacher Peter Champion, an American expatriate whose previous hippie individuality has led almost seamlessly to his career as a teacher of business models and advertising strategies. Even as Peter has devoted himself to the appreciation of the architecture of a relatively traditional India, he encourages Angie to break out of the old world and find a new life in Bangalore. The reinvented Angie arrives in Bangalore and immediately and boldly accepts a ride in an expensive car with a handsome, well-to-do stranger. This episode marks a turning point in Angie's life and is symbolic of the way Bangalore encourages a fluid, freestyle way of life that promises to fulfill hopes and dreams outside the perimeters of the inhibiting past.

Angie's impulsive decision to accept the ride is also a good example of the way that *Miss New India*, for all its modern energy, deploys a certain sense of the ancient and

(© Chip Cooper)

Bharati Mukherjee, the recipient of the 1988 National Book Critics Circle award for fiction, has written seven novels and two story collections and has co-authored two books of nonfiction. Born in Calcutta, India, she teaches English at the University of California.

the mystical. For example, Angie's story is rife with coincidences that seem to confirm that she is, as one of her friends suggests, a child of destiny. Angie's handsome stranger proves to be Mr. GG, an influential newspaper columnist called "Dynamo," whose column Angie had been coincidentally reading minutes after arriving in Bangalore. Mr. GG delivers Angie to her destination, the decayed mansion of Minnie Bagehot, a product of the British Raj who now makes a living providing room and board to enterprising young women. Minnie makes every effort to continue to live in the days of the British Raj, even as her boarders continually remind her that Indian society has changed. When Peter comes to visit his old friend Minnie, Angie is surprised to hear him also question the rise of the new India that has so beguiled her: He suggests that India has started something it cannot control and that the outcome is precarious, especially since the prosperity of Bangalore is tied to the health of the American economy and to its own status as a cheap market. Peter laments the current ethos of reinvention, but Angie has embraced the ferment of Bangalore.

Despite her enthusiasm for this new India, Angie does begin to worry her new situation is one of subtraction, rather than triumphant rebirth, a fact that is brought home to her when she finds a room in the Bagehot mansion that featured pictures of Indians murdered by the British soldiers. Although the era of the British Raj, represented by Minnie's house, is in India's past, Angie begins to wonder if modern Bangalore is not another form of colonial domination. Further doubts are raised through the stories of two other Bagehot girls, Tookie and Husseina. Tookie's friendships appear to lead to prostitution, and, even more upsetting, Husseina leads a double life as the partner of a terrorist bomber.

Revelations about other Bagehot girls lead Angie to conclude that there is a dark side to the Bangalore dream. She is unsure of both her identity and her destiny; she wonders if she too is not so much an independent career girl but someone who uses her erotic capital in a way uncomfortably similar to that of Tookie. Even worse, the surreal interchangeability of Husseina and Angie leads to disaster. Because Husseina has given Angie all her posh clothes in order to disguise herself in Angie's jeans and T-shirts, Angie is mistaken for Husseina and is arrested and charged with terrorism and treason.

Not only has Angie unwittingly enabled Husseina's involvement in the terrorist bombing, this attack has led to a retaliatory invasion of Minnie's mansion by the locals. Watching helplessly as even Minnie's loyal family retainer begins to ransack the house, Angie, now considered a fugitive from justice, hides in a locked bathroom. This episode can be said to represent the final death of the British Raj, but things may not bode well for the emerging new India if the despairing, entrapped Angie is its avatar.

Peter, who included Minnie's mansion in his appreciative study of British Raj architecture, is the influential mentor who trumpeted an India that was "catching fire," a prediction that eventually becomes disturbingly literal when Bagehot house burns to the ground. Even after Angie is exonerated, she nevertheless feels immensely vulnerable, still estranged from her old self but confused about her new identity. She spirals into a deep depression, from which she is rescued only by the sympathetic concern of Rabi Chatterjee, a photographer friend from a wealthy family who installs her in the house of his aunt, Parvati Banerji, in Dollar Colony, a luxurious Bangalore enclave for Americanized Indians. Gradually coming out of her depression, Angie takes some decisive steps toward protecting herself and taking charge of her own destiny. When the action of novel circles back to Gauripur, it becomes evident that Angie's and others' experiences have been marked as much by mutilation as by self-invention.

Ultimately, this thoughtful and entertaining novel focuses on the question of Angie's identity, which is clearly caught between two competing perspectives. At one point Mr. GG writes a column about Angie in which he suggests that she is a promising synthesis of old and new, representing a shining future for India. Her friend Rabi, on the other hand, feels there is a war going on in Angie's soul, and, by inference, in the soul of India itself. Angie's friend Monish Lahiri worries that their generation's confusion stems from its place in a "Photoshop" world in which reality has been manufactured. When Monish photographs Angie for a magazine cover, the expression on Angie's face is unreadable and she becomes "The Mona Lisa of the Mofussils." Is she happy or sad? Is life good or bad for her? Angie's final destination (and that of India itself) is inconclusive. The value in this vigorous interrogation of modern India, however, is not to be found in a last analysis but in its expert and empathic consideration of the complicated life and times of its paradigmatic title character.

Margaret Boe Birns

Review Sources

Booklist, 107, no. 12 (February 15, 2011): 48.
The New York Times Book Review, July 3, 2011 p. 8.
The Wall Street Journal, May 14, 2011, p. C8.

Modigliani
A Life

Author: Meryle Secrest
Publisher: Alfred A. Knopf (New York). Illustrated. 416 pp. $35.00
Type of work: Biography
Time: Late nineteenth to early twenty-first century
Locale: Paris

An in-depth portrait of Amedeo Modigliani, the twentieth-century master painter and sculptor, this biography aims to discern the truth about the man behind the myth.

Principal personages:

AMEDEO MODIGLIANI (DEDO, MODI; 1884–1920), a Jewish Italian painter and sculptor

EUGÉNIE GARSIN-MODIGLIANI, Modigliani's mother, the founder of a private school, and author of "L'Histoire de notre famille," an account of the Garsin and Modigliani families

FLAMINIO MODIGLIANI, Modigliani's father; co-manager of his family's mining operation

JEANNE HÉBUTERNE (1898–1920), an artist and model, Modigliani's mistress, and the mother of his daughter

JEANNE MODIGLIANI (1918–1984), daughter of Modigliani and Hébuterne, and the author of her father's biography, *Modigliani: Man and Myth* (1958)

ANNA AHKMATOVA (ANNA GORENKO) (1889–1966), a Russian poet, the wife of Nicolay Gumilyov, and Modigliani's lover

PAUL ALEXANDRE (1881–1968), a French physician, Modigliani's friend, confidant, and first patron and collector

MARIE VASSILIEFF (1884–1957), a Russian artist who ran a canteen for artists, including Modigliani, during World War I

PAUL GUILLAUME, an art dealer and Modigliani's first agent

LÉOPOLD ZBOROWSKI (1839–1932), a Polish poet, gambler, and art dealer who is also Modigliani's second agent

BEATRICE HASTINGS, a South African poet; one of Modigliani's lovers

BERTHE WEILL, an art gallery owner who organized Modigliani's first one-man show

CONSTANTIN BRANCUSI (1876–1957), a Romanian sculptor and pioneer of the modernist movement, Modigliani's mentor

In *Modigliani: A Life*, critically acclaimed biographer Meryle Secrest creates a compelling record of her search for the truth about her subject, the painter and sculptor Amedeo Modigliani, whose life appears to have followed an archetypically romantic-tragic arc through poverty, illness, alcoholism, and dissolution in the art world of turn-of-the-century Paris. Although he is "one of the most imitated and copied artists in the world," and his works have sold for tens of millions of dollars in twenty-first century auctions, he did not know much fame or fortune during his lifetime. A story of such mythic proportions had already attracted the interest of biographers and filmmakers by the time Secrest began her biography.

In her first chapter, "The Problem," Secrest writes about how her search for the truth about Amedeo Modigliani began. Secrest had "always known" about Modigliani, especially since he had been a contemporary of Romaine Brooks, the neglected painter about whom Secrest wrote in her first biography, *Between Me and Life: A Biography* (1974). Yet her fascination with him began when she saw his art in person for the first time at the East Wing of the National Gallery of Art in Washington, DC:

> I stopped first beside Modigliani's portrait of Monsieur Deleu, painted in 1916, which I had seen in reproduction but which I could almost say I had never seen, since the work itself was so startlingly different. Instead of what looked, from picture books, to be an uninteresting study of a heavyset, black-haired man with a pursed mouth in flat planes of gray, black, and russet, this was a revelation. . . . Monumentality—otherworldliness—the transcendental—such thoughts rose to the surface and whirled around in my head.

She writes further that an artist who is capable of inspiring such thoughts must be "something of a magician." Soon after her encounter described above, Secrest discovered that she was not alone in her response to his work. Secrest observes that Modigliani's biographers "were divided between those who saw him as a true pioneer of modern art, or as with Gauguin, van Gogh, and Soutine, the prototype of an artist at odds with society. He was a visionary, a poet and philosopher, even a mystic. Or he was a minor character, whose romantic life story had led some to place more importance on his work than it deserved." Secrest sets herself the challenge of finding out the truth behind these depictions, to see whether or not they are grounded in reality. Based on her research, she argues that Modigliani was a true pioneer of modern art who used his profligate behavior to mask a scandalous secret—his tuberculosis—that he was desperate to hide.

Secrest's subsequent chapters cover Modigliani's training, his art, his rise in early exhibitions, bouts with illness in adolescence, and theories about the impact of these events on his existential world view. Secrest also presents his exchange with peers such as the Chilean painter Manuel Ortiz de Zárate as well as his first unpromising attempts at sculpture as remembered in various accounts. She exposes Modigliani's willingness to lie in order to secure funds, as well as his scandalous misuse of those funds, which he spent on alcohol, a substance that "took him like a madness."

Secrest had unparalleled access to diaries of friends and family members, as well as previously published poetry, scholarship, memoirs, biographies, interviews, and correspondences from which she pieced together sequences as if looking for plots. From such sources, she was able to find reminiscences of late nineteenth- and early twentieth-century Paris by famous personages, such as George Sand. Her thorough

Meryle Secrest received a National Humanities Medal in 2006. She has written nine other biographies of artists including Salvador Dalí, Frank Lloyd Wright, and Leonard Bernstein.

research of these sources also allowed her to investigate issues such as why the number of Impressionist and Post-Impressionist artists who were drawn to Paris from around the world doubled during the period between 1870 and 1914. Records such as Rene Gimpel's *Diary of an Art Dealer* seem likely to be the most useful to researchers, especially in documenting the celebratory dizziness of the 1918 armistice period. Secrest skillfully incorporates all of this material and more in her rendering of the contextual background of her subject's life.

The tone of Secrest's anecdotes about Modigliani is particularly engaging. Readers may hear in Modigliani's own words and those of his associates how he scorned his own art and once destroyed almost everything except for a few drawings. At the time he had been half thinking of giving up painting and going back to sculpture. As Henri Gaudier-Brzeska wrote to a friend: "'Painting is too complicated with its oils and its pigments, and is too easily destroyed . . . as I've always said, I'm not a painter but a sculptor.'"

Secrest also offers anecdotes about Modigliani's associations and relationships with other artists. Many of his meetings with his peers took place in cafés such as the canteen run by Russian artist Marie Vassilieff, where painters, writers, and musicians came to huddle for warmth in the winter when their own flats had no source of heat. Once there, they conducted animated discussions of politics that, as often as not, ended up as fights about new art forms. Modigliani had a distinctive habit of undressing while drunk in front of visiting English and American women who came to partake of the scene.

Modigliani seems to have had complicated relationships with women throughout his brief life. On the one hand, Secrest writes that "to say that he was loved by women is an almost laughable understatement." According to several accounts, he was spoiled by his mother, Eugénie Garsin-Modigliani. One of his models, Aicha, is quoted as saying: "'How beautiful he was, my God, how beautiful!'" As an adult, he had many love affairs, some with women who would become well known for their own work, such as the poets Anna Ahkmatova and Beatrice Hastings. Yet in one incident the author investigated, he was reported to have thrown Hastings through a window. This incident was recalled years later in intimate detail by another woman who had once been the lover of Diego Rivera. Secrest's compiled sources also reveal hints that Modigliani may have fathered illegitimate children and that in his "height of recklessness," he ignored Board of Health advice to abstain from sexual relations in order to prevent the spread of his tuberculosis to his partners and their children. It is unclear how many children he might have fathered in this state. Modigliani's relationship with the young painter Jeanne Hébuterne, the mother of his daughter, seems particularly fraught with obsession and interdependence. "Barely two days" after he died in 1920, Hébuterne committed suicide even though she was eight-months pregnant with their second child, leaving their young daughter, Jeanne Modigliani, an orphan.

Despite Modigliani's sometimes abusive behavior towards women, he was promoted by a woman, gallery owner Berthe Weill. In her gallery at 50 Rue Taitbour, Weill displayed the works of artists such as Honoré Daumier and Pablo Picasso by hanging them "like laundry on a clothesline," unframed and unmounted. Weill played a similar role for other artists, selling Henri Matisse's work as early as 1902, supporting Raoul Dufy, and helping promote Maurice Utrillo. Likewise, she decided to represent Modigliani and exhibit his paintings of female nudes, which were considered indecent at the time because they were depicted with pubic hair. Such a nude adorns the poster that Weill used to publicize the show, which opened on December 3, 1917. Weill invited a few people, passersby dropped in, and traffic stopped outside the gallery. The police came and ordered her to remove the paintings from her gallery window. She refused to follow the order, probably so as to generate publicity. She was taken to the police office, where she gave a statement, saying that there were more such objects inside. In spite of her performance for the sake of Modigliani's work and fame, only two of his works sold at that time. Weill bought a few more for the sake of protecting Modigliani's ego.

One of the reasons so many of Modigliani's portraits of famous artists of the period survive is that he could rarely afford to pay his models. Thus his friends, many of whom were artists themselves, would oblige and sit for him. Some of them may also have commissioned portraits as a way to help Modigliani financially. For example, the painter Jacques Lipchitz and his wife asked Modigliani to paint a portrait while he was very sick with tuberculosis, as did Lunia Czechowaska in 1917.

Secrest's book continues on well after the end of her subject's life, detailing the high point for forged Modigliani art pieces, of which there are estimated to be at least one thousand on the market. This high point was between the 1950s and the 1980s. Yet, ironically, she concludes, Modigliani's name does not appear even in a footnote in *The Visual Arts, a History* by Hugh Honour and John Fleming, nor in Meyer Shapiro's *Modern Art*, a foundational text on the art of the nineteenth and twentieth centuries.

Reviews of the book have been generally positive, although some reviewers have remarked on its apparent lack of editorial supervision. While some readers applaud the detail and depth of Secrest's research, others found the author's strong presence in the text overwhelming and distracting. As one of the few biographies of Modigliani, however, this book merits attention. Moreover, Secrest's attention to primary source materials sheds new light on aspects of the artist's life and role in the Parisian art community.

Batya Weinbaum

Review Sources

Los Angeles Times, February 27, 2011 (Web).
The New Yorker, March 7, 2011 (Web).
The New York Times, May 18, 2011 (Web).
The Washington Post, March 28, 2011 (Web).

Moonwalking with Einstein
The Art and Science of Remembering Everything

Author: Joshua Foer (b. 1982)
Publisher: Penguin (New York). 320 pp.
$26.95
Type of work: Memoir, psychology
Time: 2005 to the present
Locale: Various locations in the United States

An often-humorous exploration into the human memory, this book chronicles the journey that transformed author Joshua Foer, a journalist investigating the 2005 US Memory Championship, into a participant and record-setting champion at the same event in 2006.

Principal personages:
JOSHUA FOER, a journalist who became a
   memory champion
BEN PRIDMORE , the memory champion who
   helped inspire Foer's journey
ED COOKE, Foer's memory coach
DANIEL TAMMET, a savant with sweeping memory skills
LAURENCE KIM PEEK, a savant whose life inspired the film *Rain Man*

In his 2011 work *Moonwalking with Einstein: The Art and Science of Remembering Everything*, journalist Joshua Foer tells his readers the often wild, sometimes ribald, and always entertaining story of his journey from covering the 2005 US Memory Championship—what he considered at the time to be an unenviable task—to becoming the victor of the very same event the following year. The old cliché that people are limited only by their imaginations takes on a new meaning in this book, which examines both the world of "memory athletes" and some scientific studies with bearing on the nature of memory in a careful yet lighthearted manner. Along the way, Foer offers advice on how to not only improve memory but also make life more enjoyable and fulfilling.

Despite his assurances that he is just like everyone else, Foer is clearly a man with varied interests and an insightful mind. While spending a layover visiting the Weightlifting Hall of Fame in the quaint town of York, Pennsylvania, for example, he began to ponder what would happen if the world's strongest man met the world's smartest man, and decided to find out. Locating the world's strongest man proved easy enough for Foer, but finding the smartest one proved more elusive. Intelligence, it turns out, is a rather subjective quality. In the absence of unanimity on the subject of what constitutes intelligence, the author cast about for a suitable measure. Finding the exploits of memory athletes—people who can recall a shockingly complex array of numbers, names, and other forms of minutiae—worthy of respect, Foer found himself wanting to know more. In the pages of *Moonwalking with Einstein,* he explores the science behind memory as well as the art of the discipline as practiced by those who are the sport's reigning champions.

Readers looking for a training manual for becoming the next memory champion will find this book disappointing. While Foer offers much insight into the quirky world of competitive memory, he also engages the larger, more important truth that the mind is a remarkable instrument every bit as complex as a computer. The spread of technology in the twentieth and twenty-first centuries has diminished the importance of memory through lack of use, however; with information readily available, the ability to quickly recall things has become less necessary. Despite the erosion of memorization skills, Foer asserts that anyone can improve their memory and have their productivity substantially enhanced as an added bonus (assuming the accuracy of the book's claim that the average person spends forty days a year making up for what they have forgotten). When Foer shares the nature of his memory training with his readers, it is clear that intense dedication, long hours of commitment, and mental discipline are required to produce champions. Yes, anyone can achieve enhanced memory, but only those with unusual drive will reach the pinnacle of the sport. The real value in *Moonwalking with Einstein* comes when it transcends the world of memory athletes, instead offering readers insight into those things that make life meaningful and therefore memorable.

Foer's book is as much a self-help manual as it is either a treatise on improving memory or an autobiography of his journey. In detailing what it took to achieve his enhanced memory, Foer skillfully reveals and illustrates the simple mnemonic devices utilized by most champions. Indeed, he is quick to point out that impressive memory has nothing to do with IQ, but is merely the product of a few simple tricks. One visit to Kim Peek, the man who was the real-life subject of the film *Rain Man,* underscores for Foer that a person with a below-average IQ can achieve remarkable feats of memory.

The power of memory, though attainable, is harnessed by few people. Foer refers to this tendency as the "OK plateau," noting that once a person becomes competent at something, he or she usually stops working on improvement and coasts from that point forward. Memory is no different. Most people cease improving their memorization skills once they reach the basic competency needed to perform day-to-day tasks. According to Foer, this OK plateau delimits not only memories but other aspects of life as well; people fail to achieve, or even aspire to, greatness because the standard by which they are judged is the mere attainment of proficiency. When people accept competency rather than mastery as the objective, they ensure that mediocrity flourishes. Although never fully developed by the author, the implications of Foer's assertions in this instance are powerful. By devoting time to improving characteristics like memory, people can transcend the narrow limitations that society and their own minds have placed on them. It is refreshing to see the simple values of hard work and dedication being exalted in this manner.

Although Foer's work has implications that go beyond the world of memory athletics, its central focus is on the author's journey from sidelined reporter to champion.

Joshua Foer is a freelance journalist whose articles have appeared in such publications as National Geographic, the New York Times, *and* Esquire. *He is the 2006 USA Memory Champion.*

Even in this narrow field, Foer provides suggestions that everyone, not just serious mental athletes, can employ. In his advice to readers, he states that powerful imagery is the most critical part of memory, and the more vivid and outlandish the image, the more likely it is to be remembered. The book's title, *Moonwalking with Einstein,* is a portion of the mnemonic code utilized by the author to remember the ordering of a shuffled deck of cards.

According to Foer, affixing number sequences, or anything else requiring memorization, to zany images facilitates recall. Most memory athletes utilize a similar approach, making memory more of a practiced skill than a gift. The creation of a unique "memory palace" is essential to improving one's ability to remember. This memory palace should be a very familiar place in which every detail can be visualized in mind's eye. The trick to memory is taking what needs to be recalled, whether it be a poem, a sequence of numbers, or the ordering of a deck of cards, and associating it with a specific location within the memory palace. A great deal of focus and concentration is required for this mnemonic device to be successful; one look at the outsized earphones and sunglasses worn by mental athletes during competition underscores the importance of attention.

Not content with merely explaining the art of memory, Foer also uncovers the science behind the craft. In one memorable sequence, he introduces French "chronobiologist" Michel Siffre, who once locked himself in a cave, blocking out any means of determining time. After several weeks, not only did he lose all track of time, but his memory also deteriorated to such an extent that his experiences began running together. The lesson derived from this experiment connects directly to how people remember events from their past. As Foer explains, when people are young, everything is new and exciting, and new experiences result in new and vivid memories. In youth, time passes slowly. Fast-forward twenty years and that once-wide-eyed child is working a nine-to-five job in a dead-end career, following the same routine day after day. For him, time rockets by as one year passes into the next, leaving him wondering where all the time has gone. In many ways, this hypothetical office worker is unintentionally replicating Siffre's experiment; when life becomes mundane, there are no memorable events upon which to anchor memories.

Abandoning the nine-to-five existence might not be a viable option for most, but people can usually make meaningful changes in their lives to help their routines become less routine. Changes in habits related to eating, shopping, traveling, and relaxation can all serve as triggers for mental stimulation and, by extension, memory improvement. It is here where *Moonwalking with Einstein* becomes a true self-help manual, suggesting that readers experience life rather than merely living it. Yes, there is an art to memory, but there also is a science, and for Foer, it is the science that has the widest applicability. Mnemonic devices offer people tools for developing better memory, and basic information can be retained with ease through their use. They will not necessarily make anyone smarter, but they do reveal that the path toward greater memory starts with the vividness of the memory.

Moonwalking with Einstein offers readers much to consider. Memory is a critical component of daily life, even for people who rarely give it a second thought, save for when it fails them. Many people who have struggled to remember simple, everyday things due to memory failure, such as where they left their keys or where they parked their car, will appreciate this book. The story that Foer tells is an amusing one, offering insight into a world that few readers have ever visited and filled with characters that most would otherwise never meet. Foer's suggestion that memory and perceptions of time can be improved by living a life that is not hopelessly locked in routine seems particularly salient in an age when so many are unhappy with their careers. *Moonwalking with Einstein* might not make a reader a mental athlete, but it just might make his or her days more fulfilling, and that is definitely a goal worth pursuing.

Keith M. Finley

Review Sources

Library Journal 136, no. 12 (July 1, 2011): 47.
The New York Times Book Review, March 11, 2011 (Web).
Seattle Times, March 5, 2011 (Web).
The Wall Street Journal, March 5, 2011 (Web).

Mr. Fox

Author: Helen Oyeyemi (b. 1984)
Publisher: Riverhead Books (New York).
336 pp. $25.95
Type of work: Novel
Time: Mainly the 1930s, with some stories occurring in the present day
Locale: Primarily in New York City

A novel composed of short stories, Oyeyemi's fourth book is a modern retelling of several classic fairy tales.

Principal characters:
MR. ST. JOHN FOX, a popular writer of violent novels
MARY FOXE, Mr. Fox's muse
DAPHNE FOX, Mr. Fox's wife
JOHN PIZARSKY (JP), a friend whom Mr. Fox begins to suspect is having an affair with Daphne
GRETA, Daphne's closest friend and John Pizarsky's wife

Mr. Fox, the fourth novel by Helen Oyeyemi, begins with a bit of an understatement. "Mary Foxe came by the other day—the last person on earth I was expecting to see," the eponymous narrator declares. Although he appears straight faced and calm, readers soon learn that this visit is more than a mere surprise. Mr. Fox is a novelist, one with a tendency to kill the women in his stories; Mary Foxe is the imaginary muse who first came to him in the trenches of World War I. Mr. Fox has spent years imagining her and holding conversations with her in his head, but this is the first time she has appeared of her own volition. From here, a puzzling and bizarre story begins. Mary takes issue with Mr. Fox's violence toward women in his novels and decides to take control. For the remainder of the novel, Oyeyemi alternates between two types of chapters. In one type, we follow the love triangle between Mary Foxe, Mr. Fox, and his wife, Daphne Fox. In the other, Mary Foxe and Mr. Fox write each other into short stories, falling in love and failing each other again and again. Through these stories, Mr. Fox tries to wean himself off of his habit of killing women, while Mary Foxe explores the power dynamics inherent in romance.

Unlike other novels structured as connected stories, the links between chapters and characters in *Mr. Fox* are not always clear. While early chapters tend to include characters with the familiar fox names, the narratives in later chapters are connected in more oblique ways. Similarly, Oyeyemi rarely makes each narrator's identity obvious. Instead, readers are set to the detective work of piecing together clues to determine if Mary Foxe, Mr. Fox, or both are behind the typewriter. While this structure can be dizzying and disorienting at times, it provides the author with the latitude to dip playfully in and out of familiar myths and fairy tales without being beholden to any one idea. Instead, what matters most are the driving themes and questions at the heart of the novel: the ways we control one another through romantic relationships, the violent stories and fables at the roots of culture, and the limitations of amorous roles. These are the preoccupations of *Mr. Fox*, philosophical conundrums that Oyeyemi examines from a range of narrative perspectives but does not seek to resolve.

The start of the novel eases the reader into its many conceits. Mary Foxe makes explicit many of her complaints with the man who dreamed her into existence. "You're a villain," she tells him. "You kill women. You're a serial killer." Mr. Fox makes the obvious rebuttals, claiming he is only a writer and that there is no harm in killing imaginary women, but Mary Foxe does not accept this. Instead, she launches them into a story, a sort of hallucinatory narrative in which Mr. Fox is a man who decapitates his wife, then comes to regret it. These early stories are familiar and relatively easy to follow, such as "Be Bold, Be Bold, But Not Too Bold," in which Mary is a young nanny who wants to share her short stories with the successful and inspirational writer Mr. Fox. The two correspond and jest with one another, promising to meet and then failing to do so. All the while, Mary works, taking care of a spoiled child in a rich family. Rather than having the young female writer fawn appreciatively after the older man, however, Mary becomes angry at his cruelty, calling him "vile" and "putrid." By the end of the story, when she has finally convinced him to read her stories as he promised, he has his assistant light them on fire before her eyes. These are clearly alternate versions of Mary Foxe and Mr. Fox, struggling for power both romantically and as writers, but the morals and metaphors are not so clear. Mary never truly triumphs over the cruel man, although such an ending is suggested by the title, a line taken from the classic English nursery tale about a bachelor named Mr. Fox who is outwitted by a female character. Instead, each vies for control, only to be tumbled back into the real world of Mr. Fox's life and marriage.

As the novel progresses, the real-life version of Mary Foxe asserts herself more and more, leaving notes for Daphne to find and floating in the edges of Mr. Fox's vision at inconvenient moments. The stress of her presence wears on the couple's marriage, and Daphne becomes increasingly certain that Mr. Fox is conducting an affair. Mary's intrusions test the strength of the Foxes' relationship, one in which Mr. Fox has from the start disempowered his wife (he tells Mary Foxe that he "fixed her early"). While not nearly as violent toward Daphne as he is to his fictional characters, there is a sense of brute misogyny in the way he interacts with her. As Mary Foxe becomes more present in his life, Mr. Fox is left with an important choice, one between a real relationship with a woman he has treated poorly and a fantasy relationship with an idealized but fictional partner.

Oyeyemi explores this choice less through the narrative of the love triangle itself and more through the power play of the short stories. Mary Foxe and Mr. Fox begin to collaborate, sharing the pen and further complicating an already complicated process. These later stories forgo the easy correlations of the opening pages, instead favoring

Helen Oyeyemi published her first novel, The Icarus Girl (2005), at the age of nineteen. Her work engages many literary traditions, including Cuban mythology, fairy tales, and the gothic novel. Among many other honors, she has won the 2010 Somerset Maugham Award for her novel White Is for Witching *(2009).*

narratives that resonate in unexpected ways. This includes the story of Charlie Wulf and Charles Wolfe, two boys at a sort of preparatory school meant to transform unimpressive youth into ideal husbands. The boys discover a prisoner who is magically kept at the bottom of the school's lake by the headmistress. When they defy her and release the prisoner, he goes on a misogynistic killing spree, and the boys are left to deal with their guilt. In another story, a young woman falls in love with an older psychiatrist and is forced to confront the murder of her mother by her father. These stories upset the expectations we might have had at the beginning of the novel. The love of Mary Foxe and Mr. Fox is reconfigured as the love between two teenage boys, and the male characters are both literally and figuratively imprisoned by their violence and gender. Although Oyeyemi gives some clear hints to link the narratives, such as when Daphne wonders, "Why have husbands got to keep themselves all locked up," the links are increasingly associative and elusive, and *Mr. Fox* ceases to be a simple feminist reversal of familiar fairy tales. Instead, Oyeyemi's unfamiliar narratives reveal something fresh and unexpected about her grander themes.

Eventually, the stories move so far away from the original narrative that any hint at symbolism would seem inappropriate. The most extreme departure occurs in "My Daughter the Racist," the moving story of a mother and daughter in a war-torn country who form a relationship with an occupying soldier. While it would be impossible to find any "foxes" in its narrative, "My Daughter the Racist" does signal a type of change: the remainder of the book focuses primarily on the love triangle, with only brief departures into short stories. At last, Mary Foxe presents herself to Daphne Fox, who ceases to be a minor character and steps into the focus at last. As Mary Foxe becomes real and talks to Daphne for the first time, Daphne herself gains a new agency, going out with friends and flirting with other men. This is upsetting to her controlling husband, who is forced to confront his choice between a real companion and a more copacetic fantasy. Mary and Daphne even form a sort of friendship, going out to dinner together and swapping stories about the title character. Eventually, and somewhat surprisingly, the novel returns to its original premise, becoming a love story in the truest sense. However, it is not a story of new love, but of old love renewed. As Daphne asserts herself and Mr. Fox feels challenged for one of the first times in his life, they are able to care for each other in a way they never have before.

At the conclusion, Mary Foxe takes off on her own adventure and Daphne becomes a writer, although a very different sort of writer from her husband. The final pages are devoted to fairy tales (with a hint that they were written by Daphne) that tell of a fox in love with a girl. By returning to this direct correlation, Oyeyemi is able to crystallize some of the novel's themes. The woman is in power, both as writer and as subject, and she is unwilling to accept the quick and easy solution of murder that Mary Foxe took issue with in the opening chapter. But she also reminds us that love is not easy, that the "little girl feared the fox cub, and the fox cub felt exactly the same way about her." In the end, the romance that is possible is one in which the girl and the fox care for one another, challenge one another, and hurt one another. It is about "the pleasure of biting. Or letting him. And afterwards the feel of a long, wet tongue light against the hot wound." There is nothing simple here, no pat moral to these fables, but instead an insistence on complication and an acceptance that romance often comes in a messy package.

Mr. Fox is a surprising and varied novel. In her previous work, Oyeyemi has proven herself to be an adept storyteller, able to engage with and manipulate multiple literary traditions, and it is from this skill that much of the delight to be found in *Mr. Fox* derives. Oyeyemi's prose style is simple and direct, reminiscent of fairy tales and oral storytelling, yet filled with rich images and striking details. More importantly, she draws freely from fairy tales and modern literature, quoting the macabre poet Edgar Allan Poe (1809–49) and alluding subtly to a broad range of writers. While readers looking for simple conclusions and clear narrative cohesion might be frustrated by her style, the novel comes together through the story and the poetic pleasure that she summons. Unfettered and surprising, *Mr. Fox* offers a fresh take on the joy and opportunities of storytelling.

T. Fleischmann

Review Sources

Booklist 108, no. 2 (September 15, 2011): 25.
The Guardian, June 10, 2011, p. 10.
Kirkus Reviews 79, no. 17 (September 1, 2011): 1522–23.
The New York Times Book Review, October 30, 2011, p. 16.

Music for Silenced Voices
Shostakovich and His Fifteen Quartets

Author: Wendy Lesser (b. 1952)
Publisher: Yale University Press (New Haven, CT). 368 pp. $28.00
Type of work: Music, biography
Time: 1906–1975
Locale: Soviet Union

This book, designed for the layperson rather than for the professional musician, describes the intertwining of Shostakovich's life with his string quartets.

Principal personages:
DMITRI SHOSTAKOVICH (1906–1975), one of the most prominent composers of classical music of the twentieth century
NINA VARZAR, his first wife
IRINA SHOSTAKOVICH, his third wife
GALINA SHOSTAKOVICH, his daughter
MAXIM SHOSTAKOVICH, his son, a pianist and conductor
IVAN SOLLERTINSKY, his friend, a musician
ISAAK GLIKMAN, his friend, a dramaturge
MOISEI WEINBERG AND NATALYA MIKHOELS, friends of Shostakovich and Varzar
MSTISLAV ROSTROPOVICH, cellist and conductor
YEVGENY MRAVINSKY, conductor of the Leningrad Philharmonic
KURT SANDERLING, co-conductor of the Leningrad Philharmonic and assistant to Mravinsky
DMITRI TSYGANOV, violinist and original member of the Beethoven Quartet
VASILY SHIRINSKY, violinist and original member of the Beethoven Quartet
VADIM BORISOVSKY, violist and original member of the Beethoven Quartet
SERGEI SHIRINSKY, cellist and original member of the Beethoven Quartet
NIKOLAI ZABAVNIKOV, violinist and later member of the Beethoven Quartet
FYODOR DRUZHININ, violist and later member of the Beethoven Quartet
YEVGENY ALTMAN, cellist and later member of the Beethoven Quartet

Ever since Solomon Volkov's *Testimony: The Memoirs of Dmitri Shostakovich* was published in 1979, those interested in Dmitri Shostakovich's music have been eager to decipher what external meanings, if any, reside in his works. Wendy Lesser's foray into the life and music of Shostakovich, *Music for Silenced Voices: Shostakovich and His Fifteen Quartets*, uses one of the standard approaches to his music—his biography—but from the viewpoint of a nonmusician. The result is an easy-to-read text with imaginative interpretations of the quartets. Whether these analyses are persuasive, however, is less certain.

Lesser divides the book into six chapters, each with its own subtitle: "Elegy," "Serenade," "Intermezzo," "Nocturne," "Funeral March," and "Epilogue" (the names of which also match the movements from Shostakovich's final quartet). The first five chapters cover Shostakovich's life in chronological order, while the last acts as a general essay outlining the author's opinions of the quartets, discussing the reasoning behind the critical reception of the works from both a musicological and a listener's viewpoint. This structure works particularly well because Shostakovich did not start writing quartets until he was already well known for several large-scale works and had already experienced his first major setback, the result of Joseph Stalin's scathing review of the Shostakovich opera *Lady Macbeth of the Mtensk District* (1932). Thus, Lesser is able to set the stage for the quartets using the first part of Shostakovich's life as a backdrop. The technique also allows her to set up her major premise for the book: the quartets act as a sort of "diary" for Shostakovich in a way that other, more public works could not.

Before describing each quartet, Lesser puts forth biographical details, providing a basic overview but concentrating on aspects that connect more directly to the quartet on which Shostakovich was working at the time. Indeed, in some ways, this book may be seen as a biography of Shostakovich that contains brief analyses of the quartets, thereby following in the footsteps of authors Laurel Fay and Elizabeth Wilson. Emphasis is put on the emotional state of Shostakovich more than on his other compositions or a blow-by-blow description of his activities. Again, this feeds well into Lesser's thesis about the connections between Shostakovich's emotional state and his quartets.

As Lesser states, she is not a musician, nor can she read music, and so the analyses of each quartet tend to sound more like what one would typically hear in a music-appreciation class than a musicological treatise. Consider this account of the beginning of Shostakovich's Second String Quartet:

A noticeable melody, bearing klezmerish strains of wailing or shrieking in the highest notes, yet with an essentially sardonic sensibility, appears on the first violin and stays there. This is a voice that is planning to keep us company for a while, indeed to lead us into places that we may find both fearful and enjoyable, seductive and threatening. It is a voice that throbs and scrapes, moving from tenderness to turbulence in the space of a few measures. It is a confident voice, but it invites exchange with the other instruments and finds itself often in harmony with them (though just as often at a dissonant distance from them). Whether it is happy or sad—and it is often both, or neither—it is a strong voice, capable of snappy retorts and enlightening observations. I think it is the voice of Sollertinsky.

This is considerably flowery prose that shows off the author's use of language. For her core audience of musical laypeople, it provides an accessibility to the quartets that more technical books on Shostakovich lack. By describing the section as the voice of

Wendy Lesser is the editor of the Three-penny Review *and has written several nonfiction texts and one book of fiction,* The Pagoda Garden *(2005). She is a member of the American Academy of Arts and Sciences and has received fellowships from the Guggenheim Foundation and the National Endowment for the Humanities.*

Shostakovich's close friend Ivan Sollertin-sky, who had died just before the composer started the work, she also connects it clearly to Shostakovich's biography.

In this example, we see a few of the primary strengths of Lesser's text: the emphasis on readability, rather than on a more academic style of writing, and picturesque descriptions of the quartets that are easily grasped by readers regardless of their musical aptitude. The latter aspect is particularly what sets this book apart from other books on Shostakovich. If one is looking for a close theoretical analysis, or even narratives with more precise timings, this is not the right book; if the aim is to understand the emotional ride of the piece through words, then this is the book to read.

Whether or not this is the right book for someone interested in Shostakovich and his music also depends on how one interprets the music in the first place. As the author and several other critics have noted, Shostakovich's music is notoriously tricky to interpret. One well-known illustration of this comes from the finale of his Fifth Symphony, particularly in earlier recordings. Several Western conductors would play the last portion quickly, believing it to be symbolic of rejoicing, while some Soviet conductors would slow down the same part considerably to suggest that the rejoicing is forced. Lesser admits that "the line between correct interpretations and incorrect ones is bound to be fuzzy and inconstant." Nevertheless, she believes that by using factual information, she can provide valuable insight. To do so, she concentrates on biographical information gathered not only from books such as those of Fay and Wilson but also from interviews that she has done (through an interpreter) with various people connected to Shostakovich and his quartets. Lesser uses this data to inform her readings, adding a dose of pop psychology by emphasizing what she believes to be the composer's state of mind in connection to the quartets. If, as she asserts, the quartets are meant to be a "diary," this approach makes sense logically. Unfortunately, if the reader disagrees with Lesser's assessment of Shostakovich's mental state, the musical analyses often do not have enough specificity to stand on their own.

Lesser asserts that that the quartets, and not any of Shostakovich's more "public" pieces, are the true windows to his soul. Chamber music, by its very nature, does tend to be more intimate than symphonies or other orchestral works. Also, several of the composer's programmatic works, including the obviously propagandistic cantata *The Sun Shines over Our Motherland* and pieces such as his Seventh Symphony (subtitled the "Leningrad," the symphony that made him a hero for the Allies during World War II), were designed for public consumption to put forth Shostakovich's own inner thoughts. The assumption, however, that none of the larger works could also act as a diary seems too generalized. Compare, for example, the similarities in the musical language used and the overall style in his Eighth Quartet to his Tenth Symphony. Consider, too, the use of "Jewish" themes and musical language that the composer used in a variety of works, including chamber, orchestral, and vocal, over at least a forty-year period. These shared sources suggest that Shostakovich's musical diary entries did not entirely consist of quartets. Nevertheless, as Lesser suggests, a case can be made that the quartets generally portray some of the composer's innermost thoughts.

Critically, the book has generally received good, if qualified, reviews. Edward Rothstein of the *New York Times* states that Lesser's interpretation of the quartets is "literate, sensitive, and imaginative," but that, in his opinion, "in connecting the life and the works, [she] tends to make them too personal, too apolitical and too ahistorical." Still, the book made the *New York Times* Editors' Choice list. Paul Mitchinson, writing for the *Washington Post*, notes that Lesser "usually manages to get to the heart of the matter more convincingly than many academic experts do." In the *San Francisco Chronicle*, Joshua Kosman says that the author "offers an insightful and highly readable treatment of the composer's life," but what she "doesn't do is use the composer's work to illuminate that tale." The *Guardian* critic Ed Vulliamy believes that the book's "main strength lies in Lesser's descriptions of the quartets themselves: this book is an essential companion for anyone planning to hear them." Overall, it is clear that different critics prefer different aspects of the book.

The disagreement among critics is perhaps indicative of Shostakovich studies in general. The musicological baggage associated with his life and works colors every aspect of their meaning. As Lesser astutely notes, the difficulty lies in learning what truth exists in the available sources. For instance, Shostakovich neither wrote nor signed many of the statements to which his name is ascribed. The language of the time in the Soviet Union was full of doublespeak, since even private letters could be seized by the government. Even interviews given after the fall of the Soviet Union are colored by individual and political prejudices. It would appear that finding some sort of narrative or meaning under such circumstances would be almost impossible. Nonetheless, as so many critics on both sides have stated, Shostakovich's works seem to cry out for interpretation. This is part of what makes them so interesting, not only to professional musicians, but also to those passionate about classical music in general. As one of the latter, Lesser has contributed a worthy addition to the material at hand, especially for other musical amateurs.

Lisa Scoggin

Review Sources

Nation 292, no. 19 (May 9, 2011): 35–37.
The New York Times Book Review, May 8, 2011, p. 16.
San Francisco Chronicle, May 22, 2011, p. E2.
Wilson Quarterly 35, no. 2 (Spring 2011): 106–7.

My Father's Fortune
A Life

Author: Michael Frayn (b. 1933)
Publisher: Metropolitan Books (New York).
 288 pp. $25.00; paperback $16.00
Type of work: Memoir
Time: Twentieth century
Locale: The greater London area

Author Michael Frayn recalls his father, his family life, and his own pursuits while growing up in early to mid-twentieth century London.

Principal personages:
MICHAEL FRAYN, a poet, playwright, and novelist
THOMAS FRAYN, father of Michael and his
    sister, Jill
JILL FRAYN, Michael's sister
VI FRAYN, Thomas's first wife
NANNY, Vi's mother
ELSIE SMITH, Thomas's second wife
MICHAEL LANE, schoolmate and close friend of Michael Frayn

In *My Father's Fortune: A Life*, Michael Frayn revisits his childhood and investigates the life of his father, Thomas. Early in the book, and then again later, he describes his father's first words to his mother: "I'm Tom—I suppose you're Vi!" Tom's wife and first love, Vi supported him through challenges large and small, and her influence is one that yields significant repercussions throughout the book. While he was growing up, Frayn's home life was anything but typical, with more than a dozen people seeming to reside there at any given time. The process of supporting these relatives, while also supporting their own growing family, stretched Frayn's parents thin. For all the challenges posed by middle-class life in their small, overcrowded London home, however, Frayn notes the indelible strength that appeared first in his mother and eventually passed throughout his family.

An accomplished playwright, novelist, translator, and poet, Frayn is most often recognized for his stage works, such as the farcical *Noises Off* (1982) and the historical play *Copenhagen* (1998). These works and more have been popularly and recently produced in London's West End, while *Headlong* (2000), one of Frayn's many novels, was a finalist for the Booker Prize. Frayn began his long and varied career in journalism, and so it should come as no surprise that his published work features a great deal of nonfiction. In 2010, however, and much to his own surprise, he began his first expressly autobiographical project, examining his childhood and his relationship with his father.

My Father's Fortune begins in 1969, the year Frayn's father died and the year in which Frayn wrote his first play, as he first begins to reflect on his father with a renewed sense of recognition. From here, he invites the reader back in time to explore Tom's childhood, spent in a two-room London apartment with six other family members. Tom left school at the age of fourteen to find work in the roofing business, where he supported his family by selling asbestos tiling. As a young man, Tom met Vi, though it would be eleven years before the two could finally afford to marry. Frayn recounts this early phase of his family without sentimentality or idealization. While some reviewers have criticized these passages for being routine, an appealing element of the archetypal rags-to-riches story pervades the story. Frayn himself was born in 1933, at which time the young family moved out of London and into a rented house in Ewell. Vi's mother, whom the family affectionately referred to as "Nanny," came to live there as well, assisting in housekeeping and child care, and Frayn's sister Jill was born soon after. Frayn's youth was happy, though his excellence in school but not in athletics was not entirely what Tom had anticipated.

(Eamonn McCabe)

Michael Frayn is an acclaimed playwright, novelist, screenwriter, columnist, and poet. His most prominent works include Copenhagen *(1998),* Noises Off *(1982), and* The Tin Men *(1965). He has won a wide range of awards during his career, including a Tony Award for* Copenhagen *(2000) and two New York Drama Critics' Circle Awards, in 1986 and 2000.*

The arrival of World War II, which brought about greater challenges for the Frayns, gives rise to many of the book's most vivid and memorable passages. Frayn recalls the trials of rationing, building and hiding in a bomb shelter, and many other lifestyle changes. His relatives and neighbors all joined in the war effort, even Tom, who could not fight but made significant contributions in response to the government's rising demand for asbestos. As Frayn tells it, he did not truly grasp the darkness of the war until one night when a German V-1 buzz bomb, known to Britons as a doodlebug, flew dangerously close to the family home.

Although the war led to a number of changes, Frayn reports that the true turning point came once the war had ended, when, with little warning, Vi suffered a heart attack and died. This event sent Tom into an emotional malaise that lasted for years, punctuated by his inexplicable burial of her with no headstone. Frayn is perfectly frank regarding his own narrative biases and memory lapses, especially during this period, as he describes his struggles to understand his father's grief. As far as he can recall, the family never mentioned Vi again, though the reader can detect her influence throughout the remainder of the book, even if that influence is never directly referenced.

Frayn maintains that in spite of Tom's great emotional distance, his father continued to love his children, even if he rarely demonstrated those feelings. Tom suddenly found himself the children's sole caretaker, an extremely difficult task for an already hardworking father. Frayn recalls that this period was perhaps the darkest for his family, with Tom continuing to mourn while he worked to return the Frayn household to stability. These passages are among the most strained in the book. Throughout the many struggles, however, Tom refused to let the Frayn home, which the family dubbed "Duckmore," fall apart completely.

Young Frayn began to explore his budding talent for writing during this time. Despite some subpar grades, he was able to enter a new grammar school, where a teacher opened his eyes to poetry and introduced him to the works of the nineteenth-century romantic poet Percy Bysshe Shelley, whom he quickly embraced. It is in this school that Frayn also met his first true friend, Michael Lane. The pair, known from then on as "LaneFrayn," were inseparable, reciting and writing poetry and even exploring liberal and communist ideologies together, the latter much to Tom's disapproval.

Meanwhile, Frayn continues to shape and define his portrait of Tom, showing him to have had great reserves of resilience. Tom gradually shed his lingering misery, redecorating his home and marrying Elsie, a reasonably wealthy widow with seemingly boundless energy and humor. The family moved in with Elsie at her home, Chez Nous, but over time, she began to demonstrate wild mood swings that Frayn would later learn sprang from an undiagnosed bipolar disorder. Tom dutifully stayed with Elsie for a number of years, but once both of his children had moved away, he departed from Chez Nous and eventually settled down with yet another wife.

Frayn further developed his writing skills at Cambridge University, Tom and a committed teacher of his having worked diligently to secure his admission, and ultimately landed a job as a reporter at the British daily newspaper *The Guardian*. Although he continued to write poetry and other works during this time, Frayn found relief in being able to report to his father that he held a respectable job. The observant reader will notice, however, that little mention is made of Frayn's subsequent success as a literary figure. Also evident is the element of sadness and regret that surrounds Frayn's recollections that it was his father who encouraged him to attend Cambridge and, later, to pursue work as a journalist. Moments such as these draw attention to what is quietly remarkable about the book: the modesty of Frayn's point of view and his commitment to telling a personal, straightforward account.

Frayn's younger sister, Jill, eventually married, and soon enough he did the same. Not long into Frayn's marriage, however, Tom was diagnosed with cancer. With Gladys, his third wife, by his side, Tom underwent a long period of treatment and recuperation, but as time passed, he repeatedly fell ill and grew increasingly frail. Frayn acknowledges that over the course of his life, his father had often seemed unwilling to express his love for his children, and he voices regret that in his adult years he could not recognize the subtle expressions of that love. Recalling Tom's passing in 1969, he observes that while his father left very few material goods, he did leave Frayn and his sister (and their own children as well) a "fortune" in the form of a stable childhood, a sense of humor, and a positive outlook on life.

My Father's Fortune was largely well received by critics, who found Frayn's wit, language, and storytelling enjoyable. Indeed, his retrospective draws much of its sensibility from the same lightness and humor that the author observes in his father. Sifting through family records, personal diaries, conversations, and his own memory, Frayn is often earnestly surprised by what he uncovers. He is quick to admit that the book's impetus was not his own curiosity but his daughter's, and in the eyes of certain reviewers, this lack of interest on the part of the author is perhaps too evident, with some wondering rather frankly why Frayn even bothered.

It is true that *My Father's Fortune* does not read like a historical account buttressed by facts, dates, and larger-than-life personalities, or display the character development that readers might expect from a novel. Rather, the book reads as a series of straight-forward anecdotes, the personalities and experiences of each personage remembered in the context of specific events, such as the war, Vi's death, or semesters at school. While some critics took issue with a perceived lack of depth to the project, Tom was a man who walked lightly and without pretense, "scarcely leaving a footprint, scarcely a shadow." Indeed, while Tom's modesty may prove a less-than-compelling read to some readers, his spirit informs and shapes the book. Rather than embellishing his memories or attempting a full historical chronicle, Frayn allows his book to serve as a personal, and often poignant, homage to his father. Much of his commentary, par-ticularly in the latter half of the book, seems derived from an interest that was only recently and accidentally discovered, as well as Frayn's recognition of the ways he himself carries on many of Tom's defining traits. In spite of his stature as a literary figure, Frayn narrates this memoir with a lightness of step that is very much in keeping with his father's spirit. In the end, *My Father's Fortune* is one man's self-effacing and sincere attempt to understand his own family history. It leaves the reader with what Frayn is seeking: a desire to learn more.

Michael Auerbach

Review Sources

The New Yorker 87, no. 7 (April 4, 2011): 75.
The New York Times, March 6, 2011 (Web).
NPR, February 19, 2011 (Web).
The Telegraph, September 5, 2010 (Web).
The Washington Post, March 25, 2011 (Web).

My New American Life

Author: Francine Prose (b. 1947)
Publisher: HarperCollins (New York). 320 pp.
  $25.99
Type of work: Novel
Time: Twenty-first century
Locale: New Jersey

This light-hearted look at an immigrant's pursuit of the American Dream sheds light on why so many people from other countries want to live in the United States—and why they are willing to leave their homeland for a new country.

Principal characters:
LULA, a twenty-six-year-old immigrant from
  Albania, who works as a nanny
ZEKE, the teenage son of Stanley and Ginger
STANLEY, a banker, father of Zeke, employer of
  Lula and former college professor
GINGER, the estranged wife of Stanley and mother of Zeke
DON SETTEBELLO, an immigration lawyer
ALVO, an Albanian immigrant, gangster, and object of Lula's attraction
GURI, an Albanian immigrant and member of a gang
GENTI, an Albanian immigrant and member of a gang
DUNIA, an Albanian immigrant, a former roommate and friend of Lula

My New American Life is a humorous novel that stars Lula, a twenty-six-year-old immigrant from Albania. Like many of Prose's novels, the protagonist of *My New American Life* is neither too complex nor overly simple a character. Lula's personality unfolds gradually—along with her insights about the United States, Albania, communism, capitalism, and more—revealing both a biting cynicism and a refreshing optimism. In fact, this novel is a study of contrasts: Albania versus the United States, communism versus capitalism, life under a dictatorship versus life in President George W. Bush's post-2001 United States, homeland versus new country, past versus present, legal versus illegal, inner freedom versus outer freedom, and letting go versus holding on.

The novel opens with the announcement that Lula's immigration lawyer has informed her she is "legal": her green card has been approved. Lula fervently wants to make a new life in America, and she will do almost anything—including lying to the authorities to get a visa and green card—to stay in the United States. And she will do almost anything to avoid risks that imperil her chances of staying in the United States. Despite this fervid desire, the "almost" is what poses danger and creates conflict in the novel's storyline.

After sharing an apartment with a fellow Albanian immigrant, Lula obtains a job as a nanny to high-school-age Zeke in suburban New Jersey. He does not need a baby-sitter, but in the recent aftermath of his mother Ginger's sudden departure from the family home, his father does not want him coming home to an empty house. Lula's employer, Mister Stanley, as she calls him, hires her and assigns her two tasks: to be there when Zeke comes home from school and to keep food in the house. These job duties leave her with plenty of free time, and she whiles away her days engaging in boredom-defeating activities, writing, and daydreaming.

One day, three Albanian gangsters appear at the door, claim they know her cousin George, and ask her to keep a gun for them. Despite her fear of endangering her legal status, she agrees. She also develops a crush on one of the gangsters, Alvo. A series of unusual encounters follow, threatening her livelihood, legal status, and the American life she so desires. As Lula examines her new American life and weighs her choices, she examines the lives of the Americans close to her—Stanley, Zeke, and her immigration lawyer—and ponders whether they are seeking their dreams or clinging to things that restrict them and deny them the freedom to embrace life and live it fully.

Enjoyable and easy reading, the novel at times is far-fetched and lacks credibility, as when the three Albanian gangsters target Lula and ask her to hide their gun. They claim to know her cousin and they do know intimate details about her life—such as her immigration status—but they give conflicting stories to explain this knowledge. Yet Lula allows them to enter her employer's home, accepts the obviously illicit gun without protest, and never contacts her cousin to verify their story or inquire as to who they really are and what they are doing.

The novel often requires the reader to look at the big picture and overlook minor details that are implausible and unreasonable. For example, Lula spends several months worrying about her former roommate, Dunia, and wondering whether she arrived safely in Tirana as planned. Numerous emails and phone calls have gone unanswered and un-returned, and Lula fears the worst: that Dunia has become entrapped in a sex-trafficking ring. One day, Dunia reappears mysteriously, with no explanation for her failure to answer Lula's emails, and their friendship simply resumes. This lack of logical causal relationships extends to the resolution of the conflict. Loose ends are tied up rather too conveniently and in ways that stretch plausibility. As long as one can immerse oneself in Lula's story, emotions, and thought processes, this does not create a problem.

Like many of Prose's novels, *My New American Life* is a character-driven novel. Most of the novel is a setting that plays out real events against the inner reflections of Lula's mind. The novel presents a running narrative of Lula's observations and opin-ions on the people she interacts with—primarily Zeke, Stanley, and her lawyer—and American society in general. Told through Lula's perspective, this narrative not only fleshes out her character, it creates a multidimensional representation of many im-migrants to the United States, particularly immigrants from communist or repressive countries.

Lula is a devious, egocentric woman who habitually lies and who lusts after the material riches available in her new country. She drinks alcohol every afternoon, spikes Zeke's drinks, passes off Albanian folklore as true stories about her family, and vanquishes scruples that stand in her way. Yet there is so much more to Lula. She has a finely developed, if peculiar, sense of right and wrong. She is averse to hurting others and has a strong desire to help others and make a difference in their lives. Most of all, she wants to persevere and to survive, to have a new American life and never return to the way of life she knew in Albania.

Lula's running commentary comparing Albanian life and American life helps to explain her vices and makes them seem not only understandable but even unavoidable. It also draws attention to American society and its values, highlighting how life in the United States under the George W. Bush administration is not always so different from life under a dictator and subtly interweaving information throughout the story without preaching. This creates a more comprehensive portrait of Lula, and she appears less like a conniving woman who craves the material world and more like an earnest individual who wants not only America's creature comforts but the personal freedoms and liberties it provides. Prose's novel also offers an explanation of why so many immigrants long for the life America offers—not so much because of its material wealth or job opportunities but to live free of the decay, hopelessness, and corruption prevalent in so many nations.

(Stephanie Berger)

Author, editor, and translator Francine Prose has written more than twenty novels. She has won several awards for her works, including the Dayton Literary Peace Prize in fiction and the Jewish Book Council Award. Her novel Blue Angel *(2000) was a National Book Award finalist.*

Zeke and Stanley are well-developed characters and they face a challenge similar to Lula's: how to get a new life. Life in their household has become very sterile since Ginger left, with little intimacy or communication between father and son. Zeke propels himself through the daily motions of life with the least exertion possible and exists in a perpetual state of ennui. Faced with the challenge of what he is going to do after graduating from high school, he appears unconcerned, unmotivated, and resigned to a life of drifting and boredom. Events change his perspective, however, and he transforms into a driven young adult willing to overcome obstacles and make a new life for himself.

Stanley, like his son, finds little joy or pleasure in his daily activities. He deplores his job but declines to resume his former profession, which he enjoyed. He is resigned to a life of stultifying boredom and stagnation. After his wife returns and is hospitalized in a mental health facility, his life gains focus as he becomes deeply involved in her care. Although there is little visible transformation in his life, he has found what he was seeking and is at peace with it.

In contrast to Lula, Zeke, and Stanley, Prose's minor characters are less developed and often seem to represent stock characters or stereotypes. Ginger is the woman who abandons her family and seeks meaning in New Age mysticism. Dunia is the recently divorced woman who eagerly squanders her settlement for instant yet temporary gratification. Alvo is the irresponsible playboy / gangster who eagerly embraces deportation over a prison sentence and who looks forward to having his pick of Albanian girls and his mother's cooking. Don Settebello is the liberal lawyer who advocates on behalf of the oppressed and who renounces the trappings of capitalism and corporate America despite reaping their rewards and enjoying all the advantages of an exorbitant income.

My New American Life will appeal to both young adult and adult readers. While it is narrated by a twenty-six-year-old woman, her voice sounds both older and younger than her years. Lula has a wisdom acquired from her life experiences seldom found in teens or persons in their early twenties, but in other ways she is more naive and childlike than her peers. For example, her crush on Alvo is more akin to a teenager's experience than that of a seasoned dater.

The novel has many layers. While it seems to be a simple story about a young immigrant and her new life in the United States, it also is about more complex issues, such as how the social, political, and economic conditions of a country shape a person and affect how one views the world and interacts with others. It also is a story about transformation, how people let go of the past and move on—a common theme in many of Prose's novels. In *My New American Life,* Lula seeks to become an American and live the American Dream. By the novel's end, though, she has acquired a new goal. She does not want just a new American life, she wants a new life—and she has taken steps to get that life, whatever it may be. Lula is not the only character who undergoes a transformation; so too do Alvo, Dunia, Zeke, and Stanley. While these characters experience less significant transformations, their changes provide a contrast to Lula's transformation and raise interesting questions about what it means to "get a life."

Barbara C. Lightner

Review Sources

Booklist 107, no. 11 (February 1, 2011): 31.
Kirkus Reviews 79, no. 2 (January 15, 2011): 84.
Library Journal 136 (January 1, 2011): 90.
Los Angeles Times, April 24, 2011 (Web).
The New York Times, April 21, 2011, p. C35.
The New York Times Book Review, May 1, 2011, p. L11.
Publishers Weekly 258, no. 1 (January 3, 2011): 28.
The Wall Street Journal, April 23, 2011 (Web).

Nanjing Requiem

Author: Ha Jin (Jin Xuefei, b. 1956)
Publisher: Pantheon (New York). 320 pp.
$26.95
Type of work: Novel
Time: 1937–1940
Locale: Nanjing, China

A fictionalized account of the Japanese capture of the Chinese city of Nanjing in 1937 and its effect on the Chinese population and the community of foreigners.

Principal characters:
GAO ANLING, a senior employee of the Jinling Women's College in Nanjing
MINNIE VAUTRIN, an American missionary serving as a dean at Jinling Women's College
MRS. DENNISON, the founding president of Jinling Women's College

For over two decades, Ha Jin has built a reputation as a writer of powerful stories told with exceptional craftsmanship. Most are set in his homeland of China, where he grew up during the Cultural Revolution. Ha Jin was studying in America when the Chinese government used brutal measures to crush the Tiananmen Square uprising of 1989. He decided to remain in the United States and began writing stories depicting the everyday travails of people living under Communist rule. In *Nanjing Requiem*, however, Ha Jin looks to a period in Chinese history before Mao Zedong came to power and gives himself a much harder task: to create fiction from history, recasting events surrounding the horrific Japanese invasion that led to the fall of Nanjing. The behavior of Japanese troops, well documented by Chinese and foreigners on the scene, has come to be known as the Nanjing (or Nanking) Massacre, or more graphically as the Rape of Nanjing. Abandoned by the Chinese military in December 1937, the citizens of Nanjing were left at the mercy of rapacious Japanese soldiers who slaughtered approximately 200,000 men, women, and children during the first six weeks of the occupation. As many as 20,000 women were raped. Property was wantonly destroyed, and even those in the Safety Zone, which had been hastily created to protect foreigners and other noncombatants living in the city, were not immune to the brutality of their conquerors. Japanese soldiers roamed through the area looking for deserters from the Chinese army who were trying to hide among the civilians.

The history of the invasion and the bloody aftermath has been told often and well. Eyewitness testimony and subsequent historical accounts reveal that, alongside the cruelty of many rank-and-file Japanese soldiers, there were many stories of bravery

Ha Jin (Jin Xuefei) was born and educated in Communist China; he migrated to the United States in 1989. He is the author of five collections of poetry, four collections of short fiction, six novels, and a volume of essays. He has won numerous literary awards, including the National Book Award and two PEN/Faulkner awards.

and of kindness. One figure often singled out for her indefatigable courage and energy is the American missionary Minnie Vautrin. She had been in China for two decades when the Japanese invaded the country. In December 1937, she was serving as a dean at Ginling Girls College, a school founded by American missionaries to educate young Chinese women in 1913. Vautrin turned the school grounds into a refugee camp and is credited with saving 10,000 people, almost all of them women and young girls. Sadly, the stress of the occupation took its toll on her, and in 1940, while on a furlough in the United States to receive medical attention, she committed suicide. Vautrin's story is documented in her personal diary and in Hua-ling Hu's *American Goddess at the Rape of Nanking: The Courage of Minnie Vautrin* (2000). While Ha Jin's novel also covers the story of Minnie Vautrin, it is much more besides.

On one level, Ha Jin presented a faithful portrait of Vautrin, staying close to the timeline Vautrin herself provides in her diary, and making use of nearly two dozen sources to verify historical details. The book is filled with historical characters who played a crucial role during the invasion, among them the Siemens executive (and self-proclaimed Nazi) John Rabe, German businessman Eduard Sperling, American clergyman John Magee, American professor Searle Bates, and American missionary Lewis Smythe. Their work on the International Committee of Safety helped meliorate some of the harsh conditions to which the Chinese (and foreigners) were subjected during the occupation. Also making a cameo appearance is Wu Yi-Fang, historically the first Chinese woman to become president of a college in China. The list could go on, of course, as Ha Jin wishes to root the greater emotional impact of his story in a strong sense of realism and loyalty to history. However, *Nanjing Requiem* is fiction, and its author takes some liberties in recreating accounts of the occupation, as well as Vautrin's role.

The novel opens just days before the Japanese invade Nanjing and covers the two-year period leading up to Minnie Vautrin's departure in early 1940. A brief epilogue describes the war trials held at the end of hostilities to bring to justice the Japanese officials responsible. After a day-by-day account of the Japanese invasion and seizure of the city, the narrative becomes for the most part episodic, relating Vautrin's efforts to keep her college open as a refugee camp for women and children, providing food and shelter, all while teaching women useful trades so they might make a living during and after the war. Vautrin divides her time between pleading with bureaucrats on both sides of the conflict for better treatment and fending off Japanese soldiers' attempts to enter the camp. One of the saddest and most frightening scenes involves Vautrin's negotiations with a senior Japanese officer who demands that she identify one hundred women as prostitutes so they may be taken away to a location easily accessible to soldiers. While she is vigorously defending the refugees, soldiers seize a dozen young women and spirit them out of the college. Six return later, broken and dispirited.

Further trouble is created by Mrs. Dennison, a fictionalized version of Matilda Calder Thurston, the founder of the real Ginling College, who was actually interned during the war. In *Nanjing Requiem*, Mrs. Dennison is in the United States raising funds for the college and attempting to direct activities from afar. When she returns to prepare the college for students again, she and Minnie engage in a test of wills between her rigid vision for the future of the institution and Minnie's concern for the thousands of refugees who still need assistance. Eventually, the never-ending series of conflicts eats away at Vautrin's psychological reserve until she suffers a mental breakdown and must return to the United States for treatment.

This tragic story is told by a first-person narrator, Gao Anling, a Chinese national who speaks fluent English. She is a trusted confidante of Minnie, Mrs. Dennison, and Dr. Wu. As such it is quite plausible that she would be privy to important discussions that Minnie and others have about the fate of the city and the refugee camp. She is not a major actor, however, and spends most of her time inside the college or traveling around the city in Minnie's company. Using Anling as his narrator allows Ha Jin to report on the atrocities that took place in Nanjing without having to provide gory details. Like a Greek tragedy, the bloodiest action occurs offstage, so to speak. Women come into the camp to seek refuge after their families have been assaulted. Passers-by tell Anling about what is happening, and she records somewhat dispassionately the numbers of people killed, raped, or otherwise brutalized by the conquering Japanese. While one might wonder how Anling appears unmoved by the scope of the tragedy, the technique allows readers to imagine for themselves what is happening all around the safe haven Minnie has created.

What Minnie and Anling hear is cause enough for despair. Thousands are killed, hundreds raped. Houses are destroyed, foodstuffs stolen. Women coming to the college say there is nothing left at their homes. Families are separated, and most men are rounded up and taken away by Japanese soldiers on the slight pretext that they are deserters from the Chinese army. Rumors of even worse atrocities reach the college, as Minnie and Anling learn that some of their former refugees have been sent to a camp in the northwest, where biological experiments involving germ warfare are being performed on live human subjects. These conversations reveal important facts not only about the surrounding events of the Nanjing Massacre, but also about Chinese responses to the crisis. Some act courageously, some prove to be cowards, and a few attempt to profit at the expense of fellow Chinese.

Because Anling looks up to Minnie, she is at times unable to realize the significance of what she sees or hears. Attentive readers will realize, however, that not everyone in Nanjing shares Anling's high opinion of the woman whom refugees have dubbed the Goddess of Mercy. Minnie's high profile makes her a target for both Chinese dissidents and Japanese propagandists who want to turn the people's ire on remaining foreigners. Hence, Anling is surprised when she learns that Minnie has been branded a Japanese collaborator and a traitor to the Chinese people. Perceptive readers will be able to pick up on the clues that make this revelation an expected outcome rather than a surprise. They will also notice in Anling's descriptions the subtle signs that Minnie is deteriorating emotionally and physically. Again, as in great tragedy, the end is inevitable and understandable, even if one wishes for another outcome.

Anling is a perfect narrator for other reasons as well. Through her family, Ha Jin is able to further expose some of problems facing the citizens of Nanjing after the city's capture. Her husband, Yaoping, a lecturer at Nanjing University, is educated and well respected in the community. Hence, when he chooses to flee the city rather than serve Japan's puppet government, one gets a glimpse of the hard choices some Chinese must make to save face and survive. Yaoping and Anling know that, when the Japanese leave, fellow citizens are sure to turn on those who collaborated with the enemy. Anling's daughter Liya is married to an intelligence officer in the Chinese army. He leaves the city with his unit, and Liya is left as a single parent to care for their son. Anling's son Haowen, a medical student, is completing his training in Japan, and for a long time the family has no idea how he is faring now that the Japanese are sworn enemies. Anling's anxiety for her son is replaced with dismay when she learns he has married a Japanese woman, and she fears that she will never see him again.

Nanjing Requiem is a tragedy in the classical sense of the word. It is historical, but it is more than history, as Ha Jin exercises the freedom to recreate emotions and heighten the tragic nature of events. The book is philosophical without being preachy, subtly raising questions about the nature of heroism and asking readers to contemplate the most basic tendencies of human nature: cruelty, kindness, and courage. It is a story that will haunt readers long after they have turned the last page.

Laurence W. Mazzeno

Review Sources

Booklist 107, no. 21 (July 1, 2011): 38.
Kirkus Reviews 79, no. 17 (September 1, 2011): 1517.
Library Journal 136, no. 13 (August 1, 2011): 84.
The New York Times Book Review, October 23, 2011, p. 23.
Publishers Weekly 258, no. 25 (June 20, 2011): 84.
The Wall Street Journal, October 15, 2011, p. C7
The Washington Post, October 24, 2011 (Web).

Never Say Die
The Myth and Marketing of the New Old Age

Author: Susan Jacoby (b. 1946)
Publisher: Pantheon Books (New York).
  352 pp. $27.95
Type of work: Current affairs, memoir
Time: Mid-twentieth to early twenty-first century
Locale: United States

A history of old age in the United States that challenges optimistic assumptions about aging, suggesting that only a new social contract can help prevent generational conflict as more baby boomers retire.

Principal personages:
SUSAN JACOBY, journalist, author, and public intellectual
IRMA JACOBY, her mother
ROBERT JACOBY, her father
EDWARD M. KENNEDY (1932–2009), US senator from Massachusetts, in office from 1962 to 2009
RICHARD A. MILLER, pathologist and gerontologist with the University of Michigan
BARACK OBAMA (b. 1961), the forty-fourth president of the United States
MICHELLE OBAMA (b. 1964), the first lady of the United States
WILLIAM OSLER (1849–1919), founding professor at the Johns Hopkins Hospital
RONALD REAGAN (1911–2004), the fortieth president of the United States

Susan Jacoby's depiction of the fate of the elderly in American culture is anything but comforting, but that is precisely her point. In *Never Say Die: The Myth and Marketing of the New Old Age*, she brings the same spirit of cultural critique and myth debunking that characterized her earlier books, such as *Freethinkers: A History of American Secularism* (2004) and *The Age of American Unreason* (2008). Here, she argues that for too many years, American baby boomers, the generation born in the fifteen years or so after World War II, have been harboring unrealistic expectations about what it means to grow old in the United States. As more and more baby boomers retire, they are likely to face the social, economic, and medical realities that make old age a far from pleasant time in the lives of many Americans. Any hope that old age can be postponed through the right combination of healthy living, effective drugs, and wondrous medical innovations is, Jacoby argues, a false hope. She especially challenges the misleading claims of those who push antiaging drugs and supposedly miraculous cures. She contends that the companies that make and market such drugs, as well as the journalists who often celebrate them, do a great disservice to those who are aging, misleading them about the kind of aging experience they can realistically expect. Combining personal memoir with cultural analysis and research, *Never Say Die* asserts that growing old in America is often a far from pretty experience.

Equal parts history, journalistic investigation, autobiography, and political polemic, Jacoby's book is very likely to interest older readers and those for whom aging is an immediate or relevant concern. Jacoby shows how the fates of different generations are inextricably linked and how the problems of the old are inevitably related to the problems, financial or otherwise, of the young and middle aged. As the baby boomer generation moves into retirement, the economic strain on an already strained healthcare system will become enormous, and although Jacoby has some suggestions of ways to alleviate such pressures, she is not at all sure that things will turn out well in the long run.

In the meantime, she has provided an extremely comprehensive look at the past, present, and possible future of aging in the United States. She argues that Americans have long resisted the idea of growing old and that youth culture is hardly a recent innovation, as aging has rarely been a pleasant thing to witness or experience. Throughout American history, only the very rich have been spared the worst financial, social, and medical pains of aging. Ironically, the problems faced by the elderly have become even more widespread with the increase in the average life span, usually considered a good thing. In the past, few people actually lived into their eighties or nineties, so the grim fates of many of the truly old were less common simply because they were less possible. Many baby boomers are likely to live at least that long and are therefore likely to endure much of the suffering and indignity that goes with old age. Jacoby, a baby boomer herself, is often critical of the mindless optimism of her generation, as well as of the mistakes her generation has made when preparing, or failing to prepare, for retirement. Reviewers have noted Jacoby's particularly negative criticisms of her generation's excessive pursuit of healthy lifestyles. As Jacoby argues, there is no way to turn back the clock on aging bodies and minds, regardless of what people might hope for, and likewise, there is no way for her generation to undo its mistakes. Jacoby insists that unpleasant facts have to be faced, not only by baby boomers, but also by the younger generation, for they are the ones who, if they are willing, may be responsible for footing the bill for those who preceded them.

Never Say Die is peppered with intriguing statistics and memorable factual assertions. Jacoby's sources are documented in endnotes and a bibliography, and an unusually thorough index makes the book a readily accessible compendium of highly useful if often depressing information. Yet it is not to be confused with a dry academic tome, as Jacoby's voice is lively and opinionated, and she draws on her own personal experiences with the elderly and the ill to make her book not just a sociological tract but a fairly personal memoir. She even calls attention to some of her own mistakes as a journalist, such as when she helped spread some of the misleadingly comforting claims about aging that she strongly repudiates here.

The specter of Alzheimer's disease hangs heavily over the book. Jacoby pulls no punches in describing the horrors of this particular condition, which afflicts not only the body but also the mind, destroying people long before they actually die and almost causing more pain to caregivers than to those who are afflicted. She warns readers that, regardless of the healthy lifestyles or medical regimens they may pursue, an increased likelihood of suffering Alzheimer's is an inevitable hazard of advanced age. Indeed, given the physical and neurological perils of old age, Jacoby argues that the morality of suicide deserves to be reconsidered.

Susan Jacoby is the author of nine books, including Freethinkers: A History of American Secularism *(2004),* The Age of American Unreason *(2008), and* Alger Hiss and the Battle for History *(2009). She writes the Spirited Atheist blog for the Washington Post. Her website is www.susanjacoby.com.*

Jacoby is open and frank regarding her own political bias, and accordingly, this is not the sort of book that conservatives are likely to take entirely seriously. Her comments about the Vietnam War and the ensuing holocaust in Cambodia will strike some readers as extremely simplistic, as will her depiction of the US economy in the 1970s and early 1980s (economic conditions, she notes, were bad under Gerald Ford and Richard Nixon and bad during Ronald Reagan's first term; however, Jimmy Carter's term, which resulted in Reagan's landslide victory, goes carefully and suspiciously unmentioned). She cites Jimmy Carter and Ted Kennedy as her inspiring ideals, persons who used their old age well. Henry Kissinger, of course, is the obvious counterexample. Thanks to people like Kissinger, Jacoby argues, one should never assume outright that wisdom automatically comes with old age. For conservative and libertarian readers, this claim might seem to apply to Jacoby herself, especially since she cannot seem to imagine feasible alternatives to the social programs she has long championed, programs that now seem difficult if not impossible to sustain. Medicare and Social Security, for example, will both face new challenges in the coming years as the elderly population grows.

When Jacoby deals with more recent political issues, her political biases are, once again, helpfully clear. Still, she does try to emphasize that both political parties, and ideologies on both ends of the spectrum, bear the responsibility for the existing problems as well as the absence of mutually agreed-upon solutions. Sometimes she states the obvious, like when she informs readers that the poor are more likely to favor social programs than the middle class and the rich, but at other times she expresses opinions that seem unexpected coming from a self-professed liberal. For instance, she objects to limiting the Medicare benefits of the wealthy, an option that even many conservatives support. She would also like to see the United States have the same kind of "social safety net that exists in every other developed country," but aside from the mention of benefits for the old and health insurance for the young, she does not explain how this option is actually possible, especially when most other developed countries are facing the same kind of budgetary woes as the United States, if not worse. Although Jacoby's focus is almost entirely and understandably on the US health-care system (after all, she is writing mainly for American readers), it would have been very helpful to know specifically which alternative models in which other countries Jacoby considers to be not only better but also ultimately sustainable. A quick survey of the various solutions offered by other American thinkers, encompassing ideas from liberals, conservatives, libertarians, and others, would also have strengthened the book's case. Jacoby, a skilled and lively writer, surely would have known how to present such a survey insightfully, without making it seem like a tedious C-SPAN episode.

Jacoby makes many strong points when discussing the numerous problems inherent in common American assumptions about aging, noting the social, ethical, and economic difficulties that would almost inevitably result if scientists ever did to manage to help people live well into their hundreds. She explores, for instance, the tendency to focus on highly expensive (and ultimately futile) treatments undertaken near the very end of life. Instead, she argues, there should be a focus on the kind of preventative medicine that might make aging less severe and less costly over longer periods. Still, she makes a reasonable argument that science is unlikely either to increase longevity or radically improve the health of the very old in the short term. The assumption that science can or will succeed in this regard involves an almost literal attempt to whistle past the graveyard. Jacoby's book is a sobering, sensible volume, one that young and old alike will ignore at their peril.

Robert C. Evans

Review Sources

The New Yorker 87, no. 4 (March 14, 2011): 30.
The New York Times Book Review, February 27, 2011, p. 18.
St. Petersburg Times, February 6, 2011, p. P1.
The Wall Street Journal, January 29, 2011, p. C5.
The Wall Street Journal, February 5, 2011, p. C4.
The Washington Post, February 6, 2011, p. B1.
Washington Times, March 18, 2011, p. B6.

The Night Circus

Author: Erin Morgenstern (b. 1979)
Publisher: Doubleday (New York). 387 pp.
$26.95
Type of work: Novel
Time: Late nineteenth and early twentieth centuries
Locale: primarily London, Paris, and New York

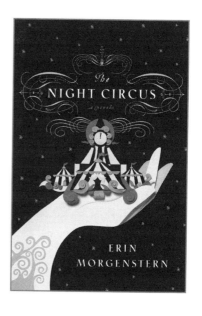

In this immersive debut novel about an intoxicatingly stylish circus and its performers, a talented pair of magicians-turned-lovers duel to the death in a competition of illusion and skill.

Principal characters:

CELIA BOWEN, known to her audiences as "the Illusionist," is a young, gifted, and beautiful magician

MARCO ALISDAIR, Bowen's studious competitor who manages the traveling circus from afar

CHANDRESH CHRISTOPHE LEFÉVRE, the circus's inventor and proprietor; Marco's boss

HECTOR BOWEN, known to his audiences as "Prospero the Enchanter," Celia's father and mentor

MR. A. H——, Marco's teacher and one of five founding circus collaborators

ETHAN BARRIS, a visionary architect and circus founder

TARA BURGESS, a circus founder who is killed when she inquires too deeply into the circus's magic

LAINIE BURGESS, Tara's sister and another circus founder, who pays great attention to detail

MADAME ANNA PADVA, a circus founder, an aging prima ballerina and skilled fashion designer

TSUKIKO, a former student of Mr. A. H—— and the circus's tattooed contortionist

ISOBEL MARTIN, the circus's tarot reader, who is in love with and dedicated to helping Marco

PENELOPE MURRAY, also known as POPPET, a seer born as the circus premieres

WINSTON MURRAY, also known as WIDGET, Penelope's twin brother, who can see the past

BAILEY CLARKE, a farm boy who befriends the Murray twins, saves the circus, and becomes its new proprietor

FRIEDRICK THIESSEN, a clock maker who creates the circus's iconic timepiece and becomes the leader of its most devoted fans, "the reveurs"

Like the best kind of party, dream, or fantasy, Erin Morgenstern's debut novel, *The Night Circus*, completely submerges the reader in its lush world of late Victoriana, placing readers squarely under the numerous big tops and tents of its Cirque des Rêves. Also like a good dream or a fantastic party, when one is surrounded by the fantasy, there seems little reason to question its logic or existence. One simply desires to keep the dream and the experience alive. Once one does emerge though, questions of function and content challenge the once seemingly perfect dream; likewise, *The Night Circus* struggles, once its final page has passed, to be more than a fantastically detailed, lovely experience.

Largely set in and around the major cities (London, Paris, Berlin, New York, and Boston) of the late nineteenth century Western world, *The Night Circus* follows two young, beautiful magicians, Celia Bowen and Marco Alisdair, who are in an ambiguous competition that could end only in death. After about a hundred pages that allude to this challenge, readers learn the characters' specific task is to use their powers to successively outdo each other in the augmentation and elaboration of the titular circus. This convenience of plot plays into Morgenstern's authorial hand, as the novel is largely more setting and imagery than plot, and this premise continues to produce plenty for Morgenstern to describe lavishly, from a labyrinth to an ice garden and a cloud maze.

Celia and Marco are the most recent in a long string of dueling pairs instructed by the magically ageless Hector Bowen and his equally timeless adversary, Mr. A. H——. Hector Bowen submits Celia, his own child, as his proxy, while Mr. A. H—— locates a suitable candidate in Marco, a young orphan he plucks up and trains in his image. The battle between Bowen and Mr. A. H—— through the centuries attempts to settle a pedagogical disagreement. Bowen dazzles audiences publically as a professional magician, "Prospero the Enchanter," and teaches Celia through direct experience and more hands-on tasks (such as slicing into her fingertips and breaking her wrists, then forcing her to heal herself), whereas Mr. A. H—— prefers a more shadowy mode of operation, both in teaching and in his personal life. Marco's education springs from constant independent study. He is a student of books, museums, linguistics, and history; his magic functions like a systematic language, and his spells are scrawled on the pages of journals, files, and ledgers. As Celia and Marco's respective educations draw to a close, Bowen and Mr. A. H—— manipulate an ambitious theatrical manager, Chandresh Christophe Lefévre, to create a suitable arena for their pupils, and thus the circus is born.

Lefévre gathers a conveniently ingenious coterie of collaborators: former ballerina and costume designer Madame Padva, architect Ethan Barris, and the Burgess sisters, Lainie and Tara, who envision a mysterious traveling circus that appears without warning, opens at dusk, and closes at dawn. Visitors wander at their leisure through an infinite structure of tents, where every spectacle comes in either black or white, from the snacks to the acrobats. The entire company, collaborators and performers, are bound to the circus by the magicians' spells. They never age or grow ill, but they also can never completely abandon the fateful project. Following in the footsteps of her father, Celia performs nightly as "The Illusionist," while Marco surreptitiously poses as Lefévre's assistant, manipulating the circus remotely from his office in London. As their illusions build and the circus and its members become all the more dependent on their manipulations, Marco and Celia resist their predetermined adversarial relationship and begin to collaborate. As their respective feats begin to intertwine, they

Erin Morgenstern studied theater and studio art at Smith College. She lives in Salem, Massachusetts. In addition to writing, she is a mixed-media artist and acrylic painter and has published a deck of tarot cards of her own design. The Night Circus, her first novel, was first drafted as part of National Novel Writing Month in November 2005.

(©Kelly Davidson)

cannot resist one another; thus, the already deadly relationship takes a romantic turn. In Celia and Marco, Morgenstern develops a precious theme of collaboration over competition, suggesting that the greatest beauty results from love and synergy, not hostility and opposition.

As the predictable master plot of the star-crossed magician-lovers develops, Morgenstern simultaneously lays the groundwork for a subplot that from its first moments alludes to an easy solution to an already too simple problem. It begins with the Murray twins, Poppet and Widget, who are born as the circus premieres, and quickly ropes in Bailey, a plucky Massachusetts farm boy who loves the circus from the moment he first visits as a young child. Years later, as a teenager at odds with his family and the future they can afford him (either as a Harvard student or as heir to the family orchard), Bailey indulges himself nightly with trips to the circus and quickly befriends the prescient Murray twins. As the Murrays predict the circus's approaching doom and as Celia and Marco's challenge begins to unravel, Poppet and Widget convince Bailey to join the circus and save them all from disaster. In a simple bit of magic, imparted by the endangered Marco and Celia, Bailey saves the circus in its moment of need and takes on its stewardship.

A classic fantasy, *The Night Circus* recycles the imagery and character tropes of everything from Roald Dahl's *Charlie and the Chocolate Factory* (1964) to J. K. Rowling's *Harry Potter* series (1997–2007). As in any indulgent fantasy, Morgenstern casts an expansive slew of characters and has clearly devoted time to calculating the rules of her surreal universe (and possibly devoted too much time to costume and set design). The border between reality and magic, a predictable theme for a fantasy novel, emerges quickly as a recurring contemplation. The book begins with an epigram from Oscar Wilde, and with its lightly gothic take on late nineteenth-century Europe, the novel continually reminds readers of Wilde's seductive *The Picture of Dorian Gray* (1890). In the towering fantasy shadow of Stephanie Meyer's *Twilight* (2005), the reader cannot help but be reminded of the electric romantic energy that defines Meyer's vampire lovers when Morgenstern begins to describe the literal sparks conjured by Marco and Celia's romance. Real-world inspiration seems to have come from the genre redefining, stylish, and narrative traveling performers of Cirque du Soleil, and Morgenstern specifically acknowledges the influence of the experimental theater group Punchdrunk in her afterword.

The Night Circus reads like a novel in some kind of literary identity crisis. Though it quotes Wilde, clothes everyone in black and white, and suggests not only the possibility of bodice-ripping but also life-threatening feats of magic, the narrative simultaneously skips along with plucky simplicity and ultimately delivers a conclusion and underdog hero of one-dimensional proportions more befitting an easily digested young-adult novel than an ambitious gothic thriller. It's unlikely that this is the aspiration of *The Night Circus*, but when a setting effortlessly outdoes both its characters and its plot, there seems to be little else *The Night Circus* ultimately can be but light, fun fare.

The experience of *The Night Circus*, from beginning to end, is typified by a sense of desire—a desire to be there, to smell the smells, to see the feats, and to taste the food. It is a desire, ultimately, to experience a plot, with twists and turns as elaborate as the costumes Morgenstern spends an exorbitant amount of time describing. Sadly, this desire goes unfulfilled: The bodice ripping never comes; the great burning romance readers are led to expect remains annoyingly lukewarm; and the young magicians, though certainly powerful, never imagine using their abilities for anything other than creating beautiful environments, technological conveniences, or simple stage-show tricks. Readers are left longing for Celia and Marco, with their dazzling wit and power, to turn on each other, at least for a bit, and then grandly unite and together turn on their exploitive, emotionally vacant guardians in a vengeance scenario that never transpires.

The Night Circus puts too much confidence in the circus as a consuming place in itself. Extending even to the syntactical level, readers are told repeatedly how enchanting and wonderful the circus is and about all the people who love and cherish it, but when it comes down to it, Morgenstern does not depict moments enchanting or memorable enough to warrant so many empty promises and baseless descriptions. Her characters are predictable, and her scenarios mechanical. *The Night Circus* requires too much set up and delivers hardly any great reveal. In the end, *The Night Circus*, though certainly a lovely and enjoyable read, does not satisfy the expectations it raises.

Grant Klarich Johnson

Review Sources

The Guardian, September 23, 2011, p. 15.
The New York Times Book Review, October 9, 2011, p. 25.
Publishers Weekly 258, no. 26 (June 27, 2011): 42–47.

Night Soul and Other Stories

Author: Joseph McElroy (b. 1930)
Publisher: Dalkey Archive (Champaign, IL).
296 pp. $14.95
Type of work: Short fiction

This is the first short story collection by a highly praised postmodernist author best known for his long, complex novels.

Since the adjectives that appear most frequently in reviews of Joseph McElroy's fiction are "radical," "avant-garde," "dense," "experimentalist," "erudite," "idiosyncratic," and "elliptical," and since the writers McElroy is often compared to are Thomas Pynchon, David Foster Wallace, Don DeLillo, William Gaddis, and Donald Barthelme, readers should be warned that when they pick up a book of his, it is not going to be an easy read. McElroy's best-known book is the twelve-hundred-page novel *Women and Men* (1987), which is reputed to be the greatest unreadable novel since James Joyce's *Finnegans Wake* (1939). However, for readers who McElroy has scared off in the past, this collection of twelve short stories, dating back to the early 1980s, might be just the primer they have been seeking. This is not to say that these stories are as transparent and accessible as those by Stephen King, but that in these stories McElroy encourages readers to make the extra effort, as he links his language to time-bound, spatially located persons and settings. After all, McElroy once remarked in an interview that rendering the difficulty of life means attending to experience and language carefully; accordingly, these stories match the difficulty of life with difficulty of prose. McElroy has said that this book represents his struggling flirtation with the short story, and his attempt to get at some reality that goes beyond language. Ever concerned with the writer's perennial problem—how to communicate something for which there are no words—McElroy is like Hemingway and Joyce in that he strives for one thing: "getting it right."

McElroy's fiction is so dependent on language that summaries are bound to be inadequate, if not misleading, but it is useful to begin with brief descriptions of the collection's relatively straightforward stories, as these may be the most accessible. For example, science-fiction fans will find familiar conventions in "The Last Disarmament but One," a doomsday-type story about a certain landlocked country that destroys itself, leaving a neat outline of the country's borders that preserves adjoining countries. However, this is not a simple cautionary tale about weapons of mass destruction. The fact that the missing country leaves a space that looks like its outline on a map is McElroy's way of emphasizing a notion that frequently appears in his fiction, that the relationship between maps and territory is not mimetic but purely formal.

"The Campaign Trail" is a political satire that places two characters that resemble 2008 presidential contenders Hillary Clinton and Barack Obama in the Canadian woods. Rather than mounting a simple criticism of the excesses of political campaigning, the story is more like a fantasy-riff on the idea of trails, exploring in a comic fashion the Wild West notion of American politics best characterized by the popular image of former Alaskan governor Sarah Palin posing with rifle in hand. Among the many erudite allusions in the story is a reference to Wallace Stevens's "Thirteen Ways of Looking at a Blackbird," a poem that suggests McElroy's broad philosophic perspective that reality itself is perspectival, a phenomenological projection of the perceiver.

"No Man's Land" is about a Muslim family in New York City being investigated by the US government for suspected terrorist activities in the aftermath of the September 11 terrorist attacks. The focus is on a friendship that develops between the family's nine-year-old son and an unemployed advertising professional and erstwhile poet. The story is less concerned with the political implications in American society after September 11 than the more general theme of displacement or nomadism, instigated by the poet's wife, the young boy's teacher, when she tells her students that everyone is a nomad. This diasporic theme of homelessness is linked to the poet's refrains of joblessness, as he finds himself lacking in purpose and identity until he accepts the "job" of identifying with the child and seeing what the boy is seeing.

Whereas "No Man's Land" is one of the most realistic stories in the collection, with its clearly identified characters and relatively simple plot, the title story and final piece in the book is a purely lyrical exploration of the challenge of communication, a central theme throughout these pieces. The central situation is clear enough: Awoken by his infant child, a man is compelled to try to understand the child, for he wants to know what the infant knows. While the nine-month-old child does not enunciate words or form sentences, the father wants to believe that his son is formulating a language of his own. The story explores the father's idealistic theory that the child knows things from the beginning of his life, things that the father, as an adult, has forgotten. Instead of training the child to imitate adult speech, the father wants to learn his son's unique language. However, since he utters during sleep, the language must spring from a source of unconsciousness and dreams rather than the consciousness of everyday life. The story poses the romantic notion that the child lives in a world in which it makes no distinctions between what he thinks and what he does, between himself and the world around him. The father wants to recapture this oneness for himself, for only when he achieves a state in which there is no separation between him and the child can he truly know what the child knows. McElroy has said that he is particularly proud of the story, as it seems emblematic of the problem all writers face of communicating something for which there are no words.

"Annals of Plagiary" begins with the narrator learning that a woman in the news has voiced a thought of his. He is astonished to read his own written words speaking to him from the newspaper page, expressing the view that the traces people leave in water are like their changing thoughts. However, at the end of the story, his wife tells him something she learned as a student from a Hindu spiritual text: water is always water, for the Ocean never changes. The man then realizes that he has obviously plagiarized the idea also, his discovery echoing the Borgesian idea that an identical phrase uttered at different times can be both the same phrase and a different phrase simultaneously. The story ends with the narrator insisting that what he has been narrating really happened, and that the account is his attempt to "get it right." For McElroy, however, the notion of getting something right does not necessarily have anything to do with fidelity to external reality. In this emblematic story, "getting it right" signifies finding the words that, like an incantation, can evoke or create the reality the author seeks.

(Peter Chin)

Joseph McElroy is the author of nine novels. He has received the American Academy of Arts and Letters Award in Literature, as well as fellowships from the National Endowment for the Arts and the Guggenheim, Rockefeller, and D. H. Lawrence foundations.

"The Man with the Bagful of Boomerangs in the Bois de Boulogne"—the shortest story in the collection and one of the earliest—is more an imaginative evocation than a tale, a *tour de force* in which a jaunt around Paris imitates the loop of the boomerang, sent on a journey that is meant to return to the beginning. Although the story begins with a visit to Paris, evoking the haunts of Hemingway and Fitzgerald, it soon becomes a poetic rhapsody about tracking the boomerang's trajectory, as it aims at some invisible destination from whence it begins a magical loop that brings it back to the beginning.

"Mister X," the longest story in the collection, and the most challenging due to its fractured syntax and structure, is about a famous architect's relationship with his friends and his ambiguous experience with an acupuncturist. As is typical in McElroy's novels, abrupt shifts in time pose challenges in following the action of the story. Thematically, it explores McElroy's fascination with the paradoxical properties of water, in this case a new form of water used as a building materials.

An unusual combination of the domestic and the experimental, "Character" plays on the fable of the city mouse versus country mouse, as a man recalls his boyhood in Vermont twenty-five years earlier, when he carved a model whaleboat out of a piece of maple found on the garage floor. The man recounts this to a woman on a job with him, but as the story progresses, McElroy moves back and forth between the past and the present without signaling the shifts, and as is often the case in McElroy's fiction, the two zones of time are blended. In a similar story, "Canoe Repair," the central character lives in the country on a lake and becomes obsessed with his neighbor's birch-bark canoe, a beautiful Native American objet d'art. The story shifts from first person to third person without warning, as if the central character is both observing and being observed at the same time.

In a famous essay on spatial form in literature, the critic Joseph Frank made the paradoxical statement that James Joyce's *Ulysses* (1922) could not be read the first time, only the second or third time. By this, Frank meant that the novel did not replicate a linear action, but rather created a spatial form in which the early parts of the novel could not be understood until one had read the entire novel and then started over again. Consequently, reading *Ulysses* is a challenge—not as great a challenge as reading his later *Finnegans Wake,* but a challenge nonetheless. Because Joyce is more concerned with the reality language creates than language's replication of action, readers have to attend to his work carefully, often to the extent of making their lips move as they read. The so-called unreadability of McElroy's fiction is due to a similar Joycean emphasis on language as a constructive dynamic device, rather than a mimetic one. The result is often such reading aggravations as a lack of transitions between paragraphs, a refusal to use quotation marks around dialogue, abrupt shifts from first person to third person, and unmarked leaps from past to present tense. Quite simply, McElroy demands that his readers take an active role in reading, making their own transitions, filling in holes where they appear, tolerating associative disruptions to chronology, and allowing that the concrete world stands aside for the dominance of thought and language. More than what characters do, McElroy is concerned with how characters think and communicate through language. The reader must be prepared to focus on words themselves, not the reality they take for granted.

Charles E. May

Review Sources

Booklist 107, no. 7 (December 1, 2010): 26.
Library Journal 136, no. 4 (March 1, 2011): 72.
The Literary Review 54, no. 3 (Spring 2011): 171–73.
Minneapolis Star Tribune, January 23, 2011, p. E13.
The New York Times Book Review, January 30, 2011, p. 9.
Publishers Weekly 257, no. 43 (November 1, 2010): 26.
The Wall Street Journal, March 26, 2011, p. C8.

Nod House

Author: Nathaniel Mackey (b. 1947)
Publisher: New Directions Books (New York).
160 pp. $15.95
Type of work: Poetry

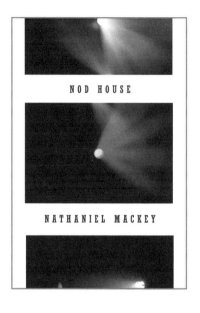

Lyric and rhythmic, the world described in Nod House *is a mythic version of our own, constantly in the process of change and reinvention. Continuing two serial poems from his previous collections,* Mackey *describes travelers, exiled from their home and wandering instead through a world of the dead, of dream states, and of music.*

Set primarily in or near a mythical land called "Quag," Nathaniel Mackey's *Nod House* continues the project that has occupied much of his writing over the past decades. In his previous collection, *Splay Anthem* (2006), the imaginary Republic of Nub came to an end, and the characters Mackey created were forced into exile. *Nod House* depicts them in their exile while also continuing Mackey's two serial poems, *"Mu"* and *Song of the Andoumboulou*, sections of which have appeared in almost all of his poetic writing. While there are narrative elements to these poems, including recurring characters and clear plotlines, *Nod House* is held together more by its stylistic and philosophical concerns than by any storyline or characterization. Mackey is a lyric poet able to write with intense beauty and music that are inseparable from the meaning of his poems. He is also known for mining a wide range of cultural and literary traditions, drawing freely from jazz music, Dogon mythology, and Bedouin poetic traditions, among many other sources. The result is less the particular story of Mackey's exiled people and more a musical elegy, a spiritual epic that probes some of the most important cultural concerns of the contemporary world.

The poems in *Nod House* can often stand on their own, sustained by their lyric qualities and musical engagement. The meaning and philosophy that Mackey explores can also be accessed through the individual works, even if that meaning can seem elusive after a first reading. However, a complete understanding of *Nod House* is found not simply through the poems in the collection but also through Mackey's previous books of poetry and his critical writing. It is in these books that readers first encounter the characters and the world that Mackey explores. For instance, his critical writing provides the best introduction to *Song of the Andoumboulou*, explaining that it is inspired by a traditional funeral song in the Dogon culture of West Africa. In his introduction to *Splay Anthem*, he writes, "the Andoumboulou are a failed, earlier form of human being in Dogon cosmogony . . ." although he sees them more as "a rough draft of human being, the work-in-progress that we continue to be." The song is a way to both recognize mortality and to celebrate spiritual rebirth. Earlier poems also give us greater context for understanding the *"Mu"* series, for the word *mu* could allude to any number of things, including the name of albums by jazz cornetist Don Cherry, the twelfth letter of the Greek alphabet, an island once thought to be in the Pacific Ocean, music, or *muthos*. It is not surprising, then, that scholars have devoted significant critical writing to Mackey's poetics, revealing the ways that jazz music, diverse cultural traditions, and multiple spiritualities are present in his texts. While many readers will miss these resonances and connections, the complexity of *Nod House* is not a reason to turn away from its poems. Instead, the evocative sense of sound and music combine with deeply felt emotions to create an immersive reading experience, one that can be explored even further by those who seek out Mackey's other writing.

Nod House opens with the poem "Sound and Somnolence—'Mu' fortieth part." In it, the exiled people are awakening, coming out of sleep to explore the world and their lives again. As is often the case in Mackey's work, the experience is tied explicitly to physicality and the sound of language; the awakening is likened to emerging from a pond. It opens:

> A light, floating slumber
> it seemed. Buoyant heads,
>   we lay like melons, the
>   pond our melon patch,
>   bobbed,
>   kept endlessly afloat . . .

Mackey is interested in liminal spaces, the experiences that cross boundaries and refuse to obey clear borders. In this opening poem, the people seem to experience death and rebirth simultaneously; they have lost their land and have been left to contemplate a new world while "kept endlessly afloat." There is both a loss of innocence and the promise of innocence, as "it / wasn't virgin earth we were on," yet there is still a "fairy tale yet to come true . . . Our / princess would come someday, soon come, / prophecy said as much." This seeming contradiction, where "World old and we / with it, new could we awake," is one of the defining modes of *Nod House*. There are many heritages of land, music, and culture, which have real effects on the modern world. Yet there is also the drive for something new and revolutionary, the potential for rebirth that is paradoxically rooted in the past. Mackey chronicles that process, finding in language the potential to transform ourselves in revelatory ways.

One of the primary ways that language operates in *Nod House* is similar to musical improvisation, especially evocative of jazz. Just as in the *Mu* album after which Mackey's series is named, he established rhythms and sounds in the poem, then repeated and played with them to see what else they could do. Rarely does a stanza go by without some sort of repetition or alliteration. In Mackey's opinion, sound play is

(© Christopher Felver/Corbis)

Nathaniel Mackey is a poet, editor, and prose writer. He has won several awards, including the National Book Award for Splay Anthem *(2006) and a Guggenheim Fellowship (2010). A professor at Duke University, he was elected to the board of chancellors of the Academy of American Poets in 2001.*

important for its own sake because "sound alone / survived," while everything else in the world was prone to death and finitude. The sound play and musicality also firmly link *Nod House* to free jazz, a musical genre from the twentieth century that is associated with revolutionary politics, especially those related to people of the African diaspora. Just as cornetist Don Cherry took the styles of jazz music and incorporated new techniques from Middle Eastern and African musical legacies, so too does Mackey take established language and play with it in new, surprising ways, informed by diverse cultural legacies. The effect is dizzying and sometimes disorienting, according to Mackey who declared, "We were there and somewhere else no / matter where we were, everywhere more / than where we were." In its story of the exiles, *Nod House* also chronicles the way people can take the language available and improvise, to see what else it can do in order to better understand experiences and find new ways to grow.

The exiled figures of *Nod House* are always in transit, both because they have been cut off from their home and because they are searching for a utopia that, according to their spirituality and culture, is their promised land. Large and mythic, like everything in Mackey's poetry, this exodus is also firmly tied to experiences of exile and migration in the real world. One of the most obvious links occurs in "Lone Coast Anacrusis—'Mu' fifty-third part" in which "Some new Atlantis known as / Lower Ninth we took leave of next." The Lower Ninth Ward is a neighborhood in New Orleans that was devastated by Hurricane Katrina, forcing out residents, many of whom were people of color. In "Lone Coast Anacrusis," the violence (political and physical) of Hurricane Katrina is one more example of "Endless letting go, endless looking / else- / where, endless turning out to be / otherwise." Tied, implicitly and explicitly, to histories of colonialism and slavery, the exile Mackey portrays is one that is filled with danger and risk. These dangers rise up again even after the promise of utopia is reinstated, or after the joy of survival and culture perseveres. This is the return to history that so often preoccupies *Nod House*. As the poem declares, we

were
them, they were there again, evacuated
we that we were . . . We were slaves or

possessed by slaves, the Alone the
indigenous ones . . . I wanted to break
free
but fell as I took a step, felt my knees
and hands hit the ground, I got back up

In the cyclical nature of *Nod House*, poems are not simply about exile, enslavement, or freedom. Instead, they are about the violence of exile and the glory and promise of something better, about falling down but also about getting up again. It is for
this reason that, even in the horrific reality of Hurricane Katrina, the people still "sang,
reprise / we broke / free from / again."

In this process of breaking free, of repetition and music, the people of *Nod House*
never quite achieve any sort of solution or conclusion. There is some sense of accomplishment reached by chronicling the exile, but even then they "wondered what
more to do but witness, / witness / nowhere near enough." There is also an undeniable
beauty in song, especially preserving the songs of your culture, but even that beauty
faces skepticism:

The one song
sang
song's inconsequence, crooned it
could not've been otherwise, song
song's own lament . . . The one
song sang song's irrelevance

The doubt, their "own lament," is an integral part of the experience of *Nod House*.
The search for beauty and meaning, for a utopian home, is a search that will never end.
The fact that it has no end, however, does not mean that the search itself is a failure.
The promised utopia "slipped /away and we slipped away and it slipped away, / Stick /
City a mirage nod concocted, not to be be- / lieved but we did though it receded." Even
places themselves are in constant motion and change, so by the end, the promised
"Quag had moved on and we moved / with it." This reality, the seeming hopelessness
that is sometimes present in the poems, is never an occasion to quit, however. Instead,
it is a further call for travel, for transformation, and for song, these redemptive forces
all the more necessary considering how unreachable utopia seems to be.

Critically, Mackey has a reputation as a poet who demands careful and sustained
attention from his readers. While *Nod House* certainly makes the demands that readers have learned to expect from him, it also offers a rich and transformative reading
experience, one well worth the investment of time. Rooted firmly in the past, richly
drawing from diverse and varied cultural histories, *Nod House* allows us to see our
own world and our contemporary concerns in a new light. He asks readers to consider
the journeys they are on, to see themselves honestly in the long march of history, and
ultimately to use that experience to understand one another. "They the two whose tale
no one / knew the whole of, the two we, two / by two, would eventually be, might /
eventually be," one poem declares, both asserting our interconnectivity and doubting

our ability to realize it. In telling a story unlike any other, through music and language that are strikingly and hauntingly unique, Mackey fills in one more piece of that "tale no one / knew the whole of."

T. Fleischmann

Review Source

Publishers Weekly 258, no. 43 (October 24, 2011).

No Regrets
The Life of Edith Piaf

Author: Carolyn Burke (b. 1941)
Publisher: Alfred A. Knopf (New York). 304 pp. $27.95
Type of work: Biography, history
Time: 1915–1963
Locale: Paris, France, and its environs; United States; parts of Europe

In this descriptive biography of the life of Édith Piaf, Burke chronicles the vocal artist's origins, meteoric career, and long struggles with cancer.

Principal personages:
ÉDITH PIAF, born ÉDITH GIOVANNA GASSION (1915–1963), French vocalist and lyricist
MARCELLIN "MARCEL" CERDAN (1916–1949), world middleweight boxing champion and Piaf's lover
YVES MONTAND (1921–1991), French singer, Piaf's most notable protégé and lover
CHARLES AZNAVOUR (b.1924), French Armenian singer and another of Piaf's protégé-lovers
MARGUERITE MONNOT (1903–1961), French composer and Piaf's most productive collaborator
SIMONE BERTEAUT, Piaf's friend and occasional performance partner
JEAN COCTEAU (1889–1963), French poet, playwright, and friend of Piaf
JACQUES PILLS (1906–1970), French songwriter and Piaf's first husband
THEOPHANIS LAMBOUKAS (1936–1970), Greek singer and Piaf's second husband

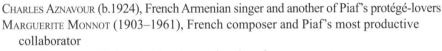

To put it in the mildest of terms, Édith Piaf was a most original personality. Her story is one of incredible, even painful, intensity, and she was one of those rare individuals who it seems could only be described in superlatives. Writing about Piaf, attempting to winnow the life from the legend, and avoiding being so dazzled by her achievements as to be blinded to the reality of her frenetic existence: These are tasks that would frustrate even the most skilled and impartial of biographers. Yet, with *No Regrets: The Life of Edith Piaf*, Carolyn Burke makes a highly competent foray into this daunting arena and can be said to have succeeded at least as well as, if not better than, anyone who has traveled this road yet.

Born in the Belleville sector of Paris on December 19, 1915, Édith Giovanna Gassion seemed destined, at face value, for an obscure life that would lead nowhere. Her mother, Annetta Giovanna Maillard (alias Line Marsa) was a freelance café singer whose family had come to France from Livorno, Italy, and her father, Louis Gassion,

was an itinerant acrobat afflicted with alcoholism. Their marriage was highly dysfunctional, the mother effectively abandoning her
daughter at the age of two, though later she
would reemerge to beg the now-famous Piaf
for money to feed her addictions and would
die of an overdose in 1945.

*Carolyn Burke, a former professor at
the Universities of California at Santa
Cruz and Davis, is the author of the biographies* Becoming Modern: The Life
of Mina Loy *(1996) and* Lee Miller: A
Life *(2005). Her work has appeared
in* Vogue *and* The New Yorker, *among
other magazines.*

One of the difficulties of tracking Piaf's
early life is the web of mythology that Piaf
deliberately wove in later years, perhaps exaggerating the obstacles she had to overcome
and thus making her rise from a difficult background seem all the more spectacular. The
author tries to cut through the layers of romanticizing to uncover the actual world in
which the young Édith lived. It is a daunting task, for Piaf was very intense (in this as
in other matters) in fostering her own personal legend, even to the point of embellish-
ment. The author sheds some doubt on Piaf's claims to having been born literally "on
the street," and similar claims about the timing of events relating to what Piaf described
as the miraculous curing of her blindness at the age of nine, which she attributed to the
intervention of Thérèse of Lisieux, her favorite saint. However, as Burke herself suc-
cinctly puts it, "her art and legend nourish each other," and untwining the strands of fact
and fiction may well be a battle that can never be won. The colorful portrait that Piaf
painted of her early years has become such an integral part of her persona, both in the
years following and long past her death, that one can never ignore it.

What seems quite certain is that after spending her early childhood in the care of
her grandmother, who ran a brothel at Bernay in Normandy, and after much time in
the company of the ladies who worked there, young Édith was "re-adopted" by her
father. He first took her on tour with the circus, then to live with him and a parade of
girlfriends in the tough working-class Paris *faubourg* of Belleville, where Édith had
been born. At Belleville, she would often perform for crowds in the street, augment-
ing her father's acrobatic stunts by singing "La Marseillaise" (and, according to her,
"L'Internationale"). During this time, she also sang *chansons realistes* depicting the
street life of Paris, largely through unrequited romantic themes, the latter forming the
dominant portion of her repertoire. She instantly gained recognition for her powerful
and expressive voice, which contrasted with her diminutive frame; she was only four
feet ten inches in height.

Leaving her father's home at the age of sixteen, Piaf embarked on her highly unconventional life as an independent songstress, teaming up with an even younger girl
named Simone Berteaut, who went by the nickname "Momone" and became her closest off and on comrade during much of her career. Piaf had her first serious sexual
liaison with a young delivery man named Louis Dupont and subsequently gave birth
to their daughter, Marcelle. The child died of meningitis two years later, by which time
Piaf and Dupont had long since drifted apart. She would have no other children.

While earning a hand-to-mouth existence and performing sporadically at the various bars, clubs, cabarets, and dives in the sleazy Pigalle district of Paris, Piaf was
noticed by entrepreneur and nightclub owner Louis Leplée, whom she credited with

giving her the break she needed and launching her into a high-profile career. It was Leplée who thought up her stage name, "La Môme Piaf" (the little sparrow), by which she would be known for the rest of her life. Leplée's potentially mob-related murder temporarily slowed Piaf's progress. In the aftermath of the murder, she was plunged into grief for the man who had been a second father to her, even finding herself grilled by the police as a suspect and excoriated as such in the tabloid press. However, the fashion in which she rebounded from the loss is indicative of the resilient spirit that would become one of her hallmarks. She would soon become an internationally re-nowned celebrity, as, from 1936–63, she entranced listeners, drove herself at a grueling pace, and shattered mores, amassing such a diverse group of lovers that the author admits to experiencing great difficulty in keeping track. This facility for acquiring and replacing the men in her life was augmented by her ability to glean skills and knowledge from some of her more mature *amants*, such as Raymond Asso and Henri Contet, both of whom also wrote songs for her. Conversely, she was also a mentor to many of her younger lovers, as in the cases of Yves Montand and Charles Aznavour, whose paths to stardom she facilitated. Piaf's most unusual and enduring relationship was with the poet-dramatist Jean Cocteau. Although Cocteau was homosexual, he was fas-cinated by Piaf, and the two maintained a deep friendship to the end; Cocteau himself died shortly after he heard the news of Piaf's demise. It was Cocteau who saw Piaf's potential as an actor, writing and offering her a role in his play *Le Bel Indifférent*.

Burke efficiently explodes the myth of Piaf's alleged cooperation with the German occupiers during World War II and instead presents compelling evidence regarding the extent of her defiance, as she worked behind the scenes to enable many targeted victims to escape from the Nazis. German authorities banned her from singing two of her most popular pieces, "Mon Légionnaire" and "Le Fanion de la Légion," deeming them to be unacceptably subversive. The postwar period saw Piaf's fame leap to even greater proportions: Her most memorable songs date from 1946–59. The most univer-sally admired of these, "La Vie en Rose," is, regrettably, given a rather summary treat-ment by the author. This is a curious omission, since the song was to become Piaf's signature tune and the title of the 2007 film on Piaf's life (released first in France as *La Môme*). Then there was "Hymne à l'amour," written for and dedicated to world middleweight boxing champion Marcel Cerdan, the only lover who Piaf continually acknowledged as being the supreme love of her life. Her liaison with the married Cer-dan came to an abrupt conclusion on October 28, 1949, when his flight to New York City, where he was scheduled for a return championship match with Jake La Motta, crashed near the Azores with no survivors. Burke somewhat cynically speculates that had Cerdan not suddenly died at the height of Piaf's passion for him, he too might have become nothing more than another of her amorous flings, rather than the object of her eternal love.

American audiences of the 1950s would have best known Piaf from her television appearances on *The Ed Sullivan Show*. Even though her health was obviously deterio-rating and her grueling pace was beginning to expose her problems, Piaf refused to slow down during this time, introducing two of her most enduring works, "Non, je ne regrette rien" and "Milord." Her love life was not neglected either; she married twice in the final years of her life, first to composer and singer Jacques Pills and next to the much younger hairstylist-turned-singer, Theophanis Lamboukas, to whom Piaf gave the stage name "Théo Sarapo." Though wracked by physical ailments and fading with each passing day, Piaf remained combative to the end and died peacefully on October 10, 1963.

Burke succeeds in illuminating some of the more obscure and little-understood elements of the Édith Piaf story. A case in point is her description and explanation of the *chansons realiste* tradition from which Piaf emerged and how she continued this rough-edged tradition, albeit honing it to a somewhat more refined format. Piaf's continuing legacy is dealt with in a concise but moving manner. That Burke holds degrees in English is made manifest in the consummate style of the book, its perfect narrative flow, and the clarity of its expression. The title is deliberately evocative, one would believe. Burke has chosen the English translation "No regrets" of Piaf's "Non, je ne regrette rien," as indicative of the woman she believes the French "sparrow" to have been—a fiercely independent and assertive woman who, rather than be dominated by the men in her life, insisted on meeting life on her own terms, and towered above and dominated those men in turn. Piaf made no apologies for her life and expected no pity from society. For the French, Piaf was the embodiment of their national situation: though battered by adversity, she never abandoned her jaunty combativeness in the face of the odds and always quested toward what was perhaps an unattainable standard of perfection.

Raymond Pierre Hylton

Review Sources

Columbia Magazine, September 2011 (Web).
New Republic, July 21, 2011 (Web).
The New York Times Book Review, March 25, 2011, p. 15.
Publishers Weekly, March 24, 2011 (Web).
San Francisco Chronicle, April 3, 2011 (Web).
The Telegraph, April 14, 2011 (Web).
The Washington Post, April 1, 2011 (Web).

Once Upon a River

Author: Bonnie Jo Campbell (b. 1962)
Publisher: W. W. Norton (New York). 348 pp.
$25.95
Type of work: Novel
Time: Late twentieth century
Locale: Rural Michigan

After her father's death, Margo Crane goes in search of her mother, setting off by herself on the Stark River.

Principal characters:
MARGO CRANE, a beautiful young girl
OLD MAN MURRAY, her grandfather
CRANE, her father
LUANNE CRANE, her mother, a depressive alcoholic
CAL MURRAY, her uncle, manager of Murray's Metal Fabricating Industries
MICHAEL, her lover

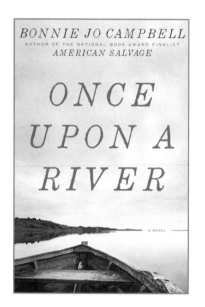

In Bonnie Jo Campbell's novel *Q Road* (2002), Rachel Crane lives outside of Kalamazoo in rural Michigan with her eccentric mother, Margo. When a local womanizer sets his sights on the young girl, Margo shoots him and disappears from her daughter's life. Rachel, in the end, marries the farmer on whose land she and her mother have always lived. In a kind of prequel, *Once Upon a River* tells the story of Margo Crane, from her earliest youth to her pregnancy with Rachel. Like her daughter, Margo is a determined individual who wishes to make her own way in a world defined both by the powerful currents of the Stark River and the pollution from Murray's Metal Fabricating Industries. The residents of the many towns adjoining the river have learned to survive in any way necessary, some setting up methamphetamine factories along the river. Likewise, the novel chronicles Margo's own grim education in survival.

Early in the novel, Margo represents the purity of the river and the unspoiled beauty of the woods surrounding it. Even when she must kill animals in order to survive, she is depicted not as an intruder despoiling nature for her own pleasure but as part of the natural order of life and death. Margo is so at one with nature that as she swims, she swallows minnows alive and feels the river move inside her. She knows the ways of the water and the woods so well that her grandfather calls her Sprite and River Nymph.

Margo's first great loss is her grandfather; after his death, the ground begins to shift imperceptibly beneath her feet, but he leaves her his greatest treasure, a teak boat called *The River Rose*, which provides her with a new freedom and the ability to explore new places along the river. Yet she can no longer hear his tales of the first inhabitants of the land, or why certain animals act the way they do in the wild. One day, after her grandfather's death, Margo witnesses a buck eating a dove and wishes her grandfather were still around to explain the deer's unusual action. She barely has time to mourn her loss, however, for in short order she loses both of her parents and finds herself alone. First, her mother, Luanne, a depressive alcoholic, decides she cannot live in the rural woods with her husband any longer, and Margo wakes one morning to find a goodbye note. While Margo does not understand why her mother has left, she realizes that she and her father are now left to survive together.

Margo once again experiences tragedy, this time at the hands of Cal, her uncle. At age fifteen, she is quite beautiful and a great huntress, always interested in learning how to shoot better, how to track more effectively, and how to skin animals more cleanly. When Cal sees her at a family picnic, he offers to take her hunting with him, and Margo jumps at the chance. Promising to show her how to skin a deer properly, he leads the girl to his shed, where he rapes her. Before Cal can get dressed, Margo's father crashes through the door and knocks Cal to the ground in anger. When Cal blames Margo for seducing him, Margo realizes that she has forever lost her uncle and her aunt Joanna, along with any promise of feeling like a part of the Murray family again.

At Thanksgiving, Margo is drawn back to the Murray place by memories of food, family, and love. At the same time, she knows her father will be unforgiving if she goes near the place. Unable to resist the sweet smell of cinnamon bread wafting across the river, Margo breaks the promise she made to her father and rows downstream, takes her rifle, and climbs stealthily into a tree near the house. When her father returns home and cannot find her, he knows where Margo has gone, and he drives madly to the Murrays' house. In the meantime, Cal walks into the yard to a place just beneath the tree to urinate. In an act of revenge, Margo shoots off the tip of Cal's penis, just as Margo's father comes charging into the yard, screaming for his daughter. In the resulting confusion, Billy, Cal's son, thinks that Margo's father has shot Cal and so he shoots and kills him. In a relatively short time, Margo has lost her closest family as well as her place in her extended family. While the Murrays then invite her to come live with them, she fiercely refuses, preferring to stay in her own house.

A few days later, having decided to go in search of her mother, Margo breaks into the Murrays' empty house and steals Cal's Marlin rifle and some cinnamon bread for the journey. She is more determined than ever to make her way in the world, to navigate the strong currents of the river and the rough waters of her life. As she rows her way upriver, she encounters several of the river's denizens, including Brian, a friend of her father's, who gives her shelter in his river house. She calls the house home for a while, becoming his lover and helper, until Brian, motivated by his dislike of Cal's management of Murray Metals as well as Cal's rape of Margo, assaults Cal and goes to jail. Margo continues to live in the house, unsure of her next move, until one day Paul, Brian's friend, appears with the makings of a meth lab. Margo remains in the house at first, but after Paul rapes her, she can no longer bear to stay there and moves in with Michael, whose house sits across the river. For once, Margo begins to feel settled, though she will never fully settle down until she finds her mother. However, her life with Michael comes to an end when she shoots and kills Paul, who has been threatening Michael's life. After disagreeing with Michael about what to do next, Margo slips away down the river, to a place near the Murrays', to figure out her future.

Although she tries to reconnect with the Murrays, meeting surreptitiously one afternoon with Joanna, she realizes that she can never again live with them because she will feel like a second-class citizen. Through a series of events, she loses her boat and, after a long journey by foot, ends up in a national park where she can camp, forage, pilfer, and survive until she figures out a way to reunite with her mother. During her stay, she meets a mysterious man who tells her he is an Indian whose family used to live in these parts.

(John Campbell)

Bonnie Jo Campbell is the author of three previous books of fiction, including American Salvage *(2009), a finalist for the National Book Award and the National Book Critics Circle Award. She was named a 2011 Guggenheim Fellow and has won numerous other awards. She teaches with the Pacific University low-residency MFA program.*

After making passionate love with her, however, the man abruptly departs, leaving Margo to deal with yet another loss. She soon discovers that she is pregnant and faces the decision of whether to keep or abort the baby.

Finally, Margo reunites with Luanne, though the reunion is short and bittersweet. Luanne marvels at her daughter's beauty and self-reliant spirit, but she is afraid to have Margo in her house, having told her new husband that she has never been married before. Margo learns that her mother really left because she was having an affair with Cal, and Joanna had discovered this and warned Luanne to get out of town or else. Luanne drops off her daughter at a local abortion clinic, promising to return soon to help her fill out the paperwork, but Margo steals away and sets out on her own once again.

Many critics have compared *Once Upon a River* to Mark Twain's *Adventures of Huckleberry Finn* (1884), since Margo's journey, like Huck's, is a dramatic American odyssey, a quintessential coming-of-age story that unfolds along a winding river fraught with peril and promise. As with Huck, Margo is shaped by the bends and shoals of the river, and she learns quickly to embrace and trust its deep, timeless wisdom. Margo's young life is marked by loss, but the healing power of the river itself soothes her losses and leads her to the next stop in life. In one of the novel's final scenes, a pregnant Margo slips easily into the river, allowing the current to carry her along as she floats in the cleansing and refreshing waters. Much like the fetus swimming in Margo's womb, Margo swims in the river's life-giving and protective waters. She is healed and at one with nature.

Campbell marvelously creates a lush, vibrant world and a young protagonist for whom readers will feel compassion and sympathy. The woods that Margo inhabits are full of animals and plants that she can shoot or pluck in order to survive, and she demonstrates a Thoreau-like quality in her solitary lifestyle. Although she regrets killing animals unnecessarily, her abilities as a sharpshooter enable her to eat meat whenever she wants. When she accidentally shoots and kills a pregnant deer, Margo feels that she has violated the spirit of nature. This incident stays with her and illustrates for her the disorder and discord that humans can bring to the natural order. Margo resolves to be more carefully attuned to nature, and her refusal to abort her child reflects her final resolve to connect to a being beyond herself, physically and spiritually. By the end of the novel, Margo has grown from a young, independent woman, out to discover herself and thinking only of her own survival, to a caring mother-to-be, still fiercely independent and preparing for her child's birth into a beautiful and cruel world.

Henry L. Carrigan Jr.

Review Sources

Booklist 107, no. 14 (March 15, 2011): 20.
Library Journal 136, no. 6 (April 1, 2011): 78.
Ms. 21, no. 3 (Summer 2011): 55–6.
The New Yorker 87, no. 22 (August 1, 2011): 69.
The New York Times Book Review, July 24, 2011, p. 11.
Poets & Writers 39, no. 4 (July/August 2011): 34–9.
Publishers Weekly 258, no. 11 (March 14, 2011): 46.

On China

Author: Henry Kissinger (b. 1923)
Publisher: Penguin (New York). Illustrated.
608 pp. $36.00
Type of work: Current affairs, history, memoir
Time: 1950 to the present
Locale: China

A key figure in US-Chinese diplomacy recounts his experience and attempts to elucidate the underlying principles of China's foreign policy in the twenty-first century.

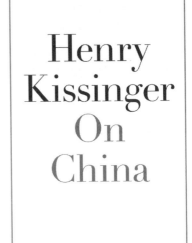

Principal personages:

HENRY KISSINGER (b. 1923), US secretary of state under Presidents Nixon and Ford

HARRY S. TRUMAN (1884–1972), thirty-third US president

RICHARD NIXON (1913–1994), thirty-seventh US president

GERALD FORD (1913–2006), thirty-eighth US president

MAO ZEDONG (1893–1976), first chairman of the Chinese Communist Party (CCP) and the People's Republic of China, architect of the Great Leap Forward and the Cultural Revolution

ZHOU ENLAI (1898–1976), first premier and foreign secretary of the People's Republic of China

DENG XIAOPING (1904–1997), paramount leader of the People's Republic of China from 1978 to 1992

HU YAOBANG (1915–1989), third chairman of the CCP, dismissed as general secretary in 1987 for failing to crack down on student protesters

JIANG ZEMIN (b. 1926), eighth general secretary of the CCP and fifth president of the People's Republic of China

HU JINTAO (b. 1942), ninth general secretary of the CCP and sixth president of the People's Republic of China

DOUGLAS MACARTHUR (1880–1964), general in the US Army

Former US secretary of state Henry Kissinger leaves his book *On China* without a subtitle, giving the reader almost no immediate indication of what it will cover or even of its genre. In fact, the book turns out to be something of a mix: part memoir, part history, part current affairs, part self-defense. After a brief historical overview, Kissinger plunges into his topic with the advent of the People's Republic of China. He then describes the famous meetings between President Richard Nixon and Chairman Mao Zedong that established de facto relationships between the Communist regime and the

United States. Kissinger, of course, played a pivotal role in these negotiations, and he writes about meetings that he had with the Chinese leadership, both official and unofficial. In all, Kissinger made some fifty trips to China. He concludes the book by trying to forecast the nature of the continuing relationship between the two superpowers.

On China is not a history per se, but Kissinger clearly believes that understanding China's past is the key to comprehending its present and making predictions about its future. In his first three chapters, he delves into Chinese attitudes toward diplomacy, strategy, and negotiation. He examines how these attitudes have developed over time, how they have become entrenched in the Chinese psyche, and how they differ from attitudes developed in the West.

Kissinger uses the Chinese game of *wei qi* to illustrate the differences between Chinese and Western statecraft. The goal of the game is to contain and surround your opponent while expanding your own territory. Kissinger contrasts *wei qi* with the "Western" game of chess, which concentrates on confrontation, elimination, and ultimate defeat. In fact, chess comes from South Asia, but nevertheless, Kissinger's point is that historically, China saw itself as the Middle Kingdom, surrounded by lesser powers that sought to contain it. China's strategy was not to conquer these powers but to contain them in turn.

Kissinger analyzes the influence of Confucius (551–479 BCE) within Chinese culture. Confucius was a Chinese government official and philosopher whose teachings evolved into the school of philosophy known as Confucianism. Essentially practical rather than mystical or spiritual, Confucianism extols balance and order and reveres hierarchy, wise men, and scholars. Kissinger contends that foreign diplomats must understand Confucianism as much as Marxism to interact successfully with Chinese leaders, whom Kissinger portrays as modern mandarins.

He also explores how Chinese nationalism hindered China's entry into the global community. He observed that the Chinese officials with whom he met often held and acted in accordance with the following nationalist beliefs: that Chinese civilization is far superior to those of the barbarian nations surrounding it; that China should always be self-sufficient and self-reliant; and that, in times of weakness, the government should adopt strategies that fool the enemy into thinking China is strong. Kissinger makes the case that only as the twentieth century drew to a close did such nationalism weaken enough for China to take its place in the international order.

Throughout the opening chapters, Kissinger expresses his admiration for politicians, Chinese or otherwise, whose politics are based on practical factors rather than theories or ethical goals. He quotes the German chancellor Otto von Bismarck (1815–98), as well as Chinese emperors who have often treated their country's inhabitants dreadfully in the name of strengthening the nation. By invoking these practitioners of realpolitik, Kissinger lays the framework for his sympathetic treatment of Mao's policy of continuous revolution and also reveals his own pragmatic stance, which proved controversial when he was secretary of state.

In the next seven chapters, Kissinger examines the establishment of China's ties with the United States during the Korean War crisis, the subsequent fallout, and the rapprochement of China and the United States in the light of Soviet hegemony. Kissinger

Henry Kissinger has served as US secretary of state (1973–77) and as national security advisor (1969–73). He has received many honors, including the 1973 Nobel Peace Prize, the 1977 Presidential Medal of Freedom, and the 1986 Medal of Liberty.

was deeply involved in the sometimes secret, always sensitive relations between the two nations during this time, and his insights about the relationship are therefore unique, although whether he has been completely forthcoming may perhaps never be known.

Kissinger makes assumptions about his audience's knowledge and understanding of the Korean War that may tax some readers. Those who do have in-depth knowledge of the war may be surprised by Kissinger's assertion that China had intended to invade Korea to help the North Korean aggressors even before the United Nations forces landed behind enemy lines or pushed across the thirty-eighth parallel. Such claims may cause historians to reevaluate General Douglas MacArthur's push to expand the war against the Chinese as well as President Harry S. Truman's desire to limit the conflict.

As Kissinger points out, the Korean War presented just one of many hurdles that China and the United States had to overcome in order to reopen diplomatic relations. Problems also rose concerning the Republic of China, which was established in 1946 by Chinese Nationalists who had fled to the island of Taiwan in 1949 when Communists took control of the mainland. Both Communist and Nationalist governments claimed to be the one and only China. The United States, with its anticommunist policies, sided with the Nationalists and was prepared to help defend them against possible Communist incursions.

The Soviet Union had also impeded closer ties between China and the United States. However, as secretary of state and special advisor to Richard Nixon, Kissinger was able to persuade China that the Soviet threat was far greater than the American one. China had been weakened by Mao's continuous revolution policy as enacted in the Great Leap Forward and the Cultural Revolution, and a rift was forming between the Chinese and the Soviets. It was a timely moment, and Kissinger and Nixon took the opportunity to extend offers of peace and understanding.

Kissinger describes in great detail the meetings he had with Mao and his prime minister, Zhou Enlai, during this time. He came to greatly admire them and felt that he had won their confidence in return. Kissinger also appreciated their successors: Deng Xiaoping, Hu Yaobang, and Jiang Zemin. They were the men who survived the disastrous Cultural Revolution and went on to succeed in politics.

The third part of the book focuses on Kissinger's dealings with these successors. The watershed for Kissinger was 1976, the year in which both Mao and Zhou died; the Ford presidency was coming to an end, and with it Kissinger's official standing in government. This section is less detailed and cohesive than the previous parts, as Kissinger's connections became more informal and infrequent. He is generous to subsequent American presidents and secretaries of state, but also appears impatient with President Carter, President Clinton, and others who made human rights issues central to US foreign policy.

In the last chapter, Kissinger makes predictions about the likely course US-Chinese relations will take in the decades to come. In the twenty-first century, the Soviet threat no longer exists as it did during the Cold War. Furthermore, with the enormous growth of China's gross domestic product (GDP) over the last two decades, the nation could reclaim its centrality in Asia or even its superiority. However, to do so would be to cut itself off from the international community. Kissinger suggests that it is within the interests of both China and the United States to pursue what he calls "co-evolution," in which they would regard each other as Pacific powers and therefore both essential for their mutual welfare and progress.

Although this is a lengthy book, there are obvious omissions. Kissinger includes very few hard facts and figures, especially concerning China's demographic and economic growth and its military strength. Without such data, readers may find it difficult to place Kissinger's account in context and weigh the merits of his opinions.

Kissinger also neglects any mention of Hong Kong's return to Chinese rule in 1997 after being leased to the British for ninety-nine years. As a British colony, it lay outside the purview of US policy toward China, but its economic success helped convince the Chinese to set up Special Administrative Regions. The publishers include a photograph of Sir Christopher Patten, the last British governor of Hong Kong, receiving the British flag as it was lowered for the last time, but no text accompanies the picture. Given that one of Kissinger's main points is that the Chinese can be trusted, his decision not to comment on the handover and China's subsequent preservation of Hong Kong's democratic institutions, albeit in circumscribed form, may seem odd to some readers.

Perhaps the most contentious omission is Kissinger's decision to abstain from a critical examination of China's human rights violations as a threat to future diplomatic relations between the United States and China. In his view, such issues should remain immune from outside interference. For example, he considers Tibet a territory that historically has always been Chinese, and is therefore an internal matter beyond the scope of international intervention. He does not mention China's treatment of Falun Gong or the Christian house church movement, though both are of great interest to many Americans. Even the Tiananmen Square massacre is downplayed and reframed; although Kissinger condemns it, he does so because it was an "overreaction" and claims that the Chinese leadership had been making great reforms when things got out of hand.

The public reception of *On China* has been mixed and therefore very much in line with how Kissinger has historically been perceived. His account, with its exoneration of the violent excesses perpetrated by the Chinese leadership on its own citizens, may confirm or even intensify the views of those who already abhor his realpolitik. At the same time, the book resonates with those who admire China's economic reforms and Beijing's rise as a bright Olympic city in 2008.

Perhaps the only thing beyond dispute is the extraordinary length and depth of Kissinger's involvement with China, his commitment to understanding the thinking and policies of its leaders, and the many patient hours he expended on diplomacy. *On China* represents a distillation of these qualities and achievements, even if Kissinger's wisdom is balanced by his desire to leave a good account of himself to posterity.

David Barratt

Review Sources

Maclean's, May 30, 2011 (Web).
The New York Times, May 9, 2011 (Web).
The New York Times Book Review, May 13, 2011 (Web).
The Wall Street Journal, May 21, 2011, p. A13.

One Day I Will Write about This Place

Author: Binyavanga Wainaina (b. 1971)
Publisher: Graywolf (Minneapolis). 272 pp. $24.00
Type of work: Memoir
Time: The 1970s to the present
Locale: Kenya, South Africa, and various other locales in Africa

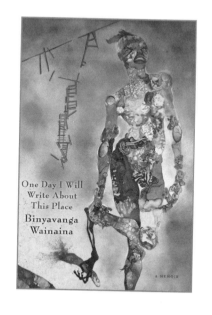

In this memoir, the author uses strong, descriptive language to depict a diverse Kenya, recounting his experiences inside and outside of his country as the political landscape in postcolonial Africa rapidly shifts.

In *One Day I Will Write about This Place*, Binyavanga Wainaina uses his acute powers of observation to transform places into evocative prose, inviting his readers into a memoir that depicts the true complexities of Africa—away from clichéd sunsets on savannahs, away from persistent stereotypes of starved and warring Africans, and away from all that is romantic and unparticular. Wainaina's Africa, which is not a country but a continent, is a dynamic and challenging place, and he uses this memoir in part to find his place in it. Using descriptive language that brings his homeland to life, Wainaina tells a compelling coming-of-age story in which Africa is as much of a presence as the author himself.

In 2005, *Granta,* an international magazine for new writing, published Wainaina's essay "How to Write about Africa," in which he caustically inventories the perennially stereotyped characters, settings, and stories that inhabit the great bulk of published writing about Africa. *One Day I Will Write about This Place* reads as the author's concerted, and successful, effort to transcend those stereotypes by contextualizing them within fresh new images of African places. More than simply a memoir of one individual's life experience, the book is a sequence of luminous illustrations of particular landscapes: urban and rural settings in Kenya, South Africa, Uganda, Ghana, and Togo, inside family homes and boardinghouses, in small-town bars and the streets of frenzied cities.

The memoir begins with Wainaina's early years in Nakuru, capital of the Rift Valley province of Kenya, and follows him through a series of boarding schools across Kenya to a stunted college career in Transkei, South Africa. In one of the book's most scintillating highlights, Wainaina returns to his mother's hometown in Uganda for an emotional family reunion. It is Wainaina's written account of his transformative trip, the short story "Discovering Home," that won him the coveted Caine Prize for African Writing in 2002. This award, given annually for the best original short story by

(Jerry Riley)

Binyavanga Wainaina is a Kenyan author and journalist. He won the Caine Prize for African Writing in 2002 and is the founding editor of Kwani? *literary magazine.* One Day I Will Write about This Place *is his first book.*

an African writer, launched a writing career that transported the newly recognized author to cities and countries throughout Africa and overseas. In the book, each of these locales is treated to Wainaina's conscientious writing about place.

For this author, and for an emergent body of theory, place is experienced space, a lived process in which those inhabiting a space make and remake it. The places of *One Day I Will Write about This Place* are depicted as lived social experiences, layered with specific objects, actions, and conversations, inhabited by beings whose identities shift against a perpetually changing political backdrop. Often, Wainaina illustrates these places through indexes of African cultural artifacts—not the exotic, traditional, or tribal, but the smells, tastes, and sounds, the products and the peddlers, the clothing and hairstyles of everyday life. Wainaina pays attention to trends and social norms; "There are things men are supposed to know . . . to belong," he writes, noting the importance of "secular things to hang on to." These are the objects that populate this author's memory, things that, when arranged next to each other, represent a place.

One of the pivotal scenes of the book revolves around a specific object, namely a painting hung in Wainaina's childhood home. As he describes the experience of returning home after several years away at college in South Africa, Wainaina recounts his changing relationship with a painting of a Nandi woman that has hung over the mantel all of his life. As a small child, he was terrified of this woman in traditional costume, with "rings on her ankles and bells on her nose." As a teenager, "set alight by the poems of Senghor and Okot p'Bitek, the Nandi woman became my Tigritude." He moved the painting to his bedroom, where he did not desire her but rather admired her with a kind of dread. When his mother moved the piece back to the mantel, he felt filled "with a fake nostalgia that was exactly what I felt I should be feeling because a lot of poetry-loving black people seemed to be spontaneously feeling this." It is not until he has spent several years away from the painting, living in an entirely different context in South Africa, that he can see the Nandi woman in a new light: as the "African Mona Lisa," wearing a smile like that of a private school girl, an impossible expression on a Nandi woman. In this one crucial object, Wainaina describes not only the paradoxes of Africa but also the contradictions in himself.

Wainaina's Africa is not the monolithic "country" of some popular Western conceptions, but rather a fragmented complex of histories, imagining and reimagining itself after the departure of its colonizers. In fact, it is contradiction itself that defines postcolonial Kenya, Wainaina writes:

> If there is a courtesy every Kenyan practices, it is that we don't question each other's contradictions; we all have them, and destroying someone's face is sacrilege . . . We know we sit on top of a rotting edifice; we are terrified of questioning anything deeply. There is nothing wrong with being what you are not in Kenya; just be it successfully.

Wainaina notices and names these contradictions early in the book and even early in his life. He was seven years old in 1978 when Kenya's President Jomo Kenyatta died. As he watched the televised memorial, he saw the diverse peoples of Kenya singing and dancing together to the music of the *nyatiti*, a traditional Luo musical instrument. He noticed that their music did not fit to the major scale he was taught in school but rather was "gibberish . . . many unrelated sounds and languages and styles and costumes, and facial expressions." He invents a word for this mix, *kimay*, to describe the confusion.

Two themes related to *kimay* appear throughout the book: music and language. The rhythm of *One Day I Will Write about This Place* is accompanied by a virtual soundtrack: Kenyan *nyatiti* music and Michael Jackson, Lionel Richie's love songs and Congolese rumba, South Africa's Mango Groove and *kwaito* house music. South African singer Brenda Fassie plays a starring role as the "Queen of African Pop," making more than one comeback after struggles with drugs. "What is up with Brenda Fassie?" asks Wainaina. "Why can't she stay dead? We have pounded her right into toothless history. We laugh and gossip-column her." More than the tribal woman of Wainaina's painting, or alongside her, Brenda Fassie is Africa, beaten down and rising back up again to record her great comeback hit, "Vulindlela," the "first real crossover song in a new South Africa." The song makes politics "disappear for a moment, as the first ten seconds of the song turns us all into mush." The song has not one word of English, but it has the power to unify the multicolored threads of Africa for one tender moment. The sound is *kimay.*

Wainaina also reflects on his increasing awareness of language and the remarkably diverse linguistic landscape of Kenya. Wainaina himself speaks both English and Kiswahili, the language of his ethnic group is Kikuyu, and the peoples of Kenya speak a total of sixty-nine languages. For young Wainaina, this cacophony of voices brings about feelings of anxiety and uncertainty. Much of his memoir is dedicated to observations about language—words and phrases, accents, and styles of speaking. In the negotiation of language and social interaction lies the author's crucial understanding of African identities. In another significant scene, Wainaina is flying by airplane to Lamu, a coastal town in Kenya, and he is seated next to a white man wearing an African shirt. The man speaks to him in "clean and elaborate" Kiswahili, while Wainaina speaks an imperfect version of Kiswahili. Between them, he feels that something is not quite right, but it is not jealousy:

> It is that he has got it all wrong. His accent is perfect; his tone, rhythm, everything. His timing is wrong. In this country, with its many languages, classes, and registers, much is

said by what is not said. There are many ways to address someone: sometimes you shift quickly into English; often you speak in a mock Kiswahili, in an ironical tone, simply to indicate that you are not dogmatic about language, that you are quite happy to shift around and find the bandwidth of the person to whom you are speaking.

This passage is about inhabiting language, as opposed to using it as a tool to perfection. The modern, postcolonial African—the *kimay* African—navigates Africa's landscape by switching, shifting, and adapting to various circumstances. Wainaina returns to the concept of *kimay* in the final breath of the book, to the music of the *nyatiti*, whose "job [it] is to follow the words, the intonation, the language and melody of the song, to maintain the integrity of the story." The music is not about the instrument; it is about the singer. "*Kimay* is people talking without words, exact languages, the guitar sounds of all of Kenya speaking Kenya's languages." Wainaina's book is extraordinary because it is not just written in English. With its original metaphors and heterogeneous references, it is written in *kimay*, the dissonant postmodern language of Africa.

Critics have lauded *One Day I Will Write about This Place* for its exuberant descriptions and astute storytelling. This fascinating memoir effectively tells the story of one individual's growth from boy into man and how he was shaped by the culture and changing conditions of Africa. Although some critics have noted that Wainaina's voice is inconsistent at times and that the memoir lacks a theme, most agree that it is a powerful, vibrant, and memorable work about a man and his home.

Amira Hanafi

Review Sources

Bookforum, July 22, 2011 (Web).
The Economist 399, no. 8742 (July 16, 2011): 86–87.
Kirkus Reviews 79, no. 8 (April 15, 2011): 17.
The New York Times Book Review, August 21, 2011, p. 30.

One Hundred Names For Love
A Stroke, a Marriage, and the Language of Healing

Author: Diane Ackerman (b. 1948)
Publisher: W.W. Norton (New York). 322 pp.
$26.95; paperback $15.95
Type of work: Memoir
Time: 2004 to the present
Locale: Ithaca, New York

Ackerman presents an account of her husband's stroke, its devastating aftermath, and her efforts to help him heal.

Principal personages:
DIANE ACKERMAN (b. 1948), a poet and naturalist
PAUL WEST (b. 1930), her husband, a novelist, poet, and critic
KELLY, his speech therapist
DR. OLIVER SACHS (b. 1933), a famed neurologist and psychologist

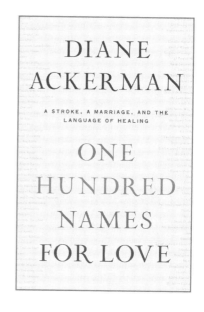

In spring 2004, writer Paul West spent three weeks in the hospital with kidney stones and a staphylococcal infection. On the eve of his release, with the promise of a return to his normal routine, West suffered a devastating stroke that damaged the area of his brain associated with key language functions. The result was global aphasia, a condition in which the stricken have difficulty processing and using language. In West's case, once he regained consciousness, all he could utter was a single unintelligible syllable, "Mem," over and over again. In *One Hundred Names for Love: A Stroke, a Marriage, and the Language of Healing*, Diane Ackerman narrates with striking beauty and warmth the ways in which both her and her husband's lives were forever changed.

As if the aphasia were not debilitating enough, West loses some of his finer motor skills. Combing his hair, turning on a faucet, and sitting on a toilet have become difficult, disorienting exertions. He is further afflicted with paralyzed muscles in his writing hand, contracting his fingers into a permanent claw. As the initial days pass, Ackerman realizes that her husband cannot read the newspaper or hold a spoon to feed himself, and that his slack jaw will not allow him to chew and swallow food or liquids. West, however, is fully aware, frustrated by his lack of coordination and inability to complete the simplest of tasks.

After six long and arduous weeks, West is allowed to return home, but his convalescence is hardly smooth. He can no longer use a telephone, write checks, or operate a stove. Friends disappear, and his struggles with language continue, as old pleasures such as writing and swimming are replaced with rounds of doctors' visits and speech therapy. West works with five speech therapists, but none of their therapies produces any success.

West's condition, his weakness and vulnerability, pose counterpoints to his earlier life. He grew up in a tiny Derbyshire mining village in northern England, and as a boy he was an avid cricket player and devotee of anything having to do with aeronautics. He had a precocious infatuation with language, learning French, Latin, and Greek by the end of high school. He later distinguished himself at the university level, attending both Oxford and Columbia for postgraduate degrees. He served his Royal Air Force (RAF) duty teaching a host of classes and then spent over thirty years teaching at the University of Pennsylvania, publishing fifty-one books ranging from poetry and novels to literary criticism and memoirs. For his facility with language to be suddenly wrested from him is thus particularly devastating.

After a visit from the renowned neurologist Oliver Sachs, Ackerman is advised to ignore the common wisdom that brains cannot recover from so much devastation. "I knew from my studies that what we used to think about the brain—that it's immutable and we're born with all the brain cells we'll ever have—was wrong. Brains are surprisingly resourceful, they can adapt and grow, forge new neural pathways, redirect signals, and sometimes even mint a handful of fresh neurons." Realizing that West is being starved of the stimulation he needs, Ackerman and his nurse embark on their own solution: "*Enrich your lab rat's environment if you want him to thrive.* To that end, Liz and I engaged Paul in 'conversation therapy' nonstop."

Diane Ackerman is a poet, naturalist, and author of twenty-one books for adults and three books for children. Her book A Natural History of the Senses *(1990) inspired PBS's five-part Nova series* Mysteries of the Senses. *She is the recipient of various awards, including a Literary Lion from the New York Public Library.*

On the surface the situation may seem reminiscent of British author Roald Dahl's treatment of his wife, American actress Patricia Neal, after her stroke. In each case, spouses minister to their partners, take control of the rehabilitation, and manage to produce remarkable results. However, where Dahl was demanding, strict, and harsh, Ackerman remains patient, sympathetic, and understanding. Performing research for her book *An Alchemy of the Mind: The Marvel and Mystery of the Brain* (2004) uniquely equipped Ackerman with insight into the obstacles West faced. She tutors her husband with deep affection through play, especially word play.

Ackerman and West, two accomplished authors, enjoy a remarkable relationship built around their mutual intoxication with language; each is the other's first and most sympathetic reader. Thus, Ackerman knows only too well what the loss of language means to a writer like West. She recalls how, before his stroke, West would frequently break out in extemporized song lyrics or write daily love missives that he would leave on the kitchen counter for her to discover. Another endearing habit of his had been to invent unique names of endearment, *piropos*, for his wife. One of Ackerman's therapeutic endeavors is to remind West of his former habit, prodding him to new inventions. He eagerly responds to the challenge, and each day he invents a new phrase: Divine Hunter of the Cobalt Blue Arena, Buoyant Hunter of the Esteemed and Cosmological Tsunami, Book-Lover of Life's Infinite Volume, and ninety-seven others, all of which are listed in the appendix.

Eventually Ackerman suggests that West attempt to write again and volunteers to transcribe his thoughts. The process is a trial, as West haltingly seeks words that refuse to present themselves and Ackerman struggles to understand her husband's often incomprehensible locutions. To their shared credit, they persevere until West eventually returns to writing his own work, no longer typing but insistently working the hand damaged from the stroke. In the years since his affliction, West has published a memoir, *My Father's War* (2005); a volume of poems, entitled *Tea with Osiris* (2006); and a deeply personal account about his experience of aphasia, entitled *The Shadow Factory* (2008). He has also completed three novels and published numerous essays in several prestigious journals.

The story follows a generally chronological order, with Ackerman tracing her husband's illness, frustration, uneven recovery, and eventual return to writing and verbal expression. However, at various key moments, Ackerman inserts reflections and observations from the patient himself, which provide revealing counterpoints to his wife's view. For example, once he recovers from his coma-like sleep, West takes stock of his condition and realizes its severity in personal, rather than medical, terms.

> I was a case of a man who had come round from delirium to find a cascade of minute changes in his world, which couldn't be ignored as the big bustle of everyday living took charge. I sensed in the complex fabric of my being that I had been remarkably altered. Changes irrevocable and final. I accepted these hammer blows from creation as overdue, as part of the mystery that people simply have to be dispatched for other people to replace them.

Surely the most emotionally wrenching of West's reflections is occasioned by Ackerman's attempt to console him. As she soothes and nurtures, he is anything but reassured.

> Here she is cuddling her overgrown baby, who had once been the terror on the cricket field. Her blue baby, her deformed baby, her armless protégé, at once older, younger, doomed, a magnet for any human task, and therefore enormously to be pitied, before being put down, buried, grave-stone naked, and maybe plundered by grave-robbers and carted away as a freak.

Ackerman does a remarkable job of navigating her way through difficult or arcane medical terms, procedures, and distinctions to present the reader with a clearly comprehensible primer on strokes and brain dysfunction. A good example occurs after she reads the terse conclusions of a speech therapist's initial assessment that hinges on daunting terms such as *apraxia* and *dysphagia*. After describing the horror of the stroke's onset, she moves into a second chapter in which she surveys the research of two pioneering nineteenth-century neurosurgeons whose names are today assigned to different neurological conditions—Paul Broca, who identified the lower-left side of the brain as the seat of language, and Carl Wernicke, who discovered that another area of the brain was responsible for language comprehension. Her treatment of these distinctions is both deft and assured, while at other moments her prose is majestic and beautifully evocative.

Her figurative tropes are clear and perceptible, as when she conjectures on what has happened to his command of language: "I imagined Paul's mind as a blackboard on which all the words had been erased, but it was more like he was being locked out of the classroom. The words were all in there, jumbled as they might be, and they had been scrambled into an alien language." As she describes the changes to the skin on her husband's fingers, Ackerman offers a lyrical description of tiny whorls of flesh that respond to the slightest sensations: "To my surprise, the stroke had brought Paul unexpected sensory bonuses. . . . The skin on his fingers had peeled as if sunburned, becoming quite raw, and in time his fingerprints simply sloughed away. But they serve a purpose, those loopy weather systems. Detecting life's finer textures, they report on a minutely sculpted world of geography and architecture too small to see."

An equally beautiful feature of the book is the descriptions of intimacy between two people who have remained fascinated by and devoted to one another. In addition to their many pet names and endearments, Ackerman recounts a silly, meandering phone conversation only a few weeks before the stroke. Similarly, after the stroke, as they snuggle in bed, the two share one of their many word games, in which they create outlandish names for each other and then imagine a trio of children named after German battleships.

However, the laughter dies out when the enormity of all that has happened sinks in. West laments his condition, yet Ackerman reassures him that he is lucky to have survived. After a pause, he tersely responds, "'And hard for you too' . . . Stroking my hair, with a faraway look in his eye . . . His voice bore a long-silenced note of regret." As she reads the manuscript of this book to him and discusses all the pain and difficulties of the ordeal, West consoles her. "A life is like an intricately woven basket, frayed, worn, broken, unraveled, reworked, reknit from many of its original pieces. As a result it has brought us much closer."

One Hundred Names for Love is a gorgeous book filled with love, acute observations, and powerful insights. Ackerman is at the top of her form here, poet and naturalist united to create a deeply moving literary experience.

David W. Madden

Review Sources

The Globe and Mail, April 23, 2011, p. R22.
Kirkus Reviews 79, no. 1 (January 1, 2011): 25.

The New York Times Book Review, April 17, 2011, p. 14.
Publishers Weekly 258, no. 5 (January 31, 2011): 38.
Science News 179, no. 77 (May 21, 2011): p. 30.
The Telegraph, May 14, 2011, p. 27.
Times Literary Supplement, no. 5651 (July 22, 2011): 10.
The Washington Post, May 1, 2011, p. B6.
Writer 124, no. 9 (September 2011): 7–8.

1Q84

Author: Haruki Murakami (b. 1949)
Publisher: Alfred A. Knopf (New York).
944 pp. $30.50
First published: *ichi-kyu-hachi-yon*, 2009, in
Japan
Translated from the Japanese by Jay Rubin and
Philip Gabriel
Type of work: Novel
Time: 1984
Locale: Tokyo and its surrounding suburbs

*Aomame finds herself pulled into an alternate
reality, which may be the fictional creation of
a seventeen-year-old girl and her ghostwriting
partner, a young man with whom Aomame had
an encounter during her childhood.*

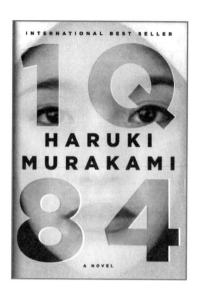

Principal characters:

MASAMI AOMAME, a fitness instructor and assassin who specifically targets abusive men
TENGO KAWANI, a math instructor and aspiring writer who secretly rewrites a novella
  titled *Air Chrysalis*
TOSHIJARU USHIKAWA, an ex-lawyer and minor criminal who works for the Sakigake cult
ERIKO FUKADA, the enigmatic seventeen-year-old original author of the novella *Air
  Chrysalis*
TAMOTSU FUKADA, her father and the Leader of the Sakigake religious cult
SHIZUE OGATA, a wealthy dowager who provides shelter for battered women and hires
  Aomame to kill the men who abused them
KOMATSU, a literary editor who persuades Tengo to rewrite the novella
MR. KAWANI, the man who raised Tengo but may or may not be his biological father
AYUMI, Aomame's policewoman friend who is violently murdered
KYOKO YASUDA, Tengo's older, married girlfriend

In the opening scene of Haruki Murakami's *1Q84*, a young woman named Aomame is
stuck in traffic on an elevated Tokyo expressway when her taxi driver suggests that she
climb down one of the expressway's emergency ladders, to make what the reader might
initially assume is a normal business appointment. The driver warns Aomame that the
world may seem a little different once she reaches the bottom, but that there is only ever
one reality at a time. Meanwhile, Tengo, a young math instructor and aspiring novelist,
is strong-armed into perpetrating literary fraud, secretly rewriting a novella submitted
to an amateur writing contest. Against his better judgment, Tengo agrees to the scheme
after meeting the inscrutable author, a seventeen-year-old girl who goes by the name
Fuka-Eri, and who has escaped from a religious cult founded by her own father.

Originally published in three volumes in Japan, *1Q84*'s first two books alternate between Aomame's and Tengo's points of view, as their lives, seemingly separate at first, become increasingly complicated and intertwined. Unlike Murakami's better-known works *The Wind-Up Bird Chronicle* (1994–95; published in English in 1997) and *Hard-Boiled Wonderland and the End of the World* (1985; 1991), this novel unfolds in third-person narration. But, much like those previous novels, nothing is as it seems. Aomame's urgent appointment turns out to be the assassination of a man who has abused his wife, an assignment from a wealthy dowager who feels that law and society have failed victims of abuse. When not working as an assassin, Aomame lives a solitary life as a fitness instructor, seeking human contact only through occasional one-night stands. After climbing down the expressway ladder, however, Aomame begins to notice small changes in the world around her, such as newsworthy events that she would not have

(Getty Images)

Haruki Murakami was born in Kyoto but currently lives in the United States. Winner of the Franz Kafka Prize for his 2002 novel, translated as Kafka on the Shore *in 2005, he has also received the Jerusalem Prize and an honorary doctorate from Princeton University.* 1Q84 *is his twelfth novel.*

missed otherwise. It is not until she sees two moons in the night sky that she accepts that she is in a new reality, which she dubs 1Q84, the "Q" standing for a question.

In the meantime, Tengo tries to return his life to normal after the interlude spent rewriting the surprise bestseller, *Air Chrysalis*, and coaching the taciturn Fuka-Eri so that she can be convincing during a press conference. He cannot quite return to normal, however, as his thoughts keep returning to the world of the novella, in which the mysterious Little People fashion chrysalises out of threads plucked from the air. Tengo learns that Fuka-Eri's guardian, Professor Ebisuno, allowed the novella's publication in order to bait the Sakigake cult into revealing the fate of Fuka-Eri's parents, whom Ebisuno suspects are imprisoned within the cult compound.

Throughout the novel, Murakami intersperses tidbits from Aomame and Tengo's childhoods. Keeping a bedside vigil for the comatose man who raised him, a man who may or may not be his biological father, Tengo reflects on his strained relationship with the elder Mr. Kawani, who spent his life working as a fee collector for Japan's public broadcasting organization. In remembering how Mr. Kawani dragged him from door to door every Sunday, cajoling and threatening money out of reluctant customers, Tengo also remembers a classmate whose mother dragged her around as a member of the Society of Witnesses, an ultraconservative religious group that practices door-to-door proselytizing. Only gradually is it revealed that this girl was Aomame. Although it is initially disconcerting to reconcile the image of this isolated little girl with the cool and competent assassin that Aomame has become, the reconciliation becomes easier as more is revealed. Most importantly, Tengo and Aomame both vividly remember the day, shortly before Aomame transferred to another school district, when she courageously and wordlessly gazed into Tengo's eyes for several moments. They have both cherished that memory over the years but have never searched for each other, perhaps because a reunion literally could not have occurred in their original reality of 1984.

As the book continues, Aomame and Tengo's paths weave tantalizingly closer to one another without actually crossing. The dowager has a special assignment for Aomame: murdering the reclusive Leader of the Sakigake cult for to his systematic raping of prepubescent girls, perhaps even his own daughter, who, the reader will not be surprised to learn, is Fuka-Eri. Both the dowager and Aomame know that this will be her last job; if she escapes alive, she will have to assume a new identity and go on the run from the cult's revenge. Meanwhile, Tengo becomes convinced that the events in Fuka-Eri's novella really happened, from the second moon to the Little People.

In the third section of the novel, another point of view is added: that of Ushikawa, a shifty ex-attorney hired by Sakigake to find Aomame after the Leader's murder. Unknown to anyone, the Leader knew she was coming, seeking death as an escape from his painful servitude to the Little People. In return for the mercy killing, he creates a portal that somehow impregnates Aomame with Tengo's child. There is no way that she and Tengo can remain safe, the Leader says, and there is no passage back to the reality she came from, but Aomame is determined to reunite with Tengo so they can protect their child.

Perhaps unsurprisingly for so lengthy and complex a novel, there are several plot threads that remain unresolved in the end, such as why Mr. Kawani's spirit roams about, knocking on doors and haunting the other characters while his body remains in a comatose state. It is not clear who or what is behind the murder of Ayumi, a policewoman that Aomame befriends. Similarly, Tengo's girlfriend disappears in a sinister fashion, but he never learns what has actually happened to her. Nonetheless, readers will likely be more than satisfied with the characters' emotional arcs and with the story's "villains," none of which are one-dimensional. Indeed, the physically and sometimes emotionally repulsive Ushikawa has a great deal in common with Aomame and Tengo, who experienced isolation and loneliness even as children within their own families. In fact, the reader may wonder whether the Ushikawa of the original 1984 might have ended up quite differently.

In addition to the engrossing plot, Murakami demonstrates exquisite timing in his revelation of information, along with a unique ability to infuse the pages with sensory-rich detail. During Aomame's fateful taxi ride, she experiences a profound memory response to Janáček's *Sinfonietta* playing on the radio. She later purchases a recording in order to study the music, which seemed somehow to portend her passage between worlds. Almost two hundred pages later, when an episode in Tengo's childhood is revealed, the reader does not need to flip back to remember the earlier chapters but rather experiences a kind of recognition akin to *déjà vu*, much as Aomame herself felt it. Other details will evoke a similar "memory sense," such as when Tengo reads passages from Anton Chekhov's *Ostrov Sakhalin* (1893; *The Island of Sakhalin*) to an enthralled

Fuka-Eri, a detail that gains significance many chapters later, when the Chekhov-quoting bodyguard, Tamaru, reveals to Aomame that he himself is from that island.

Between the intriguing plot and the rich details lie even more layers that make the novel a memorable experience. Known to be significantly influenced by Western culture, Murakami sprinkles his novel liberally with both literary and popular culture references, including a comparison drawn between the Big Brother of George Orwell's *Nineteen Eighty-Four* (1949) and his own novel's Little People. Several characters relate observations they have gleaned from authors such as Chekhov, Marcel Proust, and Isak Dinesen, and even from such movies as *On the Beach* (1959), *The Thomas Crown Affair* (1968), and *2001: A Space Odyssey* (1968). Perhaps most charmingly, while pondering the second moon that has appeared in her night sky, Aomame recalls the lyrics of the 1933 song "It's Only a Paper Moon."

Finally, adding to the reader's sense of surreal parallel worlds are the book's superior and detailed production values. The page numbers are alternately displayed forwards and backwards, while their vertical placement on successive pages meanders up and down in a manner than suggests the waxing and waning of the moon. Even the novel's title delights on multiple levels. The fact that Aomame dubs the new world 1Q84 is clever on the surface, but it also provides proof, when the Leader uses the phrase, that he and the Little People have powers that can penetrate the mind. In addition, the Western reader's eye may automatically read the first character of the title as the letter "I", suggesting "IQ.". For the Japanese reader, there is a double meaning in the fact that both the letter "Q" and the number "9" are phonetically identical, such that the names of the original world and the new world are pronounced exactly the same way: *ichi-kyu-hachi-yon*. Together with the thought-provoking plot and vivid details, these elements add up to a satisfying whole, making *1Q84* Murakami's most ambitious and far-reaching work to date.

Amy Sisson

Review Sources

Booklist 108, no. 2 (September 15, 2011): 23.
Christian Science Monitor, November 2, 2011.
Kirkus Reviews 79, no. 18 (September 15, 2011): 180.
Library Journal 136, no. 15 (September 15, 2011): 69.
The New York Times Book Review, November 6, 2011, p. 4.
Publishers Weekly 258, no. 35 (August 29, 2011): 42.

One Was a Soldier

Author: Julia Spencer-Fleming
Publisher: St. Martin's (New York). 327 pp. $24.99
Type of work: Novel
Time: 2005–2007
Locale: The Adirondack Mountains in upstate New York

This seventh novel in the Clare Fergusson and Russ Van Alstyne murder mystery series follows a group of veterans as they return home to Millers Kill from tours of duty in Iraq.

Principal characters:
CLARE FERGUSSON, rector of St. Alban's Episcopal Church, a returning veteran who served as a helicopter pilot
RUSS VAN ALSTYNE, Millers Kill's chief of police, recently widowed
ERIC MCCREA, a Millers Kill police officer and returning veteran
WILLEM ELLIS, a former high school track star and returning veteran
GEORGE "TRIP" STILLMAN, an orthopedic doctor and returning veteran
MARY "TALLY" MCNABB, a bookkeeper at Algonquin Waters Spa and Resort and returning veteran
SARAH DOWLING, the leader of the veterans' support group

One Was a Soldier is the long-awaited seventh novel in Julia Spencer-Fleming's highly popular Clare Fergusson–Russ Van Alstyne murder mystery series, and it is the first of the series to appear on the *New York Times* best-seller list. The novel focuses on a group of veterans returning from war in Iraq to Millers Kill, a fictional town in the Adirondacks. In an interview for the *Portland (ME) Press Herald*, Spencer-Fleming stated that she writes crime fiction, but the crime is not central to her work; what is critical is how the characters cope with "what life throws at them." In *One Was a Soldier*, her returning veterans cope with the aftermath of their combat experience by joining a support group at the town's community center. While one veteran, Will Ellis, has lost both his legs, the wounds of the other group members are not as easy to discern.

As do several other novels in the series, *One Was a Soldier* includes an epigraph, in this case a few lines of verse from Stephen Crane's ironic poem "War Is Kind" (1899):

> Mother whose heart hung humble as a button
> On the bright splendid shroud of your son,
> Do not weep.
> War is kind.

Crane's poem contrasts the pomp of war, the battle flags and uniforms, with the reality of death. It also contrasts the enthusiasm of those leaders who promote war with the grief of its victims, including soldiers and their families. *One Was a Soldier* focuses on those victims. Each chapter in the novel begins with a quote from the Episcopal Book of Common Prayer, and the first chapter references the "Communion of Saints" from the Apostles' Creed. In *One Was a Soldier*, the communion of saints is the group of five veterans from the area who are central to the action of the novel: Clare Fergusson, Eric McCrea, Will Ellis, Trip Stillman, and Tally McNabb. The novel opens with their first support-group meeting on September 5 and then flashes back to June 6, the date of a welcome-back party for Eric McCrea at the Millers Kill police station. McCrea, who served as an MP, assures chief of police Russ Van Alstyne that he is ready to return to work, but the formerly laid-back police officer has been changed by his experiences in Iraq. Over the course of the narrative, his inability to control his anger will be exposed.

Clare Fergusson also returns in June to Millers Kill and to her lover, Russ, after having flown combat missions in Iraq for eighteen months. Like McCrea, she claims to have no problems with reentering civilian life. She appears thinner but assures everyone that she is all right and ready to resume her duties as pastor of St. Alban's. However, it is gradually revealed in the novel that she, too, has brought back a hidden problem.

The first chapter of the novel introduces not only the principal characters but also the story of a crime that will lead to murder. On his way to the rectory with Clare, Russ is called to the Dew Drop Inn, where he encounters a fight between veterans and civilians. Clare becomes involved in the action, as is her wont in the series, and meets Tally McNabb.

In the next chapter, the time shifts ahead to September once more. Spencer-Fleming introduces the other veterans in more detail, and the plot alternates between the veterans' meetings that take place in the fall and action of the story that occurred during the summer. Readers who find Spencer-Fleming's time shifts confusing may feel more grounded once the novel reaches October and the plot begins to follow a more straightforward chronology with fewer, if any, flashbacks. At the October 3 meeting of the veterans' support group, one of the members is late. The group shortly learns that Will Ellis has tried to kill himself, and they go to the hospital to visit him. Fortunately, he survives, but two days later, it appears that Tally McNabb has succeeded in committing suicide. Clare refuses to believe that Tally could have done so and begins looking into the circumstances of her death, as she so often has in the past, much to Russ's dismay.

Prior to her death, McNabb was working as a bookkeeper at BWI Opperman, the largest employer in the county and the parent company of Algonquin Waters Spa and Resort. Clare and Russ have had bad experiences with the company's CEO, John Opperman, before, in the earlier books *A Fountain Filled with Blood* (2003) and *All Mortal Flesh* (2006). Russ hates Opperman but does not see a link between the CEO and McNabb's death. Clare, however, becomes suspicious about Tally's alleged suicide and sees a link between it and the fatal automobile accident of Ellen Bain, Opperman's previous bookkeeper.

In her effort to prove that McNabb could not have taken her own life, Clare involves the other members of their support group. McCrea has been suspended from the police department for using excessive force in an arrest, and after some initial resistance, he is eager to redeem himself by helping Clare. Ellis is encouraged by Clare to take part in

Julia Spencer-Fleming's first novel in the Clare Fergusson–Russ Van Alstyne series, In the Bleak Midwinter *(2002), won several awards, including the Agatha Award and the Anthony Award. She has written six additional Millers Kill novels since then.*

the investigation by contacting his former high school friend Olivia Bain, Ellen Bain's daughter, to obtain more information. It turns out that Ellen Bain became suspicious of activities at BWI concerning government contracts and copied incriminating evidence, which she left with her brother, Trip Stillman. However, a traumatic brain injury he received during a mortar attack in Iraq caused him to suffer short-term memory loss and forget that Ellen left the evidence with him. This short-term memory loss is his hidden wound, one that he has been desperately trying to hide. With help from a member of the support group, Clare eventually uncovers a fraud scheme involving millions of dollars, government contracts, and theft.

Since its beginning with *In the Bleak Midwinter* (2002), Spencer-Fleming's series has developed a solid fan base. Although the novels include murder, mystery, and elements of police procedurals, the strength of the series lies in its principal characters, Clare Fergusson and Russ Van Alstyne, and the open secret of their romance. Although she is an Episcopalian priest in her thirties from Virginia and he is a police chief in his fifties from Millers Kill, they share similarities. Both Russ and Clare have a military background, which is part of their initial attraction, and both are fearless in righting wrongs. Based on mutual regard, they develop a friendship that becomes a deep, growing love for each other, although the situation is complicated by Russ's marriage, even once he becomes a widower. The development of their relationship plays a central part in *One Was a Soldier*, as it does in each novel in the series.

Another important feature of the novels is the setting. Spencer-Fleming was born in Plattsburgh, New York, and her description of the towns, mountains, weather, and people all ring true. Millers Kill is physically based on the town of Hudson Falls, New York, which Spencer-Fleming has relocated to the northwestern corner of Washington County. The plots in her series often incorporate the area's problems of diminishing farms and growing crime caused by the faltering economy. Spencer-Fleming has also created an engaging group of supporting characters whose stories enhance the main plot of each novel. Some provide humor, such as Harlene, the longtime police dispatcher who "didn't believe in deferring to rank," and Russ's mother, who refers to her six-foot-four son as "Sonny." Other notable minor characters include members of the police department, the vestry at Clare's church, and various townspeople.

The recurrence of minor characters and several motifs serve to tie the novels in the series together. In the second novel, Clare saves Russ's life by not letting go of him as she pulls him to safety. The idea of their not letting go is then expressed in each subsequent novel, including *One Was a Soldier*. The final chapter of this novel shows the remaining members of the initial group of veterans in uniform as they pay their respects to Ethan Stoner, who was killed in Afghanistan. Stoner was a minor character in the first novel, and Spencer-Fleming focuses on Stoner's wife, child, and mother, echoing the verses from "War Is Kind" that show the effect of war on sweetheart, child, and mother.

What is distinctive about Spencer-Fleming's series is that she tackles a social issue in each book. The issues she has covered in previous novels have included the development of farm lands, pollution, homophobia, illegal immigrant laborers, and drug trafficking. *One Was a Soldier* shows the effects, often not initially apparent, of war on soldiers returning to the civilian lives. Using different characters, Spencer-Fleming shows the various causes, symptoms, and effects of post-traumatic stress disorder. Reviews of *One Was a Soldier* have been positive, praising Spencer-Fleming's ability to write a mystery combined with a story about the suffering of soldiers who have returned with wounds from combat; award-winning author John Hart commented that the novel made him "a shade wiser about the cost of war."

Marcia B. Dinneen

Review Sources

Booklist 107, no. 11 (February 1, 2011): 36.
Library Journal 136, no. 1 (January 1, 2011): 68.
The New York Times Book Review, April 24, 2011, p. 15.
Publishers Weekly 258, no. 9 (February 28, 2011): 37.
Portland Press Herald, May 1, 2011 (Web).
Toronto Star, July 10, 2011, p. IN7.

Open City

Author: Teju Cole (b. 1975)
Publisher: Random House (New York). 272 pp.
$25.00
Type of work: Novel
Time: 2006–2007, with flashbacks to the 1980s
Locale: New York City, Nigeria, and Brussels

This impressive debut novel provides a case history of New York City from the perspective of a Nigerian German psychiatrist finishing his residency.

Principal characters:
JULIUS, the narrator, a thirty-two-year-old psychiatrist of Nigerian German descent
NADÈGE, Julius's ex-girlfriend, who has moved to San Francisco
V., Native American author and professor at New York University
DR. SAITO, retired Maxwell College literature professor, Julius's friend and mentor
DR. MAILLOTTE, Philadelphia doctor who lives part time in Brussels
FAROUQ, a Moroccan attendant at an Internet and phone café in Brussels
KHALIL, Farouq's boss and friend, also from Morocco
MOJI KASALI, an investment banker, older sister to one of Julius's Nigerian friends

Open City is the story of Julius, a thirty-two-year-old Nigerian German psychiatrist in residency at Columbia Presbyterian Hospital in New York City. The story begins in 2006 and continues into the following year, as he wraps up research on the relationship between depression and apoplexy in the elderly. Stressed by a full schedule and professional responsibilities, Julius begins to take therapeutic walks in the evenings, exploring various neighborhoods in Manhattan, where he reflects on their architecture and history, as well as the sociopolitical issues that engulf the lives of the residents. He stops into art museums and stores, takes in an occasional movie or concert, and visits the waterfront, Ground Zero, and other significant sites, usually offering commentary with the demeanor of a tour guide but with a much deeper sensitivity and breadth of knowledge.

The novel is structured as a collection of vignettes, a blending of the narrator's peripatetic ramblings, dreams, conversations with friends and colleagues, flashbacks to his youth in Nigeria, and philosophical pontifications on a wide variety of political and social issues. It is fiction and nonfiction, essay and poetry, reading more like an elaborate, stream-of-consciousness journal than a plot-infused novel. Most reviewers noted similarities between the book and the work of J. M. Coetzee, V. S. Naipaul, and

W. G. Sebald, whose protagonist in *Die Ringe des Saturn: Eine englische Wallfahrt* (published in English as *The Rings of Saturn*, 1998) reflects on his rambles throughout the countryside of Suffolk, England. Teju Cole confirmed those observations in various interviews, claiming inspiration from many other authors as well. Endowed with Cole's passion for literature, philosophy, and history, Julius too comments on these authors' books, including Peter Altenberg's *Telegrams of the Soul* (2005), another collection of vignettes.

The novel reads so much like a diary that it is prudent to remind the reader this is a work of fiction. While Julius is a psychiatrist, Cole is an art historian and photographer. Otherwise, the similarities are such that Julius could be Cole's alter ego. They are each in their early thirties, intelligent, and professional men of Nigerian descent who came to the United States for their education and spent time in New York City, Cole at Columbia University and Julius at the fictitious Maxwell College. Like Cole, Julius has a deep appreciation for art history and a keen eye for light and detail. They are both world travelers and introverts who gain sustenance from observation and reflection. Only Cole knows where his work of imagination truly begins and ends.

The title of the book relates in part to a reference Julius makes about Brussels being an "open city" during World War II. By surrendering and negotiating with Germany, the city avoided bombardment and thus preserved its historic structures, which dated from the medieval period onward. The connotations of an open city, however, are both negative and positive. When Julius visits Brussels in search of his estranged German grandmother, he bears witness to the problems of the modern open city, especially the influx of African and Middle Eastern Muslim immigrants, whose cultural and religious values challenge the status quo. Hate crimes against nonwhites are rampant, and Julius, himself a black man, also feels his sense of security threatened. However, he is not targeted while in Brussels; instead, he is robbed and beaten when he returns to New York City, ironically by African American boys whom he had casually acknowledged just moments earlier.

The parallel between Brussels and New York City is one of the central tenets of the book. Through observation and dialogue with characters, Cole confronts the benefits and difficulties of living in a multicultural world, as well as problems related to immigration and assimilation in the post–September 11 climate. While many New Yorkers have focused their attention on preventing additional terrorist acts by Islamic fundamentalists, Cole alludes to many other threats to the open city, including ignorance, mental illness, indifference, poverty, economic recessions, and even bed bugs, those "minuscule red-coated soldier[s]," which Cole intends not merely as comic relief. Clearly, some of these threats result from openness and the ongoing access to new people, ideas, and beliefs.

The marginalization of immigrants is a prominent theme as well. As Julius wanders around New York City and Brussels, he frequently draws attention to the plight of the foreigner, alienated, impoverished, and forgotten by much of society: a Haitian shoeshine man in Penn Station; Saidu, an undocumented Liberian who, after escaping the brutal regime of Charles Taylor, was held at a detention facility in Queens for over two years; a pair of dirty, Spanish-speaking men sitting in a doorway north of Central Park,

Teju Cole is a fellow of the Chinua Achebe Center at Bard College. He has published stories in literary magazines such as the New Yorker *and* Tin House, *as well as the novella* Every Day Is for the Thief *(2007). He was raised in Lagos, Nigeria.*

one clipping the other's toenails; an unnamed cleaning woman in a Brussels church, "perhaps a refuge from . . . the Cameroons . . . Congo, or maybe even Rwanda." Like the women in Vermeer's paintings, "her silence seemed absolute." As a psychiatrist, Julius is naturally interested in the mental health of others, but his sympathy for the outcasts of society can also be seen as an extension of his own sense of alienation and "otherness."

Yet another thematic element is the exploration of place as a palimpsest, or how easily and routinely history is erased or forgotten. While visiting Ground Zero, as plans are being drawn up for new buildings and a memorial, Julius references the history of the property, the area a "bustling network of little streets . . . Robinson Street, Laurens Street, College Place," all of which had been "obliterated in the 1960s to make way for the World Trade Center." Before that, in the late nineteenth century, the area boasted "Washington Market, the active piers, the fishwives, [and] the Christian Syrian enclave." Before then, the Lenape most likely lived there, their paths "buried beneath the rubble. . . . The site was a palimpsest, as was all the city, written, erased, rewritten."

Related to the idea of palimpsests is the propensity of the expunged past to haunt successive generations. This is most evident in the case of V., a patient of Julius. V. authored *The Monster of New Amsterdam*, a scholarly book about the life of the secretary for the Dutch East India Company who bore responsibility for murdering the Canarsie Indians on Long Island and "over a hundred innocent members of the Hackensack tribe" as part of the Dutch colonists' ongoing genocide against the native people. A member of the Delaware tribe, he suffers from depressions that are largely brought on by research and assimilation of the pain and suffering, both of which continue to be felt by the greater contemporary Native American community.

As Julius walks past City Hall Park, he notices a small, rather insignificant memorial designating another repurposed site, this one having brought anguish to the African American community especially: a six-acre burial ground for African slaves from the seventeenth and eighteenth centuries. He notes that most of the coffins were found to be "oriented towards the east" and that their "excavated bodies bore traces of suffering: blunt trauma, grievous bodily harm."

While V. and a few angry African American characters exemplify the ongoing connection between modern-day individuals and collective, place-based history, Julius, on the other hand, is searching for that connection. Proud of his Nigerian past, he has all but severed those family ties and knows little about his German background. As he confronts New York City's brutal past, especially the period of slavery and the realization that the profits of slavery overlap with much of the city's origins—origins that include "the companies that later became AT&T and Con Edison"—he admits to being on a quest to find "the line that connected me to my own part in these stories." Yet Julius refuses to identify with African Americans, as he is not American or descended from slaves, and resents being called "brother" by another black person. When a cab driver states, "I'm African, just like you," Julius reveals that he was in "no mood for people who try to lay claims on me." Similarly, when an African American postal worker refers to him as "brother" and recites his own amateur, black-angst-infused poetry, Julius "makes a mental note to avoid that particular post office in the future."

Julius's trip to Brussels represents a major part of this search for identity. He has not seen his grandmother since his childhood, and he does not know if she is even alive; his father is deceased, and Julius and his mother are estranged from each other. The search for his "oma" is short-lived, though, as Julius gets distracted by the old world culture and meets new characters, who share their insight into the urban milieu. In particular, he encounters Farouq, a Moroccan graduate student who works at an Internet café, and Khalil, his employer, who together engage Julius in politically charged discussions on Islam, Palestinian American activist Edward Said, issues concerning Palestine, communitarianism, and dictators, among other subjects. The grandmother becomes little more than a pretext for the novel to expose other issues, and the reader is left without a concrete resolution.

A large portion of the book also deals with Julius trying to make sense of his Nigerian past. Through dreams, interior monologue, and dialogue with Nigerian friends, the reader learns about his schooling, family dynamics, and particular events that provide additional insight. At times, these memories seem extraneous or disparate, complicating a book already bursting with ideas, even as the memories round out the larger collection of vignettes.

However, a major revelation near the end of the book has struck certain reviewers as a stain on an otherwise compelling first book, an element of the story that was perhaps encouraged by an editor or not enough editing. Without spoiling the ending, readers should be poised to feel manipulated or deceived. For those able to accept the ending at face value, the scene demonstrates another theme; namely an individual's personal history is always evolving and can easily be compromised by new experiences, even when embracing a collective history, consciously or not. This is evident not only in Julius and V., but also in some of the other characters who have been displaced. Perhaps Julius expresses this conflict when he states, "The past, if there is such a thing, is mostly empty space, great expanses of nothing, in which significant persons and events float. Nigeria was like that for me: mostly forgotten."

Fortunately for Cole, the scene does not detract from Julius's being regarded as one of the most memorable characters in contemporary urban fiction. His astute and often poetic observations of migrating birds, paintings, and architecture will satisfy readers who appreciate a fine turn of phrase. The attention he gives to Ghanaian philosopher Kwame Anthony Appiah, French critic Roland Barthes, and a host of other intellectuals not only sets him apart from many fictional characters today but also offers stepping-stones for further intellectual inquiry. His observations on classical music, art, Austrian composer Gustav Mahler, and lesser-known artist John Brewster are insightful. Julius also gives one of the best walking tours of New York City ever to appear in fiction, stopping at the Cloisters, Chinatown, the American Folk Art Museum, and many other sites. He will be remembered favorably, and so will Cole for this masterful first novel.

Sally S. Driscoll

Review Sources

The Economist 399, no. 8744 (July 30, 2011): 76–77.
The New Yorker 87, no. 2 (February 28, 2011): 68–72.
The New York Review of Books 58, no. 12 (July 14, 2011): 25–27.
The New York Times Book Review, February 25, 2011, p.12.
World Literature Today 85, no. 4 (2011): 58–60.

Orientation
And Other Stories

Author: Daniel Orozco (b. 1957)
Publisher: Faber and Faber (New York). 176 pp. $23.00
Type of Work: Short fiction

A debut collection of nine stories about the loneliness and deadening daily life of work.

Principal characters:
ANASTASIO SOMOZA, the president of Nicaragua, living in exile in Paraguay
CLARISSA SNOW, an unhappy and lonely woman who works for a temporary employment agency
BABY, a man who witnesses a suicide while painting the Golden Gate Bridge

Whereas many short-story writers have said that they do not want to know in advance how their stories will develop, treasuring a sense of mystery as they write, Daniel Orozco once told an interviewer that with every story he writes, he tries to get at a discrete problem. For the title story of his debut collection, *Orientation: And Other Stories*, Orozco has said that he wished to explore the balance of personal identity and work identity, for in the workplace true selves are revealed. In the contributors' notes to *Best American Short Stories* (1995), Orozco wrote that after he graduated from Stanford University in 1979, he worked for a temporary employment agency for ten years, unsure of how he wanted to spend his life. By 1991, he was a full-time student again, studying creative writing and supporting himself with a temporary job at the Kaiser Building in Oakland, California. From the main hallway of the twelfth floor, Orozco could see an expanse of cubicles running the entire length of the building. When it came time to turn in a story for a writing workshop, he recalled the rat-maze image of the cubicle offices. The voice of the story's narrator came to him as an omniscient supervisor, part gossip, part god, orienting a new employee to the secret workings of the office.

With its perceptive insights into cubicle-style office life and all the restrictions and controls that come with it, "Orientation" is much more than a new office employee's introduction to his job. The story was enthusiastically received when it appeared in 1995 and has been widely anthologized since, for in it, Orozco pushes the satire to absurd and hilarious extremes. In addition to the many warnings the godlike voice gives the new employee about using the photocopier, microwave, and coffee maker, he also discloses personal information about the crazy characters who work there. One of them is a witch with dangerous powers; another is a serial killer who has mutilated people.

Instead of exploring the psychology of his characters, Orozco has said that he works from the outside in, beginning with a precise, detailed world his characters have to cope with. To infuse his stories with genuine drama, he meticulously researches his chosen settings. For "Shakers," a story about a California earthquake, Orozco consulted geological studies of California, earthquakes studies, and maps of fault lines and topography to determine the arc of the story: the journey the omniscient narrator takes across the state, which provides snapshots of the earthquake's effect on people. The story ends by zeroing in on a hiker in Joshua Tree National Park who has broken his leg and cannot move. After the quake, when night comes, a diamondback rattlesnake rests on his body, its head on his chest, and stares into his eyes. As the hiker looks up at the night sky, he feels completely separated from his previous life.

Orozco says that when he lived in the San Francisco Bay Area, his relatively short train ride to work only gave him time to read the local papers, and a fascination with the police blotter led him to wonder if he could assemble a story out of such anecdotes. The result was "Officers Weep." The police reports that make up the story are mostly insignificant, consisting of barking dogs, graffiti, petty theft, and domestic disputes. However, as the story progresses, these reports of external activity are interspersed with the police officer's thoughts as he fantasizes about his female partner, while she, in turn, begins to think about him. The story reaches its climax when they are dispatched to break up a bunch of demonstrators. Realizing that she is falling in love with her partner, the female officer beats on the demonstrators joyously. The ironic conclusion occurs when they are called to a domestic disturbance that has been developing throughout the story. As they hear sounds of screaming and violence from inside, they take out their guns and prepare to enter the scene with love in their hearts.

For "Somoza's Dream," the longest story in the collection, Orozco conducted extensive historical research on the president of Nicaragua in the 1960s and 1970s, only to discover that Anastasio Somoza was a very uninteresting man. Orozco's solution was to create characters around the dictator with whom the reader could identify, such as his driver and his mistress. Indeed, the only interesting thing Somoza does is urinate on the outside wall of the American embassy in Paraguay, and the only significant thing that happens to him is his violent assassination.

Orozco's stories are filled with lonely people trapped by their own compulsions and meaningless jobs, people who lack interesting lives inside or outside. How dispiriting is it to work at a job for ten years and still be called the "new guy"? How hopeless is it to help paint the Golden Gate Bridge, knowing that as soon as you finish, it will be time to start the task all over again? How depressing is it to work at a temp agency with the dubious assurance that you have "permanent temporary employment"? Ultimately, the only happy characters in these stories are the two police officers in "Officers Weep."

Perhaps the loneliest of Orozco's lost and alienated characters is Clarissa Snow, the central character of "Temporary Stories." Clarissa likes riding home on the bus, where no one is alone, yet she still feels alienated there. In one of her temporary jobs,

Daniel Orozco's stories have appeared in Best American Short Stories, Best American Mystery Stories, *Harper's* Magazine, *and Pushcart Prize anthologies. A former Stegner Fellow at Stanford University, he won a National Endowment for the Arts Fellowship in fiction in 2006. He teaches creative writing at the University of Idaho.*

she answers phone calls from the desperate and unemployed while collaborating with her employers to fire an entire department. "Temporary Stories" is divided into three separate stories, all focusing on Clarissa. In the first, she works as the receptionist at the human resources office of the county hospital. Every day she is besieged with phone calls from people trying to get a job at the hospital, making her so anxious that she develops an eczema rash across her body and must take aspirin continuously. In the second story, she is sent on a four-week assignment with an insurance company to type and edit a secret report for the executive vice president. Although the other workers at the company are told not to talk to her, they befriend her. But as she gets to know them, she gradually realizes what the secret report is about: a plan to dismantle the entire claims unit and outsource the work to an overseas vendor. When she completes the job, her friends, unaware that they are losing their jobs, give her a goodbye party.

There is more than a little sad irony in "Only Connect," whose title comes from the epigraph of E. M. Forster's novel *Howard's End* (1910). In this story, Orozco fashions what he calls a "narrative relay," in which the drama is handed off from one character to another. In general, *Orientation* features a few scarce instances of personal connection, a notable exception being the momentary connection the Golden Gate Bridge painter experiences with a jumper plummeting past him into the water. He is so affected by the woman's momentarily meeting him eye-to-eye that he asks his coworkers for a nickname to replace his old one, "Baby."

"Hunger Tales," like "Temporary Stories," comprises three separate stories, all about eating. The first story follows a woman who sneaks out at night to a large supermarket to buy cookies. However, the store is unusually crowded, and she is hampered by people standing around the cookie aisle. Since the key to the story is the woman's efforts to keep her cookie obsession secret, she is flummoxed when another woman gives her a smile of recognition. Like her, the stranger wears running shoes and a big, fleecy sweater. Faced with the threat of discovery, the woman becomes aware of her shame and her loneliness. The second story is about a forty-two-year-old man confined to his bed by his enormous size. Weighing over five hundred pounds, he cannot move by himself. One day, he falls while trying to ravage an empty tortilla bag and is stranded on his back like a beached whale until emergency personnel rescue him. As they laboriously get him to his feet, he has a vision of a man trotting on a beach and he laughs, but it is a laugh with no joy.

There is no joy for the man in "I Run Every Day," either, though he is fit and self-satisfied. He works at a school supplies warehouse, scorning his fellow workers for their doughnuts and mayonnaise-laden sandwiches, priding himself on his daily run. However, when he goes on a date with a new employee, he misunderstands her attention and rapes her, oblivious to any sense of wrongdoing. Although the man is a runner who watches what he eats—a model, he thinks, for the world to admire—he is completely disconnected from those around him, taking refuge in his healthy habits and deepening his isolation.

As Jane Smiley says in her introduction to the 1995 *Best American Short Stories*, Daniel Orozco's stories are both sinister and fun. They uncover the world that assaults people from both within and without, providing keen insight and more than a few chuckles. Orozco's satirical approach produces stories that are comparable to the fiction of George Saunders, especially *CivilWarLand in Bad Decline* (1996). Indeed, many reviewers have noted echoes in Orozco's work of Joshua Ferris's *Then We Came to the End* (2007) and David Foster Wallace's *The Pale King* (2011), two novels that also consider the loneliness and psychological turmoil of office life with cutting humor and keen observation. While Orozco's subject matter has received a fair share of prior exposure, his writing jumps from the page with precision and feeling that is sure to delight new readers.

Charles E. May

Review Sources

Booklist 107, no. 17 (May 1, 2011): 67.
Kirkus Reviews 79, no. 5 (March 1, 2011): 359–62.
Library Journal 136, no. 3 (February 15, 2011): 102.
Nation 292, no. 23 (June 6, 2011): 32.
The New York Times, July 24, 2011, p. 7.
Publishers Weekly 258, no. 11 (March 14, 2011): 47.

Otherwise Known as the Human Condition
Selected Essays and Reviews

Author: Geoff Dyer (b. 1958)
Publisher: Graywolf (Minneapolis). 432 pp.
$18.00
Type of work: Essays
Time: 1989–2010

This collection of Dyer's essays and critical reviews encompasses a wide range of topics, including war photography, Americana, aviation, music, and much more.

With its varied subject matter, *Otherwise Known as the Human Condition* illustrates Geoff Dyer's aptitude for writing on an astonishing variety of topics. He describes himself in the essay "My Life as a Gate Crasher" as "a literary and scholarly gate-crasher, turning up uninvited at an area of expertise, making myself at home, having a high old time for a year or two, and then moving on elsewhere," and indeed, on subjects from photography to sculpture, sports to aviation, and haute couture to comic books, Dyer makes readers feel like they are in the presence of a passionate old friend. Regardless of what prior interest one might have in the topics themselves, Dyer's enthusiasm is intoxicating, transporting the reader on an illuminating and thought-provoking ride. If Dyer is the "gate-crasher," his readers are the uninvited comrades that come along for the journey, swept along by Dyer's passion and energy.

The essays contained herein bring together the many diverse interests of a writer who has spent his life engrossed in a variety of scholarly pursuits and topics. For example, Dyer's nonfiction book *The Ongoing Moment* (2005) features the author in the role of photography critic, whereas *But Beautiful* (2009) shows him delving into the stories and mythologies of the great jazz musicians. He is also an adept fiction writer, with four novels under his belt: *The Colour of Memory* (1989), *The Search* (1993), *Paris Trance* (1998), and *Jeff in Venice, Death in Varanasi* (2009). What separates *Otherwise Known as the Human Condition* from the rest of Dyer's works is its lack of a unifying theme; rather than a novel or collection of essays on one topic, Dyer offers an introduction to his world, where one day can be spent mulling over the fortunes of the English football team and the next bemoaning the state of London city doughnuts. The passions and interests of his past, however, are never far from his focus.

As he explains in the introduction, "Almost as soon as I began writing for magazines and newspapers I hoped one day to see my articles published in book form." He has achieved this goal in *Otherwise Known as the Human Condition*, which presents twenty-one years of musings, some previously published and some not, for public consumption. Dyer invites the reader to see him as a modern-day "man of letters" as he attempts to repopularize the essay form in a twenty-first-century environment that overflows with a thousand new bloggers every day. What separates him from the flock is his apprenticeship as a writer, which allows him to transform his essays into pieces that seize his audience's imagination.

Although the book's primary focus is on subjects other than himself, Dyer is able to move more effortlessly than most essayists into very personal and profound territories. In the essay "Sacked," he describes the investigatory work and thought processes he employed in attempting to recall why he was fired from his first "proper job." Decoding his own diary scribbles from the time, Dyer recounts entertaining stories of sexual encounters, drug use, musical appreciation, and art films. After completing his detective work, he goes on to conclude that "the thing that I'm most struck by, the thing I most love and of which I am really proud, is the way that the job hardly merited a mention, either in the original diary or in this annotated commentary." Dyer's apprenticeship as a writer was to live life to the fullest, rejecting the typical career path of recent college graduates in their early twenties and instead serendipitously falling into the writing profession. As he admits, for him, writing "has always been a way of *not* having a career."

The promiscuous, drug-addled version of Geoff Dyer presented in "Sacked" stands in contrast to many facets of the writer's own story. Hailing from "the midwest"— that is, midwestern England—Dyer was a working-class boy who loved to read. Encouraged by a local Cheltenham schoolteacher, he soon turned his passion into a scholarship opportunity at Oxford University, where his love of literature only grew. "Sacked" finds Dyer during Margaret Thatcher's tenure as prime minister throughout the 1980s, a time when living off "the dole" was complemented by readings of D. H. Lawrence, Albert Camus, and W. H. Auden. This meeting of high- and lowbrow also comes out in the author's musical tastes, which run the gamut from the improvisational, free-form jazz of John Coltrane to the Ecstasy-inspired house music of the early 1990s. This dichotomy is similarly evident in the tone of Dyer's writing, which might be scholarly and melancholic in one essay, perverse and hilarious in the next. His skill lies in mastering a wide range of emotional tones, and his very best work brings all of them together.

Many of the pieces contained in this collection were previously published in newspapers and periodicals such as the *Guardian*, *Vogue*, *Esquire*, and the *American Scholar*. The fact that many are seeing their first American publication (some having previously been featured in Dyer's British-only publications, such as 2001's *Anglo-English Attitudes* and 2010's *Working the Room*) may explain the emphasis on Americana that can be found throughout the book. Whether discussing literature, food, music or film, Dyer shows an appreciation of American culture, which as a British outsider he explains in terms more exotic than many American writers could pull off. This focus on the United States is augmented by pieces that describe topics as varying and wide-reaching as Algerian holidays, Albert Camus, and battlefield musings in rural France.

Some of Dyer's essays suffer from the exuberance and enthusiasm of the author. If readers are not caught up in Dyer's passion for a topic, they can quickly find

(Matt Stuart)

Geoff Dyer is the author of several novels, essay collections, critical studies, and nonfiction titles. His nonfiction book Yoga for People Who Can't Be Bothered to Do It *(2003) won the W. H. Smith Best Travel Book Award, while his book* The Ongoing Moment *(2007) won the International Center of Photography's Infinity Award for Writing on Photography. In 2003, he was the recipient of a Lannan Literary Fellowship, and in 2005, he was elected a fellow of the Royal Society of Literature.*

themselves left high and dry. This most frequently occurs in his discussions of literature, in which his critique and praise of modern authors such as Lorrie Moore, Ian McEwan, and James Salter, to name just a few, can read like an exclusive discussion to those not familiar with their work. Dyer's discussion of photography, although featuring many fringe artists, suffers less from this criticism, as the images provided within the book offer a useful context in which the uninformed reader can understand Dyer's passion. It is in passages such as these that Dyer excels as a critical writer, as he encourages the reader to view, read, or listen to art as attentively as possible and to articulate the profound effects these media can have.

But where Dyer will shine most clearly for first-time readers is in his discussions of universal topics, such as his essay on "Sex and Hotels," a highlight of the collection. According to the author, hotels are a haven for sleaze and lasciviousness: "Cleanliness might not be next to godliness but it is certainly adjacent to horniness." Using terms derived from the theoretical work of French anthropologist Marc Augé, Dyer describes hotels as a "super-modern non-place" where the blandness and conformity of the architecture, layout, and furniture occur on such a global scale that a guest could forget whether he or she was in Seoul or London. Despite being such "non-places," however, hotels are still areas designed for and by humans, and Dyer brilliantly describes how these superclean rooms "[cry] out to be defiled. If the room is, in a sense, *virginal,* then the act of breaking the seal on bars of soap and other stealable accessories has something of the quality of breaking its hymen." The opulence, the amoral environment, the cleaners, and the do-not-disturb signs are all mundane facets of the hotel experience from which Dyer squeezes surprising insights. He makes the reader feel like a rock star who, by necessity of social status, leaves previously virginal hotel rooms in a state of used disarray. Rock stars might throw televisions out of windows, hold wild parties, and tear up interiors, but the reader's crime could be little more than spilling room-service food all over the bed and having it cleaned up by a smiling, apathetic attendant. Dyer's descriptions are a reminder that these experiences are unique and should be cherished, whether or not they are a part of mundane day-to-day lived experience.

Given the nature of Dyer's method, choice of topics, and overall lifestyle, one can be forgiven for thinking him self-indulgent on occasion. Luckily for author and reader alike, this self-indulgence is not evident in his written work. Somehow, his question of whether it would be "immodest to claim that this book gives a glimpse of a not unrepresentative way of being a late-twentieth-early-twenty-first-century man of letters" is endearing rather than off-putting. In his essay on F. Scott Fitzgerald's *Tender is the Night* (1934), Dyer compares his own use of Ecstasy to Fitzgerald's infamous alcoholism, and here it does appear that he is overstepping the mark. But through his dexterity as a writer and a critic, he is able to bring these two topics together without looking like a fool. This, again, reveals his ability to deploy a wide range of emotional tones, to meld high- and lowbrow material, and to provide readers with a sense of his own burning passion throughout.

Ultimately, what *Otherwise Known as the Human Condition* portrays is the work of an adept and seasoned author doing what he loves most. In the introduction, Dyer notes, "A distinction is often made between writers' own work—which they do for themselves—and the stuff they do for money. . . . my case is rather different. Most of the journalism I do is as much my own writing as, well, my own writing." The passion and vitality of these essays is a testament to Dyer's method: doing what you want to do, when you want to do it.

Nicholas A. Kirk

Review Sources

Los Angeles Times, April 24, 2011 (Web).
New York Observer, March 29, 2011 (Web).
The New York Times, March 22, 2011 (Web).
Publishers Weekly 257, no. 49 (December 13, 2010): 26.
The Statesman, April 10, 2011 (Web).
The Washington Post, April 6, 2011 (Web).

The Pale King

Author: David Foster Wallace (1962–2008)
Editor: Michael Pietsch (b. 1956)
Publisher: Little, Brown (New York). 560 pp. $27.99
Type of work: Fiction
Time: 1980s
Locale: Peoria, Illinois

DAVID FOSTER WALLACE

THE PALE KING

(Little, Brown and Company)

The last and unfinished novel of David Foster Wallace considers the monotony of working life and the significance of boredom through a group of IRS examiners working at the Midwest Regional Examination Center in Peoria, Illinois.

Principal characters:

LANE DEAN JR., an IRS examiner who struggles with the boredom of his job and the difficulty of sticking to his tasks

DAVID WALLACE, an examiner whose memoir is claimed to be the source for much of the book

CLAUDE SYLVANSHINE, an examiner who is a "fact psychic" and is unable to control the flow of information into his mind

LEONARD STECYK, a member of the IRS management, known for his unshakable optimism and troublesome positivity

CHRIS FOGLE, an IRS agent who is rumored to have created an algorithm that allows examiners to achieve total and complete concentration

David Foster Wallace's *The Pale King* is an unfinished work of fiction pieced together by his friend and former editor Michael Pietsch from the various chapters, notes, and scraps of summary Wallace left behind after committing suicide in 2008. In interviews regarding the book, both Pietsch and Karen Green, Wallace's widow, expressed the belief that Wallace would have wanted the book to be published despite its incomplete state, and this belief drove their decision to present the author's third and final novel to the public.

At over five hundred pages, *The Pale King* has enough breadth to convey many of Wallace's main points, though it is ultimately unclear where he might have taken the characters and the primary story arc had he finished the novel. In the end, *Pale King* feels and reads less like a complete novel and more like a series of sketches, building toward something that never occurs; and yet, as Wallace's notes on the project suggest, this may have been exactly what the author was aiming for.

The novel, such as it is, revolves around the lives of employees working for the Internal Revenue Service (IRS) in Peoria, Illinois, in a department known as the

Midwest Regional Examination Center (REC). Wallace spent much of his childhood in nearby Urbana and Champaign, Illinois, and his familiarity with Peoria and the entire "Chicagoland" area comes across in his descriptions. Action among the characters is frequently interspersed with asides regarding the setting, a banal, archetypal Midwestern hamlet in which the characters seem marooned. Peoria has a cultural significance beyond its location in the middle of the country, as it has come to represent a larger social, cultural, and geographical middle ground. The saying "Will it play in Peoria?," which developed during the vaudeville era, essentially came to mean, will this piece of art (movie, book, play, et cetera) sit well with audiences in the average American city, represented by the small and relatively boring Peoria?

Wallace's decision to base his novel in this provincial town was no accident, and the wholly unremarkable surroundings heighten the sense of malaise at the story's heart. The opening chapter contains a lengthy and vivid description of a Peoria pasture, which Wallace had previously published as a piece of

(Courtesy of Kenyon College)

David Foster Wallace was the author of three collections of short fiction, two collections of essays, and two novels, The Broom of the System *(1987) and* Infinite Jest *(1996). He was a professor of creative writing at Pomona College and the winner of a MacArthur Fellowship and* Time *magazine's Best Books of the Year award.*

short fiction. In articles about the composition of the book, Pietsch states that there was no indication that Wallace's Peoria story was supposed to lead the book, but that he felt it was an aesthetically pleasing way to introduce the more traditional (in the loosest sense of the word) section of the narrative.

As many reviewers have noted, the narrative of *Pale King* defies traditional descriptions of plot and character development; it darts between different time periods, characters, and points of view, at times leaving readers confused but also drawing them deeper into the minutiae of the novel's overarching meditations. To illustrate Wallace's approach, which in this posthumous work is also the result of the editor's choices, it is helpful to take a closer look at how the first few chapters of the book progress.

Having set the tone with a poetic description in characteristically long sentences, Wallace sets about introducing a few of his characters in chapter two. The first is Claude Sylvanshine, an IRS examiner who has recently been relocated to Peoria after a disaster befell his former station. One of the book's most unusual characters, Sylvanshine is described as a "fact psychic," one who has preternatural abilities to divine bits of factual information from the ether of collective thought. The facts that Sylvanshine obtains in this way are frequently neither germane to his situation nor relevant to the story in any meaningful way, but serve as amusing asides. As Wallace describes his abilities, "The fact psychic lives part-time in the world of fractious, boiling minutiae that no one knows or could be bothered to know even if they had the chance to know."

The next few chapters focus on seemingly disjointed subjects. Two unnamed men sit in a car and discuss their preferences for masturbation in chapter three, while chapter four relays an amusing story about Fredrick Blumquist, an IRS worker who remained at his desk for three days before any of his fellow coworkers realized he had died. The next chapter describes the childhood tribulations of future IRS manager Leonard Stecyk, whose "excruciatingly upbeat" personality arouses feelings of disgust and self-loathing in those around him. Stecyk returns later, having matured into a somewhat happier version of the boy described earlier, and joins the crew at the Peoria office in time to help craft a documentary intended to improve the public image of the IRS.

In chapter nine, Wallace introduces his readers to David Wallace, the narrator for much of the book and the person who, according to Wallace, is writing all of this down in a memoir-like fashion. The author claims that this is not entirely a work of fiction but was in fact drawn from real-life events that David Wallace experienced. Wallace, the actual author, makes little distinction as to whether he is referring to himself or the fictional character and spends most of the chapter talking about the various practical, legal, and personal issues involved in writing the memoir.

While it might seem a strange decision to place the author's foreword in the ninth chapter of the book, Pietsch has said that he initially felt the foreword should open the book, but then read some of Wallace's notes stating that it was indeed intended to appear later. From a reader's perspective, the chapter forces a complete change of focus and attention, causing him or her to reorganize all of the information given thus far in an effort to stay ahead of the rapidly shifting narrative.

In subsequent chapters, Wallace continues to introduce characters, sometimes with names and descriptions and sometimes without them. As the story winds along, dipping at times and soaring at others, Wallace never loses a sense of humor. He includes, for instance, a chapter on "phantoms," the hallucinations that accompany periods of prolonged concentration. Another chapter covers the various illnesses that plague the staff of the Peoria office, many due to long hours at desks staring at paperwork, while others are perhaps attributable to poor lifestyles, psychosomatic illnesses, and other various causes. By chapter fifty, there is a sense that the plot has been building, but in no way continuously. Each chapter seems to serve its own purpose, while the overarching plot is left unfulfilled; a chapter with insights into 1980s politics might be followed by a detailed study of minor characters, for example. While each part seems to build to a conclusion, the climax never quite arrives, and readers are left only with the underlying messages that frame Wallace's argument.

The central themes in *Pale King* are addressed again and again, in ways that run the gamut from symbolism to blunt force. In his award-winning novel *Infinite Jest* (1996), Wallace examined the many roles that entertainment plays in American culture, from hilarity to soul-wrenching tragedy, and the price that Americans pay for living a life in which entertainment is expected as the reward for citizenship. Here, Wallace again delves into a civic dimension, with unapologetic commentary on the American mindset. Wallace hints at a hypothesis that the current state of affairs may have had its origins in the 1960s, and that by the 1980s, the shift in Americans' attitudes about themselves and their role in the nation had become entrenched. In a chapter that finds several IRS examiners trapped in an elevator and debating the national culture, a character comments:

> We've changed the way we think of ourselves as citizens. We don't think of ourselves as citizens in the old sense of being small parts of something larger and infinitely more important to which we have serious responsibilities. We do still think of ourselves as citizens in the sense of being beneficiaries—we're actually conscious of our rights as American citizens and the nation's responsibilities to us and ensuring we get our share of the American pie. We think of ourselves now as eaters of the pie instead of makers of the pie. So who makes the pie?

Whereas *Infinite Jest* cemented Wallace in many critics' opinions as one of the most innovative and powerful literary voices of his generation, *The Pale King* has inspired mixed reviews. While some lauded the book as a masterpiece, others have criticized it as a mixed bag, at times brilliant and at times too scattered to have a real effect. Wallace has a way of writing that challenges readers, sometimes in the form of three-page-long sentences that barely leave room to breathe. His frequent shifts in direction, tone, and narrative style demand sharp attention and seem at times like intentional brain teasers meant to keep the reader off kilter, which is perhaps where Wallace's writing has its strongest effect, when the reader is already struggling to keep both feet on the page.

Being an unfinished work, it is perhaps unfair to speculate on the ultimate success of the novel, as it is impossible to know how Wallace might have ultimately ended it. However, of the more than one thousand pages of material found in his office, the five hundred or so pages that made it to print provide another demonstration of Wallace's considerable skill and powerful insights into modern life. The novel is left with an unfinished feel, seeming like a collection of essays, thoughts, and vignettes loosely tied together, but with a knot that seems to want to pull apart with every page. In some of his notes, Wallace hinted that the book would involve action building toward a climax that would never come, and this effect is certainly achieved, though perhaps not in the way the author intended.

Boredom plays a central role in *Pale King*, as both an obstacle that the characters confront in their daily lives and one of the main notions under Wallace's literary microscope. Even as Wallace gives painstaking descriptions of his characters' encounters with tedium, he suggests a silver lining, which is perhaps one of the novel's primary messages: that delving into mind-numbing banality can be a form of meditation, which might even lead to the elusive happiness that comes from a life lived in full clarity and consciousness. This is an issue that Wallace dealt with on more than one occasion, including his 2005 commencement speech at Kenyon College. As Wallace told the graduates:

Pay close attention to the most tedious thing you can find (tax returns, televised golf), and, in a wave, a boredom like you've never known will wash over you and just about kill you. Ride these out, and it's like stepping from black and white into color. Like water after days in the desert. Constant bliss in every atom.

Micah L. Issitt

Review Sources

Esquire, March 15, 2011 (Web).
The Guardian, April 8, 2011 (Web).
Los Angeles Times, April 15, 2011 (Web).
The New York Times, April 14, 2011 (Web).
Slant Magazine, October 31, 2011 (Web).
Time, March 31, 2011 (Web).

The Paper Garden
An Artist Begins Her Life's Work at Seventy-Two

Author: Molly Peacock (b. 1947)
Publisher: Bloomsbury (New York). Illustrat-
ed. 397 pp. $30.00
Type of work: Biography
Time: 1700–1788, with brief passages set in
the twentieth century
Locale: England and Ireland

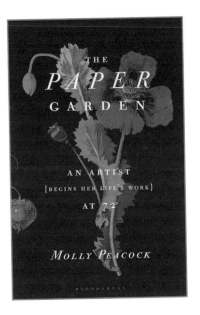

*This biography of artist Mary Delany is at once
the portrait of a fascinating woman and a meditation on creativity, womanhood, and age. Poet
Molly Peacock crafts the narrative with beautiful language, highlighted by reproductions of
Delany's flower mosaics.*

Principal personages:
MARY DELANY, an aristocratic woman who
    became a successful artist late in life
MOLLY PEACOCK, a poet who seeks parallels
    between her own life and Delany's
ALEXANDER PENDARVES, Delany's first husband
PATRICK DELANY, Delany's second husband
MARGARET CAVENDISH BENTINCK, Delany's closest friend and an early supporter of her art
RUTH HAYDEN, a Delany biographer
ANNE GRANVILLE DEWES, Delany's sister and correspondent
GEORGINA WADDINGTON, Delany's great-niece

Molly Peacock's biography of eighteenth-century English artist Mary Delany is as
much a meditation on aging and art as it is the story of Mrs. D (as Peacock affectionately calls her subject). Delany's artwork consists of paper mosaics of flowers,
meticulously crafted from a collage of stationery, decorative paper, and real flower
petals and plant leaves. Famous in their time for their striking beauty, these mosaics
have prompted modern art historians to recognize Delany as a radical innovator in
both collage and paper art.
    Although the majority of the book details Delany's life and art, Peacock also makes
frequent, sometimes substantial, detours into discussions of botany, her own life, and
the lives of others who became interested in the relatively unknown artist. These forays away from strict biography, while running the risk of distracting the reader, allow
Peacock to explore her subject matter from a fresh perspective. Why, she continually
wonders, is she so drawn to an obscure artist from centuries ago? And why are others, often with little previous artistic interest, likewise drawn to Delany? Peacock's

examination of these connections across centuries, social customs, and art forms is the focus of *The Paper Garden*. To encourage readers to look across subject matter for metaphorical connections, she prefaces the biography with a quote from poet Emily Dickinson: "The career of flowers differs from ours only in inaudibleness." While it will take the majority of the book for the full resonance of this quote to become clear, it does offer a guiding principle, suggesting that readers consider the flowers themselves as symbolic of Delany.

From here, Peacock begins the book with a rough sketch of the artist's life. Delany was born in 1700 into the aristocratic Granville family, where she was prepared for a life in the royal court of Queen Anne. When the queen died in 1714, Delany's family faced the loss of their wealth and their secure place in the court. Her parents thus arranged a marriage between Delany, who was seventeen at the time, and Alexander Pendarves, a drunken older man who would die seven years later. Delany spent many years as a widow until, at the age of forty-three, she married Dean Patrick Delany, an Irish clergyman with no title and a growing interest in gardening. It was not until 1772 that she first cut out a paper mosaic of a flower, beginning the work that would ultimately endear her to history.

This brief description of Delany's life is followed by a small number of pages devoted to historical context, basic information on paper arts, and a description of Peacock's first encounter with the artist's work. This first chapter frames the book carefully; by revealing the significant milestones of Delany's life early on, Peacock lets readers know that this biography is driven not by narrative but by metaphors, made deeper and more complicated as Delany's life is examined.

Every chapter of *The Paper Garden* is accompanied by a gorgeous recreation of one of Delany's mosaics. Each image provides readers not only an example of Delany's work but also a starting point from which to consider the themes of the chapter that it precedes. Chapter three, for instance, begins with hound's tongue, the small blue flower also known as a forget-me-not. After dramatizing Delany's creation of this mosaic and describing the careful work of cutting out paper and petals, Peacock moves into a description of the plant itself: tough, capable of living in harsh conditions, but also a beautiful flower with medicinal benefits. According to Peacock's analysis, "In placing its fragile stems and royal blue flowers above her rough and resolute leaves, Mrs. Delany created in the portrait a whiff of the plant's ambiguity—and a little of the Granville family's attitude toward child rearing, too." From here, Peacock begins to discus Delany's early life. The details are pieced together from a number of sources, with the most fruitful being a collection of Delany's correspondence, the product of her lifelong habit of writing detailed, intimate letters to her sister, Anne Granville Dewes. With these letters, Peacock is able to pepper the biography with Delany's own musical voice, increasing the intimacy of the portrait.

While Delany's early life is fleshed out somewhat in terms of historical context and family details, the greatest focus is on her experiences with art. From a young age, she was kept on a strict schedule of dancing, music playing, reading, and other artistic pursuits, all of which were emphasized further when she was sent to live with a wealthy aunt. It is when Delany's family enters a state of financial distress and this

(© Andrew Tolson, courtesy of Bloomsbury Publishing Plc)

Molly Peacock is a poet, prose writer, and educator living in Toronto. She is a president emerita of the Poetry Society of America and was one of the creators of Poetry in Motion, a program that displays poems on public buses and subways. Her collection Cornucopia *offers a critically successful retrospective of her work.*

preparation falls apart that Peacock begins to draw connections to her own life. She details the struggles of her family and the period of adolescence in which, as she says, she "hadn't discovered that I could drive this wild whatever-it-was inside me into a sonnet or a villanelle." Peacock's first boyfriend (who, decades later, would become her husband) is considered alongside Delany's first romantic suitor. Both women's early loves are understood through the metaphor of the hound's tongue. In this chapter, Peacock wonders, "Is it the fact that helps us recover—or is it the metaphor? Is it the hard knowledge of what really happened, like actual botanical material? Or is it the flesh of comparison between what happened and what that was like, the blooming of explanations?" It is this "blooming" that fills *The Paper Garden.*

Both Peacock and Delany had plenty to overcome in their early lives, with Delany being thrown into an especially deep depression by her marriage to Pendarves. However, both women also began to find joy in their middle years. After the death of Pendarves, Delany eschewed her many suitors and instead made a social and artistic life for herself. While she carried some disappointment that she never achieved an official appointment in the royal court, Delany was still a widely known and active figure, attending important events and finding ways to hone her artistic skills. Peacock celebrates this time, which allowed Delany to grow as an artist while blatantly flouting social conventions and living proudly as a single, independent woman for decades. Just as importantly, Delany's happiness seemed to be in many ways reliant on her group of female friends, many of them well-known artists and writers.

Delany's second marriage appears to have been founded on friendship, and the twenty-five years the Delanys shared together were some of the happiest in the artist's life. Their circle of friends was extensive and included the famous writer and satirist Jonathan Swift. In recounting these decades, Peacock further investigates the connections between herself and Delany. There are many similarities in their two lives, including sick husbands, international marriages, and artistic preoccupations. She does, however, stress that these similarities are not the only things that draw her to Delany's work. Peacock emphasizes the ways in which art can connect people, whether connecting Delany with her proto-feminist friends or Peacock and Delany across centuries.

Peacock also discusses biographer Ruth Hayden, who happens to be a descendent of Delany's sister. Hayden found herself becoming an expert on the artist, despite lacking any formal training. While she spoke occasionally to historical societies about Delany, Hayden was surprised when she was invited by the British Museum Press to write a biography of her ancestor. *Mrs. Delany: Her Life and Her Flowers* was first published in 1980. Like Delany with her mosaics, Hayden did not start this work until late in life, but it ultimately proved to be influential and inspirational. Peacock also takes time to detail her own friendship with Hayden; after first meeting because of their shared biographical subject, the two developed a relationship that went beyond professional collaboration.

The closing pages of *The Paper Garden* do not fixate on Delany herself, even though they discuss the time period in which the artist finally found her success. Peacock vividly describes the creation of the mosaics, as well as Delany's excitement about sharing her artwork with notable figures of the day, including England's King George III and Queen Charlotte. Some attention is also given to her relationship with Georgina Waddington, a great-niece whom she came to raise as a daughter. Peacock is just as often interested, however, in the lives of others (her own, her mother's, Hayden's) as she is in that of her subject. These threads, never quite discrete, are brought more closely together at the end of the biography. As Peacock explains in her closing, "Uncontrollable events hurtle toward us until the very moment of our deaths, yet in each instance figuring out how to go on, even on to the next world, repeats the confusion of youth. Of course we need our role models long past adolescence." To further bring the point home, she quotes the writer Virginia Woolf, who wrote in her diary of a "semi-mystic very profound life of a woman" that can be found in "one incident—say the fall of a flower."

The Paper Garden is rich with lyric descriptions, chronicling the inspirational lives of women across centuries in an engaging historical narrative. While the numerous and far-reaching modes might at times seem exhausting, Peacock's reflections on life and art ultimately redeem any missteps or strained metaphors. With the skill of a poet, she brings contemporary attention to an artist who refuses to be lost to time.

T. Fleischmann

Review Sources

Booklist 107, no. 15 (April 1, 2011): 14.
Kirkus Reviews 70, no. 2 (January 15, 2011): 119.
Library Journal 136, no. 7 (April 15, 2011): 91.
The New York Times, May 13, 2011, p. BR11.
The Washington Post, May 26, 2011 (Web).

A People of One Book
The Bible and the Victorians

Author: Timothy Larsen (b. 1967)
Publisher: Oxford University Press (Oxford).
336 pp. $55.00
Type of work: History, religion
Time: The nineteenth century
Locale: England

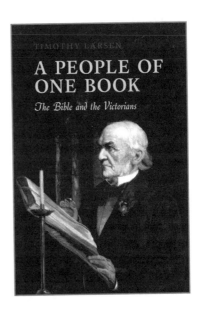

Religious studies scholar Timothy Larsen investigates how Victorians of many different Christian denominations, as well as agnostics and atheists, were influenced by the Bible.

Principal personages:
ANNIE BESANT (1847–1933), atheist and promoter of theosophy
CATHERINE BOOTH (1829–1890), cofounder of the Salvation Army
CHARLES BRADLAUGH (1833–1891), prominent Victorian atheist
JOSEPHINE BUTLER (1828–1906), feminist and social reformer
MARY CARPENTER (1807–1877), educational and social reformer
ELIZABETH FRY (1780–1845), Quaker philanthropist and social reformer
THOMAS HENRY HUXLEY (1825–1895), scientist and promoter of Darwinism
FLORENCE NIGHTINGALE (1820–1910), social reformer, considered the mother of modern nursing
EDWARD BOUVERIE "E. B." PUSEY (1800–1882), professor and leader of the Oxford movement, sometimes referred to as Tractarianism
CHARLES HADDON "C. H." SPURGEON (1834–1892), popular Baptist preacher in Victorian England
NICHOLAS WISEMAN (1802–1865), first Roman Catholic archbishop of Westminster, England, after Roman Catholic hierarchy was restored in the country

Scholarly books about the Victorians' reverence for and use of the Bible abound. Some detail individual writers' use of scripture, while others catalog its influence on the visual arts, and recent studies have described its impact on the working classes. In *A People of One Book: The Bible and the Victorians*, Timothy Larsen takes a different approach, concentrating on the Bible's place in the lives of people of various religious persuasions to show how it was, as he argues, the lens through which they marked their life experiences.

Larsen's book is a collection of case studies that present brief biographies of figures whom he considers to be representative of various faith traditions. These sketches are supplemented by careful examinations of key published works written by these men and women and, where possible, analysis of unpublished writings that offer keys to their understanding and use of biblical texts. Larsen takes pains to select women as well as men, though not simply for purposes of political correctness. He believes women played an important role in shaping religious ideas during the period, and the work they did as social reformers, often spurred by their understanding of scriptural commands to tend to the needs of others, had significant influence on the nation. Recognizing that it is always dangerous to select one person as representative of an entire population (or, in this case, a distinct religious sect), Larsen tries not to extrapolate too much in his discussions, instead letting the narrative of his subjects' lives and writings suggest how they can legitimately stand for the larger group of which they were members.

Larsen is certainly the right person to tell the story of the widespread influence of the Bible on Victorians of every sect and denomination—and on nonbelievers as well. In his 2006 study *Crisis of Doubt: Honest Faith in Nineteenth-Century England*, he turns on its head the scholarly cult examining the "crisis of faith" that caused many Victorians to lose their belief in God by his identification and description of the lives of several secular thinkers who were transformed into believers. *Crisis of Doubt* received highly favorable reviews from religious scholars and cultural critics alike and was named Book of the Year by the Christian review *Books and Culture*.

The figures Larsen selects for study are a diverse group, united only in their being well known to their contemporaries and of interest to scholars of succeeding generations. Some choices seem obvious: Nicholas Wiseman, who at the age of forty-eight became the Roman Catholic archbishop of Westminster; Oxford professor E. B. Pusey as representative of Anglo-Catholicism, the branch of Anglicanism that affiliates more strongly with Catholicism than Protestantism; and C. H. Spurgeon, the Baptist minister known not only in England but throughout the world for his powerful preaching. The women are an equally formidable group, including such figures as Catherine Booth, a Methodist who, with her husband, founded the Salvation Army; Florence Nightingale, a liberal Anglican widely known for her efforts in nursing and social reform; and Mary Carpenter, a Unitarian who was a renowned educational reformer. Larsen selects the philanthropist and reformer Elizabeth Fry as an example of the Quaker approach to applying scripture to life's challenges, and the feminist Josephine Butler to explain how Evangelicals made use of the Bible in their private and public lives. How even atheists and agnostics were influenced by the Bible is made evident by Larsen's extended discussion of the careers of Charles Bradlaugh, Annie Besant, and Thomas Henry Huxley.

One might expect to find that the lives and writings of devout Protestants such as Spurgeon, Booth, Carpenter, and Fry would be governed by the Bible. Nevertheless, Larsen's discussions of these four, and of Florence Nightingale—perhaps the most iconoclastic figure included in this study—provide subtle analysis that complements and at times corrects the work of previous scholars. For example, Nightingale insisted that the Bible was her continuing source of inspiration, yet she rejected most of the important tenets of mainstream Christianity, including the divinity of Christ. While that is well documented, Larsen points out that Nightingale's decision to remain in the Church of England must be taken as her tacit admission that organized religion, Anglican doctrine and practice in particular, has some merit and contains some truths.

Larsen may be at his best, however, in assessing the careers of figures not normally considered wedded to scripture. One of the most valuable sections of *A People of One Book* is his discussion of Archbishop Wiseman's career. Larsen's careful examination of Wiseman's published and unpublished writing explodes scholars' assumption that Roman Catholics had no interest in the Bible. In this section, Larsen explains how Wiseman, whom he describes as an excellent biblical scholar, relied heavily on scripture as a guide to his own beliefs and practices. Wiseman's defense of the role of tradition and the magisterium, the Catholic Church's teaching authority, lies in his insistence that Catholic teachings cannot be in contradiction with scripture and are in fact closer to their biblical origins than the Protestant doctrines are.

Timothy Larsen, professor of Christian thought at Wheaton College, is the author of several theological studies, including the award-winning Crisis of Doubt: Honest Faith in Nineteenth-Century England *(2006), and the editor of the* Cambridge Encyclopedia of Evangelical Theology. *He has published extensively in academic journals and is a fellow of the Royal Historical Society.*

Similarly, Larsen rescues the reputation of Anglo-Catholic E. B. Pusey, whose work as a leader of the Oxford movement earned him the title of the most hated man in England. Larsen demonstrates that Pusey, too, was a devout student of scriptural texts who believed that the Bible could be a valuable guide for people attempting to address the many challenges of the Victorian age. He also debunks the idea that Anglo-Catholics were averse to Bible reading, showing that, like Roman Catholicism, conservative Anglican Church doctrine promoted scripture interpreted by authority—though not one emanating from the Vatican—as the soundest way for the faithful to understand God's plan for salvation.

Equally intriguing are Larsen's discussions of the role of the Bible in the lives of people who were professed atheists or agnostics. Although one might expect that nonbelievers had to know the Bible in order to refute its teachings, Larsen suggests that the use of the scriptures by figures such as Bradlaugh, Besant, and Huxley was hardly so simplistic. Larsen carefully explains that Bradlaugh's works are filled with scriptural references and allusions, which are often used not simply to debunk the Bible's claims for God's existence but also in a positive way, to shore up his own arguments. Besant's work reflects the same reliance on biblical texts as a means of connecting with readers, and Huxley's writings display a constant attempt not to undermine the Bible completely but instead to turn it into a textbook promoting ethical living.

A constant refrain throughout *A People of One Book* is that many works by these representative figures have either been ignored or glossed over by other scholars. Larsen is not afraid to challenge the work of his colleagues past and present when he believes they are misguided. He expresses disappointment with Jo Manton's study *Mary Carpenter and the Children of the Streets* (1976), which to him seems grounded in an ill-formed understanding of Unitarianism, displays a naive willingness to accept common assumption as fact, and reflects a poorly conceived desire to elevate Carpenter above Victorians who were overly reliant on the Bible as a guide for life. He chastises theological scholars for ignoring Elizabeth Fry's *Texts for Every Day in the Year* (1859), a devotional book that was critically important to her. Perhaps the most interesting, if not the most important, example of Larsen's scholarly acumen is his correction of a long-standing belief that John Henry Newman, the celebrated convert to Roman Catholicism and a distinguished and influential writer in his own right, thought highly of the work of Evangelical Anglican reformer Josephine Butler; Larsen retraces the history of this idea to demonstrate that it was in fact Newman's Protestant brother, Francis, who admired Butler. This list could be expanded, but it seems sufficient to note that Larsen reads not only his subjects' writings but also the work of his colleagues with a sharp critical eye.

A valuable subtext that emerges from Larsen's study is his exceptionally good account of distinctions between the various organized religious groups that were active during the Victorian era. Whether Roman Catholic or Old Orthodox Dissenter, the people of Victorian England knew their Bible and relied on it not only for spiritual nourishment but also as a guide and comfort for everyday living. Why then, one might ask, if these were "a people of one book," should there have been such harsh divisions? Larsen argues that people of different faiths tended to provide some value-added dimension to their reading of the Bible. For Anglo-Catholics, the Bible as interpreted by the early church fathers would reveal the truth embedded in scripture, while for those like Catherine Booth, enlightenment provided by the Spirit would guarantee the veracity of her reading. These differences in approach, repeated in other denominations and often pointed out somewhat acerbically by nonbelievers, account for many of the conflicts that kept these Christians apart. What Larsen does not say, but which comes through clearly in his text, is that the Victorians were not only firm believers in the Bible but also firmly convinced that, as Shakespeare's Antonio wisely observes in *The Merchant of Venice*, "The Devil can cite scripture for his purpose." For many living in nineteenth-century England, the devil wore the garb of a Roman Catholic priest or ranted about the meaning of biblical passages from the pulpit of a Baptist or Methodist church.

In his concluding chapter, Larsen writes that he had intended this study to be published in two volumes and include a number of other traditions, notably Judaism, Spiritualism, and the Brethren (also known as the Plymouth Brethren), each of which receives an abbreviated treatment in the final text. The publisher's concern about the marketability of such a long work, along with Larsen's inability to assemble sufficient materials on these topics, led him to abandon the longer project. This is unfortunate, because the thumbnail portraits he provides of British-born Portuguese Jewish writer Grace Aguilar and the late-nineteenth-century man of letters Edmund Gosse are likely to leave readers wanting to learn more.

A People of One Book is an academic study intended for scholars, peppered with hundreds of footnotes and concluding with an extensive bibliography that lists the many sources Larsen consulted in preparing this work, including dozens of manuscript collections and nineteenth-century journals and hundreds of primary- and secondary-source publications. At the same time, the book is written in a style that makes it accessible to lay readers interested in the culture and religious life of Victorian England. Larsen's study is a testament both to the pervasiveness of the Bible in nineteenth-century English intellectual and religious life and to the scholarship of a twenty-first-century academic who has recovered the historical record with exceptional care and scholarly acumen.

Laurence W. Mazzeno

Review Sources

Christianity Today 55, no. 8 (August 2011): 69.
Historically Speaking 12, no. 4 (September 2011): 7–9.
Journal of Theological Studies 62, no. 2 (October 2011): 798–801.
Literature and Theology 25, no. 4 (December 2011): 468–71.

The Philosophical Breakfast Club
Four Remarkable Friends Who
Transformed Science and Changed the World

Author: Laura J. Snyder
Publisher: Broadway Books (New York).
448 pp. $27.00; paperback $16.00
Type of work: History
Time: Nineteenth century
Locale: Cambridge University, Great Britain

The story of four accomplished scientists who became friends while students at Cambridge in the mid-nineteenth century and formed an informal society for the discussion of science.

Principal personages:

CHARLES BABBAGE (1791–1871), mathematician and engineer, often credited with inventing the first computer in the early 1820s

JOHN HERSCHEL (1792–1871), mathematician and astronomer who completed important work on binary stars and contributed to modern star maps and the origin of photography

WILLIAM WHEWELL (1794–1866), polymath who invented the word "scientist," contributed to the study of tidal movements, and helped found mathematical crystallography

RICHARD JONES (1790–1855), mathematician who contributed to the development of the scientific application of economics

FRANCIS BACON (1561–1626), pioneering statesman and scientist, regarded as the founder of the modern scientific method

Historian Laura Snyder's detailed history reveals the unusual lives of four mid-nineteenth-century polymaths who made important and sometimes groundbreaking contributions to the development of modern science, yet whose names are virtually unknown outside of academia. Charles Babbage, John Herschel, Richard Jones, and William Whewell were among the most prominent thinkers of their day, but their significance to the history of science goes far beyond the individual achievements of each man. In fact, they were all crucial participants in the development of a new scientific paradigm that would transform the global view of science and society.

In revealing the lives of these pioneering men and their early version of an academic "journal club," Snyder casts a light on the state of science in the mid-nineteenth century. The fortunes and favors of her quartet provide insight into the politics, class relations, religious conflicts, and other social issues surrounding educated society in Great Britain. In addition, Snyder shows how these men, and others in the young scientific community, caused a paradigm shift in the discipline of science, transforming it from a socialite's dalliance into a legitimate, respected occupation. Meanwhile, the personalities of Snyder's subjects help to reveal the different traits—some laudable, some questionable—that contribute to the rare quality of true genius.

Snyder begins with the childhood of William Whewell, a boy seemingly destined for a middle-class education and a career as a carpenter, like his father. However, Whewell's considerable skill in mathematics convinced his parents to pay for him to attend the types of primary schools that sent students on to the universities. In examining Whewell's transition from state-financed schools to private college-preparatory schools to Cambridge University, Snyder paints a quick picture of the lifestyle and economics of academic students. It is from Whewell's perspective, largely revealed in letters he wrote to his father from Cambridge, that the reader is introduced to the other major players of the philosophical club.

At Cambridge, Whewell met John Herschel, the charismatic and convivial son of a well-known professor and royal astronomer at Windsor Castle. Herschel grew up in a privileged environment; he was tutored by prominent experts in the sciences and arts and followed his academic parents on a variety of intellectual adventures throughout Europe, including once being entertained by French military leader Napoleon Bonaparte. The next to join the group was Charles Babbage, the child of an upper-class family who showed prodigious skill in mathematics and had a lifelong fascination with mechanics. The last was Richard Jones, a bon vivant who attended the university to pursue a career in law and joined the club because of his love of good food and drink. Jones had suffered from a number of maladies since childhood, and because of his "uncertain health," his father soon pressed him into pursuing the life of a minister, despite the young man's desire for intellectual rigor.

In 1812, Whewell, Herschel, Babbage, and a group of like-minded students formed the Cambridge Analytical Society, an informal journal club that met weekly to discuss the latest publications in mathematics. Gentlemanly clubs were a popular pastime for the men of England in the early nineteenth century; Snyder estimates that, by the middle of the century, "as many as twenty thousand men were meeting every night in London in some kind of organized group." The Analytical Society was as much a social club as an academic concern, and its members imbibed heavily of spirits and gossiped as much as they focused on intellectual inquiry.

Whewell, Herschel, Babbage, and Jones developed a strong friendship outside of the larger Analytical Society group. At the end of 1812, they began meeting at Herschel's chambers on Sundays, after the conclusion of the compulsory chapel services, for breakfast and scintillating discussions about the state of science in England. The breakfast club only lasted until 1813 but left an indelible mark on each man, the four continuing to correspond during their subsequent major achievements. Snyder uses these breakfast meetings and the friendships that resulted as a springboard to investigate the complex evolution of science over the ensuing decades.

Among the more popular topics discussed at these philosophical breakfast meetings were the works of Sir Francis Bacon, the philosopher statesman who pushed for the idea that scientific progress should be used to shape the world and improve life

Laura J. Snyder is an associate professor of philosophy at St. John's University in New York and is president of the International Society for the History of Philosophy of Science (HOPOS). A Fulbright scholar, she has also received scholarship awards from the National Endowment for the Humanities and the American Philosophical Society. Her primary research interest is the history of inductive reasoning.

for the populace. The four friends were enamored with Bacon, taking his concept that science was often misused in its social applications to heart. Bacon had argued that men should think of science not as a "courtesan" to be used for "pleasure and vanity only" but as a "spouse, for generation, fruit, and comfort," an approach that Whewell, Herschel, Jones, and Babbage applied to the world with their scientific pursuits. Through both their own accomplishments and the lessons they imparted to their students and followers, Bacon's vision of science began to bear fruit.

Jones, who had the least mathematical inclination of the group, became a curate after university, although he continued to research legal, political, and economic issues. He went on to publish articles on taxation and the distribution of wealth, eventually becoming a prominent professor of economic policy at East India College. In this post, he worked closely with Whewell and helped to dismantle the economic thought of David Ricardo, a political economist and the author of the law of comparative advantage. Jones and Ricardo battled in the pages of academic publications, but in the end, Jones's socially conscious approach won out, forever changing the field of economics.

After university, Charles Babbage went on to make breakthroughs in the fields of mechanics, engineering, and mathematics. His most impressive feat was the design of a "difference engine," considered by many to be the first computer. Babbage's machine was capable of calculating polynomial functions using a system of gears and levers that would not be out of place in a work of steampunk fiction. Snyder says that Babbage's difference engine was the first machine "that supplanted not physical but mental labor." During his lifetime, Babbage only managed to complete a small working model of his machine, but scientists in the 1990s constructed a fully operational difference engine using Babbage's exact design and only materials that were available in the 1820s. The machine successfully executed the functions that Babbage envisioned, thereby cementing his reputation as the designer of the world's first computer.

John Herschel followed in his father's formidable footsteps, becoming a prominent astronomer whose accomplishments rivaled those of any era. He discovered and named many satellites of Saturn and Uranus and published the first catalog of double stars for the *Philosophical Transactions of the Royal Society*. Like the other members of his club, Herschel became a professor and was one of the best-known and most respected scientists of mid-century Britain. He had broad interests and also made significant contributions to other scientific fields. In the mid-1830s, Herschel retired from his academic duties and traveled to the Cape of Good Hope in South Africa, where he and his wife produced a detailed collection of illustrations and descriptions of botanical specimens. His primary accomplishment, in retrospect, may have been the influence he had over his students. At the height of his career, many prominent philosophers and scientists considered Herschel the brightest scientist of the nineteenth century.

Snyder uses the birth of William Whewell as her starting point, the narrative of his life as a frame for the book as a whole. Like Herschel, Whewell's scientific interests ranged across many fields. He was an accomplished writer and essayist whose works inspired many of the next generation's thinkers and intellectuals. He is remembered for his work in mapping the ocean tides, an important advancement in geology, as well as his works on the history of science. These accomplishments only begin to hint at his importance, however; Whewell's intellectual stamp can be found under the surface of many of the era's major discoveries, making him arguably one of the most important scientists that no one has heard of.

The Philosophical Breakfast Club is, at its core, the history of how science developed from a recreational activity into a profession. In the mid-nineteenth century, a scholar devoted to science was known as a "natural philosopher," a title that covered a variety of disciplines, from physics to theology. Scientific research was funded by individual philanthropists and was not supported at the state or national level, with universities offering instruction in science only because it was considered an essential part of a complete education.

Snyder's breakfast club realized that there was untapped potential in scientific endeavors, not just to slake the curiosity of the educated elite, but also to improve the world as they knew it. The four friends championed this new view of science through their prominent positions in academia, and they were victorious in the end, even if it took generations for their vision to emerge. Over the years, they spoke out for the public funding of scientific projects, pushed for the adoption and dissemination of the scientific method in all disciplines, and promoted the establishment of professorships dedicated to the sciences at major universities. One example of their breadth of influence can be found in the fact that Whewell himself actually invented the term "scientist," proposing it at an 1833 meeting of the British Association, where he and other club members had a reunion of sorts. Years later, Whewell formally called for the adoption of the term in his book *The Philosophy of Inductive Sciences* (1840).

Snyder's expertise in science history is evident throughout her exposition, as she draws upon myriad facts to bolster her case and offers interesting historical and social asides to help the reader understand the gravity of the events surrounding her subjects. While there are numerous historical accounts of nineteenth-century scientific history, *The Philosophical Breakfast Club* boasts a special mix of history and biography, offering the life stories of four noteworthy scientists in the context of a global perspective. As Snyder deftly pieces together history from letters, published works, and incidental descriptions, she paints a picture of four larger-than-life figures who crusaded for scientific revolution in a time when intellectual battles were as contentious as any military or political rivalry. Her subjects were pioneers of a new way of thinking as well as remnants of the world they helped society leave behind. They were, as she describes, a "strange breed: the last of the natural philosophers, who engendered, as it were with their dying breath, a new species, the scientist."

Micah L. Issitt

Review Sources

The Economist, March 17, 2011 (Web).
Library Journal, February 1, 2011 (Web).
Providence Journal, May 13, 2011 (Web).
Publishers Weekly, December 13, 2010 (Web).
Science News, March 26, 2011 (Web).
The Wall Street Journal, February 26, 2011 (Web).
The Washington Post, March 23, 2011 (Web).

Please Look After Mom

Author: Kyung-sook Shin (b. 1963)
First published: *Omma rul Put'akhae*, 2008, in South Korea
Translated from the Korean by Chi-Young Kim
Publisher: Alfred A. Knopf (New York).
256 pp. $24.95
Type of work: Novel
Time: 2007–2008, with flashbacks ranging back to 1953
Locale: Seoul and the South Korean countryside

When their elderly mother goes missing after becoming separated from her husband at a subway platform at Seoul Station, her two oldest adult children try to find her. In the course of their quest, the mother's boundless love for her children and her acceptance of a difficult husband is revealed.

Principal characters:

PARK SO-NYO, also known as MOM, a sixty-nine-year-old illiterate woman who has gone missing; a wife and mother to five adult children
CHI-HON, Park So-nyo's unmarried older daughter, a busy writer
HYONG-CHOL, Park So-nyo's eldest son, a successful salesman troubled by the fear he may have sold out his ideals in favor of material success
FATHER, Park So-nyo's husband
HONEY, Park So-nyo's second daughter, mother of three children

South Korean author Kyung-sook Shin's international best seller *Please Look After Mom* tells a moving story of a mother's unconditional love for her children, her nearly superhuman strength in enduring adversity, and her gradual self-assertion vis-à-vis her husband. Through the central characters of Park So-nyo, three of her children, and her husband, *Please Look After Mom* explores the conflict between taking care of one's family and taking care of one's self, between self-sacrifice and selfishness.

　Please Look After Mom opens with a crisis meeting held by four of So-nyo's five grown children and their father one week after their mother has gone missing at bustling Seoul Station. Even before the exact circumstances of her disappearance are narrated to the reader, the three brothers and one sister put together a missing person flier to hand out to passersby.

　So-nyo's children come to realize that their mother held quite a few secrets. They are astonished to learn from their father that their mother's official birth year was actually two years later than her actual birth year. This surprise introduces the theme that there may be a significant gap between what the children think they know about their mother and the actual facts of her life. Shin's novel has successfully set this personal experience of uncertainty and family secrets within the background of the extremely difficult period in Korean history that So-nyo lived through. In her lifetime, Korea had experienced two devastating wars on in its soil. In South Korea, traditional society had transitioned into a modern society.

To motivate people to respond to the flyer, the children offer a reward of five million South Korean won. Some readers might wish that Shin's extremely capable English translator, Chi-Young Kim, had inserted a footnote to let readers know the approximate value of this sum. In 2007, when the novel takes place, one US dollar was worth about thirteen hundred won. Thus, the promised reward comes to about just under four thousand dollars.

Once the issue of the flyers is settled, it is revealed that So-nyo got lost at sprawling Seoul Station. Arriving in the South Korean capital of Seoul by train from the countryside, her husband led her to a platform to take the subway to go to their oldest son's apartment in the city. By a fraction of a second, she missed stepping into the subway car before its doors closed and the train moved ahead. Although her husband exited the train at the next station and returned to Seoul Station, she was already gone. Some eyewitnesses described an old woman slowly moving through the maze of the station, but they were unable to tell her children where she went. From this very realistic premise of a split-second separation with grave consequences, the author has woven a complex tale.

Chi-hon, So-nyo's oldest daughter, is particularly racked by guilt over having taken her mother for granted for much of her life. Stylistically, this idea is reinforced by the author's choice of using the second-person-singular narrator to address Chi-hon in the first chapter and in the epilogue of the novel. This creates the effect of Chi-hon's guilty conscience or perhaps the internalization of her mother's voice reminding her that she put her own life far above any considerations for her mother for a long time.

After the search for the mother fails to yield results, the one thing Chi-hon comes to regret the most is that her professional life as an internationally acclaimed author gave her so little time to share with her mother. She feels guilty that she was at a writer's conference in Beijing when her mother got lost. She also realizes that her mother had begun to suffer from painful headaches and to forget things a year before her disappearance.

Changing to a more commonly used third-person-omniscient narration, the novel turns to the perspective of Hyong-chol, the oldest son, an outwardly successful contemporary South Korean white collar worker who still harbors deep resentments and disappointments about his life. As Hyong-chol follows up with his sister Chi-hon on the last promising leads of sightings of their mom, he remembers how he had always enjoyed his mother's full support and how she had shared his dream that he would become a prosecutor, a prestigious and honored profession. Despite having been the best student at his rural high school, however, he failed the university entrance exams and had to put his dream aside. Instead, he embarked on a path of menial work and

Since Kyung-sook Shin's first novella, Winter's Fable (1985), won the Munye Joongang New Author Prize, her work has won an impressive array of literary awards, including the Dong-in (1997), Isang (2001), and the second Prix de l'Inaperçu (2009). Please Look After Mom is her first work translated into English.

night study in Seoul, after which he achieved considerable material success working as a condominium salesperson.

As Hyong-chol tries to find his mother, who has apparently visited all the places in Seoul he had stayed in the course of his adult life in the city, he is joined by his sister Chi-hon. Here, the novel introduces details that the reader may find to be uncanny and unsettling. For instance, even though So-nyo had been wearing beige leather sandals when she disappeared, the people who claim to have seen her insist that she was wearing blue plastic sandals, one of which has cut deep into her foot and caused an infection. Hyong-chol and Chi-hon remember that she had worn these blue sandals when they were younger, many years ago. Brother and sister finally meet a pharmacist who claims that he saw their mother six days before. By this point, the children have come to silently acknowledge that their mother was suffering from confusion due to an earlier stroke. The kindly pharmacist reveals a picture of an old woman with an infected foot feeding from garbage cans. She disappeared from his sight before he could alert the authorities to help her. Disappointed and disheartened by their lack of progress, Hyong-chol returns home, where he takes out his frustrations on his wife and breaks down crying in front of his father, who has been staying with him since So-nyo's disappearance.

Taking yet another narrative turn, the novel then shifts to the second-person perspective of So-nyo's husband as he returns to his home in the countryside. He realizes how little he knew about the woman he had taken for granted throughout their marriage when he discovers that his wife had had quite a life of her own after their children had left home. For example, she had become a loving and respected patron of the orphanage to which she had donated most of the money she received from her children as an allowance.

Stuck with his sorrow over his own failed ambitions to leave his rural hometown, So-nyo's husband encounters his own crisis of confidence. In mental anguish, he takes a telephone call from Chi-hon, who confesses her own guilt over her shortcomings to appreciate her mother. Her father is gentle with her and reassures her that her writing was treasured by her mother, who had asked a fellow volunteer from the orphanage to read Chi-hon's novels to her because she could not read them herself. Chi-hon's father ends up imploring her to please look after her mom.

Finally, the novel turns to the mystical first-person perspective of So-nyo herself. From her perch near their window, she lovingly observes her second daughter, whom she addresses as Honey, at home with her own three children. So-nyo apologizes to Honey for being angry with her for leaving a successful career as a top-notch pharmacist to raise her children. By observing her daughter and grandchildren, So-nyo comes to understand the choice her daughter made. She remembers being a daughter herself who had been tenderly loved by her mother, just as she loved her own sons and daughters, and just as her second daughter loves her children. Motherhood has fulfilled four generations of women in this family, the narrative seems to suggest, as it will fulfill future generations.

Please Look After Mom was a huge success in South Korea and became the author's first work to be translated into English. Shin's powerful portrait of a traditional mother who puts the lives of her children above everything else while quietly emancipating herself from her unappreciative husband has moved a global readership. Though some readers might find Shin's shifting narration to be confusing or jarring, her unusual choice of a second-person-singular narrator seems to have worked well in addressing readers on a personal level. Shin has also used it as a stylistic way to suggest that So-nyo was speaking to her two daughters and her husband or to indicate that they had internalized her voice. Apart from the final chapter, which is told in first person, the only chapter in which Shin does not employ the second-person narrative is the one told mostly from Hyong-chol's third-person perspective. This may signal a certain emotional reserve between mother and son, perhaps caused by her deep respect for him and the high hopes she once had for his future.

R. C. Lutz

Review Sources

Booklist 107, no. 8 (December 15, 2010): 20.
Kirkus Reviews 79, no. 1 (January 1, 2011): 13.
Library Journal 135, no. 20 (December 1, 2010): 109.
Maclean's 124, no. 19 (May 23, 2011): 85–86.
The New York Times, March 31, 2011, p. 8.
The New York Times Book Review, April 3, 2011, p. 23.
Publishers Weekly 257, no. 48 (December 6, 2010): 27.
The Wall Street Journal, May 28, 2011, p. C14.

The Pleasures of Reading in an Age of Distraction

Author: Alan Jacobs (b. 1958)
Publisher: Oxford University Press (New
York). 176 pp. $19.95
Type of work: Memoir

*Literary and cultural critic Alan Jacobs pres-
ents an extended argument in defense of reading and offers suggestions for making the experience more enjoyable.*

Principal personages:
ALAN JACOBS, the author, a literary critic and
avid reader
MORTIMER ADLER, a philosopher and author
who published a 1940 book on reading
HAROLD BLOOM, a literary critic and writer

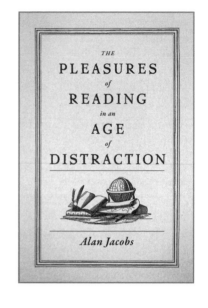

For nearly a century, one pundit after another has been predicting the death of the book.
First radio, then television, and later the personal computer were all supposed to replace books as the source of information and entertainment for the majority of people,
who would undoubtedly find reading too time consuming in a world that increasingly
values social interaction and multitasking. Books are still around, however, and sales
are increasing in some categories, such as popular fiction. Obviously, some people are
still reading. Nevertheless, literature professor and cultural critic Alan Jacobs suggests
in *The Pleasures of Reading in an Age of Distraction* that reading may have lost some
of its luster and become a distasteful chore for many who find it necessary but hardly
pleasurable. Jacobs wants to reacquaint his own readers with the joys of encountering
a text and restore some of the magic and excitement that many felt in the past when
they set aside time to spend with a good book.

Jacobs is no idealist, and *The Pleasures of Reading in an Age of Distraction* is not
intended to convince nonreaders to pick up Leo Tolstoy's *War and Peace* (1869) or the
six volumes of Winston Churchill's memoirs of World War II (1948–53). Instead, Jacobs makes it clear from the beginning of his narrative that his book is aimed at those
who have already experienced the benefits of reading—"pleasure, wisdom, joy"—but
who may have lost interest in the practice, or more likely been distracted by other
pursuits. The lure of video games and the computer is strong, and no one knows better
than Jacobs, who admits that he has spent much time on various social media sites in
recent years.

Jacobs is certainly not the first to write about the pleasures reading can bring, and
he is quick to recognize many of his predecessors. In fact, throughout *The Pleasures of
Reading*, he makes a concerted effort to acknowledge a handful of earlier books similar

to his that have helped to define the field he surveys. Most important among these is Mortimer Adler's influential 1940 treatise *How to Read a Book*. What makes Jacobs's approach different is that, where Adler and many others are prescriptive—telling people what books they ought to read in order to get the most pleasure, education, and moral benefit from reading—Jacobs is permissive about the selection of titles that can provide enjoyment. He devotes considerable attention to pointing out problems with arguments made by Adler and by the most recent self-proclaimed "Vigilant Critic," Harold Bloom, in favor of specific authors or texts; Jacobs describes how these authors' pronouncements on what books should be read (and which ones should be avoided) can stifle readers' feelings of wonder and make them feel as if they have an obligation to get through certain books. The practice of plodding through a list composed by someone else can turn reading into a grim moral exercise in which the object is to glean something important or useful from the material, rather than find delight in the act of reading itself.

Taking his cue from a comment made by the poet Randall Jarrell, Jacobs encourages people to "read at whim." By "whim" he does not mean the careless browsing of individual titles or the thoughtless selection of something to while away the time between more important activities. For Jacobs, "whim" is the act of choosing books—fiction, poetry, or nonfiction; the genre is immaterial—that catch the eye or set off a spark of curiosity in the brain. These are the books that seem to call out to a person and demand to be read "for no good reason," asking would-be readers "to do something for the plain old delight and interest of it." Jacobs argues that if one is drawn to J. K. Rowling's *Harry Potter* series, or even popular teen romances like Stephenie Meyer's *Twilight* books, it is not necessary to apologize to anyone for the preference. Of course, Jacobs is optimistic that an individual's intellectual curiosity might lead beyond lightweight texts to those he considers more meaty—and the examples he cites of works that provide a deeper pleasure are similar to those found on the lists composed by Adler and Bloom.

Where these other authors begin with a series of imperatives regarding the value of certain books, Jacobs opts for a process that lets readers discover for themselves those texts that will demand close attention and eventually prove the most pleasurable. Rather than rush through books so that they can check them off a list, he encourages readers to select materials more randomly and to reread certain books, even ones that initially did not elicit particular interest. Those who go back to books often discover something they missed on the first reading, perhaps because they were simply not ready to understand an idea or experience a certain feeling. Jacobs provides a poignant personal example of what rereading can do. He says that on a third reading of Leo Tolstoy's *Anna Karenina* (1873–77), he found tears welling up in his eyes as he read about the reaction of the Russian estate owner Nikolai Levin to the birth of his son. The book had not changed, but Jacobs had become a father shortly before taking it up again, and the effect on him proved electrifying.

Jacobs is also happy to disconnect the process of reading from the physical objects in which texts are contained. He understands why some people hold out for the continued production of traditional books for both practical and aesthetic reasons. He does

(Darrin Dueck)

Alan Jacobs is a professor of English at Wheaton College, Illinois, and the author or editor of eleven books, including a critical biography of C. S. Lewis, a study of W. H. Auden's poetry, and several studies of theology and literature. He is a frequent contributor to the New Atlantis *and other national periodicals.*

not believe, however, that twenty-first-century bibliophiles are required to argue against new technologies that provide different ways to access texts. Jacobs confesses that he found himself becoming a disaffected reader of books, drifting away from the practice in order to spend more time on the Internet. What brought him back to reading, the kind of reading he advocates in *The Pleasures of Reading in an Age of Distraction*, was the purchase of an electronic reader. A good bit of space in the book is devoted to explaining how using an e-reader can provide its own form of pleasure and actually help people accustomed to working with twenty-first-century technologies to discover, or rediscover, the joy of losing oneself in a good story or well-constructed argument. The fact that he is not holding a two-pound block of paper pasted between hard covers does not bother Jacobs in the least.

Only occasionally does Jacobs seem to overstate his case that sustained, attentive reading is important for achieving the kind of pleasure he believes reading can afford. For example, he makes the claim that no novel or play can offer "full rewards" to anyone who reads it in small chunks. One might wonder about all the nineteenth-century readers who read long novels in exactly that way as a result of serial publication. Thousands of avid fans of Charles Dickens, for example, waited with great anticipation each month (or each week, later in the novelist's career) for the next installment of novels such as *The Old Curiosity Shop* (1840–41) or *A Tale of Two Cities* (1859) to appear in booksellers' stalls. It might be more appropriate to say that different forms of reading provide different experiences, as long as one engages with the story (for fiction) or follows carefully the arguments of the writer (for nonfiction).

There are a number of qualities about Jacobs's study that make it pleasurable reading in itself. First is the author's honesty about his own reaction to individual books and writers. He admits that there are some authors he has never been fond of, others who were once favorites but who now leave him unmoved, and still others whom he once resisted but who now make sense to him. Second, he is also quick to admit that as people age, their tastes tend to contract rather than broaden, noting that he has not been immune to this phenomenon himself. Many readers who have found themselves tending to read more of the same kinds of books as they grow older will feel kinship with the author and be more inclined to agree with his conclusions. Third, *The Pleasures of Reading in an Age of Distraction* is written in a lively, conversational style that quickly engages readers and leads them gently through the subtle argument Jacobs makes in favor of attentive reading. The work is filled with vivid metaphors and lively allusions and turns of phrase. In challenging people to avoid following someone else's list of important books because they are supposed to promote intellectual health, he encourages would-be readers not to "turn reading into the intellectual equivalent of eating organic greens." Continuing the food metaphor, he encourages those who truly enjoy Great Books not to make them "your steady intellectual diet, any more than you would eat at the most elegant of restaurants every day."

Jacobs displays an exceptional command of the tradition in which he operates, and it is obvious that he has read widely and thought deeply about his subject. Information and observations from literary and cultural critics, poets, and novelists stand beside those of neurologists who have done extensive research on how reading affects the brain. Furthermore, Jacobs is not afraid to reach far outside academe to find the most apt support for his argument, as evidenced by his inclusion of a long quotation from James Murphy, lead singer for the band LCD Soundsystem, who explains how Thomas Pynchon's novel *Gravity's Rainbow* (1973) changed his ideas about reading. The pleasure Jacobs himself feels in crafting this lucid and well-reasoned defense of reading carries over even to his "Essay on Sources," which provides entertainment and profit to those who want to know where Jacobs has gone in search of support for his argument.

Jacobs's bottom-line recommendation may not win him new friends among his academic colleagues, but it is certain to appeal to the millions of adults who were once fascinated by reading but who, for one reason or another, have found themselves put off by the practice: "Read what gives you delight—at least most of the time—and do so without shame."

Laurence W. Mazzeno

Review Sources

Booklist 107, no. 18 (May 15, 2011): 4.
Christian Century 128, no. 10 (May 17, 2011): 42.
Library Journal 136, no. 7 (April 15, 2011): 92.
Publishers Weekly 258, no. 15 (April 11, 2011): 41.
The Wall Street Journal, August 8, 2011, p. A13.

The Prague Cemetery

Author: Umberto Eco (b. 1932)
First published: *Il Cimitero di Praga*, 2010, in Italy
Translated from the Italian by Richard Dixon
Publisher: Houghton Mifflin Harcourt (New York). Illustrated. 464 pp. $27.00
Type of work: Novel
Time: 1830–1898
Locale: Piedmont and Sicily, Italy; Paris, France

Set in a nineteenth-century Europe obsessed with theories of conspiracy, Umberto Eco's The Prague Cemetery *is the story of Simone Simonini, a master forger of documents who is driven by hatred.*

Principal characters:
SIMONE SIMONINI, a forger, spy, and murderer
ABBÉ DALLA PICCOLA, his other self
CAPTAIN GIOVANNI BAPTISTA SIMONINI, his grandfather, who hates Jews
ABBÉ BARRUEL, a deceased abbot to whom Simonini's grandfather wrote of Jewish conspiracy
MORDECHAI, a Jewish bogeyman who haunts Simonini's childhood
FATHER BERGAMASCHI, Simonini's tutor and later conspirator against the Jews
NOTAIO REBAUDENGO, a lawyer who introduces Simonini to forging legal documents
MAURICE JOLY, the author whose work Simonini plagiarizes
GAVIALI, an explosives expert
HERMANN GOEDSCHE, the author who plagiarizes Simonini's story about the Prague cemetery

In *The Prague Cemetery*, Umberto Eco combines elements of the historical novel, the thriller, the serial novel, the gothic novel, the psychological novel, and the memoir to create a work that explores the creation of fictions and the effects those fictions may have on individual lives as well as political and social history. Eco's Narrator, almost a character in his own right, begins the novel by describing the less-than-reputable section of Paris where Simonini keeps his junk shop, above which is located the office where he carries on his real profession as a forger of legal documents and seller of consecrated hosts. The Narrator invites the reader to look over the shoulder of an elderly man and read his diary as he writes it, withholding the man's name and stating that neither he nor the reader can possibly know who the man is at this point. In the second chapter, Simonini's diary begins. Suffering from partial amnesia, trying to figure out who he is, Simonini explains that he is writing on the advice of a German or Austrian

Jew, a psychiatrist that he met at Chez Magny. Simonini describes himself as a great lover of food but admits that he loves no one. In fact, he hates all nationalities, races, and sects, both males and females. The early pages of his diary alternate among three topics: diatribes against Germans, Frenchmen, Jesuits, Jews, Masons, and women; descriptions of and recipes for various dishes; and a discussion of nineteenth-century psychiatric theory and practice.

Then Eco complicates his novel, as Simonini is interrupted by a client and returns to his desk to find a packet of letters addressed to an Abbé Dalla Piccola. The mystery of Dalla Piccola's true identity continues through the novel as a subplot. Simonini "discovers" a mysterious corridor in which there is an array of costumes and disguises. Simonini and Dalla Piccola appear alternately in the novel and both write in the diary. Eco gives various clues that lead the reader to believe that they are the same person and Simonini is suffering from a split personality. When Simonini kills Dalla Piccola and hides the body in the sewer system under his house, Dalla Piccola continues to write in the diary and leave messages for Simonini. So the mystery continues.

In the diary, Simonini recounts the events of his life, from his childhood and youth spent in his grandfather's house in Turin, Italy. From his grandfather, he acquired his hatred of the Jews and his great love of food, as well as his fascination with the novels of nineteenth-century French writers Alexander Dumas and Eugène Sue. Simonini admits that he also discovered the pleasure of disguising himself as someone else. After his grandfather's death, Simonini is introduced to his profession of forging illegal documents by Notaio Rebaudengo, the lawyer who cheated him out of his inheritance from his grandfather. While employed by Rebaudengo, Simonini begins to work for the Piedmont secret service. Soon, however, he betrays his Carbonaro associates and Rebaudengo, falls out of favor with the secret service, and is exiled to Paris.

There, Simonini sets up a business forging legal documents. He begins working for the French secret service and eventually for the Russian secret service. The novel follows Simonini through his increasingly complicated involvement in espionage, a pursuit rife with impersonations, deceptions, betrayals, bombings, murders, and the creation of fictitious conspiracies for the aims of various governments. Simonini participates in plots to discredit the Jesuits, the Masons, and the Jews. The novel is further complicated by additional subplots, including nineteenth-century psychiatry, the story of Diana the hysteric, Leo Taxil's campaign against the Masons, and the Black Mass.

Chapter twelve is the core chapter of the novel, as Simonini discovers the existence of what he refers to as an anti-Jewish market, composed of not only Jesuits and men like his grandfather but also of revolutionaries, republicans, socialists, certain governments, and ordinary people. The French secret service contacts him and lends him to the Russians to create an anti-Jewish document. After a conversation with Jakob Brafmann, a Jew who converted to Christianity, Simonini realizes that he has the very framework necessary to create a salable document: his piece about the Prague cemetery, written in Turin. The document will depict a meeting of Jewish rabbis, not Jesuits, in the cemetery. Narrating Simonini's creation of the Prague cemetery, Eco analyzes in detail the elements that make a propaganda fiction believable and dangerous. The setting is important; it must instill fear in the reader and a sense of an unnatural power.

The abandoned Jewish cemetery, with its gravestones leaning awry, is perfect for creating the proper ambiance. The information presented in the document must be something with which people are familiar and that they can understand with ease, yet it must also appear new. Thus, Simonini creates the Jewish rabbis' conspiracy plan to take over the world through possession of the world's gold by infiltrating every profession: business, law, medicine, science, literature, the arts, agriculture, and finance. The conspiracy plan is simply usury stated in different terms, so it is both familiar and new. The scenario of the Prague cemetery conspiracy will already be familiar to many from the Masonic conspiracy for world domination presented in Dumas's *Joseph Balsamo* (1846–48). Ironically, Simonini does such an excellent job creating his document that he himself comes to believe that the conspiracy actually exists. He says that what was only an imagined hatred in his mind has become a real and identifiable hatred, as he now realizes how perverse and dangerous the Jews are.

© Guido Harari/Contrasto/Redux

Umberto Eco is renowned for his work in semiology, medievalism, philosophy, literary theory, and fiction. He is the author of the novels The Name of the Rose *(1983;* Il nome della rosa, *1980) and* Foucault's Pendulum *(1989;* Il pendolo di Foucault, *1988). He has received numerous awards and honors, including the Premio Strega and recognition as a Chevalier de la Legion d'Honneur.*

Eco adds complexity to his novel by structuring it with multiple voices. The Narrator introduces the story and at times summarizes for the reader; Simone Simonini and Dalla Piccola recount their experiences and reactions in first person, but an outside third perspective, the Narrator, also recounts the actions, words, and emotions of other characters. Eco emphasizes the switch in voices by using different typefaces for the different narrative voices. The author is also a part of the text, for at the beginning of the novel, Eco elucidates the role the Narrator will play and what the reader can and cannot expect. He includes at the end of the novel what he refers to as "Useless Learned Explanations," in which he informs the reader that Simonini is the only fictitious character and that the rest are actually drawn from history. He also presents an outline of the plot and the story chapter by chapter.

Eco's novel is also about writing fiction; it is itself a kind of compilation of nineteenth-century fictional writing. The many references to Dumas's and Sue's work, and to themes of conspiracy, subterranean chambers, cemeteries, and darkly lit rooms, all make the popular serial novels (*feuilletons*) an integral part of the text, while Eco's attention to detail and minute description of places, furniture, and foods bring to mind the realists of the period. The inclusion of the poor of Paris—the rag-and-bone men, the cigar-stub collectors, the *suiveurs* and factory girls and prostitutes, the pimps and the brothels—alludes to the work of French writer Émile Zola and the naturalist writers, with their emphasis on the lower classes and their misery. Eco further sets his novel in the nineteenth-century world of serial novels, political tracts, and conspiracy by illustrating it with engravings of the period, which add to the novel's ambiance of danger, evil intention, and monstrosity of character.

Through the very structure of the novel, Eco illustrates how fiction and reality can be intertwined and mistaken for one another. By adding one fictional character, Simonini, to historical events, he transforms reality into fiction; although the other characters did actually exist and participate in the events described, Simonini did not. Eco sets the satirical tone of his novel through the use of humorous detail. Lists, exaggeration, and absurdity abound. Eco's predilection for lists is very apparent and serves to underline the absurd quality of many devices used in nineteenth-century fiction. When Simonini takes the body of Dalla Piccola into the sewers, for instance, he discovers an enormous number of animal bodies, such as dogs, cats, chickens, goats, calves, pigs, a monkey, and even a boa constrictor. This is not the sewer of Victor Hugo's *Les Misérables* (1862). Eco also uses the exaggeration of long lists when he enumerates the titles held by various Masonic officials. He uses excess to render absurd his various characters' ravings against different sects, especially the Jews. Amassing long lists of vices and bad characteristics, the speakers and writers become carried away. Eco advances the irony of the novel in his reworking of well-known phrases; Simonini's statement "I hate, therefore I am," for example, is an amended version of French philosopher René Descartes's famous proposal "I think, therefore I am."

The Prague Cemetery is an entertaining novel filled with complex plots, impressive settings, a double identity mystery, and touches of humor and irony. However, Eco also provides a serious consideration of the human tendency toward fabrication, the deceptive power of language as communication, and the readiness of humankind to accept fiction as truth, particularly when it portrays something with which one is already familiar. The novel emphasizes how the conspiracy theory of Simonini's Prague cemetery, itself an act of plagiarism, was then plagiarized, reworked, and repeatedly used by other writers and factions to create fear, mistrust, and hatred. The satiric and ironic tone of the novel underscores the absurdity of the conspiracy theories that dominated the nineteenth century, while also warning readers against the ability of fiction to become accepted truth and result in something as harmful and devastating as *The Protocols of the Elders of Zion*, the historical tract upon which Eco bases Simonini's work, first published in Russian in 1903.

The Prague Cemetery has elicited high praise as well as harsh criticism from critics, who have both praised the novel as the definitive proof of Eco's talent as a novelist and disparaged it as a plodding and tedious compendium of erudite knowledge. The novel has also created a considerable amount of controversy, with the Vatican condemning it for its derogatory portrayal of the Jesuits. Eco has also received criticism for his postmodern, humorous depiction of fraudulent documents, especially the actual *Protocols of the Elders of Zion*, which led to persecution of the Jews during the twentieth century. Some critics have even suggested that the novel may be read as a propaganda piece for hatred and racism. However, the majority of critics have viewed this idea as absurd, for the novel is a complex and erudite work that obviously satirizes the self-serving and fanatical factions it portrays. Already an international best seller, *The Prague Cemetery* has overall been well received.

Shawncey J. Webb

Review Sources

The Guardian, November 4, 2011, p. 6
Jewish Chronicle Online, December 5, 2011 (Web).
The New York Times Book Review, November 20, 2011, p. 20.
The Observer, November 6, 2011, p. 45.
Open Letters Monthly, November 1, 2011 (Web).

The Preacher

Author: Camilla Läckberg (b. 1974)
First published: *Predikanten*, 2004, in Sweden
Translated from the Swedish by Steven T. Murray
Publisher: Pegasus Books (New York). 432 pp. $25.95.
Type of work: Novel
Time: The present
Locale: Fjällbacka, Sweden

The gruesome murder of a young woman in the small village of Fjällbacka, Sweden— and the discovery of decades-old remains located beneath her body—challenge the skills of police detective Patrik Hedström and his wife, writer Erica Falck.

Principal characters:
PATRIK HEDSTRÖM, a police detective
ERICA FALCK, a writer, Patrik's wife
ANNA MAXWELL, Erica's sister
GABRIEL HULT, a successful businessman
JACOB HULT, Gabriel's son
LINDA HULT, Gabriel's daughter
SOLVEIG HULT, Gabriel's sister-in-law
ROBERT AND STEFAN HULT, Gabriel's nephews, Solveig's sons
TANJA SCHMIDT, a traveler from Germany, missing since 1979
JENNY MÖLER, a teenage girl who goes missing

A young boy slips out of bed early to play by the water's edge outside the village of Fjällbacka on the western coast of Sweden. Attracted by a piece of red clothing protruding from a cleft in the rocks, he peers in and discovers the body of a young woman. When the police come to investigate, they discover the skeletons of two more women lying under the recently murdered woman. It quickly becomes apparent that all three were killed elsewhere and their bodies dumped at the spot where they were found.

The mystery surrounding the deaths of these three women becomes the starting point for *The Preacher*. Camilla Läckberg's tautly written police procedural brings back some faces familiar to her readers and introduces new characters, including many with dysfunctional lives, that provide Läckberg ample opportunity to do what she seems to enjoy most: combine the qualities of a traditional detective story with commentary on a society that she knows intimately.

In the second installment in her series of murder mysteries set in her hometown, Läckberg reintroduces readers to Patrik Hedström and Erica Falck, the crime-fighting protagonists of *The Ice Princess* (2003). In that novel, the writer Falck moves back to her childhood home in Fjällbacka to settle her family's estate. When she learns of an old friend's apparent suicide, she begins investigating the circumstances surrounding the tragedy with the thought of writing a fictionalized account of it. Her sleuthing uncovers hints that foul play may have been involved, however, so she seeks help from Hedström, once a high-school admirer and now a police officer. The two manage to uncover the truth and, along the way, fall in love and get married.

When *The Preacher* begins, Erica is eight months pregnant. She and Patrik are living in the Falck family home by the seashore. Limited by her pregnancy, Erica helps her husband with research into the background of the old murders and serves as a sounding board for him when the case becomes frustrating. Where *The Ice Princess* was essentially Erica's book, *The Preacher* concentrates on Patrik's work as the lead investigator of the Tanumshede police force's task force assigned to find the killer or killers. The team he heads up includes a bright young newcomer to detective work and two grizzled veterans who resent being supervised by a younger officer; the group is supervised by a chief who is clearly interested in advancing his own image with politicians and the public. This combination of personalities provides Läckberg an opportunity to explore the dynamics of a working police force during a time of crisis.

Early in his investigation, Hedström learns that the recent murder victim is Tanja Schmidt, a German tourist seen in the area of the Hult estate. The Hults, one of the region's most prominent and most notorious families, are descendants of the long-deceased Ephraim Hult, known throughout the region as "the Preacher." Ephraim's legendary ability to heal the sick had earned him the admiration of a wealthy woman who left a sizable estate to the family. His son Gabriel now lives there with his wife, while Gabriel's son Jacob and his family live nearby. Gabriel's rebellious teenage daughter, Linda, lives with her brother but spends considerable time with her cousin Stefan, son of Gabriel's deceased brother Johannes. Stefan's mother, Solveig—once a great beauty but now slovenly and bitter because her husband's family had essentially been cut out of Ephraim's will in favor of Gabriel's family—lives in squalor with her two sons, Stefan and Robert. These two are well known to the police force, having been arrested for petty crimes on numerous occasions. The two branches of the family are engaged in a long-standing and bitter feud.

As the story progresses, readers learn about the particular dysfunctions within both branches of the Hult family and receive hints as to why the Hult men are strong suspects for the more recent murder and perhaps for the older crimes as well. Readers learn that this is not the first time the Tanumshede police have visited the Hults to investigate a murder. In 1979, Johannes Hult had been identified by his brother as being with a girl on the evening she went missing. Hedström is fairly certain that one of the sets of skeletal remains belongs to the same girl. Unfortunately for the present-day investigators, after being hounded by the police at the time, Johannes committed suicide, so he could not possibly have committed the latest murder.

(Thron Ullberg)

Camilla Läckberg is the author of seven books set in her hometown of Fjällbacka on the west coast of Sweden. She received Sweden's Folket Prize in 2006, and her first mystery novel, The Ice Princess *(2003), was named International Crime Novel of the Year in 2008.*

The situation becomes more complicated for the police when Jenny Möler, a teenager visiting the area with her parents, disappears. Hedström assumes she has been taken by the same person who murdered Tanja Schmidt. The police detective's frantic search to find Jenny before she suffers the same fate dominates the second half of the book. To confuse matters even more, in the process of trying to find a likely suspect for the original murders, Hedström develops a theory that Johannes may have faked his own suicide years earlier. He orders an exhumation of the body and makes a shocking discovery that only leads to more questions. The eventual revelation of Tanja Schmidt's killer, and of the person who murdered the two girls in 1979, comes in an exciting climax that may not end as some readers hope. Nevertheless, Läckberg provides a plausible explanation and a motive for the crimes and ties up loose ends nicely, offering neat resolutions of all the problems that arise in the course of the mystery.

It is important to note, however, that *The Preacher* is not simply a straightforward whodunit. The details of Hedström's investigation are interwoven with the running narrative of the problems Erica is having with her pregnancy and with her family. A series of freeloading relatives and old friends descends on the couple's seaside house, taking advantage of their hospitality and severely taxing Erica's physical and mental stamina. How she and Patrik deal with the situation becomes an interesting test of their relationship—especially since Patrik is too busy trying to solve three murders and prevent a fourth to rescue his wife from the clutches of these demanding and insensitive parasites. Readers familiar with *The Ice Princess* will also recognize the return of Erica's sister Anna and her abusive husband, from whom she is now divorced. Despite her condition, Erica spends considerable time and energy worrying about Anna and her children. The interplay between the murder and kidnapping investigations and these domestic dramas gives *The Preacher* a richer texture than many traditional crime novels that focus exclusively on the pursuit and apprehension of the perpetrators.

Läckberg uses many traditional plot devices in order to keep the reader in suspense. Not only does she move rapidly from scene to scene, she also shifts point of view constantly, providing varying perspectives on characters and events. At one moment, readers are with Hedström as he pursues leads; in the next, they are inside a torture chamber where the missing girls are made to suffer physical and mental abuse at the hands of an unknown assailant. Flashbacks to 1979 provide a sense of the terror that the young women felt as they were slowly tortured to satisfy some inexplicable need on the part of their abductor. The eerie similarities between these earlier events and the treatment of Tanja Schmidt and Jenny Möler, a detail given to readers but unknown to detectives assigned to the case, drive readers to speculate about the relationship between these two crime sprees separated by nearly three decades. While some of the characters may seem stereotypical, quite a few are drawn with great detail and are complex and believable. The large cast of characters also makes it difficult for readers to focus on a single suspect—exactly the effect a veteran mystery writer hopes to elicit.

Furthermore, the domestic drama that serves as a subplot seems more serious than the one which ran through *The Ice Princess*. In that novel, Erica's speculations about how she might appear to Patrik and how she might eventually convince him to marry her were criticized by a number of reviewers as being heavy-handed and overdone. Some even suggested that the constant reminder of Erica's insecurities reduced Läckberg's heroine to the status of a psychological and intellectual lightweight—a judgment at odds with her considerable skills at detection and to her ability to win over Patrik on her merits rather than her appearance. The other social issue carried over from its predecessor to *The Preacher*, Erica's concern for her sister's welfare, is presented with sensitivity and insight. The new complication on the home front is also deftly handled; descriptions of houseguests taking advantage of Patrik and Erica effectively blend comedy with serious commentary on problems young couples face early in their marriage.

The Preacher and *The Ice Princess* invite comparisons with the work of other popular Swedish crime novelists, most notably Stieg Larsson and Henning Mankell. It is unlikely that, after reading only these two novels, English-speaking readers will find Hedström and Falck quite as engaging or interesting as Larsson and Mankell's iconic characters. On the evidence of the first two mysteries involving Hedström and Falck, however, there is every reason to believe that they will become household names among those who appreciate detective fiction that combines the excitement of following clues to solve a mystery with explorations of the lives of complex characters who operate on both sides of the law.

Laurence W. Mazzeno

Review Sources

Booklist 108, no. 1 (September 1, 2011): 60.
Entertainment Weekly, May 6, 2011, p. 79.
Kirkus Reviews 79, no. 6 (March 15, 2011): 447–48.
Library Journal 136, no. 3 (February 15, 2011): 103.
Publishers Weekly 258, no. 30 (July 25, 2011): 46.
Times Literary Supplement, no. 5535 (May 1, 2009): 21.
The Washington Post, June 13, 2011, p. C3.

The Psychopath Test
A Journey Through the Madness Industry

Author: Jon Ronson (b. 1967)
Publisher: Riverhead Books (New York). Il-
lustrated. 288 pp. $25.95
Type of work: History of science, medicine,
psychology
Time: Mostly the late twentieth and early
twenty-first centuries
Locale: London and the United States

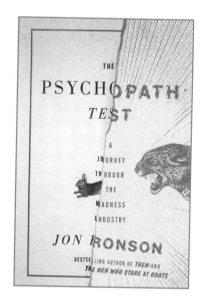

*The author offers a comic yet insightful explo-
ration of psychiatric diagnostic methods past
and present, as well as a critique of their effects
on individuals and society.*

Principal personages:

JON RONSON, investigative journalist, humorist,
documentary maker, and media personality
ROBERT "BOB" HARE, psychopathy expert who
developed the *Hare Psychopathy Check-
list—Revised* (*Hare PCL-R*) (1980)
ROBERT SPITZER, professor of psychiatry at Columbia University and editor of the
Diagnostic and Statistical Manual of Psychiatric Disorders, third edition (*DSM-
III*) (1980)
PAUL BABIAK, psychologist, researcher, and author
ELLIOT BARKER, a psychiatrist at the Oak Ridge Hospital for the Criminally Insane in
Ontario, Canada
GARY MAIER, a psychiatrist at the Oak Ridge Hospital for the Criminally Insane
EMMANUEL "TOTO" CONSTANT, a former Haitian death-squad leader convicted of mort-
gage fraud in the United States
ALBERT "CHAINSAW AL" DUNLAP, a retired Sunbeam executive and author of *Mean
Business* (1997)
DAVID SHAYLER, a British journalist, conspiracy theorist, and self-proclaimed messiah
MARTHA STOUT, a former Harvard Medical School professor and author of *The Socio-
path Next Door* (2005)

Jon Ronson opens his exposé of what he calls the madness industry with a mystery. In
2008, scores of neurologists and other academics around the world received a handmade book entitled *Being or Nothingness*. No one knew who had written it or sent it to
them. Nor did they know why they had been chosen to receive it or why some of them
had received multiple copies. They did not know if it was sent to them in earnest or if
it was a hoax. The intriguing phenomenon fueled debate, speculation, and conspiracy

theories on Internet boards and blogs. After Ronson himself was suspected of being the author of the mystery book, he offered to find out what he could about the book and its author. In the course of his investigation, he realized that "psychopaths make the world go round." He began to see madness everywhere and dedicated himself to uncovering the deeper mysteries of madness itself: what

Media personality, documentary film-maker, and newspaper columnist Jon Ronson has written two international bestsellers, Them: Adventures with Extremists *(2002) and* The Men Who Stare at Goats *(2005). The latter book inspired a popular 2009 movie starring George Clooney and Ewan McGregor.*

it is, who decides what it is and who has it, and how the diagnosis and treatment of mental illness affects individuals and society as a whole.

For *The Psychopath Test: A Journey through the Madness Industry*, Ronson has explored a variety of sources, including personal interviews, scholarly studies, declassified government reports, newspaper accounts, Goldman Sachs research reports, photographs, transcripts of broadcast media interviews, and memoirs, as well as his own experience as an investigator. Drawing from this wide range of materials, he attempts to dismantle the very foundation of the psychiatric profession.

Written in an accessible style, *The Psychopath Test* traces Ronson's investigation of the mysteries of madness and of psychopathy in particular. He begins his investigation by looking up *psychopath* in the American Psychiatric Association's revised fourth edition of the *Diagnostic and Statistical Manual of Mental Disorders* (*DSM-IV-TR*) (2000), the primary reference book that mental-health practitioners use to diagnose patients. The first edition of the manual, published in 1952, was a mere 65 pages and was not widely used. After a major expansion increased the size of the manual from a 136-page pamphlet to hefty 478-page hardbound third edition, over a million copies of the expanded *DSM-III* were sold—more than the number of psychiatrists then in existence. The *DSM-IV-TR* lists 374 mental disorders. However, much to Ronson's surprise, psychopath is not one of them.

One of Ronson's humorous tales describes how he reads the manual and identifies with twelve of the disorders. After this experience, he decides to study people in positions of power to see if they exhibit any of the disorders, particularly antisocial personality disorder, which he finds to be fascinating. He wonders if any organization has already conducted a similar sort of analysis and discovers that the Scientologist group Citizens Commission on Human Rights is dedicated to toppling psychiatry.

The Scientologists that Ronson meets introduce him to a man who faked a psychiatric disorder in order to avoid jail time. The man was then unable to prove his sanity and found himself incarcerated in a psychiatric hospital for a longer time than he would have spent in prison. Ronson is won over by the man after reading reports from the hospital about his behavior, and he subsequently visits the house of Scientology founder L. Ron Hubbard to research why the Scientologists formed their anti-psychiatry group. Ronson has also provided a detailed account of Hubbard's long-term commitment to the fight against organized psychiatry. Hubbard theorized that memory patterns of traumatic experiences can be removed without therapy or medication, concluding that both psychiatry and drug companies are therefore unnecessary and should be abolished. Hubbard also believed that the pharmaceutical companies and organized psychiatry viewed him as an existential threat and were therefore actively conspiring to destroy him. As part of his inquiry, Ronson watches the Scientology documentary *Psychiatry: An Industry of Death* (2006). From the documentary, he learns of a mental disorder, drapetomania, which was described for the first time in the United States in 1851. Evident only in slaves, the singular symptom of the disorder was "the desire to run away from slavery" and the only cure was to "whip the devil out of" sufferers to prevent the disease's development.

Ronson spends considerable time investigating a project initiated by Elliot Barker to test LSD as a cure for criminal insanity in psychopaths. Barker set up an experiment in which inmates in a Canadian hospital unit for the criminally insane were administered LSD, then stripped naked and placed together in a large cell where they were fed food through the walls with straws. Barker hypothesized that such conditions would encourage his subjects to bond with each other and feel empathy, which he hoped would prevent them from re-offending. However, a subsequent study revealed that his subjects had a higher repeat offense rate than the norm. Barker's experiment went beyond its original purpose, which was to test LSD as a cure, and instituted group Om chanting and dream work. The majority of the participants used the opportunity to study feelings and what feelings were supposed to do, which, rather than causing them to feel emotion and remorse, merely gave them new ideas for ways to manipulate other people.

During the course of his investigation, Ronson also visits Robert Hare, the inventor of the psychopath checklist test. Hare discovered in his own research that psychopaths do not release fear hormones when they are told that they are going to be administered shocks. He therefore concluded that the threat of pain does not deter psychopaths from committing further offenses. He had difficulty getting his research published, however, because of the disagreement in the profession about the morality of using electroshock therapy for research purposes. Hare also discovered that the amygdala and central nervous system do not function normally in a psychopathic brain. He theorizes that this anomaly contributes to psychopaths' lack of remorse and empathy. He regrets having done all his research in prisons rather than among the corporate elite and politicians who, in his opinion, had ruined societies. For Ronson, Hare's epiphany about the connection between psychopaths' abnormal brain physiology and their lack of remorse holds the answer to the age-old question: why is the world so unfair? Might we have savage economic injustice, brutal wars, and everyday cruelty, Ronson asks, due to the brain anomalies of our rulers, who might be psychopaths? He then wonders if that is why a disproportionate number of psychopaths occupy leadership positions in business and politics.

Ronson finds that Martha Stout, a former Harvard Medical School professor, came to this same conclusion. Stout's book, *The Sociopath Next Door* (2005), describes how she used magnetic resonance imaging (MRI) to observe the brains of sociopaths, whereupon she noticed that their emotional responses differ from the norm when they are shown pictures of cruelty and violence. Her research revealed that although sociopaths and psychopaths are more charming than most people and look normal, they do not feel love.

In order to put his newfound knowledge to the test, Ronson interviews several subjects to see if he can use the *Hare Psychopathy Checklist—Revised* to diagnose them as psychopaths. His subjects include Toto Constant, a Haitian CIA-backed murderer who was hired to influence politics; a TV talk show booker who asked people what medication they were on in order to get the right mix of madness for the show; British conspiracy theorist David Shayler; and a crime profiler who tried to get a murder confession from a suspect in unconventional ways. In Ronson's view, each of these people exhibits psychopathic traits that inspired their avocations or make them good at their jobs, but perhaps none more so than "Chainsaw Al" Dunlap, the Sunbeam executive who was lauded by the corporate community for his ability to execute harsh downsizing measures. *Fast Company* magazine wrote him up as a possible psychopath, but in Ronson's view, Dunlap earned his reputation as a psychopath well before his firing spree at Sunbeam. Dunlap had attacked his wife with a knife, refused to go to his own parents' funerals, and at one point said that he wanted to know what flesh tasted like. As a child, he had thrown darts at his sister's dolls; as an adult, he kept his mansion filled with sculptures of large predatory animals that he admired.

Ronson's final fieldwork chapter delves into pediatric psychiatry and includes his visit to a home where children are diagnosed as bipolar as early as the age of three, a practice that alarms Ronson. He also reports that a mother was charged with murder because she dispensed incorrect dosages and used psychoactive medication to try to quiet a sick child at night. Ronson questions the way psychiatrists have attempted to convince parents to give their children medications that have not been perfected on adults. He interviews an expert who says that the mass misdiagnosis of children may leave their bodies and psyches damaged for life. Such labeling may lengthen the distance between children, parents, and what they really need for a better quality of life—empathy and health. Ronson concludes his book with a three-page discussion of sources, which should prove to be valuable to readers who are interested in learning more about the history, diagnosis, and treatment of psychopathy.

Batya Weinbaum

Review Sources

Bloomberg Businessweek, July 21, 2011 (Web).
The Guardian, May 27, 2011 (Web).
Los Angeles Times, May 19, 2011 (Web).
The New York Times, May 16, 2011 (Web).

Pulphead
Essays

Author: John Jeremiah Sullivan (b. 1974)
Publisher: Farrar, Straus and Giroux (New York). 384 pp. $16.00
Type of work: Essays

John Jeremiah Sullivan presents an engaging collection of essays that provides many unexpected perspectives on American popular culture.

In the writings collected in *Pulphead: Essays*, author John Jeremiah Sullivan explores some of the more curious byways of American popular culture, ranging effortlessly from an appreciation of the artistry of Axl Rose to a eulogy for the last of the southern agrarians. Centuries from now, historians will find Sullivan an intriguing illuminator of lost worlds. Today, his readers will discover in his eclectic interests a reminder that even familiar topics can provide surprising marvels. Sullivan is a masterful commentator on popular culture because he takes it seriously. This is not to say that he approaches his subjects with the enthusiasm of a developmentally arrested fanboy; even when he writes as an aficionado, Sullivan maintains a self-consciously critical distance. What sets him apart from so many more superficial observers of the contemporary scene is his fundamental respect for the individuality and integrity of the people at the center of each essay. He concedes that musicians as diverse as Michael Jackson, Axl Rose, and obscure African American bluesmen of the 1930s were all creators who reveled in their own craftsmanship. He refuses to see his subjects simply as musical primitives, channeling their songs from some collective pool of the zeitgeist. Similarly, Sullivan avoids the temptation to caricature Tea Partiers and fans of Christian rock, something often indulged by writers with his particular political and social slant. He treats with respect people whose vision of life is alien to his own. This is made easier by the fact that Sullivan himself is deeply rooted to the predominantly conservative Middle America that is the font of much of his work.

Sullivan was born in Kentucky, his mother's ancestral home, and raised across the Ohio River in southern Indiana. As a result, he is attuned to the rhythms, manners, and mores of ordinary American life in a way that more ostensibly cosmopolitan writers are not. Even when bemused, Sullivan never sneers, for he is always ready to attempt to understand his subjects, whether or not he agrees with them. While working on a profile of Bunny Wailer, the last surviving member of Bob Marley's band, his magazine's demand for a photo shoot finally drove the aging reggae icon into rebellion;

John Jeremiah Sullivan is the author of Blood Horses: Notes of a Sportswriter's Son *(2004). He is the southern editor of the* Paris Review *and a contributing writer for the* New York Times Magazine.

Wailer refused to be photographed and denounced Sullivan, cutting off all contact. However, instead of begrudging his subject, Sullivan understood this as his final gift: he had remained true to himself.

The prose in *Pulphead* is gorgeous. A master of style, Sullivan uses language as a supple tool, both gracefully refined and raucously colloquial. One moment Sullivan may be subtly exploring a religious vision of the world; a few pages later, he might energetically evoke the Day-Glo atmosphere of a rock concert or a reality television show. His ability to effortlessly transition from the sublime to the ridiculous, and to find the right words with which to do so, places him firmly in the New Journalism literary tradition that burst onto the scene in the 1960s. New Journalism expanded and enhanced magazine reportage by bringing to bear the arsenal of literary styles that was available to novelists, freeing up prose and perspective and inaugurating a brilliantly giddy ride for readers inured to stories that settled exclusively for facts. Tom Wolfe, Hunter S. Thompson, and Norman Mailer, the pioneers of this explosive approach, lavished readers with masterpieces for over a decade before Mailer and Wolfe refocused on writing novels. The title *Pulphead* is an evocation of this movement, a reference to an epithet that Norman Mailer used in his resignation letter to a magazine editor. Though the New Journalism is no longer new, Sullivan is a gifted practitioner who boldly goes where his illustrious predecessors have not gone before. In doing so, he ensures that the best magazine writing of our day deserves to be called literature, and that it will endure beyond the ephemeral concerns of the present.

Pulphead allows Sullivan to display his versatility as a cultural observer and critic. The first essay records his experiences at the Creation Festival, an enormous gathering of Christian rock bands and fans, "a veritable Godstock" that takes place annually in rural Pennsylvania. Sullivan was willing to take on the assignment in cultural anthropology for *Gentlemen's Quarterly* on the condition that, unlike most of the festivalgoers, he did not have to camp in a tent. *GQ* could certainly afford the expense of outfitting Sullivan with a camper, but because of the festival, all the vans within one hundred miles of Philadelphia were rented, and as a result, the magazine secured for him a twenty-nine-foot RV. This led to a comedic sequence of events worthy of Lucille Ball, as Sullivan maneuvered the vehicle first along the Pennsylvania Turnpike during rush hour, then into a campground and, guided by a kid with a flashlight, up an almost vertical hill. Despite imagining that his misadventure might result in his RV rolling murderously down a hill full of Christians, Sullivan was rescued by some stalwart backwoodsmen from West Virginia, an encounter that would shape his whole experience of the festival.

At face value, Darius, Jake, Josh, Bub, Ritter, and Pee Wee were rough customers, having emerged from the world of rural poverty to live off the land in West Virginia. They were completely at home camping out at the Creation Festival, and they took Sullivan under their wing, demonstrating their born-again faith while making sure he was fed with the frog legs and other bits of game they caught. They also acted as his guides through the terra incognita of Christian rock music. Sullivan happily embraced the camaraderie of his new neighbors, and he also understood their faith on a personal level. In high school, Sullivan himself had spent several years immersed in evangelical Christianity, before doubts gradually dimmed his fire. Though unable to share the convictions of those attending the Creation Festival—or the convictions of his friends from West Virginia, whose faith had saved them from despair or worse—Sullivan could still appreciate what they wanted and what they had. The essay ends on a note of grace, with Sullivan summing up the West Virginians in the way that they would have wanted: they were crazy and they loved God. His final words describe the closing ceremony of the festival, as everyone gathered in the evening, lit a candle each, and collectively blew them out. When Sullivan drove his monstrous RV away the next morning, he had not gathered the evidence of a freak show that his editors probably expected. Instead, he had rediscovered a community that, to him, was as attractive as it was unobtainable.

Another compelling essay focuses on the year Sullivan spent living with writer and literary critic Andrew Lytle. His mother's Kentucky heritage had always impressed Sullivan, even when he was growing up in Indiana. As a young man, he was imbued with the idea of the South, and he nourished himself with the novels of William Faulkner and other literary scions of Dixie. He enrolled at the University of the South in Sewanee, Tennessee, one of the intellectual fonts of Southernism in the twentieth century. It was the home of the *Sewanee Review* as well as the base for Lytle, a leader of the southern agrarian writers' movement that made a literary stir in the 1930s. Lytle was one of the "Twelve Southerners" who contributed to *I'll Take My Stand: The South and the Agrarian Tradition* (1930), a ringing defense of southern culture and its pastoral traditions in an increasingly urban and industrial age. By the time Sullivan knew him, Lytle was the last of the agrarians. He had been close friends with Robert Penn Warren and had helped nurture the careers of Flannery O'Connor, James Dickey, and Cormac McCarthy. At almost ninety-two, he was an increasingly frail living time capsule of the southern world that no longer existed.

Sullivan had not done well academically at Sewanee. The summer after his sophomore year, he had withdrawn from the university in anticipation of being forced out and ended up working at a restaurant in Ireland with a friend. Before leaving Tennessee, however, Sullivan had become friends with Sanford, a therapeutic masseur whose list of clients included Andrew Lytle. Sanford, who knew nothing about Sullivan's standing at the university, showed Lytle some of his friend's writings. It had become the custom at Sewanee to have a student live with Lytle, to help him with everyday tasks and be there in case of emergency. As Lytle's latest student was graduating, he offered the job to Sullivan on the strength of Sullivan's writing and Sanford's recommendation. This led to a delicate complication with the university, but Lytle ultimately had his way.

What followed, during the last year of Lytle's life, was a priceless opportunity for Sullivan to learn about writing from a master. The two read Flaubert, Joyce, and other classic novelists. Lytle critiqued Sullivan's short stories, making the increasingly awed novice aware of compositional problems where he was scarcely aware that problems could exist. Sullivan also came to love Lytle in all his eccentricities, for Lytle was in many ways an anachronism, from his accent to his social attitudes. Likewise, moments of kindness, provoked memories, and amusing insights endeared Lytle to the younger man. In this way, for half a year, Sullivan became a mainstay of Lytle's home. However, Lytle's age was catching up with him, and his physical and mental condition deteriorated steadily. Sullivan found himself engaging in far more caretaking than he had expected, and this began to wear on him. He also experienced additional claims on his time as he found a new girlfriend, and Lytle was rude to her, asking her outright if she knew the proper place for a woman in an artist's life. These tensions came to a head one night in an incident that forms the essay's controversial climax. In the aftermath of the quarrel, Sullivan moved out, to be replaced by another young man. He reenrolled in the university, and when Lytle died at the age of ninety-three, he was there, helping a small team to craft the handmade cedar coffin in which Lytle was buried.

Readers will find the essays in *Pulphead* intellectually exhilarating and morally revelatory. There is not a dull page in the book. With this collection, John Jeremiah Sullivan stakes an irrefutable claim as one of the most exciting young American writers of the century.

Daniel P. Murphy

Review Sources

Booklist 108, no. 5 (November 1, 2011): 4.
Kirkus Reviews 79, no. 16 (August 15, 2011): 1449–50.
The New York Times Book Review, October 30, 2011, p. 26.
Publishers Weekly 258, no. 30 (July 25, 2011): 39.

Pym

Author: Mat Johnson (b. 1970)
Publisher: Spiegel & Grau (New York). 336 pp.
$24.00
Type of work: Novel
Time: 2011
Locale: Upstate New York, New York City, and
Antarctica

*An African American professor of literature
travels to Antarctica in order to prove that the
outlandish events related in Edgar Allen Poe's
novel* The Narrative of Arthur Gordon Pym of
Nantucket *actually took place.*

Principal characters:
CHRIS JAYNES, the narrator, a former professor
GARTH FRIERSON, Jaynes's childhood friend, an
unemployed bus driver
CAPTAIN BOOKER JAYNES, an estranged cousin
of Jaynes's, leader of the expedition
ANGELA LATHAM, Jaynes's lost love, an attorney
NATHANIEL LATHAM, Angela's new husband, an entertainment lawyer
JEFFREE, an extreme-sports enthusiast who records his exploits on his website
CARLTON DAMON CARTER, Jeffree's cameraman and lover
ARTHUR GORDON PYM, the protagonist of Poe's novel
DIRK PETERS, Pym's helper
THE TEKELIANS, a race of white, yeti-like primates
THOMAS KARVEL (MASTER OF LIGHT), a painter of treacly pastorals

Shortly after being denied tenure at the upstate New York college where he has spent the
past ten years, professor of African American literature Chris Jaynes confronts his school's
president. Jaynes, the "only black male professor on campus," was hired to "purvey the
minority perspective," and he knows that if he had served on the diversity committee
and stuck to teaching authors like Ellison and Wright, he might have retained his position. Yet for Jaynes, the broad tradition of American literature is the key to understanding
white and black America alike. He argues, "That's why I started focusing on Poe. If we
can identify how the pathology of Whiteness was constructed, then we can learn how to
dismantle it." This might be a statement of purpose for Mat Johnson's novel as a whole.
In the satiric *Pym*, Johnson dismantles the pathology of whiteness through a ribald and
inventive reworking of Edgar Allen Poe's only completed novel, *The Narrative of Arthur
Gordon Pym of Nantucket* (1838). Jaynes's journey to Antarctica becomes an exploration
of what whiteness and blackness mean in American history, literature, and culture.

Mat Johnson is the author of two previous novels, Drop *(2000) and* Hunting in Harlem *(2003), as well as two graphic novels,* Incognegro *(2008) and* Dark Rain: A New Orleans Story *(2010). He has also written* The Great Negro Plot: a Tale of Conspiracy and Murder in Eighteenth-Century New York *(2007), a history of a conspiracy hoax and its violent aftermath.*

Having lost his job, his rare book collection, and his girlfriend Angela, Jaynes finds himself at a spiritual nadir. The presence of his boyhood friend Garth Frierson, an overweight former Detroit bus driver who has come to offer solace, does little to help. Jaynes's mood and fortunes only begin to brighten when his book dealer brings him a rare, previously unpublished manuscript: *The True and Interesting Narrative of Dirk Peters.* Peters figures prominently in Poe's novel as Pym's helper, and Jaynes becomes excited at the prospect that Peters might have been a real person. For if he was not a fictional character, then some of the fantastic events narrated in *Arthur Gordon Pym* may be grounded in reality.

Johnson, in the guise of Jaynes, makes no assumption that his reader has any familiarity with Poe's novel, and launches into a funny, insightful précis. A sea story, the novel recounts its protagonist's journey to Antarctica and is replete with the familiar tropes of the genre, including mutiny, cannibalism, shipwrecks, and the inscrutable savagery of various black islanders. As bitingly satiric as Johnson can be, some of the most outrageous lines and images in *Pym* are taken directly from Poe and other nineteenth-century white authors. On the improbably warm Antarctic island of Tsalal, for example, the inhabitants have not only black skin but black teeth. If Tsalal is the proverbial heart of darkness, Poe's novel ends in an enigmatic journey into whiteness: Pym and Peters approach Antarctica, where they see "a shrouded human figure, very far larger in its proportions than any dweller among men. And the hue of the skin of the figure was of the perfect whiteness of snow." It is Poe's quasi obsession with the valences of blackness and whiteness that makes his novel such an object of fascination for Jaynes, sending him on a quest to find out if it is in fact a novel or if it is a narrative of historical events.

After seeking out a descendant of Dirk Peters and learning more about Peters's relationship with Pym and Poe, Jaynes resolves to set out for Antarctica himself. He enlists his estranged cousin, Captain Booker Jaynes, to lead the expedition. A grizzled former civil-rights activist and black nationalist, Booker has spent his years since the 1960s working as a sailor, diver, and explorer. Booker agrees to take his cousin to Antarctica, commissioning him to recruit an all-black team so that they can take advantage of a government tax break for minority-owned businesses. Booker's main purpose is to bottle Antarctic ice water for sale in the United States, but the journey will allow Jaynes to look for evidence of the people and places Arthur Gordon Pym and Dirk Peters described.

Jaynes convinces his friend Garth to join the group, playing on the big man's unlikely love of the "Master of Light," painter Thomas Karvel (a stand-in for Thomas Kinkade), who is reputed to be living in Antarctica. Jaynes's lost love Angela, an attorney, agrees to join the group, too—but to his chagrin, she brings her new husband, Nathaniel Latham. Jaynes finds the last two members of his team online: the African

American adventurer Jeffree and his lover and cameraman, Carlton Damon Carter. With his crew in place and Dirk Peters's manuscript as a guide, Jaynes sets out to verify the account of Poe's novel and, perhaps more importantly, to find Tsalal, an island paradise that might be "the great undiscovered African Diasporan homeland, might still be out there, uncorrupted by Whiteness."

Throughout his narrative, Jaynes dissects the contradictions and complexities of racial identity and culture. He is particularly intrigued by the disparity between Peters's physical traits, which Jaynes thinks might indicate his African ancestry, and Poe's description of Peters as "not a Negro but a half-breed Indian probably of the 'Upsaroka.'" *Dirk Peters* confirms Jaynes's theory when he finds that Peters was "the progeny of a free woman of European, African, and Native American heritage, and an Acadian trader." Despite his ethnically diverse heritage, Dirk Peters shares the racism of whites like Poe, yet seems oblivious to the many instances in which he is the target of such racism. Peters's descendant, Mahalia Mathis, denies her African heritage entirely, belonging instead to a group of African Americans who claim to be Native American. Jaynes himself is light-skinned enough that he is frequently taken for a white man. Garth Frierson believes that this explains Jaynes's preoccupation with race: "You so scared someone's going to kick you off Team Negro that you think everybody's got to stick to some crazy one-drop rule." Garth, for his part, is obsessed with the saccharine paintings of Karvel, works that Jaynes sees as "a Eurocentric fantasy world where black people couldn't even exist." Through a series of very funny exchanges and incidents, the six crew members challenge and belie each other's definitions of themselves and their notions of racial identity. Jaynes's mock-scholarly footnotes add another dimension to this dissection of race and culture.

The characters' identities as African Americans are thrown into sharp relief during their time in Antarctica. The crew discovers that Arthur Gordon Pym's narrative was no work of fiction; indeed, they discover Pym himself, an old man who has lived to a remarkable age. Pym resides among the Tekelians, a race of yeti-like white primates. His love of a fermented Tekelian drink seems to be the key to his longevity. Jaynes's expedition has therefore uncovered not only an unknown race but also a diet that may offer something approaching immortality. Age has not brought wisdom to Pym, however, and he is an unreconstructed racist of the most virulent and offhanded kind. He falsely assumes Chris Jaynes to be a white man leading a crew of slaves and helps him broker a deal with the Tekelians: two of the Tekelians will accompany the crew back to South America, and in exchange, the crew will provide them with a supply of the Little Debbie snack cakes that they have just introduced into their diet. In a satiric reenactment of the triangle trade, the African American crew members will trade sugar for people.

When their ship loses all communication with home, the crew must renege on the deal they made with the Tekelians, who consequently enslave them. What follows is a burlesque on the nature of slavery and differences across race lines. The monstrosity of slavery is made literal, as the slaveholders are actual monsters. Jaynes and his friends have always been conscious of the legacy of slavery, but now slavery becomes the center of their lives, and they find themselves adapting to their enslavement by taking on

Magill's Literary Annual 2012

roles that may have surprised them before their fateful trip. When former civil-rights activist Booker Jaynes becomes involved in a grotesque sexual relationship with his Tekelian mistress, his radicalism becomes twisted into a need to make the Tekelians appreciate him: "We will show them how beautiful we are. And then, then they will be forced to love us, and that is our only salvation." Nathaniel, too, is an appeaser; a corporate striver who is always looking to come out on top of any given situation, he decides he can make himself valuable to the Tekelians by cooperating with them. Chris, on the other hand, hatches an escape plan. He, Garth, and Pym will eventually make their way to the Antarctic biodome that Thomas Karvel and his wife inhabit. Here, inside a bubble painted to look like a bucolic Karvel landscape, Chris and Garth take on a role reminiscent of Reconstruction. No longer slaves, they become sharecroppers, working on a corner of Karvel's little plot of land in exchange for food and shelter.

The novel ends with a fitting inversion of the conclusion of *The Narrative of Arthur Gordon Pym of Nantucket*. Like Poe's novel, *Pym* switches to a diary format in its final pages, with Jaynes noting the events of his sea voyage. Because Johnson has taken pains to familiarize the reader with the lineaments of *Arthur Gordon Pym*, and in particular with its unresolved conclusion, the ending of his own novel feels like a true resolution. Jaynes's Antarctic journey followed in the footsteps of Poe and Pym, but now, at the end of his narrative, he is striking out into territory that has not yet been charted.

Matthew J. Bolton

Review Sources

The New York Times Book Review, March 6, 2011, p. 9.
The Washington Post, March 9, 2011 (Web).

Reading My Father
A Memoir

Author: Alexandra Styron (b. 1966)
Publisher: Scribner (New York). 304 pp.
$25.00
Type of work: Memoir
Time: 1907–2008
Locale: The United States, as well as Paris, Rome, and other European locations

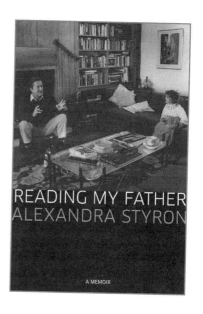

Alexandra Styron's memoir of life with her late father, American novelist William Styron, chronicles the celebrated author's achievements and struggles, as well as his lifelong battle with clinical depression.

Principal personages:
WILLIAM CLARK STYRON JR. (1925–2006), an
    award-winning American author and essayist
ALEXANDRA STYRON (b. 1966), an American
    writer; daughter of William Styron
ROSE STYRON, an American poet, journalist, and human rights advocate; wife of William and mother of Alexandra

After the death of American novelist William Styron in 2006, his youngest daughter, author Alexandra Styron, initially set out to tell his story in the pages of *Reading My Father*, a text she describes as a biographical memoir. At the memoir's outset, she embarks on the writing journey only to discover that she has, if temporarily, "mentally misplaced him," and must consult her father's archived journals, essays, letters, and photographs, in addition to her own memories, in order to properly access and reconstruct the three-dimensional intricacies of one of America's great post–World War II novelists. Throughout the process of reinventing him on the page, Alexandra Styron struggles to reconcile what appear to be the multiple personalities of her famous father: the brilliant artist, the bitter alcoholic, the codependent husband, the egomaniac, the inattentive father, the creative soul crippled by depression and an intense fear of death.

The stories of both William and Alexandra Styron run parallel to one another throughout the narrative, oftentimes complementing as well as contradicting each other in a captivating counterpoint that pits a young child's perspective of life against that of an experienced and obsessively jaded adult mind. In writing the memoir, Alexandra Styron took on the challenging task of not only attempting to accurately portray her own experiences and emotions, but also those of her father, who is, of course, unable to clarify or respond to the charges she has leveled against him in the text. Nevertheless, Alexandra Styron tells her father's story with a sense of reflective depth

(Rex Bonomelli)

Alexandra Styron penned the novel All the Finest Girls *(2002) and has contributed to such well-known publications as* Interview, the New York Times, the New Yorker, Real Simple, Vanity Fair, the Wall Street Journal *as well as various literary anthologies.*

and admiration for his creative talents while taking him to task for his emotional unavailability and selfishness when it came to his family. Her tone is by turns playful, foreboding and melancholic, apologetic, but always brutally honest. The subjectivity with which the author voices many of her memories is noticeably superseded by an occasional, and intentional, judgmental edge.

Though he eventually became an epic figure in American literature, enjoying tremendous professional and financial success, William Styron originally came from a modest Southern background. Born in 1925 in the shipyard town of Newport News, Virginia, to William Styron Sr., a marine engineer, and Pauline Styron, a musician, William Styron Jr. was destined to be an only child, which at once helped to foster the writer in him as well as to initiate what his daughter characterizes as a "chronic loneliness" that would, in many ways, stay with him over the course of his life. In 1939, just as William entered his teenage years, his mother died of breast cancer. His father, after suffering a case of nervous exhaustion, promptly married a woman named Elizabeth Buxton who, for a number of her stepson's formative years, helped to sweep the young writer's feelings of loss and loneliness "where they didn't belong: underground." Despite a relatively tumultuous childhood, he went on to attend Duke University, where he began to develop a strong literary voice and caught the attention of Professor William Blackburn, who would later introduce him to two notable New York editors, John Selby and Hiram Haydn. As a young writer living in Greenwich Village and Brooklyn, New York, Styron struggled to make ends meet as a junior editor for Manhattan publishing house McGraw-Hill; after his dismissal from this post, Styron became a full-time novelist, explaining in a letter to his father, "'Writing is a matter, really . . . of dogging both the idea and yourself to death.'"And though he was paid an advance to begin a novel he never finished, he still found himself lacking the funds he needed to survive.

Alexandra Styron relays the touching, selfless, and deeply nurturing relationship between father and son through snippets of 103 letters of correspondence between the two men. For years, William Styron Sr. sent his son a stipend of one hundred dollars a month, without question, exhibiting an almost blind faith in his son's writing abilities. At last in 1951, at the age of twenty-six, William Styron justified his father's faith when he published *Lie Down in Darkness* about a psychologically troubled, suicidal young woman from Virginia. It is without a doubt through this relationship that the reader comes to understand how he learned the importance of tolerance, faith, generosity, and love. The author credits her grandfather with single-handedly molding her father's character after his own. Furthermore, the seeds that his father planted in him early on compelled Styron to communicate the plight of the "other" in his writing. In 1967, Styron published *The Confessions of Nat Turner*, a first-person narrative based on the life of Nat Turner, the leader of a slave revolt in 1831 Virginia. Styron's said of his Pulitzer Prize–winning narrative, "my plunge into history . . . helped dissolve many of the preconceptions about race that had been my birth right as a Southerner." African American author James Baldwin, a friend of Styron's and a champion of civil rights, had repeatedly said of Styron, "'He has begun the common history—ours.'" This desire to represent and indeed speak for minority groups and the voiceless was perhaps no more evident than in Styron's portrayal of Holocaust survivor Sophie Zawistowski in his acclaimed 1979 novel *Sophie's Choice*, a work that catapulted Styron into the international literary arena and earned him the National Book Award for fiction in 1980.

As much as William Styron was both fascinated and inspired by the cultural and historical "other," he was even more haunted by and driven to write about depression, suicide, and death. His daughter writes, "*All* of his books concerned themselves with suicide." Emanating from the pages of his fictional work, emphasizes his daughter, is a manifestation of himself in many of his characters. Styron suffered two very serious bouts of clinical depression, one at the age of sixty and the other at seventy-five, and he struggled to tame what had become an unmanageable and unruly beast throughout his life. In *Reading My Father*, Alexandra Styron attempts to untangle the relationship between her father's writing and his depression, asking in several different ways throughout the narrative, "Did my father's depression steal his creative gift? Or was it the other way around . . . ?" The reader is then left to decide whether Alexandra Styron's portrait of her father answers this question. If depression was his muse, then alcohol was his loyal consultant and companion; it saw him through endless, frustrating, and often desperate writing nights and allowed him the freedom to create without judgment. Styron has said, "'Alcohol was an invaluable senior partner of my intellect, besides being a friend whose ministrations I sought daily.'" And although Alexandra Styron was always proud of her identity as the daughter of a successful writer, the writing and all that went with it were perpetually "at the center of our family's existence, playing like a constant drumbeat under everything we did." Her father's volatility, his need for positive recognition, his insecurities, and his substance abuse all contributed to the author's frequent dislike and disavowal of the man her father could become when he was fighting the silent war inside of himself.

Rose Styron, a poet from a prominent Baltimore family, married the virtually untamable William Styron Jr. in Rome, Italy, in 1953, and they produced four children (Susanna, Pauline, Tommy, and Alexandra). Alexandra Styron portrays her mother as a stoic, patient, and extremely tolerant force who quietly supported her husband throughout his career despite his moodiness, infidelities, alcoholism, and his "intermittent rejection of her" over the years. If the fickle novelist pushed his wife away during the early part of their marriage, he did just the opposite in later years, becoming increasingly and oftentimes obsessively dependent on her to care for his every physical and emotional need, especially during his most unpleasant bouts of depression.

Alexandra Styron notes that this variety of extremes actually fostered an independence in her mother that would consistently transform her "exile into adventure," allowing her to craft "a fascinating and rewarding life out of the freedom he forced on her."

William Styron joined Norman Mailer, James Jones, Kurt Vonnegut, Joseph Heller, and others in an exclusive club of, as Alexandra Styron puts it, "Big Male Writers" who "perpetuated, without apology, the cliché of the gifted, hard-drinking, bellicose writer that gave so much of twentieth-century literature a muscular, glamorous aura." By accessing childhood impressions of her father's famous friends, Alexandra Styron offers some of the book's most compelling anecdotes in her attempt to satiate gossip-hungry readers. For instance, she describes an evening of drinks and dancing with United States senators Ted Kennedy and Chris Dodd in Martha's Vineyard when she was a teenager. She writes of holidays spent with composer Stephen Sondheim and playwright Tom Stoppard, summers spent with noir novelist Dashiell Hammett, and her parents' harbor cruises with President and Mrs. Kennedy, who were eager to discuss William Styron's award-winning *Confessions of Nat Turner*. And the list of celebrities continues; however, Alexandra Styron frequently emphasizes the idea that she always thought of her parents' renowned friends as regular people complete with human faults, vices, and occasional narcissistic tendencies.

Most literary critics agree that Alexandra Styron's narrative is tightly woven, rich in detail, and presents the reader with an intimate look at the life of one of America's most respected and beloved writers. Conversely, critics chastise Alexandra Styron for her lack of restraint when it comes to divulging very personal, often embarrassing details about her family members and their behavior. Winston Groom of the the the *Wall Street Journal* places *Reading My Father* among the memoirs of other famous literary children such as James Dickey's son Christopher Dickey and J. D. Salinger's daughter Margaret Salinger, whose biographical narratives hold back few details about their famous fathers. Ultimately, *Reading My Father* portrays the fallibility of a tortured American writer and the impact that his life had on the children he left behind when he died of pneumonia (complicated by severe anxiety and unrelenting depression) in 2006. Torn between her love for her father and her need to properly examine their relationship, Alexandra Styron has memorialized the many facets of his complex personality: "Hypersensitive, aloof, unexamined, not to mention hypochondriacal, agnostic, and alcoholic. Intellectual, passionate, and infantile."

Briana Nadeau

Review Sources

The Christian Science Monitor, April 22, 2011 (Web).
Los Angeles Times, May 1, 2011 (Web).
The New York Times Book Review, April 22, 2011, p. 10.
NPR, April 28, 2011 (Web).
The Telegraph, July 29, 2011 (Web).
The Wall Street Journal, April 23, 2011 (Web).
Washington Times, April 29, 2011 (Web).

Redeemers
Ideas and Power in Latin America

Author: Enrique Krauze (b. 1947)
First published: *Los redentores*, 2011, in Spain
Translated from the Spanish by Hank Heifetz
and Natasha Wimmer
Publisher: HarperCollins (New York). 560 pp.
$29.99
Type of work: History, biography
Time: Late nineteenth through the twentieth
century
Locale: Latin America

*The author analyzes the ideas of the thinkers,
writers, and revolutionaries who have influenced politics in Latin America, making a significant contribution to the history of the region.*

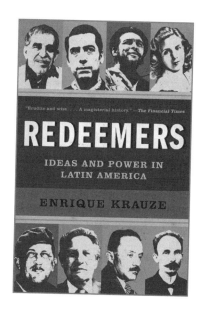

Principal personages:
JOSÉ MARTÍ, a Cuban poet and liberal revolutionary
JOSÉ ENRIQUE RODÓ, a Uruguayan essayist who
    first proposed the idea of Latin American nationalism
JOSÉ VASCONCELOS, a Mexican writer who advocated education as key to developing
    Mexican culture
JOSÉ CARLOS MARIÁTEGUI, a Peruvian Marxist who advocated socialism and indigenism
OCTAVIO PAZ, a Mexican poet and political thinker
EVA PERÓN, an Argentine political leader, the wife of Argentine dictator Juan Perón
CHE GUEVARA, an Argentine Marxist revolutionary and a comrade of Fidel Castro
GABRIEL GARCÍA MÁRQUEZ, a Colombian novelist
MARIO VARGAS LLOSA, a Peruvian writer and politician
SAMUEL RUIZ, a Mexican Catholic bishop
SUBCOMANDANTE MARCOS (RAFAEL SEBASTIÁN GUILLÉN VICENTE), a Mexican Marxist
    guerrilla fighter, the leader of the Zapatistas
HUGO CHÁVEZ, president of Venezuela

In *Redeemers: Ideas and Power in Latin America*, author Enrique Krauze examines the
development of intellectual, social, and political thought in Latin America from the late
nineteenth century through the twentieth century. Krauze combines history and biographical accounts in his text, structuring the book around twelve biographies that are divided
into six sections: "Four Prophets," "A Man in His Century," "Popular Icons," "Politics
and the Novel," "Religion and Rebellion," and "The Postmodern Caudillo." The section
entitled "Four Prophets" serves as an introduction to Krauze's topic. The four writers to
whom he refers as prophets introduced the four important concepts that have dominated

political thinking in Latin America through the end of the twentieth century: liberalism, nationalism, education as redemptive power, and a form of Marxism that combines socialism with indigenism, or native nationalism. Throughout the text, Krauze weaves together the many influences that have contributed to a turbulent political history punctuated by revolutions and dictatorships. He underscores the enormous complexity of the disparate influences and antagonistic historical situations that have played significant roles in the efforts of Latin Americans to create effective and stable social, intellectual, and political realities in various countries. In particular, he looks at the influence of Latin America's Spanish heritage and its large indigenous populations on its ideologies and systems of government.

(Miguel Dimayuga)

Historian Enrique Krauze is the editor in chief of Letras Libres *and director of Clío TV Productions. He has written several books, including* Mexico: Biography of Power *(1998). His numerous awards include a Guggenheim Fellowship, the Medalla al Mérito Historico, and the Orden Isabel la Católica.*

Krauze emphasizes the role that the expansionist policies of the United States have played in creating a strong distaste for capitalism and free-market economic systems in many Latin American countries. He points out the impact that the intellectual development in Europe had on Latin American political systems. The widespread poverty and social inequality throughout Latin America created an atmosphere in which Marxism seemed a welcome alternative. Krauze also considers at length the phenomenon of caudillismo, a reverence for a caudillo, or strongman, which has repeatedly resulted in brutal dictatorships in the region. He links this propensity to accept and admire powerful leaders to early indigenous cultures that were ruled by warrior chieftains. The Spanish conquest and the domination of the indigenous population also established a tradition of rule by power.

The close ties between political reform and education is another important theme of Krauze's study. He elaborates upon the connection between ideas, the written word, and political activity. While the political history of Latin America contains a significant number of military coups, civil wars, guerrilla activities, and dictatorships, all resulting from the use of force, it is also the history of the political journal, politically oriented literature, and the development of political theory. From José Martí to Octavio Paz to Mario Vargas Llosa, the time period Krauze analyzes abounds with political writers and their works.

As Krauze indicates in his preface, his biographical approach to his topic enables him to portray the history of ideas and political action in Latin America as a composite of human activity that has been influenced by individual experiences. Thus, the text remains securely anchored in the reality of everyday existence. Krauze's own experiences and beliefs also influence his treatment of the various thinkers, revolutionaries, writers, and politicians that he includes in his book. For example, Krauze criticizes

Gabriel García Márquez for the glorification of caudillo figures in his novels and for his close friendship with Cuban communist leader Fidel Castro. On the other hand, Krauze was a colleague and friend of Octavio Paz and worked with him as assistant editor of the journal *Vuelta*, and at 154 pages, the section on Paz is the book's longest and most central. In it, Krauze discusses Paz's revolutionary inheritance from his grandfather, Ireneo Paz, and from his father, Octavio Paz Solórzano—an inheritance of revolution carried out with both pen and sword. For Ireneo Paz, the goal of revolution was political freedom; for Octavio Paz Solórzano, who fought with Mexican revolutionary leader Emiliano Zapata, it was social justice. Krauze then analyzes Octavio Paz's role as a poet and journalist in Mexico. He also examines Paz's intellectual journey through political ideologies, which led him for a time to advocate Marxism and then liberal democracy. Krauze sees Paz's life and career as a reflection of the political experiences of Latin America from the late nineteenth century through the twentieth.

Krauze stresses the impact of personal experiences on the individuals whom he includes in his book. He analyzes at length how the violent death of Paz's father and the influence of his grandfather shaped Paz's poetry and his thinking. Later, he attributes Mario Vargas Llosa's rejection of caudillismo and Marxism to his experiences growing up with a domineering, abusive father and attending the Leoncio Prado Military School, where life was harsh and discipline was severe.

Eva Perón and Che Guevara represent the revolution at its most flamboyant. Their inclusion as "Icons of the Revolution" further elaborates upon the role of revolution in Latin America and how it has permeated all aspects of life. According to Krauze, Eva Perón's involvement in the political life of Argentina, facilitated by her meeting and captivating Juan Perón, was motivated by a personal need for fame and adulation. Krauze presents her rise to power as driven by a need to exact revenge for her illegitimacy, poverty, and marginal position in society. In his discussion of her glorification as a saintly heroine by the Argentine people, he emphasizes the connection between politics and acting. As a child, Eva Perón found her role models in the famous actresses of the time; as an adult, she became an actress who knew the importance of appearance. Through the creation of an image, Perón and her husband were able to manipulate and control the people. Krauze also attributes Perón's phenomenal success to the fact that she came from the social and financial milieu of the uneducated, impoverished masses who worshipped her for her charity on their behalf. Krauze points out that this "savior of the people" persona was a public image and that, while Perón could understand the poverty and sadness of the masses, she was not in any sense a humanitarian. He includes documentation of her acceptance of, and even participation in, the repressive tactics of Juan Perón. She considered torture and murder to be acceptable means for controlling rebellious individuals and eliminating enemies.

In his treatment of Che Guevara, Krauze portrays a revolutionary icon who deliberately created himself in defiance of his severe asthma. Determined not to be a frail young man restricted by breathing difficulties, Guevara participated in the most rigorous sport he could find: rugby. Then, as an adult, Guevara discovered two new enemies, poverty and inequality, as well as a political system with which to combat them, Marxism. Krauze presents Guevara as sincere in his belief in the redemptive power of Marxism, his faith in Castro, and his devotion to guerrilla warfare and revolution. However, the Che Guevara that he discusses was also a man inebriated by the revolution and by what it meant to be a revolutionary, a man who costumed himself as a thinking Marxist guerrilla.

In "Religion and Rebellion," Krauze discusses the Catholic Church's efforts to eliminate the inequality and discrimination suffered by the indigenous population as he examines the work of Bishop Samuel Ruiz in Chiapas, Mexico. He also discusses Ruiz's interaction with Subcomandante Marcos, the militant who led a group of Maya into armed rebellion some twenty-five years later. Krauze proposes that without Ruiz's work, Subcomandante Marcos could not have incited the rebellion.

The final biographical sketch of the book is of Hugo Chávez, the president of Venezuela, whom Krauze describes as a "postmodern *caudillo*." Krauze sees Chávez as leading Venezuela ever closer to a violent revolution as he pursues his policies of one-man rule, redemptive socialism, and his cult of the Bolivarian myth, in which he becomes the hero who controls and saves the people.

In the epilogue, Krauze expresses his own personal belief about the type of political system that should exist in Latin America. He highlights the contrasting mentalities that exist in Latin America and what he calls "Anglo-Saxon America." He reaffirms the lasting effects of the presence of Spanish monarchy and Catholicism in Latin America. The monarchy and the church imposed order based on divine right and the power of God, a situation he sees as having set the stage for "redeemers," those who believe in saving people by controlling them. For him, this mindset is also the reason it has taken so long to establish electoral democracy in Latin America. He states that all of the countries, with the dangerous exceptions of Cuba and Venezuela, have been electoral democracies since 1989. He also warns that the poverty and inequality that still exist in many of the countries could open the way for "redeemers" who may opt for totalitarianism. Krauze concludes his text with a detailed discussion of his sources, an invaluable resource for the reader interested in gaining a deeper and broader understanding of the ideas, individuals, and events that he has brought together in his book.

Redeemers: Ideas and Power in Latin America has been well received by reviewers. While some readers might find the book to be a challenge due to its panoramic treatment of political thought and action in Latin America, it is a book well worth reading. Enrique Krauze is recognized as one of the most significant Mexican historians, and his knowledge of the topic, combined with his ability to connect theory to everyday reality, makes the book a necessary read for those who wish to understand Latin America's past and present political climate.

Shawncey J. Webb

Review Sources

Commonweal, September 20, 2011 (Web).
Foreign Affairs 90, no. 5 (September/October 2011): 184.
The Financial Times, August 12, 2011 (Web).
The New York Times Book Review, August 28, 2011, p. 11.

Rodin's Debutante

Author: Ward Just (b. 1935)
Publisher: Houghton Mifflin Harcourt (New
York). 263 pp. $26.00
Type of work: Novel
Time: Mid-twentieth century
Locale: New Jesper and Chicago, Illinois

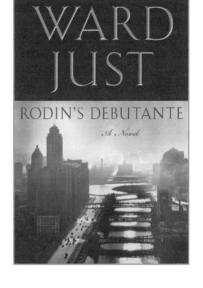

*A young man comes of age in Chicago and re-
flects on the direct and indirect events and relationships that have profoundly shaped his life.*

Principal characters:
LEE GOODELL, a small-town boy who attends
Ogden Hall School for Boys and later
becomes a sculptor
TOMMY OGDEN, an eccentric railroad heir who
donates his estate to found Ogden Hall
AUGUSTUS "GUS" ALLPRICE, the headmaster of
Ogden Hall during Lee's years there
MAGDA SERRA, Lee's classmate in New Jesper, the victim of a horrific unsolved rape
ERWIN GOODELL, Lee's father, a judge and unofficial town elder in New Jesper
MELODY GOODELL, Lee's mother
LAURA, Lee's wife, a philosophy student at the University of Chicago
BERT MARKS SR., an attorney responsible for managing Ogden Hall's finances and staffing
DOUGIE HENDERSON, Lee's childhood friend in New Jesper
CHARLES FORD, Lee's friend and roommate

The title of *Rodin's Debutante*, Ward Just's seventeenth novel, accurately reflects the
book's focus on indirect influences; just as the book has very little to do with the artist Auguste Rodin or with debutantes, many of the book's events likewise have little
direct connection to protagonist Lee Goodell's life, although they will shape him in
unexpected ways. *Rodin's Debutante* is fast-paced and unconventional coming-of-age
story that elevates the genre in its telling of a simple, yet compelling, tale.
    Part 1 of the book describes railroad scion Tommy Ogden in minute detail, from his
early love of guns and shooting animals to his intense and introverted habit of drawing, to his long-term relationships with prostitutes at an underground brothel. At fewer
than forty pages, this section seems to end abruptly because the reader has become so
intimately familiar with Ogden; even so, the section's brevity is fitting considering
that the real central character of the book—Lee Goodell—meets Ogden only once
and many years later. It is, however, a meeting that Lee will remember his entire life,
recognizing with his unusually canny introspection that Ogden actually had a great
deal of influence on his life.

In part 2, the narrative shifts from the third-person description of Tommy Ogden and his decision to found the Ogden Hall School for Boys to Lee Goodell's first-person narrative recounting the end of his childhood innocence in the small town of New Jesper, Illinois. Lee is a thoughtful, reflective boy who does well in school and enjoys rambles down by the railroad tracks with his friend Dougie Henderson. His roaming is curtailed, however, by the murder of one of the many homeless men who come through the town as a result of the Great Depression. Lee's father forbids the boy from going near the railroad tracks again, but this precaution does not shield Lee from violence as his father had hoped; only a month later, one of Lee's classmates, a young girl named Magda Serra, is raped at the high school in an attack so brutal that it renders her mute for some time. Alarmed by these violent acts, Lee's father calls for a meeting of the town's unofficial leaders. At this gathering, which Lee observes secretly, the men persuade the local newspaper reporter to downplay the incident in order to spare the girl and her mother the humiliation of having the entire town know every detail of the horrendous crime, as well as to protect their own pride and sensibilities.

Alarmed by the sudden violence in the once idyllic community, Lee's mother pressures her husband to move to Chicago, believing that New Jesper is no longer safe. Judge Goodell resists but finally gives in, and the family moves to a neighborhood on Chicago's North Side filled with attorneys, brokers, and other executives. The random and senseless violence in New Jesper affects Lee's life profoundly, although indirectly—his family never would have left their home had the attacks not taken place. These events have also left their mark on Lee's psyche, as he spends a great deal of time wondering what happened to Magda after her mother took her away from New Jesper. In another change after the move, Lee's mother decides that he should attend a private school, and Lee chooses the Ogden Hall School for Boys, several decades after its founding by Tommy Ogden. It is here that Lee encounters Rodin's marble bust of a debutante, whom the Ogden students mistakenly believe to be Tommy Ogden's wife, Marie. Lee spends hours in the library gazing at the bust, which likely inspires his eventual choice of sculpture as a vocation.

Strangely, the last fifty pages of this section of the novel switch back to a third-person narrative to describe Lee's years at Ogden Hall. These pages take a somewhat nontraditional approach to storytelling by focusing not on Lee but rather on Headmaster Augustus "Gus" Allprice, who cannot wait to leave the school, and Bert Marks Sr., an old friend of Tommy Ogden's. The reader sees Lee through Headmaster Allprice's eyes, most notably when Lee asks him for funding to run a special football training camp in the summer because the school team is tired of being a laughingstock. Allprice lends his support as a last act of kindness before he leaves the school, and the following year, the team wins the only undefeated season in the school's rather undistinguished sports history. Although he relishes the victory, Lee's characteristic gravity leads to an immediate understanding that a person can hope to set a goal and achieve it so spectacularly only once or twice in a lifetime, and he therefore needs to mentally and emotionally note the occasion. The momentous nature of this day is underscored by Lee's only in-person encounter with Tommy Ogden, who has appeared anonymously for the last game of the season and who speaks only to Lee. At this time,

(© Nina Bramhall)

Ward Just is the author of seventeen novels, including National Book Award finalist A Dangerous Friend *(1999) and Pulitzer Prize finalist* An Unfinished Season *(2004). He was also a recipient of the James Fenimore Cooper Prize for fiction and the Chicago Tribune Heartland Award.*

Tommy reveals to Lee that the Rodin bust is not of his wife, but rather some unnamed subject.

The third section of the novel begins with Lee's third year at the University of Chicago. He is living in a basement room in as unsavory neighborhood where he can make all the noise he wants when sculpting marble with a chisel and mallet. It is at this point that violence once again shapes Lee's life, although this time it is of a more direct nature. Two neighborhood hooligans attack Lee, presumably to steal his wallet and shoes. When Lee fights back, one of the attackers uses a knife and carves a vicious gash in Lee's face that will leave a noticeable scar for the rest of his life. When Lee does not go to any particular lengths to retaliate or make sure the boys are brought to justice, the neighborhood locals finally accept him as one of their own. The incident also influences Lee's long-running sculpture project, in which he has unsuccessfully been trying to coax the inner essence out of marble blocks. The first time Lee picks up his tools after his release from the hospital, he carves a gash into the stone that mirrors the one on his face, and for the first time, feels completely successfully in his artistic endeavors.

In part 4, the narrative returns to Lee's first-person point of view, relating the plans for his upcoming nuptials with Laura, a promising philosophy student whom Lee met through his former roommate, Charles. Lee also makes arrangements for his first art showing—thirteen carved marble blocks, each depicting the scar that Lee realizes is more emotional than physical. Although the art reviews are uncomplimentary, Lee's artistic debut is nevertheless quite successful, and he sells his works for a satisfactory price. The subsequent chapters go on to describe Lee's marriage and the eventual reappearance of Magda Serra, the rape victim from New Jesper. Shortly thereafter, Lee receives a call letting him know that Ogden Hall has burned down. He returns to the site while the ruins are still smoldering and recalls his meeting with the school's founder so many years before. The juxtaposition of Lee's meeting with Magda and the burning of the school serve as a message for Lee to let go of the past and concentrate on his present and future. The reader comes away with the impression that Lee will always be more thoughtful than most, though not to the point of paralysis.

One of the greatest strengths in *Rodin's Debutante* is Just's careful use of place— both New Jesper and Chicago are brought to life in such a way that they almost seem to be characters themselves rather than simply settings. Lee's father reflects on what

New Jesper represents, both before and after the transformative violent events that take away both the town's and Lee's innocence. Similarly, several characters discuss the nature of Chicago's personality in great detail, and the novel's events are so enmeshed with place that the reader ultimately feels the book could not possibly have been set anywhere else.

That said, some flaws do mar this refreshingly brief novel. The author eschews the use of quotation marks, a practice that seems affected and that in some instances leads to ambiguity as to who is actually speaking. Lee's first-person narration, so effective when it appears, is abandoned for much of the book, even when he is at the center of the action, and it is not entirely clear what this authorial choice accomplishes. Finally, characters are occasionally described as possessing attributes that seem intended to add literary effect but are ultimately contradicted by their actions. For instance, the reader is told that both Tommy and Lee have no interest in selling or even showing their artistic work to anyone, but both of them seek opportunities to display their work in galleries. Similarly, while the undefeated football season is both moving and an effective means of getting Lee and Tommy to meet in person, Lee does not exhibit the slightest interest in football for the rest of the book. Consequently, the reader is left with the impression that Just wanted to make a specific plot point but did not carry it through to make it an integrated aspect of Lee's character. Nonetheless, the novel's thoughtful nature and rich characterization make it a highly rewarding experience for readers interested in examining the meaning of life and art.

Amy Sisson

Review Sources

Booklist 107, no. 11 (February 1, 2011): 41.
Entertainment Weekly, no. 1143 (February 25, 2011): 86.
Kirkus Reviews 79, no. 1 (January 1, 2011): 6.
Library Journal 136, no. 2 (February 1, 2011): 54.
The New York Times Book Review, March 27, 2011, p. 8.
Publishers Weekly 258, no. 1 (January 3, 2011): 31.

Sacred Trash
The Lost and Found World of the Cairo Geniza

Authors: Adina Hoffman (b. 1967) and Peter Cole (b. 1957)
Publisher: Schocken Books (New York). Illustrated. 304 pp. $26.95
Type of work: History
Locale: Cambridge, United Kingdom; Cairo
Time: 1896 through the 1950s

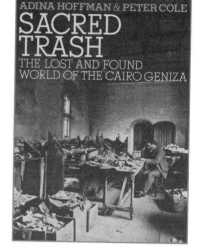

This nonfiction book delves into the work of scholars who spent over a century rediscovering lost Jewish history in the nearly 280,000 assorted documents of the Cairo Geniza, a diverse collection of documents from one Jewish community between 870 and 1880.

Principal personages:
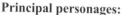
SOLOMON SCHECHTER (1847–1915), Romanian-born Talmud scholar who brought the Cairo Geniza to the attention of the scholarly world
AGNES LEWIS (1843–1926), self-taught Scottish scholar of Arabic and Syriac who, with her sister Margaret Gibson, helped bring the Geniza to Schechter's attention
MARGARET GIBSON (1843–1920), Lewis's twin sister, likewise a self-taught scholar
CHARLES TAYLOR (1840–1908), University of Cambridge biblical scholar who provided major funding for Schechter's trip to Cairo and who worked on Geniza palimpsests and other documents
SHELOMO AHARON WERTHEIMER (1866–1935), Jerusalem rabbi and independent scholar who sold manuscripts, including documents from the Cairo Geniza, and the first to knowingly transcribe and publish texts from the Geniza
FRANCIS BURKITT (1864–1935), Anglican scholar of Semitic languages and biblical history, assigned by Schechter to sort the Greek manuscripts
ISRAEL DAVIDSON (1870–1939), Lithuanian Jewish palimpsest scholar and expert in Hebrew poetry
MENAHEM ZULAY (ca. 1899–1954), Galician Jewish scholar of Hebrew poetry who pieced together coherent fragments of eight hundred poems from the Geniza
SALMAN SCHOCKEN (1877–1959), self-made German Jewish businessman and publisher of a volume of poetry translated by Zulay, one of the last Hebrew books published in Nazi Germany
ERNEST JAMES WORMAN (1871–1909), Cambridge library assistant and later curator in Asian and Middle Eastern literature, responsible for significant early organization and deciphering of the Geniza documents

JACOB MANN (1888–1940), Polish Jewish historian who wrote *The Jews in Egypt and in Palestine under the Fatimid Caliphs* (1920–1922), the first major historical work based on Geniza documents
JEFIM HAYYIM SCHIRMANN (1904–1981), scholar at the Schocken Institute for the Research of Hebrew Poetry
SHELOMO DOV GOITEIN (1900–1985), Geniza scholar who studied Mediterranean commerce and pioneered the study of everyday Judeo-Arabic documents
EZRA FLEISCHER (1928–2006), survivor of Soviet prisons and politically critical Geniza scholar
STEFAN REIF (b. 1944), Scottish Jewish scholar and bibliographer who planned the conservation, cataloging, and preservation of the Geniza and founded the Taylor-Schechter Genizah Research Unit at the Cambridge University Library
ALBERT FRIEDBERG (b. 1946), Canadian businessman and founder of the Friedberg Genizah Project, an ambitious manuscript digitization project

Adina Hoffman is an American essayist, critic, and biographer. She is the author of House of Windows: Portraits from a Jerusalem Neighborhood *(2002) and* My Happiness Bears No Relation to Happiness: A Poet's Life in the Palestinian Century *(2009), the latter about Palestinian poet Taha Muhammad Ali.*

In 1896, the eccentric Scottish scholar Agnes Lewis ran into a friend in Cambridge, the Romanian-born Talmud scholar Solomon Schechter. Neither could know at the time what would come from this chance meeting, at which Lewis asked Schechter to identify some manuscript fragments that she and her twin sister, Margaret Gibson, had purchased in Cairo.

One of the fragments turned out to be from the original Hebrew of Ecclesiasticus. Schechter and the "Giblews," as the twins were called by their friends, were ecstatic, and within months, Schechter had traveled to Cairo in search of the rest of the fragments—a spectacular cache of over 280,000 documents produced by one Jewish community between 870 and 1880, subsequently known as the Cairo Geniza.

The term *geniza* derives from the Persian *ganj*, meaning "hidden treasure" or "hoard." Variants of it appear in the biblical books of Esther and Ezra, describing royal archives. In the Talmud, *geniza* implies concealment. Jewish religious manuscripts that synagogues could no longer use required *geniza*, or ritual storage in a safe place where they might decay naturally. Over time, the term came to apply to the place itself: a burial plot, storage chamber, or cabinet. A *geniza* could store heretical as well as religious texts; it protected good texts from defilement and protected the community from bad texts.

What made the Cairo Geniza unusual is that the Palestinian Jews of the Fustat (Old Cairo) community, which later became the Ben Ezra synagogue, preserved all documents written in Hebrew letters, not just religious texts or even just texts written in the Hebrew language. Because of the reuse of writing materials, the Cairo Geniza came to contain texts written in a number of languages and writing systems, including Hebrew, Yiddish, Judeo-Arabic, Syriac, Greek, Persian, Latin, and more—even one fragment in Chinese. Besides religious texts and poetry, the documents include all the written

Peter Cole, a poet and translator, was named a MacArthur Fellow in 2007 and won an Arts and Letters Award from the American Academy of Arts in 2010. His translated anthology The Dream of the Poem: Hebrew Poetry from Muslim and Christian Spain, 950–1492 *(2007) has received many awards, including the National Jewish Book Award in Poetry.*

records of daily life, from personal letters to wills, divorces, and prescriptions. One of the most famous scholars of the Geniza, Shelomo Dov Goitein, called it "a true mirror of life, often cracked and blotchy, but very wide in scope and reflecting each and every aspect of the society that originated it."

In *Sacred Trash: The Lost and Found World of the Cairo Geniza*, authors Adina Hoffman and Peter Cole explore the history of Geniza scholarship, charting the shifting focuses of the scholarly community from an emphasis on major religious texts and famous poets to examination of the minutiae of daily life and commerce. The history of the Geniza and those who discovered and studied it is a winding and sometimes dramatic one. Before Schechter, others had made brief forays into analyzing the Geniza. Among these were Lithuanian-born adventurer Yaakov Safir, who thought the Geniza had potential but did not delve deeply; Avraham Firkovitch, who intended to explore the Geniza but instead focused on a Karaite *geniza* from Cairo; and Shelomo Aharon Wertheimer, the first to transcribe and publish some of the Geniza texts. Yet it took Schechter to bring the Cairo Geniza to the attention of the scholarly community, sparking over a century of research by numerous scholars, most of them Jewish and Eastern European.

"These scholars," write Hoffman and Cole, "have quite literally been *making* history by re-membering it, by putting it back together syllable by syllable under the intense pressure of powerfully informed and at times visionary imaginations." The Cairo Geniza documents the tenth through the thirteenth century in particular, showing a thriving community where Jews lived relatively autonomously and harmoniously, albeit heavily taxed, under Muslim rule. It was a community that produced deep religious thought and poignant poetry, as well as all the everyday detritus of civilization that changes little over the centuries: mothers admonishing sons to write more frequently, people asking rabbis for advice, and so on.

Hoffman and Cole do not provide a strictly chronological narrative of the scholarship, instead jumping back and forth between earlier and later research in a sometimes confusing fashion. *Sacred Trash* almost reads more as a book of essays than as a single narrative, with each essay focusing on the work of one or two scholars and the most attention devoted to Schechter. The authors note in the afterword that "another entire Geniza book, or three" could be written about what they left out, and this is most evident in the book's emphasis on poetry and the scholars who worked on it, likely chosen because of Cole's expertise in medieval Hebrew poetry. This focus largely produces a book that is more about scholars, the scholarly process, and poetry than about the Geniza itself. Such a focus, although certainly welcome, can be frustrating when some tantalizing bit of information found in the documents is mentioned only in passing.

It is difficult to make old documents, with their layers of cramped writing in dead languages, as exciting to the general public as tombs, monuments, and treasures. In choosing to focus on the historians and their work, Hoffman and Cole sometimes bypass the excitement of the documents themselves and the glimpses they can offer of a vanished world. The authors do convey the process of discovery and changes in scholarly attitudes and even the relationship between the world of Jewish scholars and society as a whole, as when German Jewish businessman Salman Schocken sponsored the translation and publication of a book of Hebrew poetry fragments from the Geniza under the shadow of the Holocaust.

Although Goitein figures in the narrative, his pioneering work of teasing out information about commerce and daily life in the medieval Mediterranean does not seem to fascinate Hoffman and Cole as much as the works of great poets, such as the sixth-century liturgical poet Yannai. *Sacred Trash* shines most brightly in its discussions of Yannai and other Geniza poets and of the effect that the rediscovery and translation of these poems had on Jewish intellectual life. Hoffman and Cole give short shrift to the world of the Geniza itself and how its rediscovery has changed perceptions of Jewish history and even religion. Rabbi Mark Glickman's *Sacred Treasure: The Cairo Genizah; The Amazing Discoveries of Forgotten Jewish History in an Egyptian Synagogue Attic* (2010) covers some of the same territory but is structured more chronologically and emphasizes the revelations of the Geniza itself rather than its poetry and scholars. Perhaps the place where *Sacred Trash* compares least favorably is in its relatively light analysis of the significance of the Geniza, poetry aside, to modern Jews, which Glickman reflects on extensively. Where Glickman brought the perspective of a rabbi, Hoffman and Cole bring the perspectives of a writer and a poet, respectively; they are concerned more with the literary value of the Geniza than with its religious or religious-historical significance.

The afterword of *Sacred Trash* rushes through the last few decades of Geniza scholarship—discovery after amazing discovery, despite the apparently finite nature of the cache—and the plans to digitize the entire Geniza, a staggering undertaking. It is easy to see how many more books could be written about the Geniza itself, particularly for the reader more interested in the medieval Jewish residents of Fustat than in the nineteenth- and twentieth-century scholars who are the focus of *Sacred Trash*. Although it would be impossible to write a definitive book about the Cairo Geniza, *Sacred Trash* is a fine addition to Jewish historical writing, conveying with an elegant, sometimes nearly poetic narrative at least part of the long and rich history of Jewish community, literature, and scholarship.

Melissa A. Barton

Review Sources

Kirkus Reviews 79, no. 4 (February 15, 2011): 287–88.
Maclean's, April 14, 2011 (Web).
Middle East Quarterly 18, no. 4 (Fall 2011): 96.
Nation 292, no. 25 (June 20, 2011): 27–32.
The New York Times Book Review, May 29, 2011, p. 6.

The Saturday Big Tent Wedding Party

Author: Alexander McCall Smith (b. 1948)
Publisher: Pantheon Books (New York).
224 pp. $24.95; paperback $14.95
Type of work: Novel
Time: The present
Locale: Gaborone, Botswana, in southern Africa

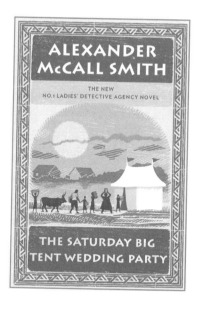

The twelfth volume of Alexander McCall Smith's series about Botswana's "No.1 Lady Detective," Precious Ramotswe, tells the story of an intriguing mystery dealing with cattle while exploring the complex daily lives of Precious's family and friends.

Principal characters:
PRECIOUS RAMOTSWE, Botswana's "No. 1 Lady Detective"
J. L. B. MATEKONI, husband of Precious and owner of Tlokweng Road Speedy Motors
GRACE MAKUTSI, abrasive associate detective in the No. 1 Ladies Detective Agency who is planning her upcoming wedding
PHUTI RADIPHUTI, fiancé of Grace and owner of a furniture store
CHARLIE, long-time apprentice to J. L. B. Matekoni, accused of abandoning his pregnant girlfriend
BOTSALO MOETI, client of the No. 1 Ladies Detective Agency and cattle farmer whose cattle are being mysteriously mutilated

Alexander McCall Smith's best-selling African novels in the No. 1 Ladies Detective Agency series provide an effective forum for powerful messages about modern society. The twelve books in the series showcase McCall Smith's ability to relate in a seemingly simplistic manner the details of daily dramas that, readers know, will be resolved in a playful tone, but that, in the meantime, present (usually minor but often significant) moral quandaries for the characters.

McCall Smith's literary output includes more than sixty books, and he is known as a writer who describes a world filled with tragedy and conflict. However, his novels are also uplifting because they demonstrate that kind and generous individuals can make the world a better place. The twelfth volume in the series, *The Saturday Big Tent Wedding Party*, reinforces McCall Smith's reputation as a writer who explores the quiet moments of life with wit and grace.

As the novel begins, Precious Ramotswe, McCall Smith's unpretentious and genial protagonist, fondly remembers her beloved "late white van," which she feels was much more than just a "collection of mechanical bits and pieces" and had become her friend.

Alexander McCall Smith is the author of several series: the No. 1 Ladies Detective Agency series, the Isabel Dalhousie series, Professor Dr. von Igelfeld series, the 44 Scotland Street series, and the Corduroy Mansions series. A professor emeritus of medical law at the University of Edinburgh, he previously taught law at the University of Botswana.

She also realizes that her "traditional build" might have been behind the dangerous tilting of the van on the driver's side that contributed to its eventual demise. Even the skillful attention of her loyal husband and mechanic, Mr. J. L. B. Matekoni, could not save it. It was replaced by a newer and more efficient blue vehicle, but it was not replaced in her heart. This plot detail seems a metaphor for McCall Smith's often nostalgic depiction of Botswana, his setting for the series and a former place of residence. The characters in the series, especially Precious, have a strong sense of and pride in their traditions. McCall Smith seems to validate this sentiment in general. The resurfacing of the van near the end of the novel expresses the importance of both the past and familiarity in McCall Smith's life and in the fictional life of his primary character.

Soon the busy life of a detective overshadows the visions that Precious has of her beloved van on the road. Grace Makutsi, her associate detective, reveals that Charlie, the eternal apprentice of Tlokweng Road Speedy Motors, is in trouble. His former girlfriend has had twins, and Charlie is the apparent father. However, he refuses to acknowledge his paternity. Grace decides to speak to him, "On behalf of girls whose boyfriends have pretended that babies have nothing to do with them." Charlie's condescending attitude toward women is revealed in his negative reaction to this discussion. He calls Grace a "warthog" and runs away to hide from his responsibilities.

Meanwhile, Precious faces her own conflicts. She has been hired by Mr. Botsalo Moeti, a wealthy rancher whose cattle are being mysteriously mutilated. The more she looks into the mystery, the less she thinks of the rancher. Not only does he abuse his workers, but also he hates his friendly neighbor, Mr. Fortitude Seleo, whose cattle are supposedly trespassing on his land. Mpho, a young boy who lives on the ranch with his mother, is the primary suspect for a time. As a result, Precious is faced with a moral dilemma.

As in previous novels in the series, problems are once again solved by following the rules of common decency and human kindness and with a sense of justice. Precious is obligated to reveal the culprit to her client, Mr. Moeti. At the same time, she realizes that she cannot identify Mpho as the culprit because then she would be responsible for whatever harm would come to him or his mother as a result. To prevent any potential backlash from Moeti, Precious, somewhat cryptically, assures him that the culprit will never kill cattle again, but she refrains from naming names.

Precious has solved one problem, only to face several others. Charlie is still missing and refusing to acknowledge his paternity. Precious visits the new mother, and what she finds out both surprises her and complicates the other characters' reactions to Charlie, whose ethics are, at least, more ambiguous than readers may have assumed.

Meanwhile, Grace faces her own problems as she prepares for her wedding to Phuti Radiphuti, the kind and generous furniture store owner. The wedding celebrations are all planned, but Grace must purchase her dress and her shoes. Readers of the series will be well aware that Grace is obsessed with shoes. On her way back from the store, she falls and breaks both the heels on the perfect new wedding shoes, for which Phuti has paid. Though this may seem like a minor dilemma, it represents a major mishap in Grace's life and illustrates McCall Smith's ability to relate the irony that happenstances that may seem minor to some are imbued with major, real-life consequences for others. As might be expected, however, given McCall Smith's track record, the predicament is resolved relatively easily and as the result of the inherent kindness of his characters.

Although McCall Smith's novel is labeled a mystery, there is little actual crime. Mr. Moeti's cattle are killed; however, when a potential culprit is found, Precious is able to solve the mystery and save face for Moeti by telling a white lie. McCall Smith's aim is not to examine the ins and outs of serious crime but to show how Precious helps people solve the problems of everyday life by using her keen sense of observation and her uncanny knowledge of human nature.

Precious is a good detective. She is experienced and intuitive in her investigative process. She often refers to Clovis Andersen's book *The Principles of Private Detection* for insight. Precious and Grace use this book as an investigative guide. Ironically, the book often gives them wise advice for their own personal lives in the process. Evidence is not always irrefutable because people's recollections of events often vary. Andersen tells readers, "'One person sees one thing, and another sees something altogether different. Both believe that they are telling the truth.'" Precious's solution to Mr. Moeti's dilemma is a great example of this philosophy.

The mystery in this novel is not the primary concern; rather, personal matters take precedence. Grace is excited and nervous about her upcoming wedding. Her "prickly behaviour" is evident in her discussions with Charlie about his treatment of his pregnant ex-girlfriend. Grace is also nervous about the actual details of the wedding celebration, particularly which shoes she is going to wear.

The final chapter describing the wedding is simply but beautifully written. McCall Smith's description of the essence of marriage is particularly memorable and encapsulates the basic philosophy undergirding the series: "A wedding was a strange ceremony . . . with all those formal words, those solemn vows made by one to another; whereas the real question that should be put to the two people involved was a very simple one. 'Are you happy with each other?' was the only question that should be asked." For all the complications that a wedding can bring, its essence is basic, a point that the No. 1 Ladies Detective Agency series repeatedly points out about myriad aspects of life.

The Saturday Big Tent Wedding Party continues McCall Smith's fascination with the peaceful yet progressive country of Botswana, where he once lived and taught law. Botswana is much more than just a place for him; it is a way of being. Precious spends many moments remembering her late father, Obed Ramotswe, who, for her, represented all that was good about her country and its past. Botswana is a country where owning cattle is a sign of great wealth and success and where everyone seems to know something about you. However, McCall Smith realizes that not everything is perfect in Botswana. As he puts it, Precious "had seen shocking things in the course of her work, even here in Botswana, a good country where things were well run and people had rights; human nature, of course, would find its way round the best of rules and regulations."

The delightful world that McCall Smith creates in his novels has its own sense of community in the tradition of authors such as Agatha Christie and P. G. Wodehouse. Kindness and the wisdom of experience are important qualities in this world. Even though everyone's life can be summed up "in a few sentences," every human being deserves love and respect. Perhaps the highest praise is reserved for Precious, "the lady to help people."

McCall Smith's novel celebrates the triumph of goodness, as conflicts are resolved and those characters at the heart of them discover the decency within. Finally, at the center of it all, Precious is rewarded for her kindness with the return of her little white van. She reminds readers what is important in life, "Did money bring any greater happiness than that furnished by a well-made cup of red bush tea and a moment or two with a good friend? She thought not."

Myra Junyk

Review Sources

Booklist 107, no. 14 (March 15, 2011): 26.
Kirkus Reviews 79, no. 6 (March 15, 2011): 457.
Library Journal 136, no. 12 (July 2011): 46.
Publishers Weekly 258, no. 9 (February 28, 2011): 37.
Seattle Times, March 24, 2011 (Web).
Washington Times, March 25, 2011 (Web).

Say Her Name

Author: Francisco Goldman (b. 1954)
Publisher: Grove (New York). 350 pp. $24.00
Type of work: Novel, memoir
Time: Mid to late 2000s, with flashbacks to the 1980s and 1990s
Locale: New York City and Mexico

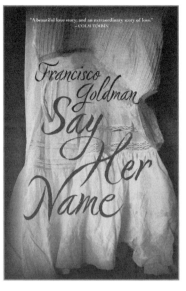

This fictionalized memoir from the award-winning journalist and novelist is a testament of the narrator's love for his deceased wife, Aura Estrada, as well as a testimony to how grief can morph into guilt.

Principal characters:
FRANCISCO GOLDMAN, the narrator, a professor and author in his late forties
AURA ESTRADA (1977–2007), Goldman's second wife, who died at the age of thirty
JUANITA, Aura's mother, an administrative assistant at a university
RODRIGO, Juanita's second husband, a public-housing consultant
HÉCTOR, Juanita's first husband, a former lawyer and leftist urban politician
LEOPOLDO, Juanita's brother, also a politician
KATIA, Aura's older stepsister

Not in a long time has a work of literature presented such a profound story of love and loss. This memoir-novel is Francisco Goldman's lament for Aura, his thirty-year-old wife, who was fatally injured on July 25, 2007, while vacationing with the author in Mexico. A novice at bodysurfing, Aura was thrown into the sand by a strong wave, breaking crucial vertebrae that left her paralyzed and unable to breathe on her own; she later slipped into a brief coma before dying. Goldman, an established novelist and journalist, first published excerpts from *Say Her Name* as "The Wave: A Tragedy in Mexico" in the *New Yorker* in February 2011. A "personal history" piece rather than this more fictionalized work, the article included photographs of Aura along with a snapshot of her with Goldman on their wedding day. With this testament of his love, Goldman and Estrada join Robert and Elizabeth Browning, F. Scott and Zelda Fitzgerald, Ted Hughes and Sylvia Plath, and other famous literary couples who immortalized their love for one another in print.

Say Her Name moves back and forth between the dreadful day in the summer of 2007 and Aura's early life growing up in Mexico and Texas, encompassing the time when Goldman first laid eyes on Aura and the couple's two years together after their wedding day. Much of the content is drawn from Goldman's own memory, often assisted by photographs of Aura, as well as her personal belongings and the household furnishings in their Brooklyn apartment. Unwilling to part with so many memories, Goldman, with support from friends, created a shrine in his home filled with Aura's books, her wedding dress, and even the bag she brought to the beach on the day of her accident, "with everything inside it just as she'd left it." He holds onto these items as tangible proof of their life together, grasping at the memory of love to withstand his grief.

(Mathieu Bourgois)

Francisco Goldman is the Allan K. Smith Professor of English at Trinity College in Hartford, Connecticut. He has written both fiction and nonfiction for such publications as Esquire *and* Outside. *His first novel,* The Long Night of White Chickens *(1992), was awarded the Sue Kaufman Prize for First Fiction.*

Goldman also draws on material from Aura's many diaries that she kept from childhood through adulthood, as well as the stories, essays, and papers she wrote during college, some already published and some in progress at the time of her death. Goldman includes some passages from these in *Say Her Name* as well. He also read or reread the Latin American literature that Aura revered, retraced the steps they had taken to restaurants and delis, and scrutinized the important and trivial moments in their relationship. He conferred with friends and relatives for other viewpoints and for help piecing together events and relationships to which he had not been privy.

Despite all the factual material and sources at his fingertips, Goldman chose to fictionalize certain elements so that the book straddles the line between imagination and reality, thus becoming a "memoir novel." This is not the first time Goldman's writing has interwoven fact and fiction; his first novel, *The Long Night of White Chickens* (1992), was based in part on his own experience growing up with a Jewish father and a Guatemalan mother. Neither is his approach entirely original. In many cases, memoir writers fictionalize characters to protect real-life identities, while other authors fictionalize works of creative nonfiction to fill in missing details.

Of course, memoirs open themselves up naturally to imaginary conversations and invented details, as they are rooted in imperfect, often selective, human memory. So which parts of *Say Her Name* are fictitious and what was Goldman's rationale for choosing this style? In various interviews, Goldman has stated that he wanted to elaborate on Aura's childhood diary entries, which required the use of his imagination. He also wanted to protect the privacy of certain friends and family members and, as a result, either changed some names and personalities or created new figures in their place. He also chose to color his own life—in part, one would assume—to draw additional empathy from the reader. By settling on fiction rather than creative nonfiction, Goldman maintained the oath undertaken by journalists to impart only facts, while also steering clear of any ensuing legal problems that might have arisen from this written account.

The legal issue was a valid one for Goldman, who began writing the book during the winter after Aura died, as Juanita, Aura's mother, was holding him responsible for her daughter's death. "*Esto es tu culpa*," she told him at the hospital where Aura died: this is your fault. He had since returned to Mexico twice—once on the first anniversary of her death to be "where it had happened, at that beach on the Pacific coast," and later that year, when he had "come home again to Brooklyn without her"—yet most readers would surmise that his trips were hardly representative of a murderer returning to the scene of the crime. Even the book jacket attests to his innocence. The confession on page one, therefore, is startling: "It's not as if I consider myself not guilty. If I were Juanita, I know I would have wanted to put me in prison, too. Though not for the reasons she and her brother gave." Goldman thus sets the stage for a bit more intrigue and tension than readers in search of a simple biography or love story might have envisioned. The book represents not only a tribute to Goldman's love but also a gut-wrenching emotional testimony to his own imagined and uncalled-for culpability.

Goldman was in his late forties when he first met Aura at a literary event in New York City. She was then just twenty-five years old, a postgraduate researcher in Latin American literature at Brown University in Providence, Rhode Island. Although Mexican, she had spent much of her childhood in Texas. She had just been accepted into the Latin American literature doctorate program at Columbia University in New York. Goldman, a divorcé of many years, was smitten with her intelligence, smile, and sweetness. As they conversed after the reading and during the dinner that followed, Goldman thought he noticed the same flicker of romantic interest in her that he felt himself. After the event, he sent her a copy of his novel, but when he did not receive an acknowledgment, he assumed that he must be of the wrong generation for her. Only several months later did he learn that there had been a misunderstanding, and that she had, indeed, sent him an engaging and perhaps opportunistic thank-you note.

From that point on, Goldman's dream began to fall into place. Aura eventually moved into his apartment, and they soon found themselves making plans for their August 2005 wedding in Mexico City. The age difference that Goldman once blamed for her seeming lack of interest in him was mostly insignificant, although Aura "pestered" him occasionally about trying "anti-aging facial creams . . . and even Botox" and insisted he dye his graying hair black for the wedding. She also dwelled occasionally on the likelihood of being widowed. Ironically, it was Goldman who found himself a widower, less than a month before their two-year anniversary.

After the accident, life for Goldman was a challenge: "Every day a ghostly ruin. Every day the ruin of the day that was supposed to have been." Two years after Aura's death, he was still wearing the tailor-made black mourning suit that he commissioned for her funeral. He had attached Aura's wedding ring to his own and wore them on a chain around his neck at all times, even when he had sex with another woman after finally summoning the strength to begin a new relationship. He was consumed with guilt, anger, and grief. Thoughts of suicide racked his brain.

While Aura represented the most intense relationship of Goldman's life, there was another significant person in her life, her mother. Juanita had separated from Aura's father, Héctor, a lawyer and rising politician, when Aura was just four years old. Aura grew up with a special closeness to her mother, while the absence of her father left a gaping hole inside. Goldman portrays Juanita in part as a controlling, ineffective, and alcoholic parent, yet he also makes it clear that she made sacrifices for Aura, working hard to pay for summer camps and other educational programs so that Aura could compete with children from wealthier families. Juniata is also credited with encouraging her precocious daughter to follow an academic path, even though later on Aura decided she favored writing over academia. In return, Aura tried hard to please her mother and was even willing to marry in a traditional Catholic ceremony despite her detachment from the Church. Aura's death sent Juanita spinning into an emotional frenzy. Unable to forgive and unable to forget, she made Goldman the target for her blame.

Most of the details about Aura's death are presented near the end of the book. Goldman's grief, however, spills onto nearly every page. Writing this book was clearly a cathartic experience for the author, serving as both a release and a way of letting go and moving on. The book also serves to promote a young author who missed out on the glory and satisfaction of success. At the time of her death, Aura had been completing a graduate degree in creative writing at Hunter College in New York, had begun to publish stories and articles in Mexican periodicals, and had been working on a novel tentatively called "Memoirs of a Grad Student." After Aura died, Goldman sent one of her stories to *Harper's Magazine*. They not only published it but also asked for more. Goldman also established the Aura Estrada Prize to be awarded biannually to a young, Spanish-speaking female writer; the prize includes a financial award as well as residences at three writers' colonies.

Say Her Name is a fitting tribute to a life that was tragically cut short. Although readers cannot presume to understand the depth of Goldman's grief, his beautiful and haunting prose will nevertheless touch whoever comes across it. Through his careful words, Goldman portrays an imperfect, intriguing young woman whose death no doubt has left a hole in the lives of her husband and the rest of her family. While treading the line between fiction and nonfiction, Goldman also meditates on memory, healing, and loss, all the while trying to balance his need to heal with his need to remember his wife. For the author, loving deeply means grieving deeply. In writing this extraordinary, often painfully sad book, Goldman has found a way to keep both Aura's memory and their love alive.

Sally S. Driscoll

Review Sources

Booklist 107, no. 13 (March 1, 2011): 28.
Library Journal 136, no. 2 (February 1 2011): 53.
The New York Times Book Review, April 10, 2011, p. 1.
Paris Review, May 3, 2011 (Web).
Publishers Weekly 258, no. 7 (February 14, 2011): 35–36.
The Wall Street Journal, April 2, 2011, p. C7.
The Washington Post, April 14, 2011, (Web).
World Literature Today 85, no. 5 (September/October 2011): 59-60.

The Seamstress and the Wind

Author: César Aira (b. 1949)
First published: *La costurera y el viento*, 1994, in Argentina
Translated from the Spanish by Rosalie Knecht
Publisher: New Directions (New York). 144 pp. $12.95
Type of work: Novel
Time: 1994; mid-to-late 1950s
Locale: Paris, France; Coronel Pringles, Argentina; Patagonia

A highly experimental, elaborate rendering of the dynamics of the imagination and the process of literary creation, The Seamstress and the Wind *presents a dream tale of a distraught mother, tracking down her missing child in the forbidding wastes of Argentina's Patagonia region.*

Principal characters:

CÉSAR AIRA, an Argentine writer, in his forties, living in Paris
OMAR SIFFONI, a childhood friend of César who one day disappeared from the neighborhood
DELIA SIFFONI, Omar's mother, a seamstress, who is a bit neurotic and an insomniac
RAMÓN SIFFONI, Delia's husband, a truck driver and gambler
SILVIA BALERO, an art teacher in her late twenties, who is pregnant and in a hurry to marry the baby's father
CHIQUITO, another truck driver, whose may have inadvertently transported Omar to Patagonia
SIR VENTARRÓN, the harsh Patagonian wind who falls in love with Delia
THE MONSTER, a hairy, pale-blue fetuslike creature, perhaps Silvia's unborn child, who roams Patagonia and may be seeking vengeance

César Aira, long a recognized master practitioner of metafiction (a genre that emerged in the 1950s and 1960s from authors' frustration over both the limitations and the conventions of psychological realism and that incorporates the author as a character in the text), reminds us in *The Seamstress and the Wind* that unconventional narration can still surprise, intrigue, amuse, and shock. *The Seamstress and the Wind* tracks two counterpointed narratives. In one, set in the late 1950s, a child, Omar Siffoni, who had been playing in the streets of the small southern Argentine town of Coronel Pringles (conveniently Aira's own hometown), does not come home one evening. His frantic mother, Delia Siffoni, a seamstress, decides in her panic that the boy has been trapped in a huge trailer truck, driven by a man named Chiquito; the truck is headed to Patagonia, the forbidding region in southern Argentina made up of nature in its most primitive—steppes, forests, pampas, mountains, and even glaciers—a desolate wasteland known to the locals as The End of the World.

Delia commandeers a taxi and its driver and heads to Patagonia, taking with her an elaborate wedding dress she has been commissioned to create for a local art teacher who is in a particular hurry to get married: She is pregnant and already showing. When Delia's husband, an inveterate gambler named Ramón, returns home that night, he is furious that his wife has left without him; he jumps in his little red truck and joins the quest to Patagonia and is followed, although he does not know it, by the art teacher desperate to secure her dress.

The plotline is, on the whole, familiar and promisingly realistic: Frantic parents are desperate to retrieve their lost child. However, around that plot is a framing narrative set in 1994; in the opening page, readers are introduced to a first-person-narrative authority, an expatriate Argentine writer, named César Aira, who sits alone in a café along the streets of Paris, notebook open, pen in hand, and restless in thought. He is, he tells us, in search of a plot. He has only a title ("The Seamstress and the Wind") and the elements of a dream he cannot forget, and he is certain that such materials contain the germ of a story. As he sips his coffee, the writer ponders two conflicting theories of fiction writing. In one, the writer draws on recollection, excavating into memory to recover traumatic moments and epiphanic experiences in order to transcribe them into language. In the other theory, the writer, finding the reservoir of individual experience thin and unpromising, liberates the imagination and trusts the crazy energy of dreams, deliberately forgetting experiences and thus freeing the kinetics of fantasy to expand rather than merely transcribe reality. The writer in the café then shares a spare memory—an afternoon when he was ten, when, playing with his best friend, Omar Siffoni, he thought he was lost, only to find that when he returned home Omar had not returned. That unsettling (and realistic) autobiographical fragment of memory triggers what quickly becomes a grand indulgence of fantasy, a most bizarre and fantastic excursion into a magical (and entirely symbolic) Patagonian landscape animated by fabulous creatures. At this point, the simple, realistic plot loses entirely its anchorage in the recognizable. However, even at the novel's most pitched moments, Aira gently and unironically returns readers to the café in Paris where the writer-narrator observes the sidewalk traffic, frets over the attention he is not receiving from the waiters, tries to settle his bill, ponders his distaste for traveling, and even inventories the characters in the novel that the readers are reading.

Effortlessly, the narrative of the missing child launches into the improbable—the surreal, boundary-free atmosphere appropriate to a dream—denying the reader the luxury of relaxing into a narrative. Aira's fervid imagination frustrates plot summary and dismisses as pedestrian the demand for explanation. As Delia pursues the tractor-trailer truck that she believes bears her missing child, the taxicab she has commandeered rear-ends the truck, killing the cab driver. The truck carries the car, with the dead cabbie and Delia, for hours until a whirlwind whips through the car and picks up the startled and terrified Delia. When the wind sets her down gently, Delia is accosted by the wind itself, who identifies itself as Sir Ventarrón (the second word is Spanish for "gale"), an endearing charmer who quickly falls in love with the seamstress in a kind of eccentric (and entirely fantastic) imitation of chivalrous romance. Meanwhile, the husband, pursued by the bride-to-be, pulls off at a hotel and gets entangled in a high-stakes poker game in which he loses his truck. The driver of the big rig, Chiquito, pulls off as well and sets his lecherous sights on the pregnant bride-to-be, who has also

In a prolific career that spans more than thirty years, Argentine author César Aira has produced nearly eighty separate titles, although only a few have been translated into English. Whatever their genre, his unclassifiable texts have testified to his gleeful interrogation of the daring of the unfettered imagination.

taken a room in the same hotel; even as that carnal interlude commences, much to Chiquito's shock, a fetuslike creature appears to emerge from the young woman, with blue skin and covered with furlike hair.

Meanwhile, Delia and Ramón each continue their search for their missing son, but one bizarre turn of events after another frustrates these efforts. In one instance, Ramón devises a sort of dinosaur-armadillo roadster in order to continue on his mission. The fetal creature sets off wreaking vengeance, destroying the hotel, and pursuing Delia, who is lovingly cared for by the wind. The wind, for his part, acts strictly in accordance with the noble code of unrequited love. And in keeping with the rest of the fantastical story, the narrative ends on a strange, somewhat ambiguous note, with Chiquito the truck driver about to sit down with the lovelorn Sir Ventarrón to play a hand of poker together.

With obvious glee, Aira resists giving his readers even the semblance of a logical plot; the slender text ruptures into a magical chaos of improbable events that pass with the animated rhythm of improvisation. The harrowing realistic premise (a missing child) concedes to the gravitational force of playful fantasy; tragedy deconstructs into comedy; apprehension gives way to delight; the need for clarity, certainty, and resolution surrenders to the liberating promise of confusion. Nothing necessarily ends the dervish of invention, save that Aira closes up his notebook and departs the Parisian café. Although any attempt to structure some point-by-point allegory for Aira's fantastic dream-tale would be frustrated by the sheer breadth of its daring, it is not a great stretch to conceive of parallels between the café writer, Aira, determined to embroider an elaborate plot, and the distraught seamstress, who refuses, despite being set upon by grievous circumstances, to abandon the elaborate dress she is creating. The seamstress-novelist defiantly, perhaps heroically, stitches together the disparate threads of a half dozen increasingly fantastic tales, caring not so much for consistency, but for the audacity of the patterning and the deft (and entirely original) construction itself, piecing together bits of narrative elements that in any other circumstance would collide in impenetrable and frustrating confusion.

Such an eccentric, elusive metanarrative is not for everyone. Aira understands that, confessing in interviews that his dozens of novels have earned readers but not an audience. Conformist readers who choose to undertake *The Seamstress and the Wind* will see only a plot that unravels, one that refuses to concede to the logic of resolution and simply ignores the most troubling issue (the whereabouts of the missing boy) in favor of a tall tale about a lovesick, talking wind, a malicious fetus, and the fossilized relics of a fabulous dinosaur. Aira is known for a signature writing process: He claims that he writes daily in intense sessions in cafés; that he never plots his novels; that his imagination, engaged by the freewheeling café environment, dares to posit unexpected directions and that his pen simply follows; and that, to maintain the integrity of invention, he never redrafts, revises, or, indeed, revisits his draft. To borrow from the deliberately inchoate metaphors of *The Seamstress and the Wind*, Aira's plot, in essence, goes where the winds of his loving, if unfettered, imagination takes it. By intruding himself at critical moments into the narrative, Aira reminds readers that even as the story line concedes to the fantastic and frustrates the traditional desire for linear plot, sympathetic characters, and tidy themes, they are to relish that spectacle show itself.

Joseph Dewey

Review Sources

Publishers Weekly 258, no. 22 (May 30, 2011): 49.
Quarterly Conversation, September 6, 2011 (Web).

The Selected Stories of Mercè Rodoreda

Author: Mercè Rodoreda (1908–1983)
First published: Three collections: *Vint-i-dos contes*, 1958, in Spain; *La meva Cristina i altres contes*, 1967, in Spain; *Semblava de seda i altres contes*, 1978, in Spain
Translated from the Catalan by Martha Tennent
Publisher: Open Letter Books (Rochester, NY). 255 pp. $15.95
Type of work: Short fiction
Time: 1930s to 1970s
Locale: Spain, France, and Switzerland

Representing over two decades of work by one of the most important Catalan authors, the stories in this collection focus on themes of obsessive love, personal loss, violence, and warfare.

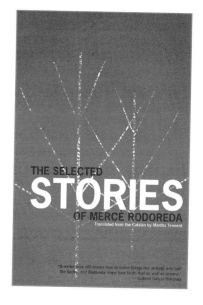

Principal characters:

MARIA LLUÏSA, a poor seamstress who contemplates murder

TERESA, a young woman who is distraught over a forgotten good-morning kiss from her lover

MARTA COLL, a newlywed woman who wishes to commit suicide to avenge her husband's lingering affection for his lost first love

MERCÈ, a preteen girl who baptizes a doll and considers her to be dead when a bath destroys the doll's cardboard body

WILSON, an African American trapped in France during World War II

LISA SPERLING, a Russian Jewish woman who commits suicide to avoid deportation to a Nazi death camp

MIXU, a cat who turns into a phantom

THE SALAMANDER, a young village woman who is burned as a witch by villagers and transformed into a salamander

The Selected Stories of Mercè Rodoreda offers a graceful English translation of some of the most remarkable short stories by Catalan author Mercè Rodoreda. Almost all of these stories have a haunting quality to them. Love is portrayed as leading easily to obsession. A strong sense of loss, either imminent or feared, deeply permeates the narratives. Most of Rodoreda's characters suffer in their lives, and quite a few encounter acts of violence, yet there is also the suggestion of a final form of redemption in many stories.

Very often Rodoreda's protagonists are women who are disappointed in love and life and are led to contemplate some astonishing solutions to their disappointment.

Mercè Rodoreda's debut novel, Aloma *(1936, revised 1968), won the Joan Crexells Prize in 1937. Her novel about the Spanish Civil War,* La plaça del diamant *(1962;* The Time of the Doves, *1980), was translated into twenty languages. Rodoreda received the Premi d'Honor de les Lletres Catalanes in 1980.*

In the first story, "Blood," the first-person narrator, a postmenopausal wife, decides to separate from her husband of many years after he plays a mean practical joke on her. To pursue separation was still a shocking act for a married woman in French and Spanish society in 1958, when the story was first published. In "Threaded Needle," the middle-aged seamstress Maria Lluïsa considers poisoning her sickly cousin, a priest, in order to inherit his money before it is all eaten up by hospital costs. He was her first love; she never married after he joined the priesthood.

The obsessive nature of love is a key subject of Rodoreda's short fiction. She explores with great narrative verve the many turns and twists an obsessive love can create. In "Happiness," Teresa seriously considers breaking up with her lover because he forgot to give her his usual good-morning kiss. In "The Mirror," a widowed grandmother of sixty remembers her one true love. After Roger G. impregnated her but married another woman, the narrator took out her revenge on the hapless Jaume Mas. After Jaume marries her, he discovers that his wife still pines for Roger.

Romantic obsession by both sexes is carried to an extreme level in "Before I Die." All seems well when Marta Coll marries the attorney Marius Roig, until she discovers that Marius is keeping love letters from his previous lover, Elisa. For revenge, Marta decides to commit suicide in the very hotel room where Marius first made love to Elisa. Here, as in other stories by Rodoreda, obsessive love becomes a lethal force.

Key traumatic events from the author's life may have inspired some of the stories collected here. "The Bath" is the only short story in which the protagonist, a little girl, shares Rodoreda's first name. The little girl and her family are leaving their home in what appears to be in Barcelona, a departure that seems to reflect Rodoreda's own exile from Catalonia at the end of the Spanish Civil War. Some of the characters in Rodoreda's other short stories, such as "Carnival," "Departure," and "On the Train," are also Catalonian exiles.

As is typical of Rodoreda's short fiction, "The Bath" is told from the protagonist's subjective point of view. On the day that young Mercè's family leaves their home, she remembers a special surprise gift from her beloved grandfather: a huge doll that stands as tall as her waist. Together with her childhood playmate, the boy Felipet, Mercè performs a play baptism for the doll. When a bath disfigures the doll's cardboard body, the children decide that she has died. They quietly add this element to their play with her. It is only the adults who react strongly when they discover the destroyed doll. On a symbolic level, at which many of Rodoreda's stories can be read, the doll represents the children's acceptance of the natural course of life, from baptism to death. In this acceptance, the children act more mature than the adults in the story.

While in exile in France, Rodoreda was caught up in France's fall to Nazi Germany in June 1940. From Paris, she and her lover, Joan Prat i Esteve, fled south trying to reach Orléans. This event is told in fictionalized form in "Orléans, Three Kilometers."

Written in a starkly realistic style that works well to depict some of the surrealism of war, Rodoreda presents the story of Roca and his unnamed wife as they try to flee into Orléans. At the village of Artenay, they meet Wilson, an African American servant to a Parisian family who also seeks to escape the advancing Germans. The couple survives a bombing raid only to find the way to Orléans blocked by destroyed bridges. Instead, they seek shelter in an abandoned estate home full of uneaten, rotting food. They meet Wilson again. During the night, he breaks down and confesses his desperate desire to return to America as the story suddenly ends on a note of desolation and uncertainty.

"Nocturnal" depicts a particularly cruel story set in occupied France during World War II. The protagonist in this story is an unnamed Spanish exile from Barcelona. When his middle-aged wife is about to give birth again, he tries to telephone a doctor for assistance with the complicated birth; however, the only working telephone in his neighborhood is located in the local brothel. Although the brothel is officially off-limits to German soldiers, when the husband enters the brothel to make his phone call he is greeted by German troops who fraternize with him and fill him with cognac and champagne. Suddenly, German military police arrive at the brothel and arrest the husband together with the troops. "Nocturnal" shows Rodoreda's creative power to write a moving piece about an ordinary man's deep personal loss in times of general turmoil and tragedy.

The Holocaust is the subject of "The Fate of Lisa Sperling." Lisa Sperling is a middle-aged Jewish woman living in France while in exile from Soviet Russia. Rather than be deported to a Nazi death camp, she decides to commit suicide. In her small rented room on the eve of her last night, she divides all her remaining personal possessions into different piles for her four friends. The story ends on this note of parting kindness in a world terrorized by the Nazis.

Most of the stories collected in this volume are told in a realistic, if often highly symbolic, fashion. Typically, Rodoreda focuses on her protagonists and tells the story from their limited, subjective, and occasionally unreliable point of view. Some stories, like "On the Train" and "Love," are told in the form of the protagonist's remarks to a silent counterpart, such as a train passenger or a haberdasher. These one-sided dialogues enable Rodoreda to explore the inner workings of her protagonists very creatively.

Among speakers and readers of Catalan, Mercè Rodoreda is revered as the most important Catalan author of the twentieth century. The thirty stories published in *Selected Stories* were taken from three different collections of her short fiction and translated into English by Martha Tennent. The first twenty were originally published in Rodoreda's 1958 collection, *Vint-i-dos contes* (Twenty-Two Stories), for which she won the prestigious Premi Víctor Català, awarded in 1957 before the book's official publication. The next seven short stories are from Rodoreda's 1978 *Semblava de seda i altres contes* (It Seemed like Silk and Other Stories). In this collection, Rodoreda employs the magical realism that characterizes much of her later work, particularly after 1972. The title story, "It Seemed like Silk," exemplifies Rodoreda's move into magical realism. Longing for her dead lover whose grave is too far away for her to visit, the protagonist selects an apparently abandoned grave in a local cemetery as a substitute. When the grave is refurbished after All Souls' Day, the narrator nearly despairs, as this threatens to dispel her illusion. In the end, she discovers a black feather on the grave, which feels like silk to her. This feather belongs to an angel who has come to visit her at the grave.

Rodoreda had already used magical realism in her second collection of her short fiction, *La meva Cristina i altres contes* (1967), which was translated into English by David Rosenthal in 1984 and published as *My Christina and Other Stories*. In her new translation of the three stories from *La meva Cristina* that round out this collection, Tennent stays very close to the original Catalan, offering a slightly different interpretation from Rosenthal's first translation.

In the last story of *Selected Stories*, "White Geranium," Rodoreda combines magical realism with the theme of obsessive love. When the narrator's wife, Balbina, dies, in part because he has deprived her of sleep, he still resents the fact that she loved his rival Cosme instead of him. After the narrator takes his resentment out on Mixu, a cat that Cosme gave to Balbina, by cruelly killing it, Mixu returns as a huge phantom to haunt him as he walks along the city limits. While Rodoreda's earlier stories rely on symbolism in a realistic setting to explore her themes, this story reflects how magical realism became her favorite style, one that she also used in her long fiction.

"The Salamander" also stands out as an example of Rodoreda's magical realism. Set in a village at an indeterminate time, its protagonist is a young woman who falls for a married man. The villagers bully her and burn her as a witch in the village square, after which the woman turns into a salamander. Her transformation, which corresponds to the European legend that salamanders can survive fire, links the story to the world of fairy tales. As the protagonist creeps into the house of her former lover, she is hunted down by his wife. With its haunting use of the cruel customs of a remote village, "The Salamander" may awaken a reader's appetite for Mercè Rodoreda's final short novel, the posthumously published *La mort i primavera* (1986), translated from the Catalan by Tennent and published as *Death in Spring* (2009), which features a novel-length exploration of similarly cruel village traditions.

The Selected Stories of Mercè Rodoreda offers a powerful survey of the author's imaginative range. Her stories develop her key themes of obsessive love, loss, and tragedy, and are told in various styles. If there is one thing a reader might wish for, it would be a translation of the occasional quotes in French, German, and Italian. Overall, Tennent's translation renders the full force of the author's original Catalan. This short story collection fully transports the reader into Mercè Rodoreda's dark, but not hopeless, universe.

R. C. Lutz

Review Sources

The Literary Review 54, no. 3 (Spring 2011): 196.
Nation 292, no. 23 (June 6, 2011): 32.
Publishers Weekly 257, no. 50 (December 20, 2010): 34.

Seven Years

Author: Peter Stamm (b. 1963)
First published: *Sieben Jahre*, 2009, in Germany
Translated from the German by Michael Hofmann
Publisher: Other Press (New York). 272 pp. $15.95
Type of work: Novel
Time: 1989–2009
Locale: Munich, Germany; Marseilles, France

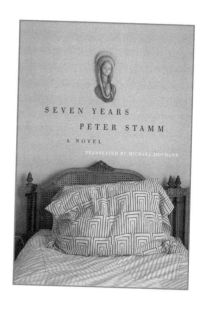

Set in Germany during reunification, this novel breathes new life into the cliché of the seven-year itch.

Principal characters:
ALEX, the narrator, an architect who is married to Sonia
SONIA, an ambitious, talented, and beautiful architect, married to Alex
IVONA, a Polish Catholic bookstore clerk who is in love with Alex
ANTJE, an older confidant of both Sonia and Alex and the character to whom Alex tells his story

Seven Years is Peter Stamm's fifth book to be translated into English. Despite being an award-winning and best-selling author in Europe, he has yet to receive wide recognition in the United States, although he began to develop an American following in 2000 with the publication of the English translation of his novel *Agnes* (1998). *Seven Years* has garnered encouraging reviews from US critics, which should continue to expand Stamm's readership outside of Europe.

Seven Years is the story of Alex's eighteen-year marriage to Sonia and his intermittent extramarital affair with Ivona. The narrative is essentially Alex's reconstruction of the events that shaped these relationships, with occasional commentary from the mature viewpoint of his friend Antje, to whom he is recounting the story. The novel begins with a quote by the French architect Le Corbusier, "Light and shadow reveal form," and Stamm's main characters seem to embody this contrast right from the start. In the very first sentence, Sonia stands in a "brightly lit space" while Alex lurks in the darkness, voyeuristically watching her through a plate glass window. They are attending an art exhibition by Antje, whom Alex has not seen for twenty years.

After Antje closes up the gallery for the night, she and Alex begin to reminisce about the details that shaped his marriage and affair. The story flashes back to 1989, at which time Alex and Sonia are both finishing their undergraduate degrees in architecture. Sonia, a beautiful and talented overachiever, hails from a privileged background, while Alex comes from a lower-middle-class family and is less motivated. His college architectural projects are admittedly rather mundane. Despite their differences, Alex and Sonia's friendship develops into a marriage as well as a business partnership. Their union grows while the Berlin Wall comes tumbling down and East and West Germany begin working toward reunification.

Alex's marriage to Sonia is much less compelling than his affair with Ivona, which is the central focus of the book. Ivona is a shy, homely, uneducated, and unsophisticated Polish Catholic bookshop clerk. She is in love with Alex, or at least has decided that he is Mr. Right, based on the portrayals of men in the romance novels she reads. In other words, the Alex she knows exists largely as a figment of her imagination. Unbeknownst to Alex, she has been following him around town and quietly waiting for him to take notice of her.

Although Alex is repulsed by Ivona's appearance and religious devotion, he nonetheless becomes sexually obsessed with her in ways that border on the pathological. This dichotomy between revulsion and compulsion represents another important theme in the story. Alex harbors thoughts of hurting Ivona, though he stops short of rape when she refuses to consent to intercourse, and they remain physically chaste with each other even as their relationship becomes more intimate. Their contrasting social, physical, and emotional qualities seem to violate the psychological laws that usually govern attraction and compatibility. Alex justifies his obsession and "his need to hurt her" by claiming to feel "strangely exhilarated" and "free and uninhibited" after being with her, terminology that evokes a darkly primitive, animalistic humanity that may leave many readers chilled.

Alex manages to break free of Ivona while he and Sonia begin to build their marriage and their architectural firm, although most of their efforts are directed toward the business. As a result, the firm becomes one of the more successful businesses in Munich. Alex chooses to let his wife do all the designing while he handles the administrative end, an arrangement that works for them on one level, but on another level reinforces Alex's old feelings of inadequacy with regard to Sonia and leaves him disconnected from his inner muse. Their marriage also appears successful when viewed as a business partnership, but in fact it is tainted by communication problems, Sonia's infertility and sexual inhibitions, and Alex's strained relationship with his in-laws.

Seven years into the marriage, Alex receives a surprise letter from Ivona requesting money, which leads to the two rekindling their affair. This time, Ivona consents to intercourse and becomes pregnant. When Sonia learns about Ivona and the baby, she insists that Alex end the affair. He complies for another seven years, but as he and Sonia enter their forties, as financial difficulties swamp their professional and personal lives, and as their discordant marriage seems to be unraveling past the point of no return, he again finds Ivona to be a distraction impossible to ignore.

As a parallel to the story of Alex, Sonia, and Ivona, Stamm introduces the biblical story of Jacob, Rachel, and Leah. The two seven-year lapses in contact between Alex and Ivona echo the two seven-year periods during which Jacob was forced to work for Rachel's father, Laban, in order to eventually marry her after being tricked into marrying her older sister Leah. Although Ivona is not Alex's wife, the love triangle depicted shares similarities with Jacob's bigamy. In each case, the man is attracted to one of the women and less attracted to or even repulsed by the other; the beloved woman is infertile, while the unloved woman bears the man's offspring.

Stamm's portrayal of Sonia and Ivona is limited mostly to Alex's perceptions, and his unreliability as a narrator becomes increasingly obvious as the story unfolds. Readers might have been suspicious of Alex's portrayal of Sonia in the first paragraph, when he suggests that Sonia enjoys being "the center of things," for if any character enjoys being the center of things, it is Alex himself. One way in which Stamm creates the sense that

(Gaby Gerster)

Peter Stamm worked in business and journalism before becoming a novelist. English translations of his novels include Agnes *(2000),* Unformed Landscape *(2004), and* On a Day Like This *(2007). He is also the author of many short stories and radio plays. His story* "Ice Moon" *was selected for the anthology* Best European Fiction *2010.*

Alex is self-centered and unreliable is by embedding dialogue in the text without using quotation marks to set it off, a technique that recalls the work of contemporary authors such as Charles Frazier and Cormac McCarthy. By choosing to forego quotation marks, Stamm makes it hard for the reader to tell which character is speaking, giving the impression that Alex may have some personal boundary issues. This technique also blurs the line between dialogue that Alex remembers and his interpretation of what is said, suggesting that his memory, and thus his reliability, may be less than perfect.

Alex's egocentrism is complicated by the often contradictory facets of his personality. He is portrayed as narcissistic, yet at times he seems to have low self-esteem. He appears at times to be depressed and yet as a rationalist he is unemotional. He suffers angst when he loses touch with himself; however, as an atheist, he believes that he lacks a soul. He claims to be good looking, but both his self-image and his unflattering portraits of Ivona may be nothing but half-truths. His immaturity stunts his personality, yet it is perhaps one of his saving graces.

While Stamm has a demonstrated ability to develop multifaceted, cerebral characters whose detachment from either society or their inner selves builds tension and depth, these same characters may also alienate some readers. It is understandably difficult to connect with ugly, reticent, or unemotional characters. However, one of the rewards of reading this novel is the challenge of piecing together all the different components of Alex's personality and trying to find redemption in his character.

In addition to having strong characters, *Seven Years* has a strong sense of place; it is very much a German story, with its setting in Munich during German reunification providing a significant layer of subtext to the narrative. The Berlin Wall can be seen as a metaphor for Alex's marriage, while the divisions between East and West are akin to those between Stamm's male and female characters. Furthermore, the novel's narrative sounds German despite being translated into English. The translator, Michael

Hofmann, collaborated with Stamm to preserve elements of German syntax in the English translation. For example, Hofmann retains the original comma splices, or run-on sentences, that are acceptable in German but grammatically incorrect in English. One such sentence reads: "It was a scene from a French movie of the fifties or sixties, our whole life was a film put together from distant shots, wide angles under white light, with little people moving through it, all very aesthetic and intellectual and cool." Grammar sticklers may rest assured that Stamm and Hoffman are making deliberate linguistic choices rather than mistakes.

Architecture is a major theme in *Seven Years* and rivals the novel's German flavor in intensity. An interest in architecture brings Sonia and Alex together but also ultimately divides them. As a devout follower of functionalism and the French architect Le Corbusier, Sonia views architecture as being transformative, capable of molding the people who live in the buildings; in contrast, Alex dislikes Le Corbusier and what he sees as the architect's arrogance: "There's something conceited about his buildings. I always get the feeling they're out to turn me into an ideal man." Instead, Alex idolizes the Italian architect Aldo Rossi, a proponent of neo-rationalism. Alex criticizes Sonia's designs, mostly urban housing projects and schools, as being too practical for his personal tastes, but it is Sonia's designs that are responsible for the growth of the company.

Architecture also functions as a frequent metaphor for Alex's internal thoughts and emotions, as he seems to draw architectural models as a way to process his desires and passions. Early in his obsession with Ivona, after she has "awakened something in him" and just days before he has to defend his final senior project, he recklessly changes the project's entire design. Although he knows there is no time to rewrite his entire thesis, he draws new, more "intuitive" blueprints that "evolved as a system of rooms, corridors, and entrances . . . more like a living creature than a building."

Stamm uses architectural metaphors in his depictions of other characters as well. The women in Alex's life are cast as different rooms in a house: Ivona is identified with a dark basement, where people hide the things they need but do not want to display upstairs, while Sonia figures as the living room or parlor, a room that is often professionally decorated and set aside for company and show.

Though firmly couched within a German setting and an architectural focus, the novel's themes of love, desire, and infidelity are universal. Even the casual reader will walk away with some insight into the meaning of true love, as well as questions about its origin, transformative powers, and social constructs.

Sally S. Driscoll

Review Sources

The New Yorker 87, no. 7 (April 4, 2011): 75.
The New York Review of Books 58, no. 12 (July 14, 2011): 43–46.
The New York Times Book Review, March 27, 2011, p. BR11.
San Francisco Chronicle, April 3, 2011, p. GF6.

The Shadow of What We Were

Author: Luis Sepúlveda (b. 1949)
First published: *La sombra de lo que fuimos,*
2009, in Spain
Translated from the Spanish by Howard Curtis
Publisher: Europa Editions (New York). 160 pp.
$15.00
Type of work: Novel
Time: The present
Locale: Santiago, Chile

A rainy day in Santiago, Chile, is the backdrop for the reunion of three aging leftists who survived the violent and oppressive Pinochet regime.

Principal characters:

CACHO SALINAS, an aging leftist who has returned to Chile after decades in exile in Paris

LOLO GARMENDIA, an aging leftist who has returned to Chile after years of exile in Europe

LUCHO ARANCIBIA, an aging leftist who remained in Chile and was tortured during the Pinochet regime

INSPECTOR CRESPO, a world-weary, independently minded police officer and contemporary of Cacho, Lolo, and Lucho

DETECTIVE ADELA BOBADILLA, Crespo's young partner, born after Pinochet's rise to power

COCO ARAVENA, an aging leftist formerly exiled to Germany

CONCEPCIÓN GARCÍA, Coco's wife

THE CHICKEN VENDOR, the proprietor of a rotisserie chicken shop, a former leftist who spent ten years in exile in Sweden

THE SHADOW / PEDRO NOLASCO GONZÁLEZ, an aging leftist and grandson of famous Chilean anarchist Pedro Nolasco Arratia

On a rainy day in Santiago, Chile, an older man is killed while on his way to meet three other men. This sophisticated reworking of a narrative cliché begins Luis Sepúlveda's *The Shadow of What We Were*, a novel that, while short in length and encompassing a simple plot, is significantly multilayered and complex. The narrative unfolds as Cacho Salinas, Lolo Garmendia, and Lucho Arancibia, three men in their early sixties, await the arrival of the dead man, Pedro Nolasco González, also known as the Shadow. The wait allows them to reflect on their personal histories, revealing that all three had been forced into prison or exile after the death of Chilean Marxist leader Salvador Allende.

(Basso Camarsa)

Luis Sepúlveda spent several years in Chilean prisons during the regime of dictator General Augusto Pinochet before going into exile. His novel The Old Man Who Read Love Stories *(Un viejo que leía novelas de amor, 1989) became an international best seller.*

Many years later, the men have reunited on July 16, which is revealed within the narrative to be a significant date in Chilean history. On that day in 1925, Pedro Nolasco Arratia, a fictionalized historical figure and grandfather of the Shadow, led the first bank robbery in Chile. The historical Pedro Nolasco Arratia became a pivotal figure in the history of the anarchist movement in Chile and inspired the formation of the Grupo Pedro Nolasco Arratia, an anarchist society composed of Chilean exiles that later expanded to become a rallying point for other groups. On the anniversary of the heist, the Shadow and his three compatriots intend to claim loot hidden in a café.

Although Sepúlveda provides readers with a basic overview of Chile's political history though the narrative, much of the story relies on an understanding of a few more detailed aspects of Chilean history that are assumed by the author to be common knowledge: In 1970, former physician Salvador Allende became the first elected Marxist leader in South America and instituted what some, including United States president Richard Nixon and the CIA, considered communist policies. On September 11, 1973, one of the most notorious days in Chilean history, Allende and his remaining loyalists were cornered in the presidential palace in Santiago during a CIA-backed military coup d'état led by General Augusto Pinochet. Hours after broadcasting his last public remarks, Allende was found dead of an apparent suicide, although some followers believed that he was assassinated. During Pinochet's totalitarian regime, which ended in 1990, thousands of citizens were killed or exiled, while many others simply disappeared.

Sepúlveda was himself a victim of the brutal and corrupt Pinochet regime. Although his background largely does not mirror that of the novel's protagonists, there are some significant intersections between the characters' related experiences and his own. In his early twenties, Sepúlveda was a political prisoner for nearly three years before going into exile in various countries in South America and Europe. Like the aging leftists in the novel, the author spent time in Sweden and Germany, before eventually settling in Spain. As a novel concerned with the aftermath of the Pinochet regime, *The Shadow of What We Were* clearly displays the influence of Sepúlveda's personal history and the collective experience of the citizens of Chile. While the novel does not provide readers with detailed knowledge of Chilean politics, it emphasizes the effects of a dictatorship on individuals and provides significant context on a personal level.

One of the most striking features of the novel is its wry humor, present throughout the narrative despite the main characters' memories of years of torture, disappearances, and political upheaval. Many of their anecdotes are remembrances of the happy times of youthful enthusiasm and excess, patriotism, and love. There is something charming about the mundane problems of these aging compatriots who have endured so much. An e-mail exchange between Cacho and Lolo, initiated as a guarded renewal of an old acquaintance, soon slips into questions about senior romance and advice about online dating services. They have retained their love, if not practice, of Marxist ideals, yet they are no longer the young revolutionaries they once were; they must find a place for themselves in the twenty-first century. Sepúlveda is fascinated by the question of what revolutionaries do and where they go after the revolution is over. For these characters, and possibly for Sepúlveda as well, post-Pinochet Chile is a strange and foreign place; after so many years in exile, they feel almost alien in their home country. This juxtaposition of old and new is both poignant and humorous, reminding the reader that even after a terrible era in a nation's history, life goes on.

Much of the humor within the novel serves to temper the horrors of the Pinochet regime. A recurring humorous concept throughout the novel is Cacho's dislike of poultry, which is first expressed in the second chapter, the beginning of the main action of the novel: "Cacho Salinas hated chickens, hens, ducks, turkeys, and any creature that had feathers." Cacho notes that he holds chickens responsible for a "lack of imagination" that afflicts those who eat them. At first, the interaction between Cacho and the chicken vendor seems to indicate that this dislike is due to the bourgeois nature of fast-food chicken restaurants, which, as the chicken vendor explains, serve processed chickens dipped in a sauce that comes from a plastic bag. Cacho and his companions eat the roasted chickens, despite repeatedly condemning them. Later, as Cacho relates one of many atrocities he experienced during the violence of the early 1970s, he reveals that he was forced to observe horrible conditions at a large chicken ranch in which the birds were being starved to death. His humorous hatred of poultry, then, is revealed to be more than it seems. For Cacho, the suffering of the chickens is analogous to the mass sufferings of ordinary Chilean citizens under Pinochet.

Another plot point that is both humorous and tragic is the manner in which the Shadow is killed. Angered by her husband's attitude, Concepción García, wife of former exile Coco Aravena, begins to throw her husband's possessions out the window of their apartment. The Shadow, en route to his meeting with Cacho, Lolo, and Lucho, is killed by a falling phonograph thrown by Concepción. In addition to being a somewhat unlikely and ridiculous cause of death, the well-designed, much-cherished phonograph seems sadly anachronistic in a world of high-tech MP3 players—as anachronistic as the Shadow himself, a revolutionary whose revolution has been over for decades. Coco's reaction to the accidental homicide further exemplifies the novel's somewhat dark humor. He concocts several amusing scenarios that he considers telling the police, all of which begin as reasonable stories but become increasingly outlandish, resembling the plots of screenplays he would like to write or movies he has seen. Coco's affinity for classic Hollywood films, from *The Man Who Shot Liberty Valance* (1962) to *Reservoir Dogs* (1992), colors his view of his situation, much to the consternation of Concepción.

An interesting counterpoint to the aging revolutionaries is Inspector Crespo, the man who must investigate the Shadow's death. A bit of a radical himself in his younger days, Crespo never fully committed to the Marxist cause and chronically wrestled with the question "Are you in?" when faced with defiance of Chile's oppressive authority. In Inspector Crespo, Sepúlveda presents a man who was not deeply involved in the revolutionary movements but was still deeply affected by the overthrow of Allende and the rise of Pinochet. His pragmatism and sense of duty, sympathies for those on the left, hatred of the Pinochet regime, and representation of an aging generation make him a particularly compelling character, one who further emphasizes the juxtaposition of old and new that propels the novel. His second-in-command, detective Adela Bobadilla, represents the new Chile and underscores the differences between the generations. As Inspector Crespo tells her, she is from a generation that is clean: too young to share the guilt of the past and too old to be swayed by the increasingly corporate mentality of the country.

A complex work ably translated into English by Howard Curtis, *The Shadow of What We Were* is a powerful examination of what it means to be a shadow, a symbol of the past in a world that has changed. To the aging protagonists, the man known as the Shadow is the embodiment of the young, idealistic men they once were, having retained his revolutionary zeal despite the passing of several decades. He remains willing to lead the other men in one last act of defiance, but their defiance lacks its previous direction. The struggles of the past are now fading memories, and Cacho, Lolo, and Lucho are diluted versions of their youthful selves, hampered by age and the hardships they have endured. Yet something of their past selves remains, and no matter how faint this shadow may be, it is a lasting, triumphant reminder of all they have accomplished and survived. "I am the shadow of what we were," the Shadow says early in the book, "and while there is light we will exist." By the end of *The Shadow of What We Were*, Sepúlveda makes one truth abundantly clear: Chile has changed, but the revolutionary spirit remains.

Patricia King Hanson

Review Sources

Huffington Post, February 11, 2011 (Web).
Library Journal 136, no. 2 (February 1, 2011): 57.
The Literary Review 54, no. 3 (Spring 2011): 197–98.

She-Wolves
The Women Who Ruled England before Elizabeth

Author: Helen Castor (b. 1968)
Publisher: HarperCollins (New York). 496 pp. $27.99
Type of work: Biography, history, women's issues
Time: The twelfth through the sixteenth century
Locale: Great Britain, France, Italy

Castor examines how perceptions of gender affected the inheritance of royal titles and access to power by medieval women who were descended from kings or related to monarchs through marriage or motherhood, analyzing how their experiences influenced the acceptance of queens in later centuries.

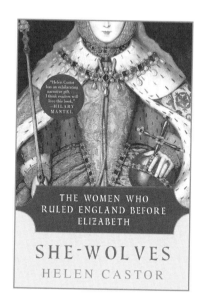

Principal personages:
MATILDA (1102–1167), empress of the Holy Roman Empire and queen consort in England
ELEANOR OF AQUITAINE (ca. 1122–1204), French queen and queen consort in England
ISABELLA OF FRANCE (ca. 1295–1358), queen consort in England
MARGARET OF ANJOU (1430–1482), queen consort in England
JANE GREY (ca. 1537–1554), queen of England
MARY I (1516–1558), queen of England
ELIZABETH I (1533–1603), queen of England
STEPHEN (ca. 1097–1154), king of England
HENRY II (1133–1189), king of England
EDWARD II (1284–1327), king of England
HENRY VI (1421–1471), king of England

She-Wolves: The Women Who Ruled England before Elizabeth depicts themes of power, control, entitlement, and loyalty associated with medieval-era women who sought the monarchical rights and authority they believed they deserved due to their descent from rulers, marriages to kings, or maternal ties to male heirs. The women featured in this book encountered opposition to their efforts, revealing social attitudes that expected women to conform to passive peripheral roles during the Middle Ages. Most men in medieval England expressed the opinion that women should not be leaders, dismissively considering them to be innately weak and incapable of ruling. Royal women were usually sidelined to positions as consorts or regents for husbands and sons who were kings. Author Helen Castor, a British historian, brings these issues to the present as she tells the story of four English queens in this well-researched and gripping work.

Throughout her text, Castor incorporates comments from male medieval writers of literary and historical treatises that indicate how people, both nobles and commoners, perceived queen consorts. These attitudes range from admiration or toleration to hatred and derision. Many chroniclers and historians, often monks, presented biased commentary designed to disseminate their agendas. Some commentators viewed these women as threats and strove to discredit them in an effort to discourage any supporters. Women who dared to seek and display power were often described as disobedient, arrogant, sinful, or unwomanly. People with this perspective sometimes referred to medieval women with unflattering imagery, such as William Shakespeare's description of Margaret of Anjou as a she-wolf. Castor also includes epigraphs from Scottish religious writer John Knox and Queen Elizabeth I, providing misogynistic viewpoints often voiced by medieval men in addition to a glimpse into a woman's thoughts as she admits flaws to appease males while framing her strengths within masculine terminology.

Castor focuses *She-Wolves* on four women—Matilda, Eleanor of Aquitaine, Isabella of France, and Margaret of Anjou—dividing her book into sections that concentrate on the biographical details of each. She introduces and concludes her examination of these four queen consorts with text describing the 1553 death of King Henry VIII's sole male heir, Edward VI; the brief, tragic reign of Jane Grey that followed it; and the acceptance of Edward VI's sisters, Mary and Elizabeth, as queens in their own right. This discussion supports Castor's thesis that the medieval predecessors she profiles established a foundation for later female succession by reshaping the concept of English rulers. In addition to consulting scholarly secondary sources, Castor incorporates quotations and information from medieval accounts, legal records, and archival documents that offer facts and examples of attitudes relevant to these women, noting that the women themselves did not leave written accounts to analyze.

Castor's narrative recognizes the strengths and ambitions of her female protagonists as they endeavored to protect and practice their royal claims despite incompatible spouses, antagonistic foes and subjects, and other adverse conditions. She depicts their marriages as legal relationships transacted for political purposes to produce legitimate heirs and secure alliances. Although Castor acknowledges the queen consorts' weaknesses and vices, such as infidelity and cruelty, she still admires them. She stresses their intelligence, bravery, and resourcefulness as they adapted to transitions and disruptions, including dissension within their families, that interfered with their responsibilities. Castor's queens sought to become empowered and prevail despite the chaos fomented by greedy kin and feudal nobility. They were confronted by opponents' accusations regarding the legitimacy of their parents' marriages in attempts to challenge political and religious requirements for attaining royal status. Foes also questioned the legitimacy of the queen consorts' sons and their eligibility to rule.

Establishing a hereditary link between the four queen consorts, Castor begins her biographical study with Matilda, whose father, Henry I, demanded his nobles recognize his daughter's legal right to rule after his death. He designated Matilda as his heir when her brother, Henry I's sole legitimate son, drowned in a ship accident in 1120. Matilda

Helen Castor, a fellow of Sidney Sussex College at Cambridge University, is the author of The King, the Crown, and the Duchy of Lancaster: Public Authority and Private Power, 1399–1461 *(2000) and* Blood and Roses: The Paston Family in the Fifteenth Century *(2004), the latter of which received the English Association's 2006 Beatrice White Prize.*

was sent to Europe to marry Heinrich V, the Holy Roman Emperor, and became empress at the age of twelve. During that marriage, she accompanied her husband on his European travels and acquired experience ruling Italian territories. After Heinrich's death in 1125, Matilda married Geoffrey of Anjou and gave birth to their son, Henry II.

When Henry I died in 1135, the English lords, who disliked Geoffrey of Anjou, resisted crowning Matilda and supported a coup by her cousin Stephen, who became king instead. Matilda departed her Normandy home in 1139 to confront Stephen in England. Depicting her as courageous and long-suffering, Castor stresses the mayhem Matilda experienced during the nineteen years of civil war she fought against the usurper Stephen and his allies, in which she was threatened by sieges, pursued, and eventually captured. During this period, Matilda acquired a network of supporters and advisers, many of whom hoped to acquire spoils and privileges if Matilda was victorious. Castor creates vivid imagery of the frozen landscape Matilda traversed in darkness after escaping from her Oxford Castle prison in 1142, emphasizing her resilience and her determination to recover and preserve the kingship established by her father for her son.

From Matilda, Castor shifts focus to her daughter-in-law, Eleanor of Aquitaine. After the annulment of her first marriage to France's Louis VII, Eleanor pursued a second marriage to Henry II in 1154. Castor suggests that Eleanor sought remarriage out of a desire for power, noting that Henry II's influential bride expanded England's territorial holdings with her rich French properties in Aquitaine, where she had gained experience as a ruler. Uninterested in the temperamental Henry II romantically, the pragmatic Eleanor nevertheless conceived and gave birth to nine children with him, reinforcing her status as queen consort and aspiring to achieve authority through her sons.

A risk taker, Eleanor implemented strategies in an attempt to gain power as the mother of a king, eventually instigating an unsuccessful military attack by her sons against their father. While Henry II overlooked his sons' actions as immature and impulsive, he forced Eleanor into confinement for fifteen years. She was released after her husband's death and witnessed her sons Richard I and John succeed him as king. In her sixties and seventies, Eleanor influenced domestic, judicial, and diplomatic policies when Richard I, participating in the Crusades, requested she represent him in England; she also performed services related to Aquitaine for John during his subsequent kingship.

In the next section of the book, Castor examines how Eleanor of Aquitaine's descendant Isabella of France secured power due to the shortcomings of her husband, Edward II, and his indifference to her. Married when she was twelve, Isabella suffered because her husband, a distant cousin who was the great-great-grandson of Eleanor of Aquitaine, chose to spend time with male companions instead of her. The queen initially defended him despite his failings as a political and military leader and helped him retain support from the English populace, but eventually she removed her son Edward III from court and began devising tactics to overthrow her husband. With the help of her lover, Roger Mortimer, and her brother, the king of France, Isabella successfully led invasion troops against her husband and his allies in 1327.

Isabella savored the influence she attained as guardian after her son became king at the age of fourteen. Encouraged by Mortimer, she provoked military conflicts with Scotland; this led to Scotland's independence from England, which enraged Edward III. The couple's deceit, deployment of spies, and intensifying strife further antagonized the young king. In 1330, Edward III had Mortimer executed, and powerless Isabella lived in various royal residences until her death.

Castor's next subject is Margaret of Anjou, a descendant of Matilda and Eleanor of Aquitaine. Margaret was married to King Henry VI, whose mental instability hindered his ability to rule and enabled his wife to assume greater authority as queen consort. Margaret was initially sympathetic to her husband's emotional decline, defending him to critics and seeking supporters while ruling independently as queen consort. Eventually, however, she became frustrated by his passivity, which escalated into immobility and unresponsiveness. Margaret focused on their son, Edward, stressing to English nobles and subjects that he was Henry VI's legitimate heir despite gossip to the contrary. She rallied Lancastrian troops during the Wars of the Roses, in which Edward, Duke of York, a rival heir for the throne, challenged Henry VI's rule.

Castor effectively depicts Edward of York as the opposite of Henry VI, emphasizing his mobility and strength. When Edward became king in 1461, Margaret was forced to flee to Scotland with her husband and son. Later, aware of divisions among her enemies, she helped her husband recover the crown in 1470. Despite Margaret's protection of her son during ongoing warfare, her aspirations for the prince ended when he was slain in combat at Tewkesbury Abbey. Henry VI died days later and Margaret was imprisoned. She was freed when France paid a ransom and returned to Anjou to live until her death in 1482.

The profiles that Castor presents of these enigmatic female leaders are detailed and informative, while still accessible to nonacademic readers who might lack prior knowledge of the times and mindsets depicted. Both scholarly and mainstream critics have recognized the quality of Castor's writing style, praising the lucidness of her vivid prose. Most reviewers admire her extensive research and how it provides details that allow readers to envision archaic settings and comprehend the motivations and dilemmas of obscure historical figures. Her study includes an annotated bibliography that is valuable for scholars but lacks citations for further research. Several critics have also stated that Castor is not entirely convincing in her argument that these women have earned their designation as she-wolves, noting that the queens in question achieved their power as a result of flawed male leaders.

Many critics have agreed that *She-Wolves* would be useful for medieval history and women's studies curricula. Aside from its academic relevance, Castor's work will also appeal to readers with an interest in the English monarchy, popular history, and powerful female figures. With its engaging narrative and solid foundation in fact, *She-Wolves* is a book worthy of the spirited and redoubtable women described in its pages.

Elizabeth D. Schafer

Review Sources

Booklist 107, no. 11 (February 1, 2011): 20.
Contemporary Review 293, no. 1701 (June 2011): 260.
History Today 60, no. 12 (December 2010): 61–62.
Kirkus Reviews 78, no. 22 (November 15, 2010): 131.
Library Journal 136, no. 1 (January 1, 2011): 106.
The New York Times Book Review, February 27, 2011, p. 19.
Publishers Weekly 257, no. 48 (December 6, 2010): 38–39.
Times Literary Supplement, no. 5618 (December 3, 2010): 26.

Silver Sparrow

Author: Tayari Jones (b. 1970)
Publisher: Algonquin Books (Chapel Hill, NC). 352 pp. $19.95; paperback $13.95
Type of work: Novel
Time: 1980s
Locale: Atlanta, Georgia

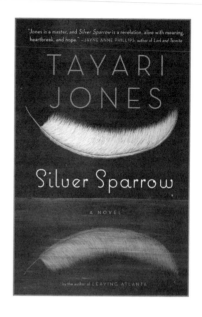

The eventual meeting of two half sisters, daughters of a bigamist father, shapes their personal identities and feelings of self-worth.

Principal characters:

DANA LYNN YARBORO, the daughter of James Witherspoon and Gwendolyn Yarboro

BUNNY "CHAURISSE" WITHERSPOON, Dana's half sister, who is unaware of her father's second family

JAMES WITHERSPOON, a bigamist, the father of Dana and Chaurisse

LAVERNE WITHERSPOON, James's first wife and Chaurisse's mother

GWENDOLYN YARBORO (GWEN), James's illegal second wife and Dana's mother

RALEIGH, James's adopted brother and best friend, whom both girls think of as an uncle

MISS BUNNY, James's mother

In the first part of Tayari Jones's third novel, *Silver Sparrow*, African American teenager Dana Lynn Yarboro reflects upon her childhood and adolescence in 1980s Atlanta—particularly the defining moment when, as a kindergartener, she learns that her father, James Witherspoon, considers her and her mother to be a second, "secret" family. Although it is years before Dana understands the full implications of her father's bigamy, even at five years old, she feels instantly threatened by Bunny "Chaurisse" Witherspoon, James's legitimate daughter from his first marriage. Dana's mother, Gwendolyn Yarboro, attempts to comfort Dana by taking her to surreptitiously observe Chaurisse, who is neither as intelligent nor as attractive as Dana: "*Surveil* was my mother's word. If he knew, James would probably say *spy*, but that is too sinister. We didn't do damage to anyone but ourselves as we trailed Chaurisse and Laverne while they wound their way through their easy lives." This spurs a somewhat unhealthy yet understandable obsession with her half sister as Dana attempts to reassure herself that her father loves her, even though she seems to receive only the leftover crumbs of his attention and affection.

In addition to the emotional burden, Dana describes the logistical implications of her life as an "outside child," as she calls herself. Although she is a promising student who enjoys science and hopes to attend medical school, she cannot enroll in the science magnet school until Chaurisse has picked a school because James is determined to prevent his two daughters from ever meeting one another. Fortunately, Chaurisse chooses a performing arts school, but there are many other occasions when Dana must skirt around Chaurisse's life, such as when she is not allowed to enroll in special Saturday classes because Chaurisse has already done so. In addition, Dana and Gwen are only guaranteed James's company for Wednesday night dinners, during which he eats sparingly because he will have to eat again after he goes back to his public family. These realities, along with Gwen's own fixation on her rival, Laverne, gradually wear down Dana's confidence and contribute to the bad choices she makes when she herself begins to date.

Jones helps prevent the reader from resenting Chaurisse as much as Dana does by shrewdly switching to Chaurisse's first-person point of view for the second half of the book. While protected and loved by her parents, Chaurisse instinctively senses that something is amiss, and her unease is fueled in part by odd but seemingly innocuous incidents whose significance she does not recognize until years later. One such occurrence takes place when Chaurisse sees her "Uncle" Raleigh in the park with Gwen one day and concludes that Gwen must be Raleigh's secret girlfriend, when in actuality Raleigh has been a longtime facilitator of James's complicated relationships. Chaurisse is more perceptive than she realizes, however, as it is gradually revealed that Raleigh loves Gwen and believes that he has been helping James for Gwen's sake. On another occasion, Chaurisse runs into Dana wearing a rabbit-fur jacket, but does not make the connection even when Dana says that her father won the coat for her in a poker game—which is precisely what James told Chaurisse when he brought an identical coat home to her.

Aside from these unsettling encounters, Chaurisse feels inferior to those she privately calls "silver" girls: natural beauties who become even more striking when they make themselves up. Chaurisse herself closely resembles her mother, a rather dumpy, plain woman whom, Chaurisse knows, James married because he got her pregnant, not because he loved her. In addition, Chaurisse cannot escape the constant reminders of how much emphasis is placed on beauty, as her mother runs a beauty salon where customers spend a great deal of time and money trying to improve their appearances. When Dana finally befriends Chaurisse, albeit without revealing the true nature of their relationship, Chaurisse admires Dana's exceptionally beautiful hair, which makes her feel more inadequate than ever.

After Dana's identity is almost revealed to Chaurisse by accident and James becomes aware of the girls' contact with one another, Gwen finally confronts Laverne, showing up with a copy of her marriage license as well as more tangible proof: a brooch given to Dana by James's mother, Miss Bunny, upon her deathbed. The climactic confrontation takes place in Laverne's hair salon, putting Gwen at an immediate disadvantage. Dana tries to dissuade Gwen from making a scene, but events have progressed too far to be stopped. Gwen and Laverne's behavior at this point, although somewhat irrational on the surface, is believable precisely because emotions often result in just such irrationality. Laverne, who has been incontrovertibly wronged, is heartbroken rather than angry,

(Marion Ettlinger)

Tayari Jones teaches creative writing at Rutgers University. Her first novel, Leaving Atlanta (2002), won numerous honors, including the Hurston/Wright Award for Debut Fiction. Her second novel, The Untelling (2005), won the Lillian C. Smith Award. Silver Sparrow *is her third novel.*

to the extent that Chaurisse becomes impatient with her. Gwen, who has actively consented to this awkward situation for almost twenty years, seems angry at Laverne rather than at James or herself. In the meantime, the daughters have complicated feelings of their own to sort through. More than anything, the end result seems to be that each girl envies the other; Dana longs for Chaurisse's legitimacy, while Chaurisse covets Dana's intelligence, beauty, and easy grace. But even while Dana envies Chaurisse, she admits that she herself has always had a distinct advantage, which is the power that knowledge brings. No matter how dissatisfied Dana may be with her father, she cannot help but feel it would be worse to be ignorant, and she even adopts a somewhat protective attitude toward Chaurisse as a result.

In addition to portraying these rich and complex relationships, Jones authenticates and grounds her novel by sprinkling it with historical tidbits. The most notable example is when Laverne crosses paths with Mary Woodson White just days before White infamously flings a pan of boiling grits on singer Al Green in a fit of jealous rage because he refused to marry her—even though she was married herself at the time. Although Laverne's salon clientele are inclined to joke about the incident, which has made the national news, Laverne does not allow them to do so in her hearing, remarking that when a woman loves a man that much, she should let him go. She also tells Chaurisse that wives should behave in a dignified manner no matter what, not lowering themselves to the lewd behavior exhibited by mistresses. Even when Chaurisse urges Laverne to give in to her desire for retribution, Laverne acts pragmatically, simply plotting the best way to get her husband to come back.

Jones's use of metaphor is further exhibited in her poignant choice of title. In an interview with NPR, Jones says, "I took sparrow from the hymn 'His Eye Is on the Sparrow'—being the sparrow is the least among us. Because I think that's what Dana is, she's a silver sparrow." In one of her perceptive observations, Chaurisse reflects upon the biblical passage regarding God's care for all creatures great and small, including the sparrow that sellers would include for free when someone bought just one bird. In addition, a single sparrow is said to be a symbol of profound loneliness, and it is clear that Chaurisse understands how lonely her beautiful "silver" half sister is and realizes that Dana has always felt like that extra, unwanted sparrow.

Ultimately, *Silver Sparrow* is an effectively subtle and realistic tragedy, one that deeply affects the lives of all of both families, with the possible exception of James himself. If the reader feels any sympathy toward James for getting into this untenable situation in the first place, that sympathy may evaporate when the reader realizes that he remains so self-centered that he cannot fathom why Dana could possibly have felt a need to know her sister. Indeed, James seems to believe that the only person he has wronged is Laverne; he cannot understand, or else refuses to consider, that he has caused Chaurisse and Dana to suffer as well. In particular, he fails to acknowledge that Gwen is the only woman in his life who was allowed to make an active choice in determining her own situation.

To some readers, *Silver Sparrow* may seem slightly incomplete. Because the confrontation between Gwen and Laverne occurs in part two, which is Chaurisse's narrative, the reader sees the climactic events only from her point of view, with little hint of the conversations that must have taken place between Dana and her mother. In addition, when Chaurisse confronts Gwen shortly after the salon showdown, Gwen tells her that Dana had actually tried to spare Chaurisse's feelings by changing the date on James and Gwen's marriage certificate, so that Chaurisse would not know that her father married his second wife while she herself lay in an incubator, a mere three days old, with an uncertain chance of survival. It is clear that Chaurisse considers the specific date of James's second marriage, as well as the possibility of Dana's kindness toward her, to be quite meaningful, but the narrative does not conclusively indicate whether or not Dana did in fact alter the date, and Chaurisse does not ask her about it when she has the chance. Finally, some readers may find the showdown and its aftermath slightly anticlimactic, having interpreted the many earlier mentions of Mary Woodson White as foreshadowing of a more violent outcome that does not materialize. Jones's resolution, however, is likely a more accurate portrayal of the majority of real-life experiences of infidelity. Overall, *Silver Sparrow* is the type of fiction that encourages the reader to examine character and motivation, and remains thought-provoking long after the book has been finished.

Amy Sisson

Review Sources

Booklist 107, no. 18 (May 15, 2011): 18.
Kirkus Reviews 79, no. 3 (February 1, 2011): 158.
Library Journal 136, no. 3 (February 15, 2011): 99.
NPR, May 19, 2011 (Web).
Publishers Weekly 258, no. 6 (February 7, 2011): 33.

A Singular Woman
The Untold Story of Barack Obama's Mother

Author: Janny Scott
Publisher: Riverhead Books (New York).
376 pp. $26.95
Type of work: Biography
Time: 1942–2010, with some reference to the
early twentieth century
Locale: Kansas, Hawaii, and Indonesia

Scott presents a meticulously researched ac-
count of the life of cultural anthropologist Ann
Dunham, whose groundbreaking contributions
had a profound impact on the lives of the poor
in Indonesia and whose values shaped the life
of her son, US president Barack Obama.

Principal personages:
STANLEY ANN DUNHAM (1942–1995), an
American anthropologist, the mother of US
president Barack Obama
STANLEY ARMOUR DUNHAM (1918–1992), Ann's
father, a furniture salesman
MADELYN PAYNE DUNHAM (1922–2008), Ann's mother, a bank executive
BARACK HUSSEIN OBAMA SR. (1936–1982), a Kenyan economist
BARACK HUSSEIN OBAMA JR. (b. 1961), son of Ann and Barack Obama Sr., the forty-
fourth president of the United States
LOLO SOETORO (1935–1987), Ann's second husband, a Javanese surveyor for an oil
company
MAYA SOETORO-NG (b. 1970), daughter of Ann and Lolo Soetoro, a writer and teacher

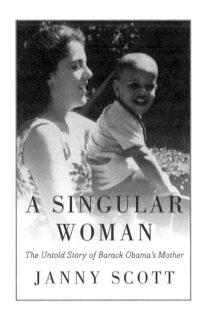

A SINGULAR
WOMAN
The Untold Story of Barack Obama's Mother

JANNY SCOTT

On March 18, 2008, presidential candidate Barack Obama Jr. declared, "I am the son
of a black man from Kenya and a white woman from Kansas." His statement no doubt
resonated with the nearly three percent of Americans who claim biracial ancestry.
When his mother, Stanley Ann Dunham, married Barack Obama Sr. on the Hawai-
ian island of Maui on February 2, 1961, interracial marriage was still illegal in some
states. It was not until 1967 that the United States Supreme Court ruled that anti-
miscegenation laws were unconstitutional. Crossing boundaries, whether they were
based on geography, race, culture, or gender, would be a recurring theme in Dunham's
life, as Janny Scott makes clear in her probing biography, *A Singular Woman*.
    Dunham's tendency toward nonconformity was established early in her life. Born
on November 29, 1942, in Wichita, Kansas, Dunham was named Stanley Ann by her
parents, Stanley and Madelyn Payne Dunham. There are conflicting stories about why

her parents chose a masculine name for their daughter. Dunham claimed that her father had always wanted a son, but "he got me" instead. In an alternate account, her mother intimated that she named her baby girl after a character in a movie played by her favorite actress, Bette Davis. Dunham lived with her parents' eccentric choice of name until she entered college, when she dropped her first name and became known as Ann.

Janny Scott was a reporter for the New York Times *from 1994 to 2008. She became interested in Ann Dunham when she wrote six biographical articles on then-Senator Obama as part of a 2007–8* Times *series on the lives of presidential candidates. She was also a member of the* Times *team that won the 2001 Pulitzer Prize for national reporting.*

The environment in which Dunham was raised was as unconventional as her name. Although it epitomized the heartland in the minds of most Americans, the Kansas of the 1940s and 1950s did not necessarily conform to its wholesome, down-home image. As Scott explores Kansan history, economics, and culture, she paints a picture of a state where opposites coexisted, a place where both conservatives and progressives lived side by side, often uneasily. Dunham's forebears were farmers, ministers, teachers, and war veterans. They were affected by oils strikes, industrial growth, and social unrest, and they put a high value on education as a means for attaining a rewarding life. As Scott describes the social and cultural milieu of Dunham's birthplace, it is plain that the Kansas she and her parents knew was a far cry from the mythical home of Dorothy in L. Frank Baum's *The Wonderful Wizard of Oz* (1900). Her vivid portrait sheds light on how Dunham, a shy girl from a small town, grew up to become an internationalist, activist, and intellectual who worked to improve the lives of people in an impoverished country half a world away.

When Dunham was two, she and her parents left Wichita and lived variously in Berkley, California; Ponca City, Oklahoma; Vernon, Texas; El Dorado, Kansas; and Seattle, Washington. Her restless father tried his hand at various jobs before becoming a furniture salesman, while her mother worked her way up the corporate ladder to become vice president of a bank. Scott comments that Dunham's numerous changes of address encouraged her to cultivate self-sufficiency, flexibility, tolerance, and a sense of humor, all qualities that would serve her well when she lived as a white, professional woman in a male-dominated Southeast Asian country. Finally, the family settled on Mercer Island, a suburb of Seattle, and Dunham attended the respected Mercer Island High School, where her intellectual gifts flourished under the guidance of first-rate educators. Philosophy teacher Jim Wichterman and humanities teacher Val Foubert, in particular, encouraged their students to think for themselves, independent of the status quo—a lesson Dunham took to heart.

If Dunham experienced an intellectual coming of age at Mercer High School, she was initiated into adulthood when she attended the University of Hawaii. Moving for the final time in 1960, the Dunham family relocated to Honolulu, where Dunham met University of Hawaii's first African student, Barack Hussein Obama. She fell in love with the charming, but sometimes arrogant, older man and married him when she discovered that she was pregnant. Though their union produced the future United States president, it did not last. When their son, Barry, was only eleven months old,

Magill's Literary Annual 2012

the elder Obama left to do graduate work at Harvard University in the fall of 1962 and then returned to Kenya and his first wife. Dunham and Obama were divorced in 1964.

Now a single mother, Dunham continued her education at the new East-West Center at the University of Hawaii, where she met her second husband, Indonesian graduate student Lolo Soetoro. They were married in 1965. After Dunham finished her undergraduate degree in anthropology in 1967, she and Barry joined her husband in Indonesia. Her second child, Maya, was born in 1970. Although a wife and mother of two, Dunham went back to the University of Hawaii to continue her education, completing her coursework for a graduate degree in anthropology in 1974. When she returned to Indonesia with her daughter, Barry having chosen to stay in Hawaii with his grandparents to attend school, she began her career in rural and economic development, working on behalf of women's rights and the poor.

Perhaps to prove her point concerning Dunham's singularity, Scott offers a nuanced description of her career and activism. Dunham focused on handicrafts and village industries in order to discover how such activities could benefit Indonesia's poor. Her pioneering research became the basis of her doctoral dissertation and eventually led to the development of a groundbreaking model of microfinancing that continues to aid disadvantaged entrepreneurs, especially women. In her capacity as a community organizer and consultant, Dunham worked for several high-profile organizations, including the Ford Foundation, the Agricultural Bank of Pakistan, and the Indonesian government.

Dunham's career is, of course, only part of who she was. In an effort to get to the core of her subject, Scott uses her skills as a reporter, drawing from more than two hundred interviews she conducted with Dunham's family, close friends, and colleagues. The result is a collage of memories that reveal a woman who was resilient, determined, plainspoken, compassionate, empathetic, resilient, nontraditional, dedicated to her children, and committed to her work.

President Obama's recollections offer some insight into the influence Dunham had on his personal development. Perhaps most telling is his choice to take a more conventional path regarding family life. He tells Scott that his mother lived a "classic expatriate life" but that her decisions were not always sound, especially with regard to financial matters. He credits his grandparents for providing him with continuity and a stable home environment. They often felt obligated to lend assistance to Ann in order to "smooth over some of her choices." However, Obama accepts his mother for who he believes she was: a woman with a big heart who loved him unconditionally and who "thought I was special"—so special, in fact, that she told a friend he could one day be president of the United States.

The people Dunham knew view her in many different ways, depending on their own unique relationships with her. Her daughter remembers her being a "softie," while a colleague recalls her as "hardheaded" and "funny." Many comment on Dunham's idealism and naïveté, while others saw her as "tough, sharp, and worldly." Her curiosity was apparently endless, which helped her develop new ways of dealing with challenges in her job. It was also said that she had an acute awareness of injustice and that she "didn't suffer fools gladly." In offering a variety of opinions of Dunham's personality, Scott strives to create an accurate portrait of who Dunham was. Yet memories can be subjective or unreliable; Charles Payne, Madelyn's brother, warns Scott, "All of this is just to tell you: Don't trust memory." It would seem that when memories are filtered through time and personal impressions, biographers can only at best approximate the essence of their subjects.

To balance the recollections of friends and family, Scott includes excerpts of letters written by Dunham that reveal unvarnished glimpses of her personality. When Dunham speaks in her own voice, the reader is able to feel a palpable connection to the woman herself. For example, Dunham's affection for her research subjects often shines through in her field notes. Scott quotes from Dunham's description of one of her interviewees: "Pak Atmo is a small, shrewd, comical man, fond of a good joke." She humorously notes that another man is "open, good-hearted, modest, and sexy." And in describing the spouse of another man, she spares no words: "Wife a bit of a twit." She could also be self-deprecating and direct. In writing to a friend to chide him about not informing her of his divorce, she says, "If you could find it in your CRABBY heart to scrawl me a note I would be overjoyed. . . . I am not such a harsh critic after all, having screwed up royally a few times myself."

Despite Scott's insistence that this is not a book about President Obama, in a way it is. The opening pages of *A Singular Woman* describe a photograph taken of Dunham and her son in 1987, in which the young man stands behind his mother with his hand casually resting on her shoulder; similarly, Obama's presence shadows Scott's account of Dunham's remarkable life. Had Dunham not been the mother of the first biracial president of the United States, her story may not have been written. Yet Scott manages to disentangle Dunham's life from that of her son and allow her to stand as an individual, a loving mother and a compassionate woman who contributed to the well-being and betterment of others.

Pegge Bochynski

Review Sources

The Christian Science Monitor, May 27, 2011 (Web).
Kirkus Reviews 79, no. 10 (May 15, 2011): 851.
Maclean's 124, no. 19 (May 23, 2011): 85.
The New Yorker 87, no. 14 (May 23, 2011): 83.

The Sly Company of People Who Care

Author: Rahul Bhattacharya (b. 1979)
Publisher: Farrar, Straus and Giroux (New
York). 288 pp. $26.00
Type of work: Novel
Time: January 2006–January 2007
Locale: Guyana and Venezuela

*Bhattacharya's engaging debut novel chroni-
cles the impressions, adventures, and realizations of a young man from India who spends a
year in Guyana.*

Principal characters:
GOOROO, a twenty-six-year-old cricket journal-
    ist visiting Guyana from India
JAN, his paramour
BABY, a confidence man and "porknocker"
FOULIS, Baby's partner in diamond prospecting
UNCLE LANCE BANARSEE, Gooroo's gossipy and
    tale-spinning neighbor
DR. RED, a mixed-race and oversexed former pimp
ROGER KHAN, a drug baron who uses force to promote East Indian interests

The Sly Company of People Who Care, Rahul Bhattacharya's first novel, augurs well
for the career of this Indian author, whose previous writing consists of journalistic reportage on cricket and *Pundits from Pakistan: On Tour with India, 2003–2004* (2005),
a book on the same subject.

Although an Indian national himself, Bhattacharya's novel is set in the South
American country of Guyana, a former colony of the Dutch and the British. Guyana's language is a kind of English characterized by Creole phrasing, grammar, and
inflection, and Bhattacharya's keen ear captures the sounds and inflections convincingly. For some readers, the dialogue may seem as off-putting as Huck Finn's did to
genteel Boston readers around the time of Mark Twain's *Adventures of Huckleberry
Finn* (1884). Guyana's colonial history, along with immigration, indentured labor, and
intermarriage, has mixed the descendants of the indigenous peoples, colonizing Europeans, African slaves, and East Indian coolies into one diverse, multiethnic society.
Into this world, Bhattacharya inserts his protagonist-narrator, a young cricket journalist from India who, after covering Test matches in Guyana four years before, decides
on a whim to spend a year in the country.

Being Indian, the narrator naturally makes many friends among East Indian Guyanese, the majority ethnic group of the country, and being impecunious, he gravitates
toward the lower stratum of Guyanese society, taking rooms in Kitty, a humble quarter

of the Guyanese capital Georgetown. Bhattacharya quickly fills his pages with characters as colorful and various as those of the novelist V. S. Naipaul, characters captured with an equally quick eye for telling details, though Bhattacharya observes them through a less jaundiced gaze than his distinguished predecessor.

The narrator's first friend in the neighborhood is Mr. Bhombal, an East Indian engineer who is incredulous that the narrator would want to spend a year in Guyana. Then there are the two busty Indian Chinese cashiers, nicknamed Curry-Chowmein, and the amiable peddler of coconut water Bibi Rashida, who is of African and East Indian descent and a Muslim. Most memorable is Uncle Lance Banarsee, the neighborhood gossipmonger, a "talkman" who can hold forth on anything from local "politricks" to Hurricane Katrina and Bollywood film stars.

Once the narrator settles in, the action of the novel picks up the pace. The trajectory of the ensuing narrative could be said to replicate the flight of a bowled cricket ball. In cricket, when the bowler releases the ball and sends it speeding toward the opposing wicket, the ball can briefly bounce off the ground, whereupon it may spin or alter momentum toward the intended destination. Similarly, the novel's storyline twists and turns. Part 1 consists of seven chapters, in which Bhattacharya describes a journey to the interior of Guyana, followed by ruminations on Guyanese society and history during the three chapters of part 2, and concluding with the ten chapters of part 3, which describe a journey to Venezuela.

The journeys of part 1 and part 3 are, of course, quite different in nature and outcome. In the first, the narrator's journey up the Essequibo River and its tributary in search of diamonds leads deep into the rain forest. The journey also leads "deep into the heart of something," signaling a kind of moral search into human motivations. In that sense, the journey hints at the journey up the Congo River in Joseph Conrad's *Heart of Darkness* (1899). Considerably different is the narrator's search for romantic and sensual gratification in Venezuela. The literary analogue for part 3 might be closer to the fiesta journey through Spain in Ernest Hemingway's *The Sun Also Rises* (1926).

In part 1, the narrator's journey starts as he strikes us a conversation with Baby, a "porknocker," or diamond prospector, who panhandles on a Georgetown street. Baby may have done jail time for killing a double-crossing partner, but when the narrator checks later, neither the court nor the prison has records on Baby. Nevertheless, when Baby sets out on his next porknocking venture, the narrator goes along, Baby serving as both a guide and a trickster figure. Their journey into the Guyanese interior brings the narrator, and the reader, into contact with a gallery of colorful characters, such as a presidential candidate canvassing anyone who will listen; Labba, who holds all natives in contempt; and Travis, their nepotistic boatman. Most interesting of all is Dr. Red ("red" meaning mixed-race in the local patois), a former pimp and gangster with a huge sexual appetite who has been celibate for years and is reinventing himself into a spiritual and herbal healer. Baby introduces the narrator himself as a master sensualist, nicknaming him Gooroo and touting him as a guru on a mission to spread the teachings of the Kama Sutra to women in the rain forest.

Meanwhile, Baby has the narrator produce fake papers so he can work as a research biologist from India in the Kaieteur National Park, and amid the brilliantly described splendors of the Kaieteur Falls and the forests along the Potaro River, Baby and the narrator team up with Foulis, another porknocker, to extract diamonds from the forest floor. After ten days of grueling labor, Baby and Foulis are dividing their spoils when an unfortunate accident transpires, after which Baby chases down the terrified Foulis. In a vividly recounted scene, Baby all but kills

Rahul Bhattacharya is the author of the cricket-tour book Pundits from Pakistan: On Tour with India, 2003–2004 *(2005). He started writing as a cricket journalist in 2000 and has since been a contributing editor with* Wisden Asia Cricket *magazine and a writer for the* Wisden Cricketers' Almanack.

him before the narrator's horrified eyes. Once Foulis is allowed to depart, the narrator discovers that Baby has been cheating Foulis all along. His realization of Baby's and, by implication, humanity's capacity for greed, violence, and treachery further intensifies the horror in his heart. Given the frequent mentions of Rastas and reggae in Bhattacharya's text, it is tempting to speculate whether Baby's name might be a reference to Babylon, a term that is emblematic of evil in the Rastafarian religion.

One feels that the narrator's horror signals a kind of moral awakening, as in part 2 he returns to Georgetown, moves to new lodgings, and ruminates on Guyana's colonial past. Guyana's history is replete with greed, violence, treachery, and the hypocritical enterprise of bringing Christian civilization to untutored indigenes. Colonialism was implemented with profit as its primary motivation; the destruction of indigenous peoples and cultures, the transporting of indentured Europeans and East Indian coolies, and the enslaving of Africans was merely collateral damage. In the midst of reading in the town library, the narrator comes across a passage in which the first three words of "Dutch East India Company," Guyana's first colonizers, have been crossed out and the word "sly" has been written in, leaving "sly company." The word is indeed redolent of the hypocrisy and self-justification with which the horrors of colonialism were carried out. Fittingly, the word also resonates in the novel's title.

If the search for material wealth was the impulse behind part 1, the search for sexual gratification is behind the journey in part 3. The narrator strikes up a relationship with Jan, a beautiful but meagerly educated young woman of East Indian descent, with whom the narrator quickly becomes infatuated. Without waiting to learn more about her and without heeding her wishes, he impatiently sweeps her off on a Christmas and New Year's trip through Venezuela. For him, the trip aspires to be a sexual holiday and a fitting climax to his year in Guyana, but for Jan, the trip represents what could be a prelude of her future away from her unhappy life in Guyana, which has been rendered miserable by a possessive and abusive boyfriend.

As they travel to Caracas, Coro, Ciudad Bolivar, and San Felix, they initially find complete gratification in their passion for each other, but gradually the cold discomforts of cheap hotels, a foreign language, and even their inability to forage for food when restaurants close for the holidays begin to wear away their budding relationship. They discover that their interests are divergent: She wants to talk about conking hair, while he wants to read V.S. Naipaul's *In a Free State* (1971), a perverse choice of reading material for a romantic journey. By the time they head back for Guyana, the petty frictions of cohabitation have taken their toll, and they have begun to quarrel. Giving each other the silent treatment, they approach the border crossing, and the narrator is piqued when suddenly Jan enters into a conversation with another man. Harassed by immigration officials that require bribing, the narrator crosses into Guyana only to realize that Jan has been detained, her new acquaintance having used her as his mule by slipping illicit drugs into her purse. Jan calls out for help, but because his visa and his ticket back to India are about to expire he is unable to stay.

Back in Georgetown, the narrator is guilt-ridden. As the title suggests, he cannot help but face his betrayal. Likewise, he must face having used Jan for the indulgence of his sexual greed. He is, after all, not much better than Baby. Perhaps his saving grace is that he has not resorted to violence. However, the narrator also knows that he is responsible for the violence that will befall Jan at the hands of others, which he has done nothing to prevent. On this bitter note of self-evaluation and disappointment, the narrator fights back tears, concluding his tale with the painful realization that all of humanity is as sly, greedy, treacherous, and hypocritical as the Dutch East India Company.

Rahul Bhattacharya's first novel has accomplished a considerable feat. It is a vivid and lively account of contemporary Guyana, with serious and worthwhile insights into human motivation, past and present. Bhattacharya successfully brings to light an obscure but fascinating corner of the world, and his narrator's moving self-realization shines important light on the darkness of human actions.

C. L. Chua

Review Sources

Booklist 107, no. 15 (April 1, 2011): 28.
Library Journal 136, no. 10 (June 1, 2011): 88.
The New York Times Book Review, May 15, 2011, p. 26.
Publishers Weekly 258, no. 8 (February 21, 2011): 109–110.
The Wall Street Journal, April 30, 2011, p. C8.

Smoking Typewriters
The Sixties Underground Press and the
Rise of Alternative Media in America

Author: John McMillian
Publisher: Oxford University Press (New
York). 304 pp. $27.95
Type of work: History
Time: 1960s
Locale: San Francisco; New York City

*McMillian offers a historical overview of the
1960s underground press and its legacy in the
modern alternative press and Internet publishing industries.*

Principal personages:
MAX SCHERR, founder of the *Berkeley Barb*,
one of the nation's earliest alternative press
publications
JOHN WILCOCK, a pioneer of alternative press
who worked on the *Village Voice* and a
variety of other publications
RAYMOND MUNGO, founding member of the Liberation News Service and a writer and
editor for a variety of Boston-area alternative news publications
STEPHEN M. MINDICH, publisher of the *Boston Phoenix* and one of the first to help
bring the alternative press style to mainstream audiences
THOMAS KING FORCADE, founder and leader of the Underground Press Syndicate and
one of the founding members and publishers of *High Times* magazine
ARTHUR KUNKIN, publisher and editor of the *Los Angeles Free Press*

"We've educated a generation that no longer buys or needs daily papers. They believe
us, not you," says Raymond Mungo, founding member of the Liberation News Service
and underground press pioneer, as quoted in social historian John McMillian's *Smoking Typewriters: The Sixties Underground Press and the Rise of Alternative Media in
America*. A professor of history at Georgia State University and a specialist in radical
politics of the 1960s, McMillian weaves together stories of the press during the early part
of that decade with prescient insights into the state of modern media in America. While
the bulk of the book focuses on the press of the 1960s and 1970s, McMillian also gives
the blogosphere a historical grounding, explaining how Internet media is following in
the steps of the radical press of the past while simultaneously exploring new territory
in a world dominated by the promise (albeit sometimes illusory) of instant information.

In McMillian's account, the underground press has its roots in the student movements of the 1960s, such as the Students for a Democratic Society (SDS). McMillian

also carefully identifies technological advancements, including the mimeograph machine, as key steps in taking control of the press away from the major news agencies.
The manifestos and newssheets of radical student organizations eventually gave way
to the "rags" (to use McMillian's terminology): small-scale, independently produced
publications that reported news from a perspective more in keeping with the attitudes,
inclinations, and overall communication style of the American youth of the age.

The 1960s underground press, which included publications like the *Berkeley Barb*,
the *Austin Rag*, the *Los Angeles Free Press*, and the *East Village Other*, was not the
model of free information that its founders envisioned. Women and minorities rarely
served as writers or editors, and the opinions proffered were most often those of college-
educated white males. Given the hierarchy and social structure of society in the 1960s,
even among the underground, it is not surprising that a somewhat different set of
prejudices and injustices still existed within an institution aimed at countering the
prejudices and injustices of the parent society.

While describing the new publications, McMillian concentrates on the stories of
the men who pioneered this new form of journalism, such as British expatriate John
Wilcock, a veteran of the mainstream media who brought his experience to the alternative press. Wilcock was a founding publisher of New York's *Village Voice* in 1955,
one of the nation's first and most successful newsweeklies. A decade later, he became
editor of the *East Village Other*, the first underground newspaper in New York and one
of the first in the nation; it was preceded only by the *Los Angeles Free Press*, which
was the brainchild of New York transplant Art Kunkin. In the Bay Area, where student
revolutionaries and hippies alike flocked in the late 1960s, publisher and former bar
owner Max Scherr started the *Berkeley Barb*, which eventually became one of the
most successful underground publications in America.

Although papers like the *Free Press* (or "Freep," as locals called it), the *Barb*,
and the *Other* were inconsistent, often poorly written, and unabashedly opinionated,
they nevertheless filled a niche that had been previously unexplored in the publishing world. Kunkin, Wilcock, Scherr, and their contemporaries sometimes tackled the
same issues as the mainstream press, but with a distinct countercultural spin. Underground papers published articles that would never have seen the light of day in the
mainstream, including how-to pieces on detecting and avoiding police surveillance
and instructional articles on drug use. They also featured reviews of films, art, and
literature that were ignored by the major newspapers. Soon, anyone with an interest in
alternative music or other social events turned to the underground papers, and the new
press became a rallying point for the evolving youth culture.

The alternative press also carried extensive coverage of political issues, most notably the Vietnam War and the associated student movement. It was openly critical of
government policies and actions, reporting on the Vietnam conflict as the "moral and
political tragedy" of the age, at a time when the mainstream press seemed paralyzed
and public opinion of the war was growing increasingly negative. The rags also promoted the philosophies of counterculture thinkers like Timothy Leary and the Diggers,
whose political rhetoric placed them in direct opposition to the government's standard
line. This political coverage, though couched in its own antiestablishment rhetoric,

was one way in which the alternative press began to expand its audience.

McMillian's history reads at times like a novel, as he delves into the intimate details of the rivalries, economic issues, and socio-political opposition that the underground papers encountered in their attempts to keep their publications going. Tumultuous waves of fortune and collapse alternated as the leaders of the new press fought among themselves over the proper role and scope of their creations. Both political leaders and representatives of the mainstream press occasionally called for government censure of the rags but found their attempts foiled by widespread popular support and issues involving the freedom of the press.

Another major figure in the movement was Thomas Forcade, who joined with a group of fellow editors and publishers to form the Underground Press Syndicate (UPS), a network of underground newspapers that included the *East Village Other*, the *Berkeley Barb*, the *Los Angeles Free Press*, and *The Paper* from Lansing, Michigan, among others. The UPS began in 1966 and

(Lenny W. Doolan V)

John McMillian is an assistant professor of history at Georgia State University and the author of Smoking Typewriters: The Sixties Underground Press and the Rise of Alternative Media in America *(2010). In 2008, he became a cofounding editor of* The Sixties: A Journal of History, Politics, and Culture.

was a major step in transforming what had been a collection of struggling papers and newssheets into a news network with the ability to spread a single story throughout the counterculture of the entire nation. It provided comics, op-ed pieces, reviews, and a variety of additional material, enabling a start-up paper to fill its pages without the cost of maintaining a large staff. The following year, publisher Ray Mungo started the Liberation News Service (LNS), a new, more encompassing attempt to provide dissemination of counterculture ideals. McMillian describes the LNS as a "kind of radical alternative to the Associated Press."

McMillian illustrates the function of the LNS and the UPS with what became known as the Great Banana Hoax of 1967. The origins of the hoax are poorly known, reports McMillian, but sometime in late 1966, a rumor spread through California's subculture that banana peels could be smoked to induce hallucinations. Soon after, the band Country Joe and the Fish, having read that banana peel smoke was an intoxicant, passed around banana joints at one of their concerts and told the assembled crowd that "smoking banana peels could get you high." The *Berkeley Barb*, which employed a staff writer who also served as a manager for Country Joe and the Fish, reported on the intoxicating effects of banana peel smoke in March of 1967. The underground syndicate helped to disseminate this rumor throughout the country in a matter of days.

While many of the authors who penned banana-smoking recipes later said they were aware it was only a hoax, consumers of the press, and of produce, clearly were not. There was a run on bananas, leading to a banana shortage in California, and soon the mainstream press was carrying articles describing bananas as the new drug craze. The song "Mellow Yellow" by counterculture crooner Donovan served to further perpetuate the myth.

According to McMillian's account, the 1960s press eventually succumbed to internal disputes among its leaders, causing many of the original newspapers and syndicates to fold. While popular with young readers, the rags suffered from insufficient revenues, and those who chose to work within the underground press were forced to labor under the almost constant threat of financial collapse.

The next generation of alternative newspapers, which came to prominence in the 1970s and 1980s, was guided by a new breed of publishers who sought a middle ground between the counterculture and the mainstream. The new papers were careful to remain inviting to advertisers in an attempt to avoid the financial problems that had plagued their 1960s counterparts, although they still benefited from the trailblazing efforts of their forebears. The 1960s press had demonstrated that there was a market for this new kind of journalism, which catered to a more specific audience with opinionated articles that often bucked mainstream perceptions of normalcy. The political gravity of the 1960s press dissolved, but the newspapers pushed forward with a more responsible and tempered sense of journalistic freedom that hovered somewhere between radicalism and conformity.

Toward the end of his analysis, McMillian turns his attention to the bloggers and Internet media outlets of the modern era. He briefly discusses the success of these groups in bringing attention to political and social issues that escape, or are purposely ignored by, the mainstream news agencies. In light of twenty-first-century developments, McMillian envisions a bleak future for the printed media, saying, "No one knows when it will happen, but eventually—in five years, or maybe ten, or sometime after that—printed daily newspapers of any type will either become rare in the United States or they will cease to exist altogether." However, he still sees hope for radical journalism in the home-baked efforts of bloggers and e-zines that keep the goals of the counterculture alive.

McMillian can perhaps be criticized for finding too clear a division between the press of the 1960s and its modern incarnations, but he presents a thoroughly researched review of history that explores radical media in the light of modern developments in the press. His affection for the material is evident and his ability to pull together historical minutiae to support his analysis in each chapter is laudable. In summing up the contributions of the 1960s press, he writes that "the underground newspapers of the late 1960s were zeitgeist touchstones by which radicals could measure the purity of their commitments to interdependence, power-sharing, and self-rule."

McMillian's history is filled with stories of the personal dramas and world-changing ambitions that drove the innovators of the age, but it is also an engrossing commentary on the birth of a form of expression in the American consciousness. McMillian asserts that, "barring some dystopian future," the underground press will never die; the values and ideals espoused by writers of the 1960s rags still inform the journalism of today, finding reflection not only in the modern alternative press but also in the literary style adopted by the mainstream in its continuing effort to remain relevant in a changing world.

Micah L. Issitt

Review Sources

American Prospect, March 25, 2011 (Web).
Berkeley Daily Planet, February 9, 2011 (Web).
Free Times, March 16, 2011 (Web).
Library Journal, January 28, 2011 (Web).
Publishers Weekly, January 17, 2011 (Web).
The Wall Street Journal, February 19, 2011 (Web).

Sobbing Superpower
Selected Poems of Tadeusz Różewicz

Author: Tadeusz Różewicz (b. 1921)
Translated from the Polish by Joanna Trzeciak
Foreword by Edward Hirsch
Publisher: W. W. Norton (New York). 368 pp.
$32.95
Type of work: Poetry
Time: Between World War II and the present
Locale: Primarily set in Poland

This extensive overview of Różewicz's poetry is drawn from over twenty individual collections. Long considered the most influential contemporary poet in Poland, Różewicz's work has been largely unread in the United States. This collection seeks to introduce new audiences to the philosophical poet's dark, stripped-down verse.

When Tadeusz Różewicz's first book was published in 1944, the Polish poet was living in the woods of his home country and working as a member of a resistance army against the occupying force of Nazi Germany. While the horrors of the war were impossible to escape, Różewicz experienced them most directly when the Gestapo executed his brother that same year. It was when he published his second book of poetry several years later that he secured his place as a major talent in Poland and a significant voice in response to the war. For the remaining decades, his poetry evolved with the history of Europe, attempting to reconcile humanity and civilization with the evil he had seen in them. Characterized as much by his philosophical stance in which despair often seems the only appropriate response to reality as by his bare, unpunctuated style, Różewicz distinguished himself as the most important poet in a generation of internationally recognized writers. Yet, while poets such as Czesław Miłosz and Zbigniew Herbert are familiar to many readers in the United States, Różewicz himself has remained relatively unread. This new collection, translated by the talented Joanna Trzeciak, attempts to remedy that situation. It is a sweeping and valuable work, including the poet's best-known individual poems while maintaining an eye on his evolution as a thinker. Through it, readers not only gain access to an important writer, but are also given the privilege of seeing his philosophy and style as he responded to age, political upheavals, and the general current of change that have marked the twentieth and early twenty-first centuries.

Considering Różewicz's tremendously prolific nature as a writer, there were by necessity only a few poems chosen from his various collections. As Trzeciak noted in her translator's note, "Trying to represent his prolific output in a volume of selected

Tadeusz Różewicz is the most influential contemporary poet in Poland. An accomplished prose writer and playwright, his work has been translated into many languages. His collection New Poems *(2007) was nominated for the National Book Critics Circle Award in 2008.*

works is like trying to sample the ocean with a sieve." From the opening poem, however, first published in 1945, a clear line of philosophical thought is established. This poem, "Rose," already features the poet's characteristic lack of punctuation, his restrained language, and his ability to test the powers of language in response to the cruelty of humanity. The first lines simply declare that "Rose is the name of a flower / or a dead girl." Simple and direct, Różewicz conflates the girl with the rose, a common poetic metaphor that he extends to uncommonly dark results. "Blood drains from the pale petal / the girl's dress hangs formless," the poem declares in its short list of violent images. The poem is nevertheless beautiful, crafted with such care and rhythm that every line resonates both on its own and as part of the whole. Like the beauty of the flower, however, the beauty of the language is powerless to alter reality. As the poem ends, "Today a rose bloomed in the garden / memory of the living and faith have died." Following the atrocities of the war, flowers continued to bloom and poets continued to write beautiful verse, but for Różewicz, these beauties did nothing to alleviate the death of faith that he and so many others experienced.

In many ways, Różewicz's work can be seen as a direct response to the philosopher Theodor Adorno's famous statement that "writing poetry after Auschwitz is barbaric," meaning that the death camps were so horrible that they negated any subsequent interest in art. Indeed, many of Różewicz's poems explicitly attempt to answer that assertion, and even when the topic of poetry is pushed beneath the surface, his stylistic choices and general philosophy are still strongly affected by the war. As he writes in "Survivor," an early poem addressing his experience as someone who lived through the occupation of Poland,

> These words are empty and equivalent:
> man and animal
> love and hate
> foe and friend
> dark and light.

These meaningful words are the same ones he often returns to in later poems, yet he sees them as meaningless, virtually the same as their dichotomous opposites. It is not so much the concepts of "man" and "love" that he challenges, but the ability of language to capture those concepts in words. Certainly, it seems odd that someone who questions the power of words made a life as a poet, or wrote a poem at all. Many people have seen in his work a total abandonment of meaning; his contemporary Miłosz (arguably the most famous Polish poet to be translated in the United States) has accused Różewicz of nihilism. Even the foreword to this collection, written by Edward Hirsch, describes Różewicz as an "antipoet," a writer who questions the act of writing even while he relies on it. While it is true that Różewicz does not accept any easy meaning or beauty, his project is less about abandoning poetry and more about salvaging whatever he can of poetry from the cruelty of humanity. As the poem "Unde Malum?" explains, "human beings are the only beings / who use words," while at the same time "evil comes from a human being / and only a human being." Having seen the massive destruction, torture, and violence that human beings have perpetrated, Różewicz's insistent need to write poetry is in some ways a struggle to be optimistic, even if the only poetry he found suitable is itself concerned with the darker sides of reality.

Różewicz's near-nihilism is also established through the voice he employs in his poems. Cool, objective, and direct, the speaker of many of these poems seems unemotional despite addressing violently emotional topics. This voice is employed for various ends: It is observational ("it's cold, foul weather / the new, 43rd president of the Superpower / is being sworn in") just as easily as philosophical ("You're right Tadeusz / it would be best to go insane / but our generation never goes insane"). His lack of ornate language and extensive commentary makes him seem resigned to what he describes, accepting the horrors for what they are. However, taken in the context of his work as a whole, these restrained observations can be understood as poetry of witness. It would be obscene in the world of Różewicz's poems to make grandiose statements of redemption or to rely on lyric, gorgeous language. Instead, he attempts a poetry that fits the reality he witnessed. It may have seemed inappropriate, as Adorno suggested, to write poetry in response to the events such as the Holocaust. However, as Różewicz writes in "Stick on Water," "whereof one cannot speak / therefore one must speak." He felt silenced by the atrocities of humanity and so it became his duty to speak through that silence.

While it is perhaps impossible to overemphasize the importance of the Holocaust in Różewicz's work, his career has continued through the twentieth century and into the twenty-first and responded to a range of different politics, ideas, and world events. As a writer who has been deeply concerned with Poland, perhaps the most significant theme in his later work is the fall of the Soviet Union and the effects that nation had on Eastern Europe. The title poem of this collection, "Sobbing Superpower," gives a characteristically succinct insight into his view of world politics. While the early twentieth century was characterized by a distrust of war, the latter half of the century made the poet distrustful of any nation that held power over another, whether politically, economically, or culturally. The world of these poems was one where capitalism, mass production, and other sources of modern power and wealth became suspect. The excess of this world is often created through lists, an almost nonsensical yet disturbing form that forces readers to confront "commissioners CEOs / tulips chimpanzees parrots / *Beware of imports!*" While still characteristically terse, sparsely punctuated, and reserved, these later poems tend to stretch across several pages and employ a voice that less clearly belongs to the poet himself. He borrows language from advertisements, political campaigns, and other writers, weaving in these disparate voices alongside his own. Likewise, these later poems are more concerned with direct political critique, questioning the authenticity and goodwill of contemporary figures such as former US president George W. Bush. While the poems that attempt to reconcile humanity with the Holocaust came to life after the horror of the war, these poems were born during what Różewicz saw as a major political and moral crisis. As such, his voice shifts a bit, becoming more confrontational and less philosophical.

Spanning his long career, Różewicz's poems were almost entirely set in Poland. For many readers in the United States, the full resonance of these works might be lost. Różewicz favors cultural and political allusions, some of which are highly specific to the region. Like many European poets, he also tends to alternate between languages, with German in particular often appearing for several lines at a time. For a work translated into English, this creates a particular challenge. In earlier poems, for instance, lines written in German often carry with them a violence derived from the occupation of Poland. However, when translated into English, this verbal violence is easily lost. While an incomplete solution, Trzeciak somewhat remedies this with an extensive section of notes that illuminate the poems themselves as well as her translation process. These notes serve as a useful guide for readers who are unfamiliar with Polish language and culture, even if some of the meaning behind Różewicz's work is lost in translation.

As an antipoet, Różewicz is an important figure in the development of world literature, and this collection is a vital introduction for English-speaking audiences. Perhaps the best explanation of his life's work may be found in "My Poetry," a short poem from early in his career. He writes that his writing "justifies nothing / explains nothing / renounces nothing" and "fulfills no hope." While in many ways a poem of negation, he also stresses that his poetry "obeys its own imperative / its own capabilities / and limitations." In the restraint he enforced on himself, then, Różewicz is a complete success, and the limits and failures of his language are one small way of respecting humanity in the face of its own limits and failures. Ultimately as much a moralist as a nihilist (a fitting contradiction for an often contradictory poet), Różewicz's poetry demands that readers see the world that humanity made and, despite how monstrous it may have seemed, insisted on our humanity after all.

T. Fleischmann

Review Sources

Pleiades 31, no. 2 (Summer, 2011): 143–149.
Publishers Weekly 257, no. 45 (November 15, 2010): 42.
Quarterly Conversation, September 6, 2011 (Web).
The Washington Post, May 26, 2011 (Web).

The Social Animal
The Hidden Sources of Love, Character, and Achievement

Author: David Brooks (b. 1961)
Publisher: Random House (New York). 448 pp.
$27.00; paperback $16.00
Type of work: Anthropology, psychology, science, sociology
Time: Late twentieth and early twenty-first centuries
Locale: United States

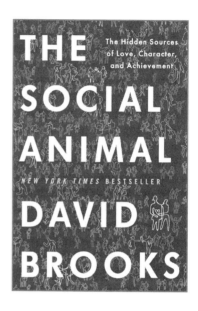

Brooks's study traces the lives of two invented characters, Harold and Erica, as a way of presenting a great deal of scientific and sociological information about how humans develop and how the mind, and especially the brain, influence this development.

Principal characters:
AMY, the mother of Erica, a second-generation Chinese American who works multiple jobs and may have bipolar disorder
ERICA, the principal female character, daughter of Amy and wife to Harold, the principal male character, who is also the son of Julia and Rob.
JULIA, the mother of Harold
ROB, the father of Harold
UNNAMED, the Mexican American father of Erica

David Brooks will be familiar to many readers as the conservative commentator who appears regularly in *The New York Times* and on National Public Radio, as well as on the Public Broadcasting System's televised program *NewsHour*. Brooks first began his dissection of the psychology of contemporary upper-class America with his 2000 "comic sociology" work *Bobos in Paradise: The New Upper Class and How They Got There*. In *The Social Animal: The Hidden Sources of Love, Character, and Achievement*, Brooks continues in this vein of inquiry and suggests that discoveries in the study of the brain, the mind, and human development help support broadly conservative insights into culture and society. Brooks is careful not to seem dogmatic, and indeed, the book both implicitly and explicitly criticizes extreme views from either the Right or the Left. In fact, Brooks's focus is not exclusively political. He is more interested in showing how much we can learn from the scientific study of personality, especially the way that personality is rooted in the brain. The book summarizes a large amount of data pertaining to the way people develop and interact with each other and the world during the course of their lives.

In order to anchor his findings as much as possible to the lives of credible human beings, and in order to prevent the book from being a dry compilation of facts and statistics, Brooks invents two characters, Harold and Erica, who come from significantly different ethnic and socioeconomic backgrounds. Harold comes of age in a white, middle-class household and enjoys a variety of social privileges. Partly as a result of her mother's mental struggles and lack of financial success, Erica grows into an ambitious woman who is determined to succeed. Eventually Harold and Erica meet when she hires him to help her set up a business that quickly becomes highly successful, at least for a period of time. Ultimately, Harold and Erica fall in love and marry, and although they face various challenges both professionally and personally, their social status, and especially Erica's social status, climbs quickly to very unusual heights. Although sometimes less than satisfied with their lives, they achieve a measure of true serenity after they retire, but due to serious health problems, Harold eventually becomes even more dependent on Erica than he had been before. In the final paragraphs of the book, Brooks depicts Harold dying peacefully while holding Erica's hand.

In certain parts, Brooks's volume becomes almost novelistic as it traces the lives of these two invented people, but the parts of his text most likely to interest readers are the parts tying the experiences of Harold and Erica to an impressive amount of solid, scientific research about typical, often predictable patterns of human nature and behavior. Brooks suggests that brain research and evolutionary psychology provide particularly valuable insights into why humans think, feel, behave, and interact as they do, especially during specific phases of their lives. The individual factors of gender, social class, ethnic background, and economic status all affect the way a person's life develops, but these factors are also highly influenced by interactions with brain chemistry, genetic inheritance, and patterns of thought and feeling rooted deep in the ancient history of the human race. Brooks's book can be seen as part of a broad trend of studies depicting "nature" as at least as important as "nurture," although it is generally agreed that the two categories cannot be easily separated.

The Social Animal is a continuously fascinating summary and application of intriguing scientific research. More than twenty pages of notes appear in small print at the back of the book and help tie Brooks's claims to various credible scientific sources. Brooks is fully aware that his book is unlikely to please readers who want their science "straight" and nuanced. However, his volume is obviously designed to interest readers who want to consider the ways in which scientific studies may be relevant to their own day-to-day experiences and to their own development from birth to death. Readers wishing to skip the sections dealing with Harold and Erica can easily do so. The persons making up Brooks's imaginary couple are not shown to be deeply complex, nor are they wholly rounded novelistic characters; rather, they are almost allegorical figures designed to illustrate the lives of intellectuals who enjoy numerous creature comforts. Brooks uses Harold and Erica in an attempt to demonstrate scientifically how their unconscious informs the choices that give rise to their success. Nevertheless, even though these characters obviously cannot represent a very wide swath of the American population, they are representative enough to make this book, especially its scientific parts, continually interesting. As finding is added to finding, the book grows

David Brooks, a social and political commentator for newspapers, magazines, radio, and television, is the author of the best-selling Bobos in Paradise: The New Upper Class and How They Got There *(2000) and* On Paradise Drive: How We Live Now (and Always Have) in the Future Tense *(2004). He was also the editor of* Backward and Upward: The New Conservative Writing *(1996).*

in persuasiveness for some readers. Many of the data Brooks reports are surprising, since they contradict various common assumptions, but in some places, the book provides empirical support for a good deal of old-fashioned common sense. This is especially true when Brooks contrasts the perspectives and teachings of the Enlightenment philosophers from France and England, contending that the English, with their emphasis on moral sentiments, have ultimately proven to be more persuasive than the French, whom Brooks characterizes by a commitment to pure reason in opposition to emotion.

It is hard not to be impressed by some of the data Brooks reports. At one point, for instance, he notes that the typical adult human brain may contain anywhere from one hundred trillion to one thousand trillion synapses, which are specific conduits of chemical information. "A mere sixty neurons," Brooks notes, "are capable of making 10^{81} possible connections with each other. (That's one with eighty-one zeroes after it.)." These kinds of data are especially suggestive, given that one of Brooks's main arguments holds that much of what goes on in our minds takes place in the unconscious, and that conscious "reasoning" is performed by only a very small part of the mind. Many of the findings Brooks cites to support these claims are striking and impressive. He offers a broad overview of the kinds of experiments social and biological scientists undertake to discover the predictable patterns of human nature. In his focus on norms, however, Brooks sometimes overlooks people who fall outside of traditional categories. There is, for instance, no reference to homosexuality anywhere in the book— which is a very surprising omission, considering the controversies surrounding that subject that have emerged during the decades of the late twentieth and early twenty-first centuries.

The book is clearly and engagingly written, and Brooks is clever at inventing terms, indeed sometimes a bit too clever. The scientific sections each contain at least a handful of thought-provoking facts and findings prominently displayed on virtually every page. Sometimes, however, assertions are not documented, and one occasionally wonders if Brooks might be presenting controversial claims as if they were settled, established facts. Footnotes, rather than the endnotes Brooks employs, would have made it easier for the reader to check the sources and reliability of Brooks's assertions, but they would also obviously have given the book a scholarly look that the publishers must have wanted to avoid. Nevertheless, Brooks has clearly read and researched widely, and his notes provide a compendium of sources that readers can easily explore on their own. As a book of popular science rather than a work intended to be read by specialists, it may introduce many readers to realms of thought they might never have explored before, or even to realms they might otherwise never have considered exploring.

Initial responses to Brooks's book were greatly mixed and were also oftentimes influenced by the political, social, and moral beliefs of the reviewers. Numerous reviewers found fault with Erica and Harold as literary characters, for example, often criticizing them as two-dimensional and even as somewhat irritating. Positive reviews often praised the book for making a great deal of scientific data easily available and for applying it to real-life situations. However, some scientists and sociologists occasionally found fault with Brooks's alleged credulity and with what they considered to be his shallow presentation of rather more complex scientific controversies. Reviewers of a more political bent were dismayed with the book for not being more explicit in presenting specific policy recommendations. Despite this sort of criticism, the book was embraced by David Cameron, the leader of the Conservative Party in Great Britain, who suggested that it be widely read by his top advisors, a fact that made some reviewers suspicious at the same times as it confirmed the value of the book in the eyes of others. Other reviewers who had religious or moral agendas of their own were often critical of the book's contention that scientific understanding alone can provide a reasonable moral guide for living. Such critics argue that an increase in knowledge does not necessarily provide answers to the most important ethical questions and social concerns and that Brooks's vision of achievement is mediocre at best and unattainable at worst. Nevertheless, Brooks's *The Social Animal* will be of great value in renewing popular debate regarding the place of reason and emotion in society, inspiring further investigation of human development and Western philosophy, and provoking thoughtful discussions of science and morality.

Robert C. Evans

Review Sources

Christianity Today 55, no. 7 (July 2011): 69.
Commentary 131, no. 3 (March 2011): 69.
Commonweal 138, no.14 (August 12, 2011): 27–30.
National Interest 114 (July/August 2011): 81.
The New York Times, March 13, 2011, p. BR6.
Science News 179, no. 9 (April 23, 1011): 34.
Wilson Quarterly 35, no. 2 (Spring 2011): 104–105.

Songs of Kabir

Author: Kabir
Translated from the Hindi by Arvind Krishna
  Mehrotra
Publisher: New York Review Books (New
  York). 144 pp. $14.00
Type of work: Poetry
Time: Fifteenth century
Locale: Northern India

*Mehrotra's translation of sixty of Kabir's po-
ems is the latest of a long line of translations
of the Indian mystic and poet. It is a sampler
done in idiomatic English, but it provides a set
of notes and a preface to give Western readers
some context.*

Principal personage:
KABIR (ca. 1440–ca. 1518), a northern Indian
  religious poet working in an oral tradition

Little is known about the Indian poet Kabir (whose poems have been translated in this
new edition by Arvind Krishna Mehrotra), apart from the fact that he was a weaver
and the son of a weaver and that he lived in the holy city of Benares (Varanasi) on the
banks of the Ganges in northern India. He composed his poetry during the fifteenth
century, though the exact dates of his birth and death are only suppositional.

Because Kabir composed in the oral tradition of the day, his poems were memorized by his disciples and only written down at a later time. However, there was never
a definitive manuscript of the poet's works. The poems were translated from Hindi
into many of the other vernacular languages of the region, and they were passed on
in a sung, oral tradition that was most likely fairly improvisational. Both the work of
translation and attempts to reproduce its improvisational quality have resulted in many
variants on the original text, over the centuries. There is some confusion about the exact number of Kabir's compositions, given the likelihood that other anonymous poets
have written similar poems and attributed them to Kabir.

A substantial number of poems were taken by proponents of the Sikh religion,
which had originated during the fifteenth century and was therefore a recent development in Kabir's world. Sikhs sought out poems that conformed to their religion's
teachings, and these poems were incorporated into Sikh scriptures, giving a particular
stability to the poems. Kabir's writings that were appropriated by Sikhism were recorded in the Punjabi language. A Hindu sect was also formed, the Kabir Panthi, which
sought to practice the kind of mysticism Kabir's poems advocated. Several thousand
poems have been attributed to Kabir, though none can be proved to be his. The general

consensus is that there are in the region of some four hundred genuine Kabir poems in the "western" or Rajasthani collection, many of which are also included in the over five hundred Kabir hymns featured in the Sikh scriptures. There is also a third, oral "eastern," or *Bijak*, tradition.

With the resurgence of interest in Indian religion in the West in the second half of the twentieth century, a new interest in its poetry also arose. Apart from the Bengali poet Rabindranath Tagore, few other Indian religious poets have been generally known or studied in the West. Kabir's poetry is clearly important to any awakening study of such poetry, both for its own particular merits and as a representative of the wider bhakti group of poets, a tradition of poetry that began in southern India in the Tamil language in the sixth century and slowly reached northern India, where Hindi was the predominant language.

One of the difficulties in dealing with Indian religion and religious poetry is the need to use the original Indian terminology, since many Indian words or phrases have no direct translation into modern Western secular language. The word "bhakti" is one such term. Roughly, it means a mystic or contemplative tradition, one in which the appearance of reality is deliberately turned upside down or inside out to show it as illusory or false and which hides a more spiritual reality. However, in the West, these terms cannot help but seem ethereal, intangible, or otherworldly.

In fact, Kabir's poetry is anything but intangible. It is concrete, confrontational, shocking, and riddling and, at the same time, it provokes readers to desire a direct experience of divine love. The nearest equivalent to Kabir's type of poetry in the English tradition would be the metaphysical poetry of the early seventeenth century, such as that of John Donne. The strength of this new translation by Mehrotra, who is a scholar and an Indian poet in his own right, is that it restores the directness and solidity of Kabir's poems in twenty-first century terms. Mehrotra justifies his freedom to use modern colloquial language by claiming the oral improvisational tradition. He quotes a modern Kabir-type song, for example, that uses railroad terms to express its spiritual truths.

Many of Kabir's previous translators have tried to adhere closely to the earliest originals and have kept the form of the Indian languages. Others have retained the poems' traditional religious symbolism and terms. In contrast, Mehrotra has broken away from these techniques, trying to keep to the fresh, in-your-face spirit of the original text.

Mehrotra has based his selection on what he considers to be the most authoritative collection of the Hindi songs, called the *Kabir Granthavali*, done by Parasnath Tiwari in 1961. To these he has added a number of other poems from other collections. He acknowledges other translations, including those done by Charlotte Vaudeville (1974, 1993), John Hawley and Mark Juergensmeyer (1988), Linda Hess (1994), Vinay Dharwadker (2003), and Robert Bly (2004). His unspoken premise in selecting such a small number of poems is to give the uninitiated reader a taste of Kabir, with regards to both style and substance.

For Mehrotra, the essence of Kabir is his individuality. He belonged to neither of the major religions of India of his time, namely Islam and Hinduism. Moreover,

Arvind Krishna Mehrotra is a poet, translator, and editor of Indian litera-ture. He was born in Lahore and is a professor of English at the University of Allahabad in northern India.

his work does not connect back to Buddhism or forward to Sikhism, though he echoes or predates both of these religions. As for Christianity, similarities and differences are left mainly to the reader to discover; these include echoes of the eroticism in the Old Testament book known as the Song of Solomon, as well as Jesus Christ's paradoxical sayings that resonate with Kabir's the "Upside Down" poems. During Kabir's time, Christianity existed only in south India in the Mar Thoma church.

Mehrotra includes a number of poems in the section "Against Pundits and Muezzins" that illustrate Kabir's iconoclastic tendencies. Kabir's strongest protest is against the Hindu caste system, but he is also against all sorts of professional holy men, spiritual teachers, and religious rituals, scriptures, and buildings. Kabir's simple thesis is that salvation cannot be earned by doing certain things or being part of a certain group; it can only be gained by loving God and becoming at one with him. Thus, he remains an unattached layman. In one poem, he talks of giving up weaving to be closer to God. When his mother protests, he states he is sure God will provide.

Mehrotra quotes the often-repeated saying that during Kabir's life both Hindus and Muslims rejected him; but that after his death, both claimed him. However, the terms Mehrotra uses for the deity are all Hindu. Presumably, he is following the original in doing so. The term "Allah" is never used, nor the more generic word "God." Typically the term used is "Rama," "Hari," or, occasionally, "Vishnu" or "the lord." The word "kabir" is Muslim, being one of the ninety-nine names attributed to Allah. Scholars suggest the poet Kabir came from a Hindu family that converted to Islam, perhaps to escape the caste system, in which weavers were low on the list.

One of the other features of Kabir's poetry is the "upside down-ness" of many of his poems, achieved through the yoking of impossible opposites, riddles, and paradoxes. This is the stuff of much religious discourse, especially of mystic traditions that interpret apparent facts as fictions and apparent realities as illusions.

In terms of the translation, Mehrotra is successful. He is a poet himself, and so the images, words, and rhythms he employs are almost without fault. Only twice does a colloquial word seem out of place, carrying the wrong force of association, and thus spoiling the poem. He overuses place names like "Deathville" or "Fearlessburg," but generally his neologisms and colloquialisms give a burst of illuminating newness to the text. Thus, terms such as "make bedroom eyes," "dreadlocked Rastas," "the smart guys," and "a buzz saw" seem quite natural. On the whole, however, Mehrotra relies on universal images and associations to convey Kabir's message, so that the poet's intent needs no further explanation.

Sometimes Mehrotra keeps the original symbolism, in which case a footnote explains the meaning. Thus in the poem "The Night Has Passed," the meaning of a heron as old age and the swan as a symbol for old age are footnoted, illuminating the poem and giving it resonance, for example, with W. B. Yeats's poem of old age, "The Wild Swans at Coole."

Often, the scholar in Mehrotra gets the better of him, as in his introduction, for example. Wendy Doniger, Mircea Eliade Distinguished Service Professor of the History of Religions at Chicago University, was engaged to write the book's preface. She supplied eighteen pages of closely knit scholarly background information. The book really does not need any more. Readers unacquainted with Indian literature will have to make an effort to absorb the preface.

In many cases, readers will most likely skip the preface and the introduction. If they do, however, they will run into terms that are simply not explained in the footnotes. A case in point is the term "maya," which Mehrotra leaves untranslated. It means "illusion" or "surface appearance," but this is only relayed to readers in Doniger's preface. In other words, the introduction is too heavy. Simple explanations about the caste system, Hindu polytheism, the relation of yoga (which readers will presumably know something about) to the bhakti tradition, and so on, would probably have been more useful than the information provided.

Having leveled that critique, the selection of poems and their arrangement into subsections is well done. The most important of the sections is perhaps "Waiting to Be Kissed" and "The Color of Rama." But the opening section on the "Upside Down" poems is also a good place to begin, and it features the riddles and paradoxes that all religious writing necessarily embraces at some stage. Readers will be immediately engaged with the riddles. They set up a pattern of reading and rereading that is part of the necessary training Mehrotra wants to take readers through to reach the heart of Kabir's message.

David Barratt

Review Sources

The New York Times Sunday Book Review, May 29, 2011, p. 14.
Religious Studies Review 37, no. 4 (December 2011): 301.

Space, in Chains

Author: Laura Kasischke (b. 1961)
Publisher: Copper Canyon Press (Port
   Townsend, WA). 113 pp. $16.00
Type of work: Poetry

A lyric and emotional exploration of grief,
Space, in Chains *focuses on the death of the
poet's parents and her own realizations of mortality and aging.*

The world of Laura Kasischke's *Space, in Chains*
is surreal and familiar, autobiographical and fantastical, direct and yet surprising in its turns.
These are qualities also found in Kasischke's previous collections, which have slowly earned her
a reputation as a leading American poet. However, with this latest collection's focus on death,
the death of her parents in particular, Kasischke's
poetic tools yield especially powerful results. Kasischke is both a mother and the daughter of two deceased parents, and while this position
is in many ways common, the realities of death, grieving, and illness make life seem, at
times, unbearable and unreal. This is the thematic basis of *Space, in Chains*, that the most
familiar and reliable things in life someday end, and with that end, life itself becomes surreal and unfamiliar. With her rare ability to manipulate rhythm and time, jumping between
narrative and lists of nouns in a way that evokes the behavior of memory, Kasischke creates a lyrical and often heartbreaking account of life as it confronts death.

While the most obvious and recurrent deaths of *Space, in Chains* are those of Kasischke's parents, a broader sense of death and aging permeates many of the poems.
The people of this collection are constantly confronting the mortality of their loved
ones, if not dying or ill themselves. They jump from planes, visit children's hospitals,
and, while happily sipping coffee, receive news of their child's sudden death. For Kasischke, however, death is not simply an occasion to mourn (although there is plenty
of mourning to be had). Instead, death inspires a spiral of poetic thought. The poem
"Time," for instance, takes as its starting point a moment when Kasischke visited her
dying mother in the hospital, a moment that lingers in her memory:

> some part of me, for all time
> stands in a short skirt in a hospital cafeteria line, with a tray, while
>
> in another glittering tower named
> for the world's richest man
> my mother, who is dying, never dies

(Patrice Normand/Opale)

Laura Kasischke is the author of several books of poetry and fiction. Among her many honors, she has won a Juniper Poetry Prize, a Pushcart Prize, and the Alice Fay Di Castagnola Award from the Poetry Society of America. She lives in Chelsea, Michigan, and teaches at the University of Michigan Master of Fine Arts in Creative Writing program.

This is not an easy acceptance of death or loss; it is a realization that death itself is frightening, illuminating, and nearly incomprehensible. The death of the mother is firmly located in the past, yet it still resonates in the present, like a "Bird / with one wing / in Purgatory, flying in circles." Even the mundane location of the hospital is made unfamiliar by the mention of the surreal "glittering tower." *Space, in Chains* is often focused on death, but it is uninterested in understanding death in any easy way, preferring instead to confront mortality as something beyond the understanding of the poet and the reader, something ineffable unless approached in the mode of poetry, song, and image.

The reality of death, although a universal truth, still seems incomprehensible. It is fitting then that in order to understand the mundane aspects of life Kasischke's poems turn to the fantastic and imaginary. "Atoms on Loan," for instance, begins with the surreal declaration that "the eyelid of a stone in my hand / flutters, and then it opens. I say, *Hello?*" Starting here, the speaker uncovers a catalogue of unreal memories, recalling absurd versions of her life, paddling down rivers of blood and imagining her husband as a Viking. The magical nature of both this list and the opening line truly show their power when Kasischke abandons the surreal and, with no transition, begins to describe real events from her life. She remembers her mother's declaration, "You'll always remember me . . . but someday you'll no longer be sad about me," while the image of her father smoking a cigarette lingers in her mind. By placing these real and mundane images in the same list as the surreal opening, she conflates the two realities. It makes no sense, in this poem, that her mother could die and that Kasischke's sadness could fade. Yet the reality is true, as shocking to her as the eyelid of a stone.

While the surreal is often employed to better understand the mundane, ordinary moments of life are often treated as sublime. In a collection so filled with quick movement and abundant imagery, quiet and calm narratives have their own magic. In "My son makes a gesture my mother used to make," a simple yet emotional moment is given careful contemplation. Here, Kasischke describes "The sun / in their eyes. / Fluttering their fingers. As if to disperse it." The fast-paced jumps of other poems are set aside and the language slows down, periods breaking the lines into incomplete phrases. At once sad and joyful, Kasischke celebrates a common gesture, "the miracle of it," even amid poems preoccupied with fabulist images and impossible feats.

Kasischke's eye for the commonplace is an important part of her project as a whole. The realities of life are as inescapable here as they are elsewhere, as "every morning we wake tethered to this planet by a rope around the ankle." Through previous poetry collections and novels, Kasischke has established herself as a writer who understands and appreciates the struggles of domestic life. By focusing on the domestic experiences common to many, though certainly not to all, she elevates these aspects of the world, treating that which is most common—death, family, loss—as that which is most significant, binding her audience together in the experience of it. Even when they depart into imagination, these poems are born out of the everyday. She announces this intention throughout the collection: "Look! I bear into this room a platter piled high with the rage my mother felt for my father! Yes, it's diamonds now. It's pearls, public humiliation, an angry dime-store clerk." There is no reason to hide the tragedies of domestic life, to turn away from the unhappiness of a married couple, or to ignore the loss of a loved one. Instead, these experiences are made the focus of Kasischke's lyric skill, set on a platter and presented to the reader like a gift.

Throughout her career, Kasischke has established several trademark styles, the noun list being the most evident here. While many of the poems operate as catalogues (the surreal memories of "Atoms on Loan" being one of the most successful examples), it is rare for more than a page or two to pass without a list of nouns. This form allows Kasischke an associative movement, with the images or ideas standing next to each other without the link of a clear explanation or action. She often forgoes any transition between her lists and the remainder of the poem. "Love poem," for instance, begins

> The water glass. The rain. The scale
> waiting for the weight. The car.
> The key. The rag. The dust. Once
> I was a much younger woman
> in a hallway, and I saw you:

The commonplace items listed at the start ring with a subtle rhythm and musicality. There are some pairings—water glass and rain, car and key, rag and dust—but for the most part Kasischke relies on these images to stand as they are. Once she has comfortably set into the list, however, she abruptly switches directions, and the rest of the poem is devoted to a meditation on her husband, their romance, and time itself. Rather than a meaningless redirection, the jump from mundane objects to an emotional outpouring is telling in and of itself. The collection is one in which daily life overflows with loss and love.

With its focus on death and despair, *Space, in Chains* definitely runs the risk of melodrama, especially in instances of straightforward narrative, when Kasischke provides moments so emotionally charged they might seem cheap to some readers. Recalling a night of teenage drinking and romance, she ends up lying

> on the damp lawn while
> the world
> made of danger, made of weight
> spun on without me
> and despite me
> for someone else's sake.

Kasischke favors these heightened moments, from the phone call announcing the death of a loved one to the scene of her own imagined death. Even in the context of the surreal, instances of near-melodrama slip in, as when her father is "in the massive shadows / of the columns / of the Museum of Griefs-to-Come." Moments such as these, along with her focus on female experience, link her clearly with confessional poets such as Sylvia Plath and Anne Sexton, whose style, while hugely influential, has fallen somewhat out of favor with contemporary poets. Certainly, Kasischke's focus on heightened emotions will deter some readers, but the collection ultimately makes a strong argument for the role of the dramatic, if not the melodramatic, in poetry; as she argues in "Life Support," "Why not the Victorians and their sentimental grief-wreaths woven from a loved one's hair?" Sentimentality, which would most often indicate a cheap emotion, is instead reclaimed as the artful "grief-wreath."

Ultimately, *Space, in Chains* is successful neither despite nor because of its emotional content. Instead, it is Kasischke's rare and powerful talent with imagery, lyricism, and form that makes the collection so successful and transforms the raw material of life into the artistry of "grief-wreaths." The poems sing with irregular rhymes, subtle word play, and inventive rhythms. Lines such as "Gall bladder, as goblin / Liver as dirty pet / Lungs panting like featherless squabs in a net" are delightful, bizarre, and memorable, inviting readers into the broken logic of death. Similarly, the illogic of "this river, / which is also the sky" and standing "on a mountaintop gulping air from a cup made of that thin stuff" are all comfortable here, earning their place in the collection if only because they are crafted with the same care and respect that Kasischke uses in crafting the news of her mother's death or the realization of her child's mortality. Her topics are massive, brimming with emotion, and, admittedly, poets have explored them countless times before. Brave and uncompromising, she still sets out to make the subject matter fresh. A cohesive collection, *Space, in Chains* showcases all of Kasischke's tools and talents, employing each one as she confronts the despair of loss and emerges lyric, energized, and alive.

T. Fleischmann

Review Sources

Library Journal 136, no. 1 (January 1, 2011): 101.
The New York Times Book Review, July 1, 2011, p. 17.
Publishers Weekly 257, no. 50 (December 20, 2010): 35.

The Splendor of Portugal

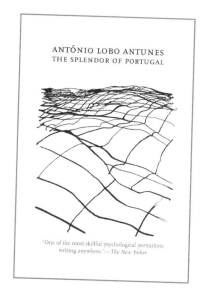

ANTÓNIO LOBO ANTUNES
THE SPLENDOR OF PORTUGAL

"One of the most skillful psychological portraitists writing anywhere."—*The New Yorker*

Author: António Lobo Antunes (b. 1942)
First published: *O Esplendor de Portugal,* 1997, in Portugal
Translated from the Portuguese by Rhett McNeil
Publisher: Dalkey Archive Press (Champaign, IL). 535 pp. $ 16.95.
Type of work: Novel
Time: July 24, 1978–December 24, 1995
Locale: Angola and Lisbon, Portugal

Another psychologically driven novel from successful storyteller António Lobo Antunes, this story examines the high price paid by a dysfunctional Portuguese settler family as they lose their African farm in the devastating postindependence civil war in Angola.

Principal characters:

ISILDA, a Portuguese woman born on a farm in Angola, wife of Amadeu and mother of Rui and Clarisse

CARLOS, the illegitimate son of Amadeu and a black Angolan woman, adopted by his father and Isilda

RUI, the epileptic son of Isilda and Amadeu

CLARISSE, the wayward daughter of Isilda and Amadeu

LENA, Carlos's working-class Portuguese wife

AMADEU, a Portuguese engineer living in Angola, husband of Isilda, and father of three, who becomes an alcoholic

EDUARDO, Isilda's father, a colonial farm owner

MARIA DA BOA MORTE, a black Angolan woman, servant of Isilda and mother figure to Carlos

JOSELIA, a black Angolan woman and devoted confidante of Isilda's mother

THE POLICE CHIEF, a colonial authority figure and Isilda's lover

The Splendor of Portugal tells the disillusioning story of a Portuguese family who loses their farm in Angola, an African country that was a colony of Portugal until 1975. While the three children, Carlos, Clarisse, and Rui, leave in 1978, their mother, Isilda, chooses to stay. Through the first-person narratives of the four major characters, author António Lobo Antunes reveals a dark, unflattering portrait of a dysfunctional family of former settlers who have lost everything, including their love for each other.

Structurally, Antunes organizes his narrative on two levels. At one level are the extended musings and flashbacks of the adult children on the occasion of Christmas

Magill's Literary Annual 2012

Eve 1995. For the first time in fifteen years, since he placed his epileptic half brother, Rui, in an institutional home and kicked out his half sister, Clarisse, Carlos has invited his siblings for Christmas Eve. He and his wife, Lena, prepare dinner together and wonder whether their guests will show up. At the other level of narration are the reflections of the children's mother, Isilda. When her children left for Lisbon, Portugal, in 1978, at the onset of the civil war engulfing Angola after its independence from Portugal, she chose to stay in Africa. The reflections of Isilda are organized chronologically, almost like a diary. They range from July 24, 1978, when her farm is occupied by Cuban invaders, to the climactic events of December 24, 1995. Throughout the novel, chapters of the children's reflections alternate with chapters told by Isilda.

From the outset, it is obvious that the main characters are neither particularly likable nor innocent. While in power in Angola, they did not treat their African workers well. As part of the Portuguese ruling class, they exploited and harassed the Africans who depended on them economically, even keeping a haughty distance from their African staff in the family home. At the same time, they suffered from major problems in their own family life.

Isilda grew up as a treasured daughter of a relatively well-off farming family. However, she knew her father, Eduardo, cheated on her mother, who retreated into her own world of religion. Tellingly, when her mother dies, Isilda seeks the comfort of her servant, Joselia, instead of members of her own family.

Isilda marries the engineer Amadeu. He is depicted as a rather weak character. Like Isilda's family and friends, readers may wonder what Isilda sees in this rather pathetic young man. Only toward the end is the suspicion raised that Isilda may have been pregnant at the time of her wedding. Isilda vehemently denies this, however, and the novel leaves this question open.

Amadeu had a premarital affair with a black African canteen worker, who bears him his son Carlos. Soon after his birth, Carlos is adopted by Amadeu and Isilda as their son. However, his partially black features, even though they are not dominant, give him a lower status in colonial society. They also show the lack of his biological bond with at least one of his white parents. In turn, Carlos gravitates to the black African household servant Maria da Boa Morte.

As the oldest son, Carlos is set to inherit the farm, which, according to his and his sibling's musings, is the reason Lena agrees to marry him. From a working-class white family at the bottom of Portuguese society in Angola, Lena views Carlos as a way out of poverty, despite his mixed ethnic heritage. In Portugal, their marriage slowly breaks apart, and Lena leaves Carlos on that fateful Christmas Eve in 1995.

Taking charge of his half siblings upon their arrival in Lisbon, Carlos soon becomes resentful of them. After two years, he puts Rui into a home for the mentally and physically disabled. Because Clarisse is rather promiscuous, Carlos kicks her out of the small apartment his family owns in Lisbon.

Even though Rui has a physical handicap, the novel depicts him as a cruel and inconsiderate person. He tortures animals and torments his family's African laborers by shooting his pellet gun at them. In the case of Rui, as with all his Portuguese characters, Antunes seeks to illustrate that the role of victim and victimizer can be embodied in one person.

With her desire for sexual fulfillment through relations with various men (from tractor drivers on the farm to a rich, older man in Lisbon), Clarisse is perhaps the character least explored psychologically in the novel. Her wild sexuality is shown as a given, and Antunes does not pursue its possible causes.

António Lobo Antunes, an award-winning Portuguese author of more than twenty novels, is known for criticizing aspects of his society. His sixth novel, Auto dos danados *(1985;* Act of the Damned, *1993), won the Portuguese Writers' Association Grand Prize. He has since received numerous other international literary prizes.*

In Angola, in the days before the civil war, Isilda began an affair with the cruel local police chief. As Amadeu descends into alcoholism, Isilda makes love with the police chief right in her home. To the chagrin of Carlos, she does not hide this affair at all. The police chief teases Carlos for his mixed ethnic heritage and occasionally abuses him physically. Because the police chief is hated by the Portuguese farmers, who resent his reckless abuse of power, nobody gives him a space on the boats leaving Angola in 1978. In scenes of karmic justice, the police chief meets his fate when he is hunted down by the Cuban soldiers sent to support the Communist side in Angola's civil war. Isilda is forced to flee the family farm with her remaining servants, and the novel leaves her ultimate fate somewhat open-ended; however, there is a strong implication that she too has been met with a violent comeuppance.

The *Splendor of Portugal* presents its readers with stylistic challenges because Antunes employs stream-of-conscious narration and renders most of the events through his characters' interior monologues and troubled memories. A trademark of the novel's style is the constant repetition of phrases, sentences, and paragraphs, which symbolizes the obsessive nature of memory and the consistent return of previously repressed traumatic events. This style has earned Antunes a justified comparison with the Nobel Prize–winning American novelist William Faulkner. Indeed, passages of *The Splendor of Portugal* read like Faulkner's famous novel *The Sound and the Fury* (1929). Like Faulkner's Benji Compson, Rui is disabled. However, unlike Faulkner's character, Rui has a dark, cruel side, which manifests in his violence toward humans and animals alike.

In Europe, and especially in his native Portugal, Antunes has become a celebrated author. His name is often mentioned as a contender for the Nobel Prize in Literature. Upon the insistence of his upper-class father, Antunes studied medicine. He served as a physician in the Portuguese army in colonial Angola from 1971 to 1973, when Portugal was fighting a war against African rebels there. His writings have often looked at Portugal's connections with its former colonies, specifically Angola. *The Splendor of Portugal* portrays the Portuguese colonials in Angola in a rather negative light. In fact, the title is an ironic reference to a line in Portugal's national anthem. There is nothing splendid about the novel's Portuguese characters, who Antunes endows with few redeeming features.

Originally written in 1997, The *Splendor of Portugal* is one of Antunes's key works; his other works are being translated into English at an increasing pace. At the time of the book's original publication, civil war between communist and anticommunist, primarily southern Angolan rebel forces, was still raging, with a high level of atrocities being committed. Only in 2002 did peace come to Angola with the killing of the rebel leader, Jonas Savimbi, whose group, UNITA, is mentioned throughout Antunes's novel. For an American readership, a brief outline of the larger conflict in Angola, perhaps in a critical introduction, would have been a helpful editorial addition. Nonetheless, interested readers can easily inform themselves about this long, brutal postindependence war in southern Africa.

Even though Antunes's Portuguese characters are far from likeable, they suffer like so many other people affected by the Angolan civil war. In one of her interior monologues toward the end of the novel, Isilda squarely blames the government of Portugal for abandoning Angola to civil war. For Isilda, the Portuguese government never liked or valued its own citizens in Angola. In her view, the government caved in to American, Russian, and other nations' interest in the African country, which resulted in a devastating civil war that was fueled by Cold War enmity between the superpowers.

The Splendor of Portugal is a demanding and deeply psychological novel. The ambiguous Portuguese characters are caught in a particularly brutal conflict that leaves them devastated emotionally. The plot highlights narrative subjectivity, and the story's narration itself echoes the endless rambling of a traumatized human mind. Indeed, the novel's refusal to present clear-cut good or evil characters (perhaps with the exception of the dictatorial police chief) represents its greatest literary strength. Readers are sure to find that in *The Splendor of Portugal* Antunes has created a literary work of great merit.

R. C. Lutz

Review Sources

The Paris Review, July 26, 2011 (Web).
Read This Next, August 29, 2011 (Web).

Steve Jobs

Author: Walter Isaacson (b. 1952)
Publisher: Simon & Schuster (New York). Illustrated. 656 pp. $35.00
Type of work: Biography, current affairs
Time: 1955–2011
Locale: United States

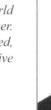

Steve Jobs by Walter Isaacson

© Albert Watson

Isaacson offers an extremely detailed and appreciative biography of Steve Jobs, the computer and marketing genius who helped transform the lives of people throughout the world through one innovative product after another. Isaacson presents Jobs as a driven, inspired, and inventive man who could be both abrasive and abusive in dealing with others.

Principal personages:

STEVE JOBS (1955–2011), one of the leaders of the technological revolution that helped transform the world in the last quarter of the twentieth century
LEE CLOW, advertising executive who helped market products designed by Jobs
TIM COOK, chief operating officer at Apple Computer Company and Jobs's successor
BILL GATES (b. 1955), software mogul and founder of Microsoft; Jobs's longtime rival
JONATHAN "JONY" IVE (b. 1967), chief designer at Apple during Jobs's second tenure there
JOHN LASSETER (b. 1957), filmmaker and partner of Jobs at the Pixar film animation company
LAURENE POWELL, Jobs's wife beginning in 1991 and the mother of three of his four children
JOHN SCULLEY, Jobs's choice as chief executive officer of Apple in 1983; in 1985, he helped fire Jobs from Apple
STEVE WOZNIAK (b. 1950), talented computer engineer who was Jobs's close friend and original partner in Apple

In 2004, six years before his death in 2011, Steve Jobs approached Walter Isaacson, a distinguished biographer, and proposed that Isaacson write the story of his life. Isaacson resisted the invitation, suggesting that it might be better to wait another ten or twenty years. Jobs was persistent, and in 2009, Jobs's wife told Isaacson that in light of a severe recurrence of Jobs's cancer, the time for writing the book had come. Jobs promised not to interfere in the project and apparently kept his word.

Committed to presenting an accurate portrait of Jobs even as he was dying, Isaacson has produced a book that is admirably frank, if also somewhat depressing in the end. The depressing aspect of this work, however, comes not because it concludes with a death but because of the basic facts of Jobs's life. He was an enormously gifted man. Indeed, Isaacson concurs with the widespread opinion that he was a creative genius whose work fundamentally transformed human life. All the sadder, then, that he was apparently so often mean (in various senses of the word) in so many other ways. Anyone who naively assumes that genius and simple decency go hand in hand need only read Isaacson's dark but illuminating volume.

Jobs was put up for adoption by his birth mother soon after he was born. He met her again only many years later, after he had become rich and famous. He never wanted to have anything to do with his birth father, and he never did (although they actually met once through a strange coincidence, without either realizing their connection). Fortunately, Jobs was adopted by a loving couple who recognized his intelligence from an early age. His birth parents—his "sperm and egg bank," as he would later call them—had let him go, but his adoptive parents showed him great love and even exceptional deference. As Isaacson puts it, summing up the first twenty years of Jobs's life: "Abandoned. Chosen. Special. Those concepts became part of who Jobs was and how he regarded himself." Jobs soon began to consider himself a genius, and the way he treated himself and others over the five-and-a-half decades of his life often reflected that lofty self-evaluation. In dealing with others, he was frequently petty, cruel, stingy, and dishonest. In pursuing his own goals, he was typically driven, determined, and often visionary, with a real and important talent for promoting himself and his products. He also had the good fortune, on several significant occasions, to run into people whose gifts supplemented his own.

First and foremost among these was Steve Wozniak, an immensely talented and slightly older engineer whom Jobs met while he was still in high school. Wozniak, who emerges in this book as in every sense a true gentleman, possessed technical skills that Jobs lacked, and it was largely the result of their initial partnership that Jobs eventually became rich and famous. Thus, it is disappointing to read that early in their relationship, when Jobs was paid a bonus for a minor innovation on which he and Wozniak had collaborated, he kept the bonus secret from Wozniak and pocketed it himself, a fact that Wozniak did not discover until a decade later. "I wish he had just been honest," Wozniak remarks. "If he had told me he needed the money, he should have known I would have just given it to him. He was a friend. You help your friends." That, at least, is how Wozniak saw circumstances. Jobs was consistently far less generous in his treatment of friends and many others. In fact, this was not the last time that Wozniak would be literally shortchanged by Jobs. Such behavior continued even after the two founded the Apple Computer Company, one of the most successful businesses in history.

Jobs had many talents that Wozniak did not possess, including an exceptional obsession with design (shapes and colors always had to be just exactly right), a flair for marketing, and a series of consistently grand and often prescient visions about what computers could and must do. Jobs was as contemptuous of competing products as he often was of other people. He also had a "gift" (if one can call it that) of appropriating others' ideas and passing them off as his own. His perfectionism was legendary, but so were his disloyalty, abrasiveness, abusiveness, and lack of generosity, both financial and otherwise. At one point, for example, an old and close friend of Jobs worked in a mid-level

(Patrice Gilbert)

Walter Isaacson, formerly a senior executive at both CNN and Time *magazine, is president of the Aspen Institute, an organization established to promote responsible public leadership. He is the author of acclaimed biographies of Albert Einstein, Benjamin Franklin, and Henry Kissinger.*

position at Apple. He had repeatedly helped Jobs before Jobs became fabulously wealthy, and he assumed that Jobs would give him some stock options before Apple went public. Instead, Jobs ignored him. Rod Holt, another friend who was entitled to options, tried to change Jobs's mind, even offering to match what Jobs would provide. Jobs snidely refused. Meanwhile, Wozniak made sure that forty different comparable colleagues would benefit handsomely from the sale of Apple shares. Jobs did give his adoptive parents, whom he genuinely loved, $750,000 worth of stock, although his own take from the initial offering was $256 million.

One phrase that appears repeatedly in Isaacson's book is "reality distortion field," a euphemism coined to describe Jobs's frequent disregard for the truth as well as his refusal to really hear others' differing ideas (unless their ideas later proved sound, in which case he often claimed he had thought of them himself). Many friends, loved ones, and colleagues found this trait, as well as his extreme temper, maddening. Partly because of such traits, Jobs was eventually ousted as head of Apple (only to return years later when the company was on the skids). Jobs possessed, or was possessed by, an extreme need for control, and clearly his various kinds of obsession helped promote the success of many, if not all, of the ventures to which he committed himself. Yet, one cannot help wondering, as one reads Isaacson's book, if Jobs might not have accomplished just as much, if not more, had he simply treated other people with a bit more decency. Isaacson shows repeatedly that Jobs believed that normal rules did not apply to him, an attitude responsible for some of both the best and worst traits of his character. Again and again, Jobs broke down and cried when he felt that he had not been treated fairly, not often realizing, it seems, the irony of such behavior.

After being booted from Apple, Jobs formed NeXT, another computer company, but his real salvation came from his involvement with Pixar, the company that revolutionized animated films. In this case, once again, he had the good fortune to partner with someone (the filmmaker John Lasseter) whose talents were crucial to the company's future. The enormous success of *Toy Story* (1995) was, in large part, the result of Pixar's devotion to its original vision of that film. Jobs's achievements at Pixar led to his reinvolvement with the floundering Apple in the late 1990s.

It was then that Jobs entered, arguably, his most creative period. His original success at Apple had depended greatly on the engineering skills of Wozniak; now, however, he was much more fully his own man, doing things that even longtime rival Bill Gates had to concede were impressive. These included not only the iMac computer but also the iPhone, iPod, and especially the iPad. Other companies had been making computers that were both more popular and more widely used than the early Apple machines, but the various "i" machines had few true competitors. In the final decade of his life, Jobs genuinely could claim to have "dented the universe"—one of his great ambitions. Here again, though, he was lucky to have a gifted and relatively unsung collaborator, Jony Ive, one of the many partners in Jobs's career who later came to feel underappreciated. The success of Apple, in the first decade of the twenty-first century, was widely, and unfairly, always attributed to Jobs alone.

Yet Jobs's final triumphs were accompanied by personal tragedies. The most obvious of these was his cancer, which was first diagnosed in 2003. It was eventually beaten back, when, after nine months of stubborn refusal, Jobs finally agreed to have surgery. In the meantime, he had relied on alternative treatments. By the time of the surgery, the cancer had spread. In 2008, it returned ferociously. This time, Jobs used his enormous wealth to ensure he could be ready for a quick liver transplant. When an organ became available, he flew in his private jet from California to Memphis to receive it. Although fawned over in Memphis, Jobs did not seem to be especially appreciative. In fact, perhaps the most depressing moment in the book occurs when Isaacson recounts how Jobs, having refused to follow his doctors' advice to have his stomach pumped before a small procedure, contracted nearly fatal pneumonia as a result. However, instead of accepting any responsibility for this outcome, he blamed medical personnel.

Coping with cancer in the final decade of his life did not particularly mellow Jobs; it seems unlikely, however, that anything ever did or ever could have. More than the cancer, readers will likely assess that the true tragedy of Jobs's last years was that he rarely treated others as well as he expected to be treated. Near the end of this book, Isaacson comments, "The nasty edge to [Jobs's] personality was not necessary. It hindered him more than it helped him. But it did, at times, serve a purpose . . . Dozens of the colleagues whom Jobs abused ended their litany of horror stories by saying that he got them to do things they never dreamed possible." This fact deserves emphasis, especially in the face of all the disappointing data this extremely honest book contains.

Many readers will close this volume feeling regret. Jobs accomplished great things. He imagined and marketed magnificent products, created many jobs, and fostered the freedom and creativity of other people. In all these ways, he benefited millions. However, it seems he did not give any real thought to ensuring his legacy beyond hoping that his company would survive and would stay at the forefront of technological innovation. At the time of his death, there was no "Steve Jobs Foundation," heavily endowed and committed to accomplishing worthy and important goals. (One thinks, in contrast, of industrialist-philanthropists Andrew Carnegie, Andrew Mellon, Henry Ford, and even Gates.) There was, perhaps most surprisingly, no Steve Jobs medical center or institute for cancer research. Also, although Jobs was thinking, at the end of his life, about ways to transform teaching and textbook marketing, he established no educational foundation before he died. In this respect, at least, Gates may be the ultimate winner of the long competition between the two to achieve, and to leave, a lasting legacy. Isaacson's biography of Jobs celebrates his accomplishments passionately and at length, without ever lapsing into shallow idolatry.

Robert C. Evans

Review Sources

Business Insider, December 10, 2011 (Web).
The Guardian, October 25, 2011 (Web).
The Independent, November 4, 2011 (Web).
Los Angeles Times, October 29, 2011 (Web).
Money Week, November 16, 2011 (Web).
The New Yorker 87, no. 36 (November 14, 2011): 32–35.
The Washington Post, October 23, 2011 (Web).

Stone Arabia

Author: Dana Spiotta (b. 1966)
Publisher: Scribner (New York). 256 pp.
$24.00
Type of work: Novel
Time: 2004, with flashbacks to the 1970s and
1980s
Locale: Primarily Los Angeles, California

*Spiotta presents a fragmented and fascinating
portrait of a brother and sister who wrestle
with the past in order to come to terms with
where they are in the present.*

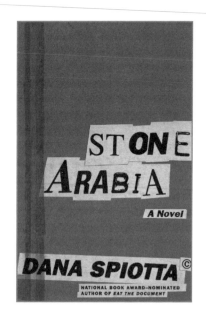

Principal characters:
NIKOLAS "NIK" THEODORE KRANIS, a reclusive
   rock musician
DENISE KRANIS, Nik's sister
ADA VOGEL, Denise's daughter
ELLA KRANIS, Nik and Denise's mother
JAY, Denise's boyfriend

Dana Spiotta first gained critical notice with her first novel, *Lightning Field* (2001),
and the critically acclaimed follow-up, *Eat the Document* (2006), a finalist for the
National Book Award in fiction. She has been praised for her thoughtful novels,
which take the time to examine how American culture radically changed from the
late twentieth to early twenty-first centuries. Spiotta herself grew up in California
and has used her knowledge of the area to add color to her fiction. With its setting
in Los Angeles, Spiotta's third novel, *Stone Arabia*, is no exception. It was made
evident in *Lightning Field* that Spiotta knows the pulse of Los Angeles extremely
well. Author Diane Leslie praised her for creating characters that "slink about in a
Los Angeles that is hazy, not with smog, but with ever-smoldering, addictive sub-
stances." Spiotta goes directly to the heart of self-obsession as it exists in an environment that itself relishes make-believe and breathes the air of fantasy. Mood is
imperative with regards to setting, and Spiotta has proven that she knows how to
get it right. Additionally, she was credited in *Kirkus Reviews* with writing "fiction as
documentary, a coruscating, heartrending fable of struggle and loss." In her novels,
the "struggle" is clearly related to the turbulence that transpires when isolated characters must reconcile their private identities with a wider, public scrutiny. The "loss"
is what almost inevitably takes place when characters cannot endure that scrutiny.
Obviously, it can pose a threatening challenge to identities that are invented in private and are, in some cases, as fanciful as a fairy tale. Spiotta is well aware of how
individuals author themselves differently in private and public, and in *Stone Arabia*,

she follows a brother and sister for whom reality and fantasy are at odds, personally and emotionally.

In writing *Stone Arabia*, Spiotta clearly immersed herself in the music of the era in order to infuse her prose. In each segment, the author found inspiration in building the narrative sentence by sentence until she had the novel she wanted. The story sheds light on a figure that never made it big as a musician, Nik Kranis, also known as Nik Worth and Nik Kat. He has suffered for his art, yet has not been rewarded with the obvious trappings of stardom. Spiotta describes Nik as someone who, having shown early promise, has chosen to live as a recluse. He is his own worst enemy. If he were truly seeking to be a phenomenon and not merely a musician, Nik would have had to chart another course of action. Unable to bring himself to do everything possible to become a rock star in reality, Nik has invented a self-contained world in which he is a success. Growing up, his only true fans were his sister, Denise, and a few close friends. It became Denise's fate to be her brother's keeper, and she has refused to give up on him no matter what happens. As a teenager in the 1970s, Nik was inspired to learn the guitar in order to join the ranks of the rock stars he admired. Since then, however, he imitated of those lifelong musicians whose delusional refusal to relinquish their dreams and ambitions has isolated them from everyone else. Nik has stopped performing music and set about creating an entire world of his own making.

At a glance, the novel appears to be a crazy quilt of different perspectives, with Spiotta narrating the story from both siblings' points of view and leaving readers to sift through the evidence and decide for themselves where the truth starts and fantasy ends. Her formal choices raise questions about the role of creative persons in society. Is the creative person supposed to follow the same sort of rule book as everyone else? The narrative structure of the novel offers no easy answers.

As he nears the age of fifty, Nik is a part-time bartender with no prospects, little money, and no outward evidence of success. Whenever he is short on funds, he must turn to his ever-loyal sister to save the day, but both siblings face complications in their lives. It is evident that Denise, who is close to financial ruin herself, cannot keep supporting her beloved brother forever. Denise is "an absorber of events," compulsively watching television and experiencing severe emotional reactions at a program's slightest provocation. Similarly, Nik has spent years and years building his own fantasy haven. He has pieced together volume after volume of "the Chronicles," a series of scrapbooks that tracks his life as a brilliant musician in detail after extraordinary detail. Spiotta produces these fragments, reviews, inside jokes, and more in order to present Nik's state of mind and the vast web of fiction that it has produced. In addition to the Chronicles, Nik has self-produced CDs of his music called "The Ontology of Worth." Denise meanwhile attempts to save her brother and herself, with varying degrees of success.

As the author moves from one narrative voice to another, the pieces of the story bleed together. Nik has his first person narrative, as does Denise. There is also a third person narration that adds clarity to the novel. With these different voices, it is obvious that Spiotta is establishing competing versions of reality for the reader. Each one bounces off the other. Each character faces memories that keep them rooted, some of which are real and some of which are manufactured, while others fall into a very gray

(Jessica Marx)

Dana Spiotta is the author of Lightning Field *(2001), a* New York Times *Notable Book of the Year, and* Eat the Document *(2006), a finalist for the National Book Award in fiction. She teaches in the Master of Fine Arts program at Syracuse University.*

area. Nik exists in his own creative and fabricated world, in which the difference between reality and fantasy has become especially difficult to define.

In each of Spiotta's novels, the reader is confronted with the idea of how a person is built for public consumption, an idea that many reviewers have traced back to similar cultural critiques in the fiction of postmodern novelist Don DeLillo. There is both self-invention and self-obsession—are these two halves of the same coin? When Nik suddenly disappears, Denise is left to fear the worst and speculate on Nik's true story. She discovers Nik's lengthy self-made newspaper obituary, which he has left for her to find. He includes an opening that reads as if it is "nearly verbatim from Elvis's *New York Times* obituary." With the mention of a "hermitage" on Skyline Drive in Topanga Canyon, Nik attributes to himself a reference to American musician Neil Young. Even in his fabricated obituary, there are inside jokes that Denise has to interpret with close scrutiny.

While Nik has barricaded himself away from the world, Denise is left to come up with a solution for her family's problems. It has become her role to make everything right and look out for everyone else. However, having to be the stable member of a family can be difficult. As Denise's mother is lost to Alzheimer disease, Spiotta examines the aging process and the way the human mind can turn on itself. Each character in the novel is impacted by this same process in different ways. Denise, for example, continues to fixate on and respond strongly to televised news stories, as it becomes increasingly difficult for her to detach herself from these tragedies. In her everyday life, she does her best to put up with Nik, her daughter, her mother, and her boyfriend, who is obsessed with the paintings of American artist Thomas Kinkade and does not believe in keeping himself clean for the benefit of others. As the novel plays out over the course of 2004, Denise seems to realize that the carefree existence that worked so well when she and Nik were younger has now become careless, even reckless. From Denise's detective-like work, it becomes clear that Nik's withdrawal from the music business can be traced back to 1979–80, when Nik gave up on his group, the Fakes (an intentionally ironic name, to be sure), and became the recluse she has to deal with today.

Spiotta has placed Denise at the center of *Stone Arabia*, performing to a tune played by others, like the dancing bear in the center ring of the circus. Ada, her twenty-something daughter, comes back to Los Angeles to make a documentary film about Nik called "Garageland" and interviews her mother about the period in the 1970s when

Nik was on the verge of a breakthrough. As Ada works on completing her film, Denise does her best to go about her life, until a tragedy on the news hits her hard. In the upstate New York village of Stone Arabia, an Amish child has gone missing. Denise feels obligated to fly back east in order to see for herself what has really happened, rationalizing the visit as a way to see Ada, who has returned to New York City after finishing the documentary. However, the journey is mandatory for Denise's well-being, signaling the degree of her involvement with her televised reality.

In the final chapter of the novel, entitled "1972," Denise remembers how she and Nik spent so much time as children without "supervision," which meant "whole evenings of uninterrupted fantasy" for the two siblings. No matter what, Nik and Denise are forever linked in this sense. In the role that fantasy played and continues to play in their lives, they are almost interchangeable.

With *Stone Arabia*, Spiotta looks behind the curtain to examine flawed characters who have not mastered how to succeed in the so-called real world. The beauty of the novel can be found in the alternate existences that the characters forge for themselves and how isolation takes its toll.

Jeffry Jensen

Review Sources

Booklist 107, nos. 19/20 (June 1/15, 2011): 37.
The Boston Globe, July 17, 2011, p. K7.
Library Journal 136, no. 9 (May 15, 2011): 81.
Los Angeles Times, July 17, 2011, p. E8.
The New York Times Book Review, July 10, 2011, p. 9.
Publishers Weekly 258, no. 14 (April 4, 2011): 28.
The Wall Street Journal, September 17, 2011, p. C8.
The Washington Post, July 25, 2011, p. C4.

The Stranger's Child

Author: Alan Hollinghurst (b. 1954)
Publisher: Alfred A. Knopf (New York).
448 pp. $27.95
Type of work: Novel
Time: 1913–2008
Locale: England

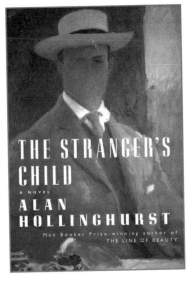

Hollinghurst's fifth novel, The Stranger's Child, *is a complex study of English society, sexual mores, literary creation, and the reliability of memory and biography told through the history of the Valance and Sawle families from 1913 to 2008.*

Principal characters:
CECIL VALANCE, aristocrat, poet, and both
    Daphne's and George's lover
DAPHNE SAWLE VALANCE RALPH JACOBS, recipi-
    ent of poem "Two Acres," thrice-married matriarch
GEORGE SAWLE, Daphne's brother and Cecil's lover
HUBERT SAWLE, Daphne's oldest brother
FREDA SAWLE, widowed mother of Daphne, George, and Hubert
HARRY HEWITT, sexually interested in Hubert
DUDLEY VALANCE, Cecil's younger brother and Daphne's first husband
MADELEINE SAWLE, George Sawle's wife
REVEL RALPH, Daphne's second husband
SEBASTIAN "SEBBY" STOKES, first biographer of Cecil Valance
CORINNA VALANCE KEEPING, Daphne's daughter
WILFRID VALANCE, Daphne's son, who takes care of her in her old age
PAUL BRYANT, second biographer of Cecil Valance
PETER ROWE, teacher at the Corley Court preparatory school and Paul's lover
JENNY RALPH, Daphne's granddaughter

The Stranger's Child by Alan Hollinghurst is a complex, multithemed novel. Hollinghurst recounts the interweaving story of the aristocratic Valance family and the middle-class Sawle family from 1913 to 2008. The novel is divided into five sections, each of which is both a self-contained story and, at the same time, an essential element in the development of the larger novel. Considerable amounts of time pass between the various sections. Thus, as each section begins, the reader has a sense of bewilderment and the pleasure of discovering how the characters' lives have changed. Hollinghurst slowly informs the reader of the new situations of the various characters.

The first section, entitled "Two Acres," introduces the two central characters of the novel, Cecil Valance and Daphne Sawle. Cecil is a student at Cambridge, a poet, and a member of the "secret" Cambridge intellectual society known as The Apostles. He is gay but retains a sexual interest in women as well. Cecil comes to Two Acres, the Sawle family's home, as a guest of the younger Sawle brother, George, who is also a student at Cambridge and Cecil's lover. George's sister, Daphne, is immediately infatuated with Cecil. She asks him to sign her autograph book, and he writes the "Two Acres" poem in her book, a poem that brings him subsequent fame.

The second section, entitled "Revel," takes place in 1926. Cecil, who was killed in France during World War I, has posthumously become famous as a poet and lies buried in a marble tomb in the family chapel at Corley Court, the three-thousand-acre family estate. Daphne has become the wife of Cecil's younger brother, Dudley, and has two children, Corinna and Wilfrid. Family members and friends arrive to be interviewed by Sebastian Stokes, who is writing a biography of Cecil. Relationships become strained. No one is pleased to be there, largely because of Dudley, a heavy drinker who takes a sadistic pleasure in sarcastically mistreating others and belittling Cecil's writing and who covers up the estate's Edwardian architecture, which he abhors.

"Steady Boys Steady," the third section, is set in 1967. Once again, the family members are coming together, this time to celebrate Daphne's seventieth birthday. As the chapters progress, readers learn that much has changed in the characters' lives. Daphne has been twice remarried since fleeing Dudley, first to artist Revel Ralph and then to a businessman named Jacobs. Corley Court has become a preparatory school. Corinna is married to an emotionally disturbed bank manager and teaches piano at Corley Court. Hollinghurst also introduces two important new characters—Paul Bryant, a clerk at the bank, and Peter Rowe, a teacher at the school, who become involved in a homosexual relationship and both adore Cecil's writing.

The next section, entitled "Something of a Poet," set in the 1970s and 1980s, depicts Paul Bryant pursuing members of the Valance-Sawle family as he writes his biography of Cecil. Bryant is more interested in Cecil's private life and on the individuals connected to him than his poetry, and he interviews Jonah Trickett, Cecil's valet during his stay at Two Acres, as well as George and Daphne.

In the final section of the novel, "Old Companions," set in 2008, Jenny Ralph and Julian Keeping are the only Valance-Sawle family members who appear. While Julian has deteriorated into a pitiful human being, Jenny, a professor of French, is definitely in control of her life. She resents the content of Bryant's biography but states that it has no importance because all of it is merely part of the faded past. At Chadwick's Antique and Second-Hand, antiquarian book dealer Rob Salter is shown a letter book belonging to Harry Hewitt, an admirer of Cecil. In the back of the book are a few transcriptions of letters from Cecil to Hewitt. The remains of Hewitt's possessions are being cleared from his house, and Rob rushes off in the hope of finding the original correspondence.

The saga of the Valance and Sawle families provides a fictional world in which Hollinghurst explores a number of themes. One of these key themes is how literary reputations are created and how they change with the passing of time. Immediately

Award-winning British novelist Alan Hollinghurst has written five books, the first of which, The Swimming Pool Library *(1988), won the Somerset Maugham Award. He received the Man Booker Prize for* The Line of Beauty *in 2004. For* The Stranger's Child, *he was chosen as the 2011 Waterstone's UK Author of the Year.*

after World War I, the deceased Cecil, who had written poems about life in the trenches, becomes a highly admired and important poet. The verses of "Two Acres" are learned and recited by the general populace throughout the country. However, as time passes, people become less fascinated with the war, and literary styles change. Cecil's fame and reputation continually dwindle. By the end of the novel, only letters and diaries containing evidence of his gay lifestyle excite any interest, and the interest in them is primarily as expensive collectors' items.

The Stranger's Child also explores the unreliability of memory and biography and shows how both distort the truth, intentionally and unintentionally. Both Sebastian Stokes and Paul Bryant write biographies of Cecil Valance. Stokes writes his in 1926, when Cecil is still valued as a talented war poet; Stokes's biography includes nothing scandalous. Bryant writes his biography in the late 1970s and early 1980s, and his text concentrates on Cecil's bisexual exploits and also reveals scandals about his friends and family, including the insistence that Cecil, not Dudley, was the father of Corinna, Daphne's daughter. George Sawle is Bryant's source, and readers are led to wonder how reliable George is. Is he seeking the attention that was denied him when Daphne was assumed to be the "you" in the poem "Two Acres" (a poem that was written for him)? The problem of reliability of memoirs and biographies is further illustrated by Daphne's admission that in her memoirs, *Short Gallery*, she invented the conversations because she could not possibly remember what everyone actually said.

The novel also elucidates the changes in attitude toward gay men and their lifestyle. In 1913, George and Cecil seek dark, secluded areas to engage in sexual activity with each other, and they always keep their relationship secret. George's mother, Freda Sawle, is appalled when she finds the letters Cecil has written to George. Still later, when Paul and Peter meet, secrecy is important. They seek privacy and assurance that no one will discover them. By contrast, when the story concludes in 2008, Peter's gay friends are united in civil partnerships and refer to their partners as husbands.

Hollinghurst is a master of detail. His lengthy and detailed descriptions of the gardens and woods of Two Acres and of the English countryside imbue the novel with a poetic ambiance that creates an impression of a pastoral poem written in prose and reflects the importance of Cecil's poem "Two Acres" in the lives of the characters. Hollinghurst also uses description as a structural device, linking the parts of the novel together and emphasizing the deterioration and animosity that fill the lives of the Valances and the Sawles. For instance, the jelly-mold domes of Corley Court reappear at several times throughout the novel. In the section "Two Acres," both George and Daphne are fascinated by the jelly-mold domes, which represent the affluence of the Valances and underline the financial and social distance between the two families. In "Revel," Dudley boxes up the molds while redecorating the mansion, a symbolic rejection of his family and the world that has preferred Cecil's writing to his. In "Steady

Boys Steady," a mishap in the house leads Peter and Paul to discover the jelly-mold domes, foreshadowing Paul's investigation into the secrets of the two families. Hollinghurst is also skilled at giving a significant amount of information about a character through a brief description. For instance, the account of Corinna bouncing, shifting, and virtually dominating the piano while playing the duet with Peter informs readers that Corinna has much in common with her grandmother, Lady Valance.

Irony is used effectively throughout the novel. Cecil Valance is heir to the extensive Corley Court, yet he writes a poem that immortalizes two acres of land, bringing him the type of fame that none of his works about Corley Court has elicited. Daphne's son, Wilfrid, will inherit his father's title and become a baron, yet he lives in Olga, a house built by Lady Caroline Messent for her old cook. From his first encounters with the Valance-Sawle family, Paul Bryant is quickly cast in a servile role. Later, however, as a biographer, he comes to wield immense power over the family's reputation.

The Stranger's Child is also a novel about writing and literature. The title is taken from a verse in Alfred, Lord Tennyson's poem "In Memoriam A. H. H.," which celebrated male friendship. Hollinghurst also prefaces three sections of the novel with literary quotes. The final one is taken from Mick Imlah's "In Memoriam Alfred Lord Tennyson." The quote proposes that everyone, even a famous writer such as Tennyson, will eventually pass from memory. Thus, the quote surrounds the novel with Tennyson, who praised men's friendship. The quote also emphasizes how writing and writers, no matter how exquisite the work is, are eventually abandoned into a shadowy past. Throughout the text, Hollinghurst mentions and alludes to many writers, including Rupert Brook, Lytton Strachey, Evelyn Waugh, and Henry James. This adds a significantly pleasing feature to the novel for those familiar with English literature. Hollinghurst also includes excerpts from the literary works, diaries, and letters of his characters, especially in "Somewhat of a Poet."

The vast majority of its critics have recognized *The Stranger's Child* as an exceptionally well-written novel. A few critics, however, have objected to the long descriptive passages and have found the characters too emotionally divided. The novel was under consideration for the 2011 Man Booker Prize but, surprisingly, was not included in the short list. Hollinghurst was chosen as the 2011 Waterstone's UK Author of the Year for his work on the novel.

Shawncey J. Webb

Review Sources

London Review of Books 33, no. 15 (July 28, 2011): 9–10.
The New York Times, November 1, 2011, p. C1.
The New York Times Book Review October 23, 2011, p. 12.

The Summer Without Men

Author: Siri Hustvedt (b. 1955)
Publisher: Picador (New York). 192 pp. $14.00
Type of work: Novel
Time: The present
Locale: Bonden, Minnesota; Brooklyn, New York

Faced with a midlife crisis and turbulence in her marriage, a poet returns to her hometown and finds strength in forging connections with teenage girls, older women, and a young mother.

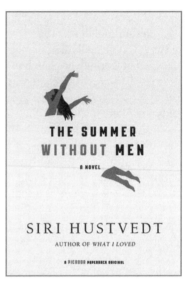

Principal characters:

MIA FREDRICKSEN, a poet and professor who must reconsider her life when her husband of thirty years requests a "pause" in their marriage

BORIS IZCOVICH, Mia's husband, a neuroscientist who has become romantically involved with a younger colleague

DAISY, Mia's adult daughter, who acts as peacemaker between Mia and Boris

THE FIVE SWANS, a group of older women living in an housing community, including Mia's mother and Abigail, a nonagenarian who creates subtly subversive needlework art

LOLA, a young woman whom Mia befriends, the harried mother of two young children

THE POETRY CLASS, a group of seven adolescent girls, including sensitive Alice

MR. NOBODY, an anonymous e-mail correspondent who sends Mia provocative messages

In *The Summer Without Men,* Siri Hustvedt weaves together overlapping stories of communities of women at the different stages of life that correspond to the tripartite goddess of legend: maiden, mother, and crone. While many of the woman are, like protagonist Mia Fredricksen, "without men," men still play a defining role in the women's lives, and their absence is itself a kind of presence. Mia is a published poet and university professor, intelligent and accomplished; yet when her husband, Boris, leaves her for a younger woman, she becomes unmoored from herself and even, briefly, from her sanity. For thirty years, Mia has lived as a wife and mother; now, she must rediscover the self that existed before her marriage. She looks for this essential self in many ways: by leaving Brooklyn, the home of her marriage, and returning to her childhood hometown in Minnesota; by keeping a notebook of sexual experiences before her marriage; by teaching a poetry class for teen girls; by spending time with her widowed mother and her mother's elderly friends; by befriending a young mother with marital troubles of her own; and by carrying on a philosophical flirtation with an e-mail correspondent who signs himself "Mr. Nobody," although his identity and even gender are uncertain. As Mia is drawn into other women's lives, she finds the integrity in her own, with or without Boris.

Siri Hustvedt is also the author of *The Shaking Woman or A History of My Nerves*, a medical memoir about her strange neurological symptoms, and she has lectured on the intersection of psychoanalysis and neuroscience. *The Summer Without Men* reflects her strong interest in neuroscience and psychology. Boris is a neuroscientist, a "rat man" who spends his days in the laboratory; Mia suffers a mental breakdown and is diagnosed with brief psychotic disorder, a "Brief Reactive Psychosis, which means that you are genuinely crazy but not for long." Her mother's elderly friends fear death, but they fear dementia more, just as Mia fears the return of her own madness. The novel's relatively brief pages touch upon issues of suicide, grief, sexuality, and the biological differences between men and women. A woman of words, Mia analyzes the breakdown of her mind and marriage through poetry and philosophy as well as psychology, making references to Emily Dickinson, Søren Kierkegaard, and Sigmund Freud throughout the first-person narrative.

The Summer Without Men is at times almost metafictional in its conscious presentation of Mia's narrative as narrative. Mia frequently steps outside her fictional frame to address the Gentle Reader in the manner of a Victorian novelist, at one point even imagining the reader throwing the book flying across the room, waiting for something to happen: "Soon, you are saying . . . There will be ACTION." Some reviewers have praised Hustvedt's stylistic quirks, such as the frequent use of capitalized words and poetic interjections (some quoted, some original) and the incorporation of e-mail exchanges and asides on various topics into the narrative, while others found them artificial and distracting.

The events of the novel take place over the course of one summer. After the breakup of her marriage and her subsequent breakdown, Mia needs a quiet place to recover, a "Yawn between Crazed Winter and Sane Fall," and she finds this place in her childhood hometown. She is hired to teach a teen poetry workshop for the local arts guild, and she also agrees to speak to the book club at Rolling Meadows East, her mother's elderly housing community. When Mia commits to these activities, she finds herself, a fifty-five-year-old woman, surrounded by both the very young and the very old. She is captivated by her mother's friends, a group of aged women she dubs the "Five Swans." She admires their tough-mindedness; all are widows, but rather than dwelling on memories of the past, they live in a "ferocious present," aware of their own mortality and prizing the independence they are still able to keep. Mia's poetry class, on the other hand, consists of "girls on the cusp" —young teens just growing into women's bodies and given to the insecurities and cliquish cruelties of adolescence. To round out the circle of women, Mia meets her neighbor, Lola, and Lola's young daughter, Flora. As Mia interacts with Lola, Flora, and the girls she teaches, she is reminded of herself at different periods of her life: as a small child, as an adolescent, and as a new mother.

The Summer Without Men is not plot driven, and at first the story seems to meander. One of the Swans, Abigail, takes Mia into her confidence, perhaps because Abigail senses

Siri Hustvedt is the author of five novels, including What I Loved *(2003). She has also written a volume of poetry and several works of nonfiction, among them the medical memoir* The Shaking Woman or A History of My Nerves *(2010). A native of Northfield, Minnesota, she attended St. Olaf College and Columbia University. Her fiction has been anthologized in* Best American Short Stories.

that, as a fellow artist, Mia will appreciate what she shows her. Abigail creates elaborate fabric artworks that contain outwardly pretty and conventional scenes subverted by the "private amusements" hidden amidst the embroidery: naked breasts behind a window, a woman vaccuming a town away, female monsters. Abigail creates her embroideries to ease her anger, but she keeps them hidden from the world. Now, nearing the end of her life, she entrusts them to Mia, and eventually shares another secret: a love affair with a woman. Abigail's "amusements" may represent all the unseen, unacknowledged truths in human lives; what she expresses in hidden tapestries, Mia attempts to convey in her poetry and journals.

The discovery and working out of secrets is a major theme in *The Summer Without Men*. Secrets abound in Mia's poetry class, of course, and while the girls' whisperings and nudges at first seem harmless, they soon take a darker turn. One of the girls, Alice, a bright but "different" young woman, becomes the target of bullying that culminates in a cruel joke. Mia eventually learns that the other girls formed a "coven" and shunned Alice, tormenting her by sending abusive text messages, secretly snapping a nude picture of her and posting it online, and eventually setting up a fake date with a boy she likes. As Mia discovers the truth, she remembers her own experience with ostracism as a young girl, being first teased and later shunned by her sixth-grade peers.

Mia decides to fight the bullying with empathy. She asks the girls to share the story of their "coven" in different voices, each time retelling the story from a different person's point of view, thus forcing the victim to speak as a victimizer and the ringleader to imagine herself as an outcast. Mia imagines the final story as a mosaic of voices combining to tell a single narrative. While Mia's solution is elegant, there is a certain distance in the telling that keeps the reader from becoming fully engaged with the girls and their adolescent drama. In one key scene, when Mia and Alice's mother are trying to find out what happened to Alice, Mia cheerfully admits that it can be "boring" to try to get the truth out of a thirteen-year-old and instead redirects her narration into a digression about a visit to a massage therapist. Such digressions, along with the fairly generic identities of the teenagers, make the girls feel more like symbolic constructs than fully developed characters.

If Mia's experience with her teenage students echoes her own youth, her friendship with her neighbor Lola makes her remember other stages in her life as well, bringing her back to her days as a new mother. Mia babysits and provides moral support for Lola, who is having her own marriage difficulties. Mia encourages Lola's artistic drive and bonds with her children, especially the innocent, imaginative Flora. Already seeing reflections of herself as a mother and as a daughter, Mia finds her memories of childhood awakened as well.

As Mia describes her interactions with the women she meets in Bonden, she also engages in a ongoing dialogue about her marriage, played out in conversations with herself, her therapist, her daughter, her husband, and a mysterious e-mail correspondent who signs himself "Mr. Nobody." At first, the question to be decided seems to be if Boris will come back; by the end of the summer, it is clear that the question has become whether Mia will take him back. To answer this, Hustvedt provides readers with an ending that is framed with a reference to classic Hollywood comedies such as Leo McCarey's 1937 film *The Awful Truth*: the difference between comedy and tragedy, she suggests, is in "stopping the story at exactly the right moment."

Hustvedt's story ends as the season does, and Mia concludes her all-female summer having meditated on her life and marriage as well as on the subjects of aging, creativity, memory, and change. The novel is simultaneously dark and humorous, often bringing wit and honesty to grim scenarios and serious issues. Though these scenarios are set off by Mia's deteriorating marriage, they also provide a broader examination of the relationships between men and women, even without the overt presence of men in the story. While *The Summer Without Men* is a story about the turmoil and instability in Mia's life, the writing itself is also slightly ungrounded. Despite any narrative inconsistencies or tangents, however, the novel remains a thought-provoking and powerful meditation on women, life, and love.

Kathryn Kulpa

Review Sources

Booklist 107, no. 16 (April 15, 2011): 22.
The Guardian, March 11, 2011, p. 11.
Kirkus Reviews 79, no. 8 (April 15, 2011): 9.
Library Journal 136, no. 9 (May 15, 2011): 75.
The New York Times Book Review, May 1, 2011, p. 9.
The Observer, February 19, 2011, p. 41.
Poets & Writers 39, no. 3 (May/June 2011): 34–42.
Publishers Weekly 258, no. 7 (February 14, 2011): 33.

Swamplandia!

Author: Karen Russell (b. 1981)
Publisher: Alfred A. Knopf (New York).
  336 pp. $24.95
Type of work: Novel
Time: Late twentieth century
Locale: The Florida Everglades and southwest
  Florida

*After the failure of their family's business, their
mother's death, and their father's abandonment, Ava Bigtree and her siblings embark on
very different journeys in strange and unfamiliar surroundings as they try to cope with their
losses.*

Principal characters:
AVA BIGTREE, a thirteen-year-old girl who
  works at her family's amusement park
HILOLA BIGTREE (SWAMP CENTAUR), her mother
CHIEF BIGTREE, her father
GRANDPA SAWTOOTH, her grandfather
OSCEOLA (OSSIE) BIGTREE, her sixteen-year-old sister
KIWI BIGTREE, her seventeen-year-old brother
THE BIRD MAN, a drifter who kills unwanted birds
LOUIS THANKSGIVING, the ghost of a former swamp dredger of the 1930s

In 2006, Karen Russell's short story "Ava Wrestles the Alligator" appeared in the
journal *Zoetrope*. Her wildly imaginative tale of a teenage girl living in an alligator
theme park in Florida won wide acclaim. A short time later, it became the lead story
in *St. Lucy's Home for Girls Raised by Wolves* (2006), a collection of nine stories
featuring other denizens of the Florida swamps as they struggle to come to terms with
the demise of the old Florida and the rampant destruction of nature, livelihood, and
values in the new Florida. Critics hailed Russell as one in a million and called her
writing vividly exuberant and absolutely irresistible. On the strength of this collection, she was on *New York* magazine's list of twenty-seven remarkable New Yorkers
under twenty-six. In 2009, she was honored by the National Book Foundation's 5
Under 35 program, and in 2010, the *New Yorker* included her in its 20 Under 40 issue
of young fiction writers.
  Russell expands on "Ava Wrestles the Alligator" in her debut novel, *Swamplandia!*,
which, like her previous work, has received well-deserved praise from many quarters.
A *New York Times* best seller, *Swamplandia!* is on the newspaper's "10 Best Books of
2011" list and has also been optioned by HBO for a comedy series. In language that is

as rich and loamy as the Florida swampland in which the novel is set, Russell weaves a colorful and fanciful tale of despair and hope, full of strange and wondrous characters.

As in "Ava Wrestles the Alligator," the novel follows the Bigtree family as they try to eke out a living in southern Florida with their alligator theme park. Ava Bigtree, the thirteen-year-old narrator, is the youngest of the family's three children. Russell also brings back Ava's older sister, Osceola (Ossie); their father, Chief; their mother, Hilola; the ninety-eight alligators that the Bigtree family fondly calls the Seths—they are all named Seth—and a bear named Judy Garland. To these, Russell has added Ava's older brother, Kiwi, the third-person narrator of several chapters. Luscious, the ghost who is Ossie's "evil boyfriend" in the story, has been transformed into the ghost of Louis Thanksgiving in the novel.

Karen Russell is the author of the story collection St. Lucy's Home for Girls Raised by Wolves *(2006). In 2009, the National Book Foundation recognized her as a 5 Under 35 fiction writer. She was also featured on the* New Yorker's *20 Under 40 list of fiction writers for 2010.*

The Bigtrees' story begins when Ava's grandfather, Ernest Schedrach, purchases the Florida land sight unseen after losing his job in an Ohio pulp mill in 1932. Looking for a big change in his life, Grandpa is lured by the promise of farmland in Florida; the flyers he sees depict a post-drainage swamp full of dairy cows, orange groves, and heavenly fields of clover. When he and his new bride arrive in this paradise, they find that their land, an island in the chain of the Ten Thousand Islands on the southwestern coast of Florida, is covered in six feet of water and nine-foot stalks of sawgrass that stretch out in the sun in all directions. Yet when a crab scuttles across his wife's shoes and she does not immediately scream, he knows that they will stay on this island and call it their home.

Ava admits that her family is not even remotely Seminole or Miccosukee, although her father always dressed them in tribal costumes for the photographs he took. To convince tourists that they were authentic denizens of the region who came by their alligator-taming skills honestly, her grandfather decided to call himself "Sawtooth" after the dense sedge that surrounded his land and "Bigtree" simply because of the strong sound of the name. On this island, Grandpa Sawtooth Bigtree's family built Swamplandia.

During its heyday, Swamplandia was advertised as the "Number One Gator-Themed Park and Swamp Café" in the area. Billboards for the park were lurid and promised a glimpse of Seth, the "FANGSOME SEA SERPENT AND ANCIENT LIZ-ARD OF DEATH!!!" Ava points out that Swamplandia advertised its attractions as boldly and as prominently as the miniature golf courses and water slide attractions in the other parts of the state. The park stayed open 365 days a year and had shows every day; it had the cheapest beer in a three-county radius as well as the Swamp Centaur—Ava's mother and Swamplandia's star attraction, Hilola Bigtree.

When Ava turns thirteen, however, it is the beginning of the end for Swamplandia. A new and larger theme park, the World of Darkness, threatens the future of her family's business. Much like Disney World, the World of Darkness attracts its hordes with a continual stream of thrill rides, water parks, and simulated natural surroundings. The

World of Darkness offers escalator tours of the rings of Hell, a water ride through the belly of a whale (the Leviathan), blood red swimming pools, and easy access to the interstate. The ads for this new park crackle over the television airwaves and into the Bigtree living room, even as the number of tourists visiting Swamplandia begins to dwindle.

The end of Swamplandia is not the only tragedy that befalls Ava in that year. Ava's mother develops cancer and ultimately succumbs to the disease, leaving the park without its main attraction and the Bigtree family without the glue that holds it together. After Hilola's death, the family must decide the fate of Swamplandia, for neither Ava nor her brother or sister is ready to step into their mother's shoes, and their father, numb with grief, refuses to admit that his wife not only held the family together but also kept Swamplandia financially afloat. However, even after Hilola's death, her presence is palpable throughout the novel, and in the end it is her spiritual presence that brings the scattered family back together. Chief Bigtree makes a shrine to Hilola in Swamplandia's gift shop and museum, and after her death, Hilola's daughters, Ava and Ossie, commune with their mother by looking through her letters, photos, and alligator-wrestling trophies. The girls even bring their mother back to life by spraying her perfume on their clothes as a substitute for washing them.

Ava, who of all the family most fervently believes in Swamplandia and hopes to bring it back to its former glory, tries to emulate her mother in all things. In several poignant scenes, Ava recognizes that she can enter alligator-wrestling championships and writes numerous letters to various agencies in an attempt to live in her mother's legacy. She tries to persuade Ossie and Kiwi, her brother, that Swamplandia, like the land around them, is worth saving, and that she is willing to be the new Hilola and swim with the Seths to attract tourists.

One afternoon, Ava watches an alligator egg hatch; out of it emerges a red alligator. The other alligators that hatch at the same time from the same lot of eggs do not survive. Every day, Ava watches over her red alligator, willing it to keep breathing and to survive. Though she does not share this secret with anyone else in her family, she nourishes her hope that this little creature will rescue the park, which will then bind her family back together again.

The rest of the Bigtrees scatter to the wind, leaving Ava to cope with the swamp on her own. Hoping to make enough money to ward off the foreclosure of Swamplandia, Kiwi sets off to the mainland to find a job, intending to send his paychecks to his father. Ironically, he ends up working for the World of Darkness, the enemy of his own family's park, and discovers just how demonic and harsh the world can be. After many months of almost indentured servitude to this new theme park—the company takes money out of his paycheck to pay for his clothes, and he must live in substandard company housing—he recognizes just how difficult the outside world is and how much his family has sustained him. Meanwhile, Chief Bigtree simply abandons Ava and Ossie, leaving no clues as to his whereabouts. Later, he surfaces as a worker in a casino on the mainland.

Ossie becomes enamored of séances and spiritualism shortly after her mother's death. She believes that she can communicate with the dead, trying several times to contact their mother. For several nights in a row, Ossie leaves the house in the middle of the night and does not return until very early in the morning. Through her séances, Ossie has met and fallen in love with a young dredgeman who lived many years earlier and died aboard a dredge in the swamps during a storm. When Ava informs Chief Bigtree that Ossie is in love with a ghost, the Chief does not respond. Ossie eventually runs away with this young man, and Ava sets off through the swamp alone in search of her. During her quest to find Ossie, Ava happens upon the Bird Man, a drifter who makes a living hunting birds. He promises to lead Ava through the swamp and help her find Ossie. Ava's journey with the Bird Man, which she describes as the Journey to the Underworld, is a harrowing ordeal.

Russell's novel offers an indictment of a world that is driven by the quest for the new and tears apart the fabric of deeply settled relationships. New Florida, with its glittering theme parks and water parks, simply bulldozes old Florida, destroying the deeply rooted beauty of the woods and swamps of the riverways and the Everglades. Even before Ava's birth, the land was threatened by the encroachment of the suburbs and Big Sugar in the south, as well as the destruction of the swamps by the melaleuca tree, an exotic invasive species. Originally planted by the Army Corps of Engineers in hopes of establishing a better means of flood control, the tree instead drained the water of nutrients, killing off many native plants and turning the swamp into dry land. When the environment on which individuals' livelihood depends shrinks, so does their world, and they are often forced to leave behind their families and homes to negotiate their way in a world with which they are emotionally and physically unfamiliar. As old Florida falls down around them and their family falls apart, the Bigtrees are forced to find ways to survive their losses and face the challenges of a new world.

Henry L. Carrigan Jr.

Review Sources

Booklist 107, no. 4 (October 15, 2010): 31.
Kirkus Reviews 78, no. 21 (November 1, 2010): 1081.
Library Journal 135, no. 17 (October 15, 2010): 69.
New Criterion 29, no. 9 (May 2011): 32–37.
The New York Times, February 16, 2011 (Web).
The New York Times Book Review, February 6, 2011, p. 1.
Publishers Weekly 257, no. 48 (December 6, 2010): 29, 30.
The Wall Street Journal, January 29, 2011, p. C8.

The Swerve
How the World Became Modern

Author: Stephen Greenblatt (b. 1943)
Publisher: W. W. Norton (New York). Illustrated. 356 pp. $26.95
Type of work: History, literary history
Time: From antiquity to the seventeenth century
Locale: Europe, especially Italy

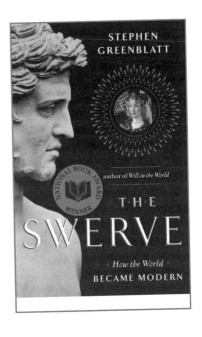

The author presents a comprehensive overview of the origins, rediscovery, and influence of a famous poem by Lucretius that foreshadowed the rise of modern thinking.

Principal personages:
GIORDANO BRUNO (1548–1600), a philosopher burned at the stake as a heretic
MARCUS TULLIUS CICERO (106–43 BCE), Roman philosopher and author
EPICURUS (341–270 BCE), ancient Greek materialist philosopher
BALDASSARE COSSA (1370–1419), Antipope John XXIII, an important patron of Poggio Bracciolini
LUCRETIUS (99–55 BCE), Roman poet and philosopher, the author of *On the Nature of Things*
THOMAS MORE (1478–1535), English humanist and statesman, the author of *Utopia*
NICCOLO NICCOLI (1364–1437), Italian humanist, a friend of Poggio Bracciolini
GIAN FRANCESCO POGGIO BRACCIOLINI (1380–1459), influential Italian humanist and book collector
LORENZO VALLA (1407?–1457), Italian humanist and educator
VIRGIL (70–19 BCE), poet and author of the *Aeneid*

Stephen Greenblatt's *The Swerve: How the World Became Modern* offers a compelling portrait of Poggio Bracciolini, the Italian humanist and book collector who, in 1417, discovered an extremely rare surviving copy of the poem *De rerum natura* (*On the Nature of Things*) by the Roman poet and philosopher Lucretius. The fact that such a poem once existed had long been known, but Poggio's discovery of the work in an obscure German monastery was an important find. Besides being a splendid Latin poem, Lucretius's work was also a major document in the history of the philosophy known as Epicureanism. Epicurus had taught that everything in the universe consisted of nothing but material particles called atoms. He also taught that pursuit of worldly pleasure was a worthy purpose of human life. The implications of Epicurus's philosophy, Greenblatt argues, made his ideas seem dangerous to other ways of thinking, especially to the thinking of medieval and Renaissance Christians. Epicureanism suggested that the soul died with the body, and that the universe was not the product of divine design but the result of the random collision of atoms. By finding, copying, and distributing Lucretius's masterfully written poem, Poggio helped to revive a philosophy that anticipated many modern beliefs, one that was often seen as heretical by Christians of his own day and later. Eventually, though, materialist beliefs began to have an increasing impact on the development of Western philosophy, and today those same ideas that once seemed so shocking are the bedrock of modern thought.

A book of popular history that synthesizes the scholarship of others, *The Swerve* takes readers on a tour of numerous times, places, and people. It surveys such topics as the lives and working conditions of the medieval monks who transcribed manuscripts, the materials and methods they used, the early life and developing career of Poggio himself, the likely details of Lucretius's life, and common methods of reading and writing in the ancient world. The increasing literacy of the ancient Romans is described, as is the survival of classical writings, the discovery of important manuscripts under the volcanic ash that destroyed Pompeii and Herculaneum, and the broad outlines of Epicurean philosophy. Greenblatt reminds the reader just how many works by ancient writers have perished, apparently forever: only seven plays by Sophocles and Aeschylus survive, of the nearly 200 they are known to have written; only eighteen of ninety-two plays by Euripides still exist; and of the forty-three plays Aristophanes composed, only eleven remain available. Of the 3,500 works by one classical author, all have disappeared, and at least 1,115 other known works have failed to survive as well. Greenblatt has clearly done his homework, in this matter as in so much else. His book is full of fascinating information about not just the Renaissance but also the classical and medieval periods. The authors who wrote books and the copyists who helped "publish" them come to life in the pages of Greenblatt's volume. Clearly, he is precisely the kind of humanist he praises: a man who is obsessed with the glories of the past and determined to help those glories flourish in the present day.

Greenblatt constantly and valuably reminds the reader of the fragility of material culture and how easily that culture can be inadvertently lost or even deliberately destroyed. He describes in detail the features of the great library of Alexandria, Egypt, which in its heyday housed more than half a million papyrus manuscripts. Yet the library, along with some of the scholars associated with it, eventually fell victim to the rise of religious fanaticism, and indeed, one of the major themes of Greenblatt's book is the damage that religion has done to learning throughout history, in particular damage perpetrated by the Christian religion. The Roman Catholic Church, especially, is presented as a highly unattractive institution. During Poggio's lifetime, schisms led to the rise of competing popes and corruption seems to have been rife, in the Vatican most of all. Poggio, who for years held high office as chief papal secretary at the Vatican, was fully aware of these many flaws, both in the institution itself as well as in many of its most prominent officials. Poggio himself had a mistress and fathered numerous illegitimate children before marrying, at a relatively old age, a much younger woman, with whom he produced a whole new set of offspring. Greenblatt admires Poggio and his contributions to learning, obviously and with good reason, but his portrait of

(Rose Lincoln–Harvard University)

Stephen Greenblatt is the John Cogan University Professor of the Humanities at Harvard University. He is the author of numerous articles and books, including Will in the World: How Shakespeare Became Shakespeare *(2004). Widely considered to be the founder of the new historicist approach to literary criticism, he is the editor of* The Norton Anthology of English Literature, *ninth edition (2012).*

the man is a warts-and-all rendering, and all the more valuable because of it. Readers will not soon forget, for example, Greenblatt's description of the vicious fistfight that once broke out between Poggio and a scholarly rival, a fight in which the two old men tried to tear out eyes, bite fingers, and inflict other highly painful damage.

In the course of describing Poggio and his rediscovery of Lucretius, Greenblatt offers vivid biographical sketches as well as intriguing depictions of Greek, Roman, medieval, and Renaissance cultural conditions. Sometimes Lucretius and his poem fall out of focus, but in general the history offered here helps the reader to understand how and why the poem was written, how and why it happened to survive and resurface, and how and why its rediscovery had such a significant impact. Especially helpful is the chapter in which Greenblatt uses bullet points and boldfaced summary sentences to outline the main arguments of Lucretius's poem. Presented in this way, Lucretius's ideas do indeed seem startling, and one can easily grasp why his poem was considered dangerous by various Renaissance-era Christians. Yet Greenblatt also shows how widely *On the Nature of Things* was read and digested by some of the most important minds of the age, including Thomas More, Niccolò Machiavelli, Giordano Bruno, Galileo Galilei, Michel de Montaigne, and Ben Jonson. In fact, copies of the poem owned by the latter two figures still survive and are full of copious annotations. Lucy Hutchinson, a learned seventeenth-century Puritan, translated the poem into English and then, shocked by its impiety, regretted having done so (or so she claimed). Greenblatt ends by noting that Thomas Jefferson, a founding father of the United States, owned numerous copies of Lucretius in Latin and in translation, and that he openly declared himself an Epicurean. One famous phrase from the Declaration of Independence, "the pursuit of happiness," may reflect the influence of Epicurus and Lucretius. This, then, is a book not just about a particular poem but about two millennia of Western culture, from the ancient Greeks to the founding of the United States.

Greenblatt makes such strong claims for the importance and beauty of Lucretius's poem that one wishes the work itself were quoted more often and discussed more explicitly as a work of art. According to Greenblatt, it is an unusually beautiful and compelling poem, simply in its phrasing and aside from any philosophical content. Poggio considered it an example of splendid Latin, and Greenblatt plainly agrees. One wishes that a literary critic of Greenblatt's talent would have included a chapter devoted to a discussion of the poem's aesthetic merits. Such a chapter might have helped arouse interest in the poem as a carefully crafted and beautiful piece of language, and indeed, since its ideas are now widely accepted, *On the Nature of Things* needs to survive as a great piece of poetry even more now and in the future than ever before. However, one highly positive effect of this stimulating book will be to send people in search of Lucretius's work. Greenblatt quotes mainly from the 2001 prose translation by Martin Ferguson Smith, though it is not completely clear which modern translation he considers to be the best at conveying the artistic excellence of the original.

Praise for Greenblatt's book was almost universal among its initial reviewers. One Catholic commentator did object to the book's unfavorable depiction of the medieval and Renaissance church, and several reviewers have suggested that Greenblatt greatly overstates the actual historical impact of Lucretius's poem. One review argues that Greenblatt makes Lucretius sound more enthusiastic about sex than he actually was, while another claims that Greenblatt makes Epicureanism sound more philosophically appealing than it has historically proved to be. Yet almost all reviewers have praised the book heartily, especially for making seemingly arcane topics both interesting and accessible to a wide readership.

Greenblatt himself writes with great clarity and verve. His book is extremely easy to read and very hard to put down. Any topic he discusses is treated lucidly, with just enough detail to satisfy most scholars but not so much that it will overwhelm general readers. This is the kind of book that will open up a number of whole new worlds for many readers, allowing them to see and experience for themselves how it felt to live in earlier times, as well as to appreciate, in every sense of the word, how those times are relevant to our own.

Robert C. Evans

Review Sources

Booklist 108, no. 1 (September 1, 2011): 18.
Catholic News Agency, October 21, 2011 (Web).
The Christian Science Monitor, October 12, 2011 (Web).
The Financial Times, September 1, 2011 (Web).
The Guardian, September 23, 2011 (Web).
New Republic 242, no. 15 (October 20, 2011): 36–39.
The New York Times Book Review, October 2, 2011, p. 18.
Slate, September 29, 2011 (Web).
The Wall Street Journal, September 26, 2011 (Web).
The Washington Post, September 21, 2011(Web).

Swim Back to Me

Author: Ann Packer (b. 1959)
Publisher: Alfred A. Knopf (New York).
225 pp. $24.95
Type of work: Short fiction
Time: The present; 1972–1973
Locale: Primarily the San Francisco Bay area

SWIM BACK TO ME

by the author of
THE DIVE
FROM
CLAUSEN'S PIER

ANN PACKER

Packer's collection of stories about Northern California bring the reader into the heart of true-to-life experiences in which ordinary suburban characters navigate their way through loss and longing.

Principal characters:
RICHARD APPLEBY, a teenager experiencing eighth grade with separated parents in the year 1972
SASHA HOROWITZ, a vivacious, strong, and witty new girl who befriends Richard
DAN HOROWITZ, an eccentric and quirky English professor whose flight from job to job keeps his family on the move
JOANIE HOROWITZ, the artistic and free-spirited mother of Sasha and Peter and wife of Dan
PETER HOROWITZ, the son of Dan and Joanie and brother of Sasha, whose wedding reunites the family

The characters in this collection of short stories give the reader a glimpse into the challenges of loss, longing, and the daily effort of dealing with heartbreak. Set mainly in the San Francisco Bay area, most of the locales and culture are familiar to author Ann Packer, a native of Northern California. Though there are mixed opinions regarding whether she is better suited for novel writing than short fiction, overall *Swim Back to Me* has been praised for its sensitively detailed plots, exceptional use of prose, and carefully and compassionately created characters.

In "Molten," Kathryn mourns the death of her teenage son, Ben, and desperately tries to reconnect with him by spending the hours that her husband is at work and her daughter is at school in Ben's room listening to his music. Nearing the point of addiction, she only tolerates the presence of others in the house in order to make it through to her next opportunity to be alone in Ben's world. It is from "Molten" that Packer derived the book's title. "Swim Back to Me" is the name of one of the songs Kathryn loses herself in as she works through Ben's absence. Beyond that, Packer explains in an interview that she liked the idea of using a phrase that encompasses the overall theme throughout the stories—someone has left who can somehow be brought back, emphasizing the importance of moving forward while not forgetting the significance of what has happened in the past.

"Her Firstborn" tells the story of another mother. Lise has already lost a baby, Jasper, at five months old and is in a second marriage and pregnant once again. It is her husband Dean's first experience with pregnancy and childbirth, and he finds himself unable to think about their baby without wondering how Lise's own anticipation is being impacted by Jasper's death. The story maps their struggle to work around her experience of loss, not knowing how to meet one another in the middle of it. One of the scenes where this feels most poignant is a childbirth class. As Dean watches and listens in amazement, Lise shares with the class a factual account of her loss. Back at home, it is still unclear how they will truly come together over what is so unique to her own experience. A connection between them is withheld, another common thread in all the stories in the collection. One character waits and longs for the emotional and sometimes physical return of another. In the case of Lise and Dean, a return does seem imminent. Their son Danny is born, and in the early days of fatherhood, Dean "feels a little space open up in his mind, for all she can tell him about her firstborn."

Ann Packer has written two other novels, the award-winning The Dive from Clausen's Pier *(2002) and* Songs without Words *(2007), as well as one other collection of short stories,* Mendocino and Other Stories *(2003).*

This theme takes on a different form in "Jump," when Carolee, a shift manager at Copy Copy, discovers that one of the employees she supervises has a life outside of the workplace completely different from what she would have imagined. To Carolee, Alejandro is a screw-up, immature and careless. Based on his accent and use of language, she assumes that he is "first-generation," which conjures certain images for her of where he might live and under what circumstances. She assumes that he is doing well for himself by having any kind of job at all, whereas her own role as a manager at the same establishment is to her a compromised kind of success. When his offer to help with her car's dead battery eventually brings them to his parents' home in the upscale town of Atherton, she is shocked. It quickly becomes clear that his efforts to project a certain image are his attempts to identify with his Latina mother and exasperate his Caucasian father, who also happens to be a successful doctor. Carolee, who is disappointed with her life at the age of nearly thirty, feels an intense sympathy for Alejandro when he opens up to her about his hatred for his father. During this experience, both realize "that wanting to be gone was one thing, but going was another."

In "Dwell Time," Laura learns that her second husband, Matt, does not make a distinction between wanting to be gone and going. In fact, he makes a habit of not doing so. The reader learns right away that Laura's first husband, Adam, was always late while Matt is reliably punctual. It is significant then that the narrative begins forty-five minutes past the time when Matt should have arrived home for the evening. Even as Laura's anxiety increases with each passing moment, her instinct is to protect both her own children and Matt's children from worry. The description of her thought process on what to make for dinner on the evening the story takes place seems to provide an apt illustration of how much responsibility she feels to please and care for everyone in the blended family. However, her two daughters reject the meal. This tangible attempt at unifying the family over food unravels just as Laura's understanding of who Matt is comes apart as well. Over the next several hours, it becomes clear that Matt is not coming home. Processing this information, she thinks back to their first date at a coffee house called Dwell Time. During the date, Matt had explained to her that dwell time is part of the coffee brewing process, an adjustable duration of time in which the water is "'in contact with the coffee grounds.'" As she reflects back on this conversation, she sees that Matt's home life is his own version of dwell time.

Framing these three stories are two novellas with shared principal characters, "Walk for Mankind" and "Things Said or Done." Opinions differ about what these two stories bring to the collection. A *New York Times* review acknowledges the challenge of balancing a collection that includes both a novella and short stories. Reviewer Lydia Peelle argues that it "drag[s] down an otherwise strong arrangement," because she feels the development of the young characters in "Walk for Mankind" is not as strong as that of the adult characters who drive the short stories. However, another review asserts that in comparison to the two framing narratives, the short stories "though well crafted and engaging, have the feel of problems solved rather than lives fully lived."

"Walk for Mankind" is told from the perspective of Richard Appleby as he experiences his eighth grade year beginning in 1972. The son of a history professor at Stanford, he becomes fascinated with a new girl at school, Sasha Horowitz. Her family has moved to Palo Alto from Connecticut so that her father can take a teaching job in the English department at Stanford, having been denied tenure at Yale. Dan and Joanie Horowitz are free-spirited parents who take Richard in as an honorary member of their household. Dan is quirky and delightful among friends and family, but evidence also suggests that these traits turn mercurial among his colleagues. The reader is able to discern the reason for the family's transient existence from Packer's clues about Dan's work life. One of Richard and Sasha's first significant experiences together is soliciting sponsors for their participation in the Walk for Mankind fundraiser. During their campaign for sponsors, Richard and Sasha meet Cal, an attractive man in his twenties whose presence in the story introduces sex, drugs, and competition for Sasha's time and attention. Though Cal alters the friendship between Sasha and Richard, it remains central to Richard. Later that summer, after previously convincing him otherwise, Sasha casually informs Richard that they are moving back to Connecticut so that her father can teach at a boarding school there. Her departure parallels the leave-taking of Richard's mother. Yet, in one final gesture, the story suggests that Richard is no longer a victim of these abandonments.

Sasha and her family appear again in "Things Said or Done." A middle-aged Sasha tells the story of mediating between her divorced parents at her brother Peter's wedding, for which all four return to California. Dan's flightiness and eccentricity are more sad than charming in his old age. Sasha herself is now divorced as well, and she reflects on the advice her mother told her before her own wedding. Joanie's perspective on faithfulness and permanence are further illustrated by her love for sketching people constantly, something Richard had observed during his young friendship with Sasha. Joanie captures moments at the wedding just as she has done throughout their family's history, a practice of commemoration adopted in response to Dan's repeated uprooting of their family. She goes on to reveal more to Sasha about the dissolution of her marriage to Dan and the role Richard's family played in it. As Joanie interrupts her story to sketch the newlyweds saying goodbye and thereby still time with her art, the collection concludes with Sasha approaching her father in a movement he still distrusts, one not of leaving but of someone coming, "swimming," back to him.

Elizabeth Bellucci

Review Sources

Booklist 107, no. 13 (March 1, 2011): 28.
Library Journal 136, no. 1 (January 1, 2011): 92.
Kirkus Reviews 79, no. 1 (January 1, 2011): 3.
The New York Times Book Review, May 20, 2011, p. 8.
Publishers Weekly 257, no. 49 (December 13, 2010): 34.
San Francisco Chronicle, April 10, 2011, p. GF1.

Tabloid City

Author: Pete Hamill (b. 1935)
Publisher: Little, Brown (New York).
288 pp. $26.99
Type of work: Novel
Time: ca. 2010
Locale: New York City

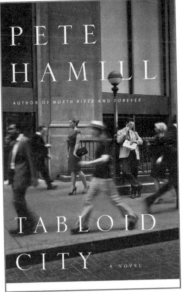

(Little, Brown and Company)

Hamill's tale about the end of a tabloid tells the story of how a man who has lived in the tabloid world far too long discovers life outside of his work. Hamill also explores the stories of a cross section of New Yorkers dealing with their own endings.

Principal characters:

SAM BRISCOE, the seventy-one-year-old editor in chief of the *New York World*

MATT LOGAN, the fifty-one-year-old managing editor of the *New York World*

BOBBY FONESCA, known as "the kid," the youngest reporter at the *New York World*

HELEN LOOMIS, an aging widow and chain-smoking "rewrite man" of the Vics and Dicks column for the *New York World*

RICHARD ELWOOD, also known as F. P., the twenty-eight-year-old son of the deceased founder of *New York World* and the current publisher of the tabloid

JOSH THOMPSON, an Iraq War veteran and double amputee with a loaded MAC-10 under his poncho, who came from Norman, Oklahoma, to New York on a mission

MALIK SHAHID, also known as MALIK WATSON, Ali Watson's homeless son and Muslim convert intent on carrying out jihad

CYNTHIA HARDING, an aging photographer, socialite, philanthropist, and longtime lover of Sam Briscoe

LEW FORREST, a widower in his nineties and a near-blind painter hoping for a comeback and living with his dog at the Chelsea Hotel

MYLES COMPTON, a hedge-fund grifter with an untraceable European Union passport in the new name of Martin Canfield; Sandra Gordon's lover

FREDDIE WHEELER, a former *New York World* employee fired by Sam Briscoe, online blogger

SANDRA GORDON, a former illiterate Jamaican orphan brought to the United States and mentored by her "second mother," Cynthia Harding; copywriter at an advertising agency

ALI WATSON, a New York Police Department sergeant on an antiterrorist squad and former Muslim; married to Mary Lou Watson, mother of Malik Shahid

BEVERLY STARR, a graphic artist with a lifelong obsession with comics and detestation
   of the misuse of the word "like"
CONSUELO MENDOZA, an undocumented immigrant and recently unemployed cleaning
   woman who was once Lew Forrest's model and lover, now a married mother of four
MARY LOU WATSON, Cynthia Harding's personal assistant and secretary
GLORIOUS BURRESS, Malik Shahid's fifteen-year-old girlfriend, who is nine-months
   pregnant and locked in a room in a vacant tenement

Tabloid City, by Pete Hamill, is a story of a dying newspaper. It is also the story of
the past, of times gone by, and of people and places that no longer exist. It is one of
revenge, of jihad. It relays a war-torn heart and body and people drifting through life
with no anchors and few connections. Set in New York, the novel is both an elegy
and a love story to a city that no longer exists. New York insiders will marvel at the
references to people, places, and customs unique to New York, such as its famed egg
creams. Nonetheless, the novel will resonate with urban dwellers anywhere, who will
recognize the references to modern-day events, such as killers shot dead on the street,
that create headlines in any American city.

   While *Tabloid City* looks at a dying industry, it is also full of characters and tells
the stories of each over a roughly twenty-four-hour span. While back-to-back snippets
of each character's life told from fourteen viewpoints make for somewhat disjointed
reading, the format slows the action and keeps the tension from rising. Rather than
creating an action-packed thriller, Hamill produces a narrative that reflects real life
with its intense moments and numbing lulls.

   The action in *Tabloid City* does not pick up until after a hundred pages, but in those
pages, Hamill provides intimate portraits of each character. Readers learn what the
characters yearn for and what makes them tick. Sam Briscoe, the editor of the *New
York World*, is stirred by the past and the newspaper industry. He considers himself a
citizen of the tabloid night, which is about to come to an end, as the publication of
the newspaper ceases and the publisher switches to an online news format. He has
little life outside the newspaper; in fact, most of his friends are (or were) people in the
newspaper industry. Briscoe therefore laments the demise of the newspaper industry
to which he has devoted his adult life, and he scorns its replacement: online websites,
where news is gleaned by armchair "reporters" who sit at home and watch events on
television, search the Internet and use gadgets for stories, and never have to leave their
homes to get the news. As he mourns *New York World*'s demise, Briscoe ponders the
glory days when he and other journalists were young and hung out in Paris after World
War II, a time when life held so much promise and opportunity. They never knew a
time would come when their days would be filled with loneliness and emptiness and
they would be warding off "conditions we never heard of in Paris."

   In *Tabloid City*, many of the characters have put their lives on the back burner to
pursue professional ambitions. They have immersed themselves in the lives of the
tabloid or in chasing criminals. Their own lives have become secondary to how they
have spent most of their days. In fact, they have forfeited spouses, families, and homes
to pursue the tales of other people's lives. Moreover, those lives take priority even

(Little, Brown and Company)

With more than fifty years in the publishing and journalism industries, Pete Hamill has worked as a writer, editor, journalist, columnist, essayist, and novelist. His many awards include the Meyer Berger Award, the Peter Kihss Award, the Mystery Writers of America Award, the Louis Auchincloss Prize, and several lifetime achievement awards.

when they encounter personal tragedy. For instance, when a police sergeant's wife dies, he buries his pain to do his job. When Briscoe's longtime lover is murdered, reporting her death takes priority for him over processing her death. Neither denies their pain, loss, or love, but their jobs take priority. This conflict is the undercurrent that dominates the novel: What is life? Is it investigating the story or living the story?

On the day when his newspaper closes and the day after his longtime lover dies, Briscoe stares at the house where she lived, and he recalls a day spent in Dublin with her long ago. He fondly thinks of showing her the sights and of her enthusiasm as she said, "Sam, I could live here." Though they inhabited homes not far from each other in New York, the two led separate lives. The text leaves readers to consider whether the characters have actually lived. Were their careers their lives, or did they have lives independent of their careers? As the night falls, Briscoe tries to pray but finds he cannot. The only word that comes is "sorry." For what he is apologizing is the central mystery of Hamill's novel, and it reflects a universal conflict for every reader.

Tabloid City examines people's raisons d'être and challenges readers to investigate how one might balance work life and personal life. Hamill's text looks at the toll work can have on people and whether life encompasses one's professional or personal pursuits; it also examines the sacrifices involved pursuing either demand. Hard-hitting and replete with references to journalism, *Tabloid City* is not so much a story of a dying newspaper as a story of loss, aging, and the conflict of work versus life. Hamill explores these themes by examining what defines people.

Reinforcing the interests of the industry in which so many characters are entrenched, Hamill uses publishing buzzwords—specifically punctuation—to create vivid imagery. For example, he uses a period to describe how Helen Loomis felt after her husband died: "All through the weeks of mourning, she felt like a dot. The kind of period that ends a sentence." He compares the generic "punctuation mark" to a gunshot. A character hears a sound and thinks, "A single blam. Like a punctuation mark. Then silence."

Hamill's tightly crafted words provide a critique of myriad aspects of modern culture, including politically incorrect language, smoking bans, the economy, pyramid schemes, illegal immigration, the rich, the homeless, the Iraq War, Muslims, terrorism, and crime, as well as the newspaper industry, the Internet, the digital age, the past, aging, loss, and death. While Hamill makes his personal opinions known, he does so without pontificating. He recognizes shades of gray and acknowledges things seldom are what they seem. He sees both the silver lining and the gloom in situations, as when he references the pilot who landed his plane in the Hudson River, commenting, "Ten years ago, he'd have smashed into a freighter. Now it's nothing but sailboats and ferries." He finds the universal in a situation and connects it to the reader: "Like people in traffic court, all of them pleading Guilty, With an Explanation. The title of every human being's autobiography."

Far from maudlin, *Tabloid City* ends on an anticlimactic note, with some ambiguity. The stories of several characters intersect as they come together at the same location, and a tragedy must unfold in the Watson family in order to avert a bigger tragedy. Detective Ali Watson offers a pain-filled apology to his wife in a bizarre kind of mirror or duplication of the one Briscoe makes after his lover's death. Hamill cuts off that story with no further details, an abrupt but fitting conclusion as additional details would be superfluous. He leaves other stories—such as that of Josh Thompson, the disabled Iraq War veteran bent on revenge against an unnamed enemy—unfinished and with no endings at all. In the book's final scene, Briscoe, who once said he never considered suicide because he wanted to know how the story turns out, walks down the street with the wind at his back. No longer part of the tabloid night, he is out to reclaim his own story.

Barbara C. Lightner

Review Sources

Booklist 107, no. 13 (March 1, 2011): 28.
Kirkus Reviews 79, no. 5 (March 1, 2011): 354–5.
Library Journal 136, no. 6 (April 1, 2011): 80.
Los Angeles Times, May 8, 2011, p. E12.
The New York Times Book Review, May 22, 2011, p. 21.
Publishers Weekly 258, no. 8 (February 21, 2011): 107.
Washington Times, June 24, 2011, p. D6.

Taller When Prone

Author: Les Murray (b. 1938)
First published: 2010, in Australia
Publisher: Farrar, Straus and Giroux (New York). 96 pp. $24.00
Type of work: Poetry

A thoughtful, mischievous, and masterful collection of poems by one of Australia's most accomplished living poets.

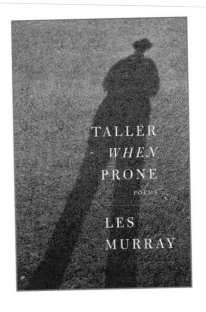

Les Murray has been one of the most respected living poets writing in the English language for several decades. His first poetry collection, *The Ilex Tree*, was published in 1965. Since then Murray has established himself as a strong advocate for the conservation of nature, of the mythical world, of the power of poetry. Born in rural New South Wales, Australia, the poet's appreciation of Australia's unique natural environment is apparent in his work, as is his interest in the myths of the Australian Aborigines. Over the years the Murray has found a way to balance his portraits of the poverty in rural Australia with the playful qualities of his writing. Murray learned how hard life can be at an early age; farm life was difficult and strained relations between family members. Clive James, a literary critic and close friend of the Murray, has stated that his friend's poetry is "truly agrarian, in the sense that the whole array of its perceptions had the rural existence for a departure point rather than a destination." While Australia can claim Murray as one of its national treasures, the rest of the world also can claim him as one of its great poets.

As he has done with several of his previous volumes of poetry, Murray has dedicated *Taller When Prone* to "the glory of God." Over the decades he has written poetry that speaks with an appreciation for both the natural world and the sacred world. Murray has saved most of his "reverence" for the wisdom that originates from the bush or wilderness and eschews the modern urbanized world. As a young man Murray converted to Catholicism and he took comfort in his newfound faith. Because of a troubled childhood the poet also has suffered from serious episodes of depression at various points during his life. Ever vigilant though, Murray has been able to make his way in the world as a man who makes his living with words. His strength with language has especially given him the ability to paint a landscape or situation with a satiric bent that can deliver quite a blow. Murray has never seemed to be willing to compromise his core principles and is truly in love with the world that has not been tarnished by civilization and development. In such striking poetry collections as *The Daylight Moon* (1987), *Translations from the Natural World* (1992), *Subhuman Redneck Poems*

(1996), *Conscious and Verbal* (1999), and *The Biplane Houses* (2006), Murray sings the praises of the natural world. The environment and the spiritual power that emanates from it are at the center of much of what inspires his poetry.

For *Taller When Prone,* Murray extends his reach beyond his beloved rural Australia, creating poems that find him in various places around the world. He opens the collection with the poem "From a Tourist Journal." As a tourist in India, Murray describes his encounter with the majestic Taj Mahal. He deftly describes his impressions of the new place and situation, including vivid images of Indian school children, camels, and the Taj itself. There is a swirl of activity around the Taj Mahal, yet Murray still is able to view "through haze, // perfection as a factory making depth, / pearl chimneys of the Taj Mahal."

Several poems in *Taller When Prone* serve as postcards for the poet as world traveler. His word pictures present readers with just enough clarity to make them want more and read further. In the poem "Bluelookout Mountain" Murray draws in his audience with lush descriptions of the outdoors, writing that "Bluelookout is the colours and smooth / texture of forest pigeons" and that "Grasses of exotic green / radiate down its ridge lines/ just how snow would lie." Throughout his entire writing career Murray has emphasized the importance of place and the meaning behind it. His globe-spanning poetic postcards will not be like any others that a careful reader could receive. Even when he has written what some might perceive as scribbles or notes, the results are no less precious, no less worth savoring. For Murray the ultimate ambition is to be the best poet that he knows how to be no matter how complicated or silly the subject at hand.

No collection by Murray could be complete without the familiar sojourns into the continent that he knows and loves. The spirit of Australia looms throughout *Taller When Prone* and readers will sense Murray's close bond with the country and the remote areas that he sees as the authentic Australia. While the poet has little regard for city life, he has a deep respect for rural Australia and all of its traditions and mythologies. For Murray, almost anything claiming to be modern is suspect; he has never been a disciple of modernism or any of its literary tributaries. Believing his homeland to be a place rich with inspiration and heritage, Murray does not see the need for Australian poets to borrow from what has become "fashionable" in faraway places. He believes that it is possible to carve out a truly Australian literary tradition that pays tribute to both its ancestors and its pioneers without the need for modern European embellishments. The poems in this collection also hint at Murray's resentment of the so-called "intelligentsia" and the group's negative opinion of white Australians who live outside the urban areas. The poet has long been a voice for what he believes are the marginalized cultures of Australia and his special brand of "conservatism" includes his support for the traditions of both Aboriginal and rural white cultures.

Taller When Prone is replete with poems that touch on the natural world that Murray loves so much. In the poem "High-speed Bird" he becomes the temporary guardian of a kingfisher that has flown into a window. Upon taking a closer look at this wonder of nature, the poet is in awe of the kingfisher's "Cobalt wings, shutting on beige / body. Gold under-eye whiskers / beak closing in recovery." Sitting together, Murray feels as if he and bird are "one on one / as if staring back or / forward toward prehistory."

Murray does not want to surrender the relationship that he has formed with the natural world in order to become "sophisticated" or to have "lofty" pretensions. This seemingly slight encounter highlights Murray's views on nature and the natural and he is perfectly content to have a rewarding encounter with this kingfisher.

Where "High-speed Bird" describes Murray's fascination with another creature, the poem "The Farm Terraces" illustrates his reverence for the environment. The poem also illustrates the complicated relationship between people and their land. In it, the poet speaks of the molding of the landscape through "Beautiful merciless work" and the wondrous things that human labor can achieve through "the orders of hunger / or a pointing lord." He describes agrarian culture and the people who must keep their "hands long in the earth," noting that these farm terraces could only be constructed by superhuman efforts and "by backwrenching slog." It is the never-ending struggle to survive through honest effort that Murray applauds.

This relationship between people and the earth is examined in the poem "Port Jackson Greaseproof Rose" as well. In it, Murray asks the questions "Which produced more civilizations, / yellow grass or green?" and "Who made poverty legal? / Who made poverty at all?" As he meditates on the human condition, he reflects on poverty and the settlement of his country as the "last human continent" wondering whether it will "rise towers of two main kinds: / new glass ones keyed high to catch money/ and brown steeples to forgive the poor." As Murray sees it this distorted form of evolution is the cruelest of all blows to humankind. This poem also illustrates the author's sympathies with the marginalized and impoverished.

Throughout *Taller When Prone* Murray shares many curious anecdotes and pointed observations with the reader, drawing from his own experiences as well as from his readings of books, pamphlets, newspapers, and the like. His good memory and ability to recall facts are especially put to use in the poem "Infinite Anthology." In this unusual poem, Murray has compiled definitions of words and phrases that were created by what he calls "single-word poets." These writers— "by far the largest class of poets," according to Murray—enrich language by adding to it. "Infinite Anthology" is, in essence, a list, but it is also an experiment in the power of words that also demonstrates that Murray is not above having some uproarious fun in his pursuit of memorable poetry. In the poem "The Conversations" Murray has likewise strung

(©Cormac Scully)

Les Murray is a prize-winning and critically-acclaimed Australian poet whose awards include the T.S. Eliot Prize and the Queen's Medal for Poetry. He is an Officer of the Order of Australia and two-time winner of the Kenneth Slessor Prize for Poetry for his collections The People's Otherworld *(1983) and* Translations from the Natural World *(1992).*

together seemingly unrelated statements of fact. The poem opens with "A full moon always rises at sunset / and a person is taller at night." From that point on the reader is presented with increasingly bizarre bits of trivia as the poem eventually takes on a surreal, and occasionally solemn, quality.

Taller When Prone finds Murray almost in a literal sense all over the map. But regardless of whether the poems in it span the globe or are rooted in Australia, this collection is incontrovertibly grounded in Murray himself. Buried deep in the list of "The Conversation," Murray writes: "A fact is a small compact faith." Indeed his faith is a thread that runs throughout the poems in *Taller When Prone*—not only in his religious faith, but also in his convictions and values about the richness of tradition and the simultaneous strength and fragility of life and nature. The collection also demonstrates Murray's versatility in both tone and topic; some critics have called it idiosyncratic, but most agree that the collection is strong as a whole. Perhaps its greatest strength is the poet's distinct and powerful voice. With it, Murray once again confirms his place as one of the most vital and vibrant poets writing in the English language.

Jeffry Jensen

Review Sources

The Guardian, January 21, 2011 (Web).
The New York Review of Books 58, no. 14 (September 29, 2011): 64–66.
The New York Times Book Review, April 3, 2011, p. 16.
Poetry 199, no. 1 (October, 2011): 57–67, 78.

The Tiger's Wife

Author: Téa Obreht (b. 1985)
Publisher: Random House (New York).
352 pp. $25.00; paperback $15.00
Type of work: Novel
Time: The 1940s to the 1990s
Locale: An unnamed Balkan country

A young doctor's humanitarian mission to the Balkans also sends her on a quest to solve the mystery of her grandfather's death.

Principal characters:
DR. NATALIA STEFANOVIĆ, a young doctor
DR. LEANDRO (GRANDPA), Natalia's grandfather
GAVRAN GAILÉ (GAVO; THE DEATHLESS MAN), a
    man doomed to never die
THE TIGER'S WIFE, a deaf and mute Muslim girl
    who befriends an escaped tiger
LUKA, the town's butcher and the human husband of the tiger's wife
AMANA, Luka's former fiancée and the sister of the tiger's wife
THE APOTHECARY, a possible ally of the tiger's wife
DURÉ, a Serbian man obsessed with giving his cousin a decent burial
BARBA IVAN, an old village fisherman

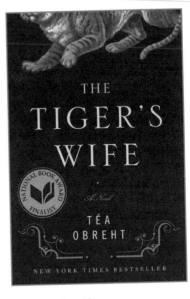

Téa Obreht has received an extraordinary amount of critical attention for her debut novel, *The Tiger's Wife*, which she published at the age of twenty-five. Many reviewers recognize Obreht as a prodigy; in her brief career as a writer, she has already achieved several milestones that may elude even the most talented and successful of writers. Her work has appeared in *The Best American Short Stories 2010* and in major national periodicals, including *The Atlantic Monthly*, *Harper's Review*, and the *New Yorker*, the latter of which featured her in its 2010 "20 Under 40" summer fiction issue celebrating twenty exceptional fiction writers under the age of forty. The National Book Foundation included her in its 2010 list of the top five writers under thirty-five and named *The Tiger's Wife* as one of four finalists for the 2011 National Book Award.

Critics have largely praised *The Tiger's Wife* as a beautifully written and richly imagined work. Obreht skillfully brings to life the history and culture of a war-torn region, despite the fact that she left it at the age of seven, before the war started, and did not witness the horrors of the conflict herself. Liesl Schillinger writes in the *New York Times* that the novel is "filled with astonishing immediacy and presence, fleshed out with detail that seems firsthand" but is imagined by the author rather than observed. Yet some reviewers take exception to the amount of detail that Obreht includes. David Ulin of the Los Angeles Times writes that fiction "is as much an art of omission as it is one of commission, and in *The Tiger's Wife* Obreht commits too much" by highlighting subplots in lieu of focusing on the main story. The poet Charles Simic shares Ulin's concern, writing that although some of these digressions are necessary to the plot, they are "too long and feel contrived at times."

Nevertheless, Simic and other reviewers laud Obreht's narrative technique, comparing it to the magical realism of Gabriel García Márquez for its blending and blurring of the ostensible facts of the story with contemporary fables. Obreht's generous incorporation of folkloric material works on a larger level to indicate the return of cultural elements suppressed by the once-powerful Soviet Union. In a 2011 interview with National Public Radio, Obreht explained that in writing *The Tiger's Wife*, she drew from traditional German and Slavic folktales and was inspired in part by the fairytale *Beauty and the Beast*.

The realistic events of the novel's main plot revolve around a mystery. Dr. Natalia Stefanović is a young doctor who lives in "the City" with her mother and her grandparents. While on a mission to deliver vaccines to Muslim orphans in a Balkan town that was once part of her Yugoslavian homeland, she learns that her grandfather, Dr. Leandro, has died in a remote village far from their home. Although Leandro's death itself does not completely surprise Natalia, who knew that he had cancer, she is perplexed by the circumstances in which he died. Why did he travel to the clinic in Zdrevkov? Why did he lie to her grandmother and say that he was going to meet Natalia to help her distribute the vaccines? Where are his personal belongings, especially his treasured copy of Rudyard Kipling's *The Jungle Book*?

As Natalia tries to solve these mysteries, she remembers the fable-like stories that her grandfather told her when she was younger. One story is about the tiger's wife of the title; the other is about Gavran Gailé, the deathless man. As the novel progresses, it becomes clear that these two distinct stories are intricately entwined with each other. At first, Natalia thinks that they are both merely fairy tales, but she soon comes to question this assumption as the stories lead her deeper into the truth about her grandfather's death and the nature of life itself.

The story of the tiger's wife begins during Leandro's boyhood in the village of Galina. Sometime during the early months of World War II, a tiger escapes from a zoo and ends up in Galina, where he is cared for by a young Muslim girl who is deaf and mute. The girl is forced into a marriage with the town butcher, who abuses her; when the butcher mysteriously disappears, the villagers assume that the girl must have fed him to the tiger. There is also a rumor that she is carrying the tiger's child. The young girl, who is indeed pregnant, is increasingly demonized by the villagers, who call her "the tiger's wife." Instinctively sympathetic to the oppressed and the wronged, and understanding that the girl's near-magical bond with the escaped tiger is a way for her to find some freedom from her unhappy circumstances, young Leandro secretly comes to her aid. The tiger's wife becomes Leandro's first love, and it is his devotion to her that will be Natalia's key to understanding her grandfather's character and integrity.

Dr. Leandro first meets the deathless man in the summer of 1954, when he is called to treat a man named Gavran Gailé who has apparently risen from his coffin, alive after all. Gavran, or Gavo, once tried to prevent his sweetheart from dying at

Téa Obreht's work has been published in the New Yorker, the Atlantic, *Best American Short Stories 2010, and* Harper's. *She is the youngest author ever to be awarded the Orange Prize (2011), which she won for her first novel,* The Tiger's Wife.

her naturally appointed time, and his uncle, Death, condemned him to a poor immortality on earth as punishment. Being a modern man of science, Dr. Leandro bets his most prized possession, a copy of Rudyard Kipling's *The Jungle Book*, that he can prove Gavran is a fraud. In turn, Gavran claims that he can survive a drowning Leandro has arranged for him in a nearby lake, wagering the magic coffee cup that allows him to determine the exact time anyone will die. Gavran survives the drowning unscathed, even though the doctor weighs him down with chains, but Leandro does not give him the book he is owed. By breaking his promise, Leandro reveals his own skeptical nature and his resistance to believing in superstition over scientific fact.

The two major stories passed on to Natalia by her grandfather speak to her of both love and loss but are situated within imaginative folktales that allow the natural world to develop a certain layer of enchantment. As a doctor like her grandfather, and as someone who thinks of herself as rational and modern, Natalia finds such enchantment to be frustrating as she tries to piece together the truth.

In the novel's last story, Natalia is infuriated by a family who insist on digging up an area of the village in order to find the corpse of their cousin. They claim that the cousin's spirit is unhappy with this burial site and is causing illness and misfortune in the family, and Natalia is unable to persuade the father, Duré, to provide his children with much-needed medical attention until she buries the cousin's heart at the crossroads. In the world of folklore, crossroads are associated with the spirit world; instead of finding a ghost there, however, Natalia meets an old local fisherman named Barba Ivan who has been pretending to be a *mora*, or spirit, to console the many grieving villagers recovering from recent wartime.

Natalia's story does not feature magic so much as explanations. Contrary to Duré's belief, there is evidently nothing supernatural going on at this crossroads. On the other hand, Barba Ivan's equable way of speaking echoes the voice of the deathless man, as if Natalia herself has had her first encounter with this eerie figure. Just as Leandro, a modern scientist, nevertheless found importance in the implausible figures of the deathless man and the tiger's wife, so his granddaughter never quite dispels her own adventure into a daytime one, instead making room for a second perspective associated with the twilight world of folklore and fantasy.

These dual perspectives—the rational and the superstitious, historical and folkloric—are both present in the storytelling of the novel, with storytelling itself being one of the novel's central themes. In particular, both Natalia and Leandro find that storytelling preserves cultural continuity during the upheaval of war. When Natalia is a teenager, and as conflict flares between different ethnic groups, Leandro takes her on a mysterious outing to see a former circus elephant being led to its new residence at the city zoo. Natalia finds this sight incredible and laments that her friends will not believe the story. Her grandfather chides her, saying, "The story of this war—dates, names, who started it, why—that belongs to everyone. Not just the people involved in it, but the people who write newspapers, politicians thousands of miles away, people who've never even been here or heard of it before. But something like this—this is yours. It belongs only to you. And me . . . You have to think carefully about where you tell it, and to whom. Who deserves to hear it?" This prompts Natalia to ask her grandfather about similar stories from the past, stories like the ones about the deathless man and the tiger's wife. By recounting these stories in the narrative of her own life story, Natalia becomes a bard, like her grandfather before her.

Natalia's visit to the crossroads parallels the critical junction she has reached in her own story. Her life so far has been shaped and perhaps thwarted by an era that spanned her grandfather's entire lifetime, an era that is now at its close. Natalia's journey, however, suggests that she will carry on her grandfather's legacy as a healer and a teller of tales, bringing these values into her own generation—perhaps as Obreht herself has by writing this richly inventive and unusually sophisticated first novel.

Margaret Boe Birns

Review Sources

Booklist 107, no. 12 (February 15, 2011): 50.
The New York Review of Books 58, no. 9 (March 26, 2011): 18–19.
The New York Times Book Review, March 13, 2011, p. 1.
Time 177, no. 10 (March 14, 2011): 64.
The Wall Street Journal, March 4, 2011, p. A11.

To End All Wars
A Story of Loyalty and Rebellion: 1914–1918

Author: Adam Hochschild (b. 1942)
Publisher: Houghton Mifflin Harcourt (New York). Illustrated. 480 pp. $28.00
Type of work: History

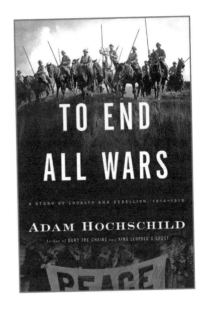

Adam Hochschild presents a brilliantly written account of Great Britain in World War I, focusing on individuals who opposed as well as supported the war.

Principle personages:
ALFRED MILNER, British statesman
JOHN FRENCH, first commander of the British army in France
CHARLOTTE DESPARD, sister of French and antiwar activist
DOUGLAS HAIG, French's successor as British military commander
SYLVIA PANKHURST, socialist and pacifist opponent of the war

World War I shaped the history of the rest of the twentieth century. It set in motion a dark age of ruthless war and mass political murder. However, none of the World War I combatants intended, much less desired, such consequences. The war was an unforeseen disaster. The forces unleashed by the conflict swiftly outran human control. Participants from kings to generals and lowly privates all came to see themselves as prisoners of events. By the time the war ended, four empires were in ruins. The victors, with the notable exception of the United States, were such in name only, drained of blood, money, and spirit. The aftershocks that followed the official cessation of hostilities—more wars and revolutions and the rise of modern totalitarianism—merely hastened the eventual European retreat from its long-held domination of the globe. A wistful nostalgia for the peace, prosperity, and moral certainties of the prewar era soon became a cultural industry. Something profound about Western civilization had come to an end, and only time would reveal the full import of the loss.

In *To End All Wars: A Story of Loyalty and Rebellion, 1914–1918*, Adam Hochschild makes a notable contribution to the attempt to understand the meaning of the World War I. His is not an analytical masterpiece like Paul Fussell's *The Great War and Modern Memory* (1975) or Modris Eksteins's *Rites of Spring* (1989); he does not dazzle the reader with sweeping generalizations or revelatory cultural insights. Instead, Hochschild draws upon his skills as a reporter. In a series of critically acclaimed books, including *King Leopold's Ghost: A Story of Greed, Terror, and Heroism in Colonial Africa* (1998), he has demonstrated a gift for narrative and a rare capacity to capture the many facets of human character. This is what he does in *To End All Wars*. Hochschild tells a human story of people wrestling with duty in the face of an all-consuming war. By taking this minimalist approach, and focusing on the plight of individuals, he breathes life into causes and beliefs that might seem mere abstractions in more topical surveys of World War I. Hochschild reminds his readers that the people caught up in the tragedy of a world-shaking conflict lacked modern society's advantage of hindsight. Sometimes with courage, sometimes with trepidation, participants had to leap into the abyss.

To End All Wars is not a comprehensive history of the war. Hochschild ably describes the broad contours of the war and the military and diplomatic strategies that shaped it. He also imposes a resolutely chronological structure in his book; following a series of chapters exploring the period before the war, he traces events year by year. Otherwise, however, Hochschild eschews the limits of more traditional military history. He focuses his story on the wartime experience of Great Britain. To do this, he develops an extensive list of historical characters, whose fates he follows during the course of the conflict. Hochschild brings to life an impressive and fascinating assortment of people, ranging from Lord Alfred Milner, an archimperialist, and by the end of the war possibly the second most powerful man in Britain, to Private Joseph Stones, who was shot for deserting his post in the line.

Hochschild takes pains to highlight the activities of the men and women who courageously took a stand against the war. He notes that, of the major warring powers, Britain alone possessed a tradition of free political discourse and civil liberties that allowed some social space for an antiwar movement during the conflict. Despite this space, opposition to the war was neither widespread nor popular. During the course of the war, twenty thousand men declared themselves conscientious objectors; six thousand were imprisoned for their beliefs. Even so well-connected an opponent of the war as the philosopher Bertrand Russell, who was descended from an earl, ended up incarcerated. The ultimate inconsequentiality of the antiwar movement, even in the face of the catastrophic casualties and enormous civilian hardship, continues to surprise and puzzle historians. Many contemporaries believed the vigorous socialist parties of Western Europe, united by an internationalist rhetoric that denounced militarism, would prove an effective barrier to the outbreak of war. When the time came, however, socialists overwhelmingly rallied to the flag. Nationalism trumped ideology. In Britain this phenomenon broke the heart of the great socialist leader James Keir Hardie; he died a little more than a year after the war began.

Despite their small numbers, the British antiwar activists are held in high esteem by Hochschild. They may not have carried much political weight in the years 1914–18, but as far as he is concerned, they were right about the war. They recognized it as a disaster for Western civilization. As might be expected of people who chose to march out of step with their times, they were a disparate group. Charlotte Despard was a wealthy widow who had embraced feminism, pacifism, Irish nationalism, and the Independent Labour Party. She threw herself into the anticonscription movement and traveled the country speaking out for peace. Ironically, Despard was the sister of Field Marshall John French, the first commander of the British Expeditionary Force on the European continent.

Adam Hochschild is a journalist who helped found Mother Jones *magazine. He is the author of numerous books, including* King Leopold's Ghost: A Story of Greed, Terror, and Heroism in Colonial Africa *(1999) and* Bury the Chains: Prophets and Rebels in the Fight to Free an Empire's Slaves *(2006). He teaches narrative writing at the University of California.*

Despard and her brother, though radically different in their politics, remained friendly.

Less fortunate in her family relations was Sylvia Pankhurst. Sylvia's mother, Emmeline Pankhurst, was the leader of the radical, and occasionally violent, women's suffrage movement in England before the war. Sylvia and her sister, Christabel, had enthusiastically supported their mother, though Sylvia also became a passionate socialist. Once the war broke out, Emmeline and Christabel became fierce advocates for the war effort; Sylvia decried the war and called for peace. As a result, she was shunned by her mother and sister, and the family was never reconciled.

Lord Lansdowne, a Conservative magnate and a former foreign minister, called for a negotiated peace midway through the war. He believed that Europe was tearing itself apart through the conflict and that nothing that might be gained from the war was worth the price being paid in blood. His reward was to be publically denounced by friends and former colleagues.

Though Hochschild's heart belongs with the antiwar minority, he is mindful that most people accommodated themselves to the war effort, either out of conviction or a sort of tribal loyalty that transcends reasoned decision. He writes of a leftist editor and critic of the war, who, upon visiting the front, found himself almost irresistibly drawn to join passing troops of British soldiers. Certainly the camaraderie enjoyed by many soldiers in the trenches, the sense of shared dangers and privations, helped them adjust to the horrific atmosphere around them. These soldiers endured a blood sacrifice almost unimaginable in retrospect. Hochschild writes movingly of the shocking losses suffered by the British in battles that made negligible territorial gains. During one attack at the Battle of Loos, in September 1915, out of ten thousand advancing British troops, more than eight thousand were killed, wounded, or taken prisoner. On a grander scale, on the first day of the Battle of the Somme, July 1, 1916, sixty thousand British soldiers became casualties; nearly twenty thousand died.

The pain of such losses was shared by all classes. The war took a bitter toll on the well-bred young men who served as officers. Five of former prime minister Lord Salisbury's ten grandsons were killed. Lady Violet Cecil's son was one of the five. Rudyard Kipling, the famous author of *The Jungle Book* (1894) and a vocal supporter of the war, lost his only son at Loos. Despite their heartbreak, these supporters of the war retained their faith in the cause. Part of the tragedy of the conflict was that an admirable sense of duty and sacrifice sustained the determination to prolong the struggle.

Hochschild is a traditionalist in one crucial aspect of the book: He is not persuaded by revisionist efforts in recent decades to rehabilitate the military reputations of the British generals of the World War I, especially that of Sir Douglas Haig. For many years these commanders were seen to be wasting the lives of their brave troops in fruitless assaults on the German trench system. Some scholars have written sympathetically of the challenges faced by these men and their often innovative attempts to overcome the military stalemate on the western front. Hochschild is too mindful of the bloody carnage in no-man's-land, and what it meant for loved ones and families, to spare any tears for men who proved excruciatingly slow to appreciate the conditions facing their men. In fact, officers whose commands took heavy casualties in combat were commended on the assumption that if they were losing lots of men, so too were the enemy. Such attitudes in the British high command intensified the horrors of trench warfare.

The first British commander in France was Sir John French, as careless with the lives of his men as he was with money and other men's wives in his private life. A bluff old cavalryman, French was good at chatting up enlisted men but out of his depth as a strategist. His successor, Haig, was the opposite in his private life, an upright and rather puritanical man. Lacking the common touch, he stayed at headquarters and cultivated relationships with the king and other influential people. This guaranteed that he was politically invulnerable when Prime Minister David Lloyd George wanted to fire him after the demoralizing failure of the Battle of Passchendaele in 1917. Haig embodied the cold, methodical qualities associated with modern industrial war; once hopes of a breakthrough dimmed, he readily embraced the military logic of attrition. He willingly bled out his own army, confident, thanks to the reports of sycophantic staff officers, that he was doing the same and more to the enemy. For Hochschild, Haig's implacable commitment to the offensive in the face of all technological or topographic reality symbolizes the tragic madness of the war.

Hochschild ends his book as he begins it, in a British cemetery near the old battlefields. The battlefields themselves are still lethal; French and Belgian farmers are occasionally blown up as they plow over unexploded shells working their way to the surface. But the cemeteries are beautifully maintained and peaceful. They are visited by family members and others who do not want to forget what these cemeteries represent. Hochschild honors the military dead. However, he likes to imagine another cemetery, filled with the people who opposed the World War I, and equally deserving of honor. By eloquently describing the bitter cost of the war unleashed in 1914, and reminding readers of the small band who courageously condemned the bloodshed, Hochschild's *To End All Wars* will deservedly win a worthy place in the extensive and often brilliant literature on World War I.

Daniel P. Murphy

Review Sources

Booklist 107, no. 15 (April 1, 2011): 17.
The Economist 399, no. 8736 (June 4, 2011): 93.
Kirkus Reviews 79, no. 3 (February 1, 2011): 183.
Library Journal 136, no. 7 (April 15, 2011): 101.
The New York Times Book Review, May 15, 2011, p. 6.
Publishers Weekly 258, no. 6 (February 7, 2011): 43.

Tolstoy
A Russian Life

Author: Rosamund Bartlett
Publisher: Houghton Mifflin Harcourt (New York). 560 pp. $35.00
Type of work: Biography
Time: Nineteenth and early twentieth centuries
Locale: Russia

Focusing on the last thirty years of Tolstoy's life, this biography vividly captures the writer's epic life and conducts readers on a fascinating journey through Russian history and culture.

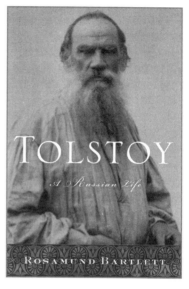

Principal personages:
LEO TOLSTOY (1828–1910), Russian novelist and man of letters
SOFYA BERS (1884–1919), a physician's daughter and Tolstoy's wife

In 2007, *Time* magazine voted Leo Tolstoy's sprawling novels of personal and public revolution, *Anna Karenina* (1877) and *War and Peace* (1869), as two of the greatest novels of all time. Over one hundred years after Tolstoy's death, his densely written and richly populated novels continue to offer deep insight into human nature, depicting the unhappiness of families, the bankruptcy of romantic love, the virtue of peasants, the hollow victories of war, and the triviality of aristocratic society. Among the writers who have voiced admiration for his work are many of the finest, including Vladimir Nabokov, William Faulkner, Anton Chekhov, and Fyodor Dostoevsky. In addition to his epic portraits of life in Russia in the nineteenth century, Tolstoy's religious writings, such as *Confession* (1882), *Resurrection* (1889), and *The Kingdom of God is Within You* (1894), continue to influence contemporary debates regarding the nature of the Christian religion and the role of pacifism in war and peace. His novella *The Death of Ivan Ilyich* (1886) appears as required reading in many philosophy classes. Perhaps more than any other nineteenth-century writer, Tolstoy can still fire the imagination and draw readers deeply into provocative conversations about the way people live in a society whose order does not always promote life, love, happiness, or peace.

Just as sprawling as Tolstoy's novels is the story of his life, which many biographies have since attempted to capture. In fact, with bookshelves already groaning under the weight of these many biographies, the reader may wonder why Rosamund Bartlett has bothered to write *Tolstoy: A Russian Life*. What new history could she possibly add to the exhaustively detailed portraits already published? What new aspects of Tolstoy's varied life as a gambler, educator, political activist, and religious thinker has she discovered?

For starters, Bartlett's book is not a literary biography, and it forgoes analysis of Tolstoy's famous works in favor of a more general contextualization of each work within the known concerns and events of his life. Bartlett approaches the biography from Tolstoy's own point of view, focusing on his life in pre-Soviet Russia and looking most closely at his last thirty years, when he became a social and religious crusader. After Tolstoy's death, the Soviet Union suppressed his spiritual legacy, which many would argue was his most important contribution to the world of letters. The subsequent relaxation of Soviet censorship has opened the floodgates to a mass of new material, and Bartlett draws extensively on the key Russian sources and materials that have since become available, thus avoiding the politically skewed picture of Tolstoy's writings that has hampered many of his previous biographers. According to Bartlett, there is much more objective information available today about Tolstoy, his family, his many followers, the activities of the Russian Orthodox Church (from which he was excommunicated in 1901), and the tsarist government.

(© Elizabeth Zeschin)

Rosamund Bartlett is the author of the acclaimed biography Chekhov: Scenes from a Life *(2005). An authority on Russian cultural history, she has also achieved renown as a translator of Chekhov's stories and letters. She is currently a visiting research fellow at Kings College, London.*

As the title suggests, Bartlett portrays Tolstoy as a quintessentially Russian genius. During his life, he embodied many prototypical Russian archetypes, such as the reckless gambler, the holy fool, the repentant nobleman, the revered elder, the anarchist, and the nihilist, and Bartlett explores his life through the lenses of these categories. Only Russia could have produced a writer like Tolstoy, Bartlett argues, and only Tolstoy could be likened to a tsar and a peasant in the same breath. From the time he was born into an aristocratic family in the idyllic surroundings of Yasnaya Polyana to the day he left that ancestral home for the last time at the age of eighty-two, Tolstoy lived a profoundly Russian life. Later critics and writers often comment that Tolstoy had no face of his own; he was the face of the Russian people, because in him the whole of Russia lived and breathed. While Bartlett conducts her book with generosity, she also holds a critical eye to her subject when necessary.

Born in 1828, Tolstoy seemed to enjoy a life of privilege and status. Although very little information exists about his earliest years at Yasnaya Polyana, Bartlett is fair in her speculations. Tolstoy likely grew up in a loving family, with a gentle, easygoing father and a mother who was modest, humble, and saintly. Tolstoy read voraciously; by his own admission, his favorite authors were Alexander Pushkin, Jean-Jacques Rousseau, Charles Dickens, and Anthony Trollope, the latter two of whom wrote sprawling social novels that explored themes like injustice, poverty, economic inequity, and the moral conduct of the privileged class. By the time he was nineteen, Tolstoy was a wealthy landowner himself and almost instantly began to exhibit tendencies typical of nobility: squandering his money on gambling and women, taking advantage of peasant girls and leaving many of them pregnant (behavior that was to continue well into adulthood). His gambling debts were so great that he had to sell off entire villages to pay them. In 1854, he even had to sell off the main house of Yasnaya Polyana, his family's estate. The house was dismantled and rebuilt in another place, but the absence of the main house left a gaping hole between the two wings of the estate.

In the same year, Tolstoy took the next step for a nobleman and became an officer in the army. Although most officers retired to the country once they received their commissions, Tolstoy used the opportunity to begin his writing career in earnest. In 1855, he wrote "Sebastopol in December," his first piece of journalism, about the harsh fighting taking place in the city of Sebastopol. Other writers received Tolstoy's sketches with great acclaim, and he soon traveled to St. Petersburg, where he met writers such as Ivan Turgenev and became recognized for his literary talents. During this period, Tolstoy began to show signs of his attraction to anarchism, alienating many of his fellow writers with his eccentric, often aggressive and argumentative nature. He refused to belong to any particular literary group and eventually parted ways with Turgenev, who did not take writing as seriously as Tolstoy thought he should.

Because of his education and the critical stance he developed toward the government, Tolstoy assumed a role in the intelligentsia. Ashamed of his participation in the immoral institution of serfdom and of his own treatment of serfs, Tolstoy adopted what Bartlett portrays as the persona of a repentant nobleman. He took a widely popularized view of the peasantry, lauding them as Russia's best class and the future of the country. In 1859, he opened a school for peasants at Yasnaya Polyana, though the endeavor, faced with the harassment of the tsarist police, did not last long. When serfdom was abolished in 1861, he established more schools so that he could teach village children how to read and write. It was during this phase of Tolstoy's life that he married the physician's daughter Sofya Bers, beginning a marriage that would become one of the most contentious in all of literary history (Tolstoy famously revealing his entire sexual history to Sofya on their wedding night, including his having fathered a child with one of his serfs).

In the first half of the 1870s, Tolstoy returned to education, reopening the school at Yasnaya Polyana and writing an alphabet book and a primer for the use of children in his schools. After teaching himself Greek, he produced his own simplified translations of Aesop's fables. By the second half of the 1870s, Tolstoy's life began to move in several directions. In 1873, while speaking out about the impoverished peasantry and the threat of impending famine, he began work on the novel *Anna Karenina*. The novel itself reflects Tolstoy's own search for meaning in a disordered world—and beyond observations such as this, Bartlett refrains from literary criticism. Out of a sense of disorder, Tolstoy began investigating several religious movements, including the monastery at Optina Pustyn, where monks separated themselves from the church hierarchy and urged a return to the ascetic spiritual practices of the early church, and the wandering peasants, who made pilgrimages to holy places, having given up everything in their spiritual quest. Tolstoy himself took to dressing like a peasant and eventually dispensed with money and private property altogether. It was during this period that he wrote *Confession*, his account of his spiritual journey; this was also when he became a nihilist, critically challenging Russian Orthodox theology. He produced his own translation of the Gospels and began preaching against the immorality of the monarchy and all other institutions of the state. By the end of the decade, Tolstoy had become the leader of a new sectarian faith that called itself the Tolstoyans. In imitation of peasant life, the Tolstoyans gave up money and property in order to live by the labor of their hands.

During the last two decades of his life, Tolstoy became the most admired and revered man in Russia, mainly for his social and religious teachings. Although the Russian Orthodox Church excommunicated him, the Russian government was powerless to stop Tolstoy from speaking out because of his immense popularity. The government could not exile or arrest him, given the international outrage such an action would inspire, as the later phase of Tolstoy's career had brought him worldwide success as his work spread in translation. Tolstoy took advantage of his popularity and political immunity, acting the "holy fool" and speaking openly and candidly about the tsar's failures as a leader. According to Bartlett, during Tolstoy's last decade, many in Russia believed that he was the "real" tsar.

Bartlett's splendid biography vividly captures Tolstoy's epic life and conducts readers on a fascinating journey through Russian history and culture. Tolstoy's changing personality reflects Russia's changing social, political, and religious landscape during the latter part of the nineteenth century. New translations of *Anna Karenina* (Bartlett's will be published in 2012) and *War and Peace* have introduced a new generation of readers to the beauty and complexity of Tolstoy's writing, just as Bartlett's brilliant portrait introduces a new generation of readers to the life and times of this maddening, contrary, and deeply admired man.

Henry L. Carrigan Jr.

Review Sources

Booklist 107, no. 19/20 (June 15, 2011): 30.
History Today 61, no. 1 (January 2011): 62.
Kirkus Reviews 79, no. 15 (August 1, 2011): 1309.
Library Journal 136, no. 12 (July 1, 2011): 81–82.
Publishers Weekly 258, no. 30 (July 25, 2011): 39.
Times Literary Supplement, no. 5637 (April 15, 2011): 7.

Tough Without a Gun
The Life and Extraordinary Afterlife of Humphrey Bogart

Author: Stefan Kanfer
Publisher: Alfred A. Knopf (New York).
304 pp. $26.95; paperback $15.95
Type of work: History
Time: Primarily 1899–1957
Locale: United States

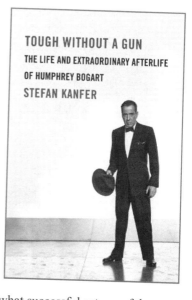

TOUGH WITHOUT A GUN
THE LIFE AND EXTRAORDINARY AFTERLIFE
OF HUMPHREY BOGART
STEFAN KANFER

Kanfer chronicles the life of Humphrey Bogart, from childhood through a struggling early career to his breakthrough as a film star in his early forties, and offers a thorough examination of the lore and legend of Bogart as a larger-than-life icon after his death.

Principal personages:

HUMPHREY BOGART (1899–1957), a famous Hollywood film star of the 1930s and 1940s

HELEN MENKEN (1901–1966), his first wife, a somewhat successful actress of the 1920s and 1930s who made the transition from Broadway to Hollywood

MARY PHILIPS (1901–1975), his second wife, a stage actress and longtime acquaintance of his

MAYO METHOT (1904–1951), his third wife, a stage and screen actress

LAUREN BACALL (b. 1924), his fourth wife, a successful film star

Of all the iconic stars of the 1930s and 1940s, Humphrey Bogart has "left the most enduring mark and remains the most forceful presence," asserts Stefan Kanfer, whose biography of Bogart attempts to determine why the legend of the Hollywood icon has endured for so many years after his death. Kanfer, who is also known for his best-selling biography *Ball of Fire: The Tumultuous Life and Comic Art of Lucille Ball* (2003), has written an unusual biography that offers a relatively brief biographical sketch, coupled with more in-depth investigations of his major roles and an insightful look at the many historical and contemporary factors that have contributed to the Bogart legend.

While he had a gift for playing miscreants, outcasts, and men who had fallen down on their luck, Bogart began his life in a privileged environment. He was born in 1899, the son of Yale-educated physician Belmont Deforest Bogart and successful illustrator Maud Humphrey. As Kanfer describes, Bogart's parents had a tumultuous and contentious relationship, complicated by his father's struggle with morphine addiction and his mother's heavy drinking. Humphrey and his two sisters, Frances and Catherine, lived in a world of both profound comfort and profound emotional turmoil.

Bogart was a poor student, despite his parents' best efforts to find an educational institution that would, either through discipline or inspiration, get their son on a more productive track. Bogart rebelled, challenging his teachers and often flouting the rules. Excited by the possibility of adventure overseas, he enrolled in the US Navy in 1918, joining the crew of the USS *Leviathan* in May, barely six months before World War I officially ended. Less than a year later, he left with the rank of seaman second class and one of his most famous physical attributes, a scar on his lip that lent the future star his characteristic slight lisp.

The story of Bogart's scar has become the subject of numerous Hollywood legends, several of which Kanfer recounts in his book. Some sources report that Bogart was struck in the mouth by a piece of shrapnel during an attack on the *Leviathan*, though this version of the story seems unlikely given that the war ended not long after Bogart enlisted. According to another story, while Bogart was escorting a naval prisoner during a transfer, the prisoner attacked him, striking him in the mouth with his manacles. Other biographers have guessed that Bogart may simply have been involved in a brawl at some point. Whatever the cause, Bogart's upper lip was badly split, and neither the initial surgery nor later plastic surgery was able to correct the deformation.

When he returned to New York, Bogart engaged in a series of jobs procured for him by his father, but he remained uninspired until he found an avenue into stage acting. He landed a series of small roles in Broadway productions, generally playing socialites, which may seem quite distant from his later, better-known roles but was not very far removed from the environment of his youth. During this time, he met and married Helen Menken, a stage actress who remained with Bogart for a little over a year before filing for divorce. The following year, Bogart married his second wife, Mary Philips, another stage actress he met in the Broadway social scene.

Bogart's first notable performance was in the 1935 play *The Petrified Forest*, where he played a hard-edged gangster. The following year, he was asked to reprise his role in a film version, and the project took him to Hollywood, where he would spend the remainder of his career. Bogart's move soon brought an end to his ten-year marriage to Philips, who preferred to remain in the East. By 1938, Bogart was married again, this time to Mayo Methot, a former stage actress who also was making the leap to the movie screen.

Bogart and Methot were contract players for Warner Bros. Studios and appeared in a variety of films over the next several years, but both struggled to find breakout roles. Even as Bogart caroused with such prominent film stars of the day as Spencer Tracy and strove for success in his career, his marriage was falling apart. Methot drank as much as her husband did and was reportedly given to violent fits of temper, which Kanfer describes in some detail.

Bogart's break finally came in 1941, when he was cast in the role of Roy "Mad Dog" Earle in the thriller *High Sierra*. In this role, Bogart showed audiences a more refined version of the criminal archetype he had been perfecting since *The Petrified Forest*. As Earle, Bogart delivered a believable blend of sympathy and scorn, giving his character dimensions that resonated with both audiences and critics. Though he was not considered famous enough to carry star billing on *High Sierra*, that same year he was given the top

Former Time *magazine editor and film critic Stefan Kanfer has worked on several anthology works, including* The Essential Groucho *(2000), a review of the comedy of Groucho Marx. He has also written several books on celebrity personalities, including a biography of Lucille Ball, and a respected history of Jewish theater entitled* Stardust Lost: The Triumph, Tragedy, and Mishugas of the Yiddish Theater in America *(2006).*

spot when he portrayed cynical detective Sam Spade in the highly successful film adaptation of Dashiel Hammett's noir novel *The Maltese Falcon* (1930). Kanfer credits Bogart's characterization of Spade, along with director John Houston's skilled treatment, for making the film a classic of the genre and turning Bogart into a household name.

Kanfer describes, with obvious admiration, the brilliance Bogart displayed during the finale of the picture, when he was called upon to give a speech with "crowded words and thoughts" that was, in Kanfer's opinion, "tautly and confidently delivered." In Hammett's book, Spade moves on as if unmoved by the events that transpired around him. While the film was initially filmed with an ending similar to that of the book, both Houston and Bogart felt that Spade's indifference detracted from the depth of the character and the significance of the "moral tragedy" that unfolded in the film's final chapter. Together with the producer, they decided to change the ending, and Kanfer repeats the Hollywood legend that claims Bogart may have had a role in penning the last reflective line of the film.

In 1942 came Bogart's most famous role, mercenary-turned-bar owner Rick Blaine in the seminal film *Casablanca.* Kanfer dedicates considerable space to a detailed discussion of the film from many angles, from directorial dilemmas and cast relations to the political and social ramifications of the film's reception. As Blaine, Bogart distanced himself from the rough gangsters of his earlier roles and carved a new niche for himself, that of the principled, romantic, yet cynical hero caught between duty and personal attainment. Bogart carried off the role with such panache that Blaine became one of the best-known and most imitated characters ever to appear on film.

Some critics have suggested that Bogart's familiarity with the etiquette and demeanor of the upper classes is precisely what allowed him to bring something unexpected and dignified to his portrayal of criminals, miscreants, and toughs. Bogart's duty-bound but battle-weary and love-worn Rick Blaine was perhaps the ultimate expression of this idea, though touches of the same set of contradictory virtues and vices sparkle from many of his more memorable roles.

Following *Casablanca,* Bogart was a major star. He socialized with the biggest celebrities in Hollywood and often spent lavishly on copious amounts of liquor, food, and cigarettes. In early 1944, with his fame at its apogee, Bogart's relationship with Methot finally disintegrated, soon after he met nineteen-year-old actress Lauren Bacall on the set of the Howard Hawks film *To Have and Have Not* (1944). The pair engaged in a secret affair that soon hit the gossip circuit as Bogart tried to reconcile with his wife. Methot, for her part, agreed to rehabilitation in an effort to control her drinking, but the relationship never stabilized; by June 1945, Bogart and Bacall were married.

Those who knew the couple describe Bacall as the perfect foil for Bogart. In her later years, Bacall herself described the marriage as a very happy one, with only minor problems arising between them. They were among the most famous icons of their day, and their relationship became established in celebrity history as one of Hollywood's greatest love stories, a legend Kanfer does not tarnish with the kind of critique he gives to Bogart's previous marriages.

In 1951, Bogart reunited with director and close friend John Houston to star in *The African Queen* alongside Katharine Hepburn. The challenging film was shot on location in the Congo and Uganda, which caused a number of problems for the cast and crew, including outbreaks of dysentery and malaria and insect attacks. Despite these setbacks, Bogart and Hepburn turned in memorable performances, and Bogart received the Academy Award for Best Actor, an honor that he took to heart despite his frequent complaints about the politics of Hollywood. Bogart later said that he considered *African Queen* to be his finest performance.

In 1956, Bogart was diagnosed with cancer, and though he tried a variety of treatment options, his health steadily declined. Over the next year, he continued to enjoy sailing, smoking, and drinking to his heart's content, comforted by his ever-present wife and their two children until his death in January 1957.

Kanfer covers the seminal events in Bogart's life more or less chronologically, as others before him have; the unique part of his presentation comes after he recounts the star's death, as he tries to unravel the elements that contribute to the Bogart mystique. Kanfer draws upon a number of examples to demonstrate how Bogart has continued to exert a force in American popular culture through the decades. He mentions, for instance, the 1960s counterculture phrase "to bogart a joint," meaning to hang a marijuana cigarette from your lip, as Bogart did in films, holding onto it for longer than your allotted time. Kanfer also devotes time to analyzing the many spoofs and send-ups of Bogart over the years in an attempt to discover what these various versions of Bogart say about the role that his legend plays in modern American culture.

Though he never quite comes to a firm answer to his central question, Kanfer does offer some interesting observations along the way. He asserts that there will never be another Bogart, partly because the era in which middle-aged actors can become major celebrities has all but passed, as the tastes of moviegoing audiences have shifted toward younger stars and story lines aimed at younger audiences. While older men still have sway in Hollywood, few of them rise to the top when already in their early forties or older. Kanfer further argues that the male archetype embodied by Bogart, with his heavy drinking and smoking and his air of emotional deportment, has been replaced by a postmodern hero, more emotionally available perhaps but lacking the classic masculinity that made Bogart an international hero. While Kanfer bemoans the loss of the "authentic" man embodied by Bogart, he celebrates the many ways that the Bogart legend continues to exert a powerful influence on American culture, seeing this as a sign that Bogart's version of "authenticity" will never truly die.

Micah L. Issitt

Review Sources

Atlantic Monthly, February 1, 2011 (Web).
Daily Mail, February 4, 2011 (Web).
Milwaukee Journal Sentinel, January 29, 2011 (Web).
Publishers Weekly 257, no. 45 (November 15, 2010): 47–48.
Slate, February 8, 2011 (Web).
The Wall Street Journal, January 29, 2011 (Web).

Townie
A Memoir

Author: Andre Dubus III (b. 1959)
Publisher: W. W. Norton (New York). 387 pp.
$25.95
Type of Work: Memoir
Time: 1970s–1990s
Locale: Haverhill, Bradford, and Newbury-port, Massachusetts, among various other towns in the surrounding Merrimack Valley

Andre Dubus III's memoir is a story of a boy who, terrified by his inability to stand up for himself and those he loves, turns to physical strength and violence as a young man and then eventually to the art of writing.

Principal personages:
ANDRE DUBUS III (b. 1959), the author, one of four siblings in a divorced family, struggling to find his voice through violence and later through writing
ANDRE DUBUS II (1936–1999), Andre's father, a writer and professor who devotes his life to his work
PATTY LOWE DUBUS, Andre's mother who struggles to provide for her family in the wake of divorce
JEB DUBUS, Andre's younger brother
SUZANNE DUBUS, Andre's older sister
SAM DOLAN, Andre's close friend with whom he initially connected over weight training and boxing

In his first walk through the student union at Bradford College, where his father was a professor, sixteen-year-old Andre Dubus III overhears a fellow student say, "That's Dubus's son. Look at him. He's such a *townie*." This memory, wherein it is apparent even to a stranger that Andre and his father are from two different worlds, resonated with the boy throughout his youth. Throughout the story of *Townie*, the Merrimack River and the Basiliere Bridge that passes over it and connects the towns of Bradford and Haverhill, Massachusetts, serve as both literal and symbolic images of the divide between Andre's gritty struggle to survive boyhood surrounded by poverty and violence and the elevated academic lifestyle of his father. Critically acclaimed as a riveting account of the ultimate triumph of peace through words over violence, *Townie* has been received with praise for the tenderness and honesty with which Dubus revisits abandonment, bullying, and becoming a writer.

After his parents' divorce, Andre, his mother, and his three siblings—Suzanne, Jeb, and Nicole—could barely meet their basic daily needs on Patty's social services salary. The family moved from one rental to another during the early 1970s, first in Newburyport, Massachusetts, and then in Haverhill. With each move and new school, all four siblings were bullied and had difficulty making friends. The repeated physical and verbal intimidation left Andre feeling helpless and weak, ashamed that he can do "nothing but run into the house and hide." As a young boy, he grew increasingly disappointed in his inability to protect himself or his family in the years following the divorce. The desire to fight back was finally roused when he saw the film *Billy Jack* (1971), in which the title character uses military skill and martial arts to avenge a brutal attack on his wife. Andre became infused with an eagerness to be able to do the same to anyone who had ever wronged him or his family up to that point. *Townie* vividly recalls the author's feeling in those days that when he "thought of the word *man*, [he] could only think of those who could defend themselves and those they loved."

Meanwhile, across the bridge, the Dubus siblings spent Wednesday and Sunday evenings with their father at his apartment in Bradford. Their worlds were foreign to one another—Andre's father did not recognize the struggles his own family faced on the other side of the Merrimack. This is poignantly illustrated in a memory of Andre when, at fourteen, he tried to play catch with his father but had no idea how to handle a baseball. He recalls recognizing that his father felt sorry for him and seemed surprised at his son's lack of knowledge and skill. For Andre, the most striking part of the memory is "being surprised that [his father] was surprised." He wonders, "What did he think the kids did in my neighborhood? What did he think we *did?* But how could I tell him anything without incriminating us all . . ." This is one of several moments in the narrative where baseball is used to illustrate the disconnect between father and son.

As a young teenager, Andre's life was marked by lack of discipline and days spent with Jeb and their friend Cleary; they spent hours drinking, smoking, and in the tree house the three of them built in the backyard. All of this changed after an incident in which Jeb was beaten up and their mother was insulted in front of their house while Andre found himself unable to do anything but plead for it to stop. Reeling from the encounter, he accused himself of being weak, small, afraid, and cowardly—a description he had applied to himself before, but on that day, "felt less like the end and more like a beginning."

From that point on, he began a strict weight training routine and even joined the cross-country team at school. His body changed, his grades improved, and he met a new friend, Sam Dolan, who was similarly disciplined and enthusiastic about bodybuilding. Training at a local boxing gym gave Andre the skills he needed to fight back and protect the vulnerable. His first opportunity to fight pitted him against another townie named Steve Lynch, and Andre knocked him out with a single punch. This moment set him on a path down which he sought healing through violence. Whether he believed he was defending a family member, friend, or even a stranger, he began to feel that each encounter was a test that brought him further from the boy he had been.

During this time, a new connection developed between Andre and his father as they bonded over weight training. In this activity, Andre was the expert and coached his father, who wanted to share in the experience of fighting other people with his fists. He even tried to fight a stranger in a bar; the result was less than successful, but the attempt was completely exhilarating. The father and son's paths also began to cross socially as the professor began to attend parties with Andre's peers on the weekends. All the while, as Andre began to meet more people and become more involved in school, he started to see his actions and violence through the eyes of others. In the aftermath of one altercation, the author remembers feeling like a "dimwitted brute" in the eyes of his girlfriend whose honor he had meant to defend.

Throughout the book, Dubus describes his ability to assert violence against another person using the image of a membrane. He notes that if a fighter can break through the membrane surrounding him, nothing holds him back from throwing the first punch and breaking through his opponent's membrane as well. However, as his circle of friends expanded and became more diverse—both at college in Bradford and in Austin, Texas—it felt to Andre as though the dissolving of the membrane separating him from others served to reveal glimpses of the

Andre Dubus III is the author of Bluesman *(1993),* House of Sand and Fog *(1999), and* The Garden of Last Days *(2008), as well as a collection of short stories,* The Cage Keeper and Other Stories *(1989). He is the recipient of such honors as The National Magazine Award, the Pushcart Prize, and a Guggenheim Fellowship.*

humanity of each individual, creating a sensitizing effect rather than a hardening one. Seeing his violent tendencies through new perspectives challenged his perception of himself and his violent actions; he slowly began to recognize that it was self-serving and that he needed a different way to "express a wound" like the ones he knew were inside of him. At twenty-two, he began to write, an act that allowed him passage into the world of processing experience through words instead of violence. It was his father's world, and one that he had previously only observed from the outside.

In the following years, as he continued to write, the author notes that he discovered a "new membrane...one between what we think and what we see, between what we believe and what is." As he describes the transformational power of writing to "dissolve" this membrane, using words to capture the intimate details of what transpires between heart, head, and the blank page, he eloquently brings the reader across the bridge and through the barrier into the center of the writer's art.

It is from this center that Andre is ultimately able to process a multitude of conflicting feelings, not the least of which are confusion, affection, and abandonment, reconciling his instincts to rage violently with his deep desire to be generous and sympathetic towards others, including his father. The author illuminates this process when he describes a culminating moment during a train ride across England with his young wife. On the train, he found himself facing multiple would-be bullies as the obvious candidate to protect the vulnerable passengers in their car. Instead of using violence, he chose to use words, eventually looking into the face of a drug dealer and decided to "trust the humanity of the other to show itself."

In the final years of his father's life, Andre's desire to trust in his father's humanity despite the years of his absence became more and more profound. The author openly describes his feelings of heartache and relief at his father's death. He reflects on how his hands, used for fighting and eventually for writing, wrapped themselves around the shovel as he dug his father's grave in the same cemetery where Cleary was buried; in this poignant scene, the impact of the memories from both sides of the river are laid bare. The author carefully punctuates these final scenes with detail that holds the tension between compassion and conviction, completing the journey for the reader in which Andre notes "what we think and what we see" and "what we believe and what is" have been challenged. Readers familiar with Andre Dubus's fiction—including the 1999 National Book Award finalist *The House of Sand and Fog*—will appreciate the insight that *Townie* provides into the author's early life. His memoir is as raw and as evocative as his novels and short stories would indicate. His candor especially shines through in his effective use of settings to enhance the anger, loss, and pain of his youth. Not only the true story of the way violence shaped a young man's life, *Townie* is also a meditation on feelings of weakness, helplessness, and regret, as well as on the power of will and discipline. In a broader respect, *Townie* is also a fascinating glimpse into notions of masculinity and male violence. Though some critics have argued that segments of the memoir are overwritten or overlong, most agree that it is an exhilarating and unforgettable book.

Elizabeth Bellucci

Review Sources

Booklist 107, no. 6 (November 15, 2010): 8.
Commonweal 138, no. 9 (May 6, 2011): 35–36.
Kirkus Reviews 78, no. 23 (December 1, 2010): 1195.
Kirkus Reviews 79, no. 1 (January 1, 2011): Special sec. 4.
The New York Times, February 25, 2011 (Web).
Publishers Weekly 257, no. 49 (December 13, 2010): 49.
Publishers Weekly 258, no. 13 (March 28, 2011): 53.

The Tragedy of Arthur

Author: Arthur Phillips (b. 1969)
Publisher: Random House (New York).
384 pp. $26.00
Type of work: Novel
Time: The present, although many passages refer
to the childhood of the narrator and his sister
Locale: Minneapolis, Prague, and New York City

This book explores the psychological character
of its narrator, his relationships with his twin
sister and criminal father, and the authentic-
ity of the manuscript of The Tragedy of Arthur,
a play purportedly penned by William Shake-
speare.

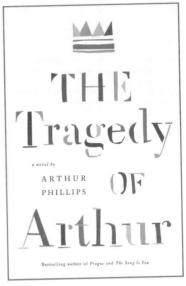

Principal characters:
ARTHUR PHILLIPS, the narrator of the fictional
   memoir
DANA PHILLIPS, Arthur's twin sister, an actress
ARTHUR EDWARD PHILLIPS, Arthur and Dana's father, a confidence man and swindler
PETRA, pseudonym of Dana's lover, object of Arthur Phillips's passion
WILLIAM SHAKESPEARE, the Elizabethan playwright, poet, and actor

Four Arthurs and three tragedies are associated with *The Tragedy of Arthur*. The Arthurs include the real Arthur Phillips, the author of this novel; Arthur Phillips, the narrator; Arthur Phillips, the narrator's father and an imprisoned swindler and confidence man; and King Arthur of Britain. The tragedies presented are the tragedies of the latter three Arthurs. Far from tragic, the real Arthur Phillips has achieved a literary tour de force through the book's unique structure.

The novel purports to be a Random House publication of a newly discovered play by William Shakespeare, *The Tragedy of Arthur.* Arthur Phillips, the fictional narrator, is the owner of the manuscript. Along with Random House, he stands to make a lot of money from the publication. Despite the opinions of many Shakespearean scholars and the scientific evidence of the authenticity of the paper and ink, Phillips has come to believe that the play is a forgery produced by his criminal father. Phillips's agreement with Random House gives him the right to write the introduction to the play. Phillips the narrator attempts to use this introduction to explain and justify his disagreement with the conclusions of the Shakespeare experts. It is this "introduction" that constitutes the body of the novel and functions as a sort of memoir, more or less closely mirroring the real Phillips's life and family history.

The memoir begins with Arthur Phillips's account of his family circumstances. He and his twin sister, Dana, had to suffer the separation and divorce of their parents at a young age, followed by the absence of their father, who has been convicted of the first of many petty crimes. He is a well-read confidence man, forger, and swindler. He loves pranks and hoaxes, and some of his tricks are very funny. However, he cannot stay out of trouble for very long and spends most of the twins' youth and adulthood in prison. Their mother remarries a faithful but very ordinary man. Arthur struggles through his childhood and youth, feeling betrayed by his father and increasingly unable to establish close relationships. He becomes a writer and publishes four successful novels. He marries a Czech woman and lives with her in Prague. Although they have children and a companionable relationship, he remains essentially isolated. His twin sister is the only person with whom he is able to share his inmost life.

Dana has become a moderately successful actress. After a certain amount of floundering, she has established an enduring romantic relationship with a woman named Petra. It is at this point in the story, perhaps halfway through the novel, that the plot begins to solidify. The father is finally released from prison. He tells Arthur that, while doing some work in an old English country house many years ago, he found a copy of a hitherto unknown play by Shakespeare. Certain that the owner of the house was unaware of the existence of the play, he had stolen and stored it in a safe-deposit box for twenty-three years. He persuades Arthur that the play is genuine and proposes that Arthur sell it; to ensure that the English family's heirs have no claim of ownership, he concocts a cock-and-bull story to account for Arthur's discovery of the play. Arthur offers *The Tragedy of Arthur* to Random House, subject to authentication, and reserves the absolute right to prepare an introduction that Random House is forbidden to alter or shorten.

Arthur, separated from his wife and children, remains in the United States. He is smitten by Petra, Dana's lover, during this period. After Dana and Petra have a spat, Arthur sleeps with Petra. He is immediately assailed by guilt that deepens when he discovers that he has impregnated Petra. He fears that he has ruined Dana's life and destroyed his relationship with her. He also comes to believe that *The Tragedy of Arthur* is a forgery perpetrated by his father and that his father has conned him again, as so often happened in his childhood. He attempts to withdraw the play, but Random House, already heavily invested in the project and enthused by the opinion of Shakespearean scholars and the authenticated paper and ink, threatens him with legal action if he withdraws from their agreement. Although he is forced to accede to the publication, he still has the right to write the introduction. He uses it to set out his memoir, in which he justifies his view of the play's fraudulence. The memoir also resolves the romantic triangle of Arthur, Dana, and Petra in a clever, unexpected, and emotionally satisfying way. Arthur's lengthy "introduction" is then followed by the text of the questionable play itself.

The resolution of the personal situations of the characters is not the only unexpected aspect of this novel. Phillips's text is heavily laden with sardonic digressions on the foibles of memoirists and their defensive maneuvers. An even more ubiquitous and satisfying underlying theme of the work is his savage debunking of several schools of Shakespearean criticism.

As children in a literate and theatrical family, Dana and Arthur have been interested in and familiar with Shakespearean plays from early in their lives, though perhaps

Arthur Phillips was born in Minneapolis and educated at Harvard University. He has been a child actor, a jazz musician, a speechwriter, an entrepreneur, and a five-time Jeopardy! *champion. His earlier novels are* Prague *(2002),* The Egyptologist *(2004),* Angelica *(2007), and* The Song Is You *(2009).*

to a lesser degree than their father has. There is much discussion of Shakespeare in the memoir; Arthur ridicules both the people who claim that someone other than Shakespeare must have written the plays as well as those who claim that Shakespeare's genius is the entire source of Western culture. Years before the suspect quarto is revealed, Dana received from their father a printed copy of *The Tragedy of Arthur* made up to look like a Modern Library edition. Because Dana likes Shakespeare far more than Arthur does, their father had given it exclusively to her. This volume plays its part in the dénouement of the plot laid out in the introduction, but the underlying question of its nature remains unresolved. It is, of course, a forgery—but is it a forgery of a forgery, or is it a forged Modern Library edition of a genuine Shakespeare play?

The play itself, as constructed by the real Arthur Phillips, could actually be a lesser work of the great Elizabethan dramatist. It is presented with learned-sounding glossary notes, and of course, there is probably not a word or expression in it outside of the accepted Shakespearean canon. Moreover, even if there were occasional blunders or inconsistencies in the text, they could probably be readily explained. The work of talented people generally fluctuates in quality around some mean or middle-line; artists with extraordinary genius sometimes create crashing disasters. In Shakespeare's case, this phenomenon might apply to *Cymbeline*. Norman Mailer's *Ancient Evenings* is another example.

The play, *The Tragedy of Arthur*, is presented in the conventional five acts. Except for a few comic scenes in which ordinary sixteenth-century language is used, it is in blank verse. As the play opens, Prince Arthur is seventeen. He is wooing a shepherd girl when the news of his accession to the throne arrives; his father, King Uter, has died, poisoned by the Saxons. The Pictish and Scottish kingdoms to the north seem to be about to rise against the British crown. Arthur reveals in a soliloquy his doubts about his fitness for the throne. Act 2 offers some comic scenes typical of a number of Shakespeare's plays. Although Arthur misses the climactic battle against the Picts and the Scots, they are defeated at Lincoln. Mordred, who has inherited the throne of Pictland, grows to hate Arthur. In act 3, Arthur marries for love rather than to establish a politic alliance with France. The Saxons invade in act 4, and King Arthur, whose military capabilities have diminished, is forced to make an alliance with Mordred, who in the final act kidnaps Arthur's wife and attempts to seize the throne. Arthur kills him in a fight but is himself mortally wounded. Because Arthur has died childless, the kingdom goes to Arthur's kinsman, Constantine.

The pattern of *The Tragedy of Arthur* is not dissimilar to that of several of Shakespeare's plays; in fact, it closely resembles a nineteenth-century Shakespeare forgery called *Vortigern and Rowena*. Yet a number of odd clues and his father's oft-proven dishonesty help convince Arthur Phillips that the play is a forgery. In the first act, Prince Arthur's dog is named Socrates. Arthur Phillips's father also had a dog named

Socrates. Additionally, one of the characters in the play is named Silvius, a name shared by Arthur Phillips's stepfather. The coincidences are too suspicious and suggest that *The Tragedy of Arthur* may not be quite what it seems. As Arthur the narrator says, "This is more than the most lenient statistician can bear."

King Arthur's fall is the final tragedy of the novel. The monarch is shown to be too fond of his wife, too peace loving, and too kind to be a successful monarch. Although portrayed as brave and strong, he has neither the gift of leadership nor the necessary ruthlessness to act in the best interests of his realm.

The first tragedy is the tragedy of Arthur Phillips's father. He has all the talents and knowledge to be successful but can only turn them into pranks, hoaxes, and unsuccessful swindles. His inability to wrap his mind around some of the Minnesota legal rules results in an extended final sentence. He has spent most of his life in prison, betraying his own potential and blighting the lives of his children.

The central tragedy is that of Arthur Phillips, the narrator. Although an accomplished novelist, his life is anguished and deception ridden. His only truly successful relationship has been with his twin sister, whom he loves dearly. He risks ruining that relationship because of his reckless infatuation with Petra.

In one of the closing paragraphs of the "introduction," Arthur Phillips, the narrator, suggests that it is up to the reader to decide whether his life's story is a tragedy or a comedy. Although some reviewers have found Phillips's inclusion of an entire play difficult to read, other readers have called this book a brilliant comedy. In addition to its sardonic humor and wit, it raises and sensibly discusses some very important questions about literature generally, the worship of Shakespeare in particular, the "science" of scholarly attributions, and contemporary popular psychology.

One test of greatness in a novel is whether it leaves the reader wishing it were true. *The Tragedy of Arthur* passes that test. It is a wonderful read.

Robert Jacobs

Review Sources

Kirkus Review 79, no. 2 (January 15, 2011): 84.
The New Yorker 85, no. 11 (May 2, 2011): 78.
The New York Times, April 27, 2011, p. C1.
The New York Times Book Review, May 1, 2011, p. 1.
The Washington Post, April 20, 2011 (Web).

Traveler

Author: Devin Johnston (b. 1970)
Publisher: Farrar, Straus and Giroux (New York). 80 pp. $23.00
Type of work: Poetry
Locale: Various locations, including the American Midwest, Scotland, and Shanghai

In poems that favor careful observation, studious details, and deliberate structure, Johnston explores travel, the natural world, and the experience of being a father.

Driving the roads of the American Midwest, strolling the shores of the sacred Scottish island Iona, arriving in Shanghai—the speaker of Devin Johnston's *Traveler* is always on the move, heading into landscapes both familiar and new. This is Johnston's fourth collection of poetry, and it builds off the strengths of his previous work. Johnston has established a reputation for himself as a nature poet, a writer deeply engaged with the imagery of the natural world. While his interest in nature writing aligns him with one of the longest traditions in literature, his preference for rhyming lines and tightly structured meters further solidifies Johnston's reputation as a poet who hearkens to traditional styles, even as he plays with modern diction. In *Traveler*, his characteristic voice and preoccupations are employed in an exploration of traveling itself. While the speaker journeys across the world, gathering cultural and natural imagery for his poems, he also begins to consider the journey of fatherhood. Although never straying far from the observational, carefully crafted poems that first brought him success, Johnston explores fresh topics in this latest book, making *Traveler* one of his most popular collections to date.

Nature is not the exclusive focus of *Traveler*, as it is in many of Johnston's earlier poems, but natural images and landscapes maintain a prominent place throughout the collection. Some of the poems operate strictly as descriptions of nature, showcasing both the beauty of the natural world and Johnston's own skill with language, as in "Tangled Yarn" when a dragonfly is a "darning needle, dancer / meadow hawk or glider." In these instances, the lines are so musical and rich with beauty that they seem to elevate the natural image, encouraging the reader to see the familiar world with fresh, appreciative eyes. More often, however, the descriptions of nature are used to evoke a broader sense of a particular place or landscape, one that metaphorically extends beyond the flower or river he describes. The American Midwest, for example, becomes a place where "a thunderstorm / trundles down the Wabash" in the poem "Storm and Sturgeon," while in "Iona," the "volcanic spilth of dawn / instantly overflows the Firth of Lorn." The natural images themselves—that of a thunderstorm and of a dawn—are commonplace, occurring in every landscape on the planet. Johnston, however, ties these regular natural events to his perception of specific places. The "trundle" of the storm reminds us of the polite, relaxed nature that is a stereotype of the Midwest, while the "volcanic spilth" makes the Firth of Lorn and its active whirlpools a place both of primordial radiance and violence. Nature, then, forms a large part of the book's imagery and lyric strength, as well as a large part of its intellectual content.

The exploration of place in *Traveler* also occurs through an exploration of culture and man-made objects. These observations are crafted with the same care and attention to detail as the natural observations, further establishing the speaker of this collection as someone who relies on reserved, thoughtful perception. He is rarely in action, interacting with the cities and landscapes, but is instead watching, taking in whatever details he can. Contractors working on construction project, for instance, are described in "Thin Place" as

> Breaking down
> dusk and dawn,
>
> housewreckers
> on horse scaffolds
>
> syncopate
> their hammers.
>
> Brick dust
> drifts like smoke,
>
> tents of habitation
> withdrawn,
>
> hinges of habit
> undone.

The image, set in some unspecified city, is as full of careful language and subtle rhyme as any other description in the collection. The meter is fairly regular, although often skipping beats, mimicking the partial construction (or deconstruction) of the building. Likewise, the rhymes are never quite exact, although they still add to the music of the poem. These descriptions are most important in the way they allow Johnston to characterize place itself; the "habit / undone," the "housewreckers," and the dusty smoke all have a feeling of melancholy to them. Untied to a particular city or country, the "thin place" of this poem becomes almost universally recognizable and familiar. As with many other poems in the collection, these moods and images are not put to a heavily rhetorical use, but instead created for their own sake, evoking a physical sense of place that the reader is encouraged to inhabit.

Regardless of where exactly Johnston is directing his observant eye, he maintains several stylistic regularities. Many contemporary writers favor verse that is written free of meter or end rhyme, instead experimenting with prose-like stanzas, sound play, and other structural devices. Johnston, however, tends to write with a style of meter and rhyme that has been established in English literature for centuries. His "Nothing Song: after William IX, Duke of Aquitaine," for instance, is composed as a variation of a Scottish ballad and a very loose translation of a similar work by the

Devin Johnston has published four books of poetry as well as a collection of essays, Creaturely and Other Essays *(2009), and a book of criticism,* Precipitations: Contemporary American Poetry as Occult Practice *(2002). His third book of poetry,* Sources *(2008), was a Book Critics Circle Award finalist.*

duke, who was also known as William the Troubadour (1071–1127). Its AAABAB rhyme scheme and iambic meter are maintained throughout the stanzas, and while this style links the poem to the classic tradition of songwriters and lyricists wandering the countryside, its subject matter is made entirely modern. The speaker is aloof from life, declaring

> For such uncertainty
> I've found no remedy
> in psychotherapy
>   or sedatives.
> I rummage through debris
>   where nothing lives.

The contemporary language of psychotherapy and sedatives is almost out of place in this strictly classic form, yet serves to move the poem away from well-trod territory and into something new and contemporary. Johnston's pairing of traditional forms with contemporary questions seems to imply that his experience as someone who "aloof, opaque—remains apart" from life is one that people have shared through the centuries. Such a combination fits well in his broader exploration of place and travel in the modern world— the speaker visits ancient locations, yet always brings along a modern sensibility.

Johnston also favors highly specific, nearly categorical language in many of these poems. While his tendency to favor specialized language might force some readers to reach for a dictionary, it also provides a unique music to the poems, the uncommon words expertly woven into the meter and rhyme of the verse. His short poems and shorter lines offer a sort of pedestal for this language, showcasing the unusual words among more recognizable turns of phrase, as in the "bedouin snap and flash / of static-electric / sparks" in "Static," and the "moist rhinarium" of the landscape in "High and Low." Such highly specific words help establish Johnston as an expert on his topics, adding further credibility to his position as the reserved observer. When describing locations, this credibility is particularly important. While the observations of Japan, for instance, are evocative and carefully constructed, it is his familiarity with the history of the land (revealed often through this specialized language) that transforms him from a gifted sightseer into someone with greater insights to offer.

On a whole, Johnston is careful to maintain his role as this observant traveler, watching the world and recreating its rich details and beauty for his readers. These descriptions are by necessity detached, the speaker very much the "aloof horseman" in "Nothing Song." The position at times makes Johnston and his poetry seem cold despite the rich beauty and deep engagement with beauty, the detachment requiring the speaker to refrain from inserting subjective emotion. In the few poems describing his experience as a father, however, subjective emotions and personal engagement find their opportunity to enter the work. The appearance of the invested, exposed speaker is somewhat surprising, even as he continues with the themes of journeying and observation that are at the heart of the book. These poems (and his role as watcher) become tender, as in "Appetites" when his three-year-old daughter "lies awake / talking in confidential tones" to herself and to her imaginary friend. Johnston is still, in many ways, an outside observer here, listening to a daughter who is unaware of his presence, picking up on the language that was meant to be "confidential." However, the deep love he feels for his family makes these poems more intimate and revealing of his inner self than the poems devoted to travel or nature ever become. In the context of the larger work, these poems of fatherhood and family both offer an important emotional counterpoint and extend in new directions the consideration of travel that is so important to the collection.

A poet traversing continents, his eye always tuned to the natural world and the plentitude of culture itself, the speaker of Johnston's *Traveler* is at once consistent, mindful, and lyric. Perhaps the best way to understand this speaker is through the title poem itself, a description of a warbler in migration. The bird flies north not to accomplish any particular goal, but rather because he is called by instinct as he

> follows Polaris
> and the Pole's magnetic field
>
> through travail
> and travel's long ordeal

The earth itself beckons the bird, even though its journey becomes an ordeal. The difficulty of travel is noted, but not lingered upon. Instead, the poem concludes with the warbler arriving to a "stationary world" where the speaker sees "against a cloud / his throat's flame." The bird, although defined by his act of travel, truly comes alive when that travel is over and he has arrived somewhere "stationary" and still, a place where the image of his red throat against a cloud is enough to close the poem. This is the quest that Johnston undertakes in *Traveler*. He is rarely concerned with the road or the adventures and challenges of entering an unfamiliar landscape. Instead, he is concerned with what happens once he arrives. It is then that he can be still, reserved, and observant, using his poetic powers to capture some moment of beauty the world offers to him. Employing brief verse with strict meter and rhyme, it is Johnston's watchful eye that drives this book forward, taking in the details of the vast world and distilling them into these carefully wrought poems.

T. Fleischmann

Review Sources

Booklist 108, no. 1 (September 1, 2011): 30.
Library Journal 136, no. 11 (June 15, 2011): 93.
Publishers Weekly 258, no. 25 (June 20, 2011): 34.

The Trouble Ball

Author: Martín Espada (b. 1957)
Publisher: W. W. Norton (New York). 66 pp.
$24.95
Type of work: Poetry

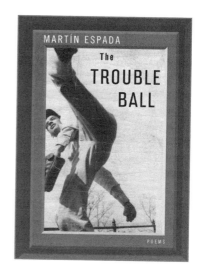

A riveting and instructive poetry collection, The Trouble Ball focuses on the personal struggles and insults that countless members of the minority community have had to endure.

With *The Trouble Ball*, Martín Espada has once again forcefully expressed himself as a poet of purpose. This does not mean that the poetry suffers under the weight of thought or subject matter, however. The poetry is both straightforward and richly textured. It is the balance of effort that is to be commended. Born in the New York City borough of Brooklyn in 1957, Espada learned at an early age how tough city life can be. His father, Frank Espada, was born in Puerto Rico and never lost his connection to the land of his birth. Growing up in public housing, the young Espada had to think on his feet in order to survive. His life experiences, coupled with his father's advice to speak up for his culture, eventually added a special vitality to his poetry. Social activism became an essential ingredient in his life. Espada had no intention of limiting his literary aspirations to esoteric realms. It was evident in his first poetry collection, *The Immigrant Iceboy's Bolero*, that Espada believed that poetry could speak to causes that were close to his heart. Published in 1984, his first collection also included photographs taken by his father.

Taking inspiration from such activist poets as Pablo Neruda and Walt Whitman, Espada has written poems that not only inform but also radiate with poetic beauty. Part of his growth as both a person and a poet was to listen to his father speak out against discrimination. He learned to appreciate his Puerto Rican heritage and to realize that, historically, mainstream American culture has not made life easy for minorities, who have had to fight for a living wage, for the right to vote, and for the right to live in a safe environment.

As a teenager, Espada began to write poetry. He wished not to merely describe a landscape or express an abstract thought, but to bring to readers' attention the plight of an oppressed people. For him, poetry can be employed as a tool to educate. In *The Trouble Ball*, Espada is no less an advocate for justice, understanding, and historical accuracy. The collection is divided into two parts. Part 1, "The Trouble Ball," includes fourteen poems that speak to poverty, racism, and the horrors of Augusto Pinochet's brutal dictatorship in Chile. Part 2, "Blasphemy," includes ten poems that speak to the power of poetry and the power of those who attempt to make a difference. Several of

Martín Espada is the author of several highly regarded poetry collections, including Rebellion Is the Circle of a Lover's Hands *(1990),* A Mayan Astronomer in Hell's Kitchen *(2000), and* The Republic of Poetry *(2006). He teaches at the University of Massachusetts, Amherst.*

the poems in part 2 are elegies to such figures as Alexander Taylor, Abe Osheroff, Adrian Mitchell, and Howard Zinn. In their own way, each of these individuals helped to make a difference as either a poet, a scholar, a historian, or an activist. In addition, the poet has included "Notes on the Poems" and a "Biographical Note."

Espada has never been considered an experimental poet. He is direct, riveting, and always to the point. There is a sincerity of language and a wedding of words with message. He does not want his message to be muddled or misunderstood. The power of the poetry is heightened by how perfectly these elements fit together. A definite rhythm of language adds certainty to each poem.

For Espada, it was only natural that he believe in the power of resistance and in the power of words. A personal remembrance can make for a strong political or social statement. Woven within a particular historical frame of reference, a poem written by Espada becomes a form of marching orders to action. He has been criticized and even threatened for his form of poetry, though. It is a poetry that pokes its nose into the political fray. The poems cause such a stir because they work so well as poetry, first and foremost. They are not merely political pamphlets posted to the wall but works of art, which makes them dangerous in some eyes.

In the title poem, Espada details his father's outing to Ebbets Field to watch the Brooklyn Dodgers play a game against the Cardinals in 1941. He points out that Satchel Paige, an African American pitcher, was not pitching in Ebbets Field on that day or any day. The institutionalized racism that kept African American players from joining the major leagues until 1947 made it impossible for Paige to show off his wicked "Trouble Ball" pitch, one that he made famous in the Negro Leagues. He could pitch "for the Brujos of Guayama" on the island of Puerto Rico. Espada reveals that "On my father's island, there were hurricanes and tuberculosis, dissidents in jail / and baseball." If someone had talent (as Paige did) then, of course, he could play baseball in Puerto Rico; this was not so in the United States in the year in which the poem is set. Later in the poem, Espada tells the reader that he was born in 1957 in Brooklyn, "when the Dodgers packed their duffle bags / and left the city." The poem incorporates the personal as well as the communal. It clues in the reader to what was going on in the United States at defined historical points in time. It is the loss of every American baseball fan that Paige was not pitching for the Dodgers, or any other major-league baseball team, in 1941. Time passes, but memory is long, and what could have happened will always be recalled. Figuratively, the "Trouble Ball" is still waiting to cross the plate.

In merely twenty-four poignant poems, Espada fills *Trouble Ball* with crucial stories. In the poem "The Spider and the Angel," the reader is introduced to a "Day camp in the summer of 1968," where "counselors steered us to the roof / of a school building in Brooklyn, / slapped down soggy mattresses / and told us to wrestle." It was necessary for a young boy to prove that he was "Puerto Rican" enough for this particular camp. Since the boy spoke only "crippled Spanish," another boy—described as being as crazy as a "spider"—attempted to "pop my eyeballs from their sockets." Authenticity counted for something in this camp. Once the boy proved himself, he earned the respect of the "spider-boy." One gets the impression that each boy was required to fend for themselves since the "counselors" merely "smoked and nodded." In the end, though, the boy was "satisfied" with the situation since they were all "Puerto Ricans, / wrestling for the approval of our keepers, / inches from rolling off the roof." This remembrance illuminates how boys in this minority strive to fit in and carve out a territory for themselves. Each boy must pass an identity test.

In the opening poem of part 2, "The *Playboy* Calendar and the *Rubáiyát* of Omar Khayyám*,*" Espada confesses that his father gave him both a *Playboy* magazine calendar and a copy of the *Rubáiyát* in "the year I graduated from high school." His father wished for his son to "Enjoy the scenery" of the calendar, but the poems of Khayyám are introduced as "an old friend." Espada shared the calendar with his best friend. Known as "The Beast," this friend was a fierce wrestler, who, on being presented with the calendar, "howled like a silverback gorilla / trying to impress an expedition of anthropologists." While Espada also became "smitten with the blonde / called *Miss January*," he memorized the poems when he was "alone at night." It is not the calendar that must remain out of sight, but it is the book of poems that is hidden "inside the folds of the *Playboy* calendar." The Beast was last seen as a Marine recruit. The calendar was last seen at the end of the year "when it could no longer tell me the week or the month." Espada states that he "last saw Omar Khayyám this morning." He was commanded by the poet to "Awake!" and without hesitation, Espada "awoke." He learned so much more than he could use in his life from his father's *"old friend"* than whatever excitement could be generated by a *Playboy* calendar. Each of these items was given to serve a purpose, but it is poetry that is lasting and can teach eternal lessons. Espada strives to teach his readership lessons that will serve them for decades to come. Poetry has the capacity to endure, to bolster the spirit, to call people to action, and to make a difference. In the title poem of part 2, "Blasphemy," the poet announces "poetry can save us."

Once again, Espada has produced a collection that illuminates, that connects to a world that needs to be made better for those who have little or no say in how things are done. In *The Trouble Ball*, Espada not only tells stories that need to be told but also tells them as only a brilliant and mature poet can.

Espada's poems are not wrapped in abstract formulas waiting to be cracked; such poems have their place, but they would not serve Espada well. In each of his collections, he has attempted to balance the "teaching moment," with the appreciation of a poem well done. Over the years, Espada has served the public good as a lawyer, a professor, a social activist, and a poet. In as many ways as possible, he has led life concerned with the well-being of the dispossessed, the invisible, and the victims of society. For him, if the American Dream means anything at all, it is supposed to serve all who strive to attain it. In his role as poet, Espada paints the portraits of those who have been forgotten, who have struggled to make a living for themselves and their family, and who have raised their voices against power. He has won several awards, including a National Endowment for the Arts Fellowship, the Paterson Poetry Prize in 1991 for *Rebellion Is the Circle of a Lover's Hands* (1990), and the American Book Award for poetry in 1997 for *Imagine the Angels of Bread* (1996). His 2006 collection, *The Republic of Poetry*, was a finalist for the Pulitzer Prize for poetry. Inspired by circumstances in both Latin America and the United States, Espada exposes the heartache of the terrorist attacks of September 11, 2001, in New York as well as the tragedy of Pinochet's coup in Chile in 1973. The poet is at his best when he can weave the personal and the political into a complete poem, which he succeeds in doing once again in *The Trouble Ball*.

Jeffry Jensen

Review Sources

Antioch Review 69, no. 2 (Spring 2011): 393–94.
Booklist 107, no. 14 (March 15, 2011): 17.
Progressive 75, no. 8 (August 2011): 43–44.

The Troubled Man

Author: Henning Mankell (b. 1948)
First published: *Den orolige mannen,* 2009, in Sweden
Translated from the Swedish by Laurie Thompson
Publisher: Alfred A. Knopf (New York). 384 pp. $26.95
Type of work: Novel
Time: 2007–2011, with passages about events that transpired in the early 1980s
Locale: Ystad, Stockholm, and other locations in Sweden; Berlin, Germany; Copenhagen, Denmark

In the tenth and final book of the author's popular series, taciturn police detective Kurt Wallander is drawn into a mystery from the Cold War when a former naval commander—the father of his daughter's fiancé—disappears.

Principal characters:
KURT WALLANDER, a sixty-year-old Ystad police detective
LINDA WALLANDER, Kurt's thirty-six-year-old daughter, a police officer
HANS VON ENKE, a financier, Linda's future husband and the father of their baby daughter, Klara
HÅKAN VON ENKE, Hans's father, a former submarine commander in the Swedish navy
LOUISE VON ENKE, Hans's mother, a retired language teacher
STEN NORDLANDER, Håkan's closest friend, a retired chief engineer in the Swedish navy
GEORGE TALBOTH, a CIA operative living in Berlin
STEVEN ATKINS, a retired American submarine captain and Håkan's friend
MONA WALLANDER, Kurt's alcoholic former wife and Linda's mother
BAIBA LIEPA, Kurt's former lover from Riga, Latvia
CHIEF INSPECTOR YTTERBERG, the Stockholm detective in charge of the von Enke case

Henning Mankell's Ystad police inspector Kurt Wallander had not appeared in any new adventures since 1999, when Mankell published *Pyramiden* (*The Pyramid,* 2008), a collection of short stories that fleshed out some of the detective's early years before he became the middle-aged, fatalistic character his fans have come to admire. The last full Wallander novel, *Brandvägg* (*Firewall,* 2002), was published in Sweden in 1998. So in 2009, it came as a welcome yet bittersweet revelation that Mankell had written a new Wallander novel, *Den orolige mannen* (*The Troubled Man,* 2011), which according to him would be his last.

Henning Mankell has written dozens of plays and books, including several children's stories set in Africa. The first novel in his Kurt Wallander mystery series, Faceless Killers (1991), won the Academy of Swedish Crime Writers Prize and the Glass Key for best Scandinavian crime novel of the year.

There are aspects of *The Troubled Man* that set it apart from the earlier novels. In this story, the mystery does not evolve from a case Wallander has been assigned by his superiors in the Ystad police force but has instead been thrust upon him by his beloved, but often emotionally distant daughter, Linda Wallander. Another difference between this novel and most of the other Wallander stories is that Mankell has not included narration from the point of view of the criminal. For at least half of the book, neither Wallander nor the readers know if a crime has even been committed.

The first section of the book is a prologue to the mystery Wallander must unravel. Linda, who also is a police officer, has become engaged to Hans von Enke, a successful Swedish financier and the father of her unborn baby. Trying to head off Wallander's well-known predilection for avoiding family and social situations, Linda insists that he travel to Stockholm to meet Hans's aristocratic father, Håkan von Enke, a retired Swedish naval commander, and his mother, Louise, a former language teacher. Linda also requests her father's attendance at Håkan's rigidly formal seventy-fifth birthday party. On the evening of the party, Håkan takes Wallander aside and confides that he is a troubled man, worried about the unresolved ramifications of something that happened long ago. Håkan then describes an incident that occurred in 1982, when he commanded a submarine patrolling the Swedish coast. He reveals details of the search for what was presumably a Soviet submarine encroaching into Swedish waters and his unease that the government may have been involved in a massive and possibly treasonous cover-up. It is suggested that the cover-up may even have extended to Prime Minister Olof Palme, the most influential Swedish leader of the twentieth century, who was assassinated in 1986.

Wallander comes to the puzzling conclusion that Håkan is desperately afraid, but he puts his momentary interest aside. Sometime later, after Wallander returns to Ystad, Håkan disappears without a trace. Linda persuades her reluctant father to help investigate the disappearance during his lengthy summer holiday. As always, Wallander takes the long road, plodding through seemingly disconnected and trivial clues, traveling throughout Sweden and into Denmark to speak with people who knew Håkan during his naval career. Eventually, he uncovers deeply troubling secrets about the family, including the fact that Hans has an older, mentally disabled sister who has been institutionalized and hidden away since early childhood. When Louise also disappears, the mystery turns into a puzzle that Wallander feels compelled to solve. When others think that the case is finally closed, Wallander keeps coming back to a small stone taken from Håkan's desk, a seemingly insignificant clue that irritates him like a speck of sand in an oyster.

While the novel's title refers to Håkan, it is also an apt description of Wallander. Throughout the long months during which he investigates Håkan's disappearance, he faces his own demons, particularly his own mortality. At the age of sixty, which

Wallander considers the threshold of old age and eventual death, he finally lives in his own house in the country, with his dog, Jussi (who is named after famed Swedish operatic tenor Jussi Björling), but his nature is no more settled than it had been in his middle years. Like many fictional detectives before him, Wallander has never been happy or even content. He has always been a troubled man, pessimistic, stubborn, solitary, and easily obsessed.

There is a constant, resigned feeling among most of Wallander's supervisors and coworkers that he is tiresome and too rigid. The notable exception is Kristina Magnusson, a female colleague with whom he has shared a close working relationship. Unfortunately, she barely appears in *The Troubled Man*. Wallander has few friends, preferring to think about his late mentor rather than tolerate the company of living people who might require more from him. He also pushes his family away, with the occasional exception of Linda, whom he recognizes as his equal in stubbornness, and Baiba Liepa, the Latvian widow and love of his life, who briefly returns to his life.

By revisiting the past, at least in Wallander's musings, even those readers who are unfamiliar with his backstory are given a glimpse into what his life has been like and who he is. The passages about the alcoholic deterioration of Mona, Wallander's former wife, recount some of his unhappy years since their divorce but also illuminate his realization that he never wants to be with her or even see her again. When Wallander travels to the town where he was brought up and sees one of his father's paintings, the images become not just his memories, but the reader's as well. A recurring theme throughout the Wallander stories has been his relationship with his difficult, now deceased father, who never understood his son's desire to be a police officer and who spent most of his life painting and repainting the same scene of flying grouse. Wallander never understood why his father continued to repaint that scene, yet Wallander himself has essentially painted the same lonely scene for his own life.

Within the mystery of Håkan's disappearance, Mankell has woven subtext about Wallander's physical deterioration. Initially the author's clues are barely discernable, but allusions to the state of Wallander's mental health periodically resurface until the implications become obvious: Like his father, he has Alzheimer's disease. Mankell has cleverly used Wallander's well-documented absentmindedness and self-absorption to mask the early symptoms. In the first incident, Wallander drinks more than usual while dining alone in a restaurant, then leaves his service revolver at the table. Readers may find it plausible that he forgot his gun because he was drunk. Three or four more seemingly inconsequential incidents, such as not being able to recall taking his diabetes medicine and forgetting where he is driving, momentarily stop the action while Wallander mentally and emotionally recovers. Soon, although a bit behind the reader, Wallander begins to realize that something is wrong. His normally pessimistic nature becomes more so as he wonders how long he can mask his memory losses and blackouts, especially from Linda and his colleagues. Later in the novel, when Wallander sees but does not recognize his beloved granddaughter, Klara, the reader is brought inside his thoughts as he wonders "who the girl running toward him was . . . what she was doing in his house he had no idea."

An underlying political theme in Mankell's novel—one that may not be appreciated by some readers—is an extremely negative vision of United States. The impression that gradually develops is that the United States' subterfuge in relation to Sweden and other allies during the Cold War was far more dangerous to the world than anything the Soviet Union had devised. Mankell brings up Sweden's participation in the US-led war in Afghanistan and their compliance in the treatment of CIA prisoners as proof of the United States' continued danger to the world. An ongoing refrain is one of mistrust of the United States' motives and, in Mankell's mind, its deceitful public relations campaign. Certainly Mankell, if not the apolitical Wallander, is not a fan of United States' foreign policy, but by the end of the novel, when the killer is revealed, some readers may not be surprised. There also remains a nagging thought that the mystery has not been solved after all. Even Wallander muses that things may not be exactly as they seem.

Laurie Thompson's English translation of *The Troubled Man* is smooth, spare, and readable. Even without knowledge of the original text, the reader is able to discern the dark tone that the author conveys with his perennially depressed hero. Wallander has been catapulted into international fame not only by Mankell's best-selling novels, but also by a popular British television series starring Kenneth Branagh. There is even a smartphone application called "In the footsteps of Wallander," which Mankell has developed in conjunction with the Ystad tourist board to guide ardent fans to visit specific locations mentioned in his mystery series. The aging, churlish Wallander will be sorely missed.

Patricia King Hanson

Review Sources

Booklist 107, no. 9/10 (January 1/15, 2011): 53.
Commonweal 138, no. 9 (May 6, 2011): 28–30.
Library Journal 136, no. 2 (February 1, 2011): 55.
Los Angeles Times, March 30, 2011 (Web).
The New York Times Book Review, March 27, 2011, p. 23.

Twice a Spy

Author: Keith Thomson
Publisher: Doubleday (New York). 336 pp. $25.95
Type of work: Novel
Time: 2011
Locale: Gstaad, Switzerland; Martinique; Paris; Mobile, Alabama

Thomson's father-son spy duo returns to grapple with a terrorist intent on detonating a nuclear device during an international economic summit in Mobile, Alabama.

Principal characters:
DRUMMOND CLARK, an accomplished Central Intelligence Agency (CIA) operative, now sixty-four and retired, edging into the early stages of Alzheimer's disease
CHARLIE CLARK, Drummond's son, a professional gambler in his thirties
ALICE RUTHERFORD, a former agent of the National Security Agency (NSA), dangerous and beautiful
J. T. BREAM, a disgruntled former Air Force intelligence officer, now a renegade international arms dealer
BILL STANLEY, a career CIA agent nearing retirement and a fierce advocate of the Agency
CHEB QATADA, an Algerian terrorist

At the height of the Cold War, the spy thriller—long established as mass-market escapism rich with suspense, cartoonish characters, breakneck action, and gratuitous violence—was co-opted by practitioners of postmodern literature such as John le Carré and Don DeLillo, who reconceived the genre as character studies in which to explore the tricky, morally complicated environment of intelligence, a deeply ironic world where the boundaries between appearance and reality, right and wrong, love and hate, trust and paranoia blur.

Keith Thomson's *Twice a Spy* makes no claim to such gravitas; indeed, it delights in its unironic sense of itself as an uncomplicated homage to the gaudy excess of classic spy thrillers. The pace is crisp, with chapters that seldom run more than a few pages, and the nonstop action includes multiple car and boat chases, shootouts, a plane wreck, jailbreaks, car crashes, and a perfectly timed grand explosion. The locales are appropriately exotic. The plot has the requisite twists and surprises. The dialogue is snappy, and the reportorial prose, unadorned with authorial flourishes, carries the reader along with its easy rhythm. The narrative itself frustrates the analytical work of excavating theme and symbols. The story's centerpiece, a nuclear device disguised as a run-down

(©Erinn Hartman)

Keith Thomson's debut spy thriller, Once
a Spy *(2010), earned lavish critical
praise and enjoyed best-seller success.
He is a columnist covering intelligence
for the* Huffington Post.

vintage washing machine, would become a
multilayered symbol in the hands of DeLillo
or le Carré, yet here it remains, well, a nuclear device disguised as a run-down vintage
washing machine. *Twice a Spy* is, in short, an
unpretentious spy thriller, comfortably and
confidently sure of its lineage.

Drummond Clark is a sixty-four-year-old
retired CIA agent, a legend in intelligence
circles for his bold Cold War initiative in
which agents disguised bogus nuclear devices as washing machines, sold them to terrorist groups, and then tracked the machines
to infiltrate the organizations. But Drummond, facing the early onset of Alzheimer's
disease, has been forced into early retirement. He understands that he has become a
target for elimination because the CIA believes it must prevent him from spilling any
state secrets as his condition inevitably worsens. In grand moments of lucidity, Drummond still manifests his Agency training, thinking smart and fighting fiercely. Charlie
Clark is Drummond's son, a college dropout in his thirties who makes a living betting
on horses. Although *Twice a Spy* works primarily as a spy romp, reanimating the best
clichés of the genre, what engages Thomson's readers—who, after all, have a surfeit
of such genre thrillers to select from—is this relationship between the father and son,
which is unique within the genre. Thomson reminds his readers of events chronicled
in the first installment, namely that Charlie is still coming to terms with his discovery
that his father, a nerdish widower and mild-mannered appliance salesman, has been
leading a secret double life as an international spy.

Reflecting Thomson's background as an editorial cartoonist and avant-garde filmmaker, the novel has a cinematic feel. The action is diced into quick-cut chapters
and Thomson splices together simultaneous events, shuttling from one cliffhanging
episode to another with an auteur's deft hand. The characters are rendered with visual
immediacy and, with the exception of the Clarks, are quickly designated as typical heroes or villains, giving the large cast the comfortable accessibility typical of film. Secondary characters are defined by surface details, such as their clothes, their hairstyle,
their skin tone, their height and weight, or the way they walk. The central premise
of the novel—an international cabal of terrorists is bent on acquiring a small nuclear
device and detonating it at an international summit of government economic advisers—has the plausibility and edge-of-the-seat suspense of big-budget action films. As
Thomson's intricate plot unfolds with galloping momentum, it is easy enough to cast
the main characters and imagine Thomson's full-throttle narrative as a film. Drummond could be played by a gracefully aging action hero such as Harrison Ford or
Sylvester Stallone; there hangs about Charlie the presence of a grizzled David Caruso
or perhaps Kiefer Sutherland. Either Angelina Jolie or Jessica Alba could feasibly play
Alice Rutherford.

Twice a Spy resists tidy summarizing; given Thomson's gift for narrative turns, such a summary would run counter to the story's clear intent to provide few opportunities for engaged readers to catch their breath. The action picks up just weeks after the close of Thomson's *Once a Spy* (2010). Framed for the murder of an agent in New York City and now on the run, the Clarks are in disguise, living outside Gstaad, Switzerland, in order to stay off the CIA's radar as they pursue an experimental drug program to treat Drummond's Alzheimer's disease. They are accompanied by a rogue NSA agent, the hauntingly beautiful and devastatingly deadly Alice Rutherford, with whom Charlie has just begun to fall in love. It is her kidnapping in the opening chapters that triggers the plot: she will be released only after a shadowy international arms dealer known as J. T. Bream has secured one of Drummond's washing machine nuclear devices, hidden in a place only Drummond knows. Bream himself is a disgruntled former intelligence agent living as a pilot-for-hire on the island of Martinique. He left intelligence shortly after the September 11 terrorist attacks due to a disagreement with his superiors, who surmised that technology had rendered human intelligence gathering irrelevant. Bream intends to teach the CIA a lesson. Of course, the CIA is still very much interested in eliminating Drummond, so he and Charlie are also dodging a ruthless covert assassination operation headed by William Stanley, a no-nonsense career agent committed to the importance of maintaining US intelligence operations. Stanley sees in Drummond's deteriorating mental condition a threat that the country cannot afford. In addition, the Clarks are the subject of vigorous pursuit in Martinique and the United States by police who believe that the two are money launderers with a $10,000 bounty on their heads.

The centerpiece of the narrative, however, is the fate of the washing machine, hidden in a cave on a remote island near Martinique. After an initial red herring involving a terrorist cell in India's Punjab, Charlie uncovers the real goal of the terrorists: to explode the device during an international economic summit in Mobile, Alabama, as a way to draw international attention to the establishment of an independent Islamic state. The narrative hurtles toward Charlie's attempt to intercept the device, which leads to a dramatic showdown with Bream. The final chapter has that palpable feeling of "to be continued," a trailing off into an ellipsis.

Although Thomson's development of the Clarks' father-son dynamic has earned critical praise, his book is first and foremost a spy novel. He demonstrates a keen familiarity with the cutting-edge technology of contemporary spy craft. His gadgets, unlike the signature devices of the James Bond series, are not outrageous science-fiction fantasies, but rather are meticulously researched and actually exist in prototype. The novel's assortment of high-tech electronic devices, including surveillance gadgets, communication interceptors, encryption software, and computer tracking systems, reflects Thomson's day job as an online columnist covering Washington's intelligence community for the *Huffington Post*. In that capacity, Thomson, who himself has no specific security clearance, has maintained a sufficient network of contacts to ensure the novel's verisimilitude. But for all the gadgetry, Thomson's characters rely on old-fashioned methodologies at critical moments. For example, when Alice attempts to escape her kidnappers, she kills one with an ordinary light-switch plate that she throws with fierce speed.

Undoubtedly the most controversial aspect of Thomson's nascent spy series is his decision to use an aging Alzheimer's patient as its hero. Thomson has recalled in promotional interviews that he initially turned to fiction when he heard about how the father of a friend had struggled with the disease, a man who in his career had run an international conglomerate but, as his condition progressed, could barely follow a football game on television. Thomson asked himself what would happen if a career CIA operative, whose mind would be stuffed with layers of critical national secrets, began to lose the ability to retain control of that information. Such a suddenly unreliable brain would draw the attention of both bad guys and good guys. Using Alzheimer's disease this way is a risk; Drummond's memory lapses come at plot-convenient moments, and readers may find that Thomson's comic touches, such as Drummond's spontaneous declarations of irrelevant trivia or Charlie's exasperated outbursts of hypothetical questions intended to spur his father's flagging memory, provoke laughter that is strained, even uneasy.

Thomson balances any pity for Drummond's fragility by giving him moments of remarkable clarity, such as when he deciphers the coded message that reveals the longitude and latitude of the remote island where the nuclear device is hidden, a code that has frustrated the concerted efforts of the terrorist cells. He also still has the ability to deliver lethal kicks and accurate gunfire during moments of tense confrontations. It remains to be seen how Thomson will handle Drummond's condition as the series continues. For now, his savvy familiarity with post–September 11 intelligence operations and his keen cinematic sense of scene and suspense provide an effective backdrop for continued development of this most intriguing father-son spy team.

Joseph Dewey

Review Sources

Booklist 107, no. 13 (March 1, 2011): 35.
Fredericksburg News, April 10, 2011 (Web).
Kirkus Reviews 79, no. 4 (February 15, 2011): 270.
Noir Journal, February 23, 2011 (Web).
Publishers Weekly 258, no. 5 (January 31, 2011): 30.
The Washington Post, March 6, 2011 (Web).

The Uncoupling

Author: Meg Wolitzer (b. 1959)
Publisher: Riverhead Books (New York).
288 pp. $25.95; paperback $15.00
Type of work: Novel
Time: The mid to late 2000s
Locale: Stellar Plains, New Jersey

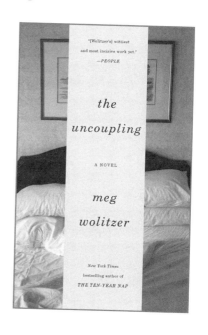

A modern fairy tale set against American involvement in Afghanistan and Iraq, Wolitzer's story uses the premise of Aristophanes' play Lysistrata *to explore the relationship between passion and love when women in suburban New Jersey suddenly become bewitched and inexplicably lose interest in sex.*

Principal characters:

DORY LANG, a popular English teacher at Eleanor Roosevelt High School in suburban New Jersey

ROBBY LANG, Dory's husband, an equally popular English teacher at the same school

WILLA LANG, their daughter, an introspective sophomore who is self-conscious about her plain looks

FRAN HELLER, the school's brash new drama teacher

ELI HELLER, Fran's gifted son, a sophomore and Willa's suitor

LEANNE BANNERJEE, the school's psychologist, who is in her late twenties and happily promiscuous

BEV CUTLER, the school's guidance counselor, in her early fifties and married to a wealthy hedge fund broker

RUTH WINIK, the school's gym teacher, a "reformed" lesbian now married to an environmental sculptor and mother of three toddlers

MARISSA CLAYBORN, an African American student, strikingly beautiful and singularly talented

From Sleeping Beauty to Cinderella, the magic energy of love has always compelled classic fairy tales centered on women. It is fitting then that Meg Wolitzer, whose novels have examined contemporary women in complex relationships through the lens of realism, would turn in this novel to the fairy tale's enduring appeal. Like a fairy tale, *The Uncoupling* is disarmingly breezy. Its premise, recalling countless classic tales, is both engaging and intriguing: An enchantment descends on an unsuspecting picture-perfect American town. An unorthodox drama teacher, new to Eleanor Roosevelt High School in Stellar Plains, New Jersey (voted among the Fifty Most Livable

Suburbs in America), selects to stage Aristophanes' *Lysistrata*, a raucous 2,500-year-old comedy about a group of determined Athenian women who withhold sex to hasten the end of the decades-long Peloponnesian War. As the rehearsals begin, a cold wind literally sweeps along the quiet streets of the suburban town, under doorstops, under comforters, and up bedclothes. The women of Eleanor Roosevelt High School soon find their sexual energy sapped; they each are suddenly gifted with unsought awareness of the oppressive burden of sexual activity. Without exactly understanding why, they each refuse their men, opting for inviolable solitude. Given the puritanical cast of the suburb, few of the women discuss their decision, and hence no one perceives the scope of the town's enchantment. So Stellar Plains quietly descends into a most forbidding winter.

The Uncoupling, then, appears poised to explore the death of desire and the difficult dynamic between passion and intimacy, sobering themes that recall landmark works of postwar suburban realism. However, unlike those fictions, which anatomized the waning of passion by probing into the darker reaches of the human psyche for some accountability, Wolitzer's narrative is shaped by the protocol of a fairy tale. Her characters do not actually fall out of love—they merely fall under a spell. Fittingly, her characters lack the dimension and specificity of psychological realism. As in fairy tales, Wolitzer uses types: the "happy wife" (Dory), who is unaware of the singular achievement of her happy marriage until it is abruptly upended by the enchantment; the "energetically promiscuous free spirit" (Leanne) who beds men, married and single, with uncomplicated gusto; the "quietly enduring nonentity" (Bev) who, at midlife, is overweight and disillusioned with love, too long married to a superficial man who has long since dismissed her as an object of desire or indeed of interest; the "frustrated house slave" (Ruth), who finds herself boxed into a conventional marriage with conventionally needy toddlers and a conventionally fawning (and pawing) husband; the "awkward woman-child" (Willa) who is just discovering the giddy transport and potent ecstasy of first love; and the "heroic isolate" (Marissa), articulate, intelligent, and independent who comes to reject relationships altogether to embrace the activist agenda of sociopolitical causes. No single character dominates the novel—we move among them guided by that most traditional of fairy tale devices, the all-knowing narrator, the voice-over who tells a (decidedly adult) bedtime story, who unironically accepts the reality of the enchantment and who comments sagaciously and gently on her characters' dilemmas as she moves about their psyches with effortless omniscience.

Even as the rehearsals for *Lysistrata* begin, the uncouplings begin one by one. The women of Stellar Plains suddenly glimpse sex in its least flattering terms and in turn coolly but firmly reject the company of husbands or lovers. The men of Stellar Plains, not touched by the enchantment, react predictably with confusion, anger, pettiness, frustration. Given the ensemble cast, Wolitzer does not dwell on any one relationship but gives us a broad sense of how these men confront the dimension of sexuality by being compelled to examine what remains when it is no longer there. The extremes of the reactions are suggested by Robby Lang, Dory's husband, and by Eli Heller, Willa's ardent lover and the son of the play's director. Given the Langs' long, happy marriage and given that, before the spell descends, they had enjoyed tireless and frequent sex,

The author of eight previous novels, Meg Wolitzer has been praised for her honest and sympathetic investigation into women and contemporary relationships, particularly marriage and family. With her cinematic sense of scene and her knack for creating authentic characters, Wolitzer has also completed several screenplays, including adaptations of her own novels.

Robby cannot understand Dory's sudden chill. Frustrated, he orders an adult board game that instructs players in erotic foreplay; tries staging an oil-scented bath together, and purchases a sort of bathrobe for two designed to encourage cuddling. Nothing works (after all, Dory is under a spell), and Robby settles into a crabby surliness even as Dory guiltily pages through marriage advice in supermarket magazines and wonders why she continues to deny her husband. Far more traumatic, however, is the reaction of young Eli Heller. Willa, long awkward with boys, finds herself catapulted into the heated throes of first love with Eli, and they begin to explore the dimensions of clothing-optional intimacy. The night when her parents are gone for the evening, even as Eli is unrolling a condom, Willa is suddenly chilled by the bewitching wind. She abruptly realizes that this relationship cannot survive graduation and curtly tells Eli to leave. The unenchanted Eli, like Robby, cannot accept the situation, however, and Willa's rejection leads him to make life-changing decisions.

Unlike the women in Aristophanes' comedy, the women of Stellar Plains do not deliberately abstain from sex to further a public agenda, but Wolitzer does give her blithesome fairy tale a sobering sociocultural context. Like Aristophanes, Wolitzer introduces war as a backdrop—specifically the American occupations of Afghanistan and Iraq. Marissa Clayborn, selected to play Lysistrata, befriends Jason Manousis, who a few years earlier had left high school and had enlisted after getting his girlfriend pregnant. Now in his early twenties, a disfigured and partially blind veteran of the war in Afghanistan, he struggles to raise his young son. As he helps Marissa practice her lines, Jason bitterly dismisses the war. Moved, Marissa stages her own protest, a bed-in inspired by the play, as she is now determined to engage the obscenity of a protracted very real war. However, hers is, on the whole, a minor plot thread. More central to the novel's sociocultural context is its biting critique of the cyber generation, the high school students who remain cut off from the wonders and complications of the real world. Wolitzer's narrator decries the younger generation's contentment with simulations; their meager attention spans; their indifference to the demands of education, communication, and relationships; their embrace of a lifestyle uncomplicated by content, detail, and nuance; and their too-easy surrender to the insulated charms of virtual worlds filled with mythological avatars.

Sociocultural context notwithstanding, Wolitzer's larger interest rests with the dynamics of those relationships tested by the sudden withdrawal of sex. The ending of *The Uncoupling*, however, resists the shattering epiphanies typical of psychological realism—here, as in any fairy tale, the lifting of the magic spell is as inevitable as it is contrived and heartwarming. In the end, Wolitzer uses the reanimated couples of Stellar Plains to offer relationship advice familiar to any fan of talk shows: A strong relationship requires communication, fidelity, gentle honesty, appreciation for the small miracles of every moment, the willingness to accept change, the consolation of memories, and perhaps most important, the promise to stay interested beyond the realm of sex. If these themes are not particularly profound (as some critics have noted), they satisfy; after all, they have become the clichés of relationship experts because each is an enduring truth. Such "common sense" messages fall neatly within the fairy tale form, known for its use of magical or implausible solutions to the characters' problems in order to draw emphasis to one to two morality lessons. And with the whimsical open-endedness of a fairy tale, *The Uncoupling*'s itinerant drama director, Fran Heller, prepares to depart Stellar Plains—and the narrative—anticipating her next town and a new opportunity to reanimate the magic of rediscovered love, a conclusion reminiscent of *Mary Poppins*, as other reviewers have been quick to point out. A psychological realist novel, it is not; neither is it a feminist tract about heterosexual relationships in which the men play the villains, nor a simple romantic fairy tale lacking in depth. Readers hoping for or expecting the book to fit solely and squarely into one of these single types will be disappointed. As a fairy tale, however, Wolitzer's unique blending of genres works, combining gender-balanced and compassionate treatment of her subjects' psychological and social struggles with a lighthearted and familiar form to structure the narrative.

Joseph Dewey

Review Sources

The Boston Globe, April 5, 2011 (Web).
Chicago Sun-Times, April 21, 2011 (Web).
The Guardian, June 18, 2011, p. 11.
Kirkus Reviews 79, no. 1 (January 1, 2011): 15–16.
Los Angeles Times, May 24, 2011 (Web).
The New Yorker 87, no. 14 (May 23, 2011): 83.
The New York Times Book Review, April 10, 2011, p. 9.

Unseen Hand

Author: Adam Zagajewski (b. 1945)
Translated from the Polish by Clare Cavanagh
Publisher: Farrar, Straus and Giroux (New
York). 128 pp. $23.00
Type of work: Poetry
Locale: Primarily Poland

Zagajewski's sixth book of poetry to be translated into English, Unseen Hand *explores memory, history, and family, all while maintaining a firm grounding in the physicality of place and everyday life.*

Many American readers first encountered the Polish poet Adam Zagajewski through "Try to Praise the Mutilated World," a poem published in the *New Yorker* that mourned the September 11 terrorist attacks. In its attempt to find beauty in a tragic event, this poem is very much in keeping with Zagajewski's body of work. Born into a country ravaged by World War II, he understands the evils of which humanity is capable and the importance of time and memory in understanding history. He is a poet who often finds hope, albeit a longing hope for what has passed. His poems are contemplative and elegiac, recovering beauty from the world despite how cruel that world may at times seem to be. These qualities are at their finest in his latest collection, *Unseen Hand*. The poems in this slim volume are quiet and restrained, yet still able to grapple with some of the hardest questions of history. Less overtly political and philosophical than his earlier work, the collection allows Zagajewski to focus his energy on physicality, family, and memory.

Throughout the collection, Zagajewski contemplates his own changes in style and outlook over the years. Once considered a member of the Polish New Wave, Zagajewski now writes with a surprising lack of concern for the political and stylistic upheaval that marked the "Generation of '68." The poem "Not Thinking about Aesthetics" notes this shift most explicitly. Here, Zagajewski imagines his father copying out one of the poet's earlier works in order to share it with friends. That particular early poem, "To Go to Lvov," is about the home from which Zagajewski's family was exiled by war; it is poetically nuanced, beautiful in its rendering of the physical city as well as its contemplation of the city's surrounding history, both familial and political. Yet "Not Thinking about Aesthetics" bypasses those qualities, imagining that the father cared not about the poem's aesthetics but "only about the city he'd loved and lost." Copying out "To Go to Lvov" is an opportunity for the father to enter that city again, and while Zagajewski acknowledges the poetic construction underlying the original creation, he is now primarily interested in his father's memory and the power of preserving, if only through words, a physical place. This task of remembrance, informed as it is by politics and aesthetics, is the primary focus of *Unseen Hand*.

Through the many poems in this collection about Zagajewski's parents, it becomes clear why memory is such an important topic for the poet. With his mother deceased and his father suffering from dementia, the history that filled his earlier work is beginning to slip away. He recalls his mother as a woman who

> forgave it all
> and how I remember that, and how I flew from Houston
> to her funeral and couldn't say anything
> and still can't.

These poems are elegies, celebrating the dead while mourning their absence. Zagajewski uses them to capture the memories of his family, praising their ability to forgive even while he acknowledges the failure that comes with not being able to "say anything" to his mother. This is the same mixture of joy and sorrow the reader sees in the father, typing again and again descriptions of a city that he has lost. While Zagajewski uses poetry to remember and preserve the irretrievable, he also mourns things that are still present, as when his father "lies submerged in darkness, sleeps, dozes, / as if he'd already taken leave." Memory can attempt to save history, perhaps, and poems can do their best to preserve the cities of the past, but time itself remains the most powerful force, unstoppable despite all attempts to restrain it.

If Zagajewski believes that time is unstoppable, with memory inevitably slipping away, it might seem futile for him to produce work so preoccupied with the act of remembrance. As he says in a poem commemorating the poet Czesław Miłosz, "Of course nothing changes / in the ordinary light of day, / when the great poet has gone." It is not only the poet who fails to change the world; those seeking poetry for guidance also fail, as "in the library a lovely girl / looks in vain for a poem that could explain it all." Yet this becomes the point of the poems, the poet insisting upon memory and language even as they fail him. The world of *Unseen Hand* is a world in which loss and beauty are intertwined and interdependent, so that even as Zagajewski crafts moments of lyric intensity, he must acknowledge that the beauty of his words will fade. He pushes continually for the brief moments he can find, those occasions (like in the poem "Lost") during which

> Still sometimes we surface for a moment,
> and the setting sun sometimes gleams
> and a short-lived certainty appears,
> nearly faith.

In what does Zagajewski maintain this "nearly faith?" The loudest and most common topic of the book is Poland itself, although some poems depart briefly to Paris, Chicago, and other locales familiar to Zagajewski. For him, Poland is a place that lives in the shadow of the trauma it faced during the twentieth century. It is a place where

"Carts full of hay / abandoned the town / in greatest quiet," the landscape deserted even as he urges "sing for it, oriole, / dance for it, little fox," pleading with the world to celebrate his home. The landscape of Poland and the history of its people are inseparable, so that sadness seems to literally hang in the air. As he describes it in "Joseph Street,"

> Years pass, I remain, memory is uncertain,
> unheard prayers lie underfoot,
> sparrows are eternity's frail emblem,
> the rain is only recollection, the silhouettes
> of unknown persons walk without casting shadows.

The figures here are unfamiliar and otherworldly, silhouettes without shadows. It is as though both the people and the land itself are gone ("rain is only recollection"), even though the speaker remains. Living in a world of ghosts, Zagajewski is a poet facing the questions age has brought him, and the fact that he addresses these mournful questions with such startling beauty and lyricism suggests hope and saves the poems from becoming maudlin. He mourns for Poland with the same words he uses to celebrate it. Yet while Zagajewski sometimes presents himself as a poet who remains in place, keeping vigil for those things that are lost, he is just as often a poet returning to a land with which he has parted ways. As he currently lives part of every year in Chicago, it is not surprising that movement between cities is mentioned in his work.

Although divided into three distinct sections, the collection includes many poems that are reminiscent of one another. There are linked poems such as "Piano Lesson" and "Piano Tuner," "The Lovely Garonne" and "And the Lovely Garonne," as well as the triad of "Self-Portrait," "Self-Portrait in Airplane," and "Self Portrait in a Little Museum." These similarly titled poems allow Zagajewski to explore the same topic from different perspectives, building on the insights of each to create a harmonious effect as he himself travels through time and place. They also allow him to emphasize the experience of returning to a place that has changed. The locale of "Joseph Street," the public square filled with silhouettes, is earlier investigated as "Joseph Street in Winter," where "few pilgrims flounder through wet snow / and don't know where they're going, to which star." While this version of the poem is more impressionistic, it also brings a heightened political history to the forefront, as the pilgrims don't "see that war / has unexpectedly erupted." Although similar in mood and topic, these paired poems allow Zagajewski an extended meditation, his thoughts moving like memory itself.

The dominant poetic mode of *Unseen Hand* is meditation, restrained and elegiac out of respect for the many losses Zagajewski describes. Yet he does, at times, include the anger and humor that were signatures of his earlier work. As he acknowledges in "I Dreamed of My City," "I realized that arguments continue, / that nothing has been settled yet." In these newer poems, however, the anger and humor are subdued, appearing only subtly so as not to distract from the rest of the work. The anger comes when "on every small square the boys / practiced their kettledrums before the Palio— / the brown city quivered like troops before battle." It is a real anger, rhythmic

(© Colin McPherson/Corbis)

Adam Zagajewski currently splits his time between Chicago and his native Poland. One of the most internationally successful contemporary Polish poets, his work has won the Kurt Tucholsky Prize and a Prix de la Liberté. The collection Without End: New and Selected Poems *(2002) offers an extensive overview of his work up to that time.*

with the drum of the boys, but it is used to inspire contemplation, the city quivering and the image resonant with meaning. Likewise, the humor comes in brief moments of relief, such as when the sun "like a worried first-grader / diligently colors in the shadows." These moments are neither ecstatic nor furious. Instead, they are modulations, used to heighten the collection's overall emotional and lyrical intensity.

That lyric intensity is distilled and pure in "Vita Contemplativa," a poem in which Zagajewski seems to come to a realization: "So this is it. What we do not know. / We live in the abyss. In dark waters. In brightness." This is the guiding principle of Zagajewski's poetry and the world it describes. The Latin title roughly translates into "the contemplative life," a way of being that emphasizes quiet understanding and acceptance. It is a world filled with "what we do not know," with both "dark water" and with "brightness." Although there are many sorrows and many joys to be experienced here, Zagajewski suggests that one's responses should be reasoned, calm, and thoughtful. Although his homeland is lost and his parents are dying, he maintains an almost religious faith in spite of his mourning, finding hope and beauty in poetry itself. A poet who has already experienced a long career and international success, Zagajewski uses this collection as an opportunity to slow down and appreciate life for the complicated and sometimes unknowable beauty it holds. As he writes in "Piano Lesson,"

> and I thought with bitterness and pleasure that I had only
> language, only words,
> images,
> only the world.

T. Fleischmann

Review Sources

The Boston Globe, June 19, 2011 (Web).
Publishers Weekly 258, no. 25 (June 20, 2011): 85.
Quarterly Conversation, June 6, 2011 (Web).

Vaclav and Lena

Author: Haley Tanner (b. 1982)
Publisher: Dial (New York). 304 pp. $25.00
Type of work: Novel
Time: Twenty-first century
Locale: Brooklyn, New York

In this debut novel, Tanner brings to life two young Russian immigrants and tells the story of how they learn to navigate the difficulties of love and life in a new land.

Principal characters:
VACLAV, a budding magician and best friend of Lena
LENA, Vaclav's best friend and assistant, an aspiring sword swallower
RASIA, a Russian immigrant, mother of Vaclav and wife of Oleg, who becomes a mother figure to Lena
OLEG, a Russian immigrant, father of Vaclav and husband of Rasia
AUNT, a Russian immigrant, caretaker of Lena

Haley Tanner's debut novel *Vaclav and Lena* is a charming story about the friendship between two young Russian immigrants. Told in three sections, it narrates the friendship when Vaclav and Lena are about nine and ten years old, when they meet again seven years later, and the period immediately before they reconnect. Often described as a love story, the novel weaves several stories of love: the love of two childhood friends, the love of two parents for their child, the love of a mother for her child's friend, and the love of a woman for her spouse. The novel is much more than a love story, though. It is also a coming-of-age story—not only in the traditional sense but also in the sense that characters reclaim their lives. The novel is also a story of immigration and of being a stranger in a new land. Finally, it is a story about the absence of love and how neglect and child abuse affect a girl and the people in her life.

The novel provides intimate glimpses of what it is like to be a Russian immigrant in the United States, including the sacrifices, struggles, and successes and failures involved in assimilating and adopting new values and customs. While the novel describes in detail the daily life in the Russian neighborhood of Brighton Beach in Brooklyn, New York, its strength lies in depicting the characters' inner thoughts about assimilation, their homeland, and their new country and showing how language affects one's ability to assimilate and relate to other people.

The novel opens with Lena and Vaclav as children, practicing for a magic show in Vaclav's bedroom. This is their main activity outside of school; magic has been the focus of Vaclav's interests since he was a toddler living in Russia, and because it is Vaclav's obsession, it becomes Lena's, too.

Although the two friends are both first-generation Americans, their similarities end there. Vaclav is the only child of two working-class Russian immigrants, Rasia and Oleg. Before he was born, a pregnant Rasia decided her son would have a better life in the United States. She endured the long wait for the emigration papers by buying English-language tapes and books and teaching her son English. She also educated him about famous Americans, such as Abraham Lincoln, Rosa Parks, and Harry Houdini, the latter of whom captures Vaclav's interest. After the family came to the United States when Vaclav was four, he was able to adapt to his new country and its language with little difficulty. While retaining Russian customs, such as eating borscht for every meal, Rasia wants her son to have the full benefit of being an American. She emphasizes education, making sure he does his homework every day and demanding he assimilate by speaking only English at home, and she adopts American attitudes and values (such as encouraging open communication between parent and child about sex) that she learns about from television. She is a concerned mother who wants both to protect her child and to give him the tools to succeed in the United States.

Lena has no hovering parent. She lives with a woman who is called her aunt but who may not have any blood relationship to her. She does not know whether she was born in Russia or in the United States, nor does she know who her parents are. Although her "aunt" is a working woman, she works nights as a prostitute and sleeps during the day. Unlike Vaclav's home, Lena's is barren and empty. When she comes home, there is no one to greet her, feed her, or tell her to do her homework. Her "aunt" is seldom home, and when she is, wants little to do with her ward, who was foisted on her after the former caretaker, called her "grandmother," died. No one in the home speaks much to Lena, but when they do speak, it is exclusively in Russian. Lena sleeps on the couch and forages for whatever food she can find.

Rather than spending the long afternoons and evenings alone, Lena spends most of her time at Vaclav's house. Since their first playdate when they were five, the two have been inseparable. Lena comes to Vaclav's house every day after school. She eats at Vaclav's house every evening, and Rasia walks her home every night. The first time she walked Lena home, Rasia went inside and saw the filthy, unkempt condition of Lena's apartment. She put her to sleep on her couch and told her the same bedtime story she told Vaclav every night, and she has loved her as if she were her own child.

While Vaclav does well in school, Lena struggles. Despite taking ESL classes, she has difficulty learning English and falls farther behind academically. This alienates her from her classmates and tightens her bond with Vaclav. However, that bond is broken when differing ideas about their magic show come between them. Then, something even more significant comes between them, and Lena disappears from school and Vaclav's life.

Seven years go by, and every night, Vaclav says good night to Lena before he falls asleep, never forgetting her and determining to protect her by keeping her in his thoughts. On the night that he decides it is time to let go of the past and to stop

Vaclav and Lena is Haley Tanner's first novel. In interviews following its publication, she cited personal experience as the inspiration for the love between the characters, specifically the love she shared with her husband, who died of cancer shortly before the book was published.

saying good night to her, Lena calls. The two meet again and reconnect. While their bond is tight, they struggle to define their friendship: Is it love? What about Vaclav's girlfriend? Who and what are they to each other? Lena asks Vaclav to go with her to Russia to find out whether her parents are dead or alive. While trying to identify his feelings for Lena, Vaclav knows he will do this for her. Their friendship (or whatever their relationship is) is tested, though, as they plan for their trip, and they discover what is enduring and what is not.

While both a coming-of-age story and a love story, the novel will also appeal to readers who have no special fondness for either type of story. Tanner's vivid storytelling and characterization distinguish this novel. Readers ultimately get the sense that they know Vaclav, Lena, and Rasia well. Moreover, Tanner makes readers want to know even more about the characters and does so without being sappy or sentimentalizing them.

Tanner brings the characters to life by narrating the novel from the viewpoints of Vaclav, Lena, and Rasia and showing their innermost thoughts as they think aloud. She reflects their observations about people, school, and the world around them as well as their mental tugs-of-war. She shows the complexity of each character, depicting both their positive traits and their flaws. She captures well the challenges of friendships and gender wars that start well before puberty. For example, after Vaclav authoritatively declares that it is impossible to use Lena's suggestion for the magic show, she asks why he is always the boss. Vaclav responds that he is the magician and she is the assistant, which is second to the magician. Lena counters that without an assistant, there is no magician. Throughout the relationship, they continue this struggle to determine who has more power, more importance, and more authority to make decisions.

Some readers may not find Lena as likable as Vaclav or Rasia. As Rasia points out, Lena is flawed. She lies and steals and is deceitful. However, these flaws highlight the effects of her childhood neglect and abuse. Tanner starkly presents other side effects of childhood abuse, such as Lena's sense of detachment from both herself and others, her sense of fragmenting, and her difficulties communicating with others. Other than in a few chapters, however, the childhood abuse is not a dominant theme. Nonetheless, the effects of the abuse underlie the entire novel as they have shaped Lena and her relationships with others. In this way, Tanner powerfully portrays the insidious nature of childhood abuse without sensationalizing or dwelling on it.

One character who is not well developed is Oleg, Vaclav's father and Rasia's husband. This lack of development is intentional, however. Unlike Rasia, Oleg yearns for the past and the land he left behind. In Russia, he was an architect. In the United States, he is a taxi driver. Despite the fact that Russia's economy crumbled and he lost his job as an architect before emigrating, he holds on to the past and makes little effort to make a new life in the United States. Instead, he works, eats, drinks vodka, and watches Russian television shows beamed in by satellite.

While one would barely describe the relationship between Vaclav's parents as a love story, their love for each other is evident through the sacrifices they have made out of their love for their son. The story makes it clear that Rasia misses the charming man she married but does not begrudge her husband for leaving that man behind.

Tanner's use of language also brings the characters to life. At the beginning of the novel, the characters use broken English. Lena's language in particular is limited to short phrases or memorized sentences. Vaclav and Rasia are more proficient in English, but their syntax is imperfect and reflects their varying levels of proficiency. During the second section of the novel, when the characters have aged, their language is more fluid and grammatically correct.

Another captivating element of the novel is its use of short, witty titles for each chapter. With just a few words, the titles capture the essence of the chapter as well as the perspective of the narrator. For example, three successive chapter titles are "Most Likely Not," "She Is Sick, Maybe," and "Secretly He Is Awake." These cryptic phrases refer to Vaclav's uncertainty about Lena's absence from school, Rasia's growing concern about Lena, and Vaclav's feigning sleep as his father tenderly carries him to bed for the first time in years while Rasia has gone to check on Lena.

The novel will appeal to both adults and teenagers. While it is a story about teenagers, its themes of love and friendship are universal, and relayed with Tanner's unique storytelling, its appeal is also universal.

Barbara C. Lightner

Review Sources

Booklist 107, no. 17 (May 1, 2011): 68.
Kirkus Reviews 79, no. 3 (February 1, 2011): 165.
Library Journal 136, no. 2 (February 1, 2011): 57–58.
National Post, June 3, 2011 (Web).
The New York Times, May 30, 2011, p. C4.
The New York Times Book Review, June 19, 2011, p. 21.
Publishers Weekly 258, no. 13 (March 28, 2011): 32.

We, the Drowned

Author: Carsten Jensen (b. 1952)
First published: *Vi, de druknede,* 2006, in Denmark
Translated from the Danish by Charlotte Barslund and Emma Ryder
Publisher: Houghton Mifflin (New York). 688 pp. $28.00
Type of work: Novel
Time: 1848–1945
Locale: Marstal, a port town on Aero Island, Denmark, and various other ports around the world

The history of a town and a way of life, this epic novel tells the story of generations of sailors from the Danish port of Marstal who went to sea to earn their living and the women and children they left behind.

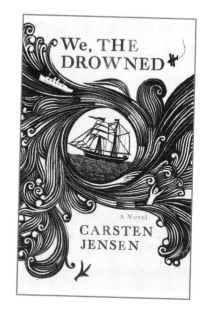

Principal characters:

LAURIDS MADSEN, a sailor who became a legend
ALBERT MADSEN, Laurids's son, a sailor, sea captain, and ship owner
KLARA FRIIS, a widow and Albert's lover, a businesswoman
KNUD ERIK FRIIS, Klara's son, a sailor and later a captain
HERMAN FRANDSEN, a sailor and a murderer, also known as the "Seagull Killer"

Translated from Danish by Charlotte Barslund and Emma Ryder, *We, the Drowned* is an epic novel and an international best seller. Narrated by the collective voice of unnamed townspersons, the novel covers a time period of over one hundred years, yet is carefully knit together by characters from the port of Marstal, the real town whose history inspired the book. Some of these characters disappear and then reappear, as do specific tokens, legends, and world events that take their places in the story. The novel centers on three sailors, beginning with Laurids Madsen, who, according to legend, went up to heaven and came back down again, thanks to his boots. In heaven, he saw Saint Peter, who "flashed his bare ass" at Laurids, leading Laurids to conclude that it was not his time to die. Both the tongue-in-cheek tone of the narration and the over-the-top nature of the story are typical of Jensen's engrossing novel.

Laurids's remarkable journey to heaven and back occurs during the Schleswig-Holstein War, when Laurids and his fellow townsmen are serving in the Danish navy in a war against Germany. Although the sailors are enthusiastic about going to war, the reality of battle changes their perspectives. Jensen's depiction of the horror of naval war demonstrates his ability to effectively combine reality with tall tales, an ongoing

(Getty Images)

Carsten Jensen is a Danish novelist, travel writer, essayist, and critic. We, the Drowned, *his fourth novel, was awarded the Danske Banks Litteraturpris in 2007. He is also the recipient of the 2009 Olof Palme Prize for outstanding achievement.*

feature of the novel. Both ships and men are destroyed and Laurids is blown up, but, as witnesses affirm, he comes down again and lands on his feet. Laurids later tells admirers that anyone wearing such heavy sea boots could not stay in heaven for long. Both Laurids and his boots become famous, but Laurids, changed by the incident, leaves his family and Marstal. He sails to Hobart Town in Van Diemen's Land, now Tasmania, where he disappears. His voyage is just one of the many worldwide journeys described in this novel of sailors from Marstal, many of whom never return.

The narrative continues with the story of the schoolmaster and his thrashing rope. Although the students in Mr. Isager's school learn little academically, they are taught to withstand physical punishment—a lesson that will aid them in their first jobs, inevitably on board a ship. Laurids's youngest child, Albert Madsen, the moral center of the novel, is introduced in these chapters. Albert's story and the impact of his life experiences on people and events recur throughout the rest of *We, the Drowned*. When Albert leaves school, he does what is expected: he goes to sea. After two years spent sailing between Baltic ports as a ship's cook, Albert is promoted to ordinary seaman and sails to the West Indies, then across the equator and around the Cape of Good Hope. His next voyage is to find his father.

In 1862, now in Hobart Town, Albert learns that Laurids once sailed with Captain Jack Lewis. He tracks Lewis to Honolulu and joins his crew on board the *Flying Scud* in exchange for Lewis's promise to take him to Laurids. While sailing to Samoa, Lewis tells tales of life in the Pacific, including the story of Captain James Cook. Eventually, Lewis shows Albert his treasure: the shrunken head of James Cook himself. While landing a cargo of slaves on a small island, the ship is attacked and Lewis is killed by natives. Albert takes command of the *Flying Scud* until it is wrecked on a reef near Apia, the port of Samoa. After an Odysseus-like journey, Alfred finds Laurids living with a new, native family. Father and son discover they have nothing to say to each other, except when Laurids notices that Albert is wearing his boots and demands them back.

The next section of the novel introduces Herman Frandsen, who, at age fifteen, kills his stepfather at sea. The townspeople suspect Frandsen of the crime, but they have no proof. Most of this section describes Marstal in the 1890s, when the shipping industry is booming. Albert Madsen, now fifty, is a shipowner and broker. He has achieved the rank of captain and is wealthy and highly respected in Marstal. On September 26, 1913, Albert begins to see visions of the future that are prophetic of war, destruction, and the end of Marstal as a center for shipping. Albert's vivid dreams frighten him; he sees Marstal ships and sailors being destroyed and the end of the prosperity for the citizens. Later, he will think of that day as the beginning of "the end."

When World War I begins, Albert's dreams start to become reality. Although Denmark remains neutral, financial circumstances dictate that Marstal ships sail from Norway to the West Indies, and even into the war zone. Once the submarine war begins, so do the losses. On June 2, 1915, the schooner *Salvador* goes down, further fulfilling Albert's vision. Marstal sailors are dying, drowned at sea. Money from shipping is still pouring into Marstal, but so is death.

Frandsen, who left years before under suspicion of murder, returns with a scheme for building steel ships. Many townspeople invest, but not Albert. Disturbed and saddened by the loss of life from the war, Albert wants to help those widows and children left at home. He befriends six-year-old Knud Erik Friis, whose father also died at sea. Albert discovers that he can share his terrible dreams, as well as his stories of his past experiences, with Knud Erik. Albert teaches the child to sail and invites him to witness the funeral he holds for James Cook's head; he has kept the shrunken head for years and feels it is time to commit it to the deep. Misfortune returns to Marstal when the proposed Marstal Steel Shipyard is proved a hoax and many lose money from their investments.

In the section "The Seagull Killer," the action shifts to young Knud Erik. Although his mother has forbidden Knud Erik to become a sailor, he does so when he is of age, serving as cook on the *Active*, where he is beaten and mistreated. Advancing to ordinary seaman aboard the *Kristina*, Knud Erik sails to Newfoundland and meets his first love. Leaving Newfoundland, the ship sails into an ice field. Since their ship is wood and not steel, it is lifted above the ice, but other ships are not as fortunate. In Newcastle, they pick up Kristina, the captain's daughter, and a new first mate, Frandsen. The voyage becomes deadly and dangerous; a crew member drowns at sea, the captain dies, and Kristina is raped by Frandsen, who again escapes the consequences of his actions.

In the final section of *We, the Drowned*, World War II has broken out and Denmark is again neutral in the conflict. Albert's haunting dreams of warfare aboard ships become Knud Erik's nightmarish reality. Jensen describes the destruction of ships as envisioned in Albert's dream and knits together the remaining pieces of the novel as ships and characters converge, united in their shared history. The novel ends where it began, in Marstal. Like a comedy, which it is not, it concludes with a dance of townspeople and those rescued. The dance is a celebration of life for those saved from the sea, for the town itself, and for those drowned but whose lives are remembered.

More than anything else, *We, the Drowned* is about a place and those who live there. Because the town is rooted in sailing the oceans and seas of the world, it is also a place many do not return to. Many sailors from Marstal never have a chance to be buried in the new cemetery; they are the drowned spoken of in the title. Women are left without husbands and children grow up without fathers. Fatherless boys are central characters in the novel. All earn their livelihood from and are defined by the sea. Despite the novel's globe-spanning story, it nevertheless remains grounded in Marstal as Jensen meditates on love, loss, and abandonment. Even more broadly, *We, the Drowned* addresses issues such as industrialization, exploration, and globalization.

The author, like many of his characters, is from Marstal, born the son of a sailor. His book, though a novel, is firmly rooted in fact and history. Jensen spent months studying the archives of Marstal in addition to researching materials on Danish involvement during the wars. He also gave readings from his manuscript at the town library, seeking input from longtime town residents. *We, the Drowned*, which took five years to write, is full of facts, yet it is the stories of life aboard ship and experiences in ports all over the world, told by the three sailors and through the collective consciousness of Marstal, that give the novel its scope and make it memorable.

Critics have lauded Jensen's work for its epic treatment of seafaring life and history. Marstal, indeed a character itself, is a fully realized town, rich in both its past and its people. Though daunting in its size, *We, the Drowned* is a powerful and readable novel that is as much about love and family as it is about adventure. In the tradition of sailor's tales, the real and the fantastic are spun together with skillful storytelling. Regardless of whether they are tempted by the allure of the open sea, readers will be enthralled by Jensen's ambitious saga.

Marcia B. Dinneen

Review Sources

Booklist 107, no. 8 (December 15, 2010): 20.
Library Journal 135, no. 15 (September 15, 2010): 60.
Los Angeles Times, April 17, 2011, p. E6.
Publishers Weekly 257, no. 40 (October 11, 2010): 23.
The Wall Street Journal, February 10, 2011, p. A17.
The Washington Post, February 22, 2011, p. C1.

We Others
New and Selected Stories

Author: Steven Millhauser (b. 1943)
Publisher: Alfred A. Knopf (New York).
387 pp. $27.95
Type of work: Short fiction

Millhauser's latest collection of short stories features selected works from his four previous collections, plus seven new and previously un-collected stories.

Principal characters:

AUGUST ESCHENBURG, the inventor of clock-work automatons

EISENHEIM, a nineteenth-century magician who creates human replicas with his mind

MAUREEN, a lonely schoolteacher who wants a relationship with the ghost haunting her attic

PAUL STEINBACH, a ghost who moves into Maureen's attic

WALTER LASHER, a normal man who one day becomes the victim of a "serial slapper"

Steven Millhauser belongs to a tradition of fabulist short-story writers that originated in the tales of Scheherazade, became more literary in the stories of Giovanni Boccaccio, and was pushed to projective psychological extremes in the nineteenth-century romantic tradition of Edgar Allan Poe. Like late-twentieth-century fabulists Jorge Luis Borges, Donald Barthelme, and John Barth, Steven Millhauser is obsessed with fictions that ignore the world of everyday reality and instead explore the world of the imagination.

In Millhauser's fiction, there are two parts to every action: the straightforward, visible part, and the convoluted inward part in which every action's true meaning resides. Millhauser is a consummate romantic; to him, surface reality is merely deception, and true reality is artifice. His short fictions are basically "what if" stories. What if a big corporation built a shopping mall that went on forever? What if someone built an amusement park that surpassed Disneyland illusions and instead created a new reality? Millhauser's most obsessive "what if" is this: What if you pushed an entertainment or a metaphor to ultimate extremes? Skeptics might say that Millhauser's stories go "too far"; however, the intensive "too far" does not exist in his vocabulary. In the title story of *The Knife Thrower* (1998), a runner-up in the 1998 O. Henry Awards, Millhauser pushes the question of how close the knife can go to unthinkable extremes. In this new collection, Millhauser's fifth, he includes a generous helping of stories from his first four collections, advising the reader in his author's note that he did not choose stories that were representative of his work, but rather stories that grabbed his attention as if they had been written by someone else. Indeed, the fourteen previously anthologized stories included here represent Millhauser's most frequent fantasies. The seven "new" stories similarly explore extremes of the creative imagination.

Millhauser is a great admirer of the short-story genre, a form that, as he has said, by excluding almost everything, is able to give perfect shape to what remains. His grand view of the short story is that if the writer concentrates attention on an apparently insignificant portion of the world, the whole world will be uncovered deep within. In one of the shortest of his new stories, Millhauser shows how a mere moment can, when pushed to extremes, reveal the basic human existential condition. "Getting Closer" is not a story about a particular happening, but rather a story about the significance of "happening." The story follows a young boy's family outing to a lake. Though excited, the boy does not rush things; he enjoys prolonging his anticipation of entering the water. As he comes closer to the moment of jumping in, however, he becomes terrified of its inevitability. Although the story appears to be about not much of anything, it is about the ultimate meaning of events. It is about what all stories are about: life in its quintessential movement in time, the basic human desire to escape time and defeat death. The boy experiences the ultimate anxiety, the sickness unto death.

In another new story, "The Slap," Millhauser takes a single metaphor—a slap—and intensifies it into a mysterious "serial slapper" who terrorizes an entire town. The story builds on the premise of a universal human fear of being assaulted by some mysterious force outside the self. The story is told in separate sections (temporal continuity seems inimical to Millhauser's stories), with the plural "we" of the town moving back and forth between accounts of those who have been mysteriously slapped and their fears and confusion. The town's voice ponders the meaning of a slap, as well as the meaning of victimhood. Given the randomness of the slap and the helplessness they feel, they cannot quite understand the extent to which they are victims. As the serial slapper becomes even more invasive and threatening—moving from nighttime assaults to broad daylight, from men to women, from outdoors to indoors—the town feels vulnerable and somehow guilty. In a section titled "Analysis of a Slap," the voice opines that a slap presents itself as assault, but an assault that signifies the withholding of greater power, which is the source of the humiliation it imposes on victims. It brings redness to the cheek but it does not bring blood. A slap, the community understands, requires submission, for even when the sting passes the invisible wound lingers. The slap is much like Millhauser's short stories, for its real work takes place in secret, on the inside.

Another new story, "White Glove," builds on a single metaphor to explore the taboo of female sexuality. Told by a high school boy who becomes friends with a young girl, the story explores how their relationship changes when a mysterious ailment compels the girl to wear a white glove on one hand. The boy becomes obsessed with the mystery of the glove and what lies hidden beneath it. At one point, the boy sneaks into the girl's bedroom while she sleeps and tries to slip the glove off, but he soon becomes ashamed and leaves without seeing what is underneath. Another time, the girl offers him her breast if he will leave the glove alone. When she finally gives in

Steven Millhauser won the Pulitzer Prize in 1997 for his novel Martin Dressler *(1996). His collection* Dangerous Laughter *(2008) was a* New York Times *Best Book of the Year. He is a professor of English at Skidmore College.*

and takes the glove off, he sees that her hand is covered with crinkly dark hair; the skin on the back of the hand is shiny as if wet, with a secretion on the thumb knuckle.

The premise of "The Next Thing," a cautionary tale the likes of which Millhauser has explored before, is a giant underground Wal-Mart, Costco, or IKEA that literally spreads and changes to become the perennial "next big thing." The Under, as the store is called, becomes an overwhelming fact of the townspeople's lives. Inside, customers choose their purchases from product display screens, and the products then tumble down in huge bins. The mysterious, invisible company buys up homes for their management personnel, moving the displaced townspeople down below, where a kind of similitude of the world is created, much like artificial landscapes in Disneyworld and Las Vegas. As the shopping center mutates, the Under deteriorates and a new world, the Over, displaces it as the next thing, and the never-ending process continues.

"We Others" is the longest of the new stories. Told from the perspective of a ghost named Paul Steinbach, who moves into the attic of a sinister schoolteacher named Maureen and her niece Andrea, the story is built on the premise that there have always been ghosts, and that sometimes they can be seen and talked with. Maureen is a lonely woman who desires a closer relationship with Steinbach's ruminant, which is impossible. When the ghost becomes involved with the young niece, Maureen tries to commit suicide, and Paul feels guilty for his interference with their lives. The story ends with the ghost cautioning his listeners/readers that he and his kind, the "others," are not good for humans. Unhappy and alone, filled with longing for connection, they bring no sense of comfort to the living.

Among the previously anthologized stories in this omnibus collection, Millhauser has included some of his best-known work. "August Eschenburg," from *In the Penny Arcade* (1986), develops Millhauser's basic premise of the attempt to create a work of art so close to reality that it becomes real. In this story, the humanlike devices are automatons, clockwork-driven robotic artifacts. The story is built in three sections: Eschenburg's childhood, as he develops his obsession with automatons; his work for a large department store creating animated shop windows; and his collaboration with an entrepreneur who wants his help in setting up automaton theaters. Eschenburg is disenchanted when, in their commercial quest, the head of the department store and the theater owner want him to devise automatons that become increasing sexually suggestive.

Millhauser's best-known story is "Eisenheim the Illusionist," from his 1999 collection *The Barnum Museum*, in which a nineteenth-century magician succeeds in creating ghostly human replicas with the projective power of his mind. The local police chief tries to arrest him, convinced that Eisenheim has crossed some forbidden boundary—in this case, the boundary between illusion and reality—but the magician disappears, revealing that he, like all reality, is a function of the mind's projective creation. In "The Eighth Voyage of Sinbad," Millhauser creates a John Barth-like tale of three parallel stories from three different perspectives of the famous Arabian Nights story:

Sinbad as an old man in retirement, Sinbad on his previously untold eighth voyage, and Sinbad as seen from the perspective of scholarly research.

The stories of Millhauser's *Dangerous Laughter* (2008) are united by his romantic quest for transcendence. Even the opening story, which uses pacing and verb tense to create the illusion that the reader is watching a Tom and Jerry cartoon, concludes with erasure of the physical and reinstatement of illusion. Similarly, "The Disappearance of Elaine Coleman" begins like a popular crime story, but what Millhauser is really interested in is posing the possibility that someone never disappears suddenly, but only gradually, as those who knew her lose sight of her image and indeed her very self. In "The Wizard of West Orange," a Thomas Edison stand-in develops a wired outfit that, when worn, replicates various feelings of touch and even creates new ones. Even though the apparatus promises transcendence, the pragmatic businessman Edison rejects it because it will not be profitable.

Unlike other modern fabulists, such as T. C. Boyle, Steven Millhauser is not interested in merely creating popular entertainments. He sees the short story as a powerful form that is uniquely capable of exploring basic human fears, hopes, and dreams. Whether his stories focus on automatons, men who marry frogs, or labyrinths underneath the everyday world, Millhauser embodies one of the most powerful traditions of short fiction: the magical story of the reality of artifice.

Charles E. May

Review Sources

Booklist 107, no. 22 (August 1, 2011): 24.
Kirkus Reviews 79, no. 14 (July 15, 2011): 1192.
The New York Times Book Review, September 4, 2011, p. 12.
Publishers Weekly 258, no. 27 (July 4, 2011): 43.
The Washington Post, September 1, 2011, p. C04.

When the Killing's Done

Author: T. C. Boyle (b. 1948)
Publisher: Viking (New York). 369 pp. $26.95
Type of work: Novel
Time: Primarily the beginning of the twenty-first century, with significant passages that describe incidents in past times, from the mid-nineteenth century to the post–World War II era
Locale: Santa Barbara and Ventura, California, and the Channel Islands off the California coast, including Anacapa and Santa Cruz

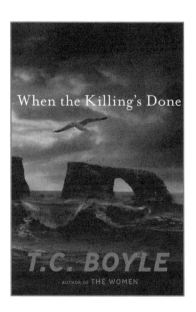

This environmental-ecological novel centers on two opposing factions, bringing to the surface the questions of who and what is right when, despite the best of intentions of both sides, fanatical adherence to principles leads to unintended consequences.

Principal characters:

ALMA BOYD TAKESUE, projects coordinator and director of information resources for the Channel Islands National Park Service and a strong proponent of restoring the indigenous ecosystem of the islands by eradicating nonnative species

TIM SICKAFOOSE, an ornithologist, Alma's boyfriend and the father of her baby

DAVE LAJOY, a successful Santa Barbara–area businessman who is a dedicated, often fanatical animal-rights activist

ANISE REED, Dave's girlfriend, a folksinger who was reared on Santa Cruz Island

BEVERLY BOYD, Alma's grandmother, who survived a horrific ordeal at sea before coming ashore on Anacapa Island in 1946

WILSON GUTIERREZ, a young carpenter and a loyal friend of Dave's

In *When the Killing's Done*, seasoned novelist and short-story author T. C. Boyle, a resident of the area in which the novel is set, weaves a story about the clashes of nature, society, and politics set against the beautiful coastal community of Santa Barbara and its offshore islands. Like many of Boyle's earlier works, *When the Killing's Done* is populated by some extreme, often unlikable characters who are at odds over nature and the environment.

Although the reader does not necessarily need to know the historical context of the novel, it is helpful to be aware that many of the incidents described in *When the Killing's Done* are based on historical fact. The passenger ship *Winfield Scott*, described early in the novel, was wrecked in the channel off Anacapa Island in December 1853 and is often cited as the inadvertent cause of the subsequent disastrous rat infestation on the island. When the *Winfield Scott* sank, rats escaping the sinking ship's hull made their way to the nearest land, which happened to be Anacapa. From that time on, the invading rat population, specifically the black rat, or *Rattus rattus*, increased to the point that it eventually dominated the environment and endangered the indigenous ecosystem. To reverse the damage, aerial bait drops conducted by the US National Park Service took place from late 2001 into 2002, with the intention of doing exactly what Boyle describes in his novel: saving the indigenous murrelet population, whose eggs were systematically being eaten by the rats. Almost ten years later, the murrelets are thriving, and the black rats reportedly have been destroyed. As in the novel, Santa Cruz Island was also earmarked by the National Park Service in a broad-based plan to destroy nonnative feral pigs, and reintroduction of the California bald eagle was the next item on the agenda.

T. C. Boyle is a distinguished professor of English at the University of Southern California. He won a Guggenheim Fellowship in 1988 and several O. Henry Awards for his short stories. Among his many other literary prizes are the 1988 PEN/Faulkner Award for Fiction and the 1999 PEN/Malamud Award for short-story writing.

There was no real-life Alma Boyd Takeuse, the lead character in the novel, but one local Santa Barbara animal-rights activist, Rob Puddicombe, could be considered a very loose inspiration for the other lead character, Dave LaJoy. Like Dave, Puddicombe attempted to mitigate the effectiveness of the aerially dropped poisons by raids on the island, spreading vitamin K–infused pellets that would be eaten by the rats and provide an effective antidote. Puddicombe's efforts, like Dave's in the novel, were ultimately unsuccessful. Puddicombe was arrested and brought up on federal charges, but he was ultimately found not guilty. In the novel, Dave faces a number of criminal charges and civil litigation, but none prove to be more than mere annoyances. Unlike the fictional loner and curmudgeon Dave, Puddicombe did not drown at sea and had many allies, especially among journalists, animals-rights activists, and libertarians. Many were disturbed as much by the government's aerial bombardment of the islands as by the idea of killing a nonindigenous species to protect another species.

Dave may at times seem to be the villain of the novel, but it is fairer to say that he is simply the antagonist to the protagonist, Alma, as his intentions are pure, even if his personality is presented as irritating and obnoxious. He feels strong dislike, and even hatred, for most of the people with whom he comes in contact, particularly those who have enough expendable income to buy the pricey sound systems he sells. He is also a fanatic, which is never an admirable trait when scrutinized. Nonetheless, Dave's conviction that no animals, no matter how lowly, should be killed, even if they themselves kill—institutionalized in his PETA-like organization, For the Protection of Animals (FPA)—is based on closely held beliefs. On the other hand, Alma, who wants to save the ecosystem on Anacapa and Santa Cruz Islands in a manner similar in intent, if not execution, to methods used when she lived and worked on Guam a few years prior to the main setting of the novel, also seems to have pure motives. While seemingly more pragmatic and, perhaps, more willing to "sell out" than Dave, she also strongly believes in the rightness of her cause.

Boyle adds a slightly ironic twist to the interaction between Alma and Dave about midway through the novel when he reveals, through Alma's thoughts, that she and Dave had once had a brief social interaction before their public disagreements began. Though it was not a relationship, but a nice initial meeting followed by an unsuccessful date, it set the stage of their antagonism. Dave can be charming, but he can turn brittle and mean, while Alma often retreats from an uncomfortable situation and is just as stubborn as Dave. Alma is as tough as her grandmother, Beverly, and perhaps the triumph of her grandmother over the unrelenting Anacapa rats is an underlying motivation for Alma's views about the island.

The first part of the book, which takes place in 1946, is a remote setup for what unfolds more than fifty years later in the main part of the story. Beverly Boyd, Alma's then-young and pregnant grandmother, is the lone survivor of the sinking of a small craft manned by her husband, a World War II veteran, and her brother-in-law. After drifting along in the channel, clinging to a buoyant Sears, Roebuck ice chest and avoiding shark attacks, she finally makes her way to shore on Anacapa Island. When Beverly enters a seemingly deserted shack, thinking she is safe, the sounds and dim sights she encounters lead her to realize that dozens, perhaps hundreds, of rats are the current occupants of the shack. Her ultimate survival depends upon her destroying the rats, or at least keeping them at bay, until she is rescued by the Coast Guard. The action then abruptly shifts to Santa Barbara, circa 2001, and Alma, whose relationship to Beverly is only gradually made clear to the reader.

Boyle's works over the years have always involved characters who are over the top and unlikable, almost unbelievably so. Though there is nothing particularly funny in *When the Killing's Done*, the reader cannot help but find some of the descriptions of the characters and situations extreme to the point of satire. By making many of the characters seem so extreme, Boyle explores the question of how to bring together two opposing forces when both have good intentions.

The female characters, including Alma, Beverly, Annabelle Yuell, and Rita and Anise Reed, are more fully drawn and, for the most part, come off better than the male characters. While both Dave and Alma's boyfriend, Tim Sickafoose, are dedicated, they have many unadmirable qualities. Tim is initially presented as a sympathetic character, seemingly the perfect, supportive boyfriend, but then reacts badly after Alma announces that she is pregnant. Prior to this, he has seemed to Alma, and perhaps the reader, to be a great life partner, but his reaction to her pregnancy—insisting that she set a date for an abortion that she clearly does not want—turns his characterization completely inside out. However, even in Tim's lack of sympathy for the pregnancy, Boyle adds a philosophical twist. Rather than just not wanting the responsibility, Tim tries to convince Alma that their strong belief in population control should take priority over her desire to go through with the pregnancy and keep the baby.

Boyle's narrative style is smooth and readable, even though he has a tendency to overwrite. No detail or thought of his characters seems too insignificant, from how eggs or coffee is savored to how slippery the floor is or what people are wearing or feeling. Boyle has a particular affinity for highly evocative sensory descriptions of tastes, textures, and smells. This reliance on long, internalized descriptions, often in the place of his characters actually speaking, somewhat bogs down the flow of the narrative and certainly adds considerable bulk to the novel. The overwriting on the small details is juxtaposed against the author's occasional tendency to abruptly stop describing important events before they completely unfold, which often leaves readers hanging. For example, late in the book, when Dave's craft goes down, the narrative abruptly shifts back to Alma. The reader's knowledge of the sinking is filled in only slightly when it is learned that Rita, Anise's mother, is about to scatter the ashes of her daughter, the only person whose body was found after Dave's boat sank.

As most reviewers have noted, and the reader comes to realize, Boyle does not pick sides in the philosophical dilemma between Alma and Dave. If anything, he is careful to present both sides as equally good and bad and as equally understandable based on the backgrounds of the characters. Although Boyle never presents a clear view of which side garners his loyalties, he does present a compelling case that do-gooders are often too blinded by their own versions of idealism to see the truth. He also seems to believe strongly in the broader societal ramifications of Sir Isaac Newton's third law: For every action, there is an equal and opposite reaction.

Patricia King Hanson

Review Sources

Atlantic Monthly 307, no. 2 (March 2011): 94.
Booklist 107, no. 7 (December 1, 2010): 27.
Library Journal 136, no. 12 (July 1, 2001): 44.
The New Yorker 87, no. 5 (March 21, 2011): 69.
The New York Review of Books 58, no. 3 (February 24, 2011): 25–26.
The New York Times Book Review, February 20, 2011, p. 17.

Widow

Author: Michelle Latiolais
Publisher: Bellevue Literary (New York).
192 pp. $14.95
Type of work: Short fiction
Time: First decade of the twenty-first century;
1960s
Locale: Mostly Los Angeles, but also Las Vegas; New York; Kalamazoo, Michigan; Massachusetts; and other places

This collection of short stories has propelled its author into the national spotlight in part for its exposé of the anger, depression, and vulnerability of widowhood that is so often misunderstood by society.

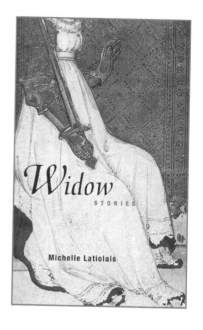

Principal characters:
THE WIDOW, a nameless, middle-aged woman identified in some stories as a literature professor; may be several different characters
BENSON, the widow's deceased husband and former drama teacher in "Crazy"
PAUL, the widow's deceased husband in "Damned Spot"
EILEEN, a baker in "Involution"
HERB, a biological anthropologist in "Gut"
JOHN, a proprietor of a knife shop in "Gut"

Widow: Stories is a slim collection of seventeen stories that range from two to twenty-two pages. Some of the stories were first published in *Absolute Disaster* (1996), *Santa Monica Review* (2000), the *Antioch Review* (2000), and other literary journals. After Michelle Latiolais's husband Paul died suddenly in 2004, she found writing to be a therapeutic way to deal with her own grief, and new stories about widowhood emerged from that darkness. Two of these, "Caduceus," published in the *Northwest Review* (2009), and "Place," published in *Green Mountain Review* (2008), were nominated for Pushcart Prizes. The collection was then published by Bellevue Literary Press, affiliated with the New York University School of Medicine, and also publisher of her second novel, *A Proper Knowledge* (2008).

Latiolais completed some of the collection's newer stories while in residency at the Ucross Foundation Ranch in Wyoming, where Pulitzer Prize–winning author Annie Proulx wrote much of her collection, *Close Range: Wyoming Stories* (1999). As with *Close Range*, *Widow* is also held together thematically, although not so much by a geography of place as of the female soul. And while Latiolais's and Proulx's writing styles bear little resemblance other than being exceptionally masterful, they share the same talent for portraying the interior emotional landscape of characters who are at odds with a harsh, exterior world. Latiolais's widow stories also lend themselves to comparison with the writing of Joan Didion and Joyce Carol Oates, whose fiction about widowhood also emerged from their own life experiences.

The title story, "Widow," opens the collection, one of just seven stories about widowhood. The widow here is a nameless, middle-aged woman who is enduring an awkward and humiliating visit with her gynecologist. While perched on the examination table in a mauve paper gown that is as comfortable as a "refrigerator box . . . all eaves and walls," she reflects on the various connotations of "widow." In Sanskrit, "widow" means "empty," while the Biblical book of Leviticus "aligns" widows with "whores and divorced women and forbids priests from marrying such defiled creatures." Although she has been submerged in grief since her husband's death two years earlier, she does manage to squeeze a bit of acerbic humor from her predicament. As she completes the medical form, noting boxes for "single" and "married" but not "widowed," she "wants very much to be able to check off the box labeled 'whore, profane, harlot, widow.'" Later, after reading self-help books at Barnes and Noble, including a dated book that advises widows to wear only black or gray pearls, she defiantly wears pink. Nevertheless, her grief is palpable and bottomless, and only her cynicism-infused moments of mania release her, and the reader, from this dark cave.

The reader next meets this same nameless widow—or perhaps it is another nameless widow—in "Pink." There, she is visiting the "Art of the Cup: A History of Design 1860–1960," a permanent exhibit tucked away at the back of an art museum. She knows the exhibit intimately and can locate it "blindfolded." She is drawn especially to the elegant, yet quirky porcelain cups, one of which is shaped like a "French champagne cork on a bistro *l'addition* saucer" while another is shaped like a "cactus flower." Her friends fail to see the attraction, able to relate only to the pedestrian Fiestaware cups, yet the widow, as she contemplates the origin of the word *porcelain*, sees so much more. At this point, Latiolais's passionate love for language sizzles on the page as a barrage of sexual connotations related to Italian food and porcelain roll off the widow's lips, heating up like Tita's sensual cooking scenes in Laura Esquivel's *Like Water for Chocolate* (1992) or Vianne as she melts chocolate in Joanne Harris's *Chocolat* (2000). The heartbreaking reality, however, is that the widow has no one with whom to share this lust. Latiolais then pushes the button further as the widow envisions a potter mixing her cremated ashes with the components of porcelain, "kaolin, china stone, silicate, lime," and creating a cup on which a man could set his lips each morning, "his tongue against the thin bone china lips her fired bones would make."

A widow appears next in "Place." It is the two-year anniversary of her husband's death and she dresses for church all in black, including black pearls. At night, she sleeps "curled around a large leather book" that is filled with her husband's ashes. She defines her life "by negation, by what she is no longer, by what she cannot have, by absence." Not only is the widow hideously trapped in the depression stage of Elisabeth Kübler-Ross's five stages of grief—modeled for cancer patients but applicable to other situations—she has backtracked to the third stage, the bargaining stage, ready to sacrifice the lives of her friends, or to "sanction their slaughter" in exchange for her husband "walk[ing] through the door from the garden."

In "Place," the reader learns that the widow is a literature professor and was married for eighteen years, details that seem to fit with, and expand upon, the characterization in the previous widow stories. These details also seem to mirror Latiolais's personal life and suddenly the bleak realization that these stories are both fiction and testimony breaks down some of the distance set by the third person point of view.

At this time, it also becomes clear that Latiolais intends to parcel out the details about the husband's death in the remaining widow stories like a good mystery, yet this

(BJ Swanson)

Michelle Latiolais is the author of three novels and codirector of the programs in writing at the University of California, Irvine. Her first novel, Even Now *(1992), received the Gold Medal for Fiction from the Commonwealth Club of California. She has also published widely in literary journals and anthologies.*

structure doesn't fall into place neatly. Not all of the widow stories seem to feature the same widow. The characterization does not hold true from story to story. Even the husbands change. Although they are mostly nameless, in "Crazy" he is Benson, while in "Damned Spot" he is named Paul, like Latiolais's late husband. The widows, however, always remain nameless.

Although the duplicity of nameless widows can be disconcerting and can be viewed as trivializing a very real, personal experience, their namelessness makes it easier to see how their characters collectively amplify the themes of love, grief, and loss across Latiolais's stories. In this postmodern society ridden with divorce and emotional platitudes, the widows here attest to having been in genuinely meaningful marriages with deep, everlasting love for their husbands. In "Caduceus," the widow keeps her husband's birthday cards in with her lingerie so that when she opens the drawer she is greeted with "Baby," "Sweetheart," and "My lover, my friend." His clothes still hang in the dark closet, where she can still smell his scent. The woman in "Widow" convinces herself that wandering around town, to malls and such, is "possibility, chance, serendipity—he might be there, that place she didn't think to look, hadn't worked hard enough to find."

After establishing the unfathomable gaps left by the departed husbands, Latiolais then explores the time constraints imposed on mourning by contemporary society. The widows are unable to shake their grief fast enough to satisfy their friends, family, and colleagues. They resent suggestions to see a therapist, take antidepressants, open themselves up to new relationships, or simply "redesign" their lives. Well-meaning suggestions are viewed more as snake oil; instead, the widows put on a good front with the hope of deflecting these interrogations and suggestions for change.

Latiolais also touches upon the contemporary taboo on public displays of emotion and "lamentation." When the widow in "Caduceus" cries at the funeral, a blogger later criticizes her behavior. She laments her inability to express anger, "the rending of clothing and the gnashing of teeth," the second stage in Kübler-Ross's model. "Only God was allowed His anger, only God."

The last widow story, "Damned Spot," offers a very different tone from the others, as if a huge fog has been lifted. There are some heartbreaking details here about the circumstances surrounding the husband's death, but the focus is not so much on the husband as it is on a dog, an English bull terrier named Damned Spot. The woman credits Damned Spot for helping her get through the year-and-a-half grieving process before he, too, dies. Rather than dwelling on emotion, the narrative is propelled by chattiness and a matter-of-fact sensibility, as if being told to a group of vacationers enjoying a round of drinks aboard a cruise ship. Witnessing this transformation from the depths of depression to acceptance—the final stage of grief in Kübler-Ross's model— is cathartic for the reader, as it was, presumably, for the author.

The other stories in the collection feature other roles filled by women: sisters, daughters, aunts, wives, grandmothers, lovers, and divorcées. The women here are victims and abusers, sexual creatures, and madonnas. Mostly, however, they are observers of the world as it spins around them, second-class citizens, and vulnerable to depression for reasons that are often beyond their control.

In "Gut," the longest story in the collection, a wife unwillingly subjects herself to a month in Africa eating leaves and bamboo shoots and throwing up constantly to please her husband, a biological anthropologist. Harvard professor Richard Wrangham and his studies, *Catching Fire: How Cooking Made Us Human* (2009) and *Demonic Males: Apes and the Origins of Human Violence* (1997), inspired Latiolais to write this farcical story. While humorous, it also exposes the vulnerability of dependent women in traditional marriages.

"Burqa" raises questions about motherhood in two contrasting societies. An American divorcée who is forced to adjust to an empty nest now that her son has moved across the country for college reminisces tenderly about her early years of motherhood. As she also questions major decisions she made during his teenage years, she reflects on an incident she observed while visiting Saudi Arabia. There, a group of women were socializing in the public square while a little boy ran "from one black shroud to another black shroud, screaming with fear and anguish, and finally a woman had stepped out in front of him and lifted her veil just enough so that he could see it was she, his own mother."

The writing in this collection is stunning, laced with vivid imagination and dotted with unusual words that shimmer and shake. In "Breathe," Latiolais plays with the metaphor of synthetic fabric as representing all that is cheap, fleeting, and even unjust in the world: the rayons, acetates, and arnels are the "tightly crowded housing tracts," while linen and cotton are the "Kentucky horse farms." She also has fun with the term *cadaverine*, "a nitrogenous material derived from human corpses," a substance rumored to have been used in the manufacture of women's nylon stockings during the 1930s. Other words that make a memorable appearance, include *marmorealize* in "Widows," *creatural anguish* in "Place," and *estrus* and *sybaritic impulses* in "Damned Spot."

Sally S. Driscoll

Review Sources

Library Journal 136, no. 3 (February 15, 2011): 102.
Los Angeles Times, January 2, 2011, p. 12.
The New York Times Book Review, February 20, 2011, p. 1.
NPR, March 4, 2011 (Web).
San Francisco Chronicle, January 23, 2011 (Web).
Star Tribune, January 30, 2011, p. 12E.

A Widow's Story
A Memoir

Author: Joyce Carol Oates (b. 1938)
Publisher: HarperCollins (New York). 432 pp.
$27.99
Type of work: Memoir
Time: February–August, 2008
Locale: Princeton, New Jersey

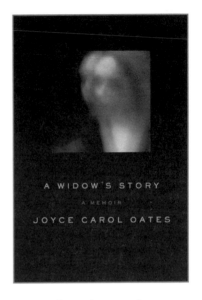

The author describes in harrowing detail her grief after the death of her husband of nearly forty-eight years.

Principal personages:
JOYCE CAROL OATES, novelist, essayist, and professor of humanities at Princeton University
RAYMOND J. SMITH, the author's husband, former editor of the *Ontario Review*

On February 18, 2008, Raymond J. Smith died unexpectedly at the age of seventy-seven, leaving Joyce Carol Oates, his wife of nearly forty-eight years, a widow. Oates is one of the best-known and most prolific living American writers, whose work has received critical acclaim and garnered numerous literary awards. Having always fiercely guarded her private life as Mrs. Smith, she exposes to public view the raw emotions of the first months after her husband's death. *A Widow's Story: A Memoir* is a dark book that begins when Raymond is in the hospital; Oates finds a note on her windshield in the hospital parking lot, a scathing comment on her bad job of parking. She sees this as evidence that her personal suffering has no meaning for others.

Oates wrote that the reason for her memoir was "to see what can be made of the phenomenon of 'grief' in the most exactingly minute of ways." In an interview, she added that she wanted to memorialize her husband, who was unknown beyond the world of publishing. Her narrative unexpectedly becomes a journey of discovery: The man she thought she had known so well had concealed an inner life of the imagination that he had not shared with his wife.

Other women have surely known the common terrors of widowhood: the guilt of the survivor, the obsessive need to telephone home to hear her husband's voice on the answering machine, anger at the thoughtless attempts at consolation from well-meaning friends, or unwanted gifts of food that are thrown into the garbage. In other ways, her grief reaches well beyond the usual experience of widowhood. Oates is not only a bereaved wife but also a creative artist whose husband had been her constant companion and inspiration. They shared a rewarding social life with an extensive group of writers and literary people and had only rarely spent a night apart in their long marriage. Raymond, eight years her elder, with his calm demeanor and quiet competence, provided the support that kept the household running, freeing Oates to create her fiction. While they worked together on the *Ontario Review*, they carefully segmented their professional lives. Raymond did not read Oates's fiction, and she never asked to see the manuscript of his unfinished novel.

She begins with a glimpse of the fragility of life, an automobile accident the previous year when she and Raymond had escaped serious injury. Perhaps both of them should have seen this as a warning, she believes. In moments of despair, she begins to suspect that Raymond, lying in his hospital bed, might have been concealing from her the foreknowledge of his death. Raymond had been hospitalized with pneumonia, usually treated with antibiotics and rarely fatal. However, within a week he succumbed to a raging infection of *E. coli* bacteria in his lungs that ended in cardiac arrest. Awakened by that dreaded nighttime summons from the hospital, Oates rushed to his side to find that Raymond had died before she could reach him.

Oates draws on the precise details recorded in her journal of those first six months after her husband's death in writing her memoir. Her prose style will be familiar to readers of her fiction: startling, often disturbing, metaphors; dashes, italics, and exclamation points; and torrents of emotional language that mirror the mental derangement of her grief. In places, she backs away from this cascade of language to refer to herself in the third person as "the widow" to comment ironically on the raw emotion of the previous passage. She includes copies of the e-mails received from her many literary friends: John Updike, E. L. Doctorow, Philip Roth, and Gail Godwin, among others. Several chapters are flashbacks of the history of the couple's shared academic positions in Beaumont, Texas; Detroit, Michigan; and Windsor, Ontario, putting their lives in context before they accepted positions at Princeton University in New Jersey, where both were on the faculty at the time of his death.

Oates's narrative is an unflinching journey of grief that offers no solace, either for those who have experienced a loss or those who are forced to recognize that they, too, must someday endure the death of a loved one. Several times the author addresses the reader directly as "you," warning of what lies in store for those who mistakenly believe they can escape the event that will forever disrupt their lives.

Guilt, overwhelming and obsessive, is a leitmotif that dominates the narrative; guilt manifests in thoughts that she might somehow have prevented his death, that she arrived at his bedside too late, that she should have taken him to New York instead of to the local hospital. A writer of fiction often described as "gothic," using images of violence and horror, Oates finds her imagination working overtime, acknowledging that her brain is "a sodden mass of gauze in which crazed thoughts teem like maggots." She imagines from the odd behavior of her two cats that they are blaming her for Raymond's absence. She fantasizes that the bacteria that killed him are evidence of a hostile world bent on destroying her. She is convinced of her own worthlessness, that although she has no religious beliefs, she is somehow being punished for having outlived her husband.

Fearing to answer the telephone calls from sympathetic acquaintances, she finds some consolation in her e-mail exchanges with literary friends who had known

(Charles Gross)

Joyce Carol Oates, Roger S. Berlind Distinguished Professor of Humanities at Princeton University, is a member of the American Academy of Arts and Letters. Her fiction has won numerous awards, including the National Book Award and the Prix Femina, and she has been nominated multiple times for the Pulitzer Prize.

Raymond. Other ordinary conversations become impossible. She stops their fitness-club membership because she cannot bear to tell the receptionist that her husband is dead. She cancels their subscription to the *New York Times*, a reminder of shared reading pleasures. Certain places call up memories that she names "sinkholes," moments of sheer terror that send her running for shelter.

Tortured by insomnia, she makes a nest of reading material in the bed they had shared. She medicates herself with prescriptions—Lorazepam, Ambien, Lunesta—as well as over-the-counter drugs. Even as she fears becoming addicted, she is tempted by the hallucination of the "basilisk," a lizardlike figure promising oblivion through suicide. Finally, on the advice of friends, she asks her doctor for Cymbalta, an antidepressant that assuages her pain but leaves her dazed.

Oates forces the reader to experience the intensity of her grief; she rejects the attempts of others to comfort her, telling no one in her professional circle of her loss. She resumes teaching her creative-writing classes at Princeton and is surprised by a student who expresses his sympathy—she had spoken to no one at the university about her husband's death. Within three weeks she has taken up her demanding schedule of speaking engagements and book signings. She has become "Joyce Carol Oates," "a flawless imitation of a writer self," convinced that her presence at the podium is a fraud. She is split between two roles: the silent, suffering widow, and the Cymbalta-dazed professional carrying out her duties in the conviction that she must not reveal to strangers the extent of her grief.

After four months, Oates steels herself to read Raymond's manuscript, fragments of an unfinished novel, "Black Mass." Recounting the early years of their marriage, Oates describes her success in her early twenties with the publication of her first book of short stories, *By the North Gate* (1963). Raymond, who had briefly tried his hand at writing fiction, shifted his focus to become an editor of the works of others.

Oates approached Raymond's novel with both anticipation and fear. She knew that he had been raised in a strict Roman Catholic family and that his father had expected him to become a priest. However, after a brief period in the seminary, Raymond had suffered a breakdown. He rejected the Catholic religion and became estranged from the family. (The couple enjoyed a warm relationship with Oates's family, however.) Both Oates and Raymond had similar events in their families: sisters who had been institutionalized as children. Oates's younger sister Lynn was severely autistic and by the age of eleven, she had become so disturbed that she was a physical danger to the family. Raymond's older sister Carol, a disruptive and troublesome child, had died of unexplained causes in an institution.

Raymond's manuscript was a compendium of partially written scenes, notes, and plot outlines. Believing that much of "Black Mass" had been written before their marriage, Oates was disturbed to discover several descriptions of places and events from their lives together. The fictional Paul had become a priest, choosing celibacy over his love for a woman, a talented poet whose life mirrored that of suicidal poet Sylvia Plath. He had also apparently withheld a vital family secret, because the institutionalized child of his novel undergoes a lobotomy, destroying the personality of the patient. This revelation explained the mystery surrounding the life and death of Raymond's sister. Although Oates acknowledged these events as fiction, she found them deeply upsetting. Raymond had lived in a world of the imagination that he had never shared with her.

Oates offers little consolation to the reader but suggests in her conclusion the beginnings of a recovery. She ends the publication of the *Ontario Review*, closing off the professional life that she and Raymond had shared. She weans herself from the antidepressants that had clouded her thinking. Raymond had been an expert gardener, so she begins the task of restoring his garden, both the place he had loved and, if anywhere, where his spirit perhaps remained. Choosing the plants (perennials, a contrast to his more colorful annuals) and digging in the soil offered Oates some solace; although she knows that she will never achieve the optimism that was Raymond's outlook on life.

Readers unfamiliar with the emotional onslaught of Oates's prose may find this memoir unsettling. Even as she demands that the reader share the shattering intensity of her experience, she seems to refute her ironic statement that her grief will have no meaning for others. However, most critics praise the work for its raw self-revelation of the author's darkest moments. Even as readers are drawn in by the intensity of her grief, there is an awareness of the artist beyond the words on the page. Her epilogue mentions, almost as an aside, meeting a man who will eventually play a part in her life. It is the only allusion to her second marriage, thirteen months after Raymond's death.

Perhaps it is the intense emotion of the memory work of Oates the writer that offers salvation and represents her reconciliation with her existence as a bereaved wife. If the author was wildly out of control in the early days of her widowhood, the completed memoir reveals Oates to be in full control of her literary art. In her epilogue she offers parting advice to a widow: She must be able to say, "I kept myself alive."

Marjorie Podolsky

Review Sources

America 204, no. 14 (April 25, 2011): 29–30.
Booklist 107, no. 3 (October 1, 2010): 13.
New Statesman 140, no. 5068 (August 24, 2011): 50–51.

The New Yorker 86, no. 40 (December 13, 2010): 70–79.
The New York Times, February 15, 2011, p. A29.
The New York Times Book Review, February 20, 2011, p. 1–10.
Publishers Weekly 257, no. 50 (December 20, 2010): 45.

Words Made Fresh
Essays on Literature and Culture

Author: Larry Woiwode (b. 1941)
Publisher: Crossway (Wheaton, IL). 192 pp.
$24.99
Type of work: Essays

This book presents an intriguing and stimulating set of essays discussing issues that are close to Woiwode's heart.

Larry Woiwode is thought of as a novelist first and foremost. His first novel, *What I'm Going to Do, I Think*, was published in 1969 and won the William Faulkner Foundation Award, as well as a Notable Book award from the American Library Association. He garnered critical acclaim for its psychological study of two people wrestling with their religious faith in the modern secular world. It has been argued that Woiwode approaches each of his narratives from a religious perspective. However, Woiwode does not wish to be considered a sermonizer or propagandist. If his ideas have any credibility at all, then they can hold up in an organic way within a narrative. While his novels and short stories have gained critical acclaim, Woiwode is a very fine essayist, poet, and literary critic as well. He has also written two illuminating memoirs. His first memoir, *What I Think I Did: A Season of Survival in Two Acts*, was published in 2000, and his second, *A Step from Death*, was published in 2008. In all of his writings it is obvious how much he cares about the subject matter he discusses. Woiwode does not shy away from the spiritual core that drives him to live and write the way he does. He is well aware of his own shortcomings as a person and has written about life choices of which he is not proud. With that said, Woiwode has clarity as to what is essential to his being and has attempted to adhere to the standards that he has set for himself.

   In some sense Woiwode comes across as an anomaly, both as a person and as a writer. He is not a modernist at heart. He is not angst-ridden or driven by a hopelessness that can only lead to despair. Woiwode is centered by a Christian reality that leads him to be hopeful. He is continually "nourished" by family and the land (more specifically, his farm). All of these aspects make him appear to be a throwback, a traditionalist, and someone who is certainly out of step with twenty-first-century literary and social trends. For him, man is not helpless. There are avenues from which anyone can find a better way. To read Woiwode is to know that he holds these moral precepts and that his literary conclusions will be based on the tenets that he holds dear. In many ways Woiwode can be seen as something of a lone voice in the wilderness. That assessment may overdramatize his situation or his standing in the American community of writers, but it cannot be too far off target.

For the collection *Words Made Fresh: Essays on Literature and Culture*, Woiwode has gathered ten essays that he feels point toward the purpose that "words" are meant to instill for the conscientious reader. Each of these essays was published at some earlier date in another incarnation. With that in mind, Woiwode presents these essays as "fresh" entities, newly configured word patterns that he hopes will lead the reader to a richer understanding of each piece. For these refashionings to be of any use to attentive readers, there must be "fresh" knowledge that was heretofore impossible to discern. Most reviewers agree that Woiwode has succeeded in rearranging his pieces for their new incarnation in *Words Made Fresh*.

Woiwode states in his introduction to *Words Made Fresh* that the title is supposed to "echo the incarnation." Presumably the writer is referencing the Incarnation of Jesus Christ, who is sometimes referred to in spiritual writings as "the Word made flesh." Woiwode explains this further by clarifying what the purpose of the Incarnation is in the first place, based on his beliefs. It is through the Incarnation, he says, that "writers outside the scope of the Hebrew or Greek texts began to understand how a metaphor of words could contain the lineaments and inner workings of a human being." For Woiwode, it is of supreme importance to make sure that each word he chooses is truly and appropriately employed. This is an important part of diligent writing in any tradition, but it has unique resonance for writers who are persons of faith. Woiwode argues forcefully that there are protocols of writing and of faith for a reason.

It is not instantly evident why these particular essays were chosen to be grouped together, but after a careful reading of each essay it becomes abundantly clear that there is a method to Woiwode's selection process. As in his 2008 memoir, there is a somewhat "scattered" feel to the essays as a whole. In the end, the meandering of subjects only goes to confirm Woiwode's brilliance as an informed observer of both literature and culture. Each essay can be looked at as a building block that only exists in this configuration to serve a greater purpose.

While in the past each essay has stood on its own merits, the urgency of the entire set can only be truly appreciated by a close examination of the structure of the whole collection. Several authors have spoken glowingly about *Words Made Fresh*, including Philip Yancey, Ellen Lansky, John L. Moore, and Thomas McGuane. Each of these authors recognizes the inventiveness and power of Woiwode's essays. He is commended for his ability to "blend" information seamlessly with an "assessment of culture." There is much to be learned in every book, paragraph, sentence, and word Woiwode writes.

The author opens the collection with a revelatory and heartbreaking essay. The essay, "Guns and Peace," was first published as "Guns" in the December 1975 issue of *Esquire* magazine. Since then it has been published in various lengths on several occasions. In its incarnation in *Words Made Fresh*, "Guns and Peace" is a very jarring essay to read. Woiwode details the day in which he killed a wounded deer with his family watching. The deer had been struck by a "delivery truck" and had "one of its rear legs torn off at the hock." This was not its only injury, but it still struggled to escape

In addition to earning critical acclaim for such novels as What I'm Going to Do, I Think *(1969),* Beyond the Bedroom Wall *(1975),* Born Brothers *(1988), and* Indian Affairs *(1992), Larry Woiwode has also secured a reputation as a brilliant writer of essays, memoirs, poetry, and literary criticism.*

its predicament. In Woiwode's eyes, it was an expression of kindness to put the deer out of its misery. However, the event did not end there; killing never seems to end when someone wants it to end. There always seem to be ripple effects. It was difficult for Woiwode to explain to his young daughter what he had done and why. He also had to justify what he did to himself over and over again. Had there been any other credible option for Woiwode to take? Did he have the right to make the decision of life or death for the wounded deer? The author expands the essay so as to explain his history with firearms and tragedy. Death may be inevitable, but is it ever possible to guarantee that it will be a "good" death? In the last paragraph of the essay, Woiwode realizes that he cannot really "refute his heritage." Even with this knowledge in hand, he doubts "that [he will] use a firearm again, certainly not in the city, and, if outside it, only in the direct emergency."

In a sense he says he will not use a firearm again in order to protect his own sanity. There are violent "fantasies" that have haunted him. The startling fact is that in his fantasies, he is not doing the shooting. For him, everything is "reversed." He is the "one being shot, or shot full of holes." The only way he can explain this turn of events to himself is that there is a "primitive portion of my imagination" that "keeps insisting this is what I deserve." Woiwode adds an afterword to the essay in which he speaks of making a good life with his wife and children, and that what he "clings" to now is the "faith" that made it possible all of their lives to "blossom and prosper in peace."

In the second essay, "Homeplace, Heaven or Hell? On the Order of Existence," the author speaks to the purpose of writing itself. For him it is the writer's responsibility to provide readers with order. Woiwode wholeheartedly believes that a writer must be able to shape "contemporary experience and phenomena into forms that illustrate a dependence on, and captivity to, ultimate form." For a Christian writer such as Woiwode, there is an even greater obligation to suggest "directions for our culture." He has little regard for writers who merely follow the crowd in order to bolster their readership. In Woiwode's eyes, writers must have respect for themselves and their purpose, for their stories (and all they entail), and for their readers (and all that writers must impart to them).

In *Words Made Fresh,* Woiwode also includes essays that describe what other writers have done to meet such an imperative standard, including Wendell Berry in "Views of Wendell Berry: On Life Against Agribusiness," John Gardner in "AmLit: On a Writer's Incorrect Views" and "Gardner's Memorial in Real Time: On the Achievement of Mickelsson," Reynolds Price in "Gospels of Reynolds Price: On Trials of Translating," John Updike in "Updike's Sheltered Self: On America's Maestro," Bob Dylan in "Dylan to CNN: On News and Not News," and William Shakespeare in "The Faith of Shakespeare: On My Favorite Actor." Woiwode also includes an essay, "Deconstructing God: On Views of Education," in which he takes issue with the way that public education is run in the United States. He speaks up for the positive aspects of homeschooling as an alternative to the broken public school system. Woiwode ends the volume with "The Faith of Shakespeare: On My Favorite Actor." In this fascinating final essay the author examines the countless ways in which Shakespeare qualifies as one whose words are fresh for every generation. This collection reveals Woiwode's masterful ability to examine and instruct, and as such it should be cherished by all attentive readers.

Jeffry Jensen

Review Source

Publishers Weekly 258, no. 24 (June 13, 2011): 46.

The Words of Others
From Quotations to Culture

Author: Gary Saul Morson (b. 1948)
Publisher: Yale University Press (New Haven, CT). 352 pp. $30.00
Type of work: History, literary criticism

This book presents a discussion of the relevance and power of the use of quotations throughout literature and culture.

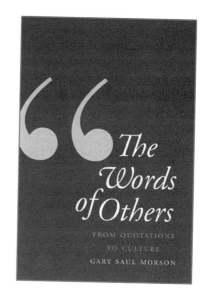

Gary Saul Morson opens his book with musings on the multitudes of "other people's words" that end up in the cultural lexicon, arguing that while iconic literary and philosophical figures like David Hume, Henry David Thoreau, and Fyodor Dostoyevsky are eminently quotable, closer inspection reveals the similarities of their ideas and verbiage to those who came before them. In fact, many of the most familiar phrases in popular culture—"stealing my thunder" and "dreams turn to dust," for example—are quotations that can be attributed to individuals, but they are often only identified as such if someone goes through the trouble of tracing them back to their original source. Morson wonders, "Can one even think without the words of others?" Morson, a known literary expert, is the author of several studies of the Russian writers Leo Tolstoy and Dostoyevsky, as well as other scholarly works. With *The Words of Others: From Quotations to Culture*, he calls upon his knowledge of novels and authors, as well as his in-depth understanding of how literature has evolved over the centuries. He also utilizes his professorial style, keeping focused on specific points while still maintaining the reader's interest.

Central to Morson's premise is the assertion that society embraces the use of quotations, and that, intentionally or not, people invoke the words of figures from every era of human history. Quotations, he argues, have been collected from ancient history to the present, and in the process they have often lost their original context and adopted a new one in the hands of the user. A quotation does not need to be from an actual historical figure; Morson points to the myriad uses of quotations from sources ranging from classic literature to recent film and television. These sources may undergo a similar transformation, as their original context is replaced with a context more suited to the speaker's perspective.

Morson begins his discussion by describing the nature and fundamentals of a quotation, differentiating it from such devices and figures of speech as the aphorism and the idiom. He argues that many writers of poetry seek a clear definition of the various forms of language and yet are unable to separate the quotation from other literary devices in a definitive way. Furthermore, he asserts that those who have described quotations correctly leave their definitions open ended, allowing the term to be subject to further interpretation. According to Morson, this approach enables the culture involved to further define the value and relevance of quotations, which are amorphous by nature. A quotation might be extracted from a piece of literature, either as an entire literary work or a mere quip from such a work. One point that echoes throughout the book is that in order to be considered a quotation, the utterance or stated idea must be memorable and display a capacity for standing on its own within the source itself.

Morson continues his analysis, noting the wide range of "verbal museums" in which quotations are preserved and transmitted across generations. These museums, mobile and not always physical, are commonly manifested in literature, particularly in the classics. Societies may collect and carry the thoughts of others in the same way an art museum collects paintings and sculptures, and Morson's concept of verbal museums is not unlike these other collections. In some cases, the quotation is the original, unaltered version of the utterance, specific in context but withstanding the test of time outside of it. In other cases, however, the quotation might be a kind of reproduction, subtly altered from its original form. Certain quotations have so heavily permeated world culture that what is believed to be an original thought may in fact be a commentary on another thought. As an example, Morson cites Miguel de Cervantes's *Don Quixote* (1605–15), in which the eponymous character chides Sancho Panza, his partner, for his frequent invocations of quotations, even though Don Quixote often unknowingly does the same. Morson's point is that the time-honored tradition of referencing quotes has evolved to the point where, much like Don Quixote, people may unwittingly utter a quotation when they believe they are expressing an original idea.

An important distinction is that quotations are not necessarily born but made. Every quotation has an author, whether it was first composed as a freestanding statement or a part of a larger work. In this regard, Morson cites the significance of anthologizers, who collect quotations from authors much in the same way that a museum displays a collection of found art. Anthologizers, and likewise biographers, may sell the quotation, presenting it in such a way that the reader embraces it, even if it has been misread or truncated in the anthology. According to Morson, the utterance itself experiences an elevation in status as it transforms from mere extract to quotation.

Coming across a text and embracing it, the reader also risks misquoting the original idea. As an example, Morson cites the phrase "blood, sweat, and tears," which is attributed to Winston Churchill and comes from a speech to the House of Commons in 1940: "I have nothing to offer but blood and toil, sweat and tears." Yet the public saw "toil" and "sweat" as redundant and embraced a misquoted version, which would evolve into the common and widely known quotation. In fact, Churchill himself eventually embraced the misquoted version of his own words, using it during wartime speeches. Morson places a great deal of emphasis on misquotation, citing in particular the literary critic Ralph Keyes, who has written several studies on well-known phrases, sayings, and statements uttered over the centuries by historical figures and fictional characters alike. Morson salutes Keyes's efforts to track commonly heard quotations back to their respective sources. At times, the invocation of a quotation out of context

Gary Saul Morson is the Frances Hooper Professor of the Arts and Humanities at Northwestern University. He is also the author of Narrative and Freedom: The Shadows of Time *(1996) and* "Anna Karenina" in Our Time: Seeing More Wisely *(2007), among other studies of Russian and Slavic literature.*

can undermine the relevance of the original literary work. Morson argues that writers like Keyes help to expose readers to the true nature of quotations.

Adding to the challenges of proper quotation use is the language barrier. Morson discusses how German-to-English translation has led to frequent misinterpretations of famed neurologist and psychoanalyst Sigmund Freud's observations. In some cases, different translations of a text can result in different manifestations of the original words, resulting in the loss of both the true context and the meaning.

Morson acknowledges the important point that many quotations are not written at all, but instead are transferred to others through oral tradition. In such instances, the original context of a quotation may have been long lost, only surfacing when academics carefully and patiently trace the utterance back to the source. For this reason and others, the words of others play a significant role in the everyday speech of historical figures and literary characters alike. In most cases, the speakers never realize that their words originated elsewhere, while others acknowledge merely a vague understanding of the origins of the utterance; for example, according to Morson, Russian literary characters frequently invoke what they believe to be biblical quotations but are not aware if these quotations are actually from the attributed source.

Morson does not limit his observations of the evolution, acceptance, and usage of quotations exclusively to literature. In addition to his attribution of quotations to such historical figures as Winston Churchill and John F. Kennedy, he highlights pop-music lyrics, discussing musicians such as the Rolling Stones, Simon and Garfunkel, and Bob Dylan. He also cites popular remarks from Andy Warhol, as well as quotes from film and television that have become part of the cultural landscape.

Although he finds enjoyment in the works of Keyes and other volumes of misquotations, Morson remains somewhat cautious about becoming immersed in the critique of quotations. He again reminds the reader of the importance of separating the extraction from the quotation. A quotation, he indicates early in the book, is the repetition of the words of another with the acknowledgment that they are the words of another. Put a different way, one who invokes a quotation uses it in the context intended by the author. Extractions, meanwhile, are taken from the author regardless of context.

Morson moves next from a discussion of the nature of quotations to a review of the places in literature, and therefore culture as well, where quotations exist in their proper context. He describes "quotations of occasion," wherein an utterance is offered relative to the author's particular situation. These occasions can include an author's dying words or words inscribed on a headstone. After this nonliterary assessment of the use of quotations, Morson returns to the development of "quotationality" in literature, both past and future. He concludes his review of the usage of quotations in literature and culture by returning to the anthology, recognizing once again the value of providing an author's original words and encouraging readers to better understand the source itself.

Ironically, Morson has spent much of his own career analyzing the words of others in varying capacities. In 2007, he published *"Anna Karenina" in Our Time: Seeing More Wisely*, in which he asserts that many of the ideas touched upon in Tolstoy's well-known novel, such as modernization, social reform, and, of course, love, are underappreciated in the modern world. Morson argues that Tolstoy's nineteenth-century work has relevance in the twenty-first century, and this kind of historical continuity is a central element of *The Words of Others* as well.

Some critics have taken issue with the fact that Morson seems to prefer that quoters use the original source material and context rather than offer their own conscious (and subconscious) interpretations of the quotation at hand. Others welcome his style but caution that his examples and critiques of modern culture are somewhat unnecessary, particularly when his knowledge of literature is so vast and relevant to his thesis. Nevertheless, *The Words of Others* is presented with a reverence for the different forms of literature and culture to which Morson has dedicated his career. He writes in a light, engaging manner that will appeal to a wide range of readers, demonstrating his awareness of the fact that not all readers will approach his book with the dedication of a scholar.

Michael Auerbach

Review Sources

Literary Review, no. 390 (August 2011): 44–45.
Times Higher Education, August 11, 2011 (Web).
Times Literary Supplement, October 14, 2011 (Web).
Weekly Standard, August 8, 2011 (Web).

The Wrong War
Grit, Strategy, and the Way Out of Afghanistan

Author: Bing West (b. 1940)
Publisher: Random House (New York). Illustrated. 336 pp. $28.00
Type of work: Current events, history

This book offers a critique of American military strategy in Afghanistan, including recommendations on how to bring the war to a successful conclusion.

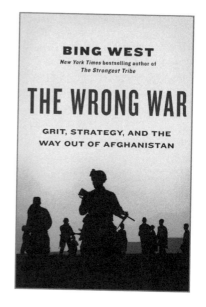

Afghanistan has been called the graveyard of empires. Alexander the Great campaigned there during the fourth century BCE and left little more than the memory of his exploits. The British in the nineteenth century and the Soviets in the twentieth century both attempted to subdue the Afghan tribesmen and failed. The United States is only the latest to wage war on this rugged battleground. Sweeping into Afghanistan in 2001, American forces initiated a brief and brilliant assault that rallied local allies and overthrew the Taliban regime, which harbored the al-Qaeda terrorists who had planned and launched the September 11 attacks on New York City and Washington, DC. A government that was friendly to the West was installed in Kabul; however, the Taliban, while defeated, had not been destroyed. Alongside other elements of al-Qaeda, they regrouped in the tribal areas of neighboring Pakistan and were soon striking back into Afghanistan, starting a guerrilla war that has waxed and waned over the years but gradually increased in intensity. Over the course of this long war, the United States and its North Atlantic Treaty Organization (NATO) allies have been engaged in both combat and nation building, but they have not achieved success on either front. The Taliban have proved a resourceful and determined enemy, and the Afghan government has failed to foster a healthy civil society or even establish its own legitimacy. It appears increasingly likely that the Taliban resistance will outlast the patience of Western electorates, who are tired of the losses suffered in the remote Hindu Kush. Few Western analysts foresee a happy outcome to the Afghan war.

In *The Wrong War: Grit, Strategy, and the Way Out of Afghanistan*, Bing West boldly offers his own strategic prescription for a military victory. West brings real expertise to his analysis. As a young Marine officer, he served with a Combined Action Platoon that garrisoned a Vietnamese hamlet for over a year. His book about the experience, *The Village* (1972), has become a classic; in it, West recounts how he and a small unit of Marines worked with Vietnamese militiamen to defend their homes against the Viet Cong and North Vietnamese. Drawing on his wartime service,

Magill's Literary Annual 2012

Bing West served in the Marines during the Vietnam War, later becoming assistant secretary of defense under President Ronald Reagan. He is the author of three award-winning books on the Iraq War, including The Strongest Tribe: War, Politics, and the Endgame in Iraq (2008).

he also authored a manual for the Marines on small unit actions. West then went on to become an expert in counterinsurgency warfare for the RAND Corporation, after which he was appointed assistant secretary of defense for international security affairs in the Reagan administration. More recently, he has studied American military policy in the Middle East and written three books about the war in Iraq. The last of these, The Strongest Tribe: War, Politics, and the Endgame in Iraq (2008), provides a brief history of American operations in Iraq until 2006, when it looked as if the war would be lost, and describes the stunning military success that came with the "surge" authorized by President George W. Bush. West attributes this victory to the skill and courage of American troops and a change in policy that emphasized the protection of the population. The heroes of the story are Generals David Petraeus and Raymond Odierno, who took American troops out of their heavily fortified bases and sent them out amongst the people. In conjunction with a popular Iraqi uprising against the terrorists and the determined efforts of the Iraqi military, American forces were able to largely quell the long-running insurgency.

As the war in Iraq wound down, however, the war in Afghanistan flared up and the security situation deteriorated. West gathered much of the data in The Strongest Tribe while embedded with American units in the field. He researched The Wrong War in the same way, visiting and going on patrol with troops from the US Army, Marines, and Special Forces, the British Army, and the Afghan National Army. Mixing with American and allied soldiers on the front lines of the war, often sharing with them the risks of combat, West writes with the authority of an eyewitness. He combines his professional judgment with an acute appreciation of the men at the sharp end of conflict. While West is severely critical of the counterinsurgency strategies promulgated by successive presidential administrations, he is unbounded in his admiration of the soldiers who are attempting to implement these strategies in the mountains and deserts of Afghanistan.

American and allied soldiers face severe constraints in their war against the Taliban. The primary goal in Afghanistan for Presidents George W. Bush and Barack Obama has been nation building. Many billions of dollars have been spent in an effort to revive civil society and to prop up the regime of President Hamid Karzai. American officers in the field have had to take on the role of regional development functionaries, supervising the construction of roads, schools, and irrigation canals. Even platoon leaders have funds to spur microlevel projects in the areas they patrol. West argues that this focus threatens to turn the American military into an armed Peace Corps, diverting it from its real mission of engaging and destroying the enemy. Worse, these expenditures and efforts have not remade Afghanistan, nor have they won the hearts and minds of its people. Instead, they have fueled massive corruption in the Afghan government and created a culture of entitlement amongst the people; Afghans now expect American largesse, with no concomitant obligations on their part. West believes that both ideological and practical considerations have prevented many Afghans from openly rallying against the Taliban. Increasingly secular Westerners underestimate the power of religion in the conflict; Islam is a political as well as a religious system, with most people in Afghanistan identifying themselves as Muslims first, Afghans second. The Taliban have been extremely effective in identifying themselves as the defenders of an Islamic homeland against "crusader" invaders. The endemic bribing of government officials lends credence to the Taliban's claims of superior virtue. The Taliban are seen as brutal but honest. Even Afghans hostile to the Taliban's religious and political pretensions are still reluctant to actively embrace outsiders. Wherever the American military goes, fighting follows, and Afghans have to calculate whether cooperation with the Americans is worth the risk to themselves and their families. The absence of a government that inspires loyalty or respect makes quiet neutrality an easy and sensible option. As a result, and despite the lavish expenditure of money, American troops can expect little from the people they are protecting.

Another consequence of American policy's emphasis on nation building has been the imposition of very strict rules of engagement upon the troops. In order to conciliate Afghan public opinion and avoid as much collateral damage as humanly possible, the overwhelming firepower of the American military can only be utilized with special authorization. The restrictions placed on air strikes often leave troops effectively without air support. Armed Taliban forces can only be engaged when there is no chance of hurting civilians. If they are unarmed, they cannot be targeted. American soldiers operating in settled areas are compelled to be exceedingly careful on their patrols. Even in more deserted areas, the initiative largely lies with the Taliban, which can attack at will with little concern for civilian casualties. These rules lead to frustrating situations wherein the Americans might see the enemy but cannot act. Soldiers on patrol often notice Taliban scouts, known as "dickers," watching them and reporting their movements by cell phone, yet these men must be left alone. Likewise, if armed Taliban forces enter a building and later emerge without a weapon, they cannot be engaged. In built-up areas of the country, unarmed Taliban fighters who use motorbikes to scoot by American units must be allowed to go on their way. Even when Taliban suspects are detained and turned over to Afghan authorities, they are often released within weeks.

Given these realities on the ground, the war is not being won. As long as the Afghan population tolerates the presence of the Taliban, West argues, it will be impossible for the American military to root them out. Regardless, West argues that the United States must stay in Afghanistan indefinitely, as a precipitous withdrawal would result in a Taliban victory and disastrous consequences for American security. Al-Qaeda would get a new lease on life in the region, Pakistan would face further destabilization, and the United States would appear weak and ineffectual before its enemies. West maintains that the United States must fight to win in Afghanistan, and the only way to end the current military stalemate is through a change in strategy. The United States and NATO must abandon their misbegotten effort at nation building through the military, and American and allied troops should focus their energies instead on defeating the enemy. This does not mean unleashing massive amounts of American firepower; rather, West advocates a significant reduction of American troop levels in Afghanistan. Large

American military formations, organized originally to fight World War II, are not what is needed to wage this war. Drawing on precedents from Vietnam and Iraq, West is emphatic that the main burden of the fight must be turned over to the Afghan army. Only Afghans will be able to win over the population and isolate the Taliban. The current Afghan army fights well when bolstered by American advisors, and West suggests a dramatic increase in this advisory role, with the majority of American forces in Afghanistan embedded with the Afghan army or providing support services. Such a war would both achieve American goals in Afghanistan and decrease costs at a time of straitened financial resources. West is confident that the American people would be willing to indefinitely support a war that was prudently economical with personnel and money. The United States has been successful at counterinsurgency warfare in the past, and if it adapts its strategy to the realities on the ground, the American military can attain victory in Afghanistan as well.

The Wrong War is a compelling read. West writes with passion, illustrating his recommendations for a new strategy with gripping accounts of American troops in combat. These alone make the book a valuable contribution to military history. West's picture of American soldiers in the field is inspiring. These young men are competent and courageous, good humored and devoted to their duty. Given a realistic mission, they can accomplish all that their country asks of them. Whether West's proposed strategy is the task these troops should be set is something that readers will have to decide for themselves. One question West does not answer is how the army of a venal and unpopular government can turn the tide against the Taliban, even with American assistance. Perhaps the answer lies in his knowledge of other wars, as the history of counterinsurgency in such places as Vietnam and Iraq demonstrates that governments do not have to be perfect to achieve military success. West's book is an important contribution to the discussion of American policy in Afghanistan. Long after this war ends, the book will endure as a rousing study of American soldiers in action.

Daniel P. Murphy

Review Sources

Kirkus Reviews 78, no. 24 (December 15, 2010): 1260.
National Review 63, no. 4 (March 7, 2011): 45–47.
The New York Times Book Review, February 27, 2011, p. 2.
Publishers Weekly 257, no. 50 (December 20, 2010): 44.
USA Today, March 3, 2011 (Web).
The Wall Street Journal, February 19, 2011, p. C8.

You and Three Others Are Approaching a Lake

Author: Anna Moschovakis (b. 1969)
Publisher: Coffee House (Minneapolis).
132 pp. $16.00
Type of work: Poetry

Largely spoken in the language of modern technology, Moschovakis's second poetry collection is an investigation into the morals and lifestyles of contemporary society.

In her second book of poetry, writer and translator Anna Moschovakis strings together four long poems that investigate the systems of modern life, both concrete and abstract: the food industry, the Internet and social networking, philosophies of death and war, and language itself. These topics are large and ponderous, often the focus of philosophy and political theory. Moschovakis understands the seriousness of her subject matter, the life-or-death nature that comes with discussing war or colonialism, and her poems are crafted with the respect and dignity of careful thinking. Yet *You and Three Others Are Approaching a Lake* is not strictly a serious book. Instead, Moschovakis is often playful and humorous, jesting while she presents dire topics to her readers. The poems deftly pull in personal narrative and lyric insights that seem somehow at home alongside the clinical language of analysis and theory. It is in this hybridization of styles and structures that *You and Three Others* ultimately succeeds, bridging cultural critique and poetry in fresh ways.

In addition to the four poems, Moschovakis's collection includes a short prologue and an epilogue. The prologue is a page-length poem, brief in comparison to the twenty- and thirty-page works that follow it. Included in its few stanzas, however, are the guiding principles for the rest of the book. From the first line, the speaker announces that she "doesn't care whether I convince you or not," offsetting any notions that this work, although political in nature, is driven by any recognizable agenda. Instead, it is a book where "everybody should always have a position on everything," where we are expected to "take our positions with us, like folding stools to the beach." Rather than trying to convince us, then, the poems that follow are there to explore the ways we carry our positions (our politics, our stances, our beliefs) with us into different systems of thought. The prologue explains this in the most abstract language possible, claiming to celebrate "each moment of courage or loss or revolution / When something pushed something and something fell down." What these "somethings" are seems less important than the effect they have on each other.

The title of the collection, sounding like the start of a word problem in math class, surfaces throughout the book. The first section, "The Tragedy of Waste," uses "You and three others are approaching a lake" not just as its opening line but as a structural device throughout. Like all sections of the collection, it is named after a political or philosophical book from the twentieth century, picked up by Moschovakis in a used bookstore or given to her by a friend. As indicated by the title, the section's theme is that waste exists in our society in problematic excess. As we approach the lake, the poem asks us, "What, precisely, is your procedure? // To be fed / To keep warm and dry." Quickly, however, it becomes clear that these are not simply questions of basic survival but fundamental concerns that must dealt with in the context of the twentieth century. "Modern industrialism / the slums of the great cities / reasonable comforts" all must be taken into account as we make our own decisions about consumption and survival. Moschovakis explores the most violent and extreme edges of life to understand the absurdity of modern survival. Considering the history of Germany in World War I and World War II, the speaker wonders,

> Suppose that instead of killing Germans
> the organization had been directed
> to the killing of malnutrition, slum dwelling,
> shoddy clothing, infant mortality, occupational disease, starved
> opportunity, illiteracy, and ignorance

As the poem continues to probe the systems of survival on which we depend, it regularly throws its initial word problem back to us. "You are approaching a lake," the speaker reminds us, so we are never far away from questions of our own survival. The effect is to transform loaded statements such as "ten men could live on the corn / where only one can live on the beef," moving them away from political theory and into something more personal and immediate.

While these same central concerns continue throughout *You and Three Others*, Moschovakis employs a wide array of techniques to explore them. The second long poem, "Death as a Way of Life," begins with a list that seems to represent the speaker's attempt to use reason to come to terms with the suffering in the world:

> 1. Life is not fair
> 2. How can I be happy while others suffer
> 3. How can I not be happy while others suffer
> 4. Others will suffer whether or not I am happy
> 5. It is not the suffering of others that causes my happiness
> 6. It is not the not-suffering of others that causes my unhappiness
> 7. The not-suffering of others would not prevent my happiness

The list is almost comical in its convoluted logic, swirling through cycles of thought without reaching any useful conclusion. It is a fitting introduction to this section, in which the speaker struggles to understand suffering, often linking it to language and language's failures. In these attempts, she becomes lyrical, describing a woman combing her hair, "threading it through her delicate fingers as it cascades in waves down her porcelain back,

(Matvei Yankelevich)

Anna Moschovakis published her debut poetry collection, I Have Not Been Able to Get Through to Everyone, *in 2006.* You and Three Others Are Approaching a Lake *is her second collection, for which she won the 2011 James Laughlin Award from the American Academy of Poets. She has also earned recognition as a translator from Le Centre National du Livre.*

which reflects the moon's silvery mood," only to realize the sorrow that the image can cause in a man. No mode, lyric or otherwise, can last long; in the same poem, she finds occasion to describe the history of guns, noting, "In the 1850s a seven-shot 'Victoria' / revolver cost $2.50." From the revolver, she leaps in a different direction again, quoting a stranger, Rick, whose internet post outlines the seven places on a woman's body that "you could shoot" with seven bullets. The link between the two stanzas (seven shots and seven bullets) suggests that there is more to blame than a violent stranger on the Internet. Instead, it is the cultural ideas that are held accountable, the very existence of violent rhetoric and violent devices. No language or voice is entirely innocent here, a natural extension of the way language itself is suspect, the speaker declaring that "naming is a form of violence" and wondering, "What does grammar kill?"

In her third long poem, "The Human Machine (Thirty Chances)," Moschovakis showcases the bizarre logic, off-kilter humor, and technological voices that make only brief appearances in the first half of the book. Continuing the investigation of the previous sections, this poem is structured around the Turing test, an early method of evaluating artificial intelligence. The identification of artificial intelligence becomes vital to Moschovakis, who begins to explore the ways in which human identity changes in a world dominated by the Internet and computers. Navigating this change, the poem features "Annabot," a guide who exists in both the digital and the physical world. As an avatar for the author, Annabot interacts with the Human Machine itself; she tells it, "I cannot feel your hand," only to have the machine respond, "I cannot feel your heart." Although sometimes humorous, Annabot's struggle to experience emotion or human connection in the artificial world is ultimately heartbreaking. It is also, much like in previous sections, a problem of language. Annabot is only a "chatbot," designed to speak "the language // of simple, obvious things." Emphasizing the reality of this linguistic shift in contemporary life, excerpts and quotes from the Internet are scattered throughout the poem, forming a core part of its voice. As the line between humanity and computers blurs, Moschovakis explores not only the effects the blurring has on our language but the effects that language eventually has on us as well.

The final section, "In Search of Wealth," is characteristically broad in its topics and styles, encompassing religion, personal narrative, and colonialism, amongst other concerns. In prose-like lines and paragraphs, Moschovakis considers the ways we compensate one another, wondering whether it is possible to take from someone without causing violence. The investigation of systems of compensation is logical and precise; Moschovakis even lists the amount she was paid for all the jobs she has held. At other moments, the poem moves distantly away from her personal experience, as in the academic writing that explores religious history:

> Scientology, on the other hand, seems to act as an apology for conspicuous consumption. Formally, it borrows from Calvin, though, with Celebrity acting as the sign of salvation and wealth its just reward. Following Weber's idea that Rationalization replaced the spiritual underpinnings of Calvinism, we could be justified in calling Scientology a kind of Calvinism 2.0.

At times including personal ads from the website Craigslist and lyric fragments ("A glass of milk / or / a cigarette / but not both"), the range in this final section is one of the widest of the book. Yet it stays cohesive, just as the four long poems complement and support one another. This cohesion is due to that central question, posed from the start of the text. "What, precisely, is your procedure?" Moschovakis asks us—how are we going to stay alive, and what are the costs of the choices we make? This is not a question projected into a void but one that must be answered in the context of our modern lives. This is the world of consumerism, constant Internet connection, and war, and Moschovakis insists that we consider ourselves as part of those powerful systems. It is a broad concern, one that she fittingly responds to with stylistic variation and innovation.

These broad concerns and moral dilemmas, rife with the injustice of contemporary society, are ultimately something we can overcome. This optimism is at the heart of *You and Three Others Are Approaching a Lake*, even at its darkest moments. "Human nature has changed since yesterday," the book declares, and while these changes are cause for concern, there is the implicit promise that we can change once more to something better. The method of change, Moschovakis believes, is through careful attention to our language and to the systems that we live in. "One letter at a time we build relationships," she observes, and while the relationships of globalization, celebrity culture, and industrialism have failed her, we can just as easily build something new. *You and Three Others* is one step toward the construction of a lyrical yet logical world in which critical analysis can become a tool of redemption.

T. Fleischmann

Review Sources

Coldfront, July 27, 2011 (Web).
Publishers Weekly 258, no. 8 (February 21, 2011): 115.

You Think That's Bad

Author: Jim Shepard (b. 1956)
Publisher: Random House (New York).
240 pp. $24.95
Type of work: Short fiction
Time: The fifteenth through the twenty-first century

Jim Shepard's new collection of short fiction examines the domestic and large-scale cataclysms that befall a wide cast of characters, from an explorer in 1930s Lebanon to a hydraulic engineer in the near future.

Principal characters:
US MILITARY ENGINEER, a "black world" operative at Los Alamos
FREYA STARK, an English autodidactic explorer in search of secret ruins in Lebanon
DUTCH HYDRAULIC ENGINEER, who struggles with a distrustful marriage as climate change threatens to flood Rotterdam
US NATIONAL GUARD RECRUIT, a young man from Wisconsin fighting the Japanese under miserable conditions in New Guinea during World War II
SWISS PORTER, accompanying a Swiss science team, "the Frozen Idiots," studying avalanches in the Alps
PARTICLE PHYSICIST, an emotionally alienated scientist whose wife is distraught following a miscarriage and from the state of their disintegrating marriage
EIJI TSUBURAYA, a film producer and special effects director in 1950s Japan, responsible for the design and story of *Godzilla, King of the Monsters*
GULF WAR VETERAN, a thirty-nine-year-old who lives with his mother in upstate New York and contends with post-traumatic stress disorder (PTSD)
ETIENNE CORILLAUT, the twenty-two-year-old page and body servant of Gilles de Rais in fifteenth-century France
POLISH MOUNTAIN CLIMBER, who struggles to the top of Nanga Parbat, the ninth tallest mountain in the world

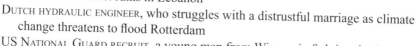

Much like his previous collection, *Like You'd Understand, Anyway* (2007), the title of Jim Shepard's newest volume of short fiction, *You Think That's Bad*, suggests a complaining, grumbling approach to life. Shepard's stories are hardly that in their examination of emotionally distant and domestically challenged men and women from across the globe who are on the brink of catastrophe. In "Your Fate Hurtles Down at You," a team of Swiss technicians studies the science of avalanches in the Alps. The narrator, the team's "touchingly passionate amateur and porter," carries the guilt of believing he was the cause of the avalanche that killed his twin brother. Near the end of the story as he imagines his team's death, he invokes a maxim that applies widely to the collection's many physicists and geniuses, technicians and loners: "We've learned more than any who've come before us what to expect, and it will do us no more good than if we'd learned nothing at all." Shepard's stories offer vibrant worlds that draw the reader into both past and present, wherein characters must confront and reckon with an "unknown value" and the inevitable disasters that follow.

"It's all infowar now," remarks the weapons engineer in "Minotaur," the collection's opening story, in which two friends reunite after working together at a military research base. Their professional lives are focused on trafficking information, but, ironically, this leads to complete secrecy within their marriages and spawns a corrosive distrust within their domestic life. "What's it like," asks the narrator's wife, "not being able to tell the people you're *closest* to anything about what you care about most?" Such a question certainly torments the women married to Shepard's distant, clueless men.

The tension between knowledge and empathy (to say nothing of the similar tensions between vocation and family, passion and loved ones) is a fascinating contradiction of terms, especially considering that Shepard himself provides a three-page bibliography of nonfictional sources. As many reviews have pointed out, Shepard is a gifted writer of the research-based "historical short story." He assembles interesting facts and details into his systems of irony and narrative. A prime example is "The Netherlands Lives with Water," in which secrecy engulfs the marriage of a Dutch hydraulic engineer and his wife. In this pointedly not-too-distant future, melting ice caps threaten to flood Rotterdam, and as the water level rises, so too does the narrator's realization that his marriage has collapsed and his wife has abandoned him. Technical descriptions of Rotterdam's dam strategy, though ample, ultimately serve to enhance the detail and metaphor of the story. The critical reception of Shepard's most recent work positions him squarely as a writer of "historical stories," and perhaps unfairly. Time and setting inform each story but do not define it. As in the best work of Flannery O'Connor (who Shepard cites as an early influence) and Ron Hansen (who Shepard names as a colleague and friend), Shepard uses time and setting as coordinates to chart emotional experiences, to reveal these experiences as occurring broadly across place and time. Shepard's first-person voice takes the reader from fifteenth-century France to Poland at a near-future point in the twenty-first century, and his formal mastery conveys all the nuances, exaggerations, traumas, and confusions of each speaker within each story. Regardless of place and time, Shepard's characters deal with similar human conflicts. In this way, Shepard's work is expressly literary and is historical only insofar as it is based in character and story.

In interviews, Shepard describes his interest in "the heartbreak of knowing that we can't be all we want or need to be for those we love." However, many of the narrators of *You Think That's Bad* are too distracted to notice that their relationships are in crisis. Shepard's men—particularly those characters who appear in early stories in the collection—are unable, or perhaps unwilling, to build common ground between their vocational knowledge and their meager knowledge of the heart. The former activates them and simultaneously propels them forward. The latter captivates them at first but

ultimately bores them and makes them restless. For example, in the collection's final
story, "Poland Is Watching," the narrator, by
his own confession, spends more time climbing Europe's highest mountains than he does
at home. He declares, "It's high time that I
stopped this kind of Russian roulette and
start thinking of someone other than myself."
The characters throughout this collection are
able to build toward such a confessional ges-
ture, toward admission of personal lack and failure, but it is a difficult journey and an
agonizing arrival.

*Jim Shepard is the author of several nov-
els, including the award-winning* Project
X *(2004). His work has been published in
numerous magazines and in Best American Short Stories and Pushcart Prize.*
Like You'd Understand, Anyway *(2007)
was a* National Book Award *finalist. He
is a professor of American history, literature, and eloquence at Williams College.*

   In "Happy with Crocodiles," a World War II solider cannot accept that his highly
attractive girlfriend instead desires his older brother. Similarly, the particle physicist of
"Low-Hanging Fruit" is oblivious to the fact that his wife is grieving their miscarried
child. The porter of "Your Fate Hurtles Down at You" speaks with a self-awareness
that is unusual for Shepard's narrators: "We'd been taught from the cradle that however much we thought we knew . . . there were always places where our ignorance
and bad luck could destroy us. " Whether real or imagined, disaster is inevitable in
Shepard's universe. Certainly for the oblivious narrators of the early stories, there is
an element of cosmic justice to the arrival of disaster, a way in which willful ignorance
is the path to certain devastation.

   Yet, the second half of the collection turns to more complicated examinations of
catastrophe, as Shepard pushes his stories to greater formal and moral extremes. "Gojira, King of the Monsters" narrates the invention of the Godzilla character at Toho
Studios in the 1950s. The inventor and special effects creator is Eiji Tsuburaya, a
"lunatic perfectionist" and "bad husband." "Gojira, King of the Monsters" is the collection's longest story and the only one told in third-person, which allows Shepard to
narrate both the production of the movie *Gojira* from Tsuburaya's point of view as
well as the Great Kanto Earthquake of 1923 from the point of view of Tsuburaya's
father. As Tokyo crumbles beneath his father's feet, the prose reaches a terrifying level
of intensity that mirrors the intensity of the earthquake: " . . . with every jolt the hotel
and adjacent bank flexed like buggy whips and cracks appeared along their walls, from
which window casings and marble avalanched into the street." The change to a third-
person point of view in the collection is crucial, as it breaks what one might call the
"formal solipsism" of the collection's first-person stories—forcing these characters,
in a sense, to consider people other than themselves. This shift also signals a change
to the darker, more confessional voices of the stories "Boys Town," "Classical Scenes
of Farewell," and "Poland Is Watching." Shepard begins to question these disasters
more closely. Who is responsible for these events? To what extent are these characters
victims? To what extent are they perpetrators of their own disastrous lives? Is one ever
able to change course, as it were, and break from a devastating path?

   "Here's the story of my life," begins the narrator of "Boys Town," a war veteran
suffering from post-traumatic stress disorder, "whatever I did wasn't good enough,

anything I figured out I figured out too late, and whenever I tried to help I made things worse." Though he is among Shepard's most troubled characters (second only to the accomplice to mass infanticide in "Classical Scenes of Farewell"), this narrator makes efforts, however distorted, to repair himself and step outside his own head. Indeed, Shepard suggests that responsibility for the character's despair and fate may rest equally with the narrator's family and with the United States government, which were the forces that directed him early in life.

Like the mountain climbers of "Poland Is Watching," all of Shepard's men seem incapable of preventing disaster or even forestalling it. They pursue their compulsive course in life as an addict would a drug, even when they recognize and acknowledge that their behavior is destructive to themselves and those around them. Yet, in true O'Connor fashion, Shepard suggests that disaster is the only way to contend honestly and morally with one's self. Each of these stories finds revelation and self-knowledge in cataclysm. In the words of the Polish mountain climber, "For people like me, winter mountaineering is just ordinary life with the polite layers shorn away . . . no one sees you with greater clarity than your teammates above eight thousand meters." Many of his teammates, however, perish in the ascent of Nanga Parbat, and the narrator's own fate is uncertain. This may suggest that the ultimate risk and the inevitable result of perspicacity is death. "Poland Is Watching," the collection's final story, leaves Shepard's readers with the troubling thought that truth goes hand in hand with ruin, that tragedy, while not heroic, is at best revelatory.

James Flaherty

Review Sources

Los Angeles Times, April 10, 2011 (Web).
The New York Times Book Review, April 1, 2011 (Web).
NPR, March 23, 2011 (Web).
Slate, April 25, 2011 (Web).

CATEGORY INDEX

AUTOBIOGRAPHY, MEMOIRS,
DIARIES, and LETTERS
Almost a Family (Darnton), 17
Book of Secrets, A (Holroyd), 107
Alfred Kazin's Journals (Cook), 9
Art and Madness (Roiphe), 41
Battle Hymn of the Tiger Mother
(Chua), 70
Blood, Bones, and Butter (Hamilton),
99
Blue Nights (Didion), 103
Conversations with Scorsese (Schickel),
184
Crazy U (Ferguson), 197
Elizabeth Bishop and the *New Yorker*
(Biele), 245
Feeding on Dreams (Dorfman), 279
H.D. Book, The (Duncan), 339
Letters of Ernest Hemingway (Spanier
and Trogdon), 442
Life Itself (Ebert), 452
Moonwalking with Einstein (Foer), 485
My Father's Fortune (Frayn), 497
Never Say Die (Jacoby), 509
One Day I Will Write About This Place
(Wainaina), 539
One Hundred Names for Love
(Ackerman), 543
Pleasures of Reading in an Age of
Distraction, The (Jacobs), 592
Reading My Father (Styron), 617
Townie (Dubus), 754
Widow's Story, A (Latiolais), 808

BIOGRAPHY
Alan Lomax (Szwed), 5
Bismarck (Steinberg), 87
Charles Dickens (Tomalin), 148
Convert, The (Baker), 188
Covert Affair, A (Conant), 193

Endgame (Brady), 262
G.K. Chesterton (Ker), 312
Great Soul (Lelyveld), 330
Heat Wave (Bogle), 343
Hemlock Cup (Hughes), 351
Immortalization Commission, The
(Gray), 367
J.D. Salinger (Slawenski), 393
Joan Mitchell (Albers), 401
Keats Brothers, The (Gigante), 413
Lee Krasner (Levin), 429
Liberty's Exiles (Jasanoff), 447
Malcolm X (Marable), 460
Modigliani (Secrest), 481
No Regrets (Burke), 526
Paper Garden, The (Peacock), 574
She-Wolves (Castor) 657
Singular Woman, A (Scott), 666
Steve Jobs (Isaacson), 699
Tolstoy (Bartlett), 745

CURRENT AFFAIRS
Fear, The (Godwin), 274
Great Stagnation, The (Cowen), 335
On China (Kissinger), 534
Wrong War, The (West), 821

ECONOMICS
Grand Pursuit (Nasar), 316

ESSAYS
Attack of the Difficult Poems
(Bernstein), 57
Believing Is Seeing (Morris), 78
China in Ten Words (Hua), 152
Otherwise Known as the Human
Condition (Dyer), 565
Pulphead (Sullivan), 609
Words Made Fresh (Woiwode), 813

ETHICS and LAW
Iphigenia in Forest Hills (Malcolm), 384

FICTION
After Midnight (Keun), 1
All Our Worldly Goods (Némirovsky), 13
Apricot Jam (Solzhenitsyn), 37
Art of Asking Your Boss for a Raise, The (Perec), 45
Art of Fielding, The (Harbach), 49
Atlas of Impossible Longing, An (Ro), 53
Bad Intentions (Fossum), 61
Binocular Vision (Pearlman), 82
Buddha in the Attic, The (Otsuka), 119
Caleb's Crossing (Brooks), 127
Call, The (Murphy), 131
Changó's Beads and Two-Tone Shoes (Kennedy), 144
Coda (Belletto), 164
Color of Night, The (Bell), 172
Curfew, The (Ball), 205
Drop, The (Connelly), 221
Drop of the Hard Stuff, A (Block), 225
11/22/1963 (King), 241
Embassytown (Mieville), 250
Emily, Alone (O'Nan), 254
Empty Room, An (Xin), 258
Evolution of Bruno Littlemore, The (Hale), 266
Fates Will Find Their Way, The (Pittard), 270
Field Gray (Kerr), 283
Fifth Witness, The (Connelly), 287
Girl in the Blue Beret, The (Mason), 304
Girl in the Polka Dot Dress, The (Bainbridge), 308
Great Night, The (Adrian), 326
Illumination, The (Brockmeier), 363
Land at the End of the World, The (Lobo Antunes), 421
Last Man in Tower (Adiga), 425

Leftovers, The (Perrotta), 434
Marriage Plot (Eugenides), 465
Micro (Crichton and Preston), 473
Miss New India (Mukherjee), 477
Mr. Fox (Oyeyemi), 489
My New American Life (Prose), 501
Nanjing Requiem (Ha Jin), 505
Night Circus, The (Morgenstern), 513
Night Soul, and Other Stories (McElroy), 517
Once Upon a River (Campbell), 530
1Q84 (Murakami), 548
One Was a Soldier (Spencer-Fleming), 552
Open City (Cote), 556
Orientation (Orozco), 561
Pale King, The (Wallace), 569
Please Look After Mom (Shin), 588
Prague Cemetery, The (Eco), 596
Preacher, The (Läckberg), 601
Pym (Johnson), 613
Rodin's Debutante (Just), 625
Saturday Night Big Tent Wedding Party, The (McCall Smith), 633
Say Her Name (Goldman), 637
Seamstress and the Wind, The (Aira), 641
Seven Years (Stamm), 649
Shadow of What We Were, The (Sepúlveda), 653
Silver Sparrow (Jones), 662
Sly Company of People Who Care, The (Bhattacharya), 670
Splendor of Portugal, The (Lobo Antunes), 695
Stone Arabia (Spiotta), 704
Stranger's Child, The (Hollinghurst), 708
Summer Without Men, The (Hustvedt), 712
Swamplandia! (Russell), 716
Swim Back to Me (Packer), 724
Tabloid City (Hamill), 728
Tiger's Wife, The (Obreht), 736

Tragedy of Arthur, The (Phillips), 758
Troubled Man, The (Mankell), 771
Twice a Spy (Thomson), 775
Uncoupling, The (Wolitzer), 779
Vaclav and Lena (Tanner), 787
We, the Drowned (Jensen), 791
We Others (Millhauser), 795
When the Killing's Done (Boyle), 799
Widow (Latiolais), 803
You Think That's Bad (Shepard), 829

FINE ARTS, FILM, and MUSIC
American Eden (Graham), 25
Electric Eden (Young), 237
Music for Silenced Voices (Lesser), 493

HISTORY
Baseball in the Garden of Eden
   (Thorn), 65
Bitter Waters of Medicine Creek, The
   (Kluger), 91
Blake and the Bible (Rowland), 95
Brilliant Disaster, The (Rasenberger),
   115
Civilization (Ferguson), 156
Eichmann Trial, The (Lipstadt), 229
Founding Gardeners (Wulf), 295
1861 (Goodheart), 233
1493 (Mann), 299
Greater Journey, The (McCullough),
   321
In the Garden of Beasts (Larson), 376
Into the Silence (Davis), 380
Jerusalem (Sebag-Montefiore), 397
Joe DiMaggio (Charyn), 405
King James Bible, The (Norton), 417
People of One Book, A (Larsen), 578
Philosophical Breakfast Club, The
   (Snyder), 583
Redeemers (Krauze), 621
Smoking Typewriters (McMillian), 674
Swerve, The (Greenblatt), 720
To End All Wars (Hochschild), 740
Tough Without a Gun (Kanfer), 749
Words of Others, The (Morson), 817

LITERARY BIOGRAPHY
And So It Goes (Shields), 33
Dante in Love (Wilson), 209
Hemingway's Boat (Hendrickson), 347
Jane Austen Education, A
   (Deresiewicz), 389
Just One Catch (Daugherty), 409

**LITERARY CRITICISM, HISTORY,
and THEORY**
Anatomy of Influence, The (Bloom), 29
Beautiful and Pointless (Orr), 74
Bowstring (Shklovsky), 111
Confessions of a Young Novelist (Eco),
   180
Forgotten Founding Father, The
   (Kendall), 291
In Other Worlds (Atwood), 371

POETRY and DRAMA
Bye-and-Bye (Wright), 123
Captain Asks for a Show of Hands, The
   (Flynn), 136
Chameleon Couch, The (Komunyakaa),
   140
Cloud of Ink (Klatt), 160
Cold War, The (Ossip), 168
Come and See (Howe), 176
Culture of One (Notley), 201
Devotions (Smith), 213
Horoscopes for the Dead (Collins), 359
Lessons, The (Diaz), 438
Life on Mars (Smith), 456
Metropole (O'Brien), 469
Nod House (Mackey), 521
Selected Stories of Mercè Rodoreda,
   The (Rodoreda), 645
Sobbing Superpower (Różewicz), 679
Songs of Kabir (Mehrotra), 687
Space, in Chains (Kasischke), 691
Taller When Prone (Murray), 732
Traveler (Johnston), 762
Trouble Ball, The (Espada), 767
Unseen Hand (Zagajewski), 783

POETRY and DRAMA (*continued*)
You and Three Others Are Approaching
   a Lake (Moschovakis), 825

SCIENCE, HISTORY OF SCIENCE,
   TECHNOLOGY, and MEDICINE
Hidden Reality, The (Greene), 355
Psychopath Test, The (Ronson), 605

SOCIOLOGY, ARCHAEOLOGY, and
   ANTHROPOLOGY
Alone Together (Turkle), 21
Don't Shoot (Kennedy), 217
Sacred Trash (Hoffman and Cole),
   629
Social Animal, The (Brooks), 683

After Midnight (Keun), 1
Alan Lomax (Szwed), 5
Alfred Kazin's Journals (Cook), 9
All Our Worldly Goods (Némirovsky), 13
Almost a Family (Darnton), 17
Alone Together (Turkle), 21
American Eden (Graham), 25
Anatomy of Influence, The (Bloom), 29
And So It Goes (Shields), 33
Apricot Jam (Solzhenitsyn), 37
Art and Madness (Roiphe), 41
Art of Asking Your Boss for a Raise, The (Perec), 45
Art of Fielding, The (Harbach), 49
Atlas of Impossible Longing, An (Ro), 53
Attack of the Difficult Poems (Bernstein), 57

Bad Intentions (Fossum), 61
Baseball in the Garden of Eden (Thorn), 65
Battle Hymn of the Tiger Mother (Chua), 70
Beautiful and Pointless (Orr), 74
Believing Is Seeing (Morris), 78
Binocular Vision (Pearlman), 82
Bismarck (Steinberg), 87
Bitter Waters of Medicine Creek, The (Kluger), 91
Blake and the Bible (Rowland), 95
Blood, Bones, and Butter (Hamilton), 99
Blue Nights (Didion), 103
Book of Secrets, A, (Holroyd), 107
Bowstring (Shklovsky), 111
Brilliant Disaster, The (Rasenberger), 115
Buddha in the Attic, The (Otsuka), 119
Bye-and-Bye (Wright), 123

Caleb's Crossing (Brooks), 127
Call, The (Murphy), 131
Captain Asks for a Show of Hands, The (Flynn), 136
Chameleon Couch, The (Komunyakaa), 140
Changó's Beads and Two-Tone Shoes (Kennedy), 144
Charles Dickens (Tomalin), 148
China in Ten Words (Hua), 152
Civilization (Ferguson), 156
Cloud of Ink (Klatt), 160
Coda (Belletto), 164
Cold War, The (Ossip), 168
Color of Night, The (Bell), 172
Come and See (Howe), 176
Confessions of a Young Novelist (Eco), 180
Conversations with Scorsese (Schickel), 184
Convert, The (Baker), 188
Covert Affair, A (Conant), 193
Crazy U (Ferguson), 197
Culture of One (Notley), 201
Curfew, The (Ball), 205

Dante in Love (Wilson), 209
Devotions (Smith), 213
Don't Shoot (Kennedy), 217
Drop, The (Connelly), 221
Drop of the Hard Stuff, A (Block), 225

Eichmann Trial, The (Lipstadt), 229
1861 (Goodheart), 233
Electric Eden (Young), 237
11/22/1963 (King), 241
Elizabeth Bishop and the New Yorker (Biele), 245
Embassytown (Mieville), 250
Emily, Alone (O'Nan), 254

Empty Room, An (Xin), 258
Endgame (Brady), 262
Evolution of Bruno Littlemore, The (Hale), 266

Fates Will Find Their Way, The (Pittard), 270
Fear, The (Godwin), 274
Feeding on Dreams (Dorfman), 279
Field Gray (Kerr), 283
Fifth Witness, The (Connelly), 287
Forgotten Founding Father, The (Kendall), 291
Founding Gardeners (Wulf), 295
1493 (Mann), 299

Girl in the Blue Beret, The (Mason), 304
Girl in the Polka Dot Dress, The (Bainbridge), 308
G.K. Chesterton (Ker), 312
Grand Pursuit (Nasar), 316
Greater Journey, The (McCullough), 321
Great Night, The (Adrian), 326
Great Soul (Lelyveld), 330
Great Stagnation, The (Cowen), 335

H.D. Book, The (Duncan), 339
Heat Wave (Bogle), 343
Hemingway's Boat (Hendrickson), 347
Hemlock Cup (Hughes), 351
Hidden Reality, The (Greene), 355
Horoscopes for the Dead (Collins), 359

Illumination, The (Brockmeier), 363
Immortalization Commission, The (Gray), 367
In Other Worlds (Atwood), 371
In the Garden of Beasts (Larson), 376
Into the Silence (Davis), 380
Iphigenia in Forest Hills (Malcolm), 384

Jane Austen Education, A (Deresiewicz), 389
J.D. Salinger (Slawenski), 393

Jerusalem (Sebag-Montefiore), 397
Joan Mitchell (Albers), 401
Joe DiMaggio (Charyn), 405
Just One Catch (Daugherty), 409

Keats Brothers, The (Gigante), 413
King James Bible, The (Norton), 417

Land at the End of the World, The (Lobo Antunes), 421
Last Man in Tower (Adiga), 425
Lee Krasner (Levin), 429
Leftovers, The (Perrotta), 434
Lessons, The (Diaz), 438
Letters of Ernest Hemingway (Spanier and Trogdon), 442
Liberty's Exiles (Jasanoff), 447
Life Itself (Ebert), 452
Life on Mars (Smith), 456

Malcolm X (Marable), 460
Marriage Plot (Eugenides), 465
Metropole (O'Brien), 469
Micro (Crichton and Preston), 473
Miss New India (Mukherjee), 477
Modigliani (Secrest), 481
Moonwalking with Einstein (Foer), 485
Mr. Fox (Oyeyemi), 489
Music for Silenced Voices (Lesser), 493
My Father's Fortune (Frayn), 497
My New American Life (Prose), 501

Nanjing Requiem (Ha Jin), 505
Never Say Die (Jacoby), 509
Night Circus, The (Morgenstern), 513
Night Soul, and Other Stories (McElroy), 517
Nod House (Mackey), 521
No Regrets (Burke), 526

Once Upon a River (Campbell), 530
On China (Kissinger), 534
One Day I Will Write About This Place (Wainaina), 539

One Hundred Names for Love (Ackerman), 543
1Q84 (Murakami), 548
One Was a Soldier (Spencer-Fleming), 552
Open City (Cote), 556
Orientation (Orozco), 561
Otherwise Known as the Human Condition (Dyer), 565

Pale King, The (Wallace), 569
Paper Garden, The (Peacock), 574
People of One Book, A (Larsen), 578
Philosophical Breakfast Club, The (Snyder), 583
Please Look After Mom (Shin), 588
Pleasures of Reading in an Age of Distraction, The (Jacobs), 592
Prague Cemetery, The (Eco), 596
Preacher, The (Läckberg), 601
Psychopath Test, The (Ronson), 605
Pulphead (Sullivan), 609
Pym (Johnson), 613

Reading My Father (Styron), 617
Redeemers (Krauze), 621
Rodin's Debutante (Just), 625

Sacred Trash (Hoffman and Cole), 629
Saturday Night Big Tent Wedding Party, The (McCall Smith), 633
Say Her Name (Goldman), 637
Seamstress and the Wind, The (Aira), 641
Selected Stories of Mercè Rodoreda, The (Rodoreda), 645
Seven Years (Stamm), 649
Shadow of What We Were, The (Sepúlveda), 653
She-Wolves (Castor) 657
Silver Sparrow (Jones), 662
Singular Woman, A, (Scott), 666
Sly Company of People Who Care, The (Bhattacharya), 670
Smoking Typewriters (McMillian), 674
Sobbing Superpower (Różewicz), 679

Social Animal, The (Brooks), 683
Songs of Kabir (Mehrotra), 687
Space, in Chains (Kasischke), 691
Splendor of Portugal, The (Lobo Antunes), 695
Steve Jobs (Isaacson), 699
Stone Arabia (Spiotta), 704
Stranger's Child, The (Hollinghurst), 708
Summer Without Men, The (Hustvedt), 712
Swamplandia! (Russell), 716
Swerve, The (Greenblatt), 720
Swim Back to Me (Packer), 724

Tabloid City (Hamill), 728
Taller When Prone (Murray), 732
Tiger's Wife, The (Obreht), 736
To End All Wars (Hochschild), 740
Tolstoy (Bartlett), 745
Tough Without a Gun (Kanfer), 749
Townie (Dubus), 754
Tragedy of Arthur, The (Phillips), 758
Traveler (Johnston), 762
Trouble Ball, The (Espada), 767
Troubled Man, The (Mankell), 771
Twice a Spy (Thomson), 775

Uncoupling, The (Wolitzer), 779
Unseen Hand (Zagajewski), 783

Vaclav and Lena (Tanner), 787

We, the Drowned (Jensen), 791
We Others (Millhauser), 795
When the Killing's Done (Boyle), 799
Widow (Latiolais), 803
Widow's Story, A (Latiolais), 808
Words Made Fresh (Woiwode), 813
Words of Others, The (Morson), 817
Wrong War, The (West), 821

You and Three Others Are Approaching a Lake (Moschovakis), 825
You Think That's Bad (Shepard), 829

AUTHOR INDEX

Ackerman, Diane
  One Hundred Names for Love, 543
Adiga, Aravind
  Last Man in Tower, 425
Adrian, Chris
  Great Night, The, 326
Aira, César
  Seamstress and the Wind, The, 641
Albers, Patricia
  Joan Mitchell, 401
Atwood, Margaret
  In Other Worlds, 371

Bainbridge, Beryl
  Girl in the Polka Dot Dress, The, 308
Baker, Deborah
  Convert, The, 188
Ball, Jesse
  Curfew, The, 205
Bartlett, Rosamund
  Tolstoy, 745
Bell, Madison Smartt
  Color of Night, The, 172
Belletto, René
  Coda, 164
Bernstein, Charles
  Attack of the Difficult Poems, 57
Bhattacharya, Rahul
  Sly Company of People Who Care,
  The, 670
Biele, Joelle
  Elizabeth Bishop and the New
  Yorker, 245
Block, Lawrence
  Drop of the Hard Stuff, A, 225
Bloom, Harold
  Anatomy of Influence, The, 29
Bogle, Donald
  Heat Wave, 343
Brady, Frank
  Endgame, 262

Brockmeier, Kevin
  Illumination, The, 363
Brooks, David
  Social Animal, The, 683
Brooks, Geraldine
  Caleb's Crossing, 127
Burke, Carolyn
  No Regrets, 526

Campbell, Bonnie Jo
  Once Upon a River, 530
Castor, Helen
  She-Wolves, 657
Charyn, Jerome
  Joe DiMaggio, 405
Chua, Amy
  Battle Hymn of the Tiger Mother, 70
Cole, Peter, and Adina Hoffman
  Sacred Trash, 629
Cole, Teju
  Open City, 556
Collins, Billy
  Horoscopes for the Dead, 359
Conant, Jennet
  Covert Affair, A, 193
Connelly, Michael
  Drop, The, 221
  Fifth Witness, The, 287
Cook, Richard M.
  Alfred Kazin's Journals, 9
Cowen, Tyler
  Great Stagnation, The 335
Crichton, Michael, and Richard Preston
  Micro, 473

Darnton, John
  Almost a Family, 17
Daugherty, Tracy
  Just One Catch, 409
Davis, Wade
  Into the Silence, 380

841

Deresiewicz, William
Jane Austen Education, A, 389
Diaz, Joanne
Lessons, The, 438
Didion, Joan
Blue Nights, 103
Dorfman, Ariel
Feeding on Dreams, 279
Dubus, Andre III
Townie, 754
Duncan, Robert
H.D. Book, The, 339
Dyer, Geoff
Otherwise Known as the Human Condition, 565

Ebert, Roger
Life Itself, 452
Eco, Umberto
Confessions of a Young Novelist, 180
Prague Cemetery, The, 596
Espada, Martin
Trouble Ball, The, 767
Eugenides, Jeffrey
Marriage Plot, 465
Ferguson, Andrew
Crazy U, 197
Ferguson, Niall
Civilization, 156

Flynn, Nick
Captain Asks for a Show of Hands, The, 136
Foer, Joshua
Moonwalking with Einstein, 485
Fossum, Karin
Bad Intentions, 61
Frayn, Michael
My Father's Fortune, 497

Gigante, Denise
Keats Brothers, The, 413
Godwin, Peter
Fear, The, 274

Goldman, Francisco
Say Her Name, 637
Goodheart, Adam
1861, 233
Graham, Wade
American Eden, 25
Gray, John
Immortalization Commission, The, 367
Greenblatt, Stephen
Swerve, The, 720
Greene, Brian
Hidden Reality, The, 355

Ha Jin
Nanjing Requiem, 505
Hale, Benjamin
Evolution of Bruno Littlemore, The, 266
Hamill, Pete
Tabloid City, 728
Hamilton, Gabrielle
Blood, Bones, and Butter, 99
Harbach, Chad
Art of Fielding, The, 49
Hendrickson, Paul
Hemingway's Boat, 347
Hochschild, Adam
To End All Wars, 740
Hoffman, Adina, and Peter Cole
Sacred Trash, 629
Hollinghurst, Alan
Stranger's Child, The, 708
Holroyd, Michael
Book of Secrets, 107
Howe, Fanny
Come and See, 176
Hua, Yu
China in Ten Words, 152
Hughes, Bettany
Hemlock Cup, The, 351
Hustvedt, Siri
Summer Without Men, The, 712

Isaacson, Walter
Steve Jobs, 699

Jacobs, Alan
Pleasures of Reading in an Age of Distraction, The, 592
Jacoby, Susan
Never Say Die, 509
Jasanoff, Maya
Liberty's Exiles, 447
Jensen, Carsten
We, the Drowned, 791
Johnson, Mat
Pym, 613
Johnston, Devin
Traveler, 762
Jones, Tayari
Silver Sparrow, 662
Just, Ward
Rodin's Debutante, 625

Kanfer, Stefan
Tough Without a Gun, 749
Kasischke, Laura
Space, in Chains, 691
Kendall, Joshua
Forgotten Founding Father, The, 291
Kennedy, David
Don't Shoot, 217
Kennedy, William
Changó's Beads and Two-Tone Shoes, 144
Ker, Ian
G.K. Chesterton, 312
Kerr, Philip
Field Gray, 283
Keun, Irmgard
After Midnight, 1
King, Stephen
11/22/1963, 241
Kissinger, Henry
On China, 534
Klatt, L. S.
Cloud of Ink, 160

Kluger, Richard
Bitter Waters of Medicine Creek, The, 91
Komunyakaa, Yusef
Chameleon Couch, The, 140
Krauze, Enrique
Redeemers, 621

Läckberg, Camilla
Preacher, The, 601
Larsen, Timothy
People of One Book, 578
Larson, Erik
In the Garden of Beasts, 376
Latiolais, Michelle
Widow, 803
Lelyveld, Joseph
Great Soul, 330
Lesser, Wendy
Music for Silenced Voices, 493
Levin, Gail
Lee Krasner, 429
Lipstadt, Deborah E.
Eichmann Trial, The, 229
Lobo Antunes, António
Land at the End of the World, The, 421
Splendor of Portugal, The, 695

Mackey, Nathaniel
Nod House, 521
Malcolm, Janet
Iphigenia in Forest Hills, 384
Mankell, Henning
Troubled Man, The, 771
Mann, Charles C.
1493, 299
Marable, Manning
Malcolm X, 460
Mason, Bobbie Ann
Girl in the Blue Beret, The, 304
McCall Smith, Alexander
Saturday Big Tent Wedding Party, The, 633

McCullough, David
Greater Journey, The, 321
McElroy, Joseph
Night Soul, and Other Stories, 517
McMillian, John
Smoking Typewriters, 674
Mehrotra, Arvind Krishna
Songs of Kabir, 687
Mieville, China
Embassytown, 250
Millhauser, Steven
We Others, 795
Morgenstern, Erin
Night Circus, The, 513
Morris, Errol
Believing Is Seeing, 78
Morson, Gary Saul
Words of Others, The, 817
Moschovakis, Anna
You and Three Others Are
Approaching a Lake, 825
Mukherjee, Bharati
Miss New India, 477
Murakami, Haruki
1Q84, 548
Murphy, Yannick
Call, The, 131
Murray, Les
Taller When Prone, 732

Nasar, Sylvia
Grand Pursuit, 316
Némirovsky, Irène
All Our Worldly Goods, 13
Norton, David
King James Bible, The, 417
Notley, Alice
Culture of One, 201

Oates, Joyce Carol
Widow's Story, A, 808
Obreht, Téa
Tiger's Wife, The, 736

O'Brien, Geoffrey G.
Metropole, 469
O'Nan, Stewart
Emily, Alone, 256
Orozco, Jesse
Orientation, 561
Orr, David
Beautiful and Pointless, 74
Ossip, Kathleen
Cold War, The, 168
Otsuka, Julie
Buddha in the Attic, The, 119
Oyeyemi, Helen
Mr. Fox, 489

Packer, Ann
Swim Back to Me, 724
Peacock, Molly
Paper Garden, The, 574
Pearlman, Edith
Binocular Vision, 82
Perec, Georges
Art of Asking Your Boss for a Raise,
The, 45
Perrotta, Tom
Leftovers, The, 434
Phillips, Arthur
Tragedy of Arthur, The, 758
Pittard, Hannah
Fates Will Find Their Way, The, 270
Preston, Richard, and Michael Crichton
Micro, 473
Prose, Francine
My New American Life, 501

Rasenberger, Jim
Brilliant Disaster, The, 115
Ro, Anuradha
Atlas of Impossible Longing, An, 53
Rodoreda, Mercè
Selected Stories of Mercè Rodoreda,
The, 645
Roiphe, Anne
Art and Madness, 41

Ronson, Jon
  Psychopath Test, The, 605
Rowland, Christopher
  Blake and the Bible, 95
Różewicz, Tadeusz
  Sobbing Superpower, 679
Russell, Karen
  Swamplandia!, 716

Schickel, Richard
  Conversations with Scorsese, 184
Scott, Janny
  Singular Woman, 66
Sebag-Montefiore, Simon
  Jerusalem, 397
Secrest, Meryle
  Modigliani, 481
Sepúlveda, Luis
  Shadow of What We Were, The, 653
Shepard, Jim
  You Think That's Bad, 829
Shields, Charles J.
  And So It Goes, 33
Shin, Kyung-sook
  Please Look After Mom, 588
Shklovsky, Viktor
  Bowstring, 111
Slawenski, Kenneth
  J. D. Salinger, 393
Smith, Bruce
  Devotions, 213
Smith, Tracy K.
  Life on Mars, 456
Snyder, Laura J.
  Philosophical Breakfast Club, The,
  583
Solzhenitsyn, Aleksandr
  Apricot Jam, 37
Spanier, Sandra and Trogden, Robert
  Letters of Ernest Hemingway, 442
Spencer-Fleming, Julia
  One Was a Soldier, 552
Spiotta, Dana
  Stone Arabia, 704

Stamm, Peter
  Seven Years, 649
Steinberg, Jonathan
  Bismarck, 87
Styron, Alexandra
  Reading My Father, 617
Sullivan, John Jeremiah
  Pulphead, 609
Szwed, John
  Alan Lomax, 5

T.C. Boyle
  When the Killing's Done, 799
Tanner, Haley
  Vaclav and Lena, 787
Thomson, Keith
  Twice a Spy, 775
Thorn, John
  Baseball in the Garden of Eden, 65
Tomalin, Claire
  Charles Dickens, 148
Turkle, Sherry
  Alone Together, 21

Wainaina, Binyananga
  One Day I Will Write About This
  Place, 539
Wallace, David Foster
  Pale King, The, 569
West, Bing
  Wrong War, The, 821
Wilson, A. N.
  Dante in Love, 209
Woiwode, Larry
  Words Made Fresh, 813
Wolitzer, Meg
  Uncoupling, The, 779
Wright, Charles
  Bye-and-Bye, 123
Wulf, Andrea
  Founding Gardeners, 295

Xin, Mu
  Empty Room, An, 258

Young, Rob
Electric Eden, 237

Zagajewski, Adam
Unseen Hand, 783